Mastering Legislation, Regulation, and Statutory Interpretation

D1557474

Mastering Legislation, Regulation, and Statutory Interpretation

THIRD EDITION

Linda D. Jellum

ELLISON CAPERS PALMER SR. PROFESSOR OF TAX LAW
MERCER UNIVERSITY SCHOOL OF LAW

CAROLINA ACADEMIC PRESS
Durham, North Carolina

See catalog.loc.gov
for Cataloging-in-Publication data

ISBN 978-1-5310-1202-1
e-ISBN 978-1-5310-1203-8

Carolina Academic Press
700 Kent Street
Durham, NC 27701
Telephone (919) 489-7486
Fax (919) 493-5668
www.cap-press.com

Printed in the United States of America

Contents

Table of Cases

Series Editor's Foreword

The Carolina Academic Press Mastering Series is designed to provide you with a tool that will enable you to easily and efficiently "master" the substance and content of law school courses. Throughout the series, the focus is on quality writing that makes legal concepts understandable. As a result, the series is designed to be easy to read and is not unduly cluttered with footnotes or cites to secondary sources.

In order to facilitate student mastery of topics, the Mastering Series includes a number of pedagogical features designed to improve learning and retention. At the beginning of each chapter, you will find a "Roadmap" that tells you about the chapter and provides you with a sense of the material that you will cover. A "Checkpoint" at the end of each chapter encourages you to stop and review the key concepts, reiterating what you have learned. Throughout the book, key terms are explained and emphasized. Finally, a "Master Checklist" at the end of each book reinforces what you have learned and helps you identify any areas that need review or further study.

We hope that you will enjoy studying with, and learning from, the Mastering Series.

Russell L. Weaver
Professor of Law & Distinguished University Scholar
University of Louisville, Louis D. Brandeis School of Law

Dedication

This edition is dedicated to my husband and best friend, Lee Jellum. It's just us now, honey, and the dog, 3 cats, 8 chickens, and 13 ducks. (We need to get better at this empty-nester thing.)

This new edition would not have been possible without help. I am extremely grateful to my dean, Cathy Cox. Without research support, my work would have been much more difficult. I would also like to thank my research assistants, Maggie Cropp, Caitlin Wise, Carley Hawkins, Stephen Poydasheff, and Melissa Caroline Sport for their invaluable help and great senses of humor. They kept me laughing at every step of the way. I also had substantial help from other academics and would like to thank the following for their insightful comments and helpful suggestions, endless reviews of draft chapters, and other assistance: Professors Michael Dimino, Erica Bristol, Benjamin Bratman, Denise Gibson, and Jeremy Kidd.

Dedication to the Second Edition

This edition is dedicated to all of my students during the last few years, but especially to the students in the Connecticut University Law School's 2012 externship program in Washington, D.C. With their help and Professor Bernard Bell's willingness to share a problem he crafted, I have added a section to each chapter called Mastering This Topic, which is based on a running hypothetical involving an ordinance prohibiting vehicles in the park. I believe the new section will greatly aid your mastery of the subject.

I would also like to thank my research assistants, Ashley Turner and Dianna Lee, for all their invaluable help and great senses of humor.

Finally, I could not have made it through this very difficult year without the help of a few very special people: Professor Dorothy Brown, Professor Nancy Levit, Terry Smith, Esq., Mary Cullen, Yuichi Miyoshi, and my husband, children, and family members. Chris, camp is finally over!

Linda D. Jellum
Bethesda, Maryland
April 2013

Dedication to the First Edition

This book is dedicated to my husband and children, who have not seen as much of me this year as they would have preferred, and to my parents, who have been there to guide and advise me for so many years.

I would like to thank the following for their insightful comments and helpful suggestions, endless review of draft chapters, and other assistance: Professor Michael Dimino, Professor Brian Slocum, Professor Steven Johnson, Professor David Ritchie, Professor Spencer Clough, Denise Gibson, Barbara Churchwell, Susan Wilson, Jamanda Turner, Chris Featherstun, Java Joe's in Hilton Head, and Mercer Law School (for research support). Each individual has made this text better with his or her involvement. Any remaining errors are mine alone.

Special thanks are due to my colleague and former co-author, Professor David Hricik. This project would have been infinitely more difficult without the foundation I gained from our earlier project. I also would like to thank Professor Russell Weaver for asking me to be involved in the Mastering Series and for supporting me in so many ways over the years.

Linda D. Jellum
Macon, Georgia
April 2008

Preface

When I graduated from law school, classes on statutory interpretation (or leg-reg) did not exist. When I started teaching at Mercer University School of Law, I was assigned to teach a mandatory course called Statutory Law and Analysis. I knew little about the topic at that time. I skimmed the books that existed but was unhappy with all of them (as law professors often are). Ultimately, I wrote my own. During that process, I learned that statutory interpretation is a skill, not doctrine. But in many schools, it is still taught like other first-year courses, using the case method and Socratic dialogue. And while cases surely do show how arguments about meaning can be made, the cases do not show how to identify the relevant language in a statute, how to explain what that language means using the various sources of meaning in a logical order, nor how to counter an opponent's arguments about meaning. Understanding these skills is essential for you to master this topic. And this book will help you do so.

Although Mercer was a pioneer in this area, after I wrote the first edition of this text, many law schools followed suit and added leg-reg courses to their curriculum. Typical leg-reg courses include a little bit of legislation, a little bit of statutory interpretation, and a little bit (often more) of administrative law. I have expanded this text during the last two editions to more comprehensively cover the administrative law piece of leg-reg so that this text will be useful to you, regardless of what your course is called.

This book is organized as follows. After an introduction, Chapter 2 describes the legislative process. Chapter 3 then explains the current approaches to separation of powers, both generally and as applied to interpretation issues. Next, Chapter 4 explains the various statutory interpretation theories and sources of meaning. Understanding theory is critical because judges approach the interpretive process in different ways (just think about Justices Ginsburg and Thomas). Then, Chapters 5 through 8 examine the various intrinsic sources of meaning, such as the text, the grammar, the punctuation, the linguistic canons, and the act's components. Chapters 9 through 11 explain the various extrinsic sources of meaning, including the legislative history and the statutory purpose. Chapter 12 surveys the policy-based sources: those based on the U.S.

Constitution and prudential considerations. The next two chapters, Chapter 13 through 14, introduce you to the administrative state. These chapters explain what federal agencies are, what they do, why they do it, and how they do it. Chapter 15 rounds out the administrative law chapters with a discussion of the standard of review a court will use to evaluate the legitimacy of an agency action, including an agency's interpretation of a statute. We have come full circle!

Finally, Chapter 16 identifies a step-by-step approach you can use to resolve questions about interpretation, whether to approach problems in class discussion, to answer questions on an exam, or to resolve a problem in practice. It is a checklist with footnoted citations you can use in your own work. I anticipate it will become your favorite chapter.

I hope you find this topic as fascinating as I do, but if not, this text will provide a blueprint for you to become a master of statutory interpretation, legislation, and regulation.

Linda D. Jellum
Macon, Georgia
2019

Mastering Legislation, Regulation, and Statutory Interpretation

Chapter 1

Preliminary Matters

Roadmap

- Learn what interpretation is and what it is not.
- Understand why most laws work as intended and interpretation is unnecessary.
- Use a hypothetical to help identify your current beliefs.

A. Introduction to This Chapter

Each chapter in this book begins with an introduction like this one, which will explain the purpose and organization of that chapter. So, let's get started. As you read this text, you will likely encounter new and unfamiliar words. There is a Glossary in Appendix A to help you learn the meanings of these new words.

While this is a book about the legislative process, statutory interpretation, and agencies, this chapter focuses primarily on statutory interpretation—what it is and why you as a future lawyer need to understand it. This chapter introduces you to statutory interpretation generally—what it is and why lawyers should master it. Next, this chapter explains the differences between a bill, an act, and a statute. To help you understand the context of interpretation, the chapter includes a sample bill so you can understand what you will be interpreting. The chapter then explains why laws, including statutes and regulations, generally work as intended and require little interpreting. But sometimes laws are unclear. This book describes the methods for interpreting unclear laws.

To help you understand how to apply these methods, this chapter includes a challenging, well-known hypothetical. The point of introducing the hypothetical in this chapter is to help you understand what you bring to interpretation before you master it. You do not come to this topic as a neophyte. Rather, you bring beliefs about the proper way to interpret legal language, the proper role for judges and legislatures, and the appropriate use of legislative history, for example. This hypothetical will help you identify your beliefs before we get started. The book as a whole will help you analyze the soundness of these beliefs.

B. Interpretation Defined

In the past, law was mostly developed in the courts through judge-made common law. Issues arose, lawyers sued, and judges resolved those issues. Law developed slowly and in piecemeal fashion. Thus, if you were a lawyer practicing in the 1800s, your practice focused on reading and understanding cases (much like first year of law school). For example, assume that a client hired you to determine whether he could sue his neighbor for cutting down a tree located on the property border. To find the answer, you would study a number of cases to determine the law. You would analyze the facts and the holdings of these cases and compare the facts of those cases to the facts of your case. You would also look at the reasoning in the cases to understand why each case was decided the way it was. After all of this research, you could answer your client's question.

Today, the process is different. If the same client came to your office, you would not start by researching case law. Rather, you would check first to see if there was a local, state, or federal statute (or regulation) on point. Assuming you found one, you would need to understand what that statute (or regulation) says. Sure, you think, that is easy. I would just read it. Not so fast. Even if the statute (or regulation) appears clear, it may not be. As you will learn, reading a statute's text is only the first step to understanding what that statute means. Because language is inherently ambiguous (for example, is "blue" a state of being or a color? Is "dust" a verb or noun?), interpreting statutes is more complex than it would seem. "In the end, much of our jurisprudential disagreement about how to interpret statutes represents a tension between our common law tradition and our democratic tradition." WILLIAM N. ESKRIDGE, JR., ET AL., LEGISLATION AND STATUTORY INTERPRETATION 17 (2d ed. 2006).

Interpretation is the process of determining the meaning of a legislative act whether that act is a statute, regulation, or other written legal language. But interpreting that law is more than simply reading the language. Interpreting law requires you to look at the enactment process, to understand the various canons of interpretation, and to make arguments about that language.

Moreover, interpretation differs greatly from common law analysis. Interpretation is different from common law analysis, in part, because the creation of the law is so different and, in part, because the reasoning behind the law's creation is mostly absent; legislatures do not always include the reasons for enacting certain laws. For example, statutes are the product of a long legislative process that includes competing interests. The final product—the statute—is a compromise arrived at only after a long political, and often controversial, process. While process is never relevant to common law interpretation, process is often relevant to statutory interpretation.

Interpretation is an art, not a science; it is a language, not a set of rules. In short, it is learning to make written and oral arguments about the meaning of words in a written law. Legislatures and lawyers do not draft perfectly; ambiguity, vagueness, omission, and mistakes are all common elements in the final product. Knowing how to interpret laws in light of these imperfections will be critical to your legal practice because most of the work lawyers do today centers on statutes and regulations, whether federal or state. While interpreting laws is not an exact science, there are canons (or rules of thumb) that guide interpretation. Recognizing the increasing importance of this topic, law schools around the country are adding statutory interpretation and legislation courses. "[A]cademic law is catching up with legal practice." ESKRIDGE ET AL., LEGISLATION AND STATUTORY INTERPRETATION, *supra*, at 2. Today, lawyers simply cannot practice law without knowing the art of interpretation. Because statutes and regulations have proliferated, reading and understanding them is a basic legal skill. Thus, mastering this skill is essential to your success as a lawyer.

This book will help you learn the art of interpretation. Because different scholars and courts use different approaches to interpretation, this text cannot definitively explain how a judge or court will interpret a statute or regulation, but it will help you learn to make arguments for your client, speak the relevant language, and anticipate how laws are likely to be interpreted. At the conclusion of this text, you should: (1) be familiar with the canons of interpretation, knowing how to use them and how to counter your opponent's use of them, (2) have an understanding of the various theories of interpretation judges use in interpreting legal language, and (3) be aware of the breadth of arguments that can be made about seemingly clear language. In short, this text will help you master the art of interpretation.

C. Defining Bills, Acts & Statutes

Before we begin, it might be helpful to understand the difference between bills, acts, and statutes. Lawyers use these terms interchangeably, but there are some differences. A bill is the written draft of a law that Congress (or a state legislature) and the president (or the governor) may enact. Before the law has been enacted, it is a bill. Often the Senate and House have companion bills that address similar topics, but these bills may not be and indeed need not be identical. Thus, a bill is a law that a legislature or the executive has or is considering but has not yet enacted.

Once both chambers of the legislature pass the bill in identical form and either the executive signs it or the legislature overrides a veto, the enacted bill becomes an act (and a law). Federal acts are published as slip laws in the *Statutes at Large*. However, because acts are placed sequentially and not topically in the *Statutes at Large*, finding the law through just a search of the *Statutes at Large* is not feasible. Hence, sections of the acts are placed into a topical code known as the *U.S. Code*. When the section of an act has been codified, as it is called, we call it a statute. Because the word "statute" is defined as meaning any written law, it is often used to refer to a section of an act as well.

Bills and acts typically include the following clauses, or provisions (see Chapter 8 for greater detail about these components and their relevance to interpretation):

- **Long Title:** Long titles typically identify the purpose of the bill and where the bill will fit within existing law. They typically start with "An Act to" or "An Act relating to."
- **Enacting Clause:** Constitutionally required language: "*Be it enacted by the Senate and House of Representatives of the United States of America in Congress assembled.*"
- **Short Title:** Short titles are used for reference. The short title typically is written as follows: "This act may be cited as the ____ Act of ____."
- **Purpose, Findings, and/or Policy Clauses:** These provisions identify the reason the law was necessary.
- **Definitions Section:** A legislature may define a word in any way the legislature wants to, and that definition is controlling. Only definitions that are applicable to the bill as a whole are included within the definitions section. Definitions used only in one particular section or subsection of a bill are usually placed within that specific section.
- **Operative Provisions:** These provisions are the heart and soul of a law. There are two types of operative provisions: (1) *substantive provisions*, which provide the rights, duties, powers, and privileges being created, and (2) *administrative provisions*, which address the creation, organization, powers, and procedures of the governmental organization that will enforce or adjudicate the law.
- **Exceptions & Provisos:** If there are any exceptions to a bill's provisions, they might appear in the same section or sentence as the pertinent operative provision or in a separate section or

sections. They typically begin with the words "except for," "provided however," and "provided that." Common phrasing at the beginning of a separately stated exception is "Nothing in this section shall be construed to."

- **Administrative Provisions:** These provisions address the creation, organization, powers, and procedures of the governmental organization that will enforce or adjudicate the law.
- **Enforcement Provisions:** These provisions identify the result if the operative provision's elements are met. Criminal statutes impose criminal penalties; civil statutes impose other penalties, such as fines or injunctions, or allow for private lawsuits.
- **Effective Date Provisions:** When the act is to be effective on a date other than the signing date, the legislature must provide that effective date in the act.
- **Saving Clause:** Such provisions "save," or exempt, behavior or legal relationships that existed before or on the effective date of a new act.
- **Sunset Clause:** A sunset provision terminates or repeals all or portions of an act after a specific date, unless further legislative action is taken to extend the act.
- **Severability/Inseverability Provisions:** These provisions address the validity of the act should any section of it be found invalid. Severability provisions allow for the remaining sections of the act to remain valid, while inseverability provisions require that the act as a whole be held invalid if any one section is invalid.

Here is an example of a bill (not an act because it has not yet been enacted), which has many of the components identified above. Can you identify which provisions are included and which are omitted?

115TH CONGRESS
2D SESSION

S. 3710

To end the unconstitutional delegation of legislative power which was exclusively vested in the Senate and House of Representatives by article I, section 1 of the Constitution of the United States, and to direct the Comptroller General of the United States to issue a report to Congress detailing the extent of the problem of unconstitutional delegation to the end that such delegations can be phased out, thereby restoring the constitutional principle of separation of powers set forth in the first sections of the Constitution of the United States.

IN THE SENATE OF THE UNITED STATES

DECEMBER 5, 2018

Mr. PAUL introduced the following bill; which was read twice and referred to the Committee on Homeland Security and Governmental Affairs

---

A BILL

To end the unconstitutional delegation of legislative power which was exclusively vested in the Senate and House of Representatives by article I, section 1 of the Constitution of the United States, and to direct the Comptroller General of the United States to issue a report to Congress detailing the extent of the problem of unconstitutional delegation to the end that such delegations can be phased out, thereby restoring the constitutional principle of separation of powers set forth in the first sections of the Constitution of the United States.

Be it enacted by the Senate *and House of Representatives of the United States of America in Congress assembled,*

SECTION 1. Short title.

This Act may be cited as the "Write the Laws Act".

SEC. 2. Constitutional authority statement.

(a) IN GENERAL.—This Act is enacted pursuant to the powers conferred by the Constitution of the United States upon Congress by—

(1) article I, section 1, which vests in Congress all legislative powers granted under the Constitution; and

(2) article I, section 8, clause 18, which vests in Congress the power to make all laws that shall be necessary and proper for executing the legislative power granted to Congress in the Constitution.

(b) OTHER AUTHORITY.—This Act is also enacted to bring the enforcement of Federal law into compliance with the guarantee under the Fifth Amendment to the Constitution of the United States that no person be deprived of life, liberty, or property without due process of law.

SEC. 3. Findings.

Congress finds the following:

(1) Article I, section 1 of the Constitution of the United States vests the legislative powers enumerated therein in Congress, consisting of a Senate and a House of Representatives, subject only to the veto power of the President as provided in article I, section 7, clause 2.

(2) Article II, section 1 of the Constitution of the United States vests the executive power of the United States in a President.

(3) Article III, section 1 of the Constitution of the United States vests the judicial power of the United States in "one supreme Court, and in such inferior courts as the Congress may from time to time ordain and establish", subject only to the jurisdictional limitations set forth in article III, section 2.

(4) As the Supreme Court of the United States has stated, "In the main, [the Constitution of the United States] has blocked out with singular precision, and in bold lines, in its three primary Articles, the allotment of power to the executive, the legislative, and judicial departments of the government [and] the powers confided by the Constitution to one of these departments cannot be exercised by another.". Kilbourn v. Thompson, 103 U.S. 168, 191 (1881).

(5) "It is ... essential to the successful working of this system, that the persons entrusted with power in any one of these branches shall not be permitted to encroach upon the powers confided to others, but that each shall by the law of its creation be limited to the exercise of the powers ... of its own department and no other.". Id.

(6) "The increase in the number of States, in their population and wealth, and in the amount of power ... [has]

present[ed] powerful and growing temptations to those to whom that exercise is intrusted, to overstep the just boundaries of their own department, and enter upon the domain of one of the others, or to assume powers not intrusted to either of them.". Id. at 191–192.

(7) Succumbing to these "powerful and growing" temptations, and beginning in the late nineteenth century with the Interstate Commerce Commission and continuing to the present time, Congress has unconstitutionally created numerous administrative agencies with blended powers, namely—

(A) the exercise of legislative power vested by the Constitution of the United States in Congress;

(B) the exercise of executive power vested by the Constitution of the United States in the President; and

(C) the exercise of judicial power vested by the Constitution of the United States in the Supreme Court and lower Federal courts.

(8) By delegating legislative, executive, and judicial power to the various administrative agencies, Congress has departed from the separation of powers structure of the Constitution of the United States, and ignored the warning of the framers of that instrument that "The accumulation of all powers, legislative, executive, and judiciary, in the same hands, whether of one, a few, or many, and whether hereditary, self-appointed, or elective, may justly be pronounced the very definition of tyranny.". James Madison, The Federalist No. 47.

(9) Further, by delegating legislative, executive, and judicial powers to various administrative agencies, Congress has unconstitutionally established a Star Chamber-like system of rules promulgated, executed, and adjudicated by administrative agencies that are functionally a part of the executive branch of the Federal Government in violation of the due process guarantee of the Fifth Amendment to the Constitution of the United States.

(10) By the very nature of legislative power, and by the express terms of article I, section 1 of the Constitution of the United States, Congress may not delegate any legislative

power to any other branch of the Federal Government or other entity, including any administrative agency. As Chief Justice John Marshall stated: "It will not be contended that Congress can delegate to the courts, or to any other tribunals, powers which are strictly and exclusively legislative.". Wayman v. Southard, 10 Wheat. (23 U.S.) 1, 42 (1825).

(11) As Chief Justice Melville Fuller explained, a "criminal offense" created or clarified by an agency in the executive branch is not valid unless the offense "is fully and completely defined by the act" of Congress. In re Kollock, 165 U.S. 526, 533 (1897).

(12) By vesting legislative power in the Congress, the Constitution requires the Senate and the House of Representatives to enact statutes containing general rules to be executed by the President, as provided in article II, section 1 of the Constitution of the United States, and to be adjudicated in a case or controversy by such inferior courts as Congress may from time to time establish, or in the Supreme Court, as provided in article III, sections 1 and 2.

(13) By abdicating its constitutional legislative responsibility to write the laws whereby the people are governed, and having unconstitutionally delegated that power to unelected bureaucrats, Congress has undermined the constitutional protections of—

(A) the checks and balances of a bicameral legislative body; and

(B) a Presidential veto.

(14) As a direct consequence of Congress having abdicated its responsibility to properly exercise the legislative power vested by the Constitution of the United States, Congress has—

(A) imposed onerous and unreasonable burdens upon the American people; and

(B) violated the constitutional principle of the separation of the legislative, executive, and judicial processes and functions.

SEC. 4. Restoring the separation of powers.

(a) In general. — Title 1 of the United States Code is amended by inserting after chapter 2 the following:

"CHAPTER 2A—
SEPARATION OF POWERS

"§ 151. Nondelegation of legislative power

"(a) Definition. — In this section, the term 'delegation of legislative powers'—

"(1) includes—

"(A) the creation or clarification of any criminal or civil offense; and

"(B) the creation or clarification of any non-criminal regulation, prohibition or limitation applicable to the public, or some subset thereof, that is not fully and completely defined in an Act of Congress, except that the executive branch of government may be delegated authority to make factual findings that will determine the date upon which such an Act is implemented, suspended, or revived; and

"(2) does not include the issuance of any Presidential proclamation, or the issuance of any rule or regulation governing the internal operation of any agency, or conditions made upon grants or contracts issued by any agency.

"(b) Prohibition. — An Act of Congress may not contain any delegation of legislative powers, whether to—

"(1) any component within the legislative branch of the Federal Government;

"(2) the President or any other member of the executive branch of the Federal Government;

"(3) the judicial branch of the Federal Government;

"(4) any agency;

"(5) any quasi-public agency;

"(6) any State or instrumentality thereof; or

"(7) any other organization or individual.

"(c) Executive actions.—No new Presidential directive, adjudicative decision, rule, or regulation, or change to an existing Presidential directive, adjudicative decision, rule, or regulation governing, limiting, imposing a penalty on, or otherwise regulating any activity of any individual or entity, other than an officer or employee of the Federal Government, may be promulgated or put into effect, unless the directive, decision, rule, or regulation is authorized by an Act of Congress that complies with subsection (b).

"(d) Report.—Not later than 6 months after the date of enactment of this chapter, the Comptroller General of the United States shall submit to Congress a report identifying all statutes enacted before the date that is 90 days after the date of enactment of this chapter which contain any delegation of legislative powers prohibited under this section.

"§ 152. Enforcement clause

"(a) In general.—An Act of Congress, Presidential directive, adjudicative decision, rule, or regulation that does not comply with section 151 shall have no force or effect and no legal, equitable, regulatory, civil, or criminal action may be brought under such an Act of Congress, Presidential directive, adjudicative decision, rule, or regulation.

"(b) Cause of action.—Any person aggrieved by any action of any officer or employee in the executive branch of the Federal Government under any Act of Congress that does not comply with section 151 may bring a cause of action under sections 2201 and 2202 of title 28 against the United States to seek appropriate relief, including an injunction against enforcement of any Act of Congress, Presidential directive, adjudicative decision, rule, or regulation that does not comply with section 151.

"(c) Standard of review.—In any action brought under subsection (b), the standard of review shall be de novo.

"§ 153. Effective date

"This chapter shall apply to any Act of Congress, Presidential directive, adjudicative decision, rule, or regulation, change to an existing Presidential directive, adjudicative decision, rule, or regulation, enacted or promulgated on or after the date that is 90 days after the date of enactment of this chapter.".

(b) Technical and conforming amendment. — The table of chapters for title 1, United States Code, is amended by inserting after the item relating to chapter 2 the following:

SEC. 5. Severability clause.

If any provision of this Act or an amendment made by this Act, or the application of a provision or amendment to any person or circumstance, is held to be invalid for any reason in any court of competent jurisdiction, the remainder of this Act and amendments made by this Act, and the application of the provisions and amendment to any other person or circumstance, shall not be affected.

You might also look at Appendices A and C. They include companion bills about loan forgiveness for law students. Can you identify which components they include?

Now that you know the components of a bill or act and understand that a statute is one section of an act inserted into a code, let's talk about how to interpret language from a section of an act or a statute.

D. Why Law Works Well Most of the Time

Before we begin, you may wonder why interpretation is necessary. After all, ordinary citizens obey laws every day. How is obeying the law possible if laws are so unclear? Most citizens do not have the luxury of hiring lawyers to help them understand the language of the law, nor do they have the time to study interpretation in the detail you will be doing. Yet these citizens are expected to know the law, whether they have read it or not, and conform their actions accordingly. Moreover, they do so more often than not. How can ordinary citizens know whether their actions conform to legal requirements if a lawyer has to take three years of law school and read books, like this one, to learn how to understand laws?

The answer to that question is actually quite simple. Many laws are intuitive and conform to societal expectations. Most of us do not need a law to tell us that killing, assaulting, or stealing from someone is wrong. Further, we also understand that there may be times when doing one of these actions, though usually wrong, would not be wrong given the particular circumstances. While most of us do not need laws to conform our behavior to societal norms, some outliers and sociopaths may need laws to prevent, or at least allow society to punish, behavior that violates social norms. Legislators write statutes, regulators write regulations, and judges write judicial opinions to explain law to the outliers and the enforcers, which then enables those in authority to punish wrongdoers and to identify the boundaries of that law.

Let's focus on statutes. How do legislators explain law clearly? Legislators follow familiar patterns. Statutes are understandable both because they conform most of the time to societal expectations, but also, because they have a familiar format. As one scholar has noted, statutes resemble dictionary definitions. LAWRENCE M. SOLAN, THE LANGUAGE OF STATUTES 18 (2010). For example, the definition of the verb "lie" is "to make an untrue statement with intent to deceive." *Lie.* MERRIAM-WEBSTER'S ONLINE DICTIONARY, http://www.merriam-webster.com/dictionary/lie (last visited June 8, 2018). If we unpack this definition, we see that people lie when they (1) make an untrue statement, and (2) have the intent to deceive. Let's compare the federal statute criminalizing perjury:

> Whoever ... having taken an oath before a competent tribunal, officer, or person, in any case in which a law of the United States authorizes an oath to be administered, that he will testify, declare, depose, or certify truly, or that any written testimony, declaration, deposition, or certificate by him subscribed, is true, willfully and contrary to such oath states or subscribes any material matter which he does not believe to be true ... is guilty of perjury.

18 U.S.C. § 1621(1). If we unpack this definition, people commit perjury when they (1) take an oath or assert in writing that they will testify truthfully, and (2) say something material that they do not believe to be true. Do you see the similarity between this statute and the definition above?

When statutes like the one above conform to societal expectations and define conduct in expected ways, statutes generally need be less clear, because most individuals will follow the law without inducement. But when statutes do not conform to societal expectations or do not define conduct in expected ways, they must be clearer; individuals and their lawyers fight by holding the legislature to the precise words it used. For example, a statute that states, "[w]hoever shall willfully take the life of another shall be punished by death" is probably both expected and clear. But a statute that requires individuals to pay thirty percent of their "income" to the federal government is unexpected (unwanted?) and, thus, must define "income" very clearly.

Let's look at another example, one closer to home. Consider your commute to work or school. You leave your house, drive a car that meets state safety standards, fill it with the appropriate kind of gas, drive on the correct side of the road, stop at stop signs, stay reasonably close to the speed limit, pay to park your car legally, and turn on your headlights when it grows dark. Daily, like all other ordinary citizens, you follow laws without thinking about whether you are doing so. You may not follow the laws perfectly (note the speed limit example), but you will follow the laws well enough to help society run smoothly. Thus, laws generally work well.

From these examples, you can see that it is only the hard cases that wind up in court and only the toughest of cases that are resolved at the Supreme Court. Remember that point because after reading this text, you will be warped into thinking that the language in all laws is malleable and ambiguous. Do not make this mistake. Let me be clear: most statutes are clear and work well. But because language is imprecise — precision is impossible with a limited number of symbols representing a multitude of concepts — ambiguity and vagueness are unavoidable. When ambiguity and vagueness arise, the question becomes how should they be resolved? That is the question that this text answers.

E. Is an Ambulance a Motor Vehicle?

Is an ambulance a motor vehicle? This question seems silly, to say the least. Of course an ambulance is a motor vehicle. But is it? You might be surprised to learn that very intelligent people disagree about whether an ambulance is a vehicle, at least within the context of a statute prohibiting "vehicles in the park." Indeed, this question is so famous and contentious that Justice Antonin Scalia and Judge Richard Posner once had a very public falling out based, in part, on their resolution of this very issue.[1]

---

1. Richard A. Posner, *The Incoherence of Antonin Scalia* (August 24, 2012), http://www.newrepublic.com/article/magazine/books-and-arts/106441/scalia-garner-reading-the-law-textual-originalism; Bryan A. Garner and Richard A. Posner, *How Nuanced Is Justice Scalia's Judicial Philosophy? An Exchange* (September 10, 2012), http://www.newrepublic.com/article/politics/107001/how-nuanced-justice-scalias-judicial-philosophy-exchange.

Below is a hypothetical city ordinance that prohibits vehicles from entering a public park. This hypothetical is based on *McBoyle v. United States*, 283 U.S. 25 (1931). The issue before the Supreme Court in *McBoyle* was whether a defendant who transported a stolen airplane across state lines violated the National Motor Vehicle Theft Act, 18 U.S.C. §408, which provided that "whoever shall transport or cause to be transported in interstate or foreign commerce a motor vehicle, knowing the same to have been stolen, shall be punished ...." According to subsection 2 of the statute, "[t]he term 'motor vehicle' shall include an automobile, automobile truck, automobile wagon, motor cycle, or any other self-propelled vehicle not designed for running on rails." While the Court acknowledged that the language of the statute was broad enough to cover an airplane, which is a self-propelled vehicle that does not run on rails, the Court reasoned that "in everyday speech, 'vehicle' calls up the picture of a thing moving on land." *Id.* at 282. Thus, the Court held that an airplane was not a motor vehicle. *Id.* The decision sparked controversy because the Court rejected the ordinary meaning of the language in the statute.

After you read the hypothetical city ordinance and its "legislative history" below, you will be asked to consider some hypothetical scenarios and decide whether you, as a new prosecutor for the city, would prosecute the individuals involved for violating the ordinance. When you answer the questions consider how, if you were to prosecute, you would explain to a judge that each of the defendant's actions violated the statute. What might a defense attorney argue in response? Why? What materials do you, as a prosecutor, find helpful, relevant, and appropriate to consider in making your decisions? What materials do you consider unhelpful, irrelevant, or inappropriate to consider? Why? What if you represented the defendant? In other words, does your answer to these questions depend on which side of the case you are on? You should think about how you would resolve these questions before you read this text and master interpretation. This hypothetical will test your beliefs about interpretation while you are still an ordinary citizen, albeit one already influenced by some legal training.

You will be tempted to skip this step; after all, no one will test you on your answers, and law school is time-consuming enough. But you will learn a lot from actually attempting the hypothetical questions and noting your answers in the margins. If you take the time, likely less than an hour to jot down your answers to these questions, you will learn quickly how you naturally approach interpretation issues, a topic we will explore in some detail in Chapter 4. Additionally, you will find your notes helpful as we return to this problem again and again throughout this text in a special section entitled: "Mastering

This Topic." So much of interpretation is intuitive and happens without your conscious thought.

Further, as you learn the rules of thumb, or the canons of interpretation, you will be tempted to think of these canons as legal rules. They are not! Legal rules are mandatory. For instance, the parol evidence rule is a legal rule. That rule prevents a party to a written contract from presenting extrinsic evidence in court if that evidence would vary the written terms of a contract. The parol evidence rule is not malleable; it applies in every case involving a contract and extra-textual evidence. In contrast, the canons of interpretation are not legal rules; rather, they are guidelines, suggestions, or even a legal language that lawyers and judges use to justify outcomes. As such, they are malleable, and for every canon that supports one party's interpretation, there is a canon that supports the opposing party's interpretation. Karl N. Llewellyn, *Remarks on the Theory of Appellate Decision and the Rules of Canons About How Statutes Are to Be Construed*, 3 Vand. L. Rev. 395, 401-06 (1950) (famously including a chart of these canons working in opposition).

Thus, know now that you are not learning law *per se*; instead, you are learning to make arguments using a new language, one that you do not master at your peril.

F. No Motor Vehicles in the Park: A Hypothetical[2]

A hypothetical local city ordinance is included below. An ordinance is like a statute, but it is just enacted by a local council instead of a state or federal legislature. Do not worry if you do not understand everything included in the hypothetical at this point. Just do your best by reading the ordinance, the accompanying legislative reports, and the mayor's signing statement. Then answer the questions that follow, noting your conclusions and reasoning in the margins. You will want to come back to your conclusions as you begin to master the material in this text. Also, note any questions you have about the

---

2. Bernard Bell graciously provided a modified version of this hypothetical to me. He describes how he uses the hypothetical in class in his article, Bernard W. Bell, *"No More Vehicles in the Park": Reviving the Hart-Fuller Debate to Introduce Statutory Construction*, 48 J. Legal Educ. 88 (1998) (citing H.L.A. Hart, *Positivism and the Separation of Law and Morals*, 71 Harv. L. Rev. 593, 607 (1958); Lon L. Fuller, *Positivism and Fidelity to Law — A Reply to Professor Hart*, 71 Harv. L. Rev. 630, 663 (1958)).

material. Later, you can see if this text helped you answer those questions. As you think about this problem, assume that this ordinance was enacted in the same way that federal legislation is enacted (a process you will learn in Chapter 2) and that the methods for interpreting ordinances are the same as the methods for interpreting federal statutes (they mostly are).

1. Hypothetical Problem Materials

Assume the following citation for the ordinance below: 27 P.P.C. § 120(B). Note that a marked-up version of this ordinance has been provided. (A marked-up version shows amendments made during the legislative process in *italics* and deletions made during that process in ~~strike-through~~ font. After a law is codified, the italics and strike-though are removed, showing the final version.)

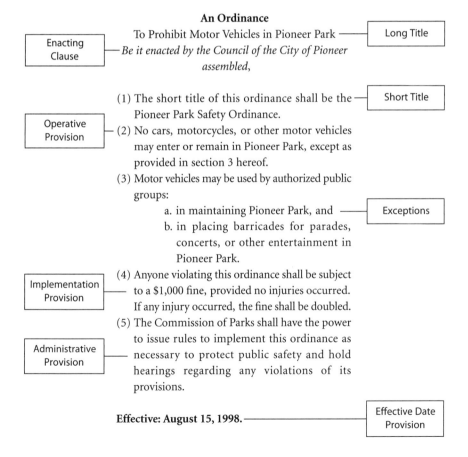

An Ordinance

To Prohibit Motor Vehicles in Pioneer Park —— Long Title

Enacting Clause —— *Be it enacted by the Council of the City of Pioneer assembled,*

(1) The short title of this ordinance shall be the —— Short Title
Pioneer Park Safety Ordinance.

Operative Provision

(2) No cars, motorcycles, or other motor vehicles may enter or remain in Pioneer Park, except as provided in section 3 hereof.

(3) Motor vehicles may be used by authorized public groups:

    a. in maintaining Pioneer Park, and —— Exceptions

    b. in placing barricades for parades, concerts, or other entertainment in Pioneer Park.

Implementation Provision

(4) Anyone violating this ordinance shall be subject to a $1,000 fine, provided no injuries occurred. If any injury occurred, the fine shall be doubled.

Administrative Provision

(5) The Commission of Parks shall have the power to issue rules to implement this ordinance as necessary to protect public safety and hold hearings regarding any violations of its provisions.

Effective: August 15, 1998. —— Effective Date Provision

Photos by Linda D. Jellum

Public Parks Committee Report: March 7, 1998

Unlike other local parks, motor vehicles are currently allowed unrestricted access to Pioneer Park. This ordinance will address the recent concerns created by a spate of accidents in Pioneer Park. In two of these accidents, a car struck a pedestrian, and another struck a bicyclist on park roads. In the third, a motorcyclist drove off road and hit a pedestrian. This ordinance, thus, bans all vehicles from entering the park, except for vehicles used in park maintenance and in setting up barricades to control crowds at park festivities and parades. All parades must be authorized before the ordinance allows the use of motor vehicles to place barricades.

The Public Parks Committee recommends that the ordinance be adopted. (Mark-up attached.)

Marked-up Version of Ordinance:

An Ordinance
To Prohibit Motor Vehicles in Pioneer Park
Be it enacted by the Council of the City of Pioneer assembled,

(1) The short title of this ordinance shall be the Pioneer Park Safety Ordinance.
(2) No cars, motorcycles, or other *motor* vehicles may enter or remain in Pioneer Park, except as provided in section 3 hereof.
(3) *Motor* vehicles may be used by authorized public groups:
    a. in maintaining Pioneer Park, *and*
    b. in placing barricades for parades, concerts, or other entertainment in Pioneer Park~~., and~~
    ~~c. Mopeds, skateboards, bicycles, and other such vehicles are exempt.~~
(4) Anyone violating this ordinance shall be subject to a $1,000 fine, provided no injuries occurred. If any injury occurred, the fine shall be doubled.
(5) The Commission of Parks shall have the power to issue rules to implement this ordinance as necessary to protect public safety and hold hearings regarding any violations of its provisions.

Effective: August 15, 1998.

Summary of the City Council Floor Debate: June 1, 1998

Debate was short and sweet. The majority of council members were in favor of the ordinance. Some discussion arose as to why bicycles, skateboards, and mopeds should be specifically exempted. For reasons that are unclear, that section was eliminated. An amendment was offered to include the word "motor" before "vehicles" in subsections (2) and (3). That amendment passed overwhelmingly. The effect on park revenue, noise, and pollution were briefly discussed. One member expressed concern that water-skiing be able to continue on Crockett Lake.

A vote was taken, with the ordinance passing.

Mayor Poordue's Signing Statement: August 14, 1998

This ordinance directly addresses the noise and pollution concerns that have increased in recent years and will make our public park much safer. The ordinance continues to allow boaters to enjoy water-skiing on the lake but bans noisy, dangerous, vehicles. I am delighted to sign it.

2. Some Hypothetical Questions

Assume that you are a prosecutor for the city, it is your first day on the job, and you have been asked to review the following cases to decide whether to prosecute or dismiss the citations. How would you resolve each of them and why? Do you need any more information to decide whether to prosecute? If so, what information do you need? Alternatively, assume you represent each of the defendants who have been charged with violating the ordinance. How do you convince the prosecutor or a judge that your client did not violate the statute?

1. An ambulance entered Pioneer Park to pick up and take to the hospital a man who had just suffered a heart attack. Did the ambulance driver violate the Pioneer Park Safety Ordinance (PPSO)? What about the man who suffered the heart attack?

2. A helicopter hovered over Pioneer Park for an hour. Was this a violation of the PPSO?
   a. What about a private jet that came in low over Pioneer Park as it approached the local airport?

3. A chapter of the local Veterans of Foreign Wars wants to put an Iraq War tank in Pioneer Park as a monument. Will this violate the PPSO?
   a. Does it matter whether the tank is operable?
   b. What if the city council had enacted another ordinance after the PPSO was enacted that assisted the VFW in the purchase of the tank on the condition that the tank be used as a monument in Pioneer Park?

4. A teenager pedaling a moped without use of its motor entered Pioneer Park. Did the teen violate the PPSO?
   a. Does it matter whether the motorized portion of the moped was operable?

5. Motorboats have been used on the lake within the park (Crockett Lake) for years. The city installed two jumps for water-skiers in 2001, and the city continues to maintain them. The jumps draw a number of water-skiers, and there is a summer competition that brings a lot of revenue into the city. Can motorboats be operated in Crockett Lake after the PPSO is enacted?
   a. If motorboats are okay, could someone use a car to bring a boat to the lake? (Assume that using some sort of land-based motorized vehicle is necessary to get a boat into the lake.)

6. Celebration Inc. scheduled a parade in Pioneer Park. The organization failed to apply for the permit required to hold the parade. Celebration Inc. used a truck to place barricades for the parade. Has Celebration Inc. violated the PPSO?

7. Citizens for a Clean Pioneer Park, a group authorized to perform maintenance work, used a riding lawnmower to cut grass in Pioneer Park. Has CCPP violated the PPSO?
   a. What if the president of CCPP drove into Pioneer Park to inspect the maintenance work performed by members of CCPP? Did the president violate the PPSO?
   b. What if Lawnworks Inc., a new group not yet authorized to perform maintenance work, used a riding lawnmower to cut grass in Pioneer Park? Have the Lawnworks employees violated the PPSO?

8. A police car entered Pioneer Park while it was chasing a car containing two people who had just robbed a bank. Have the officers violated the PPSO? What about the bank robbers?

3. More Hypothetical Questions

Assume that before you can provide the answers to the questions above to your boss, you learn that because of constant problems of interpretation that have arisen with respect to the Pioneer Park Safety Ordinance, and because the city council and the mayor cannot agree on a more detailed ordinance, the Commission of Parks (an agency) promulgated a regulation (you do not know whether formal or informal procedures were used) to interpret the PPSO regarding whether certain vehicles are permitted in Pioneer Park. Does this regulation change any of your answers to any of the questions above? Note your answers in the margins. The regulation provides as follows:

33 C.F.R. § 2300

(1) "Motor vehicle" in the PPSO means a road vehicle driven by a motor or engine used or physically capable of being used upon any public highway in this state in the transportation of persons or property, except vehicles operating wholly on fixed rails or tracks and electric trolley buses.

(2) Section 2 of the PPSO applies only to operable road vehicles (except that road vehicles may operate in Pioneer Park to the extent that they are necessary to transport boats to and from Crockett Lake).

(3) Section 3(a) of the PPSO permits vehicles to operate in Pioneer Park only if: (1) the vehicle is one that at least in part is directly used for maintenance such as lawnmowers, cherry pickers, and road surfacing equipment, or (2) the vehicle is necessary to transport materials used in maintaining Pioneer Park and is primarily used for that purpose.

(4) Section 3(b) of the PPSO permits vehicles to operate in Pioneer Park only if the vehicle is operating in conjunction with erecting barricades or other traffic control devices for a parade, concert, or other event for which the event's promoters have a valid permit.

G. Mastering This Topic

The remaining chapters of the book will include a section titled "Mastering This Topic." That section will help you learn to apply the new statutory interpretation arguments you will be learning in the context of the hypothetical presented in this chapter.

For now, remember that what you are learning is simply how to make written and oral arguments about the meaning of language. Do not ask "Can I argue X?" Ask instead, "Would a good argument to make on behalf of my client be Y?"

Checkpoints

- Interpretation is the process of determining the meaning of a written law. It is a process governed by rules of thumb, or guidelines, not law-like rules.

- Bills are written laws that have not yet been enacted.

- Acts are bills that have been enacted and become law.

- Statutes are sections of acts that have been codified into a topical code.

- Bills and acts typically have a number of components in a similar order.

- Most of the time, laws work well because they regulate behavior in ways we expect and that are familiar.

- It is the hard cases that wind up in court, and the really hard cases that end up before the Supreme Court.

Chapter 2

The Legislative Process

Roadmap

- Understand how a bill becomes a law.
- Learn about bicameralism and presentment.
- Understand the role of the various players in the legislative process.
- Learn how legislative history is created during the legislative process.
- Compare direct democracy processes.

A. Introduction to This Chapter

This chapter explains the basic process of enactment, focusing on the federal process. In addition to explaining the enactment process, this chapter also explains the roles that the various individuals in the process play, from legislators to lobbyists. Finally, as you learn how a bill becomes a law, you will discover the many ways legislative history is created. We will return to this topic in Chapter 10 when we talk about the role legislative history plays in statutory interpretation. When you finish this chapter, you should have a basic understanding of how a bill becomes law, the importance of the constitutional processes of bicameralism and presentment, and the role that politics play. Let's start with the process.

B. How a Bill Becomes a Law

This section describes the legislators and the legislative process. Further, it identifies the legislative history developed during the legislative process. The Federal Constitution governs the legislative process in a number of ways. First, Article I, Sections 2 and 3 identify the requirements for individuals to serve as legislators. Second, Article I, Section 7 contains procedural requirements for a bill to become law (think of bicameralism and presentment). Third, Article I, Section 5 authorizes each chamber of Congress to establish its own procedural rules (think of the Senate's filibuster). We will explore each topic below.

As we explore these topics, keep in mind that this section explains the *federal* legislative process rather than the state legislative process, but there are many similarities. Not all bills follow the path outlined here; for example, many legislatures have a shortcut process for non-controversial bills: the consent calendar. Bills on the consent calendar are briefly explained to the members and then voted on. They do not go through the process described below.

The chart on the following page from Linda D. Jellum & David C. Hricik, Modern Statutory Interpretation: Problems, Theories, and Lawyering Strategies 10 (2d ed. 2009), summarizes the legislative process. You may want to refer to the chart as you read the description of the legislative process below.

As you read the description below, notice that the legislative process is not an easy one. Indeed, it is much easier for a bill to fail than to be enacted. The Framers of our Constitution chose this balance because "[t]he injury which may possibly be done by defeating a few good laws, will be amply compensated by the advantage of preventing a number of bad ones." The Federalist No. 73 (Alexander Hamilton) (Clinton Rossiter ed., 1961). Difficult passage promotes consistency, avoiding dramatic changes in the law. William N. Eskridge, Jr. et al., Legislation and Statutory Interpretation 79 (2d ed. 2006). Thus, in many ways, one might say that the purpose of legislatures is to kill bills not to pass them.

1. Legislatures & Legislators

a. A Bicameral Congress

Representatives, not citizens, enact federal laws. While the Framers could have chosen a system that would have allowed citizens to enact laws directly (and some states did make that choice), the Framers opted instead for a representative system to better ensure that laws would protect all citizens, not just those in power: "Under such a regulation, it may well happen that the public voice pronounced by the representatives of the people, will be more consonant to the public good, than if pronounced by the people themselves convened for that purpose." The Federalist No. 10 (James Madison) (Clinton Rossiter ed., 1961).

Under the Articles of Confederation (the governing document that preceded the Constitution), the legislature was a unicameral body in which each state held one vote. But the larger states were not happy with the one-vote-per-state system. When the Framers drafted the United States Constitution, the legislature's

How a Bill Becomes a Law[1]

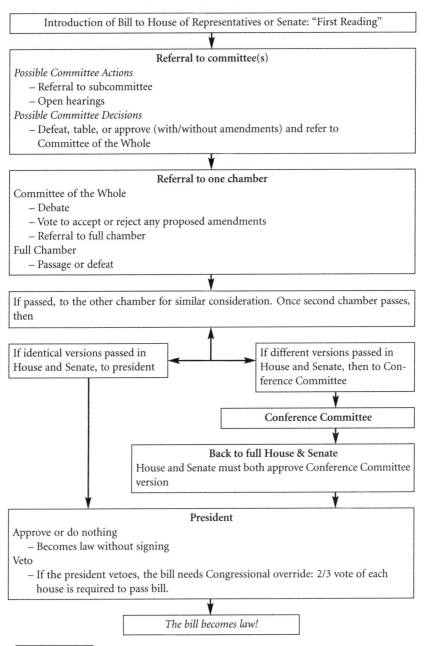

Introduction of Bill to House of Representatives or Senate: "First Reading"

Referral to committee(s)
Possible Committee Actions
　　– Referral to subcommittee
　　– Open hearings
Possible Committee Decisions
　　– Defeat, table, or approve (with/without amendments) and refer to
　　　Committee of the Whole

Referral to one chamber
Committee of the Whole
　　– Debate
　　– Vote to accept or reject any proposed amendments
　　– Referral to full chamber
Full Chamber
　　– Passage or defeat

If passed, to the other chamber for similar consideration. Once second chamber passes, then

If identical versions passed in House and Senate, to president ←→ If different versions passed in House and Senate, then to Conference Committee

Conference Committee

Back to full House & Senate
House and Senate must both approve Conference Committee version

President
Approve or do nothing
　　– Becomes law without signing
Veto
　　– If the president vetoes, the bill needs Congressional override: 2/3 vote of each
　　　house is required to pass bill.

The bill becomes law!

1. Copyright Linda D. Jellum & David Charles Hricik. Used by permission.

structure was one of the most divisive issues of the Constitutional Convention of 1787. Ultimately, the Framers selected bicameralism, a system in which there are two chambers, or houses (note the small h), which constitute one legislative body. In other words, although there is only one federal legislature, Congress, it is made up of two chambers: the House of Representatives (also called the House) and the Senate. The Framers chose bicameralism as a compromise: one chamber would represent public opinion (the House), and a second chamber would represent the views of the governments of the individual states (the Senate). State legislatures originally selected members of the Senate. Because state legislatures selected senators, they were expected to be less susceptible to mass public sentiment. Whether that was the case is unclear but irrelevant. Today, citizens of the state they represent elect senators just like representatives.

In addition to Congress, there are also fifty state legislatures, often called "general assemblies." For the most part, the state legislatures are also bicameral, but Nebraska's legislature is unicameral. While this section will focus on Congress, its legislators and legislative processes, you should learn about the process in your state. It likely differs in some way from the federal process.

Because Congress is made up of two separate chambers, each chamber has its own procedures, politics, and qualifications, all of which impact the legislative process. Because these differences affect interpretation, let's explore them for a moment.

The House is the larger of the two bodies. There are 435 representatives, and each represents a Congressional District made up of about 700,000 people. The number of representatives is currently fixed at 435 (Pub. L. No. 62–5, ch. 5, §§ 1–2, 37 Stat. 13 (1911)). Each state is represented proportionally in the House based on that state's population. California has the most representatives: fifty-three, but every state has at least one representative. Currently, seven states have only one: Delaware, Montana, North Dakota, Vermont, South Dakota, Alaska, and Wyoming. The District of Columbia, Puerto Rico, and the U.S.'s four other island territories — American Samoa, Guam, the Northern Mariana Islands, and the U.S. Virgin Islands — each sends a non-voting delegate to the House. Members of the House serve two-year terms; they are constantly running for reelection.

The Senate is the smaller of the two bodies. There are 100 senators; two senators for every state, both of whom represent the entire state. The Senate is sometimes thought to be more deliberative than the House because the Senate has fewer members. Also, senators serve a larger constituency — constituents are residents of the state that elected the individual — with many varied interests. Senators serve six-year terms; thus, they are more protected from public opinion than members of the House. Both of these factors—size and term length—encourage collegiality and discourage partisanship within the Senate. In contrast, representatives are elected from smaller (approximately 700,000 residents) and more homogenous districts than senators. The House is generally the more partisan chamber.

> Although reelection and financial considerations are important to lawmakers, most are also motivated by the desire for status and reputation and the objective of affecting policy and the national agenda in ways consistent with their ideological commitments. Empirical studies have found that a legislator's voting behavior is most related to her constituents' interests.

Eskridge et al., Legislation And Statutory Interpretation, supra, at 98 (citations omitted).

i. Legislator Qualifications

Not everyone can be a legislator. The Constitution requires that senators be thirty years old, citizens of the United States for at least nine years, and "[i]nhabitant[s]" of the state from which elected. U.S. Const. art. 1., § 3. Similarly, representatives must be twenty-five years old, citizens of the United States for at least seven years, and "[i]nhabitant[s]" of the state from which elected. U.S. Const. art. I., § 2. There is no requirement that representatives actually live in the district they represent. These minimal requirements cannot be augmented. *Powell v. McCormack*, 395 U.S. 486, 550 (1969) (rejecting Congress's attempt to refuse to seat a representative who met these qualifications but was not trustworthy). Neither Congress nor the states can alter or add to these constitutional requirements. *U.S. Term Limits, Inc. v. Thornton*, 514 U.S. 779, 837 (1995) (holding term limits imposed by many states on federal representatives in the 1990s to be unconstitutional).

Many things, including reelection, motivate legislators to vote in particular ways. Every member of Congress is up for reelection every two years (always in an even-numbered year). In contrast, senators are elected for six-year, staggered terms. Unlike the House, where every representative is up for re-election simultaneously, only one-third of senators are up for reelection at any one time. Because a senator's tenure in office is longer than a representative's tenure in the House, representatives may be more risk averse when it comes to passing new legislation than senators. Moreover, because it is considered more prestigious to be a senator, representatives from the House regularly want to "move up" to the Senate. The desire to move up may affect a representative's willingness to support unpopular legislation. Also, regular turnover negatively impacts the institutional memory of the House.

ii. Leadership

Politics matter, particularly in the House. Pursuant to Article I, Section 7, approval of both chambers is required for legislation to become law. Indeed, the legislative veto, in which one chamber could unilaterally vacate decisions of the executive, was held to be unconstitutional because such a process allowed Congress to act without following the "single, finely wrought and exhaustively considered procedures of Article I." *INS v. Chadha*, 462 U.S. 919, 951 (1983).

In the House, the party with the most seats, the majority party, has the political power to get things done. The leader in the House is the Speaker of the House, whom the members elect. House rules and customs, not the Constitution, identify the powers and duties of the speaker. Thus, these powers and duties may change over time as one party attempts to expand or reign in the speaker's political power, which can be tremendous. The speaker has many powers that affect the legislative process. For example, the speaker has the power to control the order in which members of the House speak during debate on a bill. No representative may speak or bring a motion until the speaker permits the action. This rule gives the speaker tremendous power to control the course of the debate. Additionally, the speaker rules on representatives' objections arguing that a rule has been breached (called points of order), but the speaker's decision is subject to appeal, which the whole House resolves. Further, the speaker is the chair of its party's Steering Committee, which chooses the chair of the other standing committees; these standing committees are responsible for doing the preliminary work on all bills and, thus, hold tremendous power. The speaker also decides which committee should consider bills, appoints members of the Rules Committee (which determines the rules governing debate on proposed bills), and appoints members to conference committees (which resolve any differences in the bills the House and Senate pass). All in all, the speaker has enormous political power.

After the speaker, the majority party leader, who is also elected by his or her party, has the most political power. The majority leader decides which legislation members of that party should support and which legislation the members should oppose. There is also a minority party leader who develops the minority position and negotiates with the majority party. Not surprisingly, the minority party leader holds much less political power. Both parties also elect "whips," who try to ensure that the party's members vote as the party leadership desires. Representatives generally vote as the leadership directs because otherwise they may be threatened with reduced support for reelection campaigns, pet legislation, and committee chair positions.

Leadership is slightly different in the Senate. Instead of a speaker, the vice president of the United States serves as the presiding officer, or president, of the Senate. Because the vice president does not always attend legislative sessions, the duty of presiding often falls to the president *pro tempore*, usually the most senior senator in the majority party, who may choose to delegate this task to a junior senator. Like the House, the Senate has both majority and minority party leaders and whips.

The vice president is not a senator and does not regularly vote. But in the case of a tie, the vice president may cast the tie-breaking vote. For example, John Adams, the first Vice President and President of the Senate cast tie-breaking votes twenty-nine times (more than any other vice president). He voted to protect the executive's sole authority to remove appointees, and he influenced the location of the national capital.

b. The Important Role of Committees

Both the House and Senate operate via committee and subcommittee, each of which is responsible for a particular jurisdiction or subject area. House Rule X, clause 1 and Senate Rule XXV, clause 1 specify the permanent standing committees in the chambers. All legislators serve on one or more committees. Because there are so many of them, representatives often specialize. In contrast, because of the Senate's small size, its members do not specialize the same way. Commonly, committees are broken into subcommittees, which do the messy work: hold hearings, take testimony, draft and amend bill language, and recommend whether to pass a bill on to the full committee. Not all committees have subcommittees.

While not all bills reach the floor for vote, all bills that do reach the floor are first screened by the appropriate committee. While legislators are free to sponsor a bill, any committee might examine and advocate for that bill once it reaches the floor; in reality, legislators can most effectively influence the passage of bills while they are before the committee of which the legislators are members. Moreover, legislators will be most successful when chairing that committee or, at least, when having a majority of the committee members in their party. Because the party in political power selects the chair, it is difficult for the party not in power to enact legislation. Party loyalty is strong. Legislators who adhere to the party line are rewarded while those who stray are penalized. PROFILES IN COURAGE, by John F. Kennedy, is a Pulitzer Prize-winning biography that details the bravery and integrity of eight United States Senators who suffered because of their decision to cross party lines. Hence, politics greatly influence bill passage.

c. Staffers & Lobbyists

It is not just legislators who make up Congress. Staff members surround each chamber. These staff members may also influence the legislative process; they may draft committee reports, write amendments to bills, and provide other relevant information.

Additionally, lobbyists, people who are generally paid to represent a particular point of view for a specific industry or organization, may also influence the legislative process. Interestingly, "[t]he term 'lobbying' arose from the practice of people waiting in the legislature's lobby to intercept legislators to attempt to win them over to a particular position." RONALD BENTON BROWN & SHARON JACOBS BROWN, STATUTORY INTERPRETATION: THE SEARCH FOR LEGISLATIVE INTENT 130–31 (2002). Often, lobbyists draft bills, present information during hearings, craft amendments, advocate for passage, and argue against passage. These non-legislators also affect legislation. Just how much of a role lobbyists should have is the subject of some debate. Lobbyists are paid to further the interest of those who hire them, not the public.

Lobbyists may play a role in enactment of a bill. For example, lobbyists for the biotechnology industry influenced the legislative record of the historic House debate on the Affordable Care Act (Obamacare). The *New York Times* obtained emails showing that the lobbyists drafted one statement for Democrats and another for Republicans. These remarks were then printed in the extension of remarks section of the Congressional Record under the names of forty-two different members of Congress: twenty-two Republicans and twenty Democrats.

While it is not unusual for members of Congress to submit revised or extended statements for publication in the Congressional Record after the debate, it is unusual that so many of the statements matched word for word. It is even more unusual to find clear evidence that the statements originated with lobbyists. When asked in an interview about remarks added under his name, Representative William Pascrell Jr., a Democrat of New Jersey, said: "I regret that the language was the same. I did not know it was." He said his statement came from staff members, and he "did not know where they got the information from."[2]

Lobbying is not necessarily pernicious. Lobbying is simply providing information to influence a lawmaker's decision. If you have written your congress member to advocate a position, you have lobbied. But *lobbyists* are paid to navigate the hurdles in the legislative process; they are professionals hired to represent industries or companies to influence legislation and policy. "Lobbyists inform lawmakers about constituent preferences and interests; they inform legislators about the effects of particular policies and problems that demand government solutions; they inform lawmakers about the preference of other lawmakers so that proponents of policy change can successfully negotiate the vetogates of Congress; and they inform the public about lawmakers' views and efforts regarding policies." ESKRIDGE ET AL., LEGISLATION AND STATUTORY INTERPRETATION, *supra,* at 197.

As lobbying has increased exponentially, it is viewed with more skepticism. Today, lobbyists must register with Congress and regularly file reports disclosing the identity of their clients, the issues for which they lobbied, and the amount of money they received for all lobbying efforts. 2 U.S.C. § 1603–04.

d. Office of Legislative Counsel

There is another important player in the legislative process. Legislators often seek help with the drafting and enacting process from nonpartisan lawyers who work for either the Senate or House Legislative Counsel's office.

Congress established the Legislative Drafting Service in 1918, then renamed it the Office of Legislative Counsel in 1924 (to avoid confusion with the Legislative Reference Service of the Library of Congress). Until 1970, this office included two independent arms, one under the Senate's control and one under the House's control.

In 1970, Congress gave the House Office of Legislative Counsel (HLC) its own legislative charter; thus, separating the two arms. The Senate Office of Legal Counsel (SLC) continues to operate under the 1918 Act. Notably, these offices are the only offices in Congress dedicated exclusively to drafting legislation, and they draft the majority of Congress's legislative product.

---

2. For the full story, see Robert Pear, *In House, Many Spoke with One Voice: Lobbists'*, N.Y. Times, Nov. 14, 2009, http://www.nytimes.com/2009/11/15/us/politics/15health.html?pagewanted=1&_r=2&hp&adxnnl=1&adxnnlx=1356177854-OfyR2geHJXzm3KGEGksiiA.

Lawyers in both offices aid the members of their respective chambers with various activities, such as drafting bills, resolutions, and amendments. Members of the offices also may draft conference committee reports; provide advice on process, form, procedure; and offer constitutional, legal, and technical guidance. The lawyers are impartial regarding issues of legislative policy and have an attorney-client relationship with respect to any communications with senators, representatives, or their staff members. Both offices have legislative drafting manuals.[3]

2. The Constitutionally Prescribed Process

a. Congress's Role — Bicameral Passage

Now that you understand the organizations and the players within each organization, let's turn to the legislative process. You must understand the legislative process to understand the role legislative history plays in that process and, thus, understand how to use legislative history to interpret statutes. Keep in mind that behind the neat progression described below is an "often-chaotic process of lobbying by interest groups and of assessments by legislators of the public interest and of their own, sometimes less public-regarding needs (such as reelection)." ESKRIDGE ET AL., LEGISLATION AND STATUTORY INTERPRETATION, *supra*, at 3.

Congress meets twice annually in "sessions." This word can be confusing because in addition to Congress's annual series of meetings being called a session, a meeting of the Senate or House of Representatives may be called a session. Additionally, the House and Senate are said to be in session on any particular day they meet. Congress generally has two sessions per year, although it is constitutionally mandated to assemble only once a year. U.S. CONST. art. I., § 4, cl. 2 ("The Congress shall assemble at least once in every Year, and such Meeting shall be on the first Monday in December, unless they shall by Law appoint a different Day."). Occasionally, Congress meets in an extra or special session.

Let's assume someone wants a bill passed in one of these sessions. Generally, a bill can originate in either chamber, unless it is a tax or appropriations bill, both of which must originate in the House. The first step in the process is for

---

3. The SLC's manual can be found here: https://law.yale.edu/system/files/documents/ pdf/Faculty/SenateOfficeoftheLegislativeCounsel_LegislativeDraftingManual%281997%29.pdf. The HLC's manual can be found here: https://legcounsel.house.gov/HOLC/ Drafting_Legislation/draftstyle.pdf.

one or more members of Congress to introduce, or sponsor, a bill because only a member of Congress can sponsor legislation. However, members of Congress regularly sponsor bills on behalf of their constituents or lobbyists. Often, the lobbyists write the initial draft of the bill and then submit the draft to a legislator for introduction.

Proposed legislation is generally introduced as a bill, but some legislation is introduced as a joint resolution. For our purposes, there is little practical difference between the two. Concurrent resolutions, which both chambers pass, and simple resolutions, which only one chamber passes, are not used for this purpose because they do not have the force of law. Instead, concurrent and simple resolutions regulate procedure or simply express Congress's opinion on a relevant issue.

As noted above, one or more legislators must sponsor the bill. The main sponsor is responsible for moving the bill through the legislative process; hence, choosing sponsors can be critical. The chair of the relevant committee is often a good first choice because of the power that the chair wields in getting legislation approved in committee. Having co-sponsors with varied political and geographical interests can also help ensure passage; bi-partisan bills are more likely to be enacted.

All bills go through several steps within each chamber. The first step is generally committee consideration. After a bill is introduced, the Speaker of the House or the presiding officer of the Senate (depending on where the bill originated) will refer the bill to the appropriate standing (meaning existing) committee or committees. Having the speaker or presiding member of the Senate refer one's bill to a supportive committee is helpful.

There are twenty standing committees in the House and sixteen in the Senate, each of which has a specified jurisdiction, such as foreign relations or finance. Committees have a tremendous impact on the future of a bill. Only one out of every ten bills referred to committee becomes law. ESKRIDGE ET AL., LEGISLATION AND STATUTORY INTERPRETATION, *supra,* at 72 (3d ed. 2001) (citing BURDETT LOOMIS, THE CONTEMPORARY CONGRESS 156 (1996)).

Standing committees consider, amend, reject, and report bills that come within their jurisdiction to the full chamber. A bill may fall within the jurisdiction of more than one standing committee. Committees have extensive power over bills; most importantly, committees may block bills from ever reaching the floor of the chamber. To accomplish all of their objectives, standing committees may hold hearings, subpoena witnesses, and collect evidence. In addition to their legislative responsibilities, standing committees also oversee divisions of the executive branch.

Each committee and subcommittee has one chair and one ranking member; the chair is from the majority party, while the ranking member is from the minority party. The chair has extensive power over bills because the chair controls the committee's agenda. The chair decides whether to add the bill to the committee's agenda or to refer the bill to subcommittee. Chairs can prevent a committee from considering a bill at all. The chair also decides whether to hold public hearings on the bill. If public hearings are to be held, notice of the time and location of the meeting is published. Chairs are important positions that used to be awarded based on seniority. Today, the relevant steering committee selects chairs, so chairs are often awarded to members who faithfully follow the party direction.

Assuming the chair schedules meetings, interested lobbyists and members of the public may attend those meetings; however, their testimony will be severely limited. After hearings are held, meetings take place, and amendments are or are not made, the committee has a number of choices: the committee can vote to table the bill, amend (or "mark-up" the bill), not report the bill, or approve the bill and forward it to the full chamber. A decision not to report the bill is equivalent to killing the bill. If the bill is approved and forwarded to the full chamber, staff members prepare a committee report, describing the details of the committee's work and recommendations. This committee report accompanies the bill to the floor; sometimes, it is the only part of the proposed legislation the voting members read, including the bill itself! Assuming the bill is forwarded to the full chamber, the legislative process continues.

The committee process is basically identical in both houses. From here on, however, the processes differ somewhat.

The Senate and House vary somewhat in scheduling bills for a full chamber vote. In the House, the chair of the committee that is forwarding the bill to the full House must first ask the House Rules Committee to schedule the bill for floor consideration. The Rules Committee plays a strong role in the passage of a proposed bill because the Rules Committee passes the rules governing debate on each bill, such as the time allowed for debate, how that time is allocated to each side, and the scope of possible amendments. Regarding amendments, the Rules Committee can recommend "closed rule" — allowing no amendments to the bill — "modified closed rule" — allowing limited amendments — or "open rule" — allowing all germane amendments. The Rules Committee can recommend that consideration of a bill be expedited.

The members of the House first vote on and debate the bill's rule. If the rule is accepted, the House dissolves into the Committee of the Whole. The Committee of the Whole is not a committee in the usual sense. Rather, it is simply a committee consisting of all 435 members of the House. The Committee of the Whole was developed to expedite House action. It is the largest House committee and offers a forum for debating, considering, and perfecting proposed legislation.

The Committee of the Whole follows simplified procedures to debate a bill. The Committee of the Whole debates the bill for an amount of time the House Rules Committee previously determined would be allowed, usually one to several hours. Assuming amendments are allowed, they may only be offered during this time. Further, debate and amendments (if allowed) must be germane to the bill being considered. Debate on proposed amendments is subject to the "five-minute rule," a House rule that in theory limits debate for and against an amendment offered in the Committee of the Whole to ten minutes: five minutes in support and five minutes in opposition. The Committee of the Whole may consider bills and amend them, *but it cannot pass a bill*. Instead, when the Committee of the Whole is done debating and amending a bill, "the committee rises" and reports its recommendations on the bill to the full House. Votes of the Committee of the Whole are not recorded; thus, legislators may feel freer to vote as they wish without fearing political pressure or reprisal.

Assuming the bill is forwarded to the full House (the same individuals who just debated the bill as the Committee of the Whole), more debate may ensue. Eventually, debate concludes, and the House votes on the bill or recommits (refers) the bill back to the legislative committee from which it was reported. Referral back to committee generally means the bill dies. Voting of the full House usually takes fifteen minutes, but this time may be extended if the leadership needs time to "whip" its members into shape. For example, the 2003 vote on the Prescription Drug Benefit bill remained open for three hours while the leadership worked to find the necessary votes for passage. Unlike votes in the Committee of the Whole, votes in the full House are recorded; thus, representatives may feel somewhat less free to vote against the party line.

Ties signal defeat for the bill; unlike the Senate, in which the vice president breaks ties, there is no one to cast a tie-breaking vote in the House.

In the Senate, a different process ensues. First, the Senate does not have a rules committee. Rather, senate rules, customs, and traditions govern its procedure. Moreover, the members of the Senate often waive rules by unanimous consent. Party leaders typically try to negotiate unanimous consent agreements before a bill reaches the floor because any senator may block such an agreement. Thus, while the majority party still has more power in the Senate than the minority party, a single senator theoretically can kill a bill singlehandedly; although, such objections are uncommon.

Also, unlike the House, there is no committee of the whole in the Senate; rather, the full Senate debates and amends the bill on the floor. Like representatives, senators may speak during floor debates only when the presiding officer permits. But unlike the Speaker of the House, the presiding officer of the Senate is required to recognize the first senator who rises to speak and, thus, has little control over the course of the debate. Moreover, unlike members of the House, senators may offer to amend bills at any time during floor debate.

Unlike the House, there is no germaneness rule in the Senate. Sometimes senators offer amendments simply to try to kill a bill. For example, Representative Judge Howard W. Smith offered an amendment to Title VII, in part, to kill the bill. His amendment added sex to the topics protected from employment discrimination. He added this amendment, in part, due to his own commitment to equal opportunities for women but, also, because he believed that the bill would then become so controversial that it would fail. Indeed, his amendment was welcomed with laughter from his fellow representatives. Despite the laughter, the amendment did not have the effect he was after; the bill passed the House with the amendment intact (with a vote of 168-133).

There are few restrictions on what senators may say during debate. Moreover, there are no time limits: senators may speak for as long as they please. The Senate may adopt time limits by a unanimous consent agreement, but unlimited debate is generally protected. The Senate rules allow unlimited debate of issues before the vote. So, to defeat bills and motions, senators may filibuster. Filibusters are governed by Senate customs. They are not part of the constitutional process. A filibuster is a prolonged speech offered by a senator as a delaying tactic to obstruct the legislative progress; senators may use long speeches, dilatory motions, or extensive amendments to prolong debate indefinitely.

For instance, Senator Strom Thurmond delivered one of the longest filibuster speeches in the history of the Senate when he spoke for more than twenty-four hours in an unsuccessful attempt to block passage of the Civil Rights Act of 1957. More recently, Senator Rand Paul spoke for thirteen hours to contest what he believed was the executive's policy on the use of drones against American citizens on American soil. Similarly, in the famous movie "Mr. Smith Goes to Washington," Jimmy Stewart stood on the floor of the Senate reciting the Declaration of Independence for twenty-three hours to prevent the Senate from voting on a proposed bill. Waiting for the senator to reach physical exhaustion is one of the two ways to break a filibuster. More commonly today, senators do not actually physically prevent voting; a threat is sufficient.

The primary way to defeat a filibuster is *cloture*. Senate Rule XXII, clause 2 currently provides that cloture can be invoked with the vote of sixty of the 100 senators. Because bipartisan support is almost always necessary to obtain cloture, it is rarely invoked. Indeed, since 1917, when the procedure was added to the Senate rules, cloture has been invoked successfully only twice, once during the enactment of the Civil Rights Act. If cloture is invoked, Senate debate does not end immediately; instead, further debate is limited to thirty additional hours.

The filibuster was a powerful tool that both parties protected for years. That is no longer true. During the first two years of President Obama's term, Congress was in democratic hands. Republicans were slow to approve democratic nominations to the executive and judiciary. In response, in November 2013, Senate Democrats changed the Senate rules to prevent the minority from using the filibuster for all executive branch nominations and federal judicial appointments, other than nominations to the Supreme Court. In April 2017, Senate Republicans eliminated the filibuster exception for Supreme Court nominees when Neil Gorsuch's nomination failed to overcome cloture. As of June 2018, cloture is still required to end filibusters for legislation.

Consider whether it makes any sense for Senators to eliminate the filibuster for judicial nominations, which are lifetime appointments, while maintaining it for legislation, which can be amended or eliminated at any time. Given that the process is not constitutionally mandated, perhaps the filibuster is no longer relevant.

Assuming no filibuster is offered while a bill is being considered, the members of the Senate eventually vote on the bill or send it back to committee. Senate votes are recorded. At that time, the Senate process is temporarily complete.

Once the Senate or House passes a bill, it is less than halfway towards passage because both chambers must pass the identical version of the bill and the president must approve it or a veto must be overridden. Once the first chamber passes a bill, it is *engrossed* and passed to the other chamber. The term "engrossed" is left over from a time when important documents, such as statutes, were copied onto parchment paper. Today, bills are simply printed with a laser printer, so the term no longer fits. After receiving the engrossed bill, the second chamber must pass it in identical form for it to become law; no amendments or changes are allowed. If the second chamber passes the engrossed bill, the bill returns to the first chamber where it is then *enrolled*, signed, and transmitted to the president for approval or veto.

More commonly, the second chamber will pass the same bill with an amendment representing its work product. The second chamber then sends a message to the first chamber asking the first chamber to concur with the amendment. The first chamber may agree with the amendment, in which case the bill is then enrolled.

Alternatively, the first chamber may disagree with the amendment. Because the two chambers must pass identical bills, the chambers must reconcile the differences. They can do so in two ways. The chambers can try to pass the same bill by offering amendments back and forth each time changes are made. As you can imagine, this process is cumbersome.

Alternatively, the first chamber can request a conference committee meeting. A conference committee is an ad hoc committee of select senators and representatives. Generally, the conference committee is made up of three to five members of each chamber (although there is no limit), usually the senior members of the standing committees of each chamber that originally considered the legislation. Members of the minority party must also be included. The committee meets, discusses the differences in the bills, resolves those differences, recommends amending language, and writes a report explaining its work. While the conference committee is not supposed to substantially alter the bill language, in many cases conference committees have departed significantly from both the House and Senate versions.

Conference committees can be extremely contentious, particularly when different parties control the chambers. This point may explain why the use of conference committees has declined in recent years. For example, the 104th Congress (1995–96) produced sixty-seven conference reports. In contrast, the 113th Congress (2013–14) produced only three, while the 114th Congress (2015–16) produced eight.

Once the conference committee reaches a compromise, it submits the amended bill along with its explanation in a conference committee report to both chambers. (Conference committee reports are generally issued as House Reports, meaning their citations will be H. Rpts.) At this point, the bill is not open to further amendments. While the first chamber is considering the compromise bill, a member may move to recommit it to the conference committee. However, once the first chamber passes the conference bill, the conference committee is dissolved so that members in the second chamber can no longer recommit the bill to conference. When both chambers pass the conference bill, it is sent to the president for approval.

We will discuss the president's role below, but there is one last important point regarding enrolled bills. Once the president signs an enrolled bill, courts presume conclusively that the legislature validly adopted the bill. This presumption is known as the *enrolled bill rule*. Some states follow the *journal entry rule* instead, which allows a court to determine whether constitutional requirements were met solely by looking at the journal entry. For example, under the journal entry rule, a judge could determine whether identical bills were passed, whether there were sufficient affirmative votes to override a veto, and whether a bill was subject to three readings (a holdover procedure from when some legislators were illiterate). Under the enrolled bill rule, a judge could not determine whether these procedures were actually followed.

However, because there is such a strong presumption that legislative acts are valid, the differences in the two rules are minor. Generally, under either rule, courts will not entertain challenges to the legislative process of a particular bill. This choice (1) respects the division of labor among the branches by not allowing the judiciary to police the legislature's activity, (2) promotes stability by allowing citizens to assume that filed acts are law, and (3) promotes harmony by keeping the legislative and judicial functions separate. Arguably, a legislature could choose to ignore the constitutionally required process, knowing its choice will not be subject to judicial review, but legislatures rarely do so.

Now, let's talk about the president's role.

b. The President's Role—Presentment & Signing

The final step in the legislative process is the president's approval or veto of the enrolled bill. If the president signs the bill, it becomes law. Once signed, the secretary of state files the *act* (it is no longer a bill).

If the president vetoes the bill, returning it to Congress with objections, the bill only becomes law if two-thirds of the members of each chamber vote to override the president's veto. Finally, if the president chooses not to act—neither signing nor vetoing the bill—the bill automatically becomes law after ten days (excluding Sundays). U.S. Const. art. 1, § 7. However, if Congress adjourns during this ten-day period, the bill lapses and does not become law. This process is known as a pocket veto. Because Congress adjourned, it could not override the president's veto.

If vetoed, the bill is returned to the legislature, often with a veto message. The legislature may override the president's veto only with a favorable, two-thirds vote from each chamber. Overrides are rare: less than seven percent of vetoes are successfully overridden. Eskridge et al., Legislation and Statutory Interpretation, *supra*, at 76. Indeed, as of June 2018, there have been 2,572 vetoes (both regular and pocket) with 110 overrides (four percent). Interestingly, Franklin Roosevelt had the most vetoes (635); Harry Truman was second (250). In contrast, recent presidents veto more rarely. For example, President George W. Bush vetoed ten bills, none by pocket veto; President Obama vetoed twelve bills, none by pocket veto; and President Trump has so far vetoed none.

The president must veto a bill in its entirety; the line item veto was held to be unconstitutional. *Clinton v. City of New York*, 524 U.S. 417 (1998) (finding the line item veto for appropriations bills unconstitutional). But note that forty-three states' constitutions allow governors the right to veto "items" in appropriations bills; "items" has been defined differently by each of the state courts. ESKRIDGE ET AL., LEGISLATION AND STATUTORY INTERPRETATION, *supra,* at 204.

As noted above, the president may include a veto message when vetoing a bill. A president may also sign a bill and include a signing statement. Initially, signing statements were meant to give notice of the way the president intended to implement a law. President James Monroe was the first to issue a signing statement, in which he argued that the president, not Congress, held the constitutional power to appoint military officers. His signing statement was non-controversial, which is why many believe that President Andrew Jackson, whose signing statement sparked the first controversy, was the first president to issue such a statement.

More recently, presidents have issued signing statements for other purposes. Presidents use signing statements to show disagreement with a particular bill, to narrow its effect, and to indicate how the president intends to narrow the implementation of the law. Used in this way, signing statements appear to take interpretive power away from the courts.

Indeed, under the direction of Attorney General Edwin Meese, President Ronald Reagan decided that these statements could be used to enhance the executive's influence over statutory interpretation. While working as an assistant attorney general for the Department of Justice under Meese, Samuel Alito, now Justice Alito, authored a memorandum entitled *"Using Presidential Signing Statement to Make Fuller Use of the President's Constitutionally Assigned Role in the Process of Enacting Law."*[4] In the memo, Alito argued that because bills require presidential approval in addition to approval by both chambers to become law, "it seems to follow that the President's understanding of the bill should be just as important as that of Congress." *Id.* Alito suggested that signing statements should be used to "increase the power of the Executive to shape the law" and, further, "help curb some of the prevalent abuses of legislative history." *Id.* Meese then convinced West Publishing Company to include signing statements in the legislative histories section of the *United States Code Congressional and Administrative News* (USCCAN), stating that inclusion would assist courts in the future to determine what the statute actually means. Since 1986, signing statements have been published in USCCAN.

---

4. You can find the memo here: http://www.archives .gov/news/samuel-alito/accession-060-89-269/Acc060-89-269-box6-SG-LSWG-AlitotoLSWG-Feb1986.pdf.

The use of signing statements is on the rise. In 2012, the Congressional Research Service counted the percentage of signing statements that contained "objections" to provisions of a bill being signed into law and concluded as follows:

> While the history of presidential issuance of signing statements dates to the early 19th century, the practice has become the source of significant controversy in the modern era as Presidents have increasingly employed the statements to assert constitutional and legal objections to congressional enactments. President Reagan initiated this practice in earnest, transforming the signing statement into a mechanism for the assertion of presidential authority and intent. President Reagan issued 250 signing statements, 86 of which (34%) contained provisions objecting to one or more of the statutory provisions signed into law. President George H. W. Bush continued this practice, issuing 228 signing statements, 107 of which (47%) raised objections. President Clinton's conception of presidential power proved to be largely consonant with that of the preceding two administrations. In turn, President Clinton made aggressive use of the signing statement, issuing 381 statements, 70 of which (18%) raised constitutional or legal objections. President George W. Bush has continued this practice, issuing 152 signing statements, 118 of which (78%) contain some type of challenge or objection. The significant rise in the proportion of constitutional objections made by President George W. Bush was compounded by the fact that his statements were typified by multiple objections, resulting in more than 1,000 challenges to distinct provisions of law. Although President Barack Obama has continued to use presidential signing statements, the Obama Administration has used the interpretive tools with less frequency than previous administrations — issuing 20 signing statements, of which 10 (50%) contain constitutional challenges to an enacted statutory provision.

Todd Garvey, Cong. Research Serv., RL33667, Presidential Signing Statements: Constitutional and Institutional Implications summary (2012).

As can be seen from this survey, all modern presidents use signing statements in this way; however, former President George W. Bush dramatically and controversially increased their use. His full-scale embrace of Alito's suggestion of how to use these statements garnered controversy. For example, Bush used

the statement to change sweeping mandatory provisions of the National Defense
Authorization Act into advisory provisions:

**President Bush's signing statement for H.R. 4986,
the National Defense Authorization Act
for Fiscal Year 2008**

Today, I have signed into law H.R. 4986, the National Defense Authorization
Act for Fiscal Year 2008. The Act authorizes funding for the defense of the
United States and its interests abroad, for military construction, and for
national security-related energy programs.

Provisions of the Act, including sections 841, 846, 1079, and 1222, purport
to impose requirements that could inhibit the President's ability to carry out
his constitutional obligations to take care that the laws be faithfully executed,
to protect national security, to supervise the executive branch, and to execute
his authority as Commander in Chief. The executive branch shall construe
such provisions in a manner consistent with the constitutional authority of
the President.

GEORGE W. BUSH
THE WHITE HOUSE,
January 28, 2008.

Rather than vetoing bills, President Bush used signing statements to limit
their reach; some argue that President Bush used signing statements much like
a line-item veto (to limit the sections of an act he did not like). Remember,
the Supreme Court held that the line-item veto violates separation of powers.

As noted above, President Obama acted somewhat more moderately. While
a presidential candidate, President Obama said that he thought signing
statements were legitimate when used with "restraint" — for instance, to clarify
how an ambiguous law should be interpreted. During his presidency, he issued
thirty-seven signing statements. He signed these statements when he believed
a bill would impact his constitutional powers. For example, citing his role as
commander-in-chief, he objected (1) to a provision that required thirty days'
advance notice to Congress before military exercises costing more than $100,000,
and (2) to a provision that forbade him from putting American forces under
a foreign commander as part of a United Nations' peacekeeping mission unless

another military official signed off. Below is an excerpt from a lengthy and somewhat indignant signing statement from President Obama.

President Obama's signing statement on H.R. 1540

Today I have signed into law H.R. 1540, the "National Defense Authorization Act for Fiscal Year 2012." ...

The fact that I support this bill as a whole does not mean I agree with everything in it. In particular, I have signed this bill despite having serious reservations with certain provisions that regulate the detention, interrogation, and prosecution of suspected terrorists. Over the last several years, my Administration has developed an effective, sustainable framework for the detention, interrogation and trial of suspected terrorists that allows us to maximize both our ability to collect intelligence and to incapacitate dangerous individuals in rapidly developing situations, and the results we have achieved are undeniable. Our success against al-Qa'ida and its affiliates and adherents has derived in significant measure from providing our counterterrorism professionals with the clarity and flexibility they need to adapt to changing circumstances and to utilize whichever authorities best protect the American people, and our accomplishments have respected the values that make our country an example for the world.

Against that record of success, some in Congress continue to insist upon restricting the options available to our counterterrorism professionals and interfering with the very operations that have kept us safe. My Administration has consistently opposed such measures. Ultimately, I decided to sign this bill not only because of the critically important services it provides for our forces and their families and the national security programs it authorizes, but also because the Congress revised provisions that otherwise would have jeopardized the safety, security, and liberty of the American people. Moving forward, my Administration will interpret and implement the provisions described below in a manner that best preserves the flexibility on which our safety depends and upholds the values on which this country was founded....

BARACK OBAMA
THE WHITE HOUSE,
December 31, 2011

There is no federal constitutional provision, statute, or case that explicitly permits or prohibits signing statements or veto messages. Chapter 10 discusses the role these statements play in interpretation. For now, simply be aware that they exist as part of the legislative process.

C. The Single Subject Rule

We explored a number of federal procedural rules in the last section. Here, we explore an important procedural rule in the states: the *single subject rule*. Unlike the Federal Constitution, nearly all state constitutions require bills to include just one subject. This requirement is known as the single subject rule. For example, the Illinois Constitution provides, "Bills, except bills for appropriations and for the codification, revision or rearrangement of law, shall be confined to one subject." ILL. CONST. art. IV, § 8(d). Similarly, Pennsylvania's Constitution provides, "No bill shall be passed containing more than one subject, which shall be clearly expressed in its title, except a general appropriation bill or a bill codifying or compiling the law or a part thereof." PA. CONST. art. III, § 3. Additionally, many state constitutions require a bill's title to identify the subject of the bill. To illustrate, Florida's Constitution provides, "Every law shall embrace but one subject and matter properly connected therewith, and the subject shall be briefly expressed in the title." FLA. CONST. art. III, § 6. Georgia's Constitution is similar: bills shall not "refer[] to more than one subject matter or contain[] matter different from what is expressed in the title thereof." GA. CONST. art. III, § V, ¶ III. The term "subject," in this context, is liberally construed; the subject may be very broad. "Nonetheless, the matters included in the enactment must have a natural and logical connection." *Johnson v. Edgar*, 680 N.E.2d 1372, 1379 (Ill. 1997).

The single subject rule serves two functions: (1) to prevent lawmakers from burying a controversial subject in an otherwise popular bill, and (2) to increase the likelihood that legislators will know what they are voting for or against. Thus, the rule facilitates orderly legislative procedure and ensures that the legislature addresses the difficult decisions it faces directly while subject to public scrutiny and prevents the passing of unpopular measures on the backs of popular ones.

While it is not common for state statutes to be struck down for violating the single subject rule, it does happen. For example, the Illinois Supreme Court invalidated a bill because it violated the single subject rule. *Johnson*, 680 N.E.2d at 516–17 ("While the length of a bill is not determinative of its compliance with the single subject rule, the variety of its contents certainly is.").

Because courts do not like the one subject rule, they generally interpret a single subject broadly, in part, to defer to the legislature. For example, in *Pennsylvanians Against Gambling Expansion Fund, Inc. v. Commonwealth*, 877 A.2d 383 (Pa. 2005), the court refused a single-subject challenge to a bill titled "regulation of gaming" even though the bill also established subject matter jurisdiction in the state's supreme court for the issuance of gaming licenses, among other things. *Id.* at 394–97.

Additionally, even when a court finds that a statute violates the single subject rule, courts have difficulty fashioning a remedy. While some courts have struck down the entire statute, other courts have struck just the offending sections of the statute. Arguably, the remaining statute was not what the legislature intended to enact; yet the legislature may well have wanted some law rather than no law at all.

There are other complications with the single subject rule. The rule applies equally to laws passed via initiative and referendum (*see* Section D below). Drafters of initiatives and referendums are typically less skilled in bill-drafting than lawmakers, and thus, these direct democracy laws are more often subject to attack for violating this rule. Given that the public often votes after doing little more than reading the title of a proposed law, some have argued that courts should apply the single-subject requirement more rigorously to direct legislation than to traditional laws.

For now, however, courts do not apply the rule more rigorously. For example, in 2004, Georgia voters approved an amendment to its state's constitution that prohibited gay marriage. GA. CONST. art. 1, § IV, ¶ 1. The ballot measure read, "we adopt as the amendment's objective, reserving marriage and its attendant benefits to unions of man and woman." The Georgia Constitution required that ballot measures be limited to one subject. Suit was filed alleging that the ballot measure violated the single subject provision because it prohibited both same-sex *unions* and same-sex *marriage*. The lower court agreed. *O'Kelley v. Perdue*, No. 2004CV 93434, 2006 WL 1350171 (Ga. Super. Ct. May 16, 2006). Ultimately, the Georgia Supreme Court disagreed with the lower court's opinion that civil unions and gay marriage were different topics and upheld the amendment. *Perdue v. O'Kelley*, 632 S.E.2d 110 (Ga. 2006).

While the Federal Constitution does not include a similar rule, House and Senate procedural rules do exist to combat the problem of extraneous subjects being added to bills. As we already learned, the House has the *germaneness rule* — "no motion or proposition on a subject different from that under consideration shall be admitted under color of amendment." Rules of the House of Representatives, R. XVI, H.R. DOC. NO. 109-157, at 701.

Additionally, both chambers have rules that limit what can be added to appropriations bills, which are bills that authorize the expenditure of government funds. The appropriations limit exists because if appropriations bills are not passed the government must shut down. Hence, legislators may be more willing to vote for a subject they otherwise would reject if it is attached to an appropriations bill. But internal rules can be and are waived, and courts are loath to enforce internal rules due to separation of powers concerns. The legislature and judiciary are co-equal branches of our government. Neither branch should be responsible for supervising the processes or deliberations of the other. A contrary rule would elevate one branch above the other. Hence, in *Des Moines Register & Tribunal Co. v. Dwyer*, 542 N.W.2d 491 (Iowa 1996), the majority held that a statute that allowed the public to access a legislator's phone records was a nonjusticiable rule of proceeding rather than a reviewable statute on substance. *Id.* at 502–03. The court held that the rule was not subject to review.

D. Direct Democracy: The Referendum & Initiative Process

In contrast to the legislative process described above, about one-half of the states and many local governments allow their citizens to adopt laws or amend their constitution directly using the *initiative process*. Additionally, almost all states allow their citizens to reject laws and constitutional amendments their state's legislatures propose via a *referendum*. In this country, the initiative process is more common than the referendum process and is, thus, the more important process. Both of these processes are forms of direct democracy. Each of these two processes is somewhat different, but both have in common the notion that law should come directly from the people. Note that there is no similar process at the federal level, where the legislature drafts and enacts all statutory law.

The initiative process is available in twenty-four states (mostly the western states). An initiative is a citizen-drafted statute or constitutional amendment placed on the ballot for popular vote. The process is relatively simple. First, a citizen drafts an initiative. After the initiative is drafted, the proponents of the initiative must obtain the requisite number of petition signatures to have the initiative placed on the ballot. After the initiative is placed on the ballot, the voters either approve or reject it. In this direct initiative process, the legislature and executive play no role.

In contrast, some states require that initiatives be submitted to the legislature before being placed on the ballot. If the legislature fails to approve the measure or amends it unsatisfactorily, the initiative proponents must secure more petition signatures to get the measure on the ballot. In this indirect, as opposed to direct, initiative process, the state legislature is involved. One of the more well-known state initiatives was California's Proposition 13, which severely limited the ability of state government to increase property taxes. More recently, many states have had initiatives addressing the legalization of marijuana.

The referendum process is similar to the initiative process, but the referendum process is generally used to reject proposed legislation rather than to pass new legislation. Almost every state allows some form of referendum process. There are two different kinds of referendums — popular and legislative. *Popular referendum* refers to the right of the voters, by collecting signatures on a petition, to refer specific legislation the legislature passed to the voters for approval or rejection. In contrast, *legislative referendum* refers to the ability of elected officials to submit proposed legislation or constitutional amendments to the voters for approval or rejection. Legislative referendum is constitutionally required for constitutional amendments in all states but Delaware.

As you can imagine, statutes that come about as a result of these direct voting methods present particular interpretation problems. Some argue that statutory interpretation is the art of discerning the intent of the enacting legislature (*see* Chapter 4). If so, then whose intent matters when citizens draft a statute? Those courts addressing the issue have concluded that the voters' intent controls. *See In re Littlefield*, 851 P.2d 42, 48 (Cal. 1993); *State v. Guzek*, 906 P.2d 272, 284 (Or. 1995); *Lynch v. State*, 145 P.2d 265, 270 (Wash. 1944). But which voters: those who drafted the initiative, those who petitioned to get the initiative on the ballot, or those who voted for it? Many voters are unable to understand complex, lengthy initiatives. Should their intent really matter? Concerns that we may have about legislators actually reading bills should be multiplied in the initiative arena. Moreover, voters' opinions may be formed from media portrayals, whether by news or political advertising. Indeed, some courts have looked at these sources when interpreting initiatives.

Even assuming you can decide which group's intent matters, discerning that intent can be trickier than discerning the intent of a legislative body that leaves a voluminous historical record in one location. For this reason, at least one scholar has suggested that courts should focus on the sponsor's intent. Glenn Smith, *Solving the Initiatory Construction Puzzle (and Improving Direct Democracy) by Appropriate Refocusing on Sponsor Intent*, 78 U. Colo. L. Rev. 257 (2007).

At bottom, judges are skeptical about direct democracy processes: "[For] its lack of filters to calm the momentary passions of the people and its susceptibility to use by majorities to harm disfavored groups." ESKRIDGE ET AL., LEGISLATION AND STATUTORY INTERPRETATION, *supra*, at 35. This skepticism can be seen in *Romer v. Evans*, 517 U.S. 620 (1996), in which the Supreme Court invalidated a state initiative that targeted gay individuals because the initiative was based on a "desire to harm a politically unpopular group." *Id.* at 632.

E. Mastering This Topic

Return to the hypothetical ordinance provided in Chapter 1. While the hypothetical involved a city ordinance, not a federal statute, it included information about its enactment process. Look back and see if you can identify this information on your own.

There are three areas to note. First, the hypothetical includes a committee report and a summary of the floor debates. For a judge willing to consider it, legislative history may provide insight into meaning. Some forms of legislative history are more relevant than others. In other words, there is a hierarchy of usefulness of legislative history, which you will learn in Chapter 10.

Second, the hypothetical included a marked-up version of the ordinance. Additions to the original text are italicized while deletions are in strike-through font. At the federal level, italic and strike-through text are used to indicate amendments to bills and can aid interpretation; knowing what language was added or deleted during the legislative process can be informative.

Finally, the hypothetical includes the mayor's signing statement. You may wonder how relevant executive signing statements are for interpretation. Chapter 10 will address this issue. For now, consider what weight you think they should be given. Does the signing statement attempt to rewrite the ordinance or simply inform executive enforcement? You will learn that this issue is far from settled, but generally, signing statements are considered the least relevant "legislative" history. Keep in mind that the hypothetical, which is a teaching tool, includes more legislative history than would be typical for a city ordinance or even a state statute.

Checkpoints

- It is far easier for a bill to fail than to be enacted.

- Congress, a bicameral body, is made up of the House of Representatives and the Senate.

- The legislative process begins when a legislator introduces a bill on the floor of either the House or Senate.

- A bill goes through a number of procedural steps before it is enacted. The political party in power ultimately controls the fate of the bill.

- Both the House and Senate must pass a bill in identical form for it to be presented to the president.

- The final step in the legislative process is the president's approval or veto. If the president signs the bill, it becomes law. If the president vetoes the bill, the bill fails to become law unless two-thirds of the members of both chambers override the veto.

- During the legislative process, legislative history is generated describing the bill's progress.

- The single subject rule is a state procedural rule restricting the topics to be included in a bill.

- About one-half of the states and many local governments allow citizens to adopt laws or amend the constitution directly using the initiative process. When laws are enacted via direct democracy, discerning "legislative intent" is very difficult.

Chapter 3

Separation of Powers

Roadmap

- Learn what "separation of powers" is.
- Learn the formalist and functionalist approaches to this doctrine.
- Understand the role that separation of powers plays in statutory interpretation.

A. Introduction to This Chapter

This chapter introduces you to an important constitutional principle: separation of powers. The Supreme Court's jurisprudence in this area neither definitively defines separation of powers, nor consistently applies it. Hence, you will learn about both the formalistic and functionalist approaches the justices have used either to validate or strike down innovative power arrangements. Separation of powers plays an enormously important role in statutory interpretation. Hence, we end the chapter by looking at the role of separation of powers in statutory interpretation cases.

B. Separation of Powers Generally

Separation of powers underlies all aspects of interpretation. Separation of powers is the idea that the powers of a government should be split between two or more independent groups so that no one group or person can gain too much power. The vesting clauses of the U.S. Federal Constitution split the federal governmental powers among the legislative, executive, and judicial branches. No one branch is more powerful than any other. Legislators make laws, the president executes the law, and judges interpret laws. U.S. CONST. art. I, § 1 ("All legislative Powers herein granted shall be vested in a Congress of the United States, which shall consist of a Senate and House of Representatives."); U.S. CONST. art. II, § 1, cl. 1 ("The executive Power shall be vested in a President of the United States of America."); U.S. CONST. art. III, § 1 ("The judicial Power of the United States, shall be vested in one supreme Court, and in such inferior Courts as the Congress may from time to time ordain and establish."). Yet there is overlap. Some overlap is valid. Indeed, our constitutional system is one of checks and balances. Too much overlap is invalid. Where to draw the line is a question that implicates separation of powers.

The Supreme Court has approached questions involving separation of powers issues in two different ways, one of which is more accepting of overlap than the other. Legal scholars have identified these two approaches as *formalism* and *functionalism*. As we begin this discussion of separation of powers, be aware that these categories, as well as the Court's jurisprudence in this area, are imperfect. We will touch just the surface; for additional background on the difference between formalism and functionalism, see M. Elizabeth Magill, *The Real Separation in Separation of Powers Law*, 86 VA. L. REV. 1127, 1132 (2000) (describing the formalist and functionalist approaches to separation of powers). Let's begin with formalism.

1. Formalism

The *formalist* approach to separation of powers emphasizes the necessity of maintaining three distinct branches of government, each with delegated powers: one branch legislates, one branch executes, and one branch adjudicates. These powers come from the vesting clauses of the U.S. Constitution. Article I vests in Congress "[a]ll legislative Powers herein granted." U.S. CONST. art. 1, § 1. Legislative power is the power "to promulgate generalized standards and requirements of citizen behavior or to dispense benefits—to achieve, maintain, or avoid particular social policy results." Martin H. Redish & Elizabeth J. Cisar, *"If Angels Were to Govern": The Need for Pragmatic Formalism in Separation of*

Powers Theory, 41 DUKE L.J. 449, 479 (1991). Congress, therefore, not only has the power to create law, but also, has the power to create procedural rules to ensure enforcement of those laws. Laws "alter[] the legal rights, duties, and relations of persons ... outside the Legislative Branch." *INS v. Chadha*, 462 U.S. 919, 952 (1983). Congress alters legal rights by enacting, amending, and repealing statutes.

Article II of the Constitution vests "[t]he executive Power ... in a President of the United States of America." U.S. CONST. art. II, § 1, cl. 1. Executive acts are those in which an executive official exercises judgment about how to apply law to a given situation. *Bowsher v. Synar*, 478 U.S. 714, 732–33 (1986). For the executive to execute the law there must be existing law to execute. In other words, while the legislature enacts laws, the executive enforces those laws.

Article III of the Constitution vests "[t]he judicial Power of the United States, ... in one supreme Court, and in such inferior Courts as the Congress may from time to time ordain and establish." U.S. CONST. art. III, § 1. Judicial power is the power to interpret laws and resolve legal disputes. "[T]o declare what the law is, or has been, is a judicial power, to declare what the law shall be is legislative." *Koshkonong v. Burton*, 104 U.S. 668, 678 (1881) (quoting *Ogden v. Blackledge*, 6 U.S. 272, 277 (1804)). In other words, while the legislature enacts laws, the executive enforces those laws, and the judiciary interprets those laws. Thus, "the interpretation of the laws is the proper and peculiar province of the courts." THE FEDERALIST No. 78, at 523, 525 (Alexander Hamilton) (J. Cooke ed. 1961). The judiciary interprets laws by adjudicating cases and rendering dispositive judgments based on findings of law and fact; indeed, this is the judiciary's primary power.

When confronting an issue raising separation of powers concerns, a formalist judge will use a two-step, rule-based approach. First, the judge will identify the power being exercised: legislative, judicial, or executive. Second, the judge will determine whether the appropriate branch is exercising that power in accordance with the Constitution. The chart below illustrates formalism in a very simplified way. Each branch may constitutionally perform any function that falls within its corresponding "Acts Circle" but may not constitutionally perform any function that falls within another branch's "Acts Circle." Under formalism, a branch violates separation of powers when it attempts to exercise a power that is not constitutionally delegated to it (or not within its Acts Circle). Overlap is permitted only when constitutionally prescribed. So, for example, the president and Senate both play a role in appointing principal officers without violating separation of powers, because the Constitution delegates this power to both the executive and legislative branches. U.S. CONST. art. II, § 2, cl. 2.

Formalism

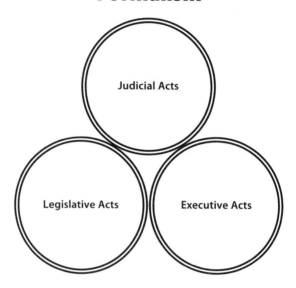

When the Supreme Court approaches a separation of powers issue under a formalist approach, the Court regularly strikes down that exercise of power. For example, in *Clinton v. New York*, 524 U.S. 417 (1998), the Court applied a formalist approach to hold that the line-item veto was unconstitutional because it enabled the executive to unilaterally amend and repeal legislation, a power delegated to the legislature. *Id.* at 447–49. Similarly, the Court struck down legislative veto provisions in *INS v. Chadha*, 462 U.S. 919 (1983). The legislative veto allowed Congress to delegate lawmaking authority to the executive branch but reserved, either to a single chamber or to a committee from a single chamber, the power to oversee and veto the executive's use of this delegated authority. The Court reasoned that the legislative veto provisions allowed one chamber of Congress to unilaterally amend legislation and, thereby, avoid constitutionally required bicameral passage and presentment. *Id.* at 954–55. Thus, the Court held that legislative veto provisions were unconstitutional. *Id.* at 955. Justice Burger's majority opinion approached the issue in a classically formalist way.

Interestingly, after the legislative veto was held to be unconstitutional, Congress passed the Congressional Review Act ("CRA"). The CRA permits Congress to pass a "resolution of disapproval." The resolution, if both houses pass and the president signs it, overrules a rule that a federal agency promulgates. Further, the CRA prohibits the agency from reissuing the rule in substantially the same form or issuing a new rule that is substantially the same "unless the reissued or new rule is specifically authorized by a law enacted after the date of the joint resolution disapproving the original rule." 5 U.S.C. § 801(b)(2). So far, the Supreme Court has not ruled on the constitutionality of the CRA.

Another example of a formalist opinion striking down the exercise of power is *Youngstown Sheet & Tube Co. v. Sawyer*, 343 U.S. 579 (1952) (the Steel Seizure Case). In that case, the Supreme Court held that President Truman's executive order seizing private steel mills during the Korean War was unconstitutional because it altered private property rights, a power reserved exclusively for Congress. *Id.* at 588–89. To prevent the steel industry from striking and potentially shutting down during the Korean War, President Truman had requested from Congress the authority to seize the mills. Congress refused. The President, in the absence of any specific statutory or constitutional authority, issued the order anyway. The industry sued. The issue for the Court was whether the President, absent any specific authority, had the *inherent* power to issue the order under his constitutional authority to act as Commander-in-Chief and to faithfully execute the laws. In Justice Black's majority opinion, the Court held that the President did not have this power. *Id.* at 582–87.

When the Supreme Court uses a formalist approach, the Court will generally reject any attempt by one branch to usurp, or take, power from another branch. For example, in *Bowsher v. Synar*, 478 U.S. 714 (1986), the Court held that Congress could not keep removal power over an agency official working within the Government Accountability Office because the agency official exercised executive authority. *Id.* at 726–27. And in *Stern v. Marshall*, 564 U.S. 462 (2011), the Court held that a Bankruptcy Court — an Article I (executive) Court — lacked constitutional power under Article III to resolve a counterclaim based on state law. *Id.* at 503. The counterclaim involved a long-running inheritance dispute regarding the estate of Texas billionaire, J. Howard Marshall. Marshall's wife of fourteen months, Anna Nicole Smith, sued Marshall's heir alleging that the ninety-year-old billionaire promised her more than $3 million.

Similarly, in *Plaut v. Spendthrift Farm, Inc.*, 514 U.S. 211, 240 (1995), the Court held that Congress could not retroactively require federal courts to reopen a judgment once it was final. Finally, in *United States v. Klein*, 80 U.S. 128, 146 (1871), the Court invalidated a statute that "prescribe[d] rules of decision" for a specific type of case. According to the Court, by prescribing a rule of decision, or an outcome, in a pending case, "Congress [] inadvertently passed the limit which separate[d] the legislative from the judicial power." *Id.*

at 147. Although Congress may amend the underlying substantive law to accomplish policy objectives, Congress may not dictate outcomes in particular cases. Because the power to decide cases by interpreting and applying existing law to a specific, factual situation is delegated to the judiciary, Congress violates separation of powers when it attempts to decide cases, reopen final cases, or interfere with a federal court's decision-making process.

As these cases show, formalists are concerned about undue accretion of power to any one branch, no matter how small. The concentration of power in any one branch is viewed as unconstitutional regardless of whether that power is being misused. Formalists believe that accretion of power in and of itself is unacceptable because once power is acquired, it can be difficult to determine whether too much power has been ceded. Perhaps, more critically, formalists are worried that once a branch acquires too much power, it would be too late to remedy the situation. Thus, formalists view separation of powers as a doctrine that is "prophylactic in nature ... designed to avoid a situation in which one might even debate whether an undue accretion of power has taken place." Redish & Cisar, *supra* at 476.

In sum, formalism is an approach that focuses on the separate, constitutionally enumerated powers delegated to each branch in the vesting clauses of the Constitution. Overlap is not permitted for fear that one branch may accrete too much power. When the Supreme Court resolves a separation of powers issue using formalism, inevitably, the Court finds the exercise of power unconstitutional.

2. Functionalism

The Supreme Court Justices have never collectively embraced formalism. Rather, the Court has oscillated between formalism and functionalism throughout its history. As the government adapted to the complexities of the twenty-first century, functionalism seemed to be winning the war. *See, e.g.*, *King v. Burwell*, 135 S. Ct. 2480 (2015) (using a functionalist approach to interpret the Affordable Care Act). More recently, with changes to the Supreme Court, formalism is making a comeback.

Functionalism's focus differs from that of formalism. While formalists focus on strict separation, functionalists focus on balancing the inevitable overlap of powers to preserve the *core functions* the Constitution assigns to each branch. To maintain a relatively balanced power distribution, functionalists believe that a complete bar against any encroachment between the branches is unnecessary. Instead, functionalists focus on limiting encroachments into the core, constitutionally appointed functions of each branch. For example, the executive's power of appointment is a core function. U.S. CONST. art. II, § 2, cl. 2. However, the executive's appointment power is limited. First, the executive's appointment of principal officers is subject to Senate approval. Second, the executive is not the only official who may appoint *inferior* officers: "Congress may by Law vest the Appointment of such inferior Officers, as they think proper, in the President alone, in the Courts of Law, or in the Heads of Departments." *Id.*

Similarly, the Constitution implicitly gives the executive the power to remove executive officers subject to conditions Congress imposes. The removal power, therefore, is similarly not absolute. Note, however, that although Congress has the authority to place limits on the executive's removal power, Congress does not have the authority to eliminate that power. *Bowsher v. Synar*, 478 U.S. 714, 725–26 (1986); *Myers v. United States*, 272 U.S. 52, 126–27 (1926). We will cover the appointment power more specifically in Chapter 14.

Like formalists, functionalists turn to the vesting clauses of the Federal Constitution to define the most central, core functions of each branch: the legislature legislates, the judiciary adjudicates, and the executive enforces the law. But unlike formalists, functionalists do not compartmentalize these core functions. For example, the legislature's power to make law is a core function. However, the judicial branch also makes law, both by developing common law and by interpreting statutes. Under formalism, this encroachment might raise a separation of powers concern, otherwise known as "judicial activism." In contrast to formalism, under functionalism, the judiciary's encroachment into a core function of the legislature does not raise concern. To trigger a separation of powers concern under functionalism, one branch would have to *unduly* encroach and aggrandize a core function of another branch.

Undue encroachment is necessary because functionalists believe that overlap between the branches is practically necessary and even desirable. Functionalists emphasize the need to maintain pragmatic flexibility to respond to the needs of modern government. Indeed, the existence of the administrative system is an example of functionalism. Agencies, which are part of the executive branch, perform all of the functions separately delegated to each of the three branches in the Constitution (*see* Chapter 13). Yet few today would suggest that agencies' exercise of authority violates separation of powers. *But see* Peter B. McCutchen, *Mistakes, Precedent, and the Rise of the Administrative State: Toward a Constitutional Theory of the Second Best*, 80 CORNELL L. REV. 1, 11 (1994) (arguing that "[u]nder a pure formalist approach, most, if not all, of the administrative state is unconstitutional").

While both formalism and functionalism share a common goal — to ensure that no one branch acquires too much unilateral power — these approaches go about meeting this goal in different ways. Whereas formalists use a two-step, bright-line-rule approach to categorize acts as legislative, judicial, or executive, functionalists use a factors approach to balance the competing power's interests with the pragmatic need for innovation. Functionalists recognize the government's need for flexibility to create new power-sharing arrangements to address the evolving needs of the modern century. Functionalists do not want to "unduly constrict Congress's ability to take needed and innovative action ...." *CFTC v. Schor*, 478 U.S. 833, 851 (1986).

To foster flexibility, functionalists focus less on maintaining the separateness of each branch and instead focus on the independence of each branch with oversight from the other branches. Independence is achieved when each branch is able to perform its core functions, while also being able to limit the accretion of power in the other branches. Justice Jackson's tripartite framework from his concurrence in the Steel Seizure Case is informative. Justice Jackson suggested that the Court review separation of powers issues differently, depending upon the level of cooperation among the other two branches. Specifically, when the executive and legislature cooperate, the Court should be more deferential than when either branch acts alone. Moreover, the Court should be especially wary when one branch acts against the wishes of the other.

Because the case involved President Truman's seizure of the steel mills, the framework specifically addressed executive power, but the analysis applies to legislative power as well:

> First, "[w]hen the President acts pursuant to an express or implied authorization of Congress, his authority is at its maximum, for it includes all that he possesses in his own right plus all that Congress can delegate." Second, "[w]hen the President acts in absence of either a congressional grant or denial of authority, he can only rely upon his own independent powers, but there is a zone of twilight in which he and Congress may have concurrent authority, or in which its distribution is uncertain." In such a circumstance, Presidential authority can derive support from "congressional inertia, indifference or quiescence." Finally, "[w]hen the President takes measures incompatible with the expressed or implied will of Congress, his power is at its lowest ebb," and the Court can sustain his actions "only by disabling the Congress from acting upon the subject."

Medellín v. Texas, 552 U.S. 491, 524–25 (2008) (quoting *Youngstown Sheet & Tube Co.*, 343 U.S. at 635–38 (Jackson, J., concurring)). Simply put, when one branch acts unilaterally against the express or implied will of the other branches, the risk of tyranny is greatest.

While formalism was depicted above as a series of separate circles with no overlap, functionalism might be pictured as a set of interlocking circles, as shown in the diagram below.

Functionalism

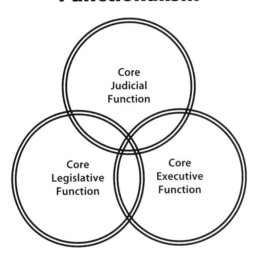

From this diagram, you can see that each branch possesses separate, constitutionally assigned, core functions. At the same time, each branch also has a penumbra of overlap (the zone of twilight) that shades gradually into the core functions of the other two branches. So long as the branches steer relatively clear of the other branches' core functions and the branches do not enlarge the size of their own circle at the expense of another branch's circle, functionalist separation of powers is maintained.

Generally, when the Supreme Court approaches a separation of powers issue under a functionalist approach, the Court approves the exercise of that branch's power. For example, in *Commodity Futures Trading Commission v. Schor*, 478 U.S. 833 (1986), the Court held that Congress can delegate to the executive the power to adjudicate a "particularized area of law," specifically common law counterclaims. *Id.* at 852–57. According to the Court, the power arrangement "raise[ed] no question of the aggrandizement of congressional power at the expense of a coordinate branch." *Id.* at 856. In other words, separation of powers was not violated simply because Congress enabled the executive to encroach on a core judicial function. The Court required a concurrent finding that Congress had correspondingly expanded, or aggrandized, the executive's power before finding separation of powers to be violated. *Id.* at 856–57.

To illustrate the difference between formalism and functionalism, we can compare this case with another case. Using a formalist approach, the Court had denied a broader judicial power grant to a non-Article III bankruptcy court. *Northern Pipeline Constr. Co. v. Marathon Pipe Line Co.*, 458 U.S. 50, 57–58 (1982). The Court in *Schor* distinguished *Northern Pipeline* by saying that "the [Act at issue] leaves far more of the 'essential attributes of judicial power' to Article III courts than did that portion of the Bankruptcy Act found unconstitutional in *Northern Pipeline*." *Schor*, 478 U.S. at 852. In short, the power transfer in *Schor* was not intrusive enough to raise concerns about aggrandizement.

To illustrate further, the Court has approved Congress's delegation of limited legislative-like powers to the judiciary. For example, in *Mistretta v. United States*, 488 U.S. 361, 368 (1989), the Court upheld the constitutionality of the U.S. Sentencing Commission, even though three of the seven proposed commissioners were sitting federal judges. The Court was unconcerned that members of the judiciary would be making law by drafting sentencing guidelines. The Court reasoned that drafting sentencing guidelines was similar to establishing court rules; therefore, "the Commission's functions … [were] clearly attendant to a central element of the historically acknowledged mission of the Judicial Branch." *Id.* at 391. Hence, the intrusion was acceptable because it was minimal and already tolerated in other areas. *See, e.g., Free Enterprise Fund v. Public Co. Accounting Oversight Bd.*, 561 U.S. 477, 519–20 (2010) (Breyer, J., dissenting) (noting that the Court has "looked to function and context, and not to bright-line rules" when resolving separation of powers cases).

In summary, functionalists take a pragmatic view of separation of powers and seek to avoid the aggrandizement of one branch at the expense of another. Whereas formalists ask what kind of power is being wielded and whether the appropriate branch is wielding that power, functionalists ask whether one branch has encroached into the core functions of another branch and thereby aggrandized power for itself. To illustrate:

> [I]f the Supreme Court were to void a presidential pardon because it was given for improper motives, ... if the Court were to void a Senate impeachment proceeding because it had defects, ... if the Court were to order the President to dismiss a Secretary of State who was facing criminal proceedings, the Court would violate the principle of separation of powers.

Aharon Barak, *Foreword: A Judge on Judging: The Role of a Supreme Court in a Democracy*, 116 HARV. L. REV. 16, 122 (2002).

In all of these examples, the issue would not be whether the Court had the power to act. The Court likely has the power to require the executive and legislature to obey the Constitution. Rather, the issue would be whether, in doing so, the Court would impede the executive or legislature's ability to carry out their respective core functions and, in the process, aggrandize the Court's own role. So, in the end, power given or taken by one branch must not "intru[de] on the authority and functions of [another] Branch." *Nixon v. Fitzgerald*, 457 U.S. 731, 754 (1982). Intrusions that impair another branch's ability to perform core functions are unconstitutional unless the "impact is justified by an overriding need to promote objectives within the constitutional authority of Congress." *Nixon v. Adm'r of General Servs.*, 433 U.S. 425, 443 (1977).

Finally, it is important to know that, while the Founders were indeed concerned about the concentration of governmental power in any one of the three branches, they were primarily concerned with congressional self-aggrandizement. *See, e.g., INS v. Chadha*, 462 U.S. 919 (1983) (using formalist reasoning to reject congressional aggrandizement).

In keeping with this concern, the Court more closely scrutinizes legislation that expands Congress's authority rather than the authority of the other branches. The Court has been more accepting of judicial and executive aggrandizement. Indeed, at least one commentator has suggested that the Court uses formalism when Congress overreaches and uses functionalism when the judiciary or executive overreach. Ronald J. Krotoszynski, *On the Danger of Wearing Two Hats:* Mistretta *and* Morrison *Revisited*, 38 WM. & MARY L. REV. 417, 460 (1997).

C. Separation of Powers & Statutory Interpretation

In the last section, you learned about separation of powers in general. Now, let's explore the role that separation of powers plays in statutory interpretation. Legislators enact statutes that the judiciary must interpret. *See, e.g., King v Burwell*, 135 S. Ct. 2480 (2015) (using a functionalist approach to interpret the term "an Exchange established by the State" in the Affordable Care Act to mean "an Exchange established by the State or federal government"). As the Supreme Court once said, "It is emphatically the province and duty of the judicial department to say what the law is." *Marbury v. Madison*, 5 U.S. (1 Cranch) 137, 177 (1803).

While separation of powers does not inform the meaning of a statute *per se*, it plays a strong supporting role. A judge's approach to interpreting statutes is based in part on his or her beliefs about separation of powers. For example, in *Yates v. United States*, 135 S. Ct. 1074, 1091 (2015), Justice Kagan criticized the plurality holding that a "tangible object" did not include fish. (Yes, you read that sentence correctly.) As Justice Kagan noted, "the ordinary meaning of 'tangible object' is 'a discrete thing that possesses physical form.' [citing the plurality's opinion]. A fish is, of course, a discrete thing that possesses physical form. *See generally* Dr. Seuss, One Fish Two Fish Red Fish Blue Fish (1960)."

Importantly for this topic, she then identified what she believed to be the proper judicial role during statutory interpretation.

But whatever the wisdom or folly [of the criminal statute at issue], this Court does not get to rewrite the law. "Resolution of the pros and cons of whether a statute should sweep broadly or narrowly is for Congress." If judges disagree with Congress's choice, we are perfectly entitled to say so—in lectures, in law review articles, and even in dicta. But we are not entitled to replace the statute Congress enacted with an alternative of our own design.

Id. at 1100 (Kagan, J., dissenting) (internal citations omitted). For Justice Kagan, rejecting the ordinary meaning of the statute violated separation of powers. But Justice Ginsburg believed that before adopting such a broad interpretation of this criminal statute, the Court should require "that Congress should have spoken in language that is clear and definite." *Id.* at 1088 (plurality opinion).

To understand why Justices Kagan and Ginsburg have differing views of the proper role of the judiciary when interpreting statutes, you must understand the history of our legal system. As you no doubt already know, our system was based, in part, on the English common law system. In early England, judges created law through case decisions. Although the King and Parliament ran the country, they rarely enacted statutes to modify this judge-made common law.

Similarly, early American judges developed law through case decisions. In the nineteenth century, law developed almost exclusively in this way. Judge-made common law was the norm. Judges were educated professionals. In contrast, legislators worked primarily part-time and were considered to be uneducated, unsophisticated, and subject to political pressure. Indeed, a holdover custom from these early days is that a bill must be read three times during the legislative process before the bill can be enacted to ensure that any representatives who are illiterate know what they are voting for.

Statutes were uncommon. Many statutes were private (meaning they applied only to specific individuals). Those statutes that were public (meaning they applied to all individuals) were broadly and succinctly written. For example, the Sherman Act, which was enacted in 1890, is a comprehensive and expansive act regulating federal antitrust activity, yet it fits onto a single page. With such breadth, Congress left significant room for judicial development.

> Statutes like the Sherman Act, the civil rights legislation, and the mail fraud statute were written in broad general language on the understanding that the courts would have wide latitude in construing them to achieve the remedial purposes that Congress had identified. The wide open spaces in statutes such as these are most appropriately interpreted as implicit delegations of authority to the courts to fill in the gaps in the common-law tradition of case-by-case adjudication.

McNally v. United States, 483 U.S. 350, 372–73 (1987) (Stevens, J., dissenting). (Notice that Justice Stevens says that gaps in statutes are implicit delegations to courts to fill in the gaps. Later, in Chapter 15 we will see that implicit delegation also serves as a rationale for allowing agencies to fill in the gaps pursuant to the *Chevron* doctrine (and Justice Stevens wrote that opinion as well).)

Also, during this time, United States legal education was developing into its current form: the case method. The "inventor" of case method instruction, Christopher Langdell, believed that statutes were not true "law" and that only judicially created common law was worthy enough to be studied. Welcome to the first year of law school.

In sum, in early American history, legislators and statutes were viewed with hostility and suspicion. Indeed, it was during this time that the judiciary developed the canon that statutes in derogation of the common law should be strictly construed (*see* Chapter 12).

However, things quickly changed. In the late nineteenth century, legislatures became more prolific and legislation became more generally applicable. As legislation proliferated, statutes began to replace common law. Indeed, this replacement intensified during the New Deal when Congress used legislation to solve social and economic problems. Additionally, as legislators became more skilled at their jobs, distrust of legislators started to fade. By the mid-twentieth century, the Supreme Court regularly heard cases involving statutes, and so, statutory interpretation became increasingly important. Similarly, during this time, regulatory agencies also proliferated. As more and more agencies drafted more and more regulations interpreting more and more statutes, courts had to grapple with the appropriate level of deference to give to those agency interpretations. This topic is currently at the forefront of legislative and judicial debate, as we will see in Chapter 15.

Today, legislation is pervasive and detailed. For example, compare the Patient Protection and Affordable Care Act (known as "the Affordable Care Act (ACA)" or (sometimes) pejoratively as "Obamacare"), which was enacted in 2010, with the Sherman Act, which was enacted in 1890. While the Sherman Act fits on one page, the ACA spans 906 pages.

Let's return to *Marbury*'s famous quote: "It is emphatically the province and duty of the judicial department to say what the law is." *Marbury*, 5 U.S. (1 Cranch) at 177. This statement is a bit simplistic; the dividing line between making law and interpreting law is blurred. When judges interpret statutes, they fill gaps, resolve ambiguity, and identify statutory boundaries. Indeed, every interpretation case requires a judge to adopt one meaning and reject at least one other meaning. Then, and because of *stare decisis*—the idea that similar cases should be decided similarly—that interpretation will apply in future cases. Thus, it is simply wrong to suggest that judges just "say what the law is"; rather, they act in concert with the legislature to develop the law. For example, consider the following issue: When courts imply a cause of action in a statute, are they "making" or "interpreting" law? Some individuals believe that when judges imply causes of action they are interpreting law, while others believe that such judges are making law. An individual's resolution of this question will be based in large part on that individual's view about the relationship between the role of the judiciary and the role of the legislature. This relationship is what we call separation of powers.

Separation of powers is at the heart of the debate regarding statutory interpretation. Some believe that only the enacted text of a statute is relevant to interpretation. This view may elevate the role of the legislature at the expense of the judiciary. Others believe that statutory purpose and legislative intent are at least as relevant. This view may elevate the judiciary's role at the expense of the legislature. The truth, of course, lies somewhere in the middle. Where in the middle is the basis of many scholarly articles and judicial debate.

All this to say, the appropriate way to interpret a statute is far from settled today. Experts disagree about the importance to be placed on the ordinary meaning of the text, the legislative history surrounding a statute's enactment, and the unexpressed purpose of the statute. Former Justice Scalia can be credited, or perhaps blamed, for the reemergence of this controversy. He has been credited with returning the judiciary's focus to the text of the statute. However, he adhered to a strict approach of interpretation that ignored legislative history and unexpressed purpose. His approach is known as "new textualism." His reason for rejecting legislative history and unexpressed purpose was based on separation of powers. Like Justice Kagan above, he believed that the legislature, not the judiciary, has constitutional authority to make law. New textualism and the other theories of interpretation will be explained in more detail in Chapter 4. You will see that the different theories reflect their adherents' views regarding separation of powers.

D. A Note About Other Legal Systems

The purpose of a legal system is to resolve public and private disputes. To resolve such disputes, a country has a number of choices.

Building on its British roots, the United States chose an adversarial legal system in which legal disputes would be resolved through a contest between the two litigants. Thus, in criminal cases, the state or federal prosecutor brings charges against a criminal defendant, accusing the defendant of violating the law. In civil cases, a plaintiff files a lawsuit against a defendant. Regardless of the type of case, the lawyers argue their client's case vigorously and fully before the neutral decision-maker, either a judge or jury.

It can be difficult for those in the United States to imagine any other system. Yet most of the rest of the world uses the inquisitorial (or nonadversarial) system. In an inquisitorial system, the judge is an active participant: investigating the facts, questioning the witnesses and lawyers, ordering evidence to be examined, researching the law, and deciding the outcome. Unlike in the United States, the judge is not a neutral decision-maker, or referee.

Many inquisitorial system countries differ from the United States in another way. The United States is a common law country. In common law countries, judges make binding law when they decide cases. Their case decisions then serve as precedent in two ways. First, when there is no statute, regulation, or constitution that applies, prior judicial decisions are the only law. Tort law and contract law are good examples. Second, even when there is a statute, regulation, or constitution, prior judicial decisions of that codified law govern interpretations in later cases. Thus, in common law systems, prior judicial opinions control future judicial decisions. Further, in a common law country the opinions of appellate courts typically bind lower courts in the same jurisdiction that address similar issues. The United States is not the only common law jurisdiction. Other common law jurisdictions include England, Australia, India, Canada, Hong Kong, Ireland, and Pakistan.

However, common law is not the only option. Many countries in continental Europe and South America have a legal system referred to as "civil" or "civilian law." Indeed, civil law is the most common legal system in the world; it is used in Louisiana, most of the European Union countries, Brazil, China, Japan, Mexico, Russia, Switzerland, Turkey, and Quebec. In civil law systems, a written code serves as the basic outline for judicial interpretation and elaboration. Civil law and common law systems differ in important ways. One important difference between them is their starting point. The civil law system typically starts with abstract principles that the legislature enacts as a code of laws. The judiciary interprets and applies these codes. A civil law judge may have more latitude when interpreting and applying a code than a common law judge because precedents are generally non-binding and, therefore, are only persuasive at best. In other words, the starting point and center of civil law analysis is the code (the statutes), not case law.

E. Mastering This Topic

Return to the hypothetical ordinance provided in Chapter 1. Remember our question: "An ambulance entered Pioneer Park to pick up and take to the hospital a man who has just suffered a heart attack. Did the ambulance driver violate the Pioneer Park Safety Ordinance (PPSO)?" Let's use the information from this chapter to help understand the meaning of the language at issue.

How would a formalist approach the interpretive question? A formalist would consider the clarity of the language of the act—motor vehicle—and its application to the facts—an ambulance. A dictionary definition or common understandings of the term point to the inescapable conclusion that an ambulance is a motor vehicle; thus, ambulances are prohibited in the park. This outcome does not make much sense; however, a formalist might conclude that the city council should fix its oversight, not the court. The formalist may try to find a reason to avoid the ordinary meaning of the language, for example by finding that an ordinance exempting ambulances from traffic rules controlled instead. Indeed, when Former Justice Scalia analyzed this question, he took a similar approach.[1] How about a functionalist? A functionalist would look at the purpose of the ordinance as a whole and conclude that the city council was trying to make the park safe from car and bike accidents. After all, the penalty increases when there is an injury. Further, there is no evidence that the council intended to prohibit ambulances from coming into the park to pick up someone who is ill. Thus, a functionalist would likely find an implicit exception in the statute for ambulances. And former Judge Posner does exactly that. *Id.* ("I call it having a pocketful of nontextual interpretive principles to draw on whenever textual originalism produces dumb results, such as barring ambulances on rescue missions from parks because the dictionary says an ambulance is a vehicle.").

Let's look at how the difference in a country's choice of legal system impacts statutory interpretation in a hypothetical case. Let's return to our park hypothetical. Let's assume that the ambulance driver receives a traffic ticket for driving his ambulance in the park. He challenges the ticket in court, arguing that ambulances should be permitted to drive in the park and the legislature just forgot to include an exception.

- Imagine the ambulance driver lives in a common law country. What sources would the court consult to evaluate his defense? If the city had

---

1. Bryan A. Garner & Richard A. Posner, How Nuanced is Justice Scalia's Judicial Philosophy? An Exchange, The New Republic, available at https://newrepublic.com/article/107001/how-nuanced-justice-scalias-judicial-philosophy-exchange (September 10, 2012) ("[Justice Scalia] and I consistently maintain that ambulances are covered by the prohibition but also explain that '[s]ome of the imperfections [in a statute] can be cured or mitigated by doctrines and devices other than the mauling of text.... For example, it may well be that the undeniable exclusion of ambulances by the text of the ordinance is countermanded by an ordinance or court-made rule exempting emergency vehicles from traffic rules.'").

no relevant ordinance, a common law court would look at prior court cases involving other vehicles or vehicle-like things that have driven in the park. Is this vehicle like the others that were either allowed or like the vehicles not allowed? However, if the city had adopted an ordinance stating, for example, "No motor vehicles in the park," the court would first see if there were other earlier judicial decisions interpreting the ordinance in similar situations. If so, the court would be bound to follow those decisions. If not, the court would determine the meaning of the words in the ordinance using traditional tools of interpretation.

• Now imagine our ambulance driver lives in a civil law country. What sources would the court consult to evaluate his defense? If there were no city ordinance directly applicable, the civil law court would look to other, related statutes. Without an ordinance specifically addressing ambulances in the park, it would turn to ordinances relating the city's traffic rules, for example. However, if the city had adopted an ordinance stating, for example, "No motor vehicles in the park," then the civil law court would consider only the ordinance itself and would not consider any prior court decision interpreting the ordinance in similar situations.

In addition to common law and civil law, other systems also exist, including Islamic Law and Socialist Law. This book, of course, focuses on the United States' approach to statutory interpretation. However, it can be useful for you to remember that lawyers from other parts of the world may approach the statutory interpretation process quite differently.

Checkpoints

- Separation of powers is the idea that the powers of a government should be split between two or more independent groups. The power distribution should be respected.

- Separation of powers underlies all aspects of statutory interpretation.

- The *formalist* approach to separation of powers emphasizes the necessity of maintaining three distinct branches of government with delegated powers: one branch legislates, one branch executes, and one branch adjudicates.

- The *functionalist* approach to separation of powers accepts some overlap so long as no one branch appropriates or takes too much constitutionally assigned power from another branch.

- The common law system is only one legal system. Other systems approach statutory interpretation differently.

Chapter 4

Statutory Interpretation: Sources & Theories

Roadmap

- Identify the three sources of evidence judges use to interpret statutes: intrinsic sources, extrinsic sources, and policy-based sources.

- Study the three main theories judges use to interpret statutes: textualism, intentionalism, and purposivism.

- Learn about other theories, such as imaginative reconstructionism, dynamic interpretation, and Alaska's sliding scale approach.

- Discover how the states and other countries approach statutory interpretation.

- Learn that constitutional interpretation differs from statutory interpretation.

- Question whether theory really matters.

A. Introduction to This Chapter

This chapter will introduce you to the building blocks underlying statutory interpretation: the sources of evidence judges use to find the meaning of statutory language and the theories of interpretation judges use when approaching an interpretation question. Most of the information in this chapter relates to the process of interpreting statutes; however, it can also be relevant to the interpretation of other legal language, regulations for example. For ease, we will use the term statutory interpretation in this chapter.

While at first glance, the information in this chapter may seem to be one designed for academics and theorists, it is not. Grasping the building blocks of statutory interpretation is essential for anyone wishing to make interpretation arguments to a judge. Theory matters, but it matters in unusual ways. These sources and theories will enable you to "talk the talk," so to speak. You will not win your case simply because you mention the text to a textualist judge, but at least that judge will understand what you are saying. Thus, in this chapter, you will learn a new language, one with which you are likely already somewhat familiar.

B. The Art of Statutory Interpretation

In its most basic form, statutory interpretation is the art of discerning the intent of the enacting legislature, for it is the enacting legislature that has the constitutional authority to make law. Theoretically then, judges should interpret statutes as the enacting legislature expected or intended. But discerning an enacting legislature's intent is extremely difficult; how does one discern the intent of a group of individuals all having potentially different goals? One cannot simply contact the legislators after the fact and ask them what they intended to accomplish. Even if they were still alive, even if they remembered having a specific intent on the issue before the court, and even if they remembered accurately, such after-the-fact rationalizations are not considered valid evidence of the intent of the legislature as a whole.

Realistically, the idea that there is one, unified intent is nonsense. While members of the legislature may share the goal of passing a bill to address a particular problem, rarely will all members have the same reason for passage or even the same expectations regarding the bill's expected effects. Rather, bills are the result of committee work and political compromise. A bill "emerges from the hubbub of legislative struggle, from the drafts of beginning lawyers, from the work of lobbyists who are casual about clarity but forceful about policy, from the chaos of adjournment deadlines." JACK DAVIES, LEGISLATIVE LAW AND PROCESS IN A NUTSHELL 307–08 (3d ed. 2007). Because of this chaos, bills are filled with ambiguity, absurdity, overbreadth, mistakes, and omissions. Legislators rarely intend to be ambiguous, absurd, overbroad, mistaken, or incomplete, but they often are.

Because of the difficulty of discerning legislative intent, judges have adopted a number of ways to resolve statutory interpretation issues. Some judges focus on the words of the text, believing that by giving words their ordinary, public meaning, they will best further the legislative agenda. Other judges focus on the stated or unstated purpose of the bill, believing that by furthering that purpose, they will best further the legislative agenda. And other judges focus on the piecemeal nature of the legislative process, believing that by comparing various versions of the bill and the legislators' statements accompanying the enactment process, they will best further the legislative agenda. Legal scholars have named these approaches the "theories of interpretation" and have exhaustively argued about which theory best accomplishes the goal of statutory interpretation. Lawyers are mostly oblivious to the differences in the theories and so approach interpretation questions based on the approach that is most intuitive to them.

So, you might wonder why this topic is in this text. After all, this text is primarily for students and practitioners of statutory interpretation, not for academics or judges. Isn't theory something of interest only to those who have time to study such abstract ideas? The simple answer to that question is "no." Perhaps more than in any other area of law, understanding theory is critical to understanding statutory interpretation because theory drives every aspect of interpretation. A judge's theory of interpretation determines what information a judge will consider when searching for meaning. For example, some judges will not look at legislative history or social context for meaning unless the text of the statute is ambiguous or absurd. To argue to one of these judges that the legislative history of the statute supports your client's position, you must first explain why it is necessary to go beyond the text for meaning. In other words, you need to learn to "talk the talk" of statutory interpretation. Indeed, you will likely lose your case unless you master this skill. Hence, this book covers theory early and in detail.

The theories are based around the three sources of information, or evidence, judges consider in construing statutory language: (1) *intrinsic sources* of evidence, (2) *extrinsic sources* of evidence, and (3) *policy-based sources* of evidence. These three sources are briefly explained below. The sources of statutory interpretation and the theories of statutory interpretation are interrelated but different. The theories, which we will study later, are based on the relevance of the sources.

C. The Evidentiary Sources of Meaning

To interpret a statute, a judge will look at a variety of sources of meaning, including intrinsic (or textual) sources, extrinsic sources, and policy-based sources. These sources are sometimes called the tools of interpretation, or *construction*, because judges use them to determine statutory meaning. For an example of a case using many of the tools, see *Tennessee Valley Authority v. Hill*, 437 U.S. 153 (1978) (analyzing text, legislative history, purpose, absurdity, and others). We explore each of these sources below.

1. Intrinsic Sources

Intrinsic sources are materials that are part of the official act being interpreted. The first step in the interpretation process for all theorists is always, "Read the statute. Read the Statute. Read the Statute." John M. Kernochan, *Statutory Interpretation: An Outline of Method*, 3 DALHOUSIE L.J. 333, 338 (1976) (citing HENRY J. FRIENDLY, BENCHMARKS 202 (1967)). Undoubtedly, the words of the statute at issue are the most important intrinsic source. But the words alone cannot be the only place a judge looks for meaning. Other intrinsic sources, such as the grammar and punctuation; the components of the act, including purpose and findings clauses, titles, and definition sections; and the linguistic canons of statutory construction may also be relevant. All of these are intrinsic sources and may be relevant to meaning.

Think of intrinsic sources as those sources coming from the pen of the legislature. They are sources that are a part of or directly related to the bill that was enacted. For example, dictionaries and the linguistic canons of construction — rules of thumb explaining how a normal English speaker understands words — are not part of the bill itself. However, both are directly related to the bill because they are used on the language in the bill.

The use of intrinsic sources is mostly non-controversial. However, one issue that arises is whether a judge should consider all of the relevant intrinsic sources in every case or just those cases in which the text is ambiguous or absurd. *See, e.g., State v. Courchesne*, 816 A.2d 562, 617 (Conn. 2003) (Zarella, J., dissenting) (arguing that "[i]f the language of a statute is plain and unambiguous, we need look no further than the words themselves, unless such an interpretation produces an absurd result"). As we will see in a moment, a judge's theory of interpretation helps resolve this issue.

2. Extrinsic Sources

Extrinsic sources are the second category of sources that judges may consider when discerning meaning. Extrinsic sources include materials that are outside of the official act but are part of the legislative process that created the act. Extrinsic sources include earlier drafts of the bill; legislative history (written and oral statements made during the enactment process); statutory purpose; legislative silence in response to judicial interpretation of a statute; interpretations from other jurisdictions of statutes patterned and borrowed from that jurisdiction; and interpretations by agencies of the ambiguous statutes they administer.

Think of extrinsic sources as those sources related to the process of enactment and subsequent interpretation of the act. The appropriate role for some of these sources — such as borrowed statutes — is relatively non-controversial. The use of others — such as legislative history — is highly controversial. Historically, intrinsic sources were regularly used to aid the interpretation process while extrinsic sources were used more sparingly. After the New Deal, this historical custom relaxed, and judges turned to extrinsic sources, especially legislative history, more readily. Today, as a result of the reemergence of a text-focused approach, consideration of extrinsic sources is once again controversial.

3. Policy-Based Sources

Third, and finally, are policy-based sources. These sources are separate from both the act and the legislative (enactment) process. These sources reflect important social and legal choices derived from the Constitution, common law, or prudence. Policy-based sources include, among others, the constitutional avoidance doctrine (the canon that if two reasonable or fair interpretations exist, one of which raises constitutional issues, the other interpretation should control); the rule of lenity (the canon that if two reasonable interpretations of a penal statute exist, the court should adopt the less penal interpretation); the remedial and derogation canons (the canons that statutes in derogation of the common law should be strictly construed, while remedial statutes should be broadly construed); and clear statement rules (the presumption that in some situations, such as ones raising federalism concerns, Congress would not intentionally alter the status quo absent a clear statement to that effect).

Additionally, certain areas of substantive law have their own policy-based sources. For example, judges should construe ambiguities in tax statutes in favor of the taxpayer, and judges should construe insurance contracts to protect the reasonable expectations of the parties. *Travelscape, LLC v. South Carolina Dep't of Revenue*, 705 S.E.2d 28, 40 (2011) (Pleicones, J., dissenting) (interpreting a tax statute); *Phoenix Control Systems, Inc. v. Insurance Co. of North America*, 796 P.2d 463, 466 (Az. 1990) (interpreting an insurance contract).

Think of policy-based sources as generally applicable doctrines not related to the act's text or its enactment process. Reliance on policy-based sources comes in and out of vogue. For example, the rule of lenity, which arises from constitutional due process concerns about providing adequate notice, has been relegated to a rule of last resort with society's current focus on penalizing criminals. In fact, some state legislatures, such as California's and New York's, have attempted to abolish the rule of lenity by statute. *See, e.g.,* Cal. Penal

CODE § 4 ("The rule of the common law, that penal statutes are to be strictly construed, has no application to this Code. All its provisions are to be construed according to the fair import of their terms, with a view to effect its objects and to promote justice."); N.Y. PENAL LAW § 5.00. However, because the rule of lenity is derived, in part, from constitutional procedural due process concerns, these state legislatures have had limited success in abolishing the rule. *See, e.g., People v. Ditta*, 422 N.E.2d 515, 517 (N.Y. 1981) ("Although [Penal Law § 5.00] obviously does not justify the imposition of criminal sanctions for conduct that falls beyond the scope of the Penal Law, it does authorize a court to dispense with hypertechnical or strained interpretations."); *People ex rel. Lungren v. Superior Court*, 926 P.2d 1042, 1053–54 (Cal. 1996) (noting that while the rule of lenity "has been abrogated ... the defendant is entitled to the benefit of every reasonable doubt ... as to the true interpretation of words or the construction of language used in a statute").

While it would be nice if the above categories were consistently and clearly defined in judicial opinions and academic circles, they are not. What one person calls a policy-based source, another might identify as an extrinsic source (agency deference, for example). Understanding exactly which category a source falls within is less important than understanding (1) that there is a breadth of sources available to judges for understating a statute's meaning, and (2) that judges vary in their willingness to look at more than intrinsic sources. What sources a judge will consider depends on that judge's theory of statutory interpretation.

D. The Theories of Interpretation

Former Justice Scalia pushed hard for a specific method of statutory interpretation:

> I thought we had adopted a regular method for interpreting the meaning of language in a statute: first, find the ordinary meaning of the language in its textual context; and second, using established canons of construction, ask whether there is any clear indication that some permissible meaning other than the ordinary one applies. If not — and especially if a good reason for the ordinary meaning appears plain — we apply that ordinary meaning.

Chisom v. Roemer, 501 U.S. 380, 404 (1991) (Scalia, J., dissenting). However, "[t]he hard truth of the matter is that American courts have no intelligible, generally accepted, and consistently applied theory of statutory interpretation." WILLIAM N. ESKRIDGE, JR. & PHILIP P. FRICKEY, INTRODUCTION TO HENRY M. HART, JR. & ALBERT M. SACKS, THE LEGAL PROCESS 1169 (William N. Eskridge, Jr. & Philip P. Frickey, eds., 1994). Though old, the Hart and Sacks quote is still accurate today. Contrary to Justice Scalia's lament, judges do not always agree on how to interpret statutes. And perhaps more concerning, you should "not expect anybody's theory of statutory interpretation ... to be an accurate statement of what courts actually do with statutes." *Id.*

So then, why study theory? Theory is relevant even if judges find it impossible to apply consistently. It is relevant because judges need a way to approach the statutory interpretation process to determine, among other things, whether to rely more heavily on the text and linguistic canons or on other, extra-textual sources of meaning; whether to consider legislative history and if so, which history; whether to consider the unexpressed purpose of the bill; and how to determine the weight to give a source that a judge will consider. Although the theories differ, they also have commonalities. All theories rely on the same sources, even if they emphasize those sources differently. *Compare United States v. American Trucking Ass'ns, Inc.*, 310 U.S. 534, 543 (1940) (applying purposivism while saying, "[t]here is ... no more persuasive evidence of the purpose of a statute than the words by which the legislature took to give expression to its wishes."), *with National Tax Credit Partners, L.P. v. Havlik*, 20 F.3d 705, 707 (7th Cir. 1994) (applying textualism while saying, "[k]nowing the purpose behind a rule may help a court decode an ambiguous text, but first there must be some ambiguity") (citations omitted). All theories are based on legislative supremacy and seek legislative intent for it is the legislature that has the power to legislate. All theorists believe they are being true to separation of powers.

So, what are these theories? Judges use a variety of methods to interpret statutes. These methods vary in their emphasis on the sources identified above. The methods are called the theories of statutory interpretation. Adherents of the different theories differ in what they believe best shows the intent of the enacting legislature and, thus, the meaning of the statute. They also differ about what role the courts and legislature should play in resolving statutory ambiguity. For example, one group of theorists, textualists, believes that judges must follow the meaning of clear text even when that meaning would contradict the statute's purpose. This approach is called the "letter of the law" approach. In contrast, another group, purposivists, believes that departing from the ordinary meaning of clear text to effectuate the purpose is sometimes necessary. This is called the "spirit of the law" approach. *See, e.g., King v. Burwell*, 135 S. Ct. 2480 (2015) (in which the majority opinion focused in large part on the purpose of the Affordable Care Act, while the dissent focused exclusively on the text); *Riggs v. Palmer*, 22 N.E. 188 (N.Y. 1889) (in which the majority opinion focused on the purpose of a law, while the dissent focused on the text).

Judges can and do blend the theories for a variety of reasons. For instance, being consistent is more difficult than it may seem. A judge may generally prefer one theory but find that for a specific case or even a specific issue, the preferred theory does not lead to the preferred outcome. Hence, that judge may adopt a different theory or meld a variety of theories. Additionally, because one judge, who may approach statutory interpretation in one way, writes an appellate opinion, and other judges, who may approach statutory interpretation differently, join the opinion, appellate opinions rarely exemplify consistency.

Debate over the appropriate theory has raged; indeed, the battle over the appropriate way to interpret statutes has left the pages of academic law journals and become center stage in judicial opinions and in legislative debates. *See, e.g., State v. Courchesne*, 816 A.2d 562, 587 (Conn. 2003) (rejecting textualism in favor of purposivism only to be legislatively overruled by Conn. Gen. Stat. Ann. § 1-2z (2017)); *Mayor of Lansing v. Michigan Public Serv. Comm'n*, 680 N.W.2d 840 (Mich. 2004) (attempting but failing to identify a theory).

Although many different theories can be found in academic writing, judges have fluctuated among three of them: textualism, intentionalism, and purposivism. These theories, and a few others, are explained in more detail below; however, here is a quick summary. Textualists believe that judges (really anyone interpreting a statute) should try to determine how ordinary people would understand the language that Congress used because looking beyond the text violates legislative supremacy. Intentionalists believe that judges should try to determine, as best as they can, the intent of the enacting legislators if they were confronted with the particular interpretive issue. Purposivists believe that legislatures enact legislation to address concerns. So, judges should identify the legislative concerns (or purposes) and then interpret statutes to further those concerns.

Importantly, none of the theories is perfect; each has its strengths and its weaknesses, its proponents and its critics. Perhaps because of the imperfections, the preferred theory has varied with time. A theory that dominated during one era often falls out of favor in the next. Purposivism is, perhaps, the oldest approach to interpretation. *Heydon's Case*, 76 Eng. Rep. 637 (Ex. 1584) (identifying the four-step process to identify the purpose of a law). It is also known as legal process theory. HENRY M. HART, JR. & ALBERT M. SACKS, THE LEGAL PROCESS: BASIC PROBLEMS IN THE MAKING AND APPLICATION OF LAW (William N. Eskridge Fr. & Philip P. Frickey eds., 1994) (tent. ed. 1958). In the middle ages, detailed statutes were difficult to produce, so it was hard to develop and circulate multiple drafts. Copiers did not exist. Thus, early English legislators voted based on the general goal, or purpose, of the statute, not on the precise text.

Like early English statutes, early American statutes were also very general. For example, the Sherman (Antitrust) Act, which was enacted in 1890, fits on only one page. During this era, Congress drafted broad statutes to allow reasoned judicial development of a particular area of law. Because there was so little guidance in the act, judges needed something other than the text to guide and unify their interpretations of different parts of the act. Purpose provided that guiding and unifying factor. Judges could easily test their decisions by discerning which interpretation best furthered the statutory purpose. By focusing on the purpose of the statute, judges were better able to fit the statute into the legal system as a whole and make public policy coherent.

In the United States, purposivism made an early appearance in 1892 in *Church of the Holy Trinity v. United States*, 143 U.S. 457 (1892). In that case, a statute made it unlawful for anyone to import any alien into the United States to "perform labor or service of any kind." *Id.* at 458. Holy Trinity Church had hired a rector from England. *Id.* Justice Brewer readily acknowledged that rectoring was "labor or service." However, the Court held that the statute did not apply because the purpose of the Act was to "stay the influx of ... cheap unskilled labor." *Id.* at 465. Rectoring was not unskilled labor. Famously stating that "[i]t is a familiar rule that a thing may be within the letter of the statute and yet not within the statute, because not within its spirit nor within the intention of its makers," the Court rejected the definitional interpretation. *Id.* at 459.

Purposivism came into vogue shortly after World War II, during a time of "relative consensus ... sustained economic growth, and burgeoning optimism about government's ability to foster economic growth by solving market failures and creating opportunities." ESKRIDGE ET AL., LEGISLATION AND STATUTORY INTERPRETATION, *supra*, at 727. Many Justices on the Supreme Court used this approach, for the most part, throughout the 1950s and 1960s. By the 1970s, however, America was changing. Economic growth had faltered and issues relating to war, family, and government were much more controversial.

Government became the enemy rather than the savior. Additionally, statutes became more complex and comprehensive. For example, the Civil Rights Act of 1964 was fifty-seven pages long.

With those changes came a change in the judicial approach to statutory interpretation. Intentionalism allowed the justices to focus on the legislative history to determine the intent of the legislature. Intentionalism reigned during the Warren Court and garnered favor with justices, such as former Chief Justices Burger and Rehnquist and Justice O'Connor.

Today, textualism has become a conservative favorite due, in large part, to former Justice Scalia's advocacy. In 1985–86, just before he was appointed to the Supreme Court, he urged judges to focus on the text of the statute and ignore legislative history entirely. When he was appointed to the Supreme Court, he continued his assault:

> I concur in the judgment rather than join the Court's opinion, however, for two reasons. First, despite having reached the above conclusion, the Court undertakes an exhaustive investigation of the legislative history of the Act. It attempts to justify this inquiry by relying upon the doctrine that if the legislative history of an enactment reveals a " 'clearly expressed legislative intention' contrary to [the enactment's] language," the Court is required to "question the strong presumption that Congress expresses its intent through the language it chooses." Although it is true that the Court in recent times has expressed approval of this doctrine, that is to my mind an ill-advised deviation from the venerable principle that if the language of a statute is clear, that language must be given effect — at least in the absence of a patent absurdity. Judges interpret laws rather than reconstruct legislators' intentions. Where the language of those laws is clear, we are not free to replace it with an unenacted legislative intent.

INS v. Cardoza-Fonseca, 480 U.S. 421, 452 (1987) (Scalia, J., concurring) (internal citations omitted). Justices Thomas, Kagan, and Alito are all textualists, although they are not all conservative. While not all of the justices have adopted textualism, former Justice Scalia should be credited with returning the Court's focus to the text of the statute.

So much for the history. As you read the explanations of these theories below, notice that an interpreter's theory determines whether and how that judge will use and emphasize the sources of meaning identified above. We will begin with textualism.

1. Textualism

a. The Theory

As noted earlier, a judge's view of separation of powers affects his or her theory of interpretation. Textualists believe that a judge's role is to be faithful to the Constitution by protecting legislative supremacy and the constitutionally prescribed enactment process. Under the federal Constitution, the legislature has the power to enact laws while the judiciary has the power to interpret laws. And the Constitution requires a specific process for enactment of statutes: bicameral passage and executive approval. Only the text goes through this process; thus, textualists argue that looking beyond the enacted text raises constitutional concerns. They "would hold Congress to the words it used.... [T]o do otherwise would permit Congress to legislate without completing the required process for enactment of legislation." Carol Chomsky, *Unlocking the Mysteries of* Holy Trinity: *Spirit, Letter, and History in Statutory Interpretation*, 100 COLUM. L. REV. 901, 951 (2000). Textualists believe judges should look for the ordinary public meaning of the words in a statute at the time it was drafted. Moreover, new textualists (defined below) believe that the text best shows the compromises reached during the legislative process.

> Textualists focus on intrinsic sources, particularly the text, to discern the public meaning of the language at the time it was used.

Textualists approach interpretation in a relatively linear fashion, starting with the ordinary meaning of the text and then turning from one source to the next in hierarchical order until meaning is found. Textualists note that legislators choose the words in a statute to express their intent. *Connecticut Nat'l Bank v. Germain*, 503 U.S. 249, 253–54 (1992) ("[C]ourts must presume that a legislature says in a statute what it means and means in a statue what it says there."); *Park 'N Fly, Inc. v. Dollar Park & Fly, Inc.*, 469 U.S. 189, 194 (1984) ("Statutory [interpretation] must begin with the language employed by Congress and the assumption that the ordinary meaning of that language accurately expresses the legislative purpose."). Of all the theorists, textualists are willing to examine the fewest sources, focusing primarily on the intrinsic sources, especially the text of a statute and its relationship to the law as a whole (*in pari materia*).

Textualism is sometimes called the *plain meaning theory* of interpretation because textualism is based on the *plain meaning canon* of interpretation. The plain meaning canon instructs that the ordinary meaning of the words in a statute should control interpretation. The plain meaning canon nicely matches textualists' interpretative goal of finding the ordinary, or public, meaning of the words in the statute because textualists presume that the legislature used words, grammar, and punctuation to communicate its intention. The more strictly a judge adheres to the plain meaning canon, the less frequently that judge will look beyond the intrinsic sources, the fewer extra-textual sources that judge will consider, and the less weight that judge will give to these other sources.

All textualists do not examine the sources in the same way. While all textualists will look first at the text of the statute, some textualists will stop at this step if they conclude that the language is clear. *See, e.g., Yates v. United States*, 135 S. Ct. 1074, 1091 (2015) (Kagan, J., dissenting) (saying, "the ordinary meaning of 'tangible object' is 'a discrete thing that possesses physical form.'… A fish is, of course, a discrete thing that possesses physical form. *See generally* Dr. Seuss, One Fish Two Fish Red Fish Blue Fish (1960)."); *General Dynamics Land Systems, Inc. v. Cline*, 540 U.S. 581, 602 (2004) (Thomas, J., dissenting) (finding that the plain language of the Age Discrimination in Employment Act to be so clear the decision "should have been an easy case.").

Other textualists will look at some, if not all, of the other intrinsic sources at this first step, including the grammar and punctuation, the act as a whole, the linguistic canons, and the text of other statutes. *See, e.g., Milner v. Department of the Navy*, 131 S. Ct. 1259, 1264 (2011) (finding the statute clear, in part, because of grammar rules).

But all textualists generally refuse to look at the extrinsic and policy-based sources unless the language of the statute is ambiguous or absurd after considering the intrinsic sources. (See Chapter 6 for a discussion of both ambiguity and absurdity.) In other words, textualists will look beyond intrinsic sources for meaning only when the intrinsic sources fail to resolve ambiguity or absurdity.

Textualism comes in gradations. While all textualists, indeed all theorists, rely foremost on the ordinary meaning of the text of the statute, the different forms of textualism differ in the willingness of their adherents to consider some of the non-intrinsic sources. For example, there are the "soft plain meaning" theorists—those who view the text as the primary, but not the exclusive, evidence of meaning. Soft plain meaning theorists are willing to consider legislative history and context in most cases. These theorists do not need to find a statute ambiguous or absurd to consider extra-textual evidence. Thus, their approach is closer to purposivism and intentionalism; yet plain meaning theorists would be unwilling to reject clear text to further purpose.

Soft plain meaning is the oldest form of textualism, one that views the text as the central but not as the solitary source of meaning. *See, e.g., State v. Grunke,* 752 N.W.2d 769 (Wis. 2008).

> If the words chosen for the statute exhibit a plain, clear statutory meaning, without ambiguity, the statute is applied according to the plain meaning of the statutory terms. However, if a statute is capable of being understood by reasonably well-informed persons in two or more senses[,] then the statute is ambiguous, and we may consult extrinsic sources to discern its meaning. While extrinsic sources are usually not consulted if the statutory language bears a plain meaning, we nevertheless may consult extrinsic sources to confirm or verify a plain-meaning interpretation. (internal quotation marks omitted).

Id. at 775. Note that to find plain meaning, dictionaries are one source that is often consulted. Newspapers, literature, and the bible are other sources.

Next are the moderate textualists. Moderates differ from the plain meaning theorists because moderates are unwilling to consider sources other than the intrinsic sources unless the text is ambiguous or absurd. When the meaning of the statute is clear from the text and dictionaries alone (or, in some cases, from the text and the other intrinsic sources), then interpretation is complete. Moderates consult no other sources. When, however, the meaning is ambiguous or absurd, moderate textualists will consider other intrinsic sources (if they have not already) and non-intrinsic sources of meaning:

> When the statute is clear and unambiguous, courts will not look behind the statute's plain language for legislative intent or resort to rules of statutory construction to ascertain intent. In such instance, the statute's plain and ordinary meaning must control, unless this leads to an unreasonable result or a result clearly contrary to legislative intent. However, if the statutory intent is unclear from the plain language of the statute, then we apply rules of statutory construction and explore legislative history to determine legislative intent.

Florida Dept. of Highway Safety & Motor Vehicles v. Hernandez, 74 So. 3d 1070, 1074–75 (Fla. 2011) (internal quotation marks omitted). Moderate textualism relies heavily on the plain meaning canon. Most textualists today are moderates.

Moderate textualism is appealing, in part, because of its inherent simplicity. Examine the text with dictionary in hand and then finish interpreting, turning to other sources only when absolutely required. But moderate textualism may favor simplicity over accuracy. One problem with the plain meaning canon is that language that seems clear to one person can be ambiguous or even mean something completely different to another person. For example, is a "buck" a male deer or a dollar? Is "bay" a body of water or a horse? Is "dust" a verb or a noun? Is a mosquito an animal? While textual context often resolves which meaning was intended when more than one meaning is possible (e.g., buck and bay), not all ambiguity is a result of multiple meanings (e.g., dust and mosquito). Moreover, litigation arises precisely because litigants and their lawyers disagree about the text's meaning. Theoretically, the plain meaning canon should never resolve an issue in any litigated case involving statutory interpretation unless one party is simply being unreasonable. If the meaning were that clear, the litigants would not be in court paying large sums of money to their attorneys to litigate the meaning of the clear words.

Moreover, the meaning of words can vary with context. For example, the word "assault" might mean one thing when it is in a criminal statute and something completely different when it is in a tort statute. Or the word "tomato" may mean one thing to someone making a salad and another thing to a botanist. Further, the linguistic capability of the readers (including judges) can affect meaning. For instance, some readers understand and apply grammar rules correctly, while others do not (consider the proper use of the word "which" and "that" or the use of the serial comma). For this reason, non-textualists argue that other non-textual sources of meaning are essential to interpretation. The New Mexico Supreme Court put it this way:

> [Textualism's] beguiling simplicity may mask a host of reasons why a statute, apparently clear and unambiguous on its face, may for one reason or another give rise to legitimate (*i.e.*, nonfrivolous) difference of opinion concerning the statute's meaning.... [T]his rule is deceptive in that it implies that words have intrinsic meanings. A word is merely a symbol which can be used to refer to different things. Difficult questions of statutory interpretation ought not to be decided by the bland invocation of abstract jurisprudential maxims.... The assertion in a judicial opinion that a statute needs no interpretation because it is "clear and unambiguous" is in reality evidence that the court has already considered and construed the act.

State ex rel. Helman v. Gallegos, 871 P.2d 1352, 1359 (N.M. 1994). Thus, despite its intuitive appeal, the plain meaning canon (the very essence of moderate textualism) cannot resolve every case. We will study more of its limitations in Chapter 5.

Finally, finishing our textualist continuum are the strict, or new, textualists. Justice Scalia was the primary crusader for this approach. He was joined by Justice Thomas and Judge Easterbrook of the Seventh Circuit. Frank Easterbrook, *Statutes' Domains*, 50 U. Chi. L. Rev. 533, 544–51 (1983). New textualism brought life back to the plain meaning theory, which had largely disappeared. New textualism simultaneously narrowed the sources that could be considered.

Professor William Eskridge coined the term "new textualist" to show that this "new" form of textualism differed from prior versions of textualism in that it was based on a strict view of separation of powers, legislative supremacy, ideological conservatism, and public choice theory. According to Professor Eskridge, however, new textualism was a radical critique of the Supreme Court's intentionalist approach to interpretation, and its use of legislative history.

New textualists, like all textualists, believe that because of legislative supremacy judges must follow the text of the statute even when it conflicts with the statute's purpose. *See, e.g., West Virginia University Hospitals, Inc. v. Casey*, 499 U.S. 83, 98 (1991) ("The best evidence of ... purpose is the statutory text adopted by both Houses of Congress and submitted to the President."). Further, new textualists argue that judges must respect the text because it shows the legislative compromises.

In terms of process, new textualists, like moderate textualists and plain meaning theorists, start with the text and dictionaries if needed. New textualists also require ambiguity or absurdity to look at sources beyond the text, including intrinsic sources. *See, e.g., Ali v. Federal Bureau of Prisons*, 552 U.S. 214, 227–28 (2008) (refusing to apply linguistic canons when the text was clear). New textualists generally examine these sources in order: intrinsic, extrinsic, and, finally, policy-based, except that Justice Scalia regularly examined the rule of lenity, a policy-based source, after finding ambiguity. *See, e.g., Smith v. United States*, 508 U.S. 223, 246 (1993) (Scalia, J., dissenting) (arguing that because there was ambiguity in a criminal statute, the rule of lenity applied).

However, new textualists differ from moderate textualists and plain meaning theorists because new textualists refuse to look at some types of non-textual sources, such as legislative history, legislative acquiescence, and unexpressed purpose. New textualists are unique in their refusal to consider these sources. New textualists offer a number of reasons for their refusal. First, new textualists suggest that it is unconstitutional to consider anything that was not subject to the formal enactment process outlined in the Constitution: namely, bicameralism and presentment. Members of Congress and the president have only enacted the text of the statute not the extrinsic material accompanying it. *See generally* Antonin Scalia, *Common-Law Courts in a Civil-Law System: The Role of United States Federal Courts in Interpreting the Constitution and Laws*, in A MATTER OF INTERPRETATION: FEDERAL COURTS AND THE LAW (Amy Gutmann ed., 1997).

Second, as Justice Scalia has explained, the concept of legislative intent is irrelevant to interpretation because the objective indication of the words is what constitutes the law:

> The meaning of terms on the statute books ought to be determined, not on the basis of which meaning can be shown to have been understood by a larger handful of the Members of Congress; but rather on the basis of which meaning is (1) most in accord with context and ordinary usage, and thus most likely to have been understood by the *whole* Congress which voted on the words of the statute (not to mention the citizens subject to it), and (2) most compatible with the surrounding body of law into which the provision must be integrated — a compatibility which, by a benign fiction, we assume Congress always has in mind.

Green v. Bock Laundry Mach. Co., 490 U.S. 504, 529 (1989) (Scalia, J., concurring). Hence, legislative history is irrelevant precisely because legislative intent is irrelevant.

Third, even if an interpreter were seeking legislative intent, legislative history would still be irrelevant in 99% of the cases that reach the court because the interpreter would not be able to find it. "If one were to search for an interpretive technique that, *on the whole*, was more likely to confuse than to clarify, one could hardly find a more promising candidate than legislative history." *Conroy v. Aniskoff*, 507 U.S. 511, 519 (1993) (Scalia, J., concurring).

Fourth, legislative history is unreliable for other reasons as well; these criticisms are detailed in Chapter 10, but here is a summary. Legislative history is often contradictory and can be manipulated to support any result a judge wants. Judges may choose which legislative history might be relevant and reject contradictory history. As Judge Harold Leventhal used to say, "[T]he trick is to look over the heads of the crowd and pick out your friends." ANTONIN SCALIA, A MATTER OF INTERPRETATION: FEDERAL COURTS AND THE LAW 36 (1997). Also, legislators often do not read committee reports. Justice Scalia said, "I frankly doubt that it is ever reasonable to assume that the details, as opposed to the broad outlines of purpose, set forth in a committee report come to the attention of, much less are approved by, the house which enacts the committee's bill." *Hirschey v. FERC*, 777 F.2d 1, 7 & n.1 (D.C. Cir. 1985) (Scalia, J., concurring) (noting that the chairman of the finance committee's response to whether he had read the committee report was: "I am working on it. It is not a bestseller, but I am working on it.").

A further criticism of legislative history is that staff members often write committee reports and even draft legislation; thus, such history should not be relied upon as articulating the intent of a body that did not write it. *Blanchard v. Bergeron*, 489 U.S. 87, 98-99 (1989) (Scalia, J., concurring) ("What a heady feeling it must be for a young staffer, to know that [information a staff member includes in a committee report] can transform [it] into the law of the land, thereafter dutifully to be observed by the Supreme Court itself."). Further, the information may be included to influence judicial interpretation. *Harrisburg v. Franklin*, 806 F. Supp. 1181, 1184 (M.D. Pa. 1992) (refusing to consider a legislator's written statements, which were made after the bill passed and were *"never actually spoken on the floor of the legislature"*).

Lastly, the Court's use of legislative history has oversold its importance to the interpreter. Again, Justice Scalia explained:

> [I]it is natural for the bar to believe that the juridical importance of [legislative history] matches its prominence in our opinions—thus producing a legal culture in which, when counsel arguing before us assert that "Congress has said" something, they now frequently mean, by "Congress," a committee report; and in which it was not beyond the pale for a recent brief to say the following: "Unfortunately, the legislative debates are not helpful. Thus, we turn to the other guidepost in this difficult area, statutory language."

Bock Laundry, 490 U.S. at 529 (Scalia, J., concurring).

Despite his assault on legislative history, the other Justices explicitly rejected Justice Scalia's suggestion that legislative history is never relevant to statutory interpretation. *See Wisconsin Pub. Intervenor v. Mortier*, 501 U.S. 597, 610 n.4 (1991) ("Our precedents demonstrate that the Court's practice of utilizing legislative history reaches well into its past. We suspect that the practice will likewise reach well into the future.") (internal citation omitted).

Supporters of new textualism argue that the approach limits judicial discretion, increases predictability and efficiency, encourages more careful legislative drafting, and limits inappropriate uses of legislative history. These supporters explain that when judges and litigants are constrained to the text of statutes, statutory meaning becomes more assured and litigation decreases. They further explain that when legislative history cannot be considered as relevant to meaning, the cost of discerning meaning lessens and certainty increases. Finally, they explain that when legislatures are held to the words they use, they are more likely to choose those words with care.

New textualism has its critics. First, some criticize the unwillingness of its adherents to consider some sources of meaning, namely legislative history and unexpressed purpose. It makes little sense to prohibit all evidence generated during the legislative process simply because that evidence was not enacted. Indeed, non-textualists do not claim that legislative history is part of the act, or even that, in any sense, it is law. While the text is authoritative and has the force of law, legislative history and purpose provide evidence of what that law means or even what the legislative compromises were. In other words, legislative history and purpose can help illuminate the meaning of the words that do make up the law and the compromises the legislators reached during the enactment process. In short, new textualists' refusal to consider legislative history or unarticulated purpose in any case seems rigid and simplistic.

Additionally, it is not clear why new textualists are willing to consult dictionaries and the linguistic canons, which similarly do not go through the legislative process, but are not willing to consult legislative history. While it may or may not be a good idea for legislators to use dictionaries or the linguistic canons when drafting, there is no proof that they do so. Abbe R. Gluck & Lisa Schultz Bressman, *Statutory Interpretation from the Inside — An Empirical Study of Congressional Drafting, Delegation, and the Canons: Part I*, 65 Stan. L. Rev. 901, 906, 932 (2013) (noting that staff who were involved with the legislative drafting process did not consult dictionaries while drafting despite knowing that Supreme Court justices regularly referred to them). If the Constitution allows judges to consider some non-textual sources, then why does it not allow them to consider all non-textual sources? What makes legislative history so untrustworthy?

Moreover, dictionaries are not the perfect reference material that textualists would have us believe. Sometimes a dictionary definition of a word differs from the ordinary meaning of a word, yet some judges rigidly adhere to the dictionary definition. For example, if a statute increases the sentence of anyone who "uses or carries a firearm" in relation to a drug offense, an ordinary reading of this language would suggest that a defendant must use the gun as a weapon to incur the additional penalty, not as an item of value to barter. But a dictionary definition of "use" is sufficiently broad to include bartering a gun for drugs. Because the dictionary definition was so broad, the majority in *Smith v. United States*, held that the statute included bartering a gun for drugs. 508 U.S. 223, 240 (1993). The dissent strongly disagreed, noting that "[t]he Court does not appear to grasp the distinction between how a word *can be* used and how it *ordinarily is* used." *Id.* at 242 (Scalia, J., dissenting). Interestingly, Justice O'Connor, who is not a textualist, wrote the majority opinion, while Justice Scalia, who is, wrote the dissent.

Regardless of his unwillingness to use legislative history, Justice Scalia properly returned judicial focus to the text of the statute as the starting point for interpretation. As a result of his and others' influence, the text of the statute has gained importance and, likely, will retain this importance in the years to come. *See, e.g., Mohamad v. Palestinian Auth.*, 566 U.S. 449, 460 (2012) ("[P]etitioners' purposivist argument simply cannot overcome the force of the plain text."); *Schindler Elevator Corp. v. United States ex rel. Kirk*, 563 U.S. 401, 412 (2011) ("In interpreting a statute, [o]ur inquiry must cease if the statutory language is unambiguous.") (citations and internal quotation marks omitted); *Ali v. Federal Bureau of Prisons*, 552 U.S. 214, 228 (2008) ("We are not at liberty to rewrite the statute to reflect a meaning we deem more desirable. Instead, we must give effect to the text Congress enacted.").

However, support for new textualism itself has waned in recent years. Thus, in the remainder of this text, when the word "textualism" is used, moderate, rather than new, textualism is intended.

To summarize, textualists examine the fewest sources, focusing primarily on the intrinsic sources. Initially, textualists will look at the text of the statute and dictionary definitions of the language at issue. Some textualists will also look at grammar and punctuation, the statute and laws as a whole, the linguistic canons, and the text of other statutes. Textualists will consider extrinsic and policy-based sources only when the statute remains ambiguous or absurd after a search of the intrinsic sources is complete. *See State ex rel. Kalal v. Circuit Court for Dane Cnty.*, 681 N.W.2d 110, 123 (Wis. 2004). "[O]ur cases generally adhere to a methodology that relies primarily on intrinsic sources of statutory meaning and confines resort to extrinsic sources of legislative intent to cases in which the statutory language is ambiguous." *Id.*

b. Textualism in the States

Although the Justices of the Supreme Court have wrestled with the appropriate approach to statutory interpretation, Congress has chosen not to provide direct guidance, although some scholars have suggested that it should. In contrast, many state legislatures have adopted statutes telling their judiciary how to interpret statutes. Not surprisingly, textualism is the most common choice. For example, as mentioned above, Connecticut has a textualist directive that reads as follows:

> The meaning of a statute shall, in the first instance, be ascertained from the text of the statute itself and its relationship to other statutes. If, after examining such text and considering such relationship, the meaning of such text is plain and unambiguous and does not yield absurd or unworkable results, extratextual evidence of the meaning of the statute shall not be considered.

CONN. GEN. STAT. § 1-2z.

Colorado, Hawaii, Iowa, North Dakota, Ohio, and Pennsylvania also have textualist directives. COLO. REV. STAT. § 2-4-203; HAW. REV. STAT. § 1-15; IOWA CODE § 4.6; N.D. CENT. CODE § 1-02-39; OHIO REV. CODE ANN. § 1.49; 1 PA. CONS. STAT. § 1921(b).

2. Intentionalist-Based Theories

While textualist theories are rooted in the belief that the text best respects legislative supremacy, intentionalist-based theories are rooted in the belief that discerning the enacting legislature's intent best respects the legislature's power to choose the policies that govern society. For intentionalist-based theorists, the court's duty is to discern the intent of that representative body and interpret statutes to further that intent. Thus, intentionalist-based theorists attempt to understand the meaning of statutes by looking for the enacting legislature's intent or goals.

There are two kinds of intent: *specific intent* and *general intent*. Specific intent is the intent of the enacting legislature on a specific issue. For example, if a court had to determine whether affirmative action programs are allowable under a statute providing that "no person shall be discriminated against on the basis of race," a judge looking for specific intent would search the sources of meaning to determine whether the enacting legislature intended the word "discriminate" to apply to affirmative action programs that promote the hiring of racial minorities. If the legislative history of the act showed that the legislators actually discussed affirmative action

> Specific intent is the intent of the enacting legislature on the precise issue presented.

programs positively or negatively during the House or Senate debates, for example, then a judge looking for specific intent would conclude that the legislature specifically intended the word "discriminate" to include or not include affirmative action programs, depending on what was said. Thus, a judge seeking specific intent looks to see whether the enacting legislature had a specific intent as to the interpretive issue before the court, in this case whether the word "discriminate" includes affirmative action programs.

In contrast, general intent is the overall goal, or purpose, of the legislature as a whole. General intent is generally much easier to find. For example, if we return to the discrimination statute in the last paragraph, a judge looking for general intent would search the sources of meaning to determine whether the enacting legislature's purpose when enacting the law was to make society color-blind or was to improve the plight of racial minorities. If the legislators wanted to improve the plight of minorities, then a judge looking for general intent would likely conclude that a statute prohibiting people from "discriminating" should not prohibit affirmative action programs. Whether the legislators actually thought about whether "discriminating" included affirmative action programs would not be the central question for a judge seeking general intent (although it may still be relevant). A judge seeking general intent is looking to see what the legislators' goal, or purpose, for enacting the law was.

> General intent is the overall goal, or purpose, the legislature had when enacting the act.

The two, prominent intentionalist-based theories are (1) intentionalism, which focuses on specific intent, and (2) purposivism, which focuses on general intent. Each of these theories is explored in detail below. A few of the less common, but related, theories are also explored.

a. Intentionalism: The Theory

Intentionalists seek out the specific intent of the legislature that enacted the statute: when the legislature enacted the act, what did that legislature have in mind in regard to the specific issue before the court? To find specific intent, intentionalists start with the statutory text. But intentionalists do not stop with the text even if the text is clear, as a textualist would do; rather, intentionalists move on and examine the other sources of meaning. In perusing other sources of meaning, intentionalists are looking for help in discerning the specific intent of the enacting legislature. Thus, intentionalists often find statements made during the

> Intentionalists focus on the text and intrinsic sources to find the specific intent of the enacting legislators in regard to the language at issue in the statute.

enactment process and early draft versions of the bill especially relevant, although intentionalists are willing to consider all sources of meaning regardless of whether ambiguity or absurdity is present. If these sources demonstrate that the legislature did not intend for the text to have its ordinary meaning, intentionalists will reject the ordinary meaning for a meaning that furthers the specific intent.

As mentioned above, a judge's understanding of separation of powers affects that judge's approach to statutory interpretation. Intentionalists believe that the judicial role is to be faithful agents of the legislature, working to ensure that the legislative policy choices are implemented. Intentionalists believe that examining sources other than the text helps constrain the judiciary and helps maintain its separate function, that of interpreting statutes. When a judge examines all sources, that judge can make a fully informed decision, rather than one based on limited information. Further, intentionalists argue that their approach furthers separation of powers because it protects the legislature's power to legislate from judicial interference: judges must implement the enacting legislature's intent and not impose their own policy preferences.

Intentionalism is not without its critics. For example, consider whether the Senate, a group of 100 individuals, all with different constituencies, can have one, unified intent (how about the House with even more members?). Probably not. Each legislator may have a unique reason for voting for a bill. For example, Title VII of the Civil Rights Act, which prohibits discrimination in the workplace, was a compromise of various competing interests: the liberal Northern and Eastern legislators (who sponsored the bill) wanted to help African American workers; the conservative Southern legislators wanted to ensure that African American workers were not helped at the expense of white workers; and finally, the conservative Midwestern legislators, the pivotal voters, wanted to limit government interference in business. With so many different legislators having so many different intentions, it is unlikely that each of these legislators would agree about whether affirmative action programs should be allowed. The liberal Northern and Eastern legislators would likely have said "yes," while the more conservative Southern and Midwestern legislators would likely have said "no." Which intent should control, "the 51st senator, needed to pass the bill, or the 67th, needed to break the southern filibuster?" WILLIAM N. ESKRIDGE, JR. ET AL., LEGISLATION AND STATUTORY INTERPRETATION 219 (2d 2006). In *United Steelworkers v. Weber*, 443 U.S. 193 (1979) (Burger, C.J., Rehnquist, J. dissenting), the Court addressed that issue. The Supreme Court's majority and dissent disagreed on whose intent was central. The purposivist majority focused on the liberal Northern and Eastern legislators, while the intentionalist dissent focused on the conservative Southern and Midwestern legislators.

Of course, intentionalists respond to that criticism by arguing that a group can have intent. While the individual members may have different, private *motives* for their own actions, the existence of private motives does not necessarily eliminate the possibility that the group has a common agenda. For example, consider a sports team as it takes the field, a political party as it enters an election, or the board of a company preparing annual strategy. The group's agenda and the members' motives might not be identical, but each group has one, overarching intent: to win. Intentionalism is, thus, less about the reality of always finding a unified intent and more about the *possibility* of finding one.

Intentionalists are also criticized for their heavy reliance on legislative history. Above you learned why new textualists criticize the use of legislative history. While these criticisms are valid, intentionalists suggest caution, not wholesale rejection, of the use of legislative history. True, legislative history is not enacted law; however, legislative history can offer insight into what some or all of the legislators may have been thinking when the law, which did go through the constitutionally prescribed process, was enacted. Because intentionalists want to know what legislators were thinking, legislative history can be useful; legislative history simply offers a fuller picture of the legislative process for a particular bill.

To summarize, intentionalists focus on finding the specific intent of the enacting legislature in regard to the specific question before the court. Judges using this approach focus first on text (do not forget this!) but, also, find legislative history and draft versions of the bill very relevant. Importantly, these theorists will examine all of the sources of meaning regardless of whether the text is ambiguous or absurd. *See, e.g., Kosak v. United States*, 465 U.S. 848 (1984) (relying on an internal Justice Department working paper, even though it was never mentioned in the legislative history, to discern intent); *Riggs*, 22 N.E. at 190 (relying on a maxim of the common law to discern intent).

b. Intentionalism in the States

Only New York has adopted intentionalism by statute. New York's statute provides as follows:

- Generally The primary consideration of the courts in the construction of statutes is to ascertain and give effect to the intention of the Legislature.

- Ascertainment of intention The intention of the Legislature is first to be sought from a literal reading of the act itself, but if the meaning is still not clear, the intent may be ascertained from such facts and through such rules as may, in connection with the language, legitimately reveal it.

N.Y. STAT. LAW § 92(a), (b). The official comment explains New York's choice:

> Since the intention of the Legislature, embodied in a statute, is the law, in the construction of statutes the basic rule of procedure and the primary consideration of the courts are to ascertain and give effect to the intention of the Legislature.... So it is the duty of courts to adopt a construction of a statute that will bring it into harmony with the Constitution and with legislative intent....
>
> The intent of the Legislature is controlling and must be given force and effect, regardless of the circumstance that inconvenience, hardship, or injustice may result. Indeed the Legislature's intent must be ascertained and effectuated whatever may be the opinion of the judiciary as to the wisdom, expediency, or policy of the statute, and whatever excesses or omissions may be found in the statute. The courts do not sit in review of the discretion of the Legislature and may not substitute their judgment for that of the lawmaking body.

Id. cmt. a.

c. Imaginative Reconstruction: An Academic's Version of Intentionalism

As noted above, discerning the specific intent of the enacting legislature is often a difficult, if not impossible, task. Moreover, limiting interpretation to a static point in time (enactment) creates its own issues. For example, how does one discern an enacting legislature's intent regarding technology that did not exist at the time the law was enacted? To address these concerns, in 1907, Dean Roscoe Pound urged courts to adopt "imaginative reconstructionism" as an approach for discerning the intent of the enacting legislature. Using imaginative reconstructionism, a judge would try to imagine what the enacting legislature would have intended had the precise interpretive issue before the court been raised during the enactment process. As Judge Learned Hand described:

> As nearly as we can, we must put ourselves in the place of those who uttered the words, and try to divine how they would have dealt with the unforeseen situations; and, although their words are by far the

most decisive evidence of what they would have done, they are by no means final.

Guiseppi v. Walling, 144 F.2d 608, 624 (2d Cir. 1944).

To imagine what the enacting legislature would do, Dean Pound proposed that judges recreate intent by examining the available historical evidence, including the statute, with a sense of morality and justice to determine what the enacting legislature likely intended given the realities of today. Roscoe Pound, *Spurious Interpretation*, 7 COLUM. L. REV. 379, 381 (1907). This approach borrows from common law analysis and civil law practice in that the language in the statute guides judicial interpretation but often does not answer the question; rather, by using reason and analogy, a judge can apply the statute to situations the language does not explicitly cover and, thus, arrive at a just result.

Imaginative reconstructionism is normative for it allows the judiciary to consider public policy when making interpretive choices. Using "practical reasoning," judges can adopt flexible interpretations based on current public norms. As seen above, Justice Learned Hand was a proponent of this theory.

Not surprisingly, imaginative reconstructionism suffers from some of the same criticisms as intentionalism: Whose intent is reconstructed? Why should unenacted information play any role in interpretation? While Dean Pound's approach has had some followers in academic circles, it garners little support among the judiciary.

d. Purposivism: The Theory

While intentionalists try to identify the specific intent of the legislature that enacted the statute, purposivists try to identify the general intent, or purpose, of the legislature that enacted the statute. Purposivists believe that law, both as a whole and specifically, is designed to solve identifiable problems; thus, every statute has a purpose or reason for its enactment. Purposivists strive to interpret the statutory language in a way that furthers this purpose. To do so, purposivists will look at all of the sources, but enacted text is the starting point.

> Purposivists examine all sources to discern the general intent, or reason, the legislature enacted the legislation.

Purposivists and intentionalists differ in what they seek when examining the various sources of meaning. As we just saw, intentionalists seek specific intent: What did the enacting legislature expect regarding the precise interpretive issue presented to the court? In contrast, purposivists seek the legislature's general intent, or purpose: What problem was the legislature trying to remedy, and how did the legislature redress that problem? Once the purpose and remedy have been identified, purposivists interpret the statute to further that purpose subject to two caveats: judges should not give words a meaning those words cannot bear, nor a meaning that would violate generally prevailing policies of law.

Remember that a judge's understanding of separation of powers affects that judge's approach to statutory interpretation. You learned above that textualists view themselves as faithful agents of the Constitution, and intentionalists view themselves as faithful agents of the legislature. In contrast, purposivists view themselves as "faithful agent[s] of a well-functioning regulatory regime." Eskridge et al., Legislation and Statutory Interpretation, *supra*, at 7 (emphasis omitted). For this reason, purposivists identify the problem the legislature was trying to address when enacting the statute. To a purposivist, a statute makes sense only when understood in light of its purpose: a rule without purpose is meaningless. For example, consider our hypothetical city ordinance prohibiting "vehicles" in the park. Is a non-motorized scooter a vehicle? To decide this question, a purposivist might ask why the city council enacted the ordinance in the first place. If the council's purpose was to limit air and noise pollution, then "vehicle" should not be interpreted to include scooters. If, instead, the city's purpose was to increase pedestrian safety, then, perhaps, "vehicle" should be so interpreted to include scooters. Thus, purposivists believe that knowing the evil, or mischief, at which the statute was aimed aids interpretation.

To discern purpose, purposivists begin with the text but do not end the analysis there:

> There is, of course, no more persuasive evidence of the purpose of a statute than the words by which the legislature undertook to give expression to its wishes. Often these words are sufficient in and of themselves to determine the purpose of the legislation. In such cases we have followed their plain meaning. When that meaning has led to absurd or futile results, however, this Court has looked beyond the words to the purpose of the act. Frequently, however, even when the plain meaning did not produce absurd results but merely an unreasonable one plainly at variance with the policy of the legislation as a whole this Court has followed that purpose, rather than the literal words. When aid to construction of the meaning of words as used in

the statute is available, there certainly can be no rule of law which forbids its use, however clear the words may appear on superficial examination.

United States v. American Trucking Ass'ns, Inc., 310 U.S. 534, 543–44 (1940) (internal citations omitted). In short, purposivists are willing to examine all relevant sources of meaning.

While purposivism and intentionalism are similar, purposivism has one advantage over intentionalism: flexibility. Purposivists can interpret statutes in situations the enacting legislature never contemplated. "Purposivism ... renders statutory interpretation adaptable to new circumstances." ESKRIDGE ET AL., LEGISLATION AND STATUTORY INTERPRETATION, *supra*, at 221. For example, in the hypothetical city ordinance prohibiting "vehicles" in the park, a purposivist judge could determine that the ordinance applied to drones even though these "vehicles" may not have been around when the ordinance was adopted. But an intentionalist judge might have more difficulty with this issue because the city council could not have intended to regulate something not in existence when the ordinance was adopted. Therefore, purposivism allows judges to interpret laws in light of technological, social, legal, and other advances—something true intentionalism is incapable of doing.

Purposivism is not without its critics. The most troublesome aspect of purposivism is, of course, how to legitimately discern a statute's purpose. Ideally, legislatures would include a findings or purpose clause in the enacted text of every act. More commonly, however, they do not. Older acts in particular often do not have such clauses. And even when an act includes a purpose clause, its wording may have been subject to controversy and political compromise during the enactment process. Thus, even when included, purpose clauses may be too general to be helpful.

For these reasons, judges often look for *unexpressed* purpose. To find unexpressed purpose, purposivists consider the text, the legislative history, the legal history, the social context, and other sources. But these sources may not be conclusive. What then? Some legal theorists have suggested that to figure out a statute's primary purpose, a judge should posit various situations. In other words, a judge should start with the situations clearly covered and radiate outward. While doing so, judges should presume that legislatures are "made of reasonable persons pursuing reasonable purposes, reasonably." HENRY HART & ALBERT SACHS, THE LEGAL PROCESS 1378 (William N. Eskridge, Jr. & Philip P. Frickey eds., 1994). You can see why this approach might concern some interpreters.

Purposivism has other criticisms. For example, even if a statutory purpose is discernible, there may be competing ideas of how to further that purpose. For example, is affirmative action the best way to achieve racial parity or is color-blindness better?

Another criticism of purposivism is that statutes often have more than one purpose, and these purposes can conflict. For example, one purpose of Title VII of the Civil Rights Act—which prohibits discrimination in the workplace—was to increase the number of African Americans in the workforce. Another purpose was to make hiring and other work-related decisions race neutral. Voluntary affirmative action programs further the first purpose but not the second. Is the fact that one purpose is furthered enough to sustain an interpretation? Purposivism does not answer the question of whether an interpretation is appropriate when one, but not another, purpose is furthered.

Similarly, a statute may have one purpose while an exception to that statute may have a conflicting purpose. For example, the purpose of the Freedom of Information Act (FOIA) (5 U.S.C. § 552) is to encourage open government. But some of the exceptions within the Act, such as prohibiting the disclosure of personnel files, exist to protect individual privacy. If a judge interprets an exception, which purpose should control: the purpose of FOIA or the purpose of the exception? In other words, should the judge interpret the exception in FOIA narrowly, to better further the purpose of the Act as a whole, or broadly, to better further the purpose of the exception? *See, e.g., Church of Scientology v. Department of Justice*, 612 F.2d 417, 425 (9th Cir. 1979) (broadly interpreting an exemption in FOIA to further the exception's purpose despite the dissent's argument that the exemption should be narrowly construed to further FOIA's purpose). Again, purposivism does not answer this question.

Finally, judges are constitutionally required to interpret statutory language, not make law. If judges make decisions based on their own policy choices, disguised as purpose, they aggrandize their own power at the expense of the legislature.

To summarize, purposivists focus on finding the general intent, or purpose, of the enacting legislature in regard to the issue before the court. Judges using this approach focus first on text (do not forget this!) but, also, find legislative history and social context very relevant. Importantly, like intentionalists, these theorists will examine all of the sources of meaning regardless of whether the text is ambiguous or absurd. *See, e.g., King v. Burwell*, 135 S. Ct. 2480, 2489–94 (2015) (using a purposivist approach to interpret a provision in the Affordable Care Act); *Yates*, 135 S. Ct. at 1088–89 (using a purposivist approach to hold that a fish is not a tangible object).

e. Purposivism in the States

Of the state legislatures that have enacted statutory directives, most legislatures have chosen textualism. It is unclear why textualism is preferred, but perhaps it is due to the lack of legislative history available in many states and the fact that state judges are often more restrained in their approach to interpretation than federal judges. Perhaps, as state legislative materials become increasingly available, this preference may be altered.

One state, Texas, does have a purposivist statute that provides as follows:

In construing a statute, *whether or not the statute is considered ambiguous on its face,* a court may consider among other matters the:

(1) object sought to be attained;

(2) circumstances under which the statute was enacted;

(3) legislative history;

(4) common law or former statutory provisions, including laws on the same or similar subjects;

(5) consequences of a particular construction;

(6) administrative construction of the statute; and

(7) title (caption), preamble, and emergency provision.

Tex. Gov't Code Ann. § 311.023 (emphasis added). But despite this clear legislative directive to look at all relevant information regardless of whether a statute is ambiguous, some members of the Texas judiciary refuse to follow it. For example, in *State v. Muller,* 829 S.W.2d 805 (Tex. Ct. Crim. App. 1992), the court said, "[W]e look to a statute's legislative history *only* if the plain meaning of the literal text of that statute is ambiguous or leads to highly improbable results." *Id.* at 811 n.7.

Similarly, a Georgia statute specifically directs courts to consider intent, purpose, and text when interpreting statutes:

(a) In all interpretations of statutes, the courts shall look diligently for the intention of the General Assembly, keeping in view at all times the old law, the evil, and the remedy....

(b) In all interpretations of statutes, the ordinary signification shall be applied to all words....

Ga. Code Ann. §§ 1-3-1(a) & (b). Though acknowledging the existence of this directive, Georgia courts generally ignore it, preferring instead to apply textualism. For example, in *Busch v. State*, 523 S.E.2d 21 (Ga. 1999), the court said, "If the words of a statute, however, are plain and capable of having but one meaning, and do not produce any absurd, impractical, or contradictory results, then this Court is bound to follow the meaning of those words." *Id.* at 23. In a later case, the Georgia Court of Appeals tried, but failed, to reconcile the court's use of textualism with the more purposivist directive of the statute:

> In construing a statute, our goal is to determine its legislative purpose. In this regard, a court must first focus on the statute's text. In order to discern the meaning of the words of a statute, the reader must look at the context in which the statute was written, remembering at all times that "the meaning of a sentence may be more than that of the separate words, as a melody is more than the notes." *If the words of a statute, however, are plain and capable of having but one meaning, and do not produce any absurd, impractical, or contradictory results, then this Court is bound to follow the meaning of those words.* If, on the other hand, the words of the statute are ambiguous, then this Court must construe the statute, keeping in mind the purpose of the statute and "the old law, the evil, and the remedy."

State v. Brown, 551 S.E.2d 773, 775 (Ga. Ct. App. 2001) (emphasis added) (citing GA. CODE APP. § 1-3-1(a)).

f. Dynamic Statutory Interpretation

An academic theory related to purposivism is dynamic statutory interpretation. Professor William Eskridge described dynamic statutory interpretation in 1987. William Eskridge, *Dynamic Statutory Interpretation*, 135 U. PA. L. REV. 1479 (1987). It is not an approach that you will find referenced in many judicial opinions. *But see Commonwealth v. Welosky*, 276 Mass. 398 (1931) (using this approach in refusing to interpret the phrase "[a] person qualified to vote for representatives" to include women). Rather, it is one academic's ideal of what should happen in interpretation. Remember that intentionalist judges typically attempt to discern legislative intent as of the time the statute was enacted and that purposivist judges typically attempt to discern statutory purpose as of the time the statute was enacted. The dynamic approach encourages judges to be more flexible and consider what the enacting legislature would have wanted when and social moral values change. For example, let's return to the Civil Rights Act of 1964, which was enacted to prohibit discrimination based on race. It is highly unlikely that the Congress of 1964 would have approved of affirmative action programs; the statute was enacted to encourage a race-blind society. Yet, years after the Act had been in effect, discrimination was still the norm. In other words, the Act was not having the intended effect. Should the Supreme Court consider this fact when interpreting the statute? The standard theories would say no; dynamic statutory interpretation would say yes. Even though no linguistic change had occurred since the Act's passage, the values of the interpreters (and society) had changed. Affirmative action programs were thought to be necessary to combat continued racism.

In general, dynamic statutory interpretation allows judges to work in concert with the legislature to accomplish its goals as times and values change. Consider statutes enacted in the 1800s that criminalize sodomy. We would define this term very differently today.

Note that a judge using this interpretive theory must identify the goals, or purposes, of the legislation. Thus, this theory is really a close cousin to purposivism. Because it is so similar to purposivism, dynamic interpretation shares some of the same weaknesses. Most notably, critics view this approach as judicial power-grabbing, which violates the Constitution's separation of powers.

3. Alaska's Sliding Scale Approach: A Compromise

As we saw above, all of the approaches have shortcomings. For this reason, the Alaska judiciary rejected all of the above approaches (especially textualism) and created its own unique approach, the "sliding scale approach." It blends textualism, intentionalism, and purposivism. It allows judges to consider a statute's meaning without first finding ambiguity or absurdity by applying a sliding scale of clarity. The sliding scale approach simply states that all evidence of meaning is relevant; however, the clearer the statutory language, the more convincing the evidence of a contrary legislative purpose or intent must be. *LeFever v. State*, 877 P.2d 1298, 1299–300 (Alaska Ct. App. 1994). You might think of a balance with text resting on one side and contrary sources on the other. The clearer the text, the heavier the contrary sources must be.

The Alaska judiciary considered moderate textualism but rejected it because that approach overly restricted the judicial inquiry. Because words are necessarily inexact and ambiguity is inherent in language, other sources of meaning often prove helpful in construing a statute. Thus, even if the statute under consideration is facially clear, the legislative history can be considered because it might reveal an ambiguity not apparent on the face of the statute. *Anchorage v. Sisters of Providence in Wash., Inc.*, 628 P.2d 22, 27 n.6 (Alaska 1981).

Alaska's sliding scale approach has inherent appeal. The approach is a kissing cousin to the soft plain meaning approach; under the sliding scale approach, the plainer the text, the more convincing the contrary indications of meaning must be to trump the text. This soft version of textualism turns the plain meaning canon into a rebuttable presumption: the plain meaning will control absent convincing evidence that the legislature intended a different meaning. In many ways, this approach blends the best of the theories above, while avoiding the difficulties; the text is always the primary, but not the exclusive, evidence of meaning. But this approach shares many of the problems of textualism and, thus, is not the perfect compromise it may appear to be. While Connecticut's Supreme Court discussed Alaska's approach with approval, to date, no other state has explicitly followed suit.

4. Theory Abroad

In case you are interested to learn how other countries approach interpretation, this section examines two other common law countries: England and Australia, starting with England.

Prior to 1965, judges from England followed a new textual approach; text was the primary consideration, and consideration of legislative history and purpose were not allowed. In 1965, the English Parliament established an independent body to determine how to make laws simpler, more accessible, fairer, modern, and more cost-effective. This independent body was the Law Commission. In 1969, the Law Commission issued a report addressing statutory interpretation. The Commission considered America's approach, among others, and concluded, "There is a tendency in our systems ... to over-emphasize the literal meaning of a provision ... at the expense of the meaning to be derived from other possible contexts; the latter include the 'mischief' or general legislative purpose ... which underlie the provision." THE LAW COMMISSION AND THE SCOTTISH LAW COMMISSION, THE INTERPRETATION OF STATUTES 49 (June 9, 1969).[1] After the report was issued, English judges became more purposivist. Purposivism expanded the sources judges could consider, including reports

---

1. Available at https://assets.publishing.service.gov.uk/government/uploads/system/uploads/attachment_data/file/228894/0256.pdf

from government bodies, the Law Commission, and the Royal Commission—a body set up to gather information about the operation of existing laws or to investigate any social, educational, or other matter.

Then, in the landmark case of *Pepper v. Hart*, [1992] 3 W.L.R. 1032, [1993] 1 All E.R. 42 (1993), a five-judge panel from the House of Lords held that judges should be able to consider legislative history when interpreting statutes that were ambiguous or absurd. In the case, John Hart and nine others were teachers at Malvern College. They benefited from a "concessionary fee" scheme that allowed their children to attend the college at one fifth of the normal price. The government attempted to tax this benefit based on the Finance Act of 1976. The issue was whether the benefit was worth the full tuition reduction (the government's position) or whether it was worth the marginal increased cost to the college (Hart's position).

The tax assessors agreed with Hart, but both lower courts agreed with the government. The majority examined statements made during the legislative process and agreed with Hart. The lords learned that during the legislative debates, the Financial Secretary to the Treasury had remarked (in response to a question about places for the children of teachers at fee-paying schools) "[N]ow the benefit will be assessed on the cost to the employer, which would be very small indeed ...." Before *Pepper*, consideration of the legislative debates known as *Hansard* would have been considered unconstitutional. In reaching their holding, the lords discussed the proper role of *Hansard* statements in the interpretation process. The lords concluded that when legislation was ambiguous or absurd, judges could refer to these statements to interpret the meaning of the legislation. Thus, they adopted moderate textualism.

Lord Mackay dissented, arguing that the legislative statements should not be considered because of the time and expense involved in a lawyer having to look up every debate and discussion on a particular statute when giving legal advice or preparing a case. The holding in *Pepper*, thus, radically transformed England's approach to interpretation from strict textualism to moderate textualism. Such a change would not seem radical in the United States!

Although the lower courts and the lords initially followed the decision, judicial acceptance of *Pepper* soon began to wane. The courts whittled down the holding. For example, in *Massey v. Boulden*, [2003] 2 All ER 87, the court held that legislative history could not be used in criminal law cases because the rule of lenity precluded its use. And in *Robinson v. Secretary of State for Northern Ireland*, [2002] UKHL 32, three of the Lords said that *Pepper*'s dissenting Lord Mackay had "turned out to be the better prophet" in noting the inefficiency and expense associated with *Pepper*'s approach. Additional criticism and limitations followed. As a result of these criticisms and limitations, Professor Stefan Vogenauer, from Oxford, concluded that "the scope of *Pepper v. Hart* has been reduced to such an extent that the ruling has almost become meaningless." Stefan Vogenauer, *A Retreat from* Pepper v Hart? *A Reply to Lord Steyn*, 25 Oxford J. Leg. Studies 629–74 (2005).

Whatever the accuracy of the criticisms, references to legislative history increased after *Pepper*'s debut. *See, e.g., Harding v. Wealands,* [2006] UKHL 32 (acknowledging that *Pepper* had been "out of judicial favour in recent years," but responding that legislative history was "perhaps especially [useful] as a confirmatory aid").

In contrast to England's choice of new textualism, the Australian Parliament adopted purposivism and rejected textualism. (These provisions come from Acts Interpretation Act 1901 (Cth).) Although the Act is dated 1901, section 15AA was added in 1982 (and amended in 2011). Section 15AB was added in 1984. Notice the breadth of sources a judge must consider.

S 15AA Interpretation best achieving Act's purpose or object

> In interpreting a provision of an Act, the interpretation that would best achieve the purpose or object of the Act (whether or not that purpose or object is expressly stated in the Act) is to be preferred to each other interpretation.

S 15AB Use of extrinsic material in the interpretation of an Act

> (1) Subject to subsection (3), in the interpretation of a provision of an Act, if any material not forming part of the Act is capable of assisting in the ascertainment of the meaning of the provision, consideration may be given to that material:
> (a) to confirm that the meaning of the provision is the ordinary meaning conveyed by the text of the provision taking into account its context in the Act and the purpose or object underlying the Act; or
> (b) to determine the meaning of the provision when:
> (i) the provision is ambiguous or obscure; or
> (ii) the ordinary meaning conveyed by the text of the provision taking into account its context in the Act and the purpose or object underlying the Act leads to a result that is manifestly absurd or is unreasonable.

(2) Without limiting the generality of subsection (1), the material that may be considered in accordance with that subsection in the interpretation of a provision of an Act includes:

    (a) all matters not forming part of the Act that are set out in the document containing the text of the Act as printed by the Government Printer;

    (b) any relevant report of a Royal Commission, Law Reform Commission, committee of inquiry or other similar body that was laid before either House of the Parliament before the time when the provision was enacted;

    (c) any relevant report of a committee of the Parliament or of either House of the Parliament that was made to the Parliament or that House of the Parliament before the time when the provision was enacted;

    (d) any treaty or other international agreement that is referred to in the Act;

    (e) any explanatory memorandum relating to the Bill containing the provision, or any other relevant document, that was laid before, or furnished to the members of, either House of the Parliament by a Minister before the time when the provision was enacted;

    (f) the speech made to a House of the Parliament by a Minister on the occasion of the moving by that Minister of a motion that the Bill containing the provision be read a second time in that House;

    (g) any document (whether or not a document to which a preceding paragraph applies) that is declared by the Act to be a relevant document for the purposes of this section; and

    (h) any relevant material in the Journals of the Senate, in the Votes and Proceedings of the House of Representatives or in any official record of debates in the Parliament or either House of the Parliament.

(3) In determining whether consideration should be given to any material in accordance with subsection (1), or in considering the weight to be given to any such material, regard shall be had, in addition to any other relevant matters, to:

    (a) the desirability of persons being able to rely on the ordinary meaning conveyed by the text of the provision taking into account its context in the Act and the purpose or object underlying the Act; and

(b) the need to avoid prolonging legal or other proceedings without compensating advantage.

5. Legislative Process Theories

In addition to the statutory interpretation theories discussed above, there are several theories that relate to the legislative process. For example, *pluralist theories* focus on the role special interest groups play in setting legislative policy. Interest group politics lead to "pluralism"—the spreading of political power across multiple political actors. The legislative process is one area in which conflicting interest groups' desires are resolved. Examples of special interest groups include political parties, churches, unions, businesses, and environmental organizations, among others. Interest groups can often accomplish what an individual cannot. Because there is strength in numbers, interest groups offer individual citizens the best possibility of meaningful participation in the legislative process. Theoretically, one benefit of a robustly pluralist system should be moderate, balanced, and well-considered legislation.

One pluralist theory is *bargaining theory*, which proposes that statutes are a compromise among various interest groups. Interest groups want a particular benefit or protection from government but often lack the clout to enact legislation absent support from other interest groups. Hence, interest groups work with other interest groups to increase their political power and get bills enacted, yet in doing so, the groups must compromise their goals. Pursuant to bargaining theory, judges should focus on furthering the compromises that produced the necessary votes for passage of the compromise legislation. For example, if we again return to Title VII (the statute prohibiting discrimination in the workplace on the basis of race), the compromise necessary to ensure passage of that bill was that white workers would not be disadvantaged to remedy black workers' plight. Bargaining theorists would have interpreted the statute not to allow voluntary affirmative action programs because such programs disadvantage white workers even while helping black workers.

Public choice theory is another pluralist theory. Public-choice theorists rely on economics to explain legislators' behavior. These theorists believe that statutes are the result of compromises among legislators that come about as a result of private interest groups bargaining. These private interest groups seek the best result for their members without regard for others. Access to the political process is disparate: business interests tend to be overrepresented, while the broad public interest and the less advantaged tend to be underrepresented. Thus, public choice theory helps explain the success of distributive legislation, legislation that rewards multiple special interests simultaneously. For example, tax bills that offer loopholes to many specialized groups or defense appropriation bills that send money to a variety of districts are both likely to be enacted for this reason. Under public choice theory, special-interest legislation and pork-barrel projects should enjoy limited support because very few special interest groups are rewarded. However, legislators may choose to support special projects for a variety of reasons, such as to gain political capital with other legislators for the future, to pay back special interest groups for financial or other support, or to increase the chances of reelection or movement within the party. Hence, contrary to intentionalist thought, public-choice theorists believe that there can be no single legislative intent; rather, each legislator may have a multitude of reasons for voting for particular legislation. Given the possibility of multiple reasons, public-choice theorists urge narrow interpretations of statutes. Additionally, these theorists suggest that judges should not fill in the statutory gaps because legislatures do not act for the public as a whole, but rather, act to reward special-interest groups and maximize their own reelection potential. As for legislative history, public-choice theorists agree with new textualists that such history should be ignored when determining statutory meaning because it shows nothing relevant. Legislation is a compromise of intentions; therefore, we cannot know exactly why legislators vote the way they do.

Public choice theory can be criticized for its skepticism. Not all legislators are opportunists looking for financial rewards from special interest groups; many are honest and have independent beliefs and goals that direct their legislative behavior. Thus, interest groups may be less effective at changing lawmakers' minds than public choice theory would have us believe. Finally, interest groups are better at blocking legislation than passing it, especially when legislation has low visibility. Hence, the theory may be inapposite for enacted legislation.

A second group of legislative theories, *proceduralist theories*, focuses on the legislative process and the political obstacles a bill must hurdle to become law. One such theory focuses on the "vetogates" of the legislative process. Eskridge et al., Legislation And Statutory Interpretation, *supra*, at

190. As you learned, it is much easier to kill a bill than to pass one because of the many steps a bill must go through before it can become law. At any one step, the bill might be choked from passage. Vetogates are the chokepoints that can prevent a bill from becoming law. Some such chokepoints include the committee process, the conference committee process, and rules of procedure such as the "germaneness rule." "Gatekeepers" are legislators that hold power at these vetogates. For example, a bill must be referred out of a committee (such as the Senate Judiciary Committee) to the full chamber (the Senate) before continuing the enactment process. The committee is a vetogate, while the members of the committee (especially the chair) are gatekeepers.

Vetogates are important for two reasons. First, gatekeepers can simply block a bill's passage at any vetogate. Second, courts often reason that statements gatekeepers made reflect the intent of the legislative body because the gatekeepers' support would have been essential to the bill's passage. But this reasoning may be flawed. Because these gatekeepers have such power, they can abuse their position. For example, the Alaska National Interest Lands Conservation Act altered the rules for access to all nonfederally owned land within the boundaries of the National Forest System. In *Montana Wilderness Ass'n v. United States Forest Service*, 655 F.2d 951 (9th Cir. 1981), *cert. denied*, 455 U.S. 898 (1981), the question for the court was whether a subsection of the Act applied nationwide or just in Alaska. *Id.* at 953. Congressman Udall, a key gatekeeper at the time the bill was enacted, had claimed in the legislative record that the subsection of the Act applied only to Alaska. *Id.* at 956 n.9 (citing 127 CONG. REC. 10376). However, other factors suggested that it was more likely that Congress intended the Act to apply nationally; thus, the Court rejected the argument that Udall's comments showed Congressional intent to limit the Act's application to Alaska.

Another legislative theory, the *best answer theory*, urges judges to interpret statutes to promote an "optimal state of affairs." Such a theory views judges as protectors of the minority, those individuals not in political power. Pursuant to this theory, a judge would likely find that Title VII did allow voluntary affirmative action programs because such programs would remedy employment practices that had a disparate impact on a less powerful group, racial minorities. Allowing an employer to enact voluntary affirmative action programs, rather than wait for possible litigation, would promote harmony, lead to positive social change, and protect minority interests. Thus, in this example, promoting the "optimal state of affairs" would support allowing limited types of affirmative action programs.

E. Constitutional Interpretation Distinguished

Judges interpret language in documents other than statutes. For example, judges often interpret constitutions, contracts, and regulations, both state and federal, and they use many of the same techniques to interpret these other types of documents.

However, there are some differences in interpretation techniques based on the text being interpreted, especially for constitutional interpretation. Just like statutory interpretation, there are many theories of constitutional interpretation including originalism and pragmatism, among others.

Pragmatists believe in a living Constitution. Justices Breyer, Brennan, Blackmun, Douglas, and Judge Posner are pragmatists. Pragmatists believe that ideas and concepts in the Constitution lack a fixed meaning; rather, their meanings are constantly shifting. For example, consider the Constitutional concepts of freedom of expression, the right to privacy, equal protection of the laws, life, liberty, and property. The meaning of these concepts is constantly shifting in today's world with social media and other advances. Justice Breyer explained his approach this way:

> Trying to apply this Constitution—with those values underlying the words—to circumstances that are continuously changing is not something that can be done by a computer. Neither [Justice Scalia nor I] thinks that. No one thinks that, and therefore it calls for human judgment.[2]

Hence, the concepts in the Constitution do not mean the same thing today as they meant when the Constitution was written. Instead, the underlying, or ancient, values in the Constitution guide interpretation, making it a living document. Viewing the Constitution as a living document allows interpretation to evolve to match new understandings about the equal treatment of minorities, the right to privacy, freedom of speech, and other concepts.

---

2. Andrea Seabrook, *Justices Get Candid about the Constitution*, NPR, (October 9, 2011, 12:58 AM), https://www.npr.org/2011/10/09/141188564/a-matter-of-interpretation-justices-open-up.

In contrast, originalists do not believe in a living Constitution. Justices Black, Scalia, Thomas, and Judge Bork are originalists. Originalists try to determine how the Framers themselves understood the rights they outlined in the Constitution. Originalists then strictly apply that understanding to today. Originalists believe that anything beyond that would allow judges to insert new rights into the Constitution (such as the right to abortion). Former Justice Scalia explained his approach this way:

> I have no problem with applying ancient values as they were understood at the time to new modern circumstances. Originalism doesn't mean that the radio is not covered by the First Amendment, but what originalism suggests is that as to those phenomenon [sic] that existed at the time, the understanding of the society as to what the constitution prohibited — at that time — subsists.

Id. For example, former Supreme Court Justice Hugo Black claimed that the First Amendment's provision that "Congress shall make no law … abridging the freedom of speech" was clear: "No law" meant absolutely no law, not even laws imposing time, place, or manner restrictions.

An important case in which these two different theories appear is *District of Columbia v. Heller*, 554 U.S. 570 (2008), in which the Supreme Court decided that the Second Amendment protects an individual's right to keep and bear arms. Justice Scalia, writing for the majority, noted that "[t]he 18th-century meaning [of the word "Arms"] is no different from the meaning today." *Id.* at 581. In contrast, Justice Breyer, in dissent, noted that he disagreed because "the District's regulation, which focuses upon the presence of handguns in high-crime urban areas, represents a permissible legislative response to a serious, indeed life-threatening, problem." *Id.* at 682. (Breyer, J., dissenting).

While it is not important that you understand constitutional theory, you should recognize that constitutional interpretation is similar to yet differs from statutory interpretation in fundamental ways and is not addressed in this text. For an interesting state case addressing the binding nature of constitutional interpretation, see *State v. Short*, 851 N.W.2d 474, 520 (Iowa 2014) (Mansfield, J., dissenting) ("Actual decisions are binding and can have stare decisis effect, but is a philosophical approach binding? Is a statement by the Iowa Supreme Court in one case that it gives no weight to United States Supreme Court interpretations of the same constitutional language binding for all future cases? I think not. Could four Justices of the Supreme Court bind this court in the future to follow 'original intent,' 'legal realism,' or 'economic analysis of the law'? I doubt it.").

F. Does Theory Matter?

Perhaps. But there is no empirical way to tell whether one theory more consistently leads to the "correct interpretation" of a statute. There is some empirical evidence that Congress overrides textualist decisions more often than intentionalist or purposivist ones. *West Virginia Univ. Hospitals, Inc.*, 499 U.S. at 113 (Stevens, J., dissenting) ("On those occasions ... when the court has put on its thick grammarian's spectacles and ignored the available evidence of congressional purpose and the teaching of prior cases construing a statute, the congressional response has been [to override them]."); William N. Eskridge, Jr., *Overriding Supreme Court Statutory Interpretation Decisions*, 101 YALE L.J. 331, 335 (1991); Michael E. Solimine & James L. Walker, *The Next Word: Congressional Response to Supreme Court Statutory Decisions*, 65 TEMP. L. REV. 425, 446 (1992). Purposivists might wish to gloat, but textualists would quickly respond that it is irrelevant what a new Congress decides. It is the enacting Congress that matters. Indeed, they would point out, congressional overrides show that the process works; when Congress disagrees with the Court's interpretation, Congress fixes it.

Only if we knew what the "right" interpretation was without applying a theory could we determine which theory most often leads to that "right" interpretation. But of course, we do not know which interpretation is right, nor do we even know what sources we are supposed to use to evaluate the correctness of any interpretation. Hence, no one theory is better at discerning the "right" meaning than any other. This point is important, for you will want to believe that your theory is right and that the others are wrong.

Academics love to debate the pros and cons of each of these theories. For example, in the famous hypothetical *Case of the Speluncean Explorers*, Professor Lon Fuller explored a hypothetical situation in which a group of explorers were trapped in a cave. Lon L. Fuller, *The Case of the Speluncean Explorers*, 62 HARV. L. REV. 616 (1949). While there, they killed one of the members of their group and ate him to survive. After they were rescued, they were tried and convicted of murder. The statute provided simply: "Whoever shall willfully take the life of another shall be punished by death." A common law self-defense exception also existed.

Professor Fuller had each judge considering the explorers' appeal draft a separate opinion, using a different statutory approach to explore the role that morality should play within the law. First, Justice Keen, a textualist, voted to uphold the conviction. According to Judge Keen, law is wholly distinct from morality; if judges believe that the law is wrong, it is not appropriate to correct that law. Instead, the legislature should fix its mistakes. Similarly, Chief Justice Truepenny also voted to affirm because he believed that the judicial role should not be concerned with morality when the other institutions are more competent to determine it. In this case, he believed the best result would be for the executive to offer clemency.

Justice Tatting withdrew from the case and refused to make any decision. For him, the tension between law and morality was unresolvable. Because he withdrew, the ultimate decision was a tie (two to affirm and two to reverse the conviction); thus, the divided court affirmed the lower court's conviction.

Justice Foster, who some have suggested was Professor Fuller in disguise, would have reversed the conviction. Using a purposivist approach, Justice Foster argued that the purpose of the murder statute was to deter wrongdoing. That purpose did not apply to the explorers because they killed their companion only as a last option to prevent the deaths of the others and because few persons facing death would be deterred by a criminal prohibition of conduct that would save their lives. He suggested that while law is not morality, the two are intertwined and cannot be separated as easily as Justice Keen suggested. Rather, the judiciary should correct legislative errors and oversights not to supplant the legislative will but, rather, to make that will effective.

Finally, Justice Handy also would have reversed. For him, law equals morality. Law should follow common sense and social norms. In this case, the public opinion supported acquittal, and Justice Handy argued that public opinion should be factored into the court's decision.

Despite the Speluncean Explorers hypothetical, the reality is that few judges rigidly adhere to just one theory. Even Justice Scalia admits, "I play the game like everybody else.... I'm in a system which has accepted rules and legislative history is used.... You read my opinions, I sin with the rest of them." Frank H. Easterbrook, *What Does Legislative History Tell Us?*, 66 Chi.-Kent L. Rev. 441, 442 n.4 (1990) (quoting Judges and Legislators: Toward Institutional Comity 174–75 (R. Katzmann ed. 1988)). Professors Eskridge, Frickey, and Garrett best summed up the reality of today's doctrine:

> We do not think the Supreme Court has entirely returned to the pre-Scalia days and suggest the following generalities about where it is today. First, the text is now, more than it was 20 or 30 years ago, the central inquiry at the Supreme Court level and in other courts that are now following the Supreme Court's lead. A brief that starts off with, "The statute means thus-and-so because it says so in the

committee report," is asking for trouble.... It remains important to research and brief the legislative history thoroughly. The effective advocate will appreciate that the presence of such materials in the briefs may influence the outcome more than the opinion in the case will indicate.

WILLIAM ESKRIDGE, JR. ET AL., CASES AND MATERIALS ON LEGISLATION: STATUTES AND THE CREATION OF PUBLIC POLICY 770–71 (3D ED. 2001).

While academics will continue rigorously to argue the legitimacy of the various approaches, few judges remain so dogmatic. Judges regularly mix approaches, fail to identify their approach, and even change approaches. Ultimately, judges want to further justice, not be dogmatically rigid. Professors Eskridge and Frickey call this *pragmatic theory*. "In deciding a question of statutory interpretation in the real, as opposed to the theoretical, world, few judges approach the interpretive task armed with a fixed set of rigid rules." John M. Walker, *Judicial Tendencies in Statutory Construction: Differing Views on the Role of the Judge*, 58 N.Y.U. ANN. SURV. AM. L. 203, 232 (2001).

To explain their pragmatic theory, Professors Eskridge and Frickey developed their funnel of abstraction in which the various sources lay on one side of the funnel, while an indicator of abstractness runs along the opposite side of the funnel. Statutory text, which is the most concrete source of meaning, anchors the bottom of the funnel. Moving up the sources side of the funnel from the bottom are specific legislative intent, then purpose, and finally current social values or morality. ESKRIDGE ET AL., LEGISLATION AND STATUTORY INTERPRETATION, *supra*, at 250–51.

Most judges do not confine themselves to the bottom of the funnel but, rather, move up and down the funnel as various sources come into play. The funnel "reflects both the multiplicity of [sources] and the conventional hierarchy ranking them against one another." *Id.* at 250. "Easy" statutory interpretation cases are those in which all the sources point in one direction (or are at least neutral). *Id.* at 251. In contrast, the "hard" cases are those in which one or more sources cut directly against another. These are the cases that reach the Supreme Court.

Perhaps, as legal realists suggest, none of this theory stuff matters. The reality is that judges decide cases based on their own personal notions of justice and the underlying equities of the case. For this reason, you should not expect to win your case simply because you use the judge's preferred theory. To win your case, you must prove to the judge that a ruling for your client would be the just and right result. But knowing a judge's preferred theory can make your job easier. For example, if you are arguing before a purposivist, you would not talk about ambiguity and absurdity before discussing legislative history or context, as you must do if you are arguing before a textualist. Thus, the theories provide legal language and seemingly impartial reasoning to help you argue your case. In this world, the Ancient Greek aphorism "know thyself" could be "know thy judge's approach."

G. Mastering This Topic

Return to the hypothetical presented in Chapter 1, regarding the city ordinance prohibiting vehicles in the park. You were asked to identify which materials you found helpful, relevant, and appropriate to consider in making your decisions as a prosecutor and which materials you considered unhelpful, irrelevant, or inappropriate to consider. If you have not completed this hypothetical already, take the time to go back and do so now.

Review your answers (which should be jotted in the margins). Identify the intrinsic sources (the text of the ordinance, the grammar and punctuation, and the title) and the extrinsic sources (the marked-up version, the committee report, the floor debates, and the governor's signing statement). Do your answers indicate whether you found intrinsic or extrinsic sources more relevant? Did you prefer one type of source exclusively, find both relevant, or find one type of source more useful? What does your answer to this question tell you about the theory you likely prefer at this point of your studies?

When you were answering the questions, did you look to the text of the ordinance first? If the text did not definitely resolve the issue for you, where did you look next? Did you find yourself pulling out your smart phone and looking up words in online dictionaries or turning to the other materials provided? As you should know by now, the more you focused on the text and turned toward dictionary definitions, the more likely you prefer some form of textualism. If you refused to look at the "legislative history" completely, then you may prefer new textualism, like Justices Scalia and Thomas. If you were willing to look at legislative history, but only when you had to, you may prefer moderate textualism. And if you looked at legislative history to confirm your understanding of the text, you may prefer the soft plain meaning approach.

If text was your starting point but not your ending point, you may lean towards intentionalism or purposivism. Can you determine which of these two better conforms to your preference? Did you find the legislative history more relevant to your interpretation process or the purpose for enacting the statute, namely safety? Were both relevant but one more so? Perhaps you are simply uncertain at this time. If so, do not let that concern you. To be honest, the more open you are to all of the theories at this point, the easier it will be for you to master the art of statutory interpretation.

Checkpoints

- Understanding theory is critical to understanding statutory interpretation because theory drives every aspect of statutory interpretation.

- To interpret a statute, a judge will look at intrinsic sources, extrinsic sources, and policy-based sources of meaning.

- Intrinsic sources are materials that are part of the official act being interpreted.

- Extrinsic sources are materials outside of the official act but within the legislative process that created the act.

- Policy-based sources are extrinsic to both the statutory act and the legislative process. They reflect important social and legal choices derived from the Constitution or existing common law ideals.

- Textualism is an interpretative approach that relies heavily on the intrinsic sources to determine meaning, particularly text.

- Intentionalism is an interpretative approach that searches all sources, particularly the legislative history, to discern the enacting legislature's specific intent.

- Purposivism is an interpretative approach that searches all sources to discern the legislative purpose.

- The judges in states and other countries also wrestle with these issues.

- Pragmatism is a constitutional theory of interpretation that recognizes the Constitution as a living document.

- Originalism is a constitutional theory of interpretation that focuses on the original understanding of concepts in the Constitution.

- Theory matters, but justice and equity matter more.

Chapter 5

Canons Based on Intrinsic Sources: The Text, Grammar & Punctuation

---

Roadmap

- Understand the plain meaning rule and its corollary, the technical meaning rule.
- Learn the difference between ordinary, definitional, and technical meanings.
- Understand that grammar and punctuation matter, except when they do not matter.
- Understand the basic grammar and punctuation rules.
- Understand special punctuation rules, such as the Doctrine of Last Antecedent.
- Learn special grammar rules relating to "and" and "or," singular and plural words, mandatory and permissive words, and masculine and feminine words.

A. Introduction to This Chapter

Finally, we begin the interpretive process. To do so, we start where all interpretation should start: with the text of the statute, including its grammar and punctuation. In this chapter, you will learn that generally, judges assume that legislatures meant words to have their ordinary, or plain, meaning. Occasionally, but much less commonly, the legislature meant words to have their technical meaning. For example, statutes are often written for lawyers, who have a technical understanding of the word "prevailing party," and not lay persons, who have an ordinary understanding of that word.

We will also consider the role that grammar and punctuation play in interpretation; after all, they are both part of the text. Laws are meant to be read as written; thus, grammar and punctuation do matter; however, they matter less than you would think. Moreover, there are a number of special grammar and punctuation rules that turn what you think you know on its head.

B. The Intrinsic Sources

In Chapter 4, you learned that there are three sources judges use to determine the meaning of statutory language: intrinsic, extrinsic, and policy-based. In the next few chapters, we will explore the relevance each of these sources has on interpretation. We begin with intrinsic sources, those sources that are part of the statute being interpreted. At this point, you should know that the words of the statute are of central importance to all judges regardless of theory. But the words are not the only intrinsic source. Grammar, punctuation, and the linguistic canons of statutory construction are also intrinsic sources. We will explore the words, grammar, and punctuation now, and we will explore the other intrinsic sources in later chapters.

C. Identifying Meaning from the Words Alone

The language of the statute, including its words, grammar, and punctuation, is the starting point for finding this meaning. "The text of a statute or rule is the primary, essential source of its meaning." UNIF. STATUTE & RULE CONSTR. ACT § 19 (1995). Thus, your job as an advocate is to identify words in the statute to support your client's position and be able to explain to opposing counsel and a court why those words mean what you say. How do you identify the relevant language and its meaning?

1. Identifying the Relevant Language

The first place to start when interpreting a statute is with the words. "We do not inquire what the legislature meant; we ask only what the statute means." Oliver W. Holmes, *The Theory of Legal Interpretation*, 12 HARV. L. REV. 417, 419 (1899). You must first identify the words in a statute that will support your client's position. I call these words the language at issue. Identifying the language at issue is not always easy. When you read cases, a court identifies the language at issue for you. When you are working with a client, you will not have the court's assistance. Instead, you must read the statute carefully to identify which words in the act will allow your client to do or not do something.

There are two types of operative provisions in an act: (1) *substantive provisions*, which identify the rights, duties, powers, and privileges being created, and (2) *administrative provisions*, which address the creation, organization, powers, and procedures of the governmental organization that will enforce or adjudicate the law. The language at issue must be found in an operative provision because only these provisions create rights and duties. So start there.

However, sometimes in the *definitions provisions* of an act, Congress will define words or phrases that are in the operative sections of the act. When Congress defines a word or phrase in a definition section, that word or phrase has the meaning Congress provided, even if it is nonsensical. *See, e.g., Commonwealth v. Plowman*, 86 S.W.3d 47, 49 (Ky. 2002) (holding that a bulldozer was a building for purposes of an arson statute, because that statute defined building as follows: "in addition to its ordinary meaning, [building] specifically includes any dwelling, hotel, commercial structure, automobile, truck, watercraft, aircraft, trailer, sleeping car, railroad car, or other structure or vehicle ...."). Thus, when an act includes definitions, you still must first identify the language at issue in the operative section of the act, for the operative section is the only section that establishes rights and duties. Then, you can turn to the act's definition of that word or phrase and apply the tools of interpretation to the language in the definition. For instance, in *Plowman*, the language at issue was "building." However, because the state legislature defined "building" to include "other ... vehicle," the court applied the canons of interpretation to "other ... vehicle."

Identifying the language at issue is a critical skill in interpretation. If you identify the "wrong" language, you may lose. For example, two cases out of Florida interpreted the same statute under almost identical facts but reached opposite results because each court focused on different words in the statute. The statute provided that traffic citations "'shall not be admissible evidence in any trial.'" *Dixon v. State*, 812 So. 2d 595, 596 (Fla. Dist. Ct. App. 2002) (quoting Fla. Stat. §316.650(9) (2000)). In both cases, the defendants gave false information to an arresting officer. The officer entered the information on a traffic citation, which the defendants then signed using false names. The defendants in both cases were arrested for forgery. At trial, the prosecutors offered the citations as evidence of the defendants' forgery (not of their traffic violations); the defendants objected, citing §316.650(9).

Despite the factual similarities, the appellate courts reached different holdings because they focused on different language in the statute. In *Dixon*, the court held that the traffic citation was inadmissible because the language of the statute was clear: "any trial" meant every trial without exception. *Id.* But in *Maddox v. State*, 862 So. 2d 783, 784 (Fla. Dist. Ct. App. 2003), the court held that the statute did not apply because the ticket was not a "traffic citation." Instead, it was "documentary evidence of Maddox's criminal conduct." *Id.* On appeal, the Florida Supreme Court agreed with the *Maddox* court, rejecting the interpretation in *Dixon*. *Maddox v. State*, 923 So. 2d 442 (Fla. 2006) (supporting its holding by considering the purpose of the statute and considering the absurdity of *Dixon*'s holding). As the appeal was pending, the Florida legislature amended the statute to allow citations to be admitted into evidence in subsequent forgery-related cases. 2005 Fla. Laws 33, c. 2005-164, § 42. (You will learn about the relevance of post-enactment legislative acts in Chapter 11.) These two cases show that identifying the appropriate language can be outcome-determinative.

2. Identifying the Language's Meaning

a. Applying the Plain Meaning Canon

After you identify the correct language, your next step is to apply the plain meaning rule, or canon, to this language. Pursuant to this rule, courts presume that words in a statute have their "plain," or "ordinary," meaning. Note the distinction: "the plain meaning rule" refers to the canon of interpretation, and "the ordinary meaning" refers to the meaning of the word that most people would think of upon hearing the word, *e.g.* a pig is a pink, round animal. Be aware that judges use these terms interchangeably when they should not.

The plain meaning rule presumes, wrongly, that native listeners and readers of language understand words to mean the same thing the speaker intended. This presumption is inaccurate because words have multiple meanings. "[W]ords do not possess intrinsic meanings and cannot be given them; to make matters worse, speakers do not even have determinative intents about the meanings of their own words." Frank H. Easterbrook, *Statutes' Domains*, 50 U. Chi. L. Rev. 533, 536 (1983). Consider the word "blue." Blue is both a color and a feeling. If I say that I am "blue" today, likely I am saying that I am sad. But I may instead be pointing out that I am wearing blue clothing. Indeed, singers and poets take advantage of language's indeterminacy regularly; consider the song title, "Don't it Make My Brown Eyes Blue." Does the author mean blue in color, blue in feeling (sad), or both? While textual context often identifies which meaning is intended, context does not always resolve ambiguity.

How does a judge find the ordinary meaning of words? Most commonly, judges turn to their own understanding of a word's meaning. People think in images. Above, I said pig. Did a picture of a cute pink animal just appear in your head?

For categories of things or ideas, people think in prototypes. Consider the word "furniture." Stop!!!

What popped into your mind? A chair? A couch? A table? I bet a lamp did not pop into your head. But you are likely willing, when you think about it, to concede that a lamp could be considered a piece of furniture. What about a bathtub? A large rock? You likely did not have to think about whether a chair, couch, or table were furniture. In contrast, you likely had to think about whether a lamp and bathtub were furniture. And again, you likely did not have to think about whether a rock was furniture.

When the language at issue is very similar to the prototype, interpretation is easiest (the chair, couch, table are all furniture). When the language at issue falls closer to the boundaries of the category, interpretation becomes harder (the lamp and bathtub). When the language at issue falls outside of the boundaries of the category, interpretation is once again easier (the rock). Thus, finding ordinary meaning is about identifying a prototype and defining its boundaries.

In addition to relying on their own understandings, judges turn to dictionaries to find the meaning of words. Dictionary definitions are offered "not as evidence, but only as aids to the memory and understanding of the court." *Nix v. Hedden*, 149 U.S. 304, 307 (1893).

Dictionaries lend an air of objectivity to the process. When a judge refers to his or her own understanding of a word to ascertain its meaning, the judge's choice appears subjective. In contrast, when a judge refers to a dictionary to identify the meaning of a word, the judge's choice appears objective.

On the contrary, a judge's use of dictionaries is not objective. For example, which dictionary should a judge choose? There is no consensus about which dictionary to use, not even which era's dictionary to use. As for era, former Justice Scalia, in his dissent in *Chisom v. Roemer*, 501 U.S. 380 (1991) (Scalia, J., dissenting), indicated that a dictionary in effect at the time legislation was drafted would be appropriate. *Id.* at 410; *see, e.g., Free Enterprise Fund. v. Public Co. Accounting Oversight Bd.*, 561 U.S. 477, 511 (2010) (examining a dictionary from 1828 to understand the meaning of the word "department"). But not all judges agree. Earlier editions of dictionaries do not account for changes in meaning over time. If the point of interpretation is to find the intent of the enacting legislature, this latter concern may not matter. But if the point is to find the ordinary meaning the audience would give the words today, it may be essential.

As for which dictionary judges should use, there is no consensus on one specific choice. Apparently, not all dictionaries are equal. In *MCI Telecommunications Corp. v. American Telephone & Telegraph Co.*, 512 U.S. 218 (1994), Justice Scalia, writing for the majority, identified a number of different dictionaries with similar definitions of the word at issue: "modify." While the majority of dictionaries suggested that "modify" meant a modest change, one dictionary, WEBSTER'S THIRD NEW INTERNATIONAL DICTIONARY, suggested that "modify" could mean either a modest or substantial change. *Id.* at 225–26. Justice Scalia rejected the latter definition and the appropriateness of that dictionary. *Id.* at 227. He noted that there was widespread criticism of this dictionary when it was published for its "portrayal of common error as proper usage." *Id.* at 228 n.3. "Virtually every dictionary we are aware of says that 'to modify' means to change moderately or in minor fashion." *Id.* at 225. Apparently, WEBSTER'S THIRD was too colloquial to be considered authoritative. But if the point of statutory interpretation is to find the ordinary meaning an audience member would likely ascribe to the language, why is colloquialism not a good thing?

Another issue is that dictionaries provide the definitional meaning of words rather than the ordinary meaning. The definitional meaning is always broader. For example, the ordinary meaning of "modify" is a modest change; while a definitional meaning of "modify" includes substantial change.

The use of dictionaries masks subjectiveness in a third way. Dictionaries generally have multiple meanings for each word. Yet the presence of multiple dictionary definitions alone is not enough to show that a word is ambiguous (you will see in a moment that ambiguity is important in interpretation). The Supreme Court started down this road in one case when it accepted the argument that the presence of multiple dictionary definitions meant that the word was inherently ambiguous. *National R.R. Passenger Corp. v. Boston & Maine Corp.*, 503 U.S. 407, 418 (1992) (stating that "[t]he existence of alternative dictionary definitions of the word 'required,' each making some sense under the statute, itself indicates that the statute is open to interpretation."). The Court quickly and correctly retreated from this unworkable definition of ambiguity in a later case when it rejected an argument, based on *National R.R. Passenger Corp.*, that the existence of multiple dictionary definitions established ambiguity. *MCI Telecomms. Corp.*, 512 U.S. at 226. Had the Court adopted this definition of ambiguity, then every word challenged in any future case would likely have been ambiguous, for it is rare, if not unheard of, for a word to have only one dictionary definition.

Another concern relating to the fact that words have more than one dictionary meaning is that there is no canon that says that the first dictionary meaning is *the* ordinary meaning. While the primacy of the definition may carry weight, it is not dispositive. *Mississippi Poultry Ass'n, Inc. v. Madigan*, 992 F.2d 1359, 1369 (5th Cir. 1993) (Reavley, J., dissenting) ("I cannot imagine that the majority favors interpreting statutes by choosing the first definition that appears in a dictionary."), *aff'd*, 31 F.3d 293 (5th Cir. 1994) (en banc). Without guidance as to which meaning to pick, how do judges know which of many dictionary definitions the legislature intended? Thus, use of dictionaries can mask the subjectiveness; choosing one dictionary over others and then choosing one meaning over others are both subjective choices.

Context helps to limit choice. Words often have different meanings in different contexts. Consider an example: the defendant "assaulted" the plaintiff. Is "assault" meant in its tortious sense, its criminal sense, or simply in its non-legal sense (meaning a violent attack)? To determine which of these possible meanings should prevail, judges look to the statute's audience. For example, a Connecticut state statute required state boards of education to indemnify personnel who were harmed "as a result of an *assault*" while working. *Patrie v. Area Coop. Educ. Serv.*, 37 Conn. L. Rptr. 470 (Conn. Super. Ct. 2004) (citing Conn. Gen. Stat. § 10-236a) (emphasis added). The plaintiff was injured when a student jumped playfully on his back. *Id.* at 470. Under the statute, the plaintiff could only recover if the playful jump was "an assault." Is a playful attack an assault?

The plaintiff argued that the legislature would have wanted "assault" interpreted broadly to further the purpose of reimbursing school personnel for injuries that were no fault of their own. *Id.* Thus, the plaintiff suggested that the term meant either an assault as defined in tort — freedom from the apprehension of a harmful or offensive contact — or as defined in that state's criminal law — an attempted but unsuccessful battery. Under either the tort definition or the criminal definition, any intent requirement would have been satisfied on these facts, for intent to harm is unnecessary under either legal theory. *Id.* at 473.

But the court rejected both legal interpretations of the word. Instead, the court said, "[t]he definition of 'assault' the plaintiff advocates forgets the audience the statute was aimed at — school administrators trying to meet budgets and run their schools and teachers concerned with their rights above and beyond workers' compensation." *Id.* Because administrators and teachers would more commonly think of an assault as being an intentionally violent attack (its non-legal meaning), the court held that the word "assault" in this statute meant an intentionally violent act. *Id.* Pursuant to this interpretation, the plaintiff could not recover for his injuries because the assault was a playful jump. *Id.* Textual context and audience were central to the court's holding.

In another case interpreting the same word in a different statute, a different court interpreted the term "assault" to have its legal, tortious meaning: specifically, freedom from the apprehension of a harmful or offensive contact. *Dickens v. Puryear*, 276 S.E.2d 325, 330 (N.C. 1981). In this case, the word "assault" was part of a statute of limitations that included other intentional torts. Using the non-legal definition in this context would have made no sense because the audience for statutes of limitations is lawyers and judges, both of whom would have a different understanding of the word "assault" than would laypersons. *Id.* at 332. Further, the surrounding words were all intentional torts.

Thus, while dictionaries can be useful guides to determining ordinary meaning, they have limitations. Judge Learned Hand cautioned judges, "not to make a fortress out of the dictionary; but [] remember that statutes always have some purpose or object to accomplish ...." *Cabell v. Markham*, 148 F.2d 737, 739 (2d Cir. 1945), *aff'd*, 326 U.S. 404 (1945); Abbe R. Gluck & Lisa Schultz Bressman, *Statutory Interpretation from the Inside: An Empirical Study of Congressional Drafting, Delegation, and the Canons: Part I*, 65 STAN. L. REV. 901, 938 (2013) (noting that a congressional staff member told them, "[n]o one uses a freaking dictionary."). Finally, dictionaries may at times be ill-suited for determining the meaning of particular language in a statute because context is often essential to meaning.

Despite these limitations, judges, particularly textualist judges, increasingly rely on both the plain meaning rule and dictionaries to determine meaning. But these judges do not always understand that there is a difference between the definitional, or dictionary, meaning of a word and the ordinary meaning of a word. The definitional meaning is the many ways a word might be used, which dictionaries show, while the ordinary meaning is how a word is ordinarily used, which some dictionaries also note. Judges do not always distinguish between these two.

Consider *Smith v. United States*, 508 U.S. 223 (1993). In that case, the majority applied the plain meaning rule to decide whether a defendant who offered to exchange his MAC-10 (a gun) for two ounces of cocaine "*use[d]* ... a firearm*" during a drug trafficking crime. *Id.* at 225. The issue for the Court was whether bartering a gun constituted "using a firearm." *Id.* The majority held that the meaning of "use" included trading the gun for drugs. *Id.* at 228–29. In so doing, the majority rejected the defendant's argument that the *ordinary* *meaning* of "using a firearm" was to use the firearm as a weapon. *Id.* at 229. The majority responded that

> [I]t is one thing to say that the ordinary meaning of 'uses a firearm' *includes* using a firearm as a weapon, since that is the intended purpose of a firearm and the example of 'use' that most immediately comes to mind. But it is quite another to conclude that, as a result, the phrase also *excludes* any other use.

Id. at 230. The majority looked to dictionary definitions to find the definitional meaning of the word "use," then interpreted the word very broadly despite the rule of lenity. *Id.* at 240. (See Chapter 12 for a discussion of this canon, which suggests that ambiguity should be resolved in a criminal defendant's favor.)

The dissent strongly disagreed and chastised the majority for failing "to grasp the distinction between how a word *can be* used and how it *ordinarily is* used." *Id.* at 242 (Scalia, J., dissenting). He pointed out that most people would not say "use a firearm" when referring to bartering a gun. *Id.* at 242–43. Justice Scalia more accurately applied the plain meaning rule in this case by identifying the ordinary as opposed to the definitional meaning.

In a subsequent case interpreting the same word in the same statute, the Court held that "use" denoted active employment, not mere possession. *Bailey v. United States*, 516 U.S. 137, 143 (1995) (holding that a defendant who carried a gun in the trunk of his car did not "use" a firearm within the meaning of the statute). Subsequently, and as a direct result of *Bailey*, the Court rejected a claim that a drug dealer who received a firearm for drugs "used" that firearm. *Watson v. United States*, 552 U.S. 74, 83 (2007). Thus, one who barters a gun for drugs *uses* that gun, but one who merely receives a bartered gun in exchange for drugs does not *use* the gun. These cases show that the plain meaning rule, though appealing in its simplicity, does not always answer the question, especially when dictionaries are consulted. Dictionaries define words broadly; thus, definitional meanings will always be broader than ordinary meanings, which textual and other context limit.

b. Applying the Technical Meaning Caveat

Some words have both ordinary and technical meanings. For example, as we just saw, "assault" can mean an intentionally violent attack—its ordinary meaning—or it can mean freedom from the apprehension of a harmful or offensive contact—a technical (in this case legal) meaning. Legislatures generally intend words to have their ordinary meaning; occasionally, legislatures intend words to have their technical meaning.

The plain and technical meaning rules provide that

> [U]nless a word or phrase is defined in the statute or rule being construed, its meaning is determined by its context, the rules of grammar, and common usage. A word or phrase that has acquired a technical or particular meaning in a particular context has that meaning *if it is used in that context.*

Unif. Statute & Rule Constr. Act § 2 (1995) (emphasis added).

Together, these rules reflect the reality that most often the legislature intended the words to have their ordinary meaning. However, the rule allows for those few times the legislature intended the words to have their technical meaning. Thus, the ordinary meaning will generally prevail when both an ordinary and technical meaning co-exist, absent any indication that the word was used in its technical sense.

For example, is a tomato a vegetable—its ordinary meaning—or a fruit— its technical meaning to a botanist and linguist? Believe it or not, this issue was litigated before the Supreme Court! Confounding botanists around the world, the Court held that a tomato is a vegetable. *Nix v. Hedden*, 149 U.S. 304, 306 (1893). At issue in *Nix* was whether a statute that taxed vegetables at a higher rate than fruits applied to tomatoes. Perhaps, unsurprisingly, the Court held that the statute did apply, and the Government got its money despite the canon that ambiguities in tax and tariff statutes should be construed in favor of the taxpayer. *Id.*

Why did the Court choose to apply the ordinary meaning rather than the technical? To determine which meaning was intended—technical or ordinary— a judge will look at two things: (1) whether the surrounding words are technical, and (2) whether the statute was directed to a technical audience. *St. Clair v. Commonwealth*, 140 S.W.3d 510, 569 (Ky. 2004), is illustrative of the first point, that surrounding words matter. In *St. Clair*, the court had to determine whether the word "conviction" in a sentence enhancing statute was used in "its ordinary or popular meaning, [meaning] a finding of guilt by plea or verdict, [or] its legal or technical meaning, [meaning] the final judgment entered on plea or verdict of guilty." *Id.* at 568 (quoting 21A Aм. Jur. 2d Criminal Law § 1313, at 571 (1998)). The difference meant life or death to the criminal defendant. Looking at the language surrounding the word "conviction" in the statute, the court held that "conviction" was meant in its ordinary sense because the legislature had used the phrase "prior record of conviction" and not "judgment of conviction." *Id.* at 563. Thus, in this case, the other words in the statute provided textual context for determining that the ordinary meaning was intended. *Contra Dickens v. Puryear,* 276 S.E.2d 325, 330 n.8 (N.C. 1981) (holding the word "assault" was used in its technical, legal sense (specifically, as an intentional tort), because the listed words in the statute were all intentional torts).

O'Hara v. Luckenbach Steamship Co., 269 U.S. 364 (1926), is illustrative of the second point, that audience matters. The statute at issue in that case involved the safety and welfare of those at sea. Because the statute was directed solely to individuals and companies in the maritime trade, the Court interpreted the statutory language to have a technical meaning, the meaning that would be understood by those in the maritime trade. *Id.* at 370–71; cf. Felix Frankfurter, *Some Reflections on the Reading of Statutes,* 47 Colum. L. Rev. 527, 536 (1947) ("If a statute is written for ordinary folk, it would be arbitrary not to assume that Congress intended its words to be read with the minds of ordinary [people]. If they are addressed to specialists, they must be read by judges with the minds of specialists.").

In *Dickens* and *O'Hara,* the technical meaning was a legal meaning. Legal audiences have unique understandings of some words and phrases. And statutes are sometimes intended for lawyers and judges. Thus, sometimes, when words have legal meanings, these meanings apply. However, even when a statute uses a term that has a unique legal meaning, that is no guarantee that Congress intended the legal meaning to control. *See, e.g., Moskal v. United States,* 498 U.S. 103, 114 (1990) (interpreting the term "falsely made" in its ordinary sense because that interpretation furthered the purpose of the statute).

One last point before we leave this topic. While judges generally use textual context and audience to determine whether ordinary or technical meaning applies, judges are not limited to these sources when determining which meaning was intended. Other indicia of meaning may also inform the court such as titles, purpose, and legislative history. We will cover these other sources in later chapters.

Let's turn from the words of the statute to its punctuation and grammar.

D. Identifying Meaning from Punctuation & Grammar

1. The General Punctuation & Grammar Rule

In England, "until 1849 statutes were enrolled upon parchment and enacted without punctuation. No punctuation appearing upon the rolls of Parliament such as was found in the printed statutes simply expressed the understanding of the printer." *Taylor v. Inhabitants of Caribou*, 67 A. 2 (Me. 1907). Because the "printer," or clerk, added punctuation after the statute was enacted, English judges refused to consider punctuation when interpreting a statute.

In contrast, in the United States, Congress passes bills with the punctuation included; hence, "[t]here is no reason why punctuation, which is intended to and does assist in making clear and plain the meaning of all things else in the English language, should be rejected in the case of the interpretation of [American] statutes." *Id.* at 2. American legislators are presumed to know and apply common rules of grammar and punctuation (syntactic rules). Because the plain meaning rule presumes that legislators use grammar and punctuation appropriately, the general rule provides that punctuation and grammar matter unless the plain meaning rule suggests that they should be ignored. 2A JABEZ GRIDLEY SUTHERLAND, STATUTES AND STATUTORY CONSTRUCTION § 47.15 at 346 (Norman Singer ed., 7th ed. 2007) ("[A]n act should be read as punctuated unless there is some reason to do otherwise. ….").

> The plain meaning rule presumes that grammar and punctuation are relevant, unless there is a reason to ignore them.

Sometimes, there is a reason for ignoring grammar entirely. For example, in *U.S. National Bank of Oregon v. Independent Insurance Agents of America, Inc.*, 508 U.S. 439, 455 (1993), the Supreme Court ignored the placement of quotation marks to conclude that a specific section of a statute had not been repealed. In so doing, the Court said,

> A statute's plain meaning must be enforced, of course, and the meaning of a statute will typically heed the commands of its punctuation. But a purported plain-meaning analysis based only on punctuation is necessarily incomplete and runs the risk of distorting a statute's true meaning…. No more than isolated words or sentences is punctuation alone a reliable guide for discovery of a statute's meaning. Statutory

construction is a holistic endeavor and, at a minimum, must account for a statute's full text, language[,] as well as punctuation, structure, and subject matter.

Id. at 455.

When grammar and punctuation are used correctly and consistently, a reader's understanding of written material is enhanced. However, not everyone uses grammar and punctuation correctly or consistently, not even legislators. Indeed, some syntactic rules are optional. Let's look at just such an example: the serial comma rule (also known as the Oxford or Harvard comma rule). The serial comma rule directs that when a comma separates a series of items, each item is distinct from the others. This is the rule, but not every English writer follows it. Indeed, while the Chicago Manual of Style insists on its use, the Associated Press considers it superfluous.

Let's see why the serial comma is important for clarity. Serial comma adherents use a comma to separate each item in a list (yellow, blue, red, and white), while non-serial comma adherents use a comma to separate all but the final two items in a list (yellow, blue, red and white). It is unclear whether the second phrase includes only three types of items: (1) those that are yellow, (2) those that are blue, and (3) those that are red and white. Or whether it includes four types of items: (1) those that are yellow, (2) those that are blue, (3) those that are red, and (4) those that are white. Without knowing whether the writer uses the serial comma, the reader cannot know which meaning the writer intended. But when the serial comma is included, ambiguity disappears. Thus, because the serial comma aids clarity, legal writers should always use serial commas when writing.

> The serial comma should be used to separate each item in a list of three or more items.

Indeed, the lack of a serial comma was outcome determinative in *O'Connor v. Oakhurst Dairy*, 851 F.3d 69 (1st Cir. 2017). The plaintiff dairy drivers argued that they should have been paid approximately $10 million in overtime for distributing agricultural products. The defendant company disagreed and refused to pay the plaintiffs. The relevant statute provided that individuals engaged in the following activities were not entitled to overtime pay: "The canning, processing, preserving, freezing, drying, marketing, storing, packing for shipment or distribution of ... [food products]...." ME. STAT. tit. 26 §664(3)(F) (2017). The dairy drivers *distributed* milk, but they did not *pack* it. *O'Connor*, 851 F.3d at 71.

The issue for the court was whether "packing for shipment or distribution of [food products]" was one activity [packing (packing for shipment of or packing for distribution of)] or whether "packing for shipment" was a separate activity from "distribution of." The district court found for the employers; however, the First Circuit reversed. *Id.* at 70. Had the legislature included a serial comma after "packing for shipment," there would have been no ambiguity. *Id.* However, because no such comma was included, the First Circuit found the language ambiguous. The court reasoned that under "Maine law, ambiguities in the state's wage and hour laws must be construed liberally in order to accomplish their remedial purpose." *Id.* Hence, the dairy farmers won based on the remedial statute canon (*see* Chapter 12). Ironically, Maine's Legislative Drafting Manual specifically provided "when drafting Maine law or rules, don't use a comma between the penultimate and the last item of a series." *Id.* at 73 (quoting Maine Legislative Drafting Manual 113 (Legislative Council, Maine State Legislature 2009), http://maine.gov/legis/ros/manual/Draftman2009.pdf). Ultimately, the case settled for $5 million.

As the case above shows, when grammar and punctuation are used incorrectly, the reader can be confused. For example, one familiar and fun example is the following: "With gratitude to my parents, the Pope and Mother Teresa." Without the serial comma after the word "Pope," the sentence suggests that the writer's parents are the Pope and Mother Teresa, rather than additional recipients of the writer's gratitude.

Thus, punctuation is a fallible standard of meaning and is used more as a last resort in construing doubtful statutes. "Punctuation is a minor, and not a controlling, element in interpretation, and courts will disregard the punctuation of a statute, or re-punctuate it, if need be, to give effect to what otherwise appears to be its purpose and true meaning." *United States v. Ron Pair Enter., Inc.*, 489 U.S. 235, 250 (1989) (O'Connor, J., concurring) (internal quotation marks omitted). Hence, punctuation and grammar matter, but only when viewed within their textual context.

2. Special Punctuation Rules

a. Commas: The General Rule

Commas are particularly troubling in the English language—their use is "exceedingly arbitrary and indefinite." *United States v. Palmer,* 16 U.S. (3 Wheat.) 610, 638 (1818) (separate opinion of Johnson, J.). Commas are troubling, in part, because comma rules are not consistently followed, yet their placement can be critical to meaning. Lynne Truss famously pointed out: "[A] panda eats shoots and leaves" means something very different from "a panda eats, shoots, and leaves." LYNNE TRUSS, EATS, SHOOTS & LEAVES: THE ZERO TOLERANCE APPROACH TO PUNCTUATION (2003). The two sentences vary by only two commas. But their meanings are entirely different. The phrase "the panda eats shoots and leaves" tells us what the panda has for dinner. The phrase "the panda eats, shoots, and leaves" tells us in what order the panda had his dinner, shot his companions, and left the party. Note that the second sentence again illustrates the importance of the serial comma rule that we saw above: when a comma separates a series of items, each item is distinct from the others. Another example: a single comma makes a critical difference between "Let's eat, Grandma!" and "Let's eat Grandma!"

In statutes, comma placement can be critical. For example, in *Peterson v. Midwest Security Insurance Co.*, 636 N.W.2d 727 (Wis. 2001), a recreational immunity statute provided immunity to owners of "real property and buildings, structures and improvements thereon, and waters of the state." *Id.* at 728–29 (citing WIS. STAT. §895.52(1)(f) (1997-1998)). The plaintiff had fallen from the insured's tree stand. The insured did not own the land beneath his tree stand, so the defendant's insurance company argued that the defendant was immune from suit based on the recreational immunity statute. The plaintiff responded that the statute protected only owners of structures who also owned the real property on which the structure was located; thus, the insured was not immune from suit. Resolution of the case centered on the absence of a serial comma between the words "real property" and "buildings" in the statute; if the legislature intended to protect three, rather than two, categories of property, then the legislature should have included a serial comma after "structures." *Peterson*, 636 N.W.2d at 731.

Despite the absence of this comma (and the presence of the word "thereon"), the majority found the language to be clear and broadly interpreted the statute to provide immunity to (1) owners of real property, (2) owners of buildings, structures, and improvements on *any* real property, and (3) owners of the waters of the state. *Id.* at 732 & n.7. In ignoring the punctuation, the majority stated, "[w]e decline to give the absence of a comma such interpretive significance." *Id.* at 731.

The dissent disagreed. Noting that the drafter had regularly not used a serial comma in other parts of the statute, the dissent questioned "whether the legislature's choice of punctuation in a statute could be dismissed so easily." *Id.* at 736 (Bradley, J., dissenting). The dissent observed that the missing comma and the word "thereon" allowed for four possible interpretations. First, the statute could be read as the majority had suggested. *Id.* at 737. Second, the statute could be read to provide immunity to (1) owners of real property along with the buildings, structures, and improvements *on that* real property, and (2) the waters of the state. *Id.* Third, the statute could be read to provide immunity to (1) owners of real property, (2) owners of buildings, structures, and improvements *on that* real property, and (3) owners of the waters of the state. *Id.* Fourth, and most consistently with the serial comma rule, the statute could be read to provide immunity to (1) owners of real property and buildings, (2) owners of structures, and improvements *on that* real property or buildings, and (3) owners of waters of the state. *Id.* (Note that the legislature could also have avoided the ambiguity simply by inserting numbers before each category or by using semicolons to separate each category, as I have done.) Finding the language ambiguous, the dissent turned to the purpose of the statute — encouraging property owners to allow *outdoor* recreational activities. *Id.* at 739. In light of this purpose, the dissent concluded that the majority's interpretation — that owners of *any* building or structure were protected — was simply too broad to further the purpose of the statute even if that interpretation made sense in this particular case. *Id.*

b. Commas: The Doctrine of Last Antecedent

Reddendo singula singulis means "rendering each to his own." This canon is appropriate when a complex sentence has multiple subjects and either multiple verbs or objects that are incorrectly placed. "Under the canon *reddendo singula singulis*, [w]here a sentence contains several antecedents and several consequents they are to be read distributively. [In other words, t]he words are to be applied to the subjects that seem most properly related by context and applicability." *In re Macke Intern. Trade, Inc.*, 370 B.R. 236, 251–52 (9th Cir. 2007) (internal quotation marks omitted).

By "rendering," or associating, each object or verb to its appropriate subject, the sentence can be understood correctly. To illustrate, assume that a will provides, "I devise and bequeath my real property and personal property to State University." The term "devise" is more appropriate for real property, while the term "bequeath" is more appropriate for personal property. The sentence would have been clearer if written as follows: "I devise my real property and bequeath my personal property to State University." Notice that this second sentence is longer, even while being clearer and more accurate. *Reddendo singula singulis* allows a reader to interpret the first sentence as if it were written like the second. In other words, the canon allows readers to ignore grammar and interpret the language as intended. To illustrate again, a contract might say "for money or other good consideration paid or given." *Reddendo singula singulis* tells us that the phrase really means "for money paid or other good consideration given."

The *doctrine (or rule) of last antecedent* is a subset of *reddendo singular singulis*. Jabez Sutherland created the doctrine of last antecedent in 1891, when he wrote his famous treatise on interpreting contracts and statutes. He created the doctrine to help interpreters derive the meaning of contract clauses that contained multiple obligations or conditions with a modifying phrase.

The doctrine states that when a qualifying word or phrase is used with a group of obligations or conditions, the qualifying words are presumed to modify only the condition or obligation that immediately precedes it (the "last antecedent"). For example, Article II of the United States Constitution provides, "No person except a natural born Citizen, or a Citizen of the United States, at the time of the Adoption of this Constitution, shall be eligible to the Office of President...." The phrase "at the time of the Adoption of this Constitution" is a modifying phrase. This phrase modifies only the phrase "a Citizen of the United States." If instead the modifying phrase were understood to modify both "a natural born Citizen" and "a Citizen of the United States" — then the U.S. would have run out of presidential candidates long ago because no one would be left alive who meets the criteria. One point to note is that the phrase would be clearer yet if commas were omitted altogether: "No person except [1] a natural born Citizen_ or [2] a Citizen of the United States_ at the time of the Adoption of this Constitution_ shall be eligible to the Office of President...." U.S. CONST. art. II, § 1, cl. 4. The framers did not always use punctuation as we use it today.

The doctrine (or rule) of last antecedent provides that if a comma separates a modifying phrase from a list of prior antecedents, then the modifying phrase modifies each of the prior antecedents. Conversely, if there is no comma (as in my redrafted example), then the modifying phrase modifies only the final antecedent. Thus, if a statute applied to "dentists, nurses, and doctors in a hospital," pursuant to the doctrine of last antecedent, the limiting phrase "in a hospital" would modify only "doctors" and not "dentists [and] nurses," unless a

> The doctrine of last antecedent states that if a modifying phrase is separated by a comma from a list of prior items, then the modifying phrase modifies each item, not just the last item in the list.

contrary legislative intent were found. In contrast, if the statute applied to "dentists, nurses, and doctors, in a hospital," the modifying phrase "in a hospital" would modify all of the professionals because a comma separates "in a hospital" from all three antecedents. Notice how one, simple comma can significantly affect meaning.

Importantly, this doctrine is not absolute because it conflicts with general comma rules (which is why the term "doctrine" is used here, rather than "rule"). *Lessee v. Irvine*, 3 U.S. (3 Dall.) 425, 444 (1799). The choice to put a comma between the qualifying phrase and the preceding list of antecedents is grammatically optional. *United States v. Bass*, 404 U.S. 336, 340 n.6. (1971). For this reason, judges will ignore the doctrine when applying it would result in an absurd result or an interpretation that make no sense because, for example, the legislature has been unclear.

Two cases illustrate what happens when a legislature is unclear about comma placement: *Matter of Forfeiture of 1982 Ford Bronco*, 673 P.2d 1310 (N.M. 1983), and *State v. One 1990 Chevrolet Pickup*, 857 P.2d 44 (N.M. Ct. App. 1993). In both cases, the state was attempting to take vehicles from owners who had used the vehicles to transport drugs. The forfeiture statute subjected the following property to forfeiture: "all ... vehicles..., which are used, or intended for use, ... to transport, or in any manner to facilitate the transportation *for the purpose of sale of [drugs]* .... *Ford Bronco*, 673 P.2d at 1312 (quoting N.M. STAT. ANN. 30-31-34(D) (N.M. 1978)) (emphasis and underlines added). The modifying phrase is "for the purpose of sale of [drugs]...." The issue for the court was whether that phrase modified "to transport" *and* "to facilitate the transportation" or modified just "to facilitate the transportation." For ease of reference, the statutory language is in the text box above.

> [A]ll ... vehicles..., which are used, or intended for use, ... to transport, or in any manner to facilitate the transportation **for the purpose of sale of [drugs]....**
>
> *Ford Bronco*

In both cases, the car owners acknowledged that they transported drugs, but did not do so to sell the drugs. In the *Ford Bronco* case, the car owner argued that the drug sale had already taken place prior to his arrest so the transportation of the drugs could not have been *for the purpose of* selling the drugs. 673 P.2d at 1311–12. In the *Chevrolet* case, the owner argued that the drugs were for personal use so the transportation of the drugs could similarly not have been for the purpose of selling drugs. 857 P.2d at 46.

Notice that (1) a comma separates these two phrases ("or in any manner to facilitate the transportation" and "to transport"), (2) the relevant language appears with the second phrase, and (3) there is no comma in the second phrase between "or in any manner to facilitate the transportation" and "for the purpose of sale." Applying the doctrine of last antecedent, the court found the absence of a comma between the phrases "or in any manner to facilitate the transportation" and "for the purpose of sale" to be fatal to the car owner's claim. *Ford Bronco*, 673 P.2d at 1312. Transporting drugs alone without intending to sell the drugs satisfied the statute. In other words, the language "for the purpose of sale" modified only "to facilitate the transportation."

Unhappy with the result in the *Ford Bronco* case, the legislature amended the statute by deleting the comma between the words "transport" and "or." (The two commas surrounding "or intended for use" were also removed.) The amended version provided: "[A]ll … vehicles…, which are used_ or intended for use_ … to transport_ or in any manner to facilitate the transportation *for the purpose of sale of [drugs]*…." *Chevrolet Pickup*, 857 P.2d at 46 (quoting N.M. STAT. ANN. § 30-31-34(D) (1981)) (emphasis added). The modifying phrase is "for the purpose of sale of [drugs]…." The issue for the court was whether that phrase modified "to transport" *and* "to facilitate the transportation" or modified just "to facilitate the transportation." For ease of reference, the statutory language is in the text box above. Underlines have been added to the excerpt so that you can see where the commas were removed.

> [A]ll … vehicles…, which are used_ or intended for use_ … to transport_ or in any manner to facilitate the transportation *for the purpose of sale of [drugs]*….
>
> *Chevrolet Pickup*

The issue before the court in the new case was the same as in the *Ford Bronco* case: What did the phrase "for the purpose of sale" modify—"to transport" or "in any manner to facilitate the transportation"? *Id.* The City argued that the relevant language still modified only the latter phrase ("in any manner to facilitate the transportation") and that the removal of the commas was irrelevant because the legislature did not amend the statute in the way that the *Ford Bronco* court had recommended. *Id.* Pursuant to *Ford Bronco*, the legislature needed to add a comma between "in any manner to facilitate the transportation" and "for the purpose of sale" for the modifying phrase to modify "to transport." The legislature did not correctly modify the statute. Why? It is unclear; however, even educated lawyers do not always know how to use commas properly.

The *Chevrolet* court rejected the City's argument. *Id.* at 48. Applying "a less technical version of the 'last antecedent rule,'" the court held that "for the purpose of sale" modified all three clauses connected by the term "or." *Id.* In other words, forfeiture was applicable only to those vehicles, (1) which are used to transport drugs for the purposes of sale, (2) which are intended for use to transport drugs for the purposes of sale, and (3) which are used in any manner to facilitate the transportation of drugs for the purposes of sale. *Id.*

The court held that the forfeiture statute applied only when a car owner possessed drugs and planned to sell them. *Id.* at 49. Having drugs for personal use did not qualify. *Id.*

While the court said it applied "a less technical version" of the doctrine, the reality is that the court simply ignored the doctrine altogether. Assuming the legislature wanted to criminalize the actions of those persons trying to sell drugs, the legislature did a poor job drafting the statute in the first place. And the legislature's subsequent attempt to fix the statute by removing all the commas did not fix the initial error. If the legislature wanted the forfeiture statute to apply only when a defendant intended to sell drugs, the legislature should have written the statute as directed by the *Ford Bronco* court by adding one comma. Likely, the *Chevrolet* court recognized that the legislature simply did not understand the doctrine of last antecedent and its relationship to commas. The court, thus, interpreted the statute to further the legislative intent to change the holding in the *Ford Bronco* case.

Let's look at another example. To make the discussion easier for you to follow I have modified the statutory language. Assume that a statute provided "that alcohol shall not be sold between eleven at night and six in the morning, nor on Sunday *except if the licensee is a hotel.*" The modifying phrase in this statute is in italics. According to the doctrine of last antecedent, the phrase "except if the licensee is a hotel" should only qualify the phrase "on Sunday" because there is no comma between "Sunday" and "except." The highlighted phrase should not be understood to qualify the phrase "between eleven at night and six in the morning." Thus, pursuant to the doctrine of last antecedent, hotels can sell alcohol on Sundays, but not between 11:00 PM and 6:00 AM.

This modified statute is similar to the statute at issue in *Commonwealth v. Kelly,* 64 Mass. (10 Cush.) 69 (Mass. 1852). In that case, the court applied the doctrine of last antecedent and held that the statute did not allow the defendants, presumably hotel owners, to sell alcohol after eleven. *Id.* at 71. As in most cases involving the last antecedent, other arguments also supported the court's holding. The court relied on the title of the Act, "An act to prohibit the sale of spirituous and intoxicating liquors between the hours of eleven at night and six in the morning" and the purpose of the Act. *Id.*

What if a drafter would prefer to have the qualifying phrase apply to all the preceding antecedents? As noted above, all a drafter would have to do to have a phrase modify all the preceding nouns is add a comma between the modifier and the last antecedent. "A qualifying phrase separated from antecedents by a comma is evidence that the qualifier is supposed to apply to all the antecedents instead of only to the immediately preceding one." 2A JABEZ GRIDLEY

Sutherland, Statutes and Statutory Construction § 47.33 (Norman Singer ed., 7th ed. 2007). Thus, if the Massachusetts's statute had provided "that alcohol shall not be sold between eleven at night and six in the morning, nor on Sunday, *except if the licensee is a hotel*," then the qualifying phrase "except if the licensee is a hotel" would modify both the phrase "between eleven at night and six in the morning" and the phrase "on Sunday." A hotel could sell alcohol all the time, with no exceptions. All other businesses would be unable to sell alcohol either on Sundays or on any day between 11:00 PM and 6:00 AM. The addition of one simple comma between the words "Sunday" and "except" would completely change the meaning of the statute.

As textualism has gained currency and the linguistic canons have gained favor, this doctrine has become more of a hard-and-fast rule than a rule of thumb. In 2003, Justice Scalia brought the doctrine to the forefront of judicial attention. In *Barnhart v. Thomas*, 540 U.S. 20 (2003), a social security claimant appealed the denial of her application for disability insurance benefits and supplemental security income on the ground that the administrative law judge should have taken into account that opportunities to perform her previous work no longer existed in significant numbers within the national economy. She had worked as an elevator operator. The statute provided:

> An individual shall be determined to be under a disability only if his physical or mental impairment or impairments are of such severity that he is *not only unable to do his previous work but cannot*, considering his age, education, and work experience, *engage in any other kind of substantial gainful work which exists in the national economy.* ...

Id. at 20 (quoting 42 U.S.C. § 423(d)(2)(A) (1999) (emphasis added)). Writing for the majority, Justice Scalia applied the doctrine of last antecedent to hold that the clause "which exists in the national economy" modified only the phrase "any other kind of substantial gainful work." *Id.* at 26–27. Justice Scalia acknowledged that "this rule is not an absolute and can assuredly be overcome by other indicia of meaning," but that "construing a statute in accord with the rule is quite sensible as a matter of grammar." *Id.* at 26 (quotations omitted). More interestingly, he provided the following, humorous example:

> Consider, for example, the case of parents who, before leaving their teenage son alone in the house for the weekend, warn him, "You will be punished if you throw a party or engage in any other activity that damages the house." If the son nevertheless throws a party and is

caught, he should hardly be able to avoid punishment by arguing that the house was not damaged. The parents proscribed (1) a party, and (2) any other activity that damages the house. As far as appears from what they said, their reasons for prohibiting the home-alone party may have had nothing to do with damage to the house. For instance, the risk that underage drinking or sexual activity would occur. And even if their only concern was to prevent damage, it does not follow from the fact that the same interest underlay both the specific and the general prohibition that proof of impairment of that interest is required for both. The parents, foreseeing that assessment of whether an activity had in fact "damaged" the house could be disputed by their son, might have wished to preclude all argument by specifying and categorically prohibiting the one activity—hosting a party—that was most likely to cause damage and most likely to occur.

Id. at 27–28. Importantly, *Barnhart* represents the first time a justice of the Supreme Court chose to explain the doctrine's application in some detail rather than simply apply or not apply it. But has Justice Scalia automated application of the doctrine too much? Admittedly, he is likely correct in his interpretation of the teenager admonishment above; however, consider the following example:

> [A] law firm partner instructs her associate to review a client's file "for emails or documents written by the CEO." Although [the sentence is] ambiguous, an astute associate would not apply the [doctrine], but would read the modifying clause, "written by the CEO," as modifying both the first and last antecedent and search for both emails written by the CEO and documents written by the CEO.

Jeremy L. Ross, *A Rule of Last Resort: A History of the Doctrine of the Last Antecedent in the United State Supreme Court*, 39 Sw. L. Rev. 325 (2009).

Finally, in *Jama v. Immigration & Customs Enforcement*, 543 U.S. 335 (2005), Justices Scalia and Souter debated whether the doctrine should apply to a statute that contained a number of itemized subsections when only the final subsection included the language at issue. Because each subsection ended with a period and the qualifying language was contained only in the final subsection, Justice Scalia, writing for the majority, applied the doctrine of last antecedent to limit the qualifier to apply only to the final subsection. *Id.* at 344. Justice Souter disagreed with the majority's decision to apply the doctrine, finding instead that other indicia of legislative intent militated in favor of applying the modifying clause to each subsection. *Id.* at 355–57 (Souter, J., dissenting).

Thus, as with all the canons but even more so with this canon, the doctrine of last antecedent must be used, not robotically, but with common sense and an understanding of context. Indeed, one might say that to call the doctrine a "rule" as many judges do is, at best, "oxymoronic." Ross, *supra*, at 336.

3. Special Grammar Rules

We turn now from punctuation rules to the general grammar rule and its exceptions. Keep in mind that the same two general rules apply: (1) grammar matters, unless the plain meaning canon suggests that it should be ignored, and (2) courts presume that legislatures use grammar accurately and consistently. For example, in *Robinson v. City of Lansing*, 782 N.W.2d 171 (2010), grammar was dispositive. In that case, the plaintiff tripped on a sidewalk, fracturing her wrist and requiring surgery. Both parties agreed that the portion of the sidewalk where she tripped was less than two inches above the lowered portion. The Michigan legislature had codified a common law rule, known as the two-inch rule, which relieved municipalities of liability when the difference in a sidewalk joint was less than two inches. The statute provided:

(1) Except as otherwise provided by this section, a municipal corporation has no duty to repair or maintain, and is not liable for injuries arising from, a portion of *a county highway* outside of the improved portion of the highway designed for vehicular travel, including a sidewalk, trailway, crosswalk, or other installation....

(2) A discontinuity defect of less than 2 inches creates a rebuttable inference that the municipal corporation maintained the sidewalk, trailway, crosswalk, or other installation outside of the improved portion of *the highway* designed for vehicular travel in reasonable repair....

Id. at 178 (quoting MICH. COMP LAWS § 691.1402a) (1999) (emphasis added). The plaintiff sued, claiming that the City had failed to maintain the sidewalk in reasonable repair. In response, the City raised the two-inch rule as an affirmative defense. The issue for the court was whether subsection 2 of the statute—which created a rebuttable inference that a discontinuity defect of less than two inches in a sidewalk meant that the municipality maintained the sidewalk in reasonable repair—applied to sidewalks adjacent to state highways or only to sidewalks adjacent to county highways. *Id.* at 174. The court focused on the definite article "the" preceding the word "highway" in subsection 2 to conclude that the highways referred to in subsection 2 were "county highways," which were first identified in subsection 1 and were not highways "in general." *Id.* at 179–80. Grammatically, this outcome was correct. Had the legislature used the indefinite article "a," the result may well have been different.

Thus, courts generally presume that legislatures use grammar appropriately, and grammar can be outcome determinative. Let's explore some specific grammar issues that you may face; some of these cases follow this general rule while others specifically do not.

a. The Meaning of "And" & "Or"

Two simple words that are typically used to connect items and phrases in sentences can be critical. These words are "and" and "or." Generally, they mean different things. The word "or" means *either.* In contrast, the word "and" means *all.*

But sometimes the word "and" is used to mean *either* and the word "or" is used to mean *all.* For example, consider the phrase: "Would you like cream *or* sugar?" Surely, you could choose both cream and sugar, or you could choose neither cream nor sugar. In the last sentence, the writer used the word "or" to mean none, one, the other, or both. Similarly, sometimes the word "and" is used to mean either. Consider the phrase, "She was forced to choose between getting gas *and* making it to class on time." In this sentence, "and" does not mean both. It means one or the other; either she would have time to get gas and be late for class or she could choose not to get gas and arrive at class on time. When drafting, it can be difficult to know whether to use "and" or "or." To counteract this conundrum, many legal drafters have resorted to using the imprecise wording "and/or;" a practice that should be discouraged as imprecise and lazy.

When legislators draft statutes, they generally do not use "and/or." Instead, they use the conjunctive "and" when the law requires that two or more requirements be fulfilled. Where failure to comply with any one requirement would not be fatal, the disjunctive "or" is generally used. 1A JABEZ GRIDLEY SUTHERLAND, STATUTES AND STATUTORY CONSTRUCTION § 21:14 (Norman Singer ed., 7th ed. 2007).

Ordinarily, "and" and "or" are not interchangeable in statutes. But because the use of these two terms baffles legislators as much as other legal writers, judges sometimes will construe the word "and" to mean "or" whenever such a conversion is mandated to effectuate the obvious intention of the legislature. Often, just as in both examples above, textual or other context can help determine which meaning was intended.

In some cases, however, discerning whether "and" truly means and can be difficult. In *Comptroller of Treasury v. Fairchild Industries, Inc.*, 493 A.2d 341, 343–44 (Md. 1985), the court rejected the state's argument that "and" meant "or." In that case, a taxpayer incurred a net operating loss that the taxpayer was legally entitled to "carry back" to a prior year. In essence, the taxpayer would get a refund on taxes it had already paid because the taxpayer incurred a loss in a subsequent year. The issue was whether the taxpayer was also entitled to receive the interest on the money paid that was later refunded. *Id.* at 342. A state tax statute required that interest be paid on income tax refunds except where the tax, as originally paid, was due to "a mistake or error on the part of the taxpayer *and* not attributable to the State ...." *Id.* at 343 (emphasis added). The state argued that the word "and" in this statute really meant "or." In other words, the state argued that the conditions in the statute were disjunctive: so long as an error was not the state's fault, the state did not have to pay the taxpayer interest on the refund regardless of whether the taxpayer made the error. *Id.* Rejecting that argument, the court said that there was nothing in the statute or legislative history to suggest that "and" meant anything other than what it normally means. *Id.* Thus, unless the taxpayer made an error *and* that error was the state's fault, the taxpayer was entitled to interest. In this case, the taxpayer had not made an error.

In summary, generally "and" and "or" are understood as intended; however, occasionally, they are not.

b. Singular & Plural

Unlike the canon above, the canons relating to number usage do not follow general grammar rules; just the opposite is true. For ease of drafting, statutes are typically written in the singular. But for statutory interpretation, a legislature's use of the singular is assumed to include the plural, and the legislature's use of the plural is assumed to include the singular. The *United States Code* provides, "In determining the meaning of any Act [or resolution] of Congress, unless the context otherwise indicates, words importing the singular include and apply to several persons, parties, or things; words importing the plural include the singular ...." 1 U.S.C. § 1. Many states have similar statutes, for example, Minnesota and Pennsylvania. MINN. STAT. § 645.08(2); 1 PA. CONS. STAT. §§ 1921–28.

In *Homebuilders Ass'n of Central Arizona v. City of Scottsdale*, 925 P.2d 1359 (Ariz. Ct. App. 1996), the court explained why courts ignore grammar in this instance.

The historical purpose of construing plural and singular nouns and verbs interchangeably is to avoid requiring the legislature to use such expressions as "person or persons," "he, she, or they," and "himself or themselves." Under this principle, the plural has often been held to apply to the singular in a statute, absent evidence of contrary legislative intent.

Id. at 1366 (citation omitted). In *Homebuilders Ass'n*, the court interpreted the words "council men" to include the singular "council man." *Id.* at 1367. The statute at issue had provided that the number of signatures required to place a referendum petition on the ballot would be determined based on the percentage of those voting at the city election "at which a mayor or council *men* were chosen last." Id. at 1364 (quoting ARIZ. REV. STAT. § 19-142(a)) (emphasis added). After finding the statute ambiguous, the court applied the singular-plural canon and held that the signature requirement should be calculated as a percentage of those voting at the last city election, even if only one council man were elected. *Id.* at 1368.

> A legislature's use of the singular includes the plural, and the legislature's use of the plural includes the singular.

As with the other canons of statutory construction, a judge will ignore this canon when the court finds a contrary legislative intent. For example, in *Van Horn v. William Blanchard Co.*, 438 A.2d 552 (N.J. Sup. Ct. 1981), the court rejected an interpretation that would have resulted from application of this canon. In that case, the court analyzed New Jersey's Comparative Negligence Act and held that the singular "person" did not include the plural "persons." *Id.* at 554. Despite the existence of a statutory directive urging that "any word importing the singular number ... shall be understood to include and apply to several persons or parties as well as to one person or party," the majority rejected the plaintiff's argument that the word "person" should include the plural "persons." *Id.* at 554–55. The context, according to the court, illustrated that the legislature had intended the singular to be used in this specific situation; thus, the directive was inapposite. Perhaps the court accurately discerned the legislative intent, perhaps not; in direct response to this case, the New Jersey legislature promptly amended the statute to reflect the interpretation the plaintiff advocated, and the majority rejected: that person and persons were both covered. *Id.* (citing N.J. STAT. ANN. § 2A:15-5.3 (West 2012)).

c. Words with Masculine, Feminine & Neuter Meaning

The third grammar canon relates to masculine, feminine, and neuter words; it too defies typical grammar rules. Until the 1980s or so, statutes were generally written using the masculine gender because the masculine pronoun was used as a "generic" pronoun reference. Legislators did not intend to refer only to men when using the masculine pronoun; rather, this grammatical practice was just accepted as a language norm of the time. Thus, for statutory interpretation purposes, the masculine pronoun is generally interpreted to include the feminine and the neuter. For example, 1 U.S.C. § 1, provides, "words importing the masculine gender include the feminine as well." Most states have similar provisions. "Words used in the masculine gender may include the feminine and the neuter." OR. REV. STAT. 174.127(2).

A simple application of the canon can be seen in *Commonwealth. v. Henninger*, 25 Pa. 3d D. & C. 3d. 625 (Pa. Ct. Com. Pl. 1981). In that case, the court applied the gender canon when it held that females can commit statutory rape. The statute provided, "A person who is 18 years of age or older commits statutory rape, a felony of the second degree, when *he* engages in sexual intercourse with another person not *his* spouse who is less than 14 years of age." *Id.* at 626 (citing 18 PA. CONS. STAT. § 3122) (emphasis added). The female defendant argued that the gender-based language "he" demonstrated an "intent on the part of the legislators to protect only women." *Id.* Citing the gender canon, the court rejected the defendant's argument. *Id.*

> A legislature's use of the masculine gender includes the feminine and neuter.

Notice that the statutes above only allow for the masculine to include the feminine and neuter, but not the feminine to include the masculine and neuter. Remember that the canon exists because the masculine pronoun was thought to be gender-neutral. The feminine pronoun had not been used in the same way. Should the canon be used interchangeably such that the feminine pronoun should be understood to include the masculine? Perhaps, especially today. However, in *Matter of Compensation of Williams*, the court refused to interpret the word "woman" to include men. 635 P.2d 384, 386 (Or. Ct. App. 1981), *aff'd,* 653 P.2d 970 (Or. 1982). The statute at issue in that case provided that an unmarried woman was entitled to compensation when the man with whom the woman was cohabiting was accidentally injured. *Id.* at 385 n.1 (citing OR. REV. STAT. § 656.226). In the case, it was a woman who was injured and the cohabiting man who sought compensation. The court reasoned that the word "woman" in the statute did not include men because "woman" was not a word used "in the *masculine* gender." *Id.* at 386. Because Oregon's gender directive (quoted above) allowed masculine words to be interpreted to include the feminine, but not feminine words to be interpreted to include the masculine, the court held that the canon was inapplicable. *Id.* However, note that reading a gender limitation into a statute might raise a constitutional question regarding whether the statute violates equal protection. To avoid the constitutional question that would be raised (*see* Chapters 6 and 12), a court might apply the canon despite the gender specific nature of the statute.

d. Mandatory & Discretionary Words

While some of the preceding canons did not follow grammar usage, this last canon does. One issue that may arise when a court interprets a statute is whether the action at issue is required or allowed, in other words, are the statutory requirements mandatory or discretionary. To resolve this question, courts will most commonly examine the form of the verb used in a statute. For example, a court will look to see whether something "may," "shall," "must," or "should" be done. The legislature's verb choice is the most important consideration in determining whether a statute is mandatory. Ordinarily, "may" is considered discretionary, "shall" is considered mandatory, "must" is considered mandatory when a condition precedent is present, and "should" is considered discretionary. *Daniel v. United Nat'l Bank*, 505 S.E.2d 711 (W. Va. 1998).

When the legislature uses "shall" or "must," judges generally interpret those words as excluding judicial or executive discretion to take into account equity or policy. *Escondido Mut. Water Co. v. La Jolla Band of Mission Indians*, 466 U.S. 765, 772 (1984) ("The mandatory nature of the language chosen by Congress [shall] appear[] to require that the Commission include the Secretary's conditions in the license even if it disagrees with them."). Sometimes, though, "shall" can mean *may*:

> Ordinarily, the use of the word "shall" in a statute carries with it the presumption that it is used in the imperative rather than in the directory sense. But this is not a conclusive presumption. Both the character and context of the legislation are controlling.... The mandatory sense to the word "shall" should not be given, if by so doing the door to miscarriages of justice should be opened.

Jersey City v. State Bd. of Tax Appeals, 43 A.2d 799, 803–04 (N.J. 1945) (refusing to interpret "shall" in a statute to be mandatory); *Cobb Cnty. v. Robertson*, 724

S.E.2d 478, 479 (Ga. Ct. App. 2012) ("Even though the word 'shall' is generally construed as mandatory, it need not always be construed in that fashion"), *cert. denied*, (Sept. 10, 2012).

Conversely, "may" sometimes means *shall* or *must*. As one court said, "The word 'may' generally denotes a discretionary provision while the use of the word 'shall' suggests that the provision is mandatory. However, when the context indicates otherwise, 'may' can have the effect of 'must' or 'shall.'" *Fink v. City of Detroit*, 333 N.W.2d 376, 379 (Mich. Ct. App. 1983) (holding that "may" was mandatory) (internal citations omitted).

One way to determine whether a statute is mandatory or discretionary is to see if the statute provides a penalty for the failure to comply with its terms. If it does, the terms are likely mandatory; if not, the terms are likely discretionary. *Christian Disposal, Inc. v. Village of Eolia*, 895 S.W.2d 632, 634 (Mo. Ct. App. 1995) ("Although 'shall' when used in a statute will usually be interpreted to command the doing of what is specified, the term is 'frequently used indiscriminately and courts have not hesitated to hold that legislative intent will prevail over common meaning.'"). When the meaning cannot be ascertained from the text alone, judges may look to other sources to discern the legislative intent.

E. Mastering This Topic

Return to the hypothetical ordinance provided in Chapter 1. The first question was the following: "An ambulance entered Pioneer Park to pick up and take to the hospital a man who has just suffered a heart attack. Did the ambulance driver violate the Pioneer Park Safety Ordinance (PPSO)?" How should you, as prosecutor, attempt to answer that question?

Recall that the first step in the interpretive process is to identify the language at issue in the operative section of the statute or ordinance. The answer to this question should be easy, for we already told you that the language at issue is "motor vehicle." Keep in mind that identifying language in a statute is often more challenging.

Next, let's apply the plain meaning rule and its technical corollary. What is the ordinary meaning of "motor vehicle" to you? What prototype did you envision? Likely, a picture of a car or truck came to mind. What are the boundaries of this prototype? Is an ambulance like a car or truck? Yes; it is nearly identical to either of these prototypes. Hence, the ordinary meaning of motor vehicle includes an ambulance.

What about definitional meaning; did you take that approach? Perhaps you opened your dictionary to find the definitional meaning of motor vehicle, and likely you did this after a car or truck appeared in your head (what does that tell you regarding the use of dictionaries?). You probably had to look up each word independently. Does meaning change when you join two words that are joined as one phrase?

Let's assume the definition of "vehicle" is the following: "any means in or by which someone travels or something is carried or conveyed; a means of conveyance or transport...."[1] The definition of "motor" is the following: "any of various power units that develop energy or impart motion: such as ... a small compact engine...."[2]

Does an ambulance fit within the definitional meanings of "motor" and "vehicle"? An ambulance is something that has a "power unit to impart motion, such as small compact engine" and is something in which people are "carried or conveyed," so, yes, an ambulance fits within the definitional meaning of motor vehicle.

Before leaving the plain meaning rule, we should consider whether its technical corollary applies: Is there a technical meaning of "motor vehicle" that applies in this case? No. Even if a technical meaning existed (which it does not), this ordinance was written for the general public, not a specialized audience. Thus, even if "motor vehicle" had a technical meaning, it likely would not apply here. Again, remember legislatures rarely intend technical meaning.

Let's turn to the punctuation and grammar. Does the grammar or punctuation of the statute help clarify the meaning? Section 2 of the Ordinance provides:

> (2) No cars, motorcycles, or other motor vehicles may enter or remain in Pioneer Park, except as provided in section 3 hereof.

You might be tempted to turn to the doctrine of last antecedent for the language "may enter or remain in Pioneer Park," for a comma does not separate it from the words "cars" and "motorcycles." Thus, you might incorrectly conclude that the phrase does not apply to these items. You would be incorrect because

---

1. Vehicle, Dictionary.com, http://dictionary.reference.com/browse/vehicle (last visited Sept. 15, 2018).

2. *Motor*, Merriam-Webster, *https://www.merriam-webster.com/dictionary/motor* (last visited Sept. 15, 2018).

the phrase "may enter or remain in Pioneer Park" is not a modifying phrase needing one or more antecedents. Rather it is the predicate (or verb portion) of the sentence. The doctrine does not apply to verb phrases. Be careful.

But wait, there is a modifying clause, can you identify it? The phrase "except as provided in section 3 hereof" modifies the items preceding it. There is a comma between the final item "other motor vehicles" and the modifier "except as provided in section 3 hereof." The doctrine of last antecedent tells us that the modifier would apply to all of the antecedents, cars, motorcycles, and other motor vehicles. Here is the exception:

(3) Motor vehicles may be used by authorized public groups:
a. in maintaining Pioneer Park, and
b. in placing barricades for parades, concerts, or other entertainment in Pioneer Park.

None of the exceptions applies in the case of the ambulance, so the doctrine of last antecedent does not help you resolve the ambiguity.

Note that there is a modifier in subsection (3)(b) above: "in Pioneer Park." There is no comma after "other entertainment." The rule of last antecedent might tell us that in placing barricades only the other entertainment must actually occur "in Pioneer Park." Parades and concerts could take place anywhere, and a motor vehicle could drive through the park to place the barricades for those off-site concerts. Does it seem likely that the legislature intended this outcome? This interpretation borders on absurd, which we will talk about in the next chapter.

Are there any other relevant grammar or punctuation issues? You might have noticed that the plural form of vehicle was used. You now know that the plural includes the singular, so it is irrelevant that only one ambulance was used. Likely, you knew this intuitively, but the grammar canon helps you confirm your intuition.

Ultimately, the grammar and punctuation in this statute provide little aid to interpretation, which is often true. As mentioned at the start of this chapter, grammar and punctuation play a relatively small role in interpretation, especially when used correctly. Thus, grammar and punctuation matter, but they matter substantially less than the words of the statute because grammar and punctuation are not used consistently or even correctly by English writers and legislators. In the next chapter, we consider ways in which you might avoid what seems to be an odd outcome: prohibiting an ambulance from entering the park to save a dying man.

Checkpoints

- The language of the statute, including its words, grammar, and punctuation, is always the starting point for interpretation.

- Typically, courts presume that words in a statute have their "plain," or "ordinary," meaning. This presumption is known as the "plain meaning rule."

- To find the ordinary meaning of words, people think in images.

- To find the ordinary meaning of categories, people think in prototypes. The closer the statutory language is to the prototype, the more likely the statute applies.

- Ordinary meaning differs from definitional meaning, which is found by using dictionaries. Definitional meaning is usually much broader than ordinary meaning.

- A word or phrase that has acquired a technical or unique meaning in a specific context has that meaning if the word or phrase is used in that context. This corollary to the plain meaning rule is known as the "technical meaning rule."

- The general grammar and punctuation rule provides that both grammar and punctuation matter unless clear legislative intent suggests that they should be ignored.

- In statutes, comma placement can be critical. Commas are troubling, in part, because comma rules are not consistently followed. Yet their placement can be critical to meaning.

- The Doctrine of the Last Antecedent directs that modifying words and phrases modify only the immediately preceding noun or noun phrase in a list of items. All a drafter need do to have a phrase modify all the preceding nouns is add a comma between the modifier and the last antecedent.

- Generally, the word "and" has a conjunctive meaning, while the word "or" has a disjunctive meaning. However, when context dictates, courts will interchange these two words.

- For ease of drafting, statutes are typically written in the singular. But for statutory interpretation, the legislature's use of the singular is assumed to include the plural, and the legislature's use of the plural is assumed to include the singular.

- Also, for ease of drafting, the masculine pronoun is generally interpreted to include the feminine or neuter. The feminine pronoun may be interpreted to include the male or neuter.

Chapter 6

Canons for Choosing or Avoiding Ordinary Meaning

Roadmap

- Discover that there may be multiple ordinary meanings.
- Learn how judges define and resolve ambiguity.
- Understand that the ordinary meaning may be absurd.
- Learn how judges define and resolve absurdity.
- Learn how judges resolve interpretations that contain a scrivener's error or raise a constitutional question.

A. Introduction to This Chapter

In the last chapter, you learned that judges assume that legislatures meant words to have their ordinary, sometimes called plain, meaning. You also learned that occasionally the legislature meant words to have their technical meaning. Because technical meaning is rarely intended, the remainder of this chapter will address ordinary meaning. So, what should a judge do when there is more than one ordinary meaning? Or when that ordinary meaning is absurd or might violate the state or federal constitution?

This chapter explains the four situations when judges choose between or avoid ordinary meaning: ambiguity, absurdity, scrivener's error, and constitutional avoidance. When these situations arise, judges will turn to sources of meaning beyond the text, such as other intrinsic sources, extrinsic sources, and policy-based sources.

Ambiguity is most common reasons judges look beyond text, so we will start there.

B. Choosing Among Multiple Ordinary Meanings

1. Ambiguity

While some judges are willing to look at all the sources of meaning even when the text is clear (meaning that the text has one ordinary meaning), more commonly, judges may need to have a reason to look beyond allegedly clear text. Indeed, textualist judges refuse to look beyond the ordinary meaning of clear text unless there is a reason to do so. *See, e.g., Goswami v. American Collections Enters., Inc.*, 377 F.3d 488, 492 (5th Cir. 2004) ("In interpreting statutes we do not look beyond the plain meaning of the statute unless the statute is absurd or ambiguous."). The most common reason judges look beyond the ordinary meaning of the words is that the words do not have one ordinary meaning; rather, they have multiple ordinary meanings.

When words and phrases have multiple ordinary meanings, they are ambiguous. "Ambiguous" means "open to or having several possible meanings or interpretations; equivocal."[1]

Ambiguous words and phrases may be likened to optical illusions in that both parties legitimately claim to see — or in the case of words and phrases, understand — the same thing in a different way. Consider the famous optical illusion in the text box to the left. Do you see a young or old woman? Many people see the young woman first, but if you look at the picture long enough, you should be able to make out the old woman as well. The young woman's necklace is the old woman's mouth. The young woman's chin is the old woman's nose. The young woman's ear is the old woman's eye. They share the hair, fur, and feather.

Anyone viewing the picture can legitimately say it is a picture of either a young or old woman. Both "interpretations" are legitimate because the picture is equivocal, or "ambiguous," intentionally so in this case. Ambiguous words

---

1. *Ambiguous*, Dictionary.com, http://dictionary.reference.com/browse/ambiguous (last visited Sept. 15, 2018).

are similar to optical illusions; they have more than one ordinary meaning. Children love to joke using ambiguous words. For example, how did the baker get rich? She made a lot of dough! Or what kind of bagel can fly? A plane bagel. (I did not say they were good jokes!)

Unfortunately, judges do not define ambiguity consistently. The most common articulation of ambiguity is that statutory language is "ambiguous if it is capable of being understood by reasonably well-informed persons in two or more senses." *State ex rel. Kalal v. Circuit Court for Dane County,* 681 N.W.2d 110, 124 (Wis. 2004). In other words, a statute is ambiguous when it has more than one meaning when applied to the facts of a particular case. For example, in *Church of the Holy Trinity v. United States,* 143 U.S. 457, 459 (1892), the Court had to interpret the word "labor." The statute could have included all types of labor or it could have included only unskilled, physical labor. The text of the statute alone (the word "labor" and its surrounding words) did not resolve the ambiguity, at least to the Court. Thus, the word "labor," in this context, was ambiguous. To resolve the ambiguity, the Court turned to other sources, namely the title and purpose of the act, to choose between the two possible meanings. *Id.*

Although the "reasonable people disagree" standard is often articulated, it is likely incorrect because every case involving a statutory interpretation issue would involve ambiguity under this standard. Litigants always disagree as to the meaning of the statutory language, and judges often disagree as well. If the "reasonable people disagree" definition were correct, then most litigants, their lawyers, and many judges would be unreasonable people. An alternative definition is that one or more interpretations are *equally plausible. Florida Dep't of Revenue v. Piccadilly Cafeterias, Inc.,* 554 U.S. 33, 41 (2008); *Mayor of Lansing v. Michigan Pub. Serv. Comm'n.,* 680 N.W.2d 840, 847 (Mich. 2004); (stating that "a provision of the law is ambiguous only if ... it is *equally* susceptible to more than a single meaning."). This definition is much narrower. A judge who defines ambiguity in this way is less likely to find words ambiguous.

A judge's approach to interpretation might affect that judge's willingness to define "ambiguity" broadly ("reasonable people disagree") or narrowly ("equally plausible"). Possibly, a judge's desire to look beyond the text could affect this choice. A broader definition of ambiguity allows judges to review extra-textual evidence of meaning more readily, while a narrower definition constrains judicial review of such evidence. Hence, we might expect textualist judges to define ambiguity narrowly while non-textualist judges, if they define it at all, might choose a broader definition. Indeed, in *Florida Dep't of Revenue,* Justice Thomas, a textualist, defined ambiguity narrowly (equally susceptible to more than a single meaning), while Justice Breyer, a purposivist, defined ambiguity broadly (the statute can be read either way). 544 U.S. at 41, 54.

Be aware that simply because a word has more than one meaning does not mean that the word is ambiguous. For example, in *State ex rel. Kalal*, an employer allegedly stole retirement funds from his employee. 681 N.W.2d at 115. A statute allowed the district court to bring a criminal action directly if the district attorney "refuse[d]" to issue the complaint. *Id.* at 114 (quoting Wis. Stat. § 968.02(3) (2001–02)). The district attorney told the employee that she "was free to proceed legally in whatever manner she believed necessary." *Id.* After being told she was free to proceed, the employee filed a motion for a criminal complaint, which the court granted. *Id.* The issue in the case was whether the word "refuse" required an explicit refusal or merely an indication of unwillingness to do something. *Id.* at 115. The court concluded that the language was not ambiguous, despite the two, possible interpretations, because the second interpretation better furthered the purpose of the statute. *Id.*

There are two types of ambiguity: lexical ambiguity and structural ambiguity. *Lexical ambiguity* occurs when a word or phrase has multiple meanings. Everyday examples include nouns like "bay," "pen," and "suit"; verbs like "dust," "draw," and "run"; and adjectives like "hard" and "blue." Textual context typically, but not always, resolves this type of ambiguity. As Justice Scalia has explained, "If you tell me, 'I took the boat out on the bay,' I understand 'bay' to mean one thing; if you tell me, 'I put the saddle on the bay,' I understand it to mean something else." ANTONIN SCALIA, A MATTER OF INTERPRETATION 26 (1997).

Structural ambiguity occurs when a phrase or a sentence can be interpreted in more than one way due to an ambiguous structure. Some examples include "the Tibetan history teacher," "short men and women," "the girl hit the boy with a book," and "visiting relatives can be boring." Each phrase can be represented in two structurally different ways, e.g., "[Tibetan history] teacher" and "Tibetan [history teacher]"; [visiting relatives] can be boring and [visiting] relatives can be boring. Here is another example of structural ambiguity: "Will you call me a taxi?" "Sure, you are a taxi." Judges resolve lexical and structural ambiguity in the same way; however, you will need to explain why language is ambiguous, so knowing the difference between these two will be helpful to you.

Additionally, ambiguous is not the same as vague, broad, and general. First, ambiguity is not the same as vagueness. Vague means "not clearly or explicitly stated or expressed."[2] Vagueness means that the boundaries of meaning are

---

2. *Vague*, DICTIONARY.COM, http://dictionary.reference.com/browse/vague (last visited Sept. 15, 2018).

indistinct. For example, if I say I want the report next week sometime, "next week sometime" is vague, not ambiguous. If language is vague, it is susceptible to multiple meanings.

Second, ambiguity is not the same as broadness. "Broad" means "of great breadth; of great extent; large."[3] If I say that I want a ten- to fifty-page report, that range may be broad, but it is not ambiguous. If language is broad, it is susceptible to multiple meanings.

Third, ambiguity is not the same as generalness. "General" means "of or relating to all persons or things belonging to a group or category."[4] If I say I want a report on birds, the topic "birds" may be general, but it is not ambiguous. If language is general, it is susceptible to multiple meanings.

Although vague, broad, and general do not mean the same thing as ambiguous, judges regularly use the term "ambiguous" whenever a word is susceptible to multiple meanings. Again, knowing why the language is susceptible to multiple meanings can help you explain to a judge why a word is ambiguous and your meaning is the correct one.

When a judge determines that language in a statute is ambiguous, however defined, that judge opens the door to sources other than just the words. Which sources a judge will consider continues to be influenced by that judge's theory of interpretation. We will consider the other sources in later chapters.

C. Rejecting the Ordinary Meaning of Words

1. The Absurdity Doctrine (The Golden Rule)

While ambiguity applies when words have more than one ordinary meaning, absurdity applies when words have one ordinary meaning, but that ordinary meaning seems odd given the circumstances of the case.

Absurdity offers a way for judges to reject the ordinary meaning of the language when a statute would be absurd if implemented according to the ordinary meaning. The *absurdity doctrine* allows the judges to correct legislative policy mistakes; thus, it is compatible with intentionalism and purposivism. Judges should reject the ordinary meaning of the language in the statute when

---

3. *Broad*, DICTIONARY.COM, http://dictionary.reference.com/browse/broad (last visited Sept. 15, 2018).

4. *General*, DICTIONARY.COM, http://dictionary.reference.com/browse/general (last visited Sept. 15, 2018).

necessary to implement the will of the legislators or the purpose of the act. Yet textualists, even the new textualists, accept this doctrine. *See, e.g., Barnhart v. Sigmon Coal Co., Inc.* 534 U.S. 438, 459 (2002) (Thomas, J.) (acknowledging the doctrine's existence while rejecting its application when the text was clear and unambiguous); *INS v. Cardoza-Fonseca*, 480 U.S. 421, 452 (1987) (Scalia, J., concurring) ("[I]f the language of a statute is clear, that language must be given effect—at least in the absence of a patent absurdity."); *Kerr v. Puckett*, 138 F.3d 321, 323 (7th Cir. 1998) (Easterbrook, J.) ("Instead of relying on 'common sense', which is an invitation to treat the law as if one side or the other had its way, a court should implement the language actually enacted— provided the statute is not ... absurd.").

The absurdity doctrine made an early appearance in this country in 1868. In *United States v. Kirby*, 74 U.S. (7 Wall.) 482 (1869), the Supreme Court dismissed an indictment charging a sheriff with violating a statute that prohibited anyone from "knowingly and willfully obstruct[ing] or retard[ing] the passage of the mail, or of any driver or carrier." *Id.* at 485–86. The defendant sheriff had arrested a mail carrier wanted for murder while the mail carrier was delivering mail. Although the defendant violated the clear terms of the statute, the Court dismissed the indictment. *Id.* at 487. In doing so, the Court explained:

> All laws should receive a sensible construction. General terms should be so limited in their application as not to lead to injustice, oppression, or an absurd consequence. It will always, therefore, be presumed that the legislature intended exceptions to its language, which would avoid results of this character. The reason of the law in such cases should prevail over its letter.

Id. at 486–87.

In support of its decision to reject the ordinary meaning, the Court referenced two early decisions from Europe. First, a medieval Italian court had refused to punish a surgeon "who opened the vein of a person that fell down in the street in a fit" for violating a law punishing anyone "who[] drew blood in the streets." *Id.* at 487. Second, an English court had refused to punish a prisoner who had escaped from a prison that was on fire under a statute prohibiting prison escapes. *Id.* In these two cases, the courts deviated from the ordinary meaning of the statutes because application of the statute to the particular facts in each case led to a result the legislature would not have intended. "[T]he absurdity doctrine therefore rests on the premise that if legislators had foreseen the problems raised by a specific statutory application, 'they could and would have revised the legislation to avoid such absurd results.'" Glen Staszewski, *Avoiding Absurdity*, 81 IND. L.J. 1001, 1007 (2006) (quoting John F. Manning, *The Absurdity Doctrine*, 116 HARV. L. REV. 2387, 2394 (2003)) (citation omitted). Relying on the rationale in these prior cases, the Supreme Court in *Kirby* applied the absurdity doctrine to reach a result that seems just and fair.

In 1892, the Supreme Court explained that the rationale for absurdity was to avoid a result that was contrary to legislative intent. *Church of the Holy Trinity v. United States*, 143 U.S. 457, 459 (1892) ("[F]or frequently words of general meaning are used in a statute, words broad enough to include an act in question, and yet a consideration of the whole legislation, or of the circumstances surrounding its enactment, or of the absurd results which follow from giving such broad meaning to the words, makes it unreasonable to believe that the legislator intended to include the particular act."). The act at issue in *Holy Trinity* prohibited businesses from bringing anyone into the country "to perform labor or service of any kind." *Id.* at 458. The defendant contracted with an individual from England to immigrate to the United States to serve as a pastor in its church. In response and pursuant to the ordinary meaning of the Act, the federal government sued the church to recover a statutory penalty. The Supreme Court rejected the government's argument that "labor or service of any kind" covered pastoral services. *Id.* at 459. Stating that "[i]t is a familiar rule that a thing may be within the letter of the statute and yet not within the statute, because not within its spirit, nor within the intention of its makers," the Court found the government's interpretation was absurd after looking at the legislative history. *Id.* The legislative history showed that the legislature had intended the word "labor" or "service" to mean *manual* labor. *Id.* at 462–63.

The Supreme Court's use of absurdity in light of such clear text has been solidly criticized, perhaps because textualism has gained currency. The Court has suggested that the doctrine is one of last resort, "rarely invoke[d] … to override unambiguous legislation." *Barnhart*, 534 U.S. at 441. As Justice Kennedy noted, "the potential of this doctrine to allow judges to substitute their personal predilections for the will of the Congress is so self-evident from the case which spawned it [(*Holy Trinity*)] as to require no further discussion of its susceptibility to abuse." *Public Citizen v. DOJ*, 491 U.S. 440, 474 (1989) (Kennedy, J., concurring).

Today, the Court turns to the absurdity doctrine occasionally to reject the ordinary meaning of clear statutory text. While the justices of the Supreme Court turn to the doctrine increasingly rarely, to date, none have ever rejected the doctrine outright. Indeed, in rejecting the application of the doctrine in particular cases, the justices have reaffirmed the doctrine's continued vitality.

Furthermore, the doctrine, despite its flaws, is alive and well in the lower federal and state courts. *See, e.g., Robbins v. Chronister*, 402 F.3d 1047 (10th Cir. 2005), *rev'd*, 435 F.3d 1238 (10th Cir. 2006).

Given that the doctrine is alive and well, let's look at how it has been applied. In *Public Citizen*, the Court invoked the absurdity doctrine to avoid the ordinary meaning of the Federal Advisory Committee Act (FACA). 491 U.S. at 454. The issue in the case was whether a committee of the American Bar Association (ABA) was subject to FACA. *Id.* at 448. The Act required disclosure and open meetings for all federal "advisory committee[s]." *Id.* at 446–47. "Advisory Committee" was defined in the Act as any committee "utilized by the President ... in the interest of obtaining advice or recommendations." *Id.* at 451 (quoting 5 U.S.C. §3(2) (1982)). Thus, pursuant to the ordinary meaning of the statute, the ABA was an advisory committee because the president routinely sought the recommendations of the ABA regarding judicial nominees.

Citing *Holy Trinity*, however, the majority refused to give the statute its ordinary meaning. *Id.* at 454. Because the ordinary meaning of the statute "compel[led] an odd result," the Court searched "for other evidence of congressional intent to lend the term its proper scope." *Id.* According to the majority, the statute was enacted to cure two specific ills—namely the "wasteful expenditure of public funds for worthless committee meetings and biased proposals" made by special interest groups. *Id.* at 453. The Court thought it unlikely that Congress intended FACA to cover every formal and informal meeting between the president and a group rendering advice. *Id.* Citing the absurdity doctrine, the Court held that FACA did not apply to the ABA despite the ordinary meaning of the words of the statute. *Id.* at 454.

Here's another example. In *Green v. Bock Laundry Mach. Co.*, 490 U.S. 504, 528–29 (1989) (Scalia, J., concurring), Justice Scalia reasoned that former federal Rule of Evidence 609(a)(1) was absurd, perhaps even unconstitutional, because it allowed a court to weigh the prejudice of impeachment evidence for civil defendants but not for civil plaintiffs. Plaintiff Green, an inmate, worked at a car wash while on work release. His arm was torn off while he was using a laundry machine, so he sued the manufacturer. The defendant manufacturer wanted to make the jurors aware that the plaintiff was an inmate in jail. Rule 609, as then in effect, required a court, when admitting evidence that a witness had been convicted of a felony, to balance "the probative value of admitting th[e] evidence [with] the prejudicial effect to *the defendant*." *Id.* at 509 (quoting FED. R. EVID. 609(a)(1) (emphasis added)).

In Green's case, there would have been no prejudicial effect to the defendant manufacturer in admitting Green's conviction into evidence, but it was tremendously prejudicial to Green, the plaintiff, to have his status known. Based on the ordinary meaning of the rule, the trial court allowed the information in, and Green lost.

Green appealed. While the ordinary meaning of "defendant" is any defendant, Justice Scalia reasoned that that meaning would be absurd because such an interpretation would deny a civil plaintiff the same right to impeach a witness that a civil defendant would have. *Id.* at 528–29. He found this interpretation to be absurd and perused the legislative history solely to determine whether Congress had intended the absurd result. Concluding that Congress had not intended the outcome, Justice Scalia interpreted the word "defendant" to mean "criminal defendant." Green lost his appeal.

One difficulty in using the absurdity doctrine is that absurdity, like ambiguity, is not consistently defined in the jurisprudence. For example, in *Holy Trinity*, the Supreme Court never explicitly defined absurdity. Instead, the Court merely suggested that a meaning that conflicts with congressional intent would be absurd. In *Bock Laundry*, Justice Scalia equated absurd with "irrational" and "likely unconstitutional." 490 U.S. at 528. More recently, in *King v. Burwell*, Justice Scalia defined an absurd result as "a consequence 'so monstrous, that all mankind would, without hesitation, unite in rejecting the application.'" 135 S. Ct. 2480, 2505 (2015) (Scalia, J., dissenting) (quoting *Sturges v. Crowninshield*, 17 (4 Wheat.) 122, 203 (1819)).

Moreover, choosing a definition of absurdity can be outcome determinative. For example, in *Robbins v. Chronister*, the majority used *Holy Trinity*'s broad definition of absurdity—contrary to congressional intent—while the dissent used a narrower definition—shocking to one's conscience. 402 F.3d 1047 (10th Cir. 2005), *rev'd*, 435 F.3d 1238 (10th Cir. 2006).

Which is the most accurate definition of absurdity? Perhaps none. The definitions of absurdity used in *Holy Trinity* and *Bock Laundry* were so broad that they would essentially open the door for consideration of extra-textual evidence in almost every case. A broad definition might be appealing to non-textualist judges willing to look to extra-textual sources relatively readily, but less appealing to textualist judges. Yet Justice Scalia's definition of absurdity in *Burwell* is little improved. It sets a standard that will rarely, if ever, be met. The correct definition of absurdity must lie between these two extremes. Just where is not clear, and the jurisprudence is of little help. Most commonly, instead of defining absurdity, judges simply list other cases that have found absurdity, thereby suggesting that the instant case is like or unlike those in the list. What does that mean for you as a lawyer? You should pick the definition that best helps your client.

2. Scrivener's Error Doctrine

The scrivener's error doctrine is a subset of the absurdity doctrine. While the absurdity doctrine applies when the legislative policy choices seem odd given the circumstances of the case, the scrivener's error doctrine applies when the act contains an obvious drafting error. The scrivener's error exception to the plain meaning rule permits judges to correct obvious clerical or typographical errors. For example, in *United States National Bank of Oregon v. Independent Insurance Agents of America, Inc.*, 508 U.S. 439, 462 (1993), the Court corrected misplaced punctuation. Similarly, in *United States v. Coatoam*, 245 F.3d 553, 557 (6th Cir. 2001), the Sixth Circuit corrected a cross-reference to the wrong subsection of an act. And in *United States v. Scheer*, 729 F.2d 164, 169 (2nd Cir. 1984), the Second Circuit changed the word "request" in a statute to "receipt" where the statute had erroneously provided that a certificate be furnished "upon request of the ... request." *Id.*

In the past, judges may have turned to this doctrine more readily to correct substantive, rather than drafting errors. *See, e.g., Shine v. Shine*, 802 F.2d 583, 588 (1st Cir. 1986) ("While the wording of the statute may have given rise to some confusion, '[t]he result of an obvious mistake should not be enforced, particularly when it overrides common sense and evident statutory purpose.'" (quoting *In re Adamo*, 619 F.2d 216, 222 (2d Cir. 1980), *cert. denied*, 449 U.S. 843 (1980)) (internal quotation marks omitted)). Today, however, the scrivener's error exception is understood to be a narrow exception, which is not used simply because the court believes a policy error might have been made; "[i]t is beyond [a court's] province to rescue Congress from its drafting errors, and to provide for what we might think ... is the preferred result." *United States v. Granderson*, 511 U.S. 39, 68 (1994). For example, in *United States v. Locke*, 471 U.S. 84, 93 (1985), the Court refused to interpret "prior to December 31" as including December 31. In that case, the Locke family needed to file papers to retain its right to mine gravel on federal lands. The Lockes were told by the relevant agency personnel that the papers had to be filed on or before December 31. *Id.* at 89 n.7. So the Lockes filed on that date. The agency then rejected the papers, claiming that the papers had to be filed on or before December 30.

When the Lockes sued, the Court agreed with the agency because the language was clear and "a literal reading of Congress' words is generally the only proper reading of [filing deadlines]." *Id.* at 93. The Court explained when it had leeway to alter statutory text pursuant to the scrivener's error doctrine: "[t]here is a basic difference between filling a gap left by Congress' silence and rewriting rules that Congress has affirmatively and specifically enacted." *Id.* at 95 (quotations omitted). While the phrase "prior to" was clumsy, its meaning was clear. *Id.* at 96. Luckily for the Lockes, the Court remanded on other grounds, and the Lockes kept their mineral rights.

In sum, the scrivener's error doctrine does not give courts *carte blanche* to redraft poorly written statutes to correct legislative "mistakes"; rather, it is a doctrine that allows courts limited authority to fix obvious drafting errors. Finally, be aware that the doctrine is not *carte blanche* for judges to forgive obvious grammatical errors (*see* Chapter 5).

3. The Constitutional Avoidance Doctrine

While the scrivener's error doctrine allows courts to reject ordinary meaning because of an obvious drafting error, the *constitutional avoidance doctrine* (also known as the avoidance canon) allows courts to reject ordinary meaning to avoid having to consider the constitutionality of a statute. The constitutional avoidance doctrine provides that when there are two reasonable interpretations of statutory language, one which raises a constitutional issue and one that does not, the statute should be interpreted in a way that does not raise the constitutional issue. *Murray v. Schooner Charming Betsy*, 6 U.S. (2 Cranch) 64, 118 (1804). As just described, this formulation is the modern avoidance canon; it allows courts to avoid the constitutional issue altogether when another fair interpretation exists. However, there is another formulation of this doctrine: the classical avoidance canon. This formulation directs courts to interpret statutes to avoid a construction that actually is unconstitutional; it does not allow courts to avoid addressing the constitutional question like the modern approach does. Here, we will focus on the modern avoidance canon.

For example, in *Bock Laundry*, explained above, the Court turned to the modern doctrine to reject the ordinary meaning of the text of Rule 609 of the Federal Rules of Evidence. You will recall that Rule 609, as then in effect, required a court to balance "the probative value of admitting th[e] evidence [that a witness had been convicted of a felony with] the prejudicial effect to *the defendant* . . . ." *Bock Laundry*, 490 U.S. at 509 (quoting FED. R. EVID. 609(a) (emphasis added)). While the ordinary meaning of "defendant" is a civil or criminal defendant, the majority held that this meaning would be "odd" because such an interpretation would deny a civil plaintiff the same right to impeach a witness that a civil defendant would have. *Id.* In other words, the interpretation would raise a question about whether the statute violated due process. After reviewing the legislative history, the Court concluded that the legislature more likely intended the word "defendant" to mean "criminal defendant," and so avoided the ordinary meaning, which would have raised this constitutional question. *Id.* at 509.

The avoidance canon is justified in two ways. First, some believe that the canon accurately reflects congressional intent. They say that Congress tries to respect the limits of its constitutional authority and does not legislate in ways that test those bounds unintentionally. *Clark v. Martinez*, 543 U.S. 371, 381 (2005) (noting that "one of the canon's chief justifications is that it allows courts to avoid resolving constitutional questions. It is a tool for choosing between competing plausible interpretations of a statutory text, resting on the reasonable presumption that Congress did not intend the alternative which raises serious constitutional doubts.").

Second, some argue that the canon aids judicial restraint. *See, e.g., Three Affiliated Tribes of the Fort Berthold Reservation v. Wold Engineering, P.C.*, 467 U.S. 138, 157 (1984) ("It is a fundamental rule of judicial restraint, however, that this Court will not reach constitutional questions in advance of the necessity of deciding them."). Moreover, because it is much harder for Congress to overturn a Supreme Court case holding a statute to be unconstitutional, judicial restraint furthers the relationship between the Court and Congress.

Given these justifications, the avoidance canon should be used only when there are two *fair* and *reasonable* interpretations of a statute. *Ashwander v. Tennessee Valley Auth.*, 297 U.S. 288, 348 (1936) (Brandeis, J., concurring) ("When the validity of an act of the Congress is drawn in question, and even if a serious doubt of constitutionality is raised, it is a cardinal principle that this Court will first ascertain whether a construction of the statute is *fairly possible* by which the question may be avoided.") (emphasis added). Limiting the choice to interpretations that are fair and reasonable confines the judiciary to its proper constitutional role of interpreting rather than legislating.

In reality, however, some judges may adopt an interpretation that is not reasonable or fair simply to avoid the constitutional question. For example, in *NLRB v. Catholic Bishop*, 440 U.S. 490 (1979), the majority refused to adopt an interpretation of the National Labor Relations Act that might violate the First Amendment of the Constitution. *Id.* at 507. In that case, the Court was asked to determine whether the National Labor Relations Board had jurisdiction over lay teachers who taught at church-operated schools. By its terms, the Act applied to all "employer[s]," defined as "any person acting as an agent of an employer, directly or indirectly ...." *Id.* at 510 (Brennan, J., dissenting) (quoting 29 U.S.C. § 152(2) (1978)). Citing the avoidance canon, the Court said it could reject the ordinary meaning "if *any other possible construction* remain[ed] available." *Id.* at 500 (emphasis added). The majority then looked for "a clear expression of Congress' intent to [raise Constitutional questions involving] the First Amendment Religion Clauses." *Id.* at 507. Not finding any such clear statement, the majority refused to use the ordinary meaning of "employer" and instead concluded that "employer" must mean all employers *except* church-operated schools. *Id.* at 499. In sum, the majority misquoted the doctrine and rewrote the statute to include an implied exception to avoid reaching the constitutional issue.

Similarly, in *Public Citizen*, the Supreme Court construed FACA narrowly to avoid "formidable constitutional difficulties." 491 U.S. at 466. FACA requires advisory committees to file a charter; provide notice of meetings; open those meetings to the public; and make minutes, records, and reports available for public inspection and copying. *Id.* at 447. The issue for the Court was whether a committee of the ABA was "an advisory committee" when the Justice Department sought the committee's views on prospective judicial nominees. *Id.* at 443.

FACA defined "advisory committee" as "any committee, board, commission, council, conference, panel, task force, or other similar group, or any subcommittee ... which is ... *utilized* by the President ...." *Id.* at 451 (citing 5 U.S.C. § 3(2) (1982) (emphasis added)). Recognizing that the Justice Department and president did "utilize" the committee in a broad sense, the Court nevertheless rejected the ordinary meaning of the text because that meaning would raise a serious constitutional question: namely whether the statute "infringed unduly on the President's Article II power to nominate federal judges and [thus] violated the doctrine of separation of powers." *Id.* at 466. Rather than decide the constitutional issue, the majority adopted an interpretation that did not raise the issue and was consistent with the purpose of the statute, even though the interpretation was at odds with the ordinary meaning of the text. *Id.* at 464.

The justices in these cases applied the doctrine too readily. In contrast, in *United States v. Marshall*, 908 F.2d 1312, 1335 (7th Cir. 1990) (en banc), *aff'd sub nom. Chapman v. United States*, 500 U.S. 453 (1991), Judge

Easterbrook refused to apply the doctrine at all in a case in which the doctrine's application was more appropriate. In *Marshall*, the court had to interpret the federal sentencing guidelines, which set mandatory minimum terms of imprisonment for individuals who were caught selling drugs. *Id.* at 1315. According to these guidelines, anyone selling more than ten grams of a "mixture or substance containing a detectable amount" of a drug would be sentenced to a minimum of ten years, while those selling less than ten grams would be subject to a minimum of five years. The defendant was convicted of selling more than ten grams of LSD and was sentenced to twenty years. *Id.* at 1314.

The issue for the court was whether the language of the statute—"mixture or substance containing a detectable amount of"—meant that the weight of a carrier mixed with the drug was included. *Id.* at 1315. Unlike other drugs such as cocaine, LSD is sold in a very heavy carrier such as orange juice, blotter paper, or gelatin cubes. If the weight of the carrier were included, then LSD dealers would be subject to a higher penalty than other drug dealers even if the LSD dealers sold a smaller total amount of LSD. In fact, the weight of LSD itself is so small in comparison to its carrier that LSD dealers would be sentenced entirely based on the weight of the carrier. *Id.* at 1315.

The defendant argued that interpreting the statute to include the weight of the blotter paper or other carrier would raise two constitutional questions: (1) whether the statute violated substantive due process by penalizing individuals without regard to the severity of the crime, and (2) whether the statute violated equal protection by treating some drug dealers differently than others based on a nonsensical distinction. *Id.* at 1320, 1322.

Writing for the majority, Judge Easterbrook concluded that "[s]ubstance or mixture containing a detectable quantity" was not ambiguous, so avoidance was not "fairly possible." *Id.* at 1318. Because he did not find the language ambiguous, he chose the interpretation that raised the constitutional questions, then answered both questions in the negative.

But Judge Easterbrook misunderstood the doctrine. He suggested that judges should use the constitutional avoidance canon only "when *the language is ambiguous* and a construction of the statute is fairly possible by which the question may be avoided." *Id.* (emphasis added) (citation omitted). The latter point is correct. But the requirement of ambiguity is wrong. Judge Easterbrook conflated ambiguity and the constitutional avoidance doctrine. If the language were ambiguous, then the avoidance canon is unnecessary. It is only when the language is clear that the avoidance canon is applicable. And then, the alternative interpretation must be reasonable and fair.

Judge Posner dissented and argued that the majority should have avoided the constitutional questions altogether by interpreting the language to exclude the carrier. Although admitting that his interpretation was not the *best* interpretation of the language, he concluded that Congress likely did not understand how LSD was sold and, thus, probably did not intend to raise the constitutional questions that the majority's interpretation raised. *Id.* at 1331 (Posner, J., dissenting). He said that judges should use the constitutional avoidance canon when "there is not merely a constitutional question about, *but a constitutional barrier to*, the statute when interpreted literally." *Id.* at 1335–36 (emphasis added). Under this articulation, judges must first conclude that a statute is unconstitutional, and then adopt an alternative interpretation. Thus, Judge Posner applied the classical avoidance formulation rather than the modern formulation. Under the modern formulation, the point of the *avoidance* canon is to avoid having to resolve the constitutional question.

Let's summarize what you have learned in this chapter. When one or more ordinary meanings are equally plausible, then the language is ambiguous and judges will have to choose one meaning over another. Also, there are three situations in which judges avoid the ordinary meaning of words altogether: (1) if the ordinary meaning of the text is absurd, however absurdity is defined; (2) if there is an obvious scrivener's error; or (3) if the ordinary meaning would raise a constitutional question. When any of these four situations is present, judges look beyond the words to determine meaning. In the next chapter, we continue our exploration of the intrinsic sources of meaning, turning first to the linguistic canons.

D. Mastering This Topic

Return to the hypothetical ordinance provided in Chapter 1. The first question was the following: "An ambulance entered Pioneer Park to pick up and take to the hospital a man who has just suffered a heart attack. Did the ambulance driver violate the Pioneer Park Safety Ordinance (PPSO)?" How should you, as prosecutor, attempt to answer that question?

You have already identified the language at issue, rejected technical meaning, and settled on an ordinary meaning. You should have concluded that the ordinance prohibits ambulances from driving within the park to pick up heart attack victims. Therefore, the driver should be fined, right? Does this outcome seem odd to you? Do you find yourself squirming, knowing you will have to fine the driver, who was only doing his job and helping an ill person? Perhaps there is a way to avoid this ordinary meaning. Let's see if any of the exceptions to the plain meaning rule apply.

First, is there ambiguity? Are there two equally plausible, ordinary meanings of the words "motor vehicle"? Not really. An ambulance is a motor vehicle, as we discovered in Chapter 5. The term "motor vehicle" may be vague, broad, or general, but it is not ambiguous; it covers ambulances. Thus, there is no ambiguity in this ordinance. Let's skip absurdity for the moment.

Second, is there a scrivener's error? No. There is no obvious drafting error.

Third, is there a constitutional question that could be avoided? No. The ordinance does not raise constitutional questions. It would not be unconstitutional to fine the driver for driving in the park.

Finally, is there absurdity? Ah ha! That must be it. But let's see if the absurdity doctrine is truly satisfied. How would you define absurdity? If you define absurdity as "shocking to one's conscience," then this situation likely does not fit within your definition. If, instead, you define absurdity as meaning an "odd result" or "contrary to legislative intent," then this situation likely fits within your definition of absurdity. It seems highly unlikely that the city council intended to prohibit ambulances from coming into the park to rescue critically ill people especially if it is a very large park (it does include a lake after all). Moreover, the ordinance was enacted to promote safety in the park. Doesn't rescuing a heart attack victim promote safety? Well, you decide, the ordinary meaning of the statute is absurd because it leads to an odd result and that result is likely contrary to legislative intent. Absurdity is the only legitimate reason to avoid the ordinary meaning of the text of this ordinance.

If you self-identified as a textualist, using the absurdity doctrine should not be an easy choice. But it is the only way you can avoid applying the statute as written, if that is what you want to do. If, instead, you self-identified as a purposivist or intentionalist, this analysis may have seemed very formalistic, simplistic, and unnecessary. Your turn to squirm is coming.

Checkpoints

- When language has more than one ordinary meaning, we say that the language is ambiguous.

- Ambiguity is not consistently defined in the cases. Some say that language is ambiguous when the words are capable of being understood by reasonable people in more than one way, while others say that language is ambiguous when two or more interpretations are equally plausible.

- A litigant wishing to have the court consider sources of meaning other than the text should use the easier to meet definition (reasonable people), while those wishing to constrain judges to the text should use the harder to meet definition (equally plausible).

- When language is ambiguous, judges look at sources of meaning other than text, such as other intrinsic sources, extrinsic sources, and policy-based sources.

- Absurdity is not consistently defined in the cases. Some say that an interpretation is absurd when it would lead to odd results that conflict with the legislative intent or statutory purpose; others say an interpretation is absurd when it is shocking to one's conscience.

- When an interpretation is absurd, judges look at sources of meaning other than text, such as other intrinsic sources, extrinsic sources, and policy-based sources.

- The scrivener's error doctrine allows judges to correct obvious clerical or typographical errors, or drafting errors. It is a subset of absurdity and a very narrow exception.

- The constitutional avoidance doctrine allows a court to avoid the ordinary meaning of the text when that meaning would raise serious doubts about the constitutionality of the statute.

- The constitutional avoidance canon allows judges to avoid having to decide the constitutionality of one interpretation only to adopt a different interpretation.

Chapter 7

Canons Based on Intrinsic Sources: The Linguistic Canons

Roadmap

- Learn *in pari materia*: both the whole act and whole code aspects.

- Learn the linguistic canons including the presumption of consistent usage and meaningful variation, the rule against surplusage, *noscitur a sociis*, *ejusdem generis*, and *expressio unius est exclusio alterius*.

- Understand that the linguistic canons are simply rules reflecting commonly understood agreements about language usage.

A. Introduction to This Chapter

If language in an act is ambiguous, the ordinary meaning of that language would be absurd or raise a constitutional question, or if the act has a scrivener's error, a judge must turn to other sources to discern meaning. In this chapter, we examine one of the first intrinsic sources judges turn to when continuing to search for meaning: the linguistic (or semantic) canons. Because many of the linguistic canons have Latin names, they seem scary. In reality, these canons reflect common-sense rules native to English speakers and are, for the most part, quite simple, despite their intimidating names. Antonin Scalia, *Common-Law Courts in a Civil-Law System: The Role of United States Federal Courts in Interpreting the Constitution and Laws*, in A MATTER OF INTERPRETATION 3, 26 (Amy Gutmann ed., 1997) (describing the linguistic canons as "so commonsensical that, were the canons not couched in Latin, you would find it hard to believe anyone could criticize them").

Two points about when these canons should apply. Point one: the justices were the most enthusiastic about using legislative history to discern legislative intent in the mid-1900s, following the New Deal. At that time, the Court typically concluded that these linguistic canons should yield to persuasive evidence of intent or purpose as found in the legislative history. JOHN F. MANNING & MATTHEW C. STEPHENSON, LEGISLATION AND REGULATION 215 (2d ed. 2013) (citing *Andrus v. Glover Constr. Co.*, 446 U.S. 608, 616–17 (1980); *Nat'l R.R. Passenger Corp. v. Nat'l Ass'n of R.R. Passengers*, 414 U.S. 453, 458 (1974)). However, with the recent judicial focus returning to text and increased criticism of legislative history and unarticulated purpose, the justices more regularly turn to these canons before examining such extrinsic sources. *Id.* (citing *Barnhart v. Sigmon Coal Co.*, 534 U.S. 438, 457 & n.15 (2002); *United States v. Gonzales*, 520 U.S. 1, 5–6 (1997)).

Point two: some judges, notably Justice Thomas, refuse to apply these canons absent linguistic ambiguity. *See, e.g., Ali v. Federal Bureau of Prisons*, 552 U.S. 214, 247–48 (2008) (refusing to consider *ejusdem generis* or *noscitur a sociis* because the language was clear). Other judges, notably former Justice Kennedy, use the linguistic canons to identify the ordinary meaning of language in a statute. *See, e.g., Gustafson v. Alloyd Co., Inc.*, 513 U.S. 561, 575–76 (1995) (applying the linguistic canons to find the ordinary meaning of the word "prospectus" in the Securities Act of 1933); *State v. Peters*, 263 Wis. 2d 475, 491 (2003) (Abrahamson, C.J., concurring) ("The canon [*ejusdem generis*] is an 'intrinsic aid' that is germane to a textualist approach to statutory interpretation; that is, it is both compatible with and necessary to the plain meaning rule."). As you read this material and learn that the canons are merely commonsense principles of linguistic interpretation, consider whether Justice Thomas's or Kennedy's approach makes more sense. Should interpreters turn to the linguistic canons only when language is ambiguous, or should they apply the linguistic canons to discern ordinary meaning?

B. The Linguistic Canons: Our Latin Friends

The linguistic canons are rules of thumb that help judges understand the meaning of the language of an act. These canons are not hard and fast rules, but rather are guides or presumptions to which judges turn to further help them discern the legislative intent from the words used, or if textualists, to determine the public meaning of the words used. The linguistic canons simply reflect shared assumptions about the way English speakers and writers use language.

These canons were once the bedrock of early Anglo-American statutory interpretation, and many early treatises were organized around them. Although the canons fell out of favor with the federal courts when purposivism edged out textualism as the preferred statutory interpretation approach, the linguistic canons remained important to state court judges. Indeed, many states have codified these canons. For example, both Minnesota and Pennsylvania have statutory construction acts that codify some of these various canons. Minn. Stat. Ann. §§ 645.001–645.51; 1 Pa. Cons. Stat. Ann. §§ 1921–39. Today, the linguistic canons have enjoyed a comeback with the reemergence of textualism. Textualists especially like these canons because, like dictionaries, the linguistic canons appear to be a neutral source. Moreover, textualists believe that turning to the linguistic canons early in the interpretive process will help further the drafting process. If legislators know that courts will apply the canons and if courts apply the canons predictably, then legislators can more easily enact text that will be interpreted as they intended. The linguistic canons serve a communication function, if you will, one that aids predictability.

These canons presume common understandings regarding how English speakers speak and write. Some of the canons are merely weak presumptions that act as tiebreakers (*e.g.*, the rule against surplusage). Others are strong presumptions that regularly inform meaning (*e.g.*, *in pari materia*). While rigid application of these canons can make interpretation somewhat mechanical and simplistic, judges love them anyway. However, these canons should be used cautiously for many reasons. First, and most importantly, using the linguistic canons makes sense only when both the drafter and the interpreter are aware of them, understand them, and correctly use them. If a drafter is unaware of a particular canon and did not use it while drafting, then it makes little sense to apply that canon to that drafter's final product. In truth, legislatures rarely consciously think about these canons while drafting; thus, it makes little sense to apply them religiously. However, legislatures may unconsciously think about these canons; hence, it makes sense to consider them as presumptions.

Second, the canons are presumptions based on how *ordinary* English speakers and writers use language. The canons may be unsuitable in legal drafting because *legal* writers are trained to write differently than ordinary English writers. Legal writing is replete with redundancy and wordiness. Legal writers are less concerned with repeating themselves than with covering all their bases (think of "cease and desist" and "will and testament"). For example, legal writers learn to include a comprehensive list of items with a general catch-all phrase to ensure that no circumstance is omitted or overlooked. Yet one of the linguistic canons — the rule against surplusage — directs that every word in a list should have independent meaning. Here, the writers' legal training and the linguistic canon directly conflict; legal writers expect that their drafting may have overlap; indeed, legal drafters prefer such overlap to inadvertent omission.

Third, the canons presume that the legislature carefully considered every word in the statute and included each word for a reason. Hence, the presumption is that the linguistic canons should apply because the legislature chose its words carefully. The reality is that legislatures are far more concerned with the big picture than with the small details. Legislation is the result of compromise. Fighting over one word could halt the enactment process entirely. Thus, legislators cannot be concerned with the exact wording of a statute, or their job would never be done. Rather, legislators must choose their battles.

Fourth, the linguistic canons mask subjectivity. The canons are appealing, in part, because, like dictionaries, they appear to offer a neutral method of resolving the meaning of language. In other words, these canons provide the appearance of neutrality for decision-making. They "do not, on their face at least, express any policy preference, but simply purport to be helpful ways of divining the nature and limits of what the drafters of the legislation were trying to achieve." David L. Shapiro, *Continuity and Change in Statutory Interpretation*, 67 N.Y.U. L. REV. 921, 927 (1992).

But this apparent objectivity masks subjectivity. The linguistic canons, like every method of interpretation, are merely rebuttable presumptions. As such, they can be manipulated to produce a desired result. Liberal justices can use the canons to further liberal agendas, while conservative justices can use the canons to further conservative agendas. "[T]he canons [do not have] an independent, constraining effect on the Justices' decisionmaking—in particular, they are not functioning as a set of overarching 'neutral principles' in the hands of either liberal or conservative Justices." James J. Brudney & Corey Ditslear, *Canons of Construction and the Elusive Quest for Neutral Reasoning*, 58 VAND. L. REV. 1, 59 (2005). In 1949, Professor Karl Llewellyn suggested that for every canon of construction (the "thrust") there is an equal but opposing canon (the "parry"). Karl N. Llewellyn, *Remarks on the Theory of Appellate Decision and the Rules or Canons About How Statutes Are to Be Construed*, 3 VAND. L. REV. 395, 404 (1949) (juxtaposing the thrust that "[e]very word and clause must be given effect" with the parry that "[i]f inadvertently inserted or if repugnant to the rest of the statute, they may be rejected as surplusage"). His point was to debunk the myth that application of the canons was an unbiased, useful method of interpretation; judges can easily use the canons to mask the real reason for deciding a case in a particular way.

Perhaps Llewellyn's critique was overstated, but it derailed "intellectual debate about the canons ... for almost a quarter of a century." Jonathan R. Macey & Geoffrey P. Miller, *The Canons of Statutory Construction and Judicial Preferences*, 45 VAND. L. REV. 647, 647 (1992). In any event, the canons merely set forth *rebuttable presumptions* about statutory meaning. The very nature of such a presumption is that it can be overcome by other evidence. Indeed, Llewellyn's "parries" identify the circumstances when the "thrusts," or presumptions, should fail. This ability to be rebutted allows judges to use discretion when applying the canons, which, of course, makes their application somewhat unpredictable but not unexplainable.

There is another subjectivity issue. Often, more than one canon may apply. When that happens, which linguistic canon should a judge apply? There is no hierarchy of linguistic canons; thus, selecting which canon to argue may simply depend on which better leads you to your client's preferred outcome. *See* James J. Brudney, *Canon Shortfalls and the Virtues of Political Branch Interpretive Assets*, 98 CAL. L. REV. 1199, 1231 (2010) ("The Court's failure to develop any interpretive rubric for prioritizing or ordering its reliance on different canons may well stem from an implicit understanding that such a creation would be both arbitrary and unproductive.").

Moreover, not only is there no hierarchy, the choice of one canon can be outcome determinative. Often, the canon that furthers the interpreter's choice of meaning is the one selected. One famous example involving multiple, conflicting canons is the case of *Babbitt v. Sweet Home Chapter of Communities*, 515 U.S. 687 (1995). In that case, the majority and dissenting justices used many of the linguistic canons, including *in pari materia, noscitur a sociis, ejusdem generis, expressio unius*, the rule against surplusage, and the presumption of consistent usage. The majority and dissent focused on different canons to reach their holdings.

The issue in the case was whether the Secretary of the Interior could promulgate a regulation making it unlawful for anyone to significantly modify the habitat of an endangered species. *Id.* at 690 (citing 16 U.S.C. § 1532(9)(a)(1)). The Endangered Species Act of 1973 prohibited anyone from "tak[ing]" any endangered species. The Act defined "take" as meaning "to harass, *harm*, pursue, hunt, shoot, wound, kill, trap, capture, or collect, or to attempt to engage in any such conduct." *Id.* at 691 (citing 16 U.S.C. § 1532(19)) (emphasis added). The Secretary interpreted the word "harm" to include "significant habitat modification or degradation where it actually kills or injures wildlife." *Id.* (citing 50 C.F.R. § 17.3 (1994)). The majority found the Secretary's interpretation reasonable, using *in pari materia* (which allows a court to look at the act in its entirety) and the rule against surplusage (which suggests that every word in a statute must have independent meaning). *Id.* at 701–02.

In contrast, the dissent focused on the other listed words in the statute surrounding the word "harm" (*noscitur a sociis*) to conclude that Congress intended the word "harm" to mean "affirmative conduct intentionally directed against a particular animal or animals." *Id.* at 720–21 (Scalia, J., dissenting). The dissent concluded that, because the Secretary's interpretation included non-affirmative conduct, such as the logging targeted in the case, that interpretation was unreasonable. *Id.* Interestingly, both the majority and dissent specifically rejected the other side's argument that the identified canon was controlling. Specifically, the majority criticized the dissent for denying the word "harm" any independent meaning. *Id.* at 688. The dissent accused the majority of ignoring the realities of legal drafting. *Id.* at 721 (Scalia, J., dissenting).

For all these reasons, the linguistic canons should be used with common sense and a realization that lawyers often draft differently than the canons presume. The canons are, for the most part, presumptions, gap-fillers, and tiebreakers. When there is better evidence of legislative intent, the canons should take a back seat. Also, because the canons counter each other, it is important to remember that, as a litigant, you will win your case based on the underlying equities, not based on a linguistic canon. Like the theories in Chapter 4, the linguistic canons simply give you the language to *help* the judge interpret the statute in your client's favor. In other words, it is still up to you to make the judge *want* to rule in your client's favor.

Below are the contemporary linguistic canons. While other canons may have been used in the past, they have not been included because they are rarely used today.

C. The Contemporary
Linguistic Canons: Explained

1. *In Pari Materia*

The most popular and least controversially used linguistic canon is *in pari materia*. Unlike the linguistic canons we will cover next, *in pari materia* is not a canon about how words are used, but because it has a Latin name, it is generally included with the other linguistic canons. *In pari materia* is a canon that identifies the legal material that judges may legitimately consider in order to discern meaning or fill gaps. *See, e.g., Fla. Dep't of Highway Safety & Motor Vehicles v. Hernandez*, 74 So. 3d 1070, 1076 (Fla. 2011) (noting that a statute that allowed the state to suspend the driver's license of any person who refused to submit to a "lawful" breathalyzer test must be read *in pari materia* with a different statute that defined the parameters of a lawful breath-alcohol test).

Many judges (and academics) incorrectly equate *in pari materia* and the presumption of consistent usage. It is true, these two linguistic canons work in harmony and are commonly used together; however, they are different. *In pari materia* identifies the material to be considered (the act and acts with similar purposes), while the presumption of consistent usage explains what to do with that material (interpret identical words similarly and different words differently).

In pari materia answers the question of which parts of an act or statutes in the entire code are relevant to the meaning of language in a particular statute. As such, this canon works in tandem with the other linguistic canons. So, for example, a judge might very well apply the canon of consistent usage (that identical words should have identical meanings) to interpret a word that appears in more than one section of an act, even though only the one section of the act is applicable to the facts before the court. Such was the case in *Mohasco Corp. v. Silver*, 447 U.S. 807 (1980). In that case, the Supreme Court held that Congress intended the word "filed" to have the same meaning in subsections (c) and (e) of section 706 of the Civil Rights Act of 1964; subsection (e) was the only subsection at issue in the case. *Id.* at 809. As you can see from this example, *in pari materia* is the canon that allowed the Court to look for meaning in language beyond the narrow language being interpreted.

In Latin, *"in pari materia"* means "part of the same material." This canon has two aspects—the whole act aspect and the whole code aspect. First, the *whole act* aspect directs that a section of a legislative act should not be interpreted in isolation. Rather, the entire act is relevant. Second, the *whole code* (or related acts) aspect directs that statutes should be interpreted harmoniously with other statutes concerning the same subject. *In pari materia* promotes coherence. Both aspects of *in pari materia* together attempt to ensure internal consistency across acts, related statutes, and even the code as a whole. Let's look at each aspect in turn, starting with the less controversial aspect: the whole act aspect.

a. The Whole Act Aspect of In Pari Materia

When a bill is enacted, the ensuing act is not simply placed *in serum* (in order) in the code; rather, sections of the act are codified (placed into the code) where appropriate. For example, sections of the U.S.A. Patriot Act can be found throughout the *United States Code*. The U.S.A. Patriot Act created nine new sections in the Code and amended more than 100 others. It addressed things from foreign intelligence, to money laundering, to immigration, to library usage. When the U.S.A. Patriot Act was codified, those sections that addressed foreign intelligence surveillance were placed in one part of the Code, while those sections that addressed immigration law were placed in another section of the Code. Yet the U.S.A. Patriot Act was one bill that became an act: a package of statutes, if you will. Hence, all of the sections of the U.S.A. Patriot Act should be interpreted to work together. If the word "terrorist" is used in more than one section of the U.S.A. Patriot Act, then "terrorist" should have the same meaning throughout the U.S.A. Patriot Act (pursuant to the presumption of consistent usage), unless the legislature clearly indicated that it had a different intent. The *whole act aspect* of *in pari materia* presumes that although the sections of an act may not be codified together, the act's sections should be interpreted harmoniously.

For example, in *Rhyne v. K-Mart Corp.*, 594 S.E.2d 1, 20 (N.C. 2004), the court used the whole act aspect of *in pari materia* to interpret a punitive damages limitation. K-Mart's employees had roughed up two individuals who were apparently looking through the store's dumpster. The dumpster-divers sued. Each was awarded punitive damages of $11.5 million. *Id.* at 6. The trial court reduced each award from $11.5 million to $250,000 based on a state statute that limited punitive damages:

> Punitive damages awarded against *a defendant* shall not exceed ... [$250,000]. If a trier of fact returns *a verdict* for punitive damages in excess of the maximum amount specified under this subsection, the trial court shall reduce *the award* and enter judgment for [the maximum amount].

Id. at 7 (quoting N.C. Gen. Stat. § 1D-25(b) (1996)) (emphasis added). K-Mart argued that the ordinary meaning of "a defendant" in this statute was each defendant, meaning K-Mart in this case. In other words, K-Mart argued that pursuant to the ordinary meaning, the total K-Mart had to pay in punitive damages was $250,000 to both plaintiffs, not $500,000 ($250,000 per plaintiff). *Id.* at 19.

The appellate court disagreed, stating, "[W]e construe statutes *in pari materia*, giving effect, if possible, to every provision." *Id.* at 20. The court reasoned that in the same section of the statute being interpreted, the legislature had referred to "*a* verdict" and to "*the* award" (see that language italicized above). *Id.* Because plaintiffs receive verdicts and awards, not defendants, the court held that the $250,000 limit applied to a plaintiff's *verdict* or *award*, not to a defendant's damages. *Id.* Thus, in this case, the dumpster-divers each received $250,000 in punitive damages, rather than splitting one $250,000 award.

To rebut the presumption that *in pari materia* is applicable, a litigant could argue that the whole act aspect of *in pari materia* is based on the idea that there was a single drafter for the bill, whether that drafter was an individual legislator or a committee. Yet the single-drafter assumption does not reflect the political reality. Legislation comes about from the compromises of many legislators from different political parties, different constituencies, and with different agendas. Even the president has a role. To suggest that one drafter (whether it be a unified group or an individual) wrote the bill with internal consistency simply ignores the reality of the legislation process. " 'No man should see how laws or sausages are made.'" *Community Nutrition Inst. v. Block*, 749 F.2d 50, 51 (D.C. Cir. 1984) (internal quotations omitted).

b. The Whole Code Aspect of In Pari Materia

Judges will also consider the relevance of other acts and statutes within the whole code. This aspect of *in pari materia* is known as the *whole code aspect*. The whole code aspect of *in pari materia* directs that statutes should be interpreted harmoniously with other statutes in the code *concerning the same subject*. This aspect of *in pari materia* presumes that the legislature was aware of all related, existing statutes when it enacted the one in question; thus, the new statute should be interpreted harmoniously with all related, existing statutes. In other words, if a statute criminalizes certain behavior, that statute should be interpreted consistently with other statutes criminalizing the same or similar behavior. This aspect of *in pari materia* helps the judiciary ensure the law's coherence. As former Justice Scalia once said:

> Where a statutory term presented to us for the first time is ambiguous, we construe it to contain that permissible meaning which fits most logically and comfortably into the body of both previously and subsequently enacted law. We do so not because that precise accommodative meaning is what the lawmakers must have had in

mind (how could an earlier Congress know what a later Congress would enact?), but because it is our role to make sense rather than nonsense out of the *corpus juris.*

West Va. Univ. Hosps., Inc. v. Casey, 499 U.S. 83, 100–102 (1991) (holding that a statute allowing an award for "a reasonable attorney's fee" did not allow an award for expert fees). As Justice Scalia notes, practically speaking, it is highly unlikely that the legislature was aware of every statute, yet the presumption persists and actually makes some sense. Legislators should be aware of the limits of existing law when they enact new law.

One challenge with this aspect of the canon is defining what statutes concern the same or similar subject matter. To make this determination, a court should look to see whether the related statutes share similar purposes such that the legislature was likely aware of the existing statute when it drafted the newer statute and, thus, intended harmony. *Smith v. City of Jackson*, 544 U.S. 228, 233–34 (Miss. 2005) (interpreting the Age Discrimination in Employment Act of 1967 harmoniously with the Civil Rights Act of 1964 because were enacted for similar reasons). In *Commonwealth v. Smith*, 728 N.E.2d 272, 278–79 (Mass. 2000), the court held that the definition of sexual intercourse used in a rape statute did not apply to an incest statute because the statutes did not concern sufficiently similar subject matters and were located in separate chapters in the state's code. However, location in the same chapter of a code (*e.g.,* Taxation), while relevant, should not be controlling.

> [T]he mere fact that the statutes appear in the same chapter [does not show the statutes relate to a common subject matter.] The Legislature may choose to employ a term differently in two different statutes. In each statute, the term should be construed to effectuate the purposes of that particular statute.

Id. at 280 (Ireland, J., dissenting).

2. The Presumption of Consistent Usage & Meaningful Variation

After *in pari materia*, the next most commonly used and least controversial linguistic canon is *the presumption of consistent usage and meaningful variation* (also known as the identical words presumption). This canon presumes that when the legislature uses the same word in different parts of the same act or a related act, the legislature intended those words to have the same meaning (consistent usage). And contrariwise, if the legislature uses a word in one part of an act or a related act, then changes to a different word in another part of the same or related act, the legislature intended to change the meaning (meaningful variation). *Robinson v. City of Lansing*, 782 N.W.2d 171, 182 (Mich. 2010) ("[U]nless the Legislature indicates otherwise, when it repeatedly uses the same phrase in a statute, that phrase should be given the same meaning throughout the statute."); *see, e.g., West Va. Univ. Hosps., Inc.*, 499 U.S. at 92 (reasoning that expert fees and attorney's fees are distinct items because "dozens of statutes refer[] to the two separately").

The purpose of this canon, like the purpose of *in pari materia*, is to promote internal consistency. Thus, in *Gustafson*, former Justice Kennedy relied on this canon to narrow language Congress had defined broadly. 513 U.S. at 575. The facts of the case are quite complicated. Defendant Gustafson and two other individuals ("Gustafson") were the sole shareholders of Alloyd Company, Inc. ("Alloyd") *Id.* at 564. In 1989, Gustafson sold shares in Alloyd to Wind Point Partners. *Id.* The sales contract stated that revenue figures from the prior year would be used to value Alloyd and that if those figures were incorrect, an adjustment would be available to either party. *Id.* at 565. Not surprisingly, the revenue figures were incorrect. *Id.* Pursuant to the adjustment clause, Gustafson paid Wind Point (now Alloyed) $815,000 plus interest, but Alloyd sued. *Id.* at 566.

Alloyd sued Gustafson under section 12(2) of the Securities Act of 1933, seeking rescission of the contract. *Id.* at 565–66. Section 12(2) allows buyers to undo, or rescind, such a transaction if the seller "offers or sells a security ... by means of a *prospectus* ... which includes an untrue statement of material fact." *Id.* at 567 (quoting Securities Act of 1933 § 12(2), as amended, 15 U.S.C. § 77l (2)) (emphasis added). Wind Point alleged that the sales contract was a "prospectus" and that the incorrect revenue figures were a material misstatement. *Id.* at 566. The Court assumed that the misstatements were material. *Id.* at 567. Hence, the issue for the Court was whether the misstatements "were made 'by means of a prospectus.'" *Id.* at 566–67 (quoting § 12(2)). The parties argued about the breadth of the word "prospectus": (1) did it include all written communications involving the sale of a security, including secondary sales (Alloyd's argument), or (2) did it include only documents relating to initial public stock offerings (Gustafson's argument). *Id.* at 568.

Using the identical words presumption, Justice Kennedy concluded that "prospectus" referred only to documents relating to initial public offerings.

Id. at 571. He noted that the term appeared in three different sections of the Act: § 2(10) which defines "prospectus," § 10, which identifies the information required to be included in a prospectus, and § 12(2), which imposes liability for misstatements in a prospectus. *Id.* at 568. Kennedy reasoned that the term "'prospectus' must have the same meaning under §§ 10 and 12" and that "§ 10 [provides] guidance and instruction for giving the term a consistent meaning throughout the Act." *Id.* at 570. Using two other linguistic canons (the rule against surplusage and *noscitur a sociis*), Kennedy then rejected Alloyd's argument that the word "communication" in the definition of "prospectus" in § 2(10) was broad enough to include secondary sales. *Id.* at 574–75.

Justice Thomas dissented. *Id.* at 584 (Thomas, J., dissenting). He reasoned that the identical words presumption canon was inapplicable because the definition in § 2(10) controlled, the language in that definition was not ambiguous, and two different meanings for "prospectus" were acceptable because the preface to the definition section stated "unless the context otherwise requires." *Id.* at 588–89. (quoting Securities Act of 1933 § 2, 15 U.S.C. § 77b). Here, according to Justice Thomas, context required that the meaning in §§ 10 and 12(2) be different. *Id.* at 588.

Justice Ginsburg agreed, called the majority's approach backwards, and criticized the opinion for ignoring Congress's broad definition in favor of an operative section that was inapplicable to the facts of the case. *Id.* at 597 (Ginsburg, J., dissenting) (suggesting that the identical words presumption has "'all the tenacity of original sin and must constantly be guarded against.'" (quoting Walter Wheeler Cook, *Substance and Procedure in the Conflict of Laws*, 42 YALE L.J. 333, 337 (1933)).

Like all the linguistic canons, this canon can be overcome with evidence that the legislature intended a different meaning. In *Gustafson*, Justices Thomas and Ginsburg found that evidence in the definition of the language at issue. For another example, in *Travelscape, LLC v. S.C. Dep't of Revenue*, 705 S.E.2d 28 (S.C. 2011), the majority and dissent disagreed about whether the canon applied or was rebutted by other language in the statute. Expedia, aka Travelscape, helped customers book hotel rooms online to stay in South Carolina; however, the company did not pay state accommodations taxes to South Carolina. The state wanted the lost taxes. *Id.* at 95–96. The court addressed two issues: what to tax and who to tax. The court explained:

> Section 12–36–920(A) sets forth what is subject to the tax—"the gross proceeds derived from the rental or charges for any rooms ... or sleeping accommodations *furnished* to transients by any hotel ...

or any place in which rooms, lodgings, or sleeping accommodations are *furnished* to transients for a consideration." (emphasis added). In turn, section 12–36–920(E) establishes who is subject to the tax — "every person engaged ... in *the business of furnishing accommodations* to transients for consideration." (emphasis added).

Id. *at 97.*

As for what to tax, subsection (A) of the statute taxed the gross proceeds from the rental of any "furnished" accommodations. *Id.* As for who to tax, subsection (E) of the statute required that anyone "in the business of furnishing" accommodations pay the tax. *Id.* Travelscape argued that it did not physically "furnish" accommodations; therefore, it did not have to pay the tax. *Id.* The state responded that Travelscape indirectly furnished accommodations so it did have to pay tax. *Id.* at 96.

The majority agreed with the state. *Id.* at 97. The majority reasoned that "furnish" actually did not mean the same thing in subsections (A) and (E) of the act. *Id.* at 101. Subsection (E) contained additional language "in the business of," which modified the word "furnishing" and broadened it to include activities other than directly providing the hotel rooms. *Id.* Thus, the majority concluded that the identical words presumption was rebutted here because the additional words modifying "furnishing" broadened the meaning of the word "furnished." *Id.* The dissent disagreed, arguing that the identical words presumption required the court to interpret the words "furnish" and "furnishing" identically, despite the additional language in subsection (E). *Id.* at 112. *See also Jensen v. Elgin, Joliet & Eastern Railway Co.*, 182 N.E.2d 211, 213 (Ill. 1962) (holding that the canon was not applicable to the word "children," which was included in both sections 1 and 9 of the Federal Employers' Liability Act, because the two sections allowed recovery for different types of injuries: *injuries the deceased employee sustained* and *losses the dependents of the deceased employee suffered directly* (emphasis added)).

As a practice pointer, lawyers should avoid varying words; lawyers are taught that a change in word usage signifies a new meaning. For example, do not use "agreement" in one sentence and "contract" in another. While variety of language is highly praised in some disciplines, it is not in law. For a lawyer, a change in the words signals a change in meaning. For example, "shall" and "will" mean very different things in law, although a thesaurus identifies these words as synonyms. Legal concepts are difficult enough to understand; do not make your reader work harder by varying words unnecessarily.

3. *Noscitur a Sociis*

The next four canons are more controversial and interrelated: *noscitur a sociis, ejusdem generis,* the rule against surplusage, and *expressio unius.* These canons often conflict with one another and, like the other canons, do not always reflect the reality of legal drafting. Let's take a closer look at each, starting with two related canons: *noscitur a sociis* and *ejusdem generis.*

Most words have multiple meanings. *Noscitur a sociis* and *ejusdem generis* are fancy, Latin terms for a commonsense notion: that words can best be understood in their textual context. In Latin, *noscitur a sociis* means "it is known from its associates." This canon is based on the simple presumption that when a word has more than one meaning, the appropriate meaning should be gleaned from the words surrounding the word being interpreted, in other words, from the textual context. 2A Jabez Gridley Sutherland, Statutes and Statutory Construction § 47:16 (Norman Singer ed., 7th ed. 2007).

In practice, we use this canon all the time when we communicate. For example, Justice Scalia has famously said: "If you tell me, 'I took the boat out on the bay,' I understand 'bay' to mean one thing; if you tell me, 'I put the saddle on the bay,' I understand it to mean something else." Antonin Scalia, A Matter of Interpretation: Federal Courts and the Law 26 (1987). And as one of my students suggested, if you tell me that "Fido bays at the moon," I might understand "bay" to mean a third thing altogether. Similarly, the word "answer" might mean a legal document that responds to a complaint or it might mean a response to a question. *Noscitur a sociis* helps identify which meaning was intended. Without *noscitur a sociis,* we would need a new word for each situation identified above. The English language is wordy enough already!

While *noscitur a sociis* has force when any word is being interpreted (as we saw with "bay" above), judges explicitly use the canon most commonly when they are interpreting words in a list, especially one without a catch-all. When applying *noscitur a sociis,* judges try to find the shared trait, called the unifier, in the list of items. Thus, in the following list of items: "yellow, blue, red, chartreuse, and white," all of the items are colors; color is the unifier. Even if you did not know what "chartreuse" was, you would likely surmise that it was a color.

Notice that when judges identify a unifier and then interpret the word in light of that unifier, judges interpret the language in dispute more narrowly. Hence, *noscitur a sociis* narrows a statute's application. This canon prevents a court from "ascribing to one word a meaning so broad that it is inconsistent with its accompanying words, thus giving 'unintended breadth to the Acts of Congress.'" *Gustafson*, 513 U.S. at 575 (quoting *Jarecki v. G.D. Searle & Co.*, 367 U.S. 303, 307 (1961). Yet legislators as legal writers are trained to draft broadly, to include every possibility. Thus, the presumption behind the canon and the reality of legislative drafting conflict. For example, in *People v. Vasquez*, 631 N.W.2d 711 (Mich. 2001), the majority applied *noscitur a sociis* to determine whether a defendant who lied to a police officer about his age "obstruct[ed], resist[ed], oppose[d], assault[ed], beat, or wound[ed]" that officer. *Id.* at 714 (quoting MICH. COMP. LAWS § 750.479). Applying *noscitur a sociis*, the majority concluded that the words shared the common trait of threatened or actual *physical* interference. *Id.* at 716. Because lying was not *physical* interference, the majority concluded that the defendant had not violated the statute when he lied to the police about his age. *Id.* Query: would not the legislature likely have preferred to penalize someone who lied to the police?

The dissent thought so for two reasons. First, the dissent thought the term "obstruct" was clear: obstructing an officer includes lying to the officer. *Id.* at 731 (Corrigan, C.J., dissenting). Further, because it was inappropriate to turn to the linguistic canon absent ambiguity, the dissent said that the majority unnecessarily narrowed the term "obstruct" by resorting to *noscitur a sociis*. *Id.* Second, the dissent argued that even if the canon were appropriate, the majority incorrectly identified the unifier. *Id.* The dissent suggested that the unifier was simply *interference*, not *physical* interference. *Id.* And lying was interference.

This case nicely illustrates one problem with this canon—how similar must items in a list be? At times, *noscitur a sociis* and the rule against surplusage may conflict. *Noscitur a sociis* directs that words share meaning, while the rule against surplusage directs that each word should have a different meaning (see below). Arguably, the majority in *Vasquez* violated the rule against surplusage by interpreting the terms in the statute so similarly that they lost independent meaning. What, under the majority's interpretation, is the difference between "obstruct" and "resist" if physical interference is required? The dissent's interpretation preserved the distinction better than the majority's interpretation.

Similarly, in *G.C. Timmis & Co. v. Guardian Alarm, Co.*, 662 N.W.2d 710 (Mich. 2003), the dissent refused to apply the canon because the language in the statute was not ambiguous. *Id.* at 720. The case is somewhat complicated, but there is a marvelous discussion between the majority and dissent about whether *noscitur a sociis* would be appropriate to apply to the list "Duck, Goose, Pig, Swan, Heron." *Id.* at 723 (Young, J., dissenting). The dissent thought not; a pig is what it is: a swine. If *noscitur a sociis* were applied, the court would have to interpret "pig" to be some type of waterfowl. *Id.* But the majority thought that the word "pig" could have multiple meanings (including someone who eats too much); thus, *noscitur a sociis* would help identify which of the many possible meanings was intended: the animal meaning. *Id.*

Who was right? Both. A reader of the language above would intuitively interpret the word "pig" to mean a pink animal that oinks because animal is the unifier. If the list instead said, "cop, fuzz, pig," a different meaning for "pig" would likely suggest itself. English speakers intuitively understand which meaning a legislature intended because of *noscitur a sociis.* We intuitively apply the canon whether we admit it or not. Indeed, in *G.C. Timmis & Co.* and *Vasquez,* the majority and dissent disagreed about the degree of similarity *noscitur a sociis* demanded to the listed items. For example, if "pig" is included with a list of waterfowl, must "pig" be interpreted to be a kind of waterfowl? Of course not.

Judges also disagree about when to apply *noscitur a sociis.* Should the canon be used only when ambiguity remains after applying the plain meaning canon, or should the canon be used in conjunction with the plain meaning canon? *Compare Stryker Corp. v. Director, Div. of Taxation,* 773 A.2d 674, 684 (N.J. 2001) (refusing to apply the canon because the text was clear), *with G.C. Timmis & Co.,* 662 N.W.2d at 714–15 (applying the canon without first finding ambiguity). *See also Gustafson,* 513 U.S. at 575–76 & 586–87 (majority applies *noscitur a sociis* without first finding ambiguity while the dissent refuses to apply the canon because the language is clear). As noted earlier, the canon *noscitur a sociis* should not apply only after a court first finds ambiguity. The basic notion that textual context aids interpretation is inarguable. Any language in which words have multiple meanings, like English, requires such a rule; in fact, you could not understand either the written or spoken word without using this canon. For this reason, *noscitur a sociis* should apply when a judge searches for ordinary meaning regardless of ambiguity. Indeed, it is likely that judges intuitively apply the canon whether they say they are applying it or not. Yet the rhetoric continues.

4. *Ejusdem Generis*

Our next canon is *ejusdem generis,* which in Latin means "of the same kind, class, or nature." *Ejusdem generis* directs that when general words are near specific words, the general words should be limited to include only things similar in nature to the specific words. *Ejusdem generis* presumes that if the legislative body had intended the general words to be used in their unrestricted and broadest sense, the specific words would not have been included. *Cf., Begay v. United States*, 553 U.S. 137, 153 (2008) (using the rule against surplusage for the point that Congress would not have included items in a list preceding a catch-all if Congress had intended the catch-all to have its broadest possible meaning).

Ejusdem generis is a subset, or type of, noscitur a sociis. Both canons are used to limit words in a list. While noscitur a sociis is used to narrow the meaning of items in a list, ejusdem generis is used to narrow the meaning of broad catch-alls following a list. For example, assume a state tax applied to "lemons, limes, grapefruits, and others." "Lemons, limes, and grapefruits" are the listed items, "and others" is the catch-all. Applying *ejusdem generis* to the general catch-all "and others," a judge would conclude that the catch-all "and others" would include other citrus fruits like oranges but would not include vegetables like broccoli. When used to interpret a general catch-all phrase, ejusdem generis limits the catch-all by implication to include "everything else of the same type as those in the list."

Here are two examples of courts applying the canon. First, in *McBoyle v. United States*, 283 U.S. 25, 25–26 (1931), the Supreme Court used *ejusdem generis*, without naming it, to reason that the general catch-all "any other self-propelled vehicle not designed for running on rails" did not include an airplane because the listed items preceding the catch-all—"automobile, automobile truck, automobile wagon, [and] motorcycle"—limited the word "vehicle" in the catch-all to "vehicle[s] running on land." Second, in *People v. Smith*, the court held that an M-1 rifle was not a "dangerous weapon." 225 N.W.2d 165, 167 (Mich. 1975). The statute prohibited individuals from carrying concealed weapons, such as "a dagger, dirk, stiletto, or [o]ther dangerous weapon except hunting knives." *Id.* at 166 (quoting MICH. COMP. LAWS 750.227). The court reasoned that because a rifle was not a "stabbing weapon," the statute did not prohibit its concealment. *Id.* at 167. Notice how in both cases, the courts used *ejusdem generis* to narrow an otherwise very broad catch-all: "other self-propelled vehicle" and "dangerous weapon."

Are you wondering why we need two canons for one similar concept? Lawyers do occasionally confuse these two canons. *See, e.g., Babbitt v. Sweet Home Chapter Communities*, 515 U.S. 687, 720 (1995) (Scalia, J., dissenting) (noting that the Solicitor of the Fish and Wildlife Service incorrectly identified the relevant canon as *ejusdem generis* rather than *noscitur a sociis*). The confusion is understandable. Both canons share the same principle—when there are several items in a list that share a common attribute, the listed item (*noscitur a sociis*) or the catch-all phrase (*ejusdem generis*) should be interpreted as possessing that same attribute. To avoid confusing the two, remember these rules: *Ejusdem generis* should be applied only when there is a general term or catch-all that is being interpreted. "The *ejusdem generis* rule is generally applied to general and specific words clearly associated in the same sentence in a pattern such as '[specific], [specific], or [general]' or '[general], including [specific] and [specific].'" *State v. Van Woerden*, 967 P.2d 14, 18 (Wash. Ct. App. 1998). In contrast, *noscitur a sociis* is applied when an item in the list or a specific word in the statute is being interpreted rather than the catch-all.

In addition to keeping the two canons distinct, there are numerous other difficulties with *ejusdem generis*, including determining (1) what the unifier among the listed items is, and (2) how narrowly to limit the catch-all. In other words, in the hypothetical tax statute above ("lemons, limes, grapefruits, and others"), is the unifier "fruit," "citrus fruit," or "sour citrus fruit"? At some point, a unifier limits a catch-all so much that the rule against surplusage is violated. *See, e.g., Circuit City Stores, Inc. v. Adams*, 532 U.S. 105, 114 (2001) ("Construing the residual phrase to exclude all employment contracts fails to give independent effect to the statute's enumeration of the specific categories of workers which precedes it; there would be no need for Congress to use the phrases 'seamen' and 'railroad employees' if those same classes of workers were subsumed within the meaning of the [language at issue]"). Moreover, sometimes, application of *ejusdem generis* can lead to an interpretation at odds with the ordinary meaning of words. *See, e.g., Commonwealth v. Plowman*, 86 S.W.3d 47, 49 (Ky. 2002) (finding a defendant guilty of committing arson of a "building" after he set fire to a bulldozer); *McKinney v. Robbins*, 892 S.W.2d 502, 599 (Ark. 1995) (refusing to interpret the phrase "domesticated animals" to include kittens).

Another difficulty with this canon is that it does not reflect the reality of legal drafting, at least as it relates to catch-alls. Legislatures use catch-alls for fear that "they would not be able to imagine, in advance, every possible kind of [activity] that should be included." Stephen Breyer, *On the Uses of Legislative History in Interpreting Statutes*, 65 S. CAL. L. REV. 845, 854 (1992). Thus, legislatures use catch-alls to broaden statutes, not narrow them. Hence, legislatures would likely prefer that catch-alls be interpreted broadly, not narrowly, to cover all possible, but similar, activity. If a legislature wishes to ensure that a statute applies only to the items listed or only to very similar items, then the legislature should not include a broad catch-all.

Ejusdem generis, like all the linguistic canons of construction, is not an iron-clad rule, but rather is a guide to meaning. When the list of things is not sufficiently similar, *ejusdem generis* should not apply. *Cf. Ali v. Federal Bureau of Prisons*, 552 U.S. 214, 245 (2008) (Breyer, J., dissenting) (saying, "And it is because these particular canons simply crystallize what English speakers already know, namely, that lists often (but not always) group together items with similar characteristics. That is why we cannot, without comic effect, yoke radically different nouns to a single verb, *e.g.*, 'He caught three salmon, two trout, and a cold.'").

Moreover, some judges refuse to apply the canon absent ambiguity. For example, in *Ali*, the majority refused to apply the canon. 552 U.S. at 224. The petitioner had been a federal prisoner at one federal penitentiary and was moved to another penitentiary. During the move, some of his personal belongings disappeared. *Id.* at 216. He sued. *Id.* While the Federal Government is generally immune from suit absent a clear statement to the contrary (*see* Chapter 12), in the Federal Tort Claims Act (the "FTCA") Congress had waived immunity for claims arising out of torts committed by federal employees. *Id.* at 217–18 (citing 28 U.S.C. § 1346(b)(1)). However, the FTCA specifically exempted "any claim arising in respect of … the detention of any goods, merchandise, or other property by any officer of customs or excise or *any other law enforcement officer*." *Id.* at 218 (quoting 28 U.S.C. § 2680(c)) (emphasis added). The issue for the Court was whether "any other law enforcement officer" included *all* law enforcement officers or just law enforcement officers acting in a customs or excise capacity. *Id.*

Rejecting petitioner's *ejusdem generis* and *noscitur a sociis* arguments, the majority held that the word "any" was clear on its face and meant exactly that: "Congress' use of 'any' to modify 'other law enforcement officer' is most naturally read to mean law enforcement officers of whatever kind." *Id.* at 220. The majority refused to apply linguistic canons to "clear" text.

The dissent disagreed and relied heavily on the linguistic canons. *Id.* at 243–45 (Breyer, J., dissenting). Justice Breyer explained that the issue for the Court was "not the *meaning* of the words," but was instead "the statute's *scope*." *Id.* at 243. And *ejusdem generis* and *noscitur a sociis* were essential to that inquiry:

> The word "any" is of no help because all speakers (including writers and legislators) who use general words such as "all," "any," "never," and "none" normally rely upon context to indicate the limits of time and place within which they intend those words to do their linguistic work. And with the possible exception of the assertion of a universal truth, say, by a mathematician, scientist, philosopher, or theologian, such limits almost always exist. When I call out to my wife, "There isn't any butter," I do not mean, "There isn't any butter in town." The context

makes clear to her that I am talking about the contents of our refrigerator. That is to say, it is context, not a dictionary, that sets the boundaries of time, place, and circumstance within which words such as "any" will apply.

Context, of course, includes the words immediately surrounding the phrase in question. And canons such as *ejusdem generis* and *noscitur a sociis* offer help in evaluating the significance of those surrounding words.

Id. at 243–44.

Who was right? The word "any" standing alone is very broad and indeterminate. Hence, the dissent correctly looked to the surrounding words to limit the breadth of that word, which is exactly the purpose of this canon: to narrow an otherwise overly broad catch-all. Thus, *ejusdem generis* helped show that Congress intended to limit the waiver of immunity for a specific group of law enforcement officers: those involved in customs and tax collection. Here, Congress provided a clear statement waiving immunity for these types of claims but included an exception to the waiver. Because exceptions are narrowly construed (*see* Chapter 8), Breyer's approach makes more sense. *See also People v. Fields*, 105 Cal. App. 3d 341, 344–45 (1980) (refusing to apply the canon to limit a general catch-all in a statute prohibiting "the knowing destruction … of any book, paper, record, instrument in writing, or *other matter or thing*" because the statute was not ambiguous and reasoning that the statute applied to "an unending variety of physical objects" including the marijuana the defendant flushed down the toilet).

5. The Rule Against Surplusage (or Redundancy)

According to the *rule against surplusage*, the proper interpretation of a statute is one in which every word has meaning; nothing is redundant or meaningless. There are two separate aspects to this canon: (1) every word must have an independent meaning, and (2) two different words cannot have the same meaning. If different words had the same meaning, then the second word would be surplusage, or unnecessary. Note that this canon compliments the identical words presumption in that both canons direct that the same words in a statute should mean the same thing and that different words in a statute should mean different things, absent contrary legislative intent. *See, e.g., Feld v. Robert & Charles Beauty Salon*, 459 N.W.2d 279, 284 (Mich. 1990) (applying the canon to conclude that a workers' compensation claimant could not bring an attorney to a medical exam where the statute explicitly allowed claimants to bring "a physician," because the word "physician" would be unnecessary if anyone were allowed to attend).

The rule against surplusage presumes three things: (1) that the statute was drafted with care, (2) that each word was the result of thoughtful deliberation, and (3) that if the legislature had found extra words, it would have removed them during the deliberation process. In other words, the canon presumes that the legislature would not include surplus language to communicate its meaning. But these presumptions are flawed. Statutes are not always carefully drafted. Legal drafters often intend to include redundant language to cover any unforeseen gaps, and legislatures simply fail to identify the redundancy timely. Legislators are not likely to waste time or energy arguing to remove redundancy when there are more important issues to address. Thus, the presumptions simply do not match drafting reality. "[A] statute that is the product of compromise may contain redundant language as a by-product of the strains of the negotiating process." Richard A. Posner, *Statutory Interpretation — In the Classroom and in the Courtroom*, 50 U. Chi. L. Rev. 800, 812 (1983) (saying, "No one would suggest that judicial opinions or academic articles contain no surplusage; are these documents less carefully prepared than statutes?"). For these reasons, not all judges use this canon. *Mayer v. Spanel Int'l Ltd.*, 51 F.3d 670, 674 (7th Cir. 1995) ("Redundancy is common in statutes; we do not subscribe to the view that every enacted word must carry independent force.").

But many judges do. For example, in *Begay v. United States*, 553 U.S. 137, 140 (2008), the defendant had twelve convictions for driving under the influence of alcohol (DUI) in New Mexico. Each DUI after the first three was considered a felony. *Id.* When he was arrested by local police during a domestic dispute, he had a firearm. *Id.* Under federal law, it is illegal for a convicted felon to possess a firearm. The defendant pleaded guilty in federal court to unlawful possession of a firearm. *Id.* The issue on appeal involved his sentence: if felony DUI was a "violent felony" under the Armed Career Criminal Act, then a higher sentence applied. *Id.* at 139.

The statute provided that an offender who had three prior convictions "for a *violent felony*" was subject to a 15-year mandatory minimum sentence. *Id.* at 139 (quoting 18 U.S.C. § 924(e)(1)). The statute defined a *violent* felony as one that "is burglary, arson, or extortion, involves use of explosives, or *otherwise involves conduct that presents a serious potential risk of physical injury to another.*" 18 U.S.C. § 924(e)(2)(B) (emphasis added). The U.S. District Court for the

District of New Mexico concluded that DUI was a "violent felony." The Tenth Circuit panel affirmed. *Begay*, 553 U.S. at 140. The Supreme Court reversed. *Id.* at 148.

Writing for the majority, Justice Breyer applied *ejusdem generis* and said that the conduct included within the catch-all ("otherwise involves conduct that presents a serious potential risk of physical injury to another") must be similar in nature to the listed items. *Id.* at 143. He reasoned that the commonality shared amongst the listed words was "purposeful, violent, and aggressive conduct." *Id.* at 143–44. (One could ask why drunk driving isn't purposeful, violent, and aggressive conduct.) He then turned to the rule against surplusage. *Id.* at 144–45. He reasoned that the words in the list ("burglary, arson, or extortion, involves use of explosives") preceding the broad catch-all narrow it, otherwise, he asked, why would Congress have included the listed words at all? They would be surplusage. *Id.*

Justice Scalia concurred in the judgment but disagreed with the majority's use of the rule against surplusage both because he did not find the language ambiguous and, in any event, he did not believe the majority's interpretation eliminated the surplusage. *Id.* at 148 (Scalia, J., concurring). For Scalia, the rule of lenity was determinative. *Id.* Justice Alito in dissent focused on the word "otherwise" introducing the catch-all to conclude that included offenses must simply be performed "in a different manner"; they need not be "'purposeful,' 'violent,' or 'aggressive.'" *Id.* at 159. He did not address the majority's rule against surplusage reasoning.

Like many of the other linguistic canons, this canon is a rebuttable presumption and yields to contrary legislative intent. *Cf. Ransom v. FIA Card Servs., N.A.*, 562 U.S. 61, 81 (2011) (Scalia, J., dissenting) (saying, "The canon against superfluity is not a canon against verbosity. When a thought could have been expressed more concisely, one does not always have to cast about for some additional meaning to the word or phrase that could have been dispensed with."). Thus, courts can reject words "as surplusage" when they are "inadvertently inserted or if repugnant to the rest of the statute ...." *Chickasaw Nation v. United States*, 534 U.S. 84, 94 (2001) (quoting KARL N. LLEWELLYN, THE COMMON LAW TRADITION 525 (1960)). In *Chickasaw Nation*, the Court held that the rule against surplusage did not apply when the rule produced an interpretation that conflicted with the intent of Congress. 534 U.S. at 94–95. The canon was particularly inappropriate in the Court's view because the surplus words were simply a numerical cross-reference in a parenthetical. *Id.* Such minor surplusage should not overcome the ordinary meaning of the rest of the text.

6. *Expressio Unius Est Exclusio Alterius*

Our final linguistic canon, *expressio unius* (also known as *inclusio unius*), is a rule of negative implication: it literally means "the inclusion of one thing means the exclusion of the other." Young children (and as I learned, teenagers) use *expressio unius* all the time. For a simple example, let's assume that a mother tells her child not to "hit or push" any of the other children. When that child then kicks another child on the playground and gets in trouble, the child argues, "But you didn't tell me I couldn't *kick* anyone!" Parents learn early to try to anticipate every contingency in their communications. Judges presume that legislatures do the same.

Expressio unius is implicated when a statute has a gap. The existence of the gap permits two very different inferences: either the legislature intended to omit the circumstance, or the legislature never considered the circumstance. *Expressio unius* presumes the former: that when the legislature includes some circumstances explicitly, then the legislature intentionally omitted other similar circumstances that would logically have been included. In other words, the canon presumes that the legislature considered and rejected every related possibility. It further presumes that if the legislature had intended to cover every circumstance, then the legislature would have included a general catch-all. Logically, however, *expressio unius* should apply only when the items in the list "are members of an 'associated group or series,' justifying the inference that items not mentioned were excluded by deliberate choice, not inadvertence." *Barnhart v. Peabody Coal Co.*, 537 U.S. 149, 168 (2003) (quoting *United States v. Vonn*, 535 U.S. 55, 65 (2002)).

If we return to a modified version of our hypothetical tax statute from the last section "lemons, limes, and grapefruits," *expressio unius* would tell us that oranges, which are not specifically included, are specifically omitted because (1) they are not specifically included, although they are sufficiently similar to the other items that a drafter likely would have thought about including them, and (2) there is no general word or catch-all following the list. While the presumption is that the legislature intentionally left out anything omitted, the reality is that the legislature may never have considered the omitted circumstance at all.

For example, in *Dickens v. Puryear*, 276 S.E.2d 325, 330 n.8 (N.C. 1981), the court used *expressio unius* to determine the appropriate statute of limitations in a tort case. The primary issue before the court was whether the defendant committed assault or intentional infliction of emotional distress when he threatened to kill the plaintiff if the plaintiff did not leave the state. *Id.* at 330. The court held that this threat of future harm was a claim for intentional infliction of emotional distress, not for assault. *Id.* at 336. The relevant statute provided that a one-year statute of limitations applied to actions involving "libel, slander, assault, battery, or false imprisonment." *Id.* at 330 n.8. The plaintiff had filed suit more than one year after the threat. *Id.* at 330. Applying *expressio unius*, the court reasoned that because intentional infliction of emotional distress was not listed with the other torts in the statute, it was not subject to the one-year limitation. *Id.* at 330 n.8. Hence, another statute of limitations applied instead.

Similarly, in *Silvers v. Sony Pictures Entertainment, Inc.*, 402 F.3d 881, 899 (9th Cir. 2005), the Ninth Circuit considered whether an assignee of an accrued cause of action for copyright infringement had standing to sue for that infringement when the assignee had no legal or beneficial interest in the copyright itself. *Id.* at 883. The relevant statute provided that only "[t]he *legal or beneficial owner of an exclusive right under a copyright* is entitled … to institute an action for infringement." *Id.* at 884 (quoting 17 U.S.C. §501(b) (emphasis added)). "Exclusive right" was defined in another section of the Act, which listed a number of such rights. *Id.* at 884–85. The list did not include the right to sue for an accrued infringement claim. *Id.* at 885. The majority reasoned that because the right to sue for an accrued infringement was not specifically included in the list, Congress intended to exclude it, pursuant to the doctrine of *expressio unius est exclusion alterius*. *Id.*

The dissent reasoned that although the language was ambiguous the doctrine was inapplicable because it should be applied only when "Congressional intent cannot be discerned." *Id.* at 899 (Bea, J., dissenting). The dissent explained that the canon is best "[u]nderstood as a descriptive generalization about language rather than a prescriptive rule of construction," explaining that " 'My children are Jonathan, Rebecca and Seth' means 'none of my children are Samuel' " but that " 'get milk, bread, peanut butter and eggs at the grocery' probably does not mean 'do not get ice cream.' " *Id.* (quoting *Longview Fibre Co. v. Rasmussen*, 980 F.2d 1307, 1313 (9th Cir. 1992)). Because the drafting and legislative history demonstrated that Congress intended to enlarge, not limit, the ability of owners to copyrights to bring suit, the dissent would have allowed the assignee to sue. *Id.* at 900–02.

This canon, like the others, presumes something about legislative drafting that may not reflect reality. *Expressio unius* presumes that the legislature actually considered all the possible options and included those options it wanted. Nonsense! "[*Expressio unius*] is increasingly considered unreliable, for it stands on the faulty premise that all possible alternative or supplemental provisions were necessarily considered and rejected by the legislative draftsmen." *Nat'l Petroleum Refiners Ass'n v. FTC*, 482 F.2d 672, 676 (D.C. Cir. 1973). In reality, legislatures omit things for a variety of reasons, some intentional, some not. Despite the canon's limitations, many judges still use this canon. Hence, you need to be aware that it exists and know how it is used.

In conclusion, the linguistic canons provide common sense guidelines for understanding how English speakers and writers use language. As such, these canons serve as rebuttable presumptions and should yield when there is either evidence that the drafter did not follow the canons or evidence that the drafter did not intend for a particular canon to apply to a specific situation. Because these canons help us understand how English writers ordinarily use language, the canons may not accurately reflect how legal writers use language and should be used with some caution. Finally, it is simply illogical, as some judges argue, to apply the canons only when ambiguity exists. The point of the canons is to help a reader understand the ordinary meaning of the words used; hence, the canons should be used as part of the search for ordinary meaning. Despite the limitations of using these canons, they have come back into vogue with the renewed emphasis on the text.

In the next chapter, we move to the final intrinsic source to be covered: the other components in the bill. Surprisingly, with the exception of definitions, these components play a less-central role in interpretation than the intrinsic sources we have covered so far.

D. Mastering This Topic

Return to the hypothetical ordinance provided in Chapter 1. Assuming you think the term "motor vehicles" is ambiguous as applied to the various hypotheticals and especially the ambulance hypothetical, do the linguistic canons help resolve the ambiguity? The ordinance (in non-marked up form) provides:

An Ordinance

To Prohibit Motor Vehicles in Pioneer Park

*Be it enacted by the Council of the City of Pioneer
assembled,*

(1) The short title of this ordinance shall be the Pioneer Park Safety Ordinance.
(2) No cars, motorcycles, or other motor vehicles may enter or remain in Pioneer Park, except as provided in section 3 hereof.
(3) Motor vehicles may be used by authorized public groups:
      a. in maintaining Pioneer Park, and
      b. in placing barricades for parades, concerts, or other entertainment in Pioneer Park.
(4) Anyone violating this ordinance shall be subject to a $1,000 fine, provided no injuries occurred. If any injury occurred, the fine shall be doubled.
(5) The Commission of Parks shall have the power to issue rules to implement this ordinance as necessary to protect public safety and hold hearings regarding any violations of its provisions.

Effective: August 15, 1998.

Let's look at each of the linguistic canons in turn starting with *in pari materia*. Remember that this canon identifies the statutory material that is relevant to the interpretive process. Here, the whole act aspect lets us know that we should look at the ordinance as a whole (in the bill form), so the whole ordinance is included above. We do not have other related ordinances from this city's code, so the whole code aspect is inapplicable to our problem. But as a prosecutor, you might have looked to see if there were special ordinances related to ambulances and traffic laws, for example, that might provide insight.

Turning to the presumption of consistent usage and meaningful variation, you should note that the phrase "motor vehicles" is used twice. Thus, because the council did not alter the phrase at all, you can assume that the phrase was meant to have the same meaning in sections 2 and 3. This canon does not resolve the ambiguity regarding ambulances, however.

Does the rule against surplusage help resolve the ambiguity? This canon directs that all words and phrases must have independent meaning. In other words, "motor vehicles" does not mean "vehicles." Also, "motor vehicles" must mean more than just cars and motorcycles. But the canon does not seem to resolve the ambiguity in the statute as it applies to ambulances.

How about *noscitur a sociis* or *ejusdem generis*; do either of these canons resolve the ambiguity? First, you must determine which canon is appropriate. Because the language being interpreted is the catch-all, "other motor vehicles," you know that *ejusdem generis* is the appropriate canon, not *noscitur a sociis*. Next, you need to identify the attribute the items share so that you can interpret the catch-all to be of the same type as the items listed. Cars and motorcycles are vehicles that people drive to get places. They have motors, and they carry people. Does an ambulance share these attributes? Yes, hence, your application of *ejusdem generis* should suggest that the council would have intended that an ambulance be included within the general catch-all, and, thus, the ambulance driver should be cited. While this may not be the outcome you would prefer, the canon does suggest this outcome.

Finally, let's turn to *expressio unius est exclusio alterius*. Is this canon appropriate? After all, ambulances were not specifically included in the listed items; therefore, could one argue that the legislature intended to omit them (or allow them to be driven in the park)? Actually, no, the ambulance driver cannot make this argument for the simple reason that the legislature included a general catch-all, which shows that the council did not intend to identify in the ordinance every possible type of vehicle that was prohibited from driving in park. The canon should not apply to section 2.

But the canon would apply to section 3. Section 3 specifically identifies two vehicles that can be driven in the park and does not include a catch-all. Ambulances are not included within this list. Therefore, *expressio unius* would suggest that ambulances are not excepted because the council showed that it knows how to exclude certain vehicles when it wants to do so, and it chose not to exclude ambulances. Further, it chose not to include a general catch-all to broaden the exceptions. Again, this may not be the outcome you would prefer, but the canon does suggest it.

In summary, after applying the linguistic canons, you should conclude that while many of them do not help resolve the ambiguity, two are applicable: *ejusdem generis* and *expressio unius*. Applying these two canons, you should conclude that the ambulance driver must be cited. Helpfully, both canons point to the same result. Perhaps you are satisfied with this result, and if you are a textualist, you may well be. If the council wants to exclude ambulances, then it should say so (and also exclude helicopters, airplanes, and other similar vehicles). But if you are dissatisfied with this result and are a textualist, there is one final intrinsic source that may provide help in resolving the ambiguity: the components. We turn to this topic next.

Checkpoints

- The linguistic canons simply reflect shared assumptions about the way English speakers and writers use language. These canons are rules of thumb that help judges draw inferences from the words of the statute.

- The linguistic canons should be used with common sense and a realization that lawyers draft differently than the canons presume. When there is better evidence of legislative intent, the canons should take a back seat.

- While the linguistic canons were less favored in the last century, they have made a strong comeback with the renewed focus on the text.

- *In pari materia* directs judges to look at an entire act and related acts in the whole code to determine meaning. The canon helps ensure internal consistency across acts, statutes, related statutes, and even the code as a whole.

- The presumption of consistent usage and meaningful variation presumes that when the legislature uses the same word in different parts of the same act, the legislature intended those words to have the same meaning (consistent usage). And, contrariwise, if the legislature uses a word in one part of the act, then changes to a different word in the same act, the legislature intended to change the meaning (meaningful variation).

- *Noscitur a sociis*, meaning "it is known from its associates," directs that when a word has more than one meaning, the appropriate meaning should be gleaned from the textual context, meaning the other words in the statute. The canon is often used when a statute includes a list with no catch-all.

- *Ejusdem generis*, meaning "of the same kind, class, or nature," directs that when general words are near specific words, the general words should be limited to include only things similar in nature to the specific words. This canon is a subset of *noscitur a sociis* and is generally used when a statute includes a list with a catch-all.

- According to the rule against surplusage, the proper interpretation of a statute is the one in which every word and phrase has meaning; nothing is redundant or meaningless.

- *Expressio unius* presumes that when the legislature includes some circumstances explicitly, then the legislature intentionally omitted other similar circumstances that should logically have been included.

Chapter 8

Canons Based on Intrinsic Sources: The Components

Roadmap

- Learn the codification process.
- Identify the three parts of the bill, including the beginning provisions, the purview, and the closing provisions.
- Understand that the operative and enforcement sections include the general rule, any exceptions to that rule, and methods for enforcing the rule.
- Learn to start the interpretive process by finding language within the purview.
- Learn that the other components, such as headings, titles, enacting clauses, preambles, and definitions, may aid interpretation but do not establish rights, duties, or legal obligations.

A. Introduction to This Chapter

In this chapter, we survey our final intrinsic source: the remaining components of a bill or act. Some components of an act are critical to interpretation, such as definition sections. Some components of an act may be relevant to interpretation, such as titles and purpose clauses. Some components of an act play no role in interpretation, such as enacting clauses.

This chapter follows the chapter on linguistic canons although the two are intimately connected. The canon *in pari materia*, the whole act aspect, makes clear that the entire act is relevant to interpretation. Now that you understand that point, we can talk about the relevance to interpretation of the various parts of the act, known as the components. You already know what to do with the language you find in these components. For example, you might apply the identical words presumption or the rule against surplusage.

Using a simple bill that was never enacted, this chapter will identify the various bill components and explore the canons surrounding their relevance to the interpretation of the ensuing statute. The House bill and the Senate's companion bill are reproduced in full in Appendices B and C. For ease of reference, however, each section in this chapter includes the relevant component from the sample bill or another bill so that you can see actual bill language.

B. Codification

To understand the role components play in interpretation, you must first understand what codification is. In early American history, acts were not codified; rather, they were simply placed in books sequentially. RONALD B. BROWN & SHARON J. BROWN, THE SEARCH FOR LEGISLATIVE INTENT 150 (2002). During this time there were far fewer statutes; hence, codification was less necessary.

As you might imagine, researching the *Statutes at Large* would be time consuming and frustrating because the acts are arranged chronologically, not topically. Moreover, statutes are regularly amended and repealed; thus, extensive cross-referencing would be essential. Eventually, smart entrepreneurs figured out that codifying statutes — placing statutes with similar subject matters together — would be profitable. *Id.* These entrepreneurs were right. Today, all federal and state acts are codified: rearranged and published in a topical code. The process of inserting sections of an act into a code is called *codification*.

Codification is simple. When Congress passes a bill, it becomes an enrolled bill and is presented to the president for approval. If the president signs (or fails to effectively veto the bill), the bill becomes an act. The act is delivered to the Archivist of the United States; duplicates of the act are published chronologically in official pamphlets called "slip laws," which the Government Printing Office publishes. An example of a simple slip law extending the Patriot Act is included below. Ultimately, slip laws are officially bound chronologically into "session laws" and placed into the *Statutes at Large*. Acts may be only one page long or hundreds of pages in length. They may cover just one topic or a variety of topics.

Sample Slip Law

---

125 STAT. 216   PUBLIC LAW 112–14—MAY 26, 2011

Public Law 112–14
112th Congress
An Act

May 26, 2011

[S. 990]

To provide for an additional temporary extension of programs under the Small Business Act and the Small Business Investment Act of 1958, and for other purposes.

Be it enacted by the Senate and House of Representatives of the United States of America in Congress assembled,

PATRIOT Sunsets Extension Act of 2011. 50 USC 1801 note.

SECTION 1. SHORT TITLE.

This Act may be cited as the "PATRIOT Sunsets Extension Act of 2011".

SEC. 2. SUNSET EXTENSIONS.

(a) USA PATRIOT IMPROVEMENT AND REAUTHORIZATION ACT OF 2005.—Section 102(b)(1) of the USA PATRIOT Improvement and Reauthorization Act of 2005 (Public Law 109–177; 50 U.S.C. 1805 note, 50 U.S.C. 1861 note, and 50 U.S.C. 1862 note) is amended by striking "May 27, 2011" and inserting "June 1, 2015".

50 USC 1805 and note, 1861, 1862.

(b) INTELLIGENCE REFORM AND TERRORISM PREVENTION ACT OF 2004.—Section 6001(b)(1) of the Intelligence Reform and Terrorism Prevention Act of 2004 (Public Law 108–458; 50 U.S.C. 1801 note) is amended by striking "May 27, 2011" and inserting "June 1, 2015".

Approved May 26, 2011.

The official code for federal statutes is the *United States Code*, which is divided into more than forty different "titles" based on subject matter. Title 18, for example, contains all statutes related to "Crimes and Criminal Procedure." Title 26 contains all statutes related to "the Internal Revenue Code." Titles are further divided into "articles" or "chapters," which are themselves broken down into "sections." Sections are broken down into subsections. For example, Title 18, Crimes and Procedures, has Chapter 55, Kidnapping, which includes § 1201, the elements of the crime of kidnapping. This section includes subsections (a)–(h). 18 U.S.C. § 1201. A minority of states use "chapters" rather than "titles." Chapters are broken down into "articles," which are broken down into sections. *See, e.g.,* NEB. REV. STAT. § 28–312 (2018).

The code is much simpler to search than the *Statutes at Large*. But you cannot search the code for a named act, such as the Patriot Act. Sections of the Patriot Act are scattered throughout the code. But you can find the Patriot Act in the *Statutes at Large*.

The Office of the Law Revision Counsel of the U.S. House of Representatives ("OLRC") maintains the *United States Code*. OLRC determines which acts in the *Statutes at Large* should be codified. It also determines whether a new statute amends or repeals any existing statutes and whether any existing statutes have lapsed.

Because the legislature originally had nothing to do with the placement of a statute in a particular section of the code, placement itself was considered irrelevant to meaning. Even when the states and federal government began officially codifying statutes, the legislature continued to have no role in this process; hence, where a statute was located in a code continued to be irrelevant to meaning. Today, however, the legislature often specifically indicates where sections or parts of an act should be placed in the code. When the legislature does so, placement may affect meaning. *See, e.g., Commonwealth v. Smith*, 728 N.E.2d 272, 275 (Mass. 2000) (holding that the term "sexual intercourse" in an incest statute did not mean the same thing as the term "sexual intercourse" in a rape statute because the two statutes were located in different sections of the code).

Codification is imperfect. Many statutes cover more than one subject. For example, tax evasion is a felony. But the relevant statute criminalizing tax evasion can be found in the tax chapter of the code, not the criminal chapter. *See, e.g.,* 26 U.S.C § 7201 (2012) (providing, "Any person who willfully attempts in any manner to evade or defeat any tax imposed by this title or the payment thereof shall, in addition to other penalties provided by law, be guilty of a felony"). The statute cannot be placed in both (consider how enormous the code would become), yet arguably tax evasion relates to both subjects.

Regardless of the relevancy of placement in the code, relying solely on the code and ignoring the *Statutes at Large* can be foolhardy. First, codification is imperfect. For the most part, the code is accurate, but occasionally, there have been transpositions or other errors. While the code is *prima facie* evidence of the law, the text of the *Statutes at Large* is "legal evidence" of the law as enacted. *Stephan v. United States*, 319 U.S. 423, 426 (1943). Thus, on the rare occasion when there is conflict, the *Statutes at Large* controls. "[T]he very meaning of 'prima facie' is that the Code cannot prevail over the *Statutes at Large* when the two are inconsistent." *Id.* For example, 12 U.S.C. § 92 was omitted from the *United States Code* for decades. Despite that fact, Congress amended § 92 in 1982. In *U.S. National Bank of Oregon v. Independent Insurance Agents of America, Inc.*,

508 U.S. 439 (1993), the parties disputed whether §92 had remained valid law. Despite omission from the *U.S. Code*, the Supreme Court held that the section was still valid law because the *Statutes at Large* so dictated. *Id.* at 440.

Importantly, not every section (or component) of an act is codified. Acts have a variety of components. Some components are required, such as enacting clauses and titles; many are optional, such as findings clauses and short titles. Generally, only those components that follow the enacting clause, which we will address in a moment, are codified. The enacting clause itself is not codified, only the language following it. Moreover, "[w]hile the enacting clause is required for the act to become law, it does not itself become law ...." *State v. Phillips*, 560 S.E.2d 852, 856 (N.C. Ct. App. 2002). Long titles and preambles, which precede the enacting clause, are not codified. Similarly, provisions for the effective date of amendments to existing laws may not be codified. When not codified, these titles, preambles, and effective date provisions can only be found by looking at the full act in the *Statutes at Large* or the state equivalent. Perhaps surprisingly, codification does not affect the relevance components have on meaning. Components that are not codified can affect interpretation, while components that are codified may have little to no effect.

Typically, an act is organized in the following order. First is the beginning section, which includes the heading, the act's name, legislative findings, statutory purpose, the scope of the act, and any definitions. Following the beginning section is the purview, which includes operative and enforcement provisions. Operative provisions provide the general rule, any exceptions to that rule, and the consequences for violating that rule. Enforcement provisions identify the methods the government will use to enforce the rule. Finally, the act may conclude with a closing section, which includes provisions identifying the effective date of the act, whether the rule will sunset at a specific time, and whether the act is severable or not. Let's now take a look at each of the sections.

C. The Components & Their Canons

1. Beginning Section

The beginning section includes some or all of the following: the heading, the enabling clause, the act's short title, if any, legislative findings, statutory purpose, the scope of the act, and any definitions. These provisions in the beginning section have no legal effect alone. However, they may be useful in understanding the meaning of language in an operative or enforcement provision.

a. Heading

In the box below, you will see the heading of a sample bill (it was not passed, so technically, it is not an act; the term "act" should be used to refer to an enacted bill only). You can find the entire bill in Appendix B. This heading identifies the Congress responsible for enacting the bill (the 110th), the session in which the bill was debated (the first), the bill designation number (H.R. 916), the Chamber from which the bill came (H.R. identifies it as House bill, S. would be a Senate bill), the primary sponsor (Representative Scott of Georgia) and the other sponsors of the bill, what happened to the bill, and when it happened (the bill was referred to the Committee on the Judiciary on February 8, then sent to the Committee of the Whole on May 14, 2007). Note that a sponsor signs a bill before introducing it; a bill number is assigned when the bill is introduced.

Union Calendar No. 88

110TH CONGRESS

1ST SESSION   H. R. 916

[Report No. 110–148]

To provide for loan repayment for prosecutors and public defenders.

———

IN THE HOUSE OF REPRESENTATIVES

FEBRUARY 8, 2007

Mr. SCOTT of Georgia (for himself, Mr. GORDON of Tennessee, Mr. LEWIS of Georgia, Mr. PAYNE....) introduced the following bill; which was referred to the Committee on the Judiciary

MAY 14, 2007

Additional sponsors: Mr. LINCOLN DAVIS of Tennessee, Mr. COOPER, Mr. CHANDLER, Mr. UDALL of Colorado....

MAY 14, 2007

Reported with an amendment, committed to the Committee of the Whole

House on the State of the Union, and ordered to be printed

———

A BILL

None of the information in this heading is codified, but some of the information might be useful for further research; for example, the sponsors of the bill are identified. For the most part, none of this information is relevant to statutory interpretation. Following the heading are the components relevant to interpretation, beginning with titles: long titles, short titles, and section titles.

After the heading, each section of a bill must be separately numbered. 1 U.S.C. § 104. Additionally, "as nearly as may be" each section must contain only a single proposition of enactment. *Id.*

The sample bill begins section numbering with the *short* title. Thus, if you wanted to cite this section in the bill, you would cite the bill by name (if relevant), the abbreviated name of the chamber, the number of the bill, the number of the Congress, the relevant section number, and year of publication (John R. Justice Prosecutors and Defenders Incentive Act, H.R. 916, 110th Cong. § 1 (2007)).

b. Titles

There are three types of titles in a bill: (1) long titles, (2) short titles, and (3) section titles. The canon for using any one of the three in interpretation is identical and simple: titles are not controlling. But the rationale differs depending on which title is relevant, so let's look at each in more detail. We will start with the long title because it precedes the other two.

i. Long Titles & Enacting Clauses

Every bill has a long title. Look in the box below. The long title immediately follows the words "A Bill." Generally, all long titles begin with the words "to" or "relating to"; they then identify the purpose of the bill and where the bill will fit within existing law. Does the bill contain new statutes? Does this bill amend, repeal, or replace existing statutes? One purpose of the long title is to answer these questions. Another purpose of the long title is to provide the reader, including legislators, with a convenient way to determine what topics the bill addresses without having to read the whole bill. Both federal and state law require titles, in part, to prevent a legislator from including extraneous provisions in a bill while attempting to avoid legislative or public notice.

Component: Long Title & Enacting Clause

A BILL
To provide for loan repayment for prosecutors and public defenders.
Be it enacted by the Senate and House of Representatives of the United States of America in Congress assembled,

The long title of our bill is "To provide for loan repayment for prosecutors and public defenders." This long title is actually very short! A more illustrative long title follows:

> A BILL ... To amend Chapter 12 of Title 16 of the Official Code of Georgia Annotated, relating to offenses against health and morals, ... to provide for definitions; to require that a female give her informed consent prior to an abortion; to require that certain information be provided to or made available to a female prior to an abortion; to require a written acknowledgment of receipt of such information; to provide for the preparation and availability of certain information; to provide for procedures in a medical emergency; to provide for reporting; ... and for other purposes.

H.B. 364, 144th Cong. (1997).

To understand the limited role that long titles have in statutory interpretation, we must turn to our English heritage. In England, the clerks in parliament historically added long titles to bills; thus, the early English rule prohibited judges from considering the long title during interpretation. For the most part, that rule still holds true in England.

In contrast, in the United States, the legislature writes its own long titles; therefore, a different rule developed. Here, "[t]he title of an act cannot control its words, but may furnish some aid in showing what was in the mind of the legislature." *Church of the Holy Trinity v. United States,* 143 U.S. 457, 462 (1892). In other words, a judge may look at a long title to resolve ambiguity or correct drafting errors. In *Holy Trinity,* the Supreme Court did just that. In that case, Holy Trinity Church hired a pastor from England. However, a federal statute prohibited employers from importing any foreigner "to perform labor or service of any kind." *Id.* at 463. While suggesting that the word "labor" in the statute was clear, the Court nevertheless looked to the long title of the Act to determine whether Congress intended to prohibit manual labor or all forms of labor. *Id.* The long title was "[a]n act to prohibit the importation and migration of foreigners and aliens under contract or agreement to perform labor in the United States." *Id.* From the legislative history and this title, the Court concluded that Congress had intended the Act to "reach[] only to the work of the manual laborer, as distinguished from that of the professional man." *Id.*

If a legislature writes the long title, why would such a title be less controlling than the words of the statute? One reason might be that long titles are not codified because they precede the enacting clause. But this reason alone is not sufficient because short titles, which follow the enacting clause and may be codified, similarly do not carry as much weight as other text. Hence, codification alone cannot be the answer. More likely, the reluctance to give weight to titles stems from our English heritage, where titles are not considered in interpretation.

Following the long title in a bill is the enacting or resolving clause. Enacting clauses are used for bills, both at the federal and state levels, while resolving clauses are used for joint resolutions. In the United States, enacting clauses are required, and their language is prescribed. 1 U.S.C. §§ 101, 102. Enacting clauses are so foundational that in Texas, a "bill" without an enacting clause cannot be amended by adding an enacting clause, nor may "such a bill" be referred to committee under that state's house and senate rules. Texas legislators must get it right the first time.

For a federal bill, the required language of the enacting clause is "*Be it enacted by the Senate and House of Representatives of the United States of America in Congress assembled ....*" 1 U.S.C. § 101. Notice that the enacting clause in the text box from earlier has this magic language. For a joint resolution, the language differs slightly: "*Resolved by the Senate and House of Representatives of the United States of America in Congress assembled ....*" 1 U.S.C. § 102. There are no interpretation issues surrounding enacting clauses because the language is prescribed and never varies.

The components following the enacting clause are generally codified; the components preceding the enacting clause are not. *See* 1 U.S.C. § 103. Thus, the components we have studied up to this point are not codified. The ones we are about to study generally are codified.

ii. Short Titles

For some bills, a short title may also be included, even if the long title is not all that long. The short title is located in a separate section of the statute, usually the first section. The short title typically is written as follows: "This act may be cited as the _____ Act of _____." The short title of our sample bill is the "John R. Justice Prosecutors and Defenders Incentive Act of 2007."

Component: Short Title

SECTION 1. SHORT TITLE.

This Act may be cited as the "John R. Justice Prosecutors and Defenders Incentive Act of 2007".

One Hundred Eleventh Congress
of the
United States of America

AT THE SECOND SESSION

Begun and held at the City of Washington on Tuesday, the fifth day of January, two thousand and ten

An Act

To modernize the air traffic control system, improve the safety, reliability, and availability of transportation by air in the United States, provide for modernization of the air traffic control system, reauthorize the Federal Aviation Administration, and for other purposes.

Be it enacted by the Senate and House of Representatives of the United States of America in Congress assembled,

SHORT TITLE

SECTION 1. This Act may be cited as the "_____ Act of _____".

In this case, the short title is almost as long as the long title! So why would a legislature include one? Legislatures include short titles for a variety of reasons. One obvious reason is that, when a title is truly long, a short title eases reference. However, short titles are used for other reasons as well. Short titles are often used to persuade either legislators or the public to support the bill. For example, consider the following two short titles: "The No Child Left Behind Act" and "The Patriot Act." A legislator would be hard-pressed to vote against children and patriotism!

In addition to persuasion, a short title can be used, as in this case, to honor someone involved in either the bill process or the subject. In this case, John R. Justice was the Solicitor (the highest state prosecutor) of South Carolina; the bill's title was chosen to honor his public service work. Some acts earn their short name (not a true short title) only after enactment, *e.g.* the Sherman Act, which was originally called the "Act of July 2, 1890." For an excellent discussion of short names, see Mary Whisner, *What's in a Statute Name?*, 97 LAW LIBR. J. 169 (2005).

Interestingly, sometimes during the drafting process, errors can occur. In 2010, Congress enacted and President Obama signed into law the "The __[blank]__ Act of __[blank]__." See the text box on the preceding page and note the short title.

Although the short title follows the enacting clause and, thus, may be codified, the canon remains the same: "the name given to an act by way of designation or description ... cannot change the plain import of its words." *Caminetti v. United States*, 242 U.S. 470, 490 (1917). In *Caminetti*, the defendants were convicted of violating the "White Slave Traffic Act" for bringing their mistresses across state lines. *Id.* at 482–83. The statute prohibited the transportation of any woman for the purpose of prostitution, debauchery, or "*any other immoral purpose.*" *Id.* at 485. The Court found the listed word "debauchery" and the text of the catch-all clear; debauchery and any immoral purpose included bringing women across state lines to be mistresses. *Id.* Thus, the majority refused to consider the defendants' argument that Congress intended the Act to reach only commercial trafficking of women (meaning prostitution). *Id.* at 485. The dissent disagreed. Finding that the short title of the Act "[gave] more than a title; it [made] distinctive the purpose of the statute," the dissent argued that the short title should be used to narrow the expansive meaning of the broad catch-all in this case. *Id.* at 497 (McKenna, J., dissenting).

In *Holy Trinity*, the Court allowed purpose and the long title to prevail over clear text; the dissent in *Caminetti* would have done the same. In contrast, the majority in *Caminetti* refused to consider the short title in light of the clarity of statute's text. Why the difference? It's hard to know, but it would appear that the judges' approaches to statutory interpretation may have been outcome determinative here. The majority opinion in *Caminetti* followed the title canon.

iii. Section Titles

Almost all bills have section titles or headings to aid the reader in finding content within a particular section of a bill. A section title is merely a short-hand reference to the general subject matter in the section. Earlier, you might have noticed that a section title preceded the short title of the John R. Jones Prosecutor and Defenders Incentive Act. The section title reads: *Section 1: Short Title.* If not, go back and find this section title; while it is not hugely helpful to a reader, it does provide some focus. Generally, section titles do no more than indicate the content of the section in a general manner, especially when text is complicated and prolific. It would be impossible for the legislature to attempt to capture everything contained within a section within one short section title. Thus, section titles were never meant to take the place of the detailed provisions of the text; hence, they offer little to judges who are interpreting statutory language.

The canon for section titles is identical to that of the other titles: the section title cannot prevail over the ordinary meaning of the text. For interpretative purposes, section titles are relevant when the text is ambiguous or absurd. In other words, section titles "are but tools available for the resolution of a doubt. But they cannot undo or limit that which the text makes plain." *Brotherhood of R.R. Trainmen v. Baltimore & O.R. Co.*, 331 U.S. 519, 529 (1947); *accord, Yates v. United States*, 135 S. Ct. 1074, 1083 (2015) ("While [section] headings are not commanding, they supply cues."); *Almendarez-Torres v. United States*, 523 U.S. 224, 234 (1998) ("[T]he title of a statute and the heading of a section are tools available for the resolution of a doubt about the meaning of a statute.") (internal quotation marks omitted).

Some state legislatures do not write section titles in bills; instead, the publisher of their code does so. Such was the case in *Michigan Ave. National Bank v. County of Cook*, 732 N.E.2d 528 (Ill. 2000). In that case, the plaintiff relied on a caption, or section title, that was not in the official version of the statute, but rather was added by West when it published the statute. Not surprisingly, the court rejected the argument that this caption should carry any interpretative weight. *Id.* at 536.

iv. Code Chapter & Heading Titles

As noted above, acts have various titles. Additionally, codes have titles, chapters, subchapters, and sections identifying the general subject matter within them. For example, the title of 26 U.S.C. is "Internal Revenue Code." Within title 26, Subtitle A is titled "Income Taxes." Within Subtitle A, Chapter 2 is titled "Tax on Self-Employment Income." Within Chapter 2 is section 1401 titled "Rate of Tax." One would expect to find the tax rates for self-employment income in this section, and, indeed, one would so find. The *United States Code* currently has more than fifty different titles.

The Office of the Law Revision Council ("OLRC") prepares and publishes the Code. When Congress specifies amendments and repeals of statutes, OLRC makes the changes. Sometimes, bills create new statutes and OLRC must decide where to place these new laws. It is the job of the OLRC's classifying attorneys to determine whether and how to classify new sections of the Code if Congress fails to do so. Sometimes, the codifiers provide the title. Hence, these various Code titles are generally irrelevant to its meaning.

In 1873, when Congress enacted the *Revised Statutes of the United States of America*, our very first code, Congress include the following provision, known as Section 5600:

> The arrangement and classification of the several sections of the revision have been made for the purpose of a more convenient and orderly arrangement of the same, and therefore no inference or presumption of a legislative construction is to be drawn by reason of the Title, under which any particular section is placed.

18 Stat. 1085. This provision cannot be found in the Code today because OLRC decided years ago to drop it. But its guidance is still valid. Further, Congress has made this point explicitly for a number of titles. *See, e.g.*, 26 U.S.C. § 7806(b) ("No inference, implication, or presumption of legislative construction shall be drawn or made by reason of the location or grouping of any particular section or provision or portion of this title, nor shall any table of contents, table of cross references, or similar outline, analysis, or descriptive matter relating to the contents of this title be given any legal effect.").

Thus, the rule is quite simple: when trying to determine the meaning of a statute, the title and heading under which the provision was placed are irrelevant. For example, in *United States v. Dixon*, 347 U.S. 381, 385–86 (1954), the Supreme Court rejected the defendant's argument that the relevant statute allowed only that he be subject to forfeiture and not to criminal prosecution, because, in part, the heading was "forfeitures and seizures." *See also, Fla. ex rel. Attorney Gen. v. U.S. Dep't of Health and Human Servs.*, 648 F.3d 1235, 1319 (11th Cir. 2011) (rejecting the government's argument that the individual mandate operated as a tax because it is housed in the Internal Revenue Code because "the Code itself makes clear that Congress's choice of where to place a provision in the Internal Revenue Code has no interpretive value."), *aff'd in part and rev'd in part sub nom. Nat'l Fed'n of Indep. Bus. v. Sebelius*, 567 U.S. 519 (2012); *but see Yates v. United States*, 135 S. Ct. 1074, 1083 (2015) (relying on the heading and placement of the relevant statute to conclude that a fish is not a "tangible object" even though a provision in the relevant chapter specifically directed that "[n]o inference of a legislative construction is to be drawn by reason of the chapter in Title 18, Crimes and Criminal Procedure.").

State law is similar. For example, in *State v. Bussey*, 463 So. 2d 1141 (Fla. 1985), the court found that a statute penalizing the sale of drugs was a criminal statute despite being located in the "Fraudulent Practices" section of the state code. The court reasoned,

> The arrangement and classification of laws for purposes of codification in the Florida Statutes is an administrative function of the Joint Legislative Management Committee of the Florida Legislature. The classification of a law or a part of a law in a particular title or chapter of Florida Statutes is not determinative on the issue of legislative intent.

Id. at 1143 (internal citation omitted).

c. Preambles, Purpose Clauses & Legislative Findings

After either the short title, if there is one, or the enacting/resolving clause if there is no short title, there may be a section called legislative findings or purpose. These provisions are called preambles, findings clauses, or purpose clauses. These provisions are generally called preambles when they precede the enacting clause and findings, purpose, or policy clauses (or some combination) when they follow the enacting clause. Findings clauses and purpose clauses differ somewhat from each other. Findings clauses identify the legislative facts that lead the legislature to enact the new law, while purpose clauses identify the purpose of the act. While findings and purpose clauses can be separate sections of a bill, or one can be included and the other not included, the common practice is to include both clauses together in one section.

While preambles, legislative findings, and purpose clauses are not required, they can be informative. The sample bill has a simple purpose clause, which is in the box below. While the language of the clause would suggest it applies only to one section of the bill (it says "[t]he purpose of this section"), there is really only one relevant subsection in the bill; thus, the purpose clause applies to all the important provisions in this bill.

Component: Purpose Clause

> "SEC. 3111. GRANT AUTHORIZATION.
>
> "(a) PURPOSE.—The purpose of this section is to encourage qualified individuals to enter and continue employment as prosecutors and public defenders.

Commonly, findings and purpose clauses are much longer and more detailed. A highly edited sample findings and purpose clause from The Rehabilitation Act appears in the box below. Notice that this example clause contains findings, purposes, and policy.

Component: Finding & Purpose Clause

Sec. 2. Findings; Purpose; Policy

(a) **Findings**

Congress finds that— ...

    (3) disability is a natural part of the human experience and in no way diminishes the right of individuals to—

    (A) live independently;

    (B) enjoy self-determination;

    (C) make choices;

    (D) contribute to society;

    (E) pursue meaningful careers; and

    (F) enjoy full inclusion and integration in the economic, political, social, cultural, and educational mainstream of American society;

...

(b) **Purpose**

The purposes of this Act are— ...

    (2) to ensure that the Federal Government plays a leadership role in promoting the employment of individuals with disabilities....

(c) **Policy**

It is the policy of the United States that all programs, projects, and activities receiving assistance under this Act shall be carried out in a manner consistent with the principles of—

    (1) respect for individual dignity ...

Increasingly, Congress is placing its findings and purposes within the section of the bill to be codified to increase the likelihood that a judge will use the findings or purpose to interpret it. Whether a judge is willing to consider such clauses depends largely on that judge's approach to interpretation. Some judges are willing to consider findings and purpose clauses only when the statute is ambiguous. *See, e.g., Knebel v. Hein*, 429 U.S. 288, 292 n.9 (1977) ("The salutary purpose and the broad outlines of the federal food stamp program are well known."). The canon for preambles and findings and purpose clauses is identical to the titles' canon: they cannot trump clear, enacted text, but they can help resolve ambiguity, if a judge is willing to consider them. For example, in *Sutton v. United Air Lines, Inc.*, 527 U.S. 471 (1999), the Supreme Court turned to the findings provision to limit the reach of the Americans with Disabilities Act (the "ADA"). In that case, two severely myopic sisters sued United Airlines when it denied their application to become commercial pilots. *Id.* at 475–76. Claiming that they were not disabled under the ADA because the sisters' vision could be corrected, United Airlines sought dismissal. *Id.* at 476. The term "disability" was not defined in the statute. *Id.* at 478. Thus, the Court turned to the findings clause. *Id.* at 484. The findings clause provided that "some 43,000,000 Americans have one or more physical or mental disabilities, and this number is increasing as the population as a whole is growing older." *Id.* (citing U.S.C. § 12101(a)(1)). According to the Court, the "findings enacted as part of the ADA require the conclusion that Congress did not intend to bring under the statute's protection all those whose *uncorrected* conditions amount to disabilities." *Id.* In other words, if correctable conditions were included, that number would have been much larger. Hence, Congress must have intended to include only uncorrectable disabilities within the statute's protection.

A state case that highlighted the role of a findings clause is *Commonwealth v. Besch*, 674 A.2d 655 (Pa. 1996). In that case, the defendants sold marijuana and cocaine to each other. *Id.* at 656. The State of Pennsylvania charged the defendants with violating its Corrupt Organizations Statute (the State equivalent of the Racketeer Influenced and Corrupt Organizations Act (RICO)). The issue for the court was whether the state could prosecute a wholly illegitimate drug conspiracy under the Act. *Id.* at 655. The language at issue in the statute was "enterprise," which the statute defined as any "legal entity." *Id.* at 658 (quoting 18 PA. CONN. STAT. § 911(h)(3)). The court did not find this definition dispositive, so it turned to the findings clause, which stated that the Act was designed to prevent "organized crime [from] infiltrate[ing] and corrupt[ing] *legitimate businesses* ...." *Id.* at 659 (quoting § 18 PA. CONN. STAT. § 911(a) (emphasis added)). Because the statute was aimed at protecting legitimate businesses from money laundering, the defendants did not violate the act. *Id.* at 661. In essence, the court concluded that the defendants were too guilty to be guilty! It took the state legislature only two months to overturn this decision legislatively.

d. Definitions

Codes may have definitions that apply globally. For example, 1 U.S.C. § 1 defines a number of words—including signature, oath, and writing—for all federal statutes. "In determining the meaning of any Act of Congress, [these definitions control] unless the context indicates otherwise." *Id.* States also have global definitional statutes. *See, e.g.,* ALA. CODE § 1-1-1 (2018) ("The following words, whenever they appear in this Code, shall have the signification attached to them in this section unless otherwise apparent from the context ....")

However, most statutory definitions are contained within the relevant act in a separate section of that act, known as the definitions section. The definitions section, if one is included, is the most important section of the beginning sections. As we will see below, if Congress includes a definition of a word or phrase, that definition is controlling, even if it makes no sense.

If an act includes a definition section, then the definitions should precede the purview. Only definitions that are applicable to the act as a whole are included within the definitions section. Definitions that apply only in one particular subsection of the act are usually placed within that specific subsection. Sometimes, legislatures do not follow this rule, so a competent attorney will search the entire act for definitions. The sample bill has a definition section contained within section 3 (see below). Because this bill only has three sections, this definition section likely applies to all of the relevant sections of the bill. But it would have been clearer had Congress placed the definition section in its own separate section. As drafted, section 3 of the bill is unwieldy. In a different, longer act, misplacement might create interpretation issues: Does the definition apply to all sections of the act or just the section in which it is located?

Component: Definitions Section

"SEC. 3111. GRANT AUTHORIZATION....

"(b) DEFINITIONS.—In this section:
    "(1) PROSECUTOR.—The term 'prosecutor' means a full-time employee of a State or local agency who—
    "(A) is continually licensed to practice law; and
    "(B) prosecutes criminal or juvenile delinquency cases (or both) at the State or local level, including an employee who supervises, educates, or trains other persons prosecuting such cases....

For statutory interpretation, definitions are critical and controlling. Often, the interpretation of a statute depends on the words in the statute. If the legislature has defined those words, then that definition controls over all other interpretations, *even if the legislature's definition makes no sense*. And sometimes, a legislature's definitions make no sense. In *Commonwealth v. Plowman*, 86 S.W.3d 47 (Ky. 2002), the court had to decide whether a defendant who set fire to a bulldozer "start[ed] a fire ... with intent to destroy or damage a building." *Id.* at 49 (quoting KY. REV. STAT. ANN § 513.030). While one would normally not understand the word "building" to include bulldozers, in this case, the legislature had specifically defined "building" as follows: "'Building' in addition to its ordinary meaning, specifically includes any ... automobile, truck, watercraft, aircraft, ... or other ... vehicle ...." *Id.* (quoting KY. REV. STAT. ANN. § 513.010). Because of the definition, the issue for the court was whether a bulldozer was a "vehicle." *Id.* at 48. The court decided that the bulldozer was a vehicle, thus, holding that a bulldozer was a building. *Id.* at 50. This odd result occurred entirely because of the definition in the statute at issue.

One famous, but fictional, criminal case showing the importance of definitions is *Regina v. Ojibway*, 8 Crim. L.Q. (Can.) 137 (Sup. Ct. 1965) (Blue, J.). In that case, the defendant was riding his pony in a public park. He was using a pillow filled with down as a saddle. After the pony broke its leg, the defendant shot it. He was then charged with having violated the Small Birds Act, which stated: "Anyone maiming, injuring or killing small birds is guilty of an offence and subject to a fine not in excess of two hundred dollars." The trial court dismissed the charges, finding that the defendant had killed a horse and not a small bird. On appeal, the court disagreed, stating:

> In light of the definition section my course is quite clear. Section 1 defines "bird" as "a two-legged animal covered with feathers." There can be no doubt that this case is covered by this section.... We are not interested in whether the animal in question is a bird or not in fact, but whether it is one in law.... Different things may take on the same meaning for different purposes. For the purpose of the Small Birds Act, all two-legged, feather-covered animals are birds. This, of course, does not imply that only two-legged animals qualify, for the legislative intent is to make two legs merely the minimum requirement. The statute therefore contemplated multi-legged animals with feathers as well.... Therefore, a horse with feathers on its back must be deemed for the purposes of this Act to be a bird, and *a fortiori*, a pony with feathers on its back is a small bird.

Id.

It is important to remember that definitions do not provide rights or remedies. As such, they are not part of the operative section of the act. Only language from an operative or enforcement section, which we will discuss below, can create a right, remedy, or obligation. Think of it this way: If a federal act included only a title, purpose clause, and definitions, the act would provide no rights or duties. The government would not be able to enforce it. Private parties similarly could not sue to enforce it. Operative and enforcement sections provide the rights, duties, and obligations necessary for a law to have legal effect. For this reason, as a lawyer, you should begin with the operative and enforcement sections of the statute to find the language at issue, and then look to see whether Congress provided a definition for the relevant language. Do not start with the definitions, but do not ignore them either.

For an example of a case in which the Court approached the interpretive question backwards, let's look at *Gustafson v. Alloyd Co., Inc.*, 513 U.S. 561 (1995). In that case, the majority ignored the definition of the language at issue in the operative section (§ 12(2)) of the Securities Act of 1933. *Id.* at 571. The language at issue was "prospectus," which Congress had broadly defined to include "any prospectus, notice, circular, advertisement, letter, or *communication*, written or by radio or television, *which offers any security for sale.*" *Id.* at 573 (quoting Securities Act of 1933 § 2(10)) (emphasis added). The document in question was a contract for the secondary sale of securities, which fit comfortably within Congress's very broad definition as a communication offering any security for sale. *Id.* at 564.

Instead of finding the relevant language in the enforcement section of the Act—§ 12(2)—and then turning to the definition of that language in the definitions section—§ 10(2)—to understand the meaning of that language as used in the enforcement section, the majority turned to another operative section of the Act—§ 10. *Id.* at 568. Section 10 was not relevant to the case before the Court. Only after applying the identical words presumption to conclude that "prospectus" must have the same meaning in both the operative (§ 10) and the enforcement (§ 12(2)) sections, did the majority reject the plaintiff's argument that the contract was a communication offering a security for sale pursuant to the definitions section. *Id.* at 571. Both dissents rightly criticized the majority's backwards approach to the interpretive question. *Id.* at 584, 596 (Thomas, J. & Ginsburg, J., dissenting).

Including definitions for every word might seem to be the perfect answer to avoiding ambiguity. If the legislature simply defined every word it used, wouldn't ambiguity disappear? Actually, no. It is not possible, nor even desirable, for the legislature to define every word used in a bill, for a number of reasons.

First, bills would become unwieldy to say the least! Also, defining words can be challenging. Legislatures may not know in advance every circumstance they would want covered. Hence, the ambiguity would simply move from the operative section of the act to the definitions section. Finally, where would drafters draw the line? Should they define common words like "the"? Less common words like "any"? Only very uncommon words? For all these reasons, legislators should only define those words and phrases (1) that have a unique, technical meaning (*e.g.*, "summary judgment"), (2) that they wish to have a meaning broader, narrower, or different from the ordinary or dictionary definition (*e.g.*, "discrimination"), or (3) that have been created to refer to a complex or wordy idea in a simpler way (*e.g.*, "Department" for "Department of Health and Human Services").

2. The Purview

The purview follows the beginning section identified above. The purview includes the substantive provisions. The order of the substantive provisions is generally predictable: principal operative provisions first, exceptions second (or included within the primary provision), and enforcement provisions third. When this expected order is not followed, ambiguity may result. For example, in *Bank One Chicago, N.A. v. Midwest Bank & Trust Co.*, 516 U.S. 264 (1996), the Supreme Court had to determine whether it had jurisdiction under the Expedited Funds Availability Act to hear a case one bank brought against another. *Id.* at 266. The Act was poorly drafted because the section authorizing interbank litigation—an enforcement provision—was placed in the wrong section of the Act. *Id.* at 268. As Justice Stevens noted, "[w]hen Congress creates a cause of action, the provisions describing the new substantive rights and liabilities typically precede the provisions describing enforcement procedures; [this act] does not conform to this pattern." *Id.* at 277 (Stevens, J., concurring).

The substantive provisions are the essence of the bill. Indeed, it is likely that the language that is being interpreted comes from one of these sections. For the most part, there are no unique canons that apply to these sections. Rather, the canons throughout this text help resolve the meaning of text in these subsections. Let's look at the substantive sections in more detail.

a. Operative Provisions

Following the definitions section are the principal operative provisions, which provide the rights, responsibilities, powers, obligations, and privileges being created. Generally, the purpose for enacting a bill is to change conduct.

There are two types of provisions within this category: (1) *substantive provisions*, which provide the general rule, and (2*) exceptions and provisos*, which provide exclusions and exceptions from the statute's general rule. If the law is drafted well, operative provisions with general applicability will precede operative provisions with specific applicability and general rules will precede any exceptions to those rules. In the sample bill, the operative and administrative provisions are combined, so here is an example of an operative section from another act. This is a criminal act, identifying new duties and obligations.

Component: Operative Provision

"SEC. 201. PROHIBITION ON INTERNET SALES OF DATE RAPE DRUGS.
    Section 401 of the Controlled Substances Act (21 U.S.C. 841) is amended by adding at the end the following:
"(g) INTERNET SALES OF DATE RAPE DRUGS.—
    "(1) Whoever knowingly uses the Internet to distribute a date rape drug to any person, knowing or with reasonable cause to believe that—
    "(A) the drug would be used in the commission of criminal sexual conduct; or
    "(B) the person is not an authorized purchaser; shall be fined under this title or imprisoned not more than 20 years, or both." …

Title II—Federal Criminal Law Enhancements Needed to Protect Children from Sexual Attacks and Other Violent Crimes, Pub. L. No. 109–248, §201 (July 27, 2006), 120 Stat. 612.

b. Exceptions & Provisos

Exceptions and *provisos* are provisions or clauses that create an exception or limit the effect of the general rule. They are called exceptions when they begin "except for" and provisos when they begin "provided however" and "provided that." Unlike exceptions, provisos often include special rules related specifically to the situations within the proviso. Savings clauses similarly except matters from a new law's reach but are more commonly located in the closing section.

Because exceptions and provisos exempt something from an act's reach or qualify something within the act, these clauses are generally narrowly interpreted. Narrow interpretation makes sense because the statute provides a general rule while the exception or proviso limits that general rule or provides an exception to it. *See State ex rel. Crow v. St. Louis*, 73 S.W. 623, 629 (1903) ("The proviso should be confined to what immediately precedes, unless a contrary intent clearly appears, and should be construed with the section with which it is connected. This rule is not, however, absolute …."). Thus, any limit or exception should be confined to its express and clear terms. Otherwise, the proviso's exception could swallow the general rule. An example of an exception from the sample bill is below; the exception has been italicized.

Component: Exception

(d) TERMS OF LOAN REPAYMENT.—….
  "(3) LIMITATIONS.—
  "(A) STUDENT LOAN PAYMENT AMOUNT.—Student loan
      repayments made by the Attorney General under this
      section shall be made subject to the availability of
      appropriations, and subject to such terms, limitations,
      or conditions as may be mutually agreed upon by the
      borrower and the Attorney General in an agreement under
      paragraph (1), *except that the amount paid by the Attorney
      General under this section shall not exceed*—
  "(i) $10,000 for any borrower in any calendar year; or
  "(ii) *an aggregate total of $60,000 in the case of any
      borrower.*"

The proviso canon is somewhat similar to *expressio unius* in that both are canons of negative implication. However, application of the proviso canon leads to a result that is opposite to that of the application of *expressio unius*. With *expressio unius*, that which is omitted in the statute is *omitted* in the statute's application; in contrast, with exceptions and provisos, that which is omitted in the exception or proviso is *included* in statute's application. *See, e.g., Gay & Lesbian Law Students Ass'n v. Board of Trustees*, 673 A.2d 484, 494–95 (Conn. 1996).

One famous proviso, the Wilmot Proviso, was introduced by Representative David Wilmot in the House of Representatives in 1846 as a rider to a $2 million appropriations bill, which President Polk had introduced to facilitate negotiations with Mexico over the settlement of the Mexican-American War. The proposed language read:

> Provided, That, as an express and fundamental condition to the acquisition of any territory from the Republic of Mexico by the United States by virtue of any treaty which may be negotiated between them, and to the use by the Executive of the money herein appropriated, neither slavery nor involuntary servitude shall ever exist in any part of said territory except for crime, whereof the party shall first be duly convicted.

Louise Weinberg, *Dred Scott and the Crisis of 1860*, 82 CHI.-KENT L. REV. 97, 99 (2007) (quoting CHAPLAIN W. MORRISON, DEMOCRATIC POLITICS AND SECTIONALISM: THE WILMOT PROVISO CONTROVERSY 18 (1967)). Wilmot's purpose in submitting the proviso was to prevent slavery from being introduced into any territory the United States acquired from Mexico. While the House approved the bill with the proviso included, Congress adjourned before the Senate could vote on it; thus, the bill and its proviso failed. Yet some commentators have suggested that this proviso may have been a cause of the Civil War.

c. Administrative & Enforcement Provisions

The final sections in the purview of an act are administrative and enforcement provisions. Administrative provisions address the creation, organization, powers, and procedures of the governmental organization that will enforce or adjudicate the law, usually an *agency*. The administrative provisions identify how government will implement the law. In these provisions, the legislature will create or identify the governmental organization or organizations that will be responsible for administering and enforcing the law and explain how the government will administer and enforce the law. In the sample bill, the Department of Justice would have been in charge of administering the bill had it passed and would have had the authority to issue regulations (rules) to carry out the law. An excerpt is in the box below.

Component: Administrative Provision

"SEC. 3111. GRANT AUTHORIZATION.

"(c) PROGRAM AUTHORIZED.—The Attorney General shall ... establish a program by which the Department of Justice shall assume the obligation to repay a student loan ...

(d), for any borrower who—

"(1) is employed as a prosecutor or public defender; and
"(2) is not in default on a loan for which the borrower seeks forgiveness.

(g) REGULATIONS.—The Attorney General is authorized to issue such regulations as may be necessary to carry out the provisions of this section." ...

Enforcement provisions are also necessary because the legislature can best affect conduct by prescribing either a punishment for noncompliance or a reward for compliance with an enacted rule. The rule is included within the operative provisions, while the consequence (reward or punishment) is included within the enforcement provisions. The more common enforcement provisions include (1) the potential for criminal, civil, and administrative penalties; and (2) the availability of injunctive relief. Notice that in the enforcement provision excerpted below, the federal government would have had the power to recover funds owed to it by any legal means.

Component: Enforcement Provision

"SEC. 3111. GRANT AUTHORIZATION.

"(d) TERMS OF LOAN REPAYMENT.—
"(1) BORROWER AGREEMENT.—

"(C) if the borrower is required to repay an amount to the Attorney General under subparagraph (B) and fails to repay such amount, a sum equal to that amount shall be recoverable by the Federal Government from the employee (or such employee's estate, if applicable) by such methods as are provided by law for the recovery of amounts owed to the Federal Government.

---

3. The Closing Section

The final provisions in an act are often omitted and even when included generally offer fewer interpretation issues. These provisions include effective date provisions, savings provisions, sunset provisions, and severability and inseverability provisions. Each is addressed below.

a. Effective Date Provisions

Often, a bill expressly provides a starting date, known as the *effective date*. If it does not, a federal statute is effective on the date the president signs the bill or on the date that Congress overrides a veto. Because of this default rule, many federal bills, like the John R. Justice Prosecutor and Defenders Incentive Act, do not include an effective date provision. But if an act is to be effective on a date other than the signing date, Congress must provide that effective date in the bill. Below is an example of effective date provisions from a recent bill Senator Rand Paul introduced called the "Write the Laws Act."

Component: Effective Date Provision

> "**§ 153. Effective date**
> "This chapter shall apply to any Act of Congress, Presidential directive, adjudicative decision, rule, or regulation, change to an existing Presidential directive, adjudicative decision, rule, or regulation, enacted or promulgated on or after the date that is 90 days after the date of enactment of this chapter."

S. 3710, 115th Cong. § 153 (2018).

States take a variety of approaches to this issue. Most commonly, a state's constitution or a statute will provide a default date for any statute not containing an effective date provision. For example, in Alaska, a bill takes effect at 12:01 a.m. on the ninetieth day after the governor signs it, unless the legislature specifies a different date. ALASKA CONST. art. II, § 18; ALASKA STAT. ANN. § 01.10.070. The Texas Constitution states that a bill becomes effective 91 days from the date of the legislature's final adjournment. TEXAS CONST. art. III, § 39.

Generally, effective date provisions raise few interpretation issues. *But see Fowler v. State*, 70 P.3d 1106, 1109 (Alaska 2003) (holding that an act with a provision identifying the effective date as one that preceded the governor's signature was effective the day after the governor actually signed the bill, even though that day was a state holiday); *Sims v. Adoption Alliance*, 922 S.W.2d 213, 215 (Tx. Ct. App. 1996) (applying a new waiting time period to a pending adoption because the effective date provision was clear that the law "applies to a pending suit ... without regard to whether the suit was commenced").

b. Saving & Grandfather Provisions

Related to effective date provisions are *saving provisions*. When a new law would affect existing rights, obligations, and procedures that the legislature does not intend to affect, the legislature may include a saving, or Grandfather clause, to limit the application of the new law. Such clauses except something specific from the application of the new rule. In other words, they allow the old rule to continue to apply to some existing situations while the new rule will apply to all future situations. *See, e.g.*, U.C.C. §4-10-101 ("(1) This title shall take effect at 12:01 a.m. on July 1, 1966. The provisions of this title apply to transactions entered into and events occurring after such date. (2) Transactions validly entered into prior to the effective date of this title and the rights, duties, and interests flowing from them remain valid thereafter and may be terminated, completed, consummated, or enforced as required or permitted by any statute or other law amended or repealed by the enactment of this title as though such repeal or amendment had not occurred."). Because saving clauses are similar to exceptions in that they limit a law's application, they too should be construed narrowly. *State ex rel. Crow v. St. Louis*, 73 S.W. 623, 629 (Mo. 1903).

Saving clauses are most commonly used to restrict the breadth of a repealing act to maintain existing rights, pending proceedings, and penalties. *Id.* They are common in zoning ordinances, for example, when a city changes the zoning of a particular section of town to residential but grandfathers in existing businesses. Such businesses may continue to operate even though no new businesses may start up. Another example of grandfathering occurred in the 1980s, when states increased the legal drinking age from 18 to 21; those individuals who had already turned 18 and could drink legally when the new laws passed were grandfathered in so they could continue to drink legally despite being under age 21.

Our sample bill does not have a saving provision. Another example has been provided in the box on the following page.

Component: Saving Provision

SECTION 9. SAVING PROVISION

(a) The change in law made by this Act applies only to an offense committed on or after the effective date of this Act. For purposes of this section, an offense is committed before the effective date of this Act if any element of the offense occurs before that date.

(b) An offense committed before the effective date of this Act is covered by the law in effect when the offense was committed, and the former law is continued in effect for that purpose.

---

c. Sunset Provisions

A sunset provision provides that an act or some of its provisions shall no longer have effect after a specific date, unless further legislative action is taken to extend the act. *Acree v. Republic of Iraq*, 370 F.3d 41, 61–62 (D.C. Cir. 2004) (Roberts, J., concurring) ("'[s]unsetting laws does not mean repealing them. Laws would only expire if Congress failed to meet its responsibility to reexamine and renew these statutes within a specified period of time.'") (quoting S. Rep. No. 104-85, at 64 (1995)). Most laws do not have sunset provisions; in such cases, the law goes on indefinitely. The John R. Justice Prosecutor and Defenders Incentive Act does not have a sunset provision.

Idaho has an unusual sunset statute that requires the legislature or governor to reauthorize all agency regulations annually. Idaho Code Ann. §67-5292(1) (West 2017) ("Notwithstanding any other provision of this chapter to the contrary, every rule adopted and becoming effective after June 30, 1990, shall automatically expire on July 1 of the following year unless the rule is extended by statute."). In 2019, the state's legislature adjourned without passing a renewal statute, allowing the governor to pick which rules to keep and which to jettison.

At the federal level, tax statutes often have sunset provisions. *See, e.g.,* Economic Growth and Tax Relief Reconciliation Act of 2001 (Pub. L. 107–16, 115 Stat. 38, June 7, 2001); *cf.* Violent Crime Control and Law Enforcement Act of 1994 (Pub. L. 103-322, 108 Stat. 1796, September 13, 1994). One famous act that includes a sunset provision is the U.S. Patriot Act. Under the sunset provision, many of the surveillance and criminal sections were set to expire in December of 2005. Congress has temporarily extended these sections repeatedly (see the slip law above). Here's the original provision:

Component: Sunset Provision

SEC. 224. SUNSET.

(a) IN GENERAL.— Except as provided in subsection (b), this title and the amendments made by this title (other than sections 203(a), 203(c), 205, 208, 210, 211, 213, 216, 219, 221, and 222, and the amendments made by those sections) shall cease to have effect on December 31, 2005.

(b) EXCEPTION.— With respect to any particular foreign intelligence investigation that began before the date on which the provisions referred to in subsection (a) cease to have effect, or with respect to any particular offense or potential offense that began or occurred before the date on which such provisions cease to have effect, such provisions shall continue in effect.

U.S. Patriot Act, Pub. L. 107-56, § 224, 115 Stat. 272 (2001).

d. Severability & Inseverability Provisions

Sometimes courts find a section of an act to be unconstitutional. Does that mean the entire act is invalid or only that section of the act? If the unconstitutional section of an act is "severable" from the rest of the act, then only that section is invalid. But if the unconstitutional section cannot be severed, meaning it is "inseverable," then the entire act is invalid.

Legislatures may include provisions to address issues relating to the severability of various sections of an act. Severability and inseverability (also known as non-severability) provisions address the validity of the act should any section of it be found invalid. Severability provisions are a type of saving clause because they save parts of an act when any part is found to be invalid. Severability provisions allow for the remaining sections of the act to remain valid, while inseverability provisions require that the act as a whole be held invalid if any one section is invalid.

Inseverability provisions come in two types: "general" and "specific." *General inseverability provisions* provide that *none* of the provisions of an act are severable; in contrast, *specific inseverability provisions* provide that *specific* provisions of an act are not severable from one another.

Early acts had neither severability nor inseverability provisions; however, in response to judicial interpretations of acts not having these provisions, severability clauses began to appear in bills in the early 1900s. Inseverability provisions are a more modern, less utilized creature.

If a severability or inseverability provision is included in an act, it generally is placed at the end of the act. The John R. Justice Prosecutor and Defenders Incentive Act contains neither a severability nor an inseverability provision. Instead, two sample provisions are provided in the box below.

Component: Severability & Inseverability Clauses

SEC. 10A. SEVERABILITY.

If any provision of this Act or its application to any person or circumstance is held invalid, the invalidity does not affect other provisions or applications of this act that can be given effect without the invalid provision or application, and to this end the provisions of this Act are declared to be severable.

SEC. 10B. INSEVERABILITY.

Section 1 of this Act, prohibiting the sale of alcohol without a license, and Section 2 of this Act, imposing a tax on the sale of alcohol, are not severable, and neither section would have been enacted without the other. If either provision is held invalid, both provisions are invalid.

---

i. Severability Provisions

Severability provisions raise many issues including constitutional, relevance, and effectiveness issues. Constitutional issues arise when a court strikes one part of an act, but not another. By altering the law as written, some argue that the court has effectively rewritten the act in violation of the Constitution. Under the Constitution, it is the legislature's job to write laws. By striking some sections of the act and not others, the court has effectively redrafted the law. Would the legislature have wanted the act to become law as redrafted? Possibly not. Thus, separation of powers concerns arise when the judiciary alters the law as written. Even though the text of these clauses is clear, effectiveness and relevance issues arise because the ordinary meaning often does not control.

The *doctrine of severability* is simple: statutes are presumed to be severable. The Supreme Court has said repeatedly that severability provisions are merely presumptions about what the legislature intended. In other words, it matters little whether or not Congress includes a severability clause. When Congress includes a clause indicating that sections in the act are severable, this severability clause provides a rebuttable presumption that provisions in the act are severable; however, that presumption can be overcome "by strong evidence that Congress intended otherwise." *Alaska Airlines, Inc. v. Brock,* 480 U.S. 678, 686 (1987). For example, in *Alaska Airlines,* the act at issue—The Airline Deregulation Act of 1978—did not contain a severability provision, although the Act it amended did have one. *Id.* at 683.The Supreme Court did not care, noting that the test for whether a section of an act is severable is the same regardless of whether the act includes a severability provision. *Id.* at 684–85. The Court described the test as follows: "the unconstitutional provision must be severed unless the statute created in its absence is legislation that Congress would not have enacted." *Id.* at 685. Severability is presumed, although a provision makes such a finding easier. *Id.* at 686.

That presumption of severability is overcome in two situations. First, the presumption fails if the statute, without its unconstitutional provisions, cannot function. Illustrative of this situation is *Warren v. Mayor & Aldermen of Charlestown,* 68 Mass. (2 Gray) 84 (1854). In that case, the Massachusetts Supreme Court held that a state statute that would have annexed Charlestown to Boston violated the U.S. Constitution because the statute would deny the citizens of Charlestown effective federal representation. *Id.* at 99. The court then invalidated the statute as a whole, concluding that "various provisions of the act ... are so connected with each other" that the legislature could not have intended the remaining, constitutional statutory remnants to remain in force. *Id.* at 100.

Second, the severability presumption is overcome when the legislature "intended otherwise," meaning that the legislature would have preferred no legislation at all to the enacted legislation without its unconstitutional provisions.

Thus, a legislature's inclusion of a severability clause does not resolve the question. Rather, a severability clause merely preserves the general severability presumption just outlined. Why? Commonly and much like boilerplate language in contracts, legislatures include severability provisions with little thought about their true impact, partly because their true impact can be unknowable. Rather than carefully consider whether some provisions in a bill should survive if others do not, legislatures, without thought, simply include a severability clause directing that all provisions remain valid regardless of what the act might actually look like after litigation has excised some provisions. Thus, the doctrine that severability provisions are rebuttable presumptions makes sense; if the legislature does not think about what it is doing, then courts should not rubber-stamp the decision to include such a provision.

In situations where there is evidence that Congress actually thought about this issue and wanted the legislation to be severable or inseverable that intent should control. For example, the Bipartisan Campaign Finance Reform Act (the "McCain-Feingold Act") resulted from a legislative bargain: members of Congress agreed that in exchange for a ban on soft-money contributions, then-existing hard-money contribution limits would be increased. Without this compromise, the Act would have failed. But the compromise raised a potential conflict: If a court found the soft-money ban to be unconstitutional, should the increase in allowable hard-money contributions remain in effect?

To anticipate this issue, Congress specifically included a severability provision. Bipartisan Campaign Reform Act of 2002, Pub. L. No. 107–155, § 401, 116 Stat. 112 (2002). But it did not do so without considering the issue thoroughly. After two Republican senators attempted to include an *inseverability* provision, the bill's sponsors and the Democratic leadership effectively inserted a severability provision. Michael D. Shumsky, *Severability, Inseverability, and the Rule of Law*, 41 Harv. J. on Legis. 227, 229–30 (2004). The debate over whether to include the provision was long and arduous. Given that Congress actually considered and fought over the severability provision in the McCain-Feingold Act, that unambiguously expressed intent of Congress should control that question if it is ever litigated. Parenthetically, in *Citizens United v. FEC*, 558 U.S. 310, 365 (2010), the Supreme Court held that the First Amendment of the Federal Constitution prohibits the government from restricting independent political expenditures by corporations and unions.

Regardless of their validity, severability provisions are actually unnecessary because courts uniformly construe statutes as severable regardless of whether there is a severability provision in them. Indeed, some states even provide as much by statute. For example, Texas has a statute that says all statutes are severable unless the statute specifically indicates that it is not. Tex. Gov't Code Ann. §§ 311.032 & 312.013. Thus, if the Texas legislature wishes for an entire act or specific sections of an act to be held invalid, the legislature must so provide.

Virginia's history with severability provisions is interesting. In that state, the legislature changed the presumption in 1986 by statute. Before 1986, courts presumed that statutes were not severable. In 1986, the legislature changed that presumption. Currently, the law provides that provisions in that state's statutes are severable unless either (1) the statute specifically provides that its provisions are not severable, or (2) it is apparent that two or more statutes or provisions must operate in accord with one another. Va. Code. Ann § 1-243 (2005) (formerly cited as Va. Code. Ann § 1-17.1 (1986)). As a result, all statutes, not just those enacted after 1986, without severability provisions are presumed to be severable in Virginia. *Elliott v. Commonwealth*, 593 S.E.2d 263, 267 (Va. 2004). You should identify the presumption in your own state.

ii. Inseverability Provisions

In contrast to the commonness and, thus, thoughtlessness of including severability provisions, inseverability (or non-severability) provisions are included much less frequently. Arguably, these provisions demonstrate more clearly a legislature's intent. "A non-severability [provision] is almost unheard of and constitutes a legislative finding that every section [of an act] is so important to the single subject that no part of the act can be removed without destruction of the legislative purpose." *Farrior v. Sodexho, U.S.A.*, 953 F. Supp. 1301, 1302 (N.D. Ala. 1997).

Inseverability clauses are different from severability clauses for another reason as well. If an inseverability clause is included in a bill, its very presence likely represents proof that the bill was a compromise of competing interests:

> When Congress includes an inseverability clause in constitutionally questionable legislation, it does so in order to insulate a key legislative deal from judicial interference. Such clauses are iron-clad guarantees — clear statements by Congress that it would not have enacted one part of a statute without the others. Legislation containing an inseverability clause can thus be conceived of as a contract among competing political interests containing a structural enforcement mechanism designed to alleviate the concerns of those legislators who were willing to vote for ... a particular statutory scheme *only* if credibly assured that certain limiting provisions would be secure in the enacted legislation.

Shumsky, *Severability, Inseverability, and the Rule of Law, supra* at 267–68.

Congress rarely uses inseverability provisions; thus, the Supreme Court has not yet addressed their validity. *Id.* at 243–44. Because there is no guidance from the Supreme Court, lower courts have tended to treat inseverability clauses in the same way that the Court treated severability clauses; "a non-severability clause cannot ultimately bind a court, it establishes [only] a presumption of non-severability." *Biszko v. RIHT Financial Corp.*, 758 F.2d 769, 773 (1st Cir. 1985). Thus, again, "[d]espite the unambiguous command of ... inseverability clauses ... they create only a rebuttable presumption that guides — but does not control — a reviewing court's severability determination." Shumsky, *Severability, Inseverability, and the Rule of Law, supra* at 230. So, for example, in *Louk v. Cormier*, 622 S.E.2d 788 (W. Va. 2005), the relevant act included both a severability and a non-severability provision because the state legislature intended that some sections be severable, and others not. *Id.* at 802. The non-severability provision was the one at issue in the case. *Id.* Stunningly, the majority looked at the severability and non-severability provisions, rejected their clear language, rejected evidence in the legislative history that the provisions were included in the act as legislative compromises, and decided on a case by case basis whether each provision in the act was severable. *Id.* at 803–04. The majority and dissents disagreed about which branch should decide whether unconstitutional provisions in a statute are severable: the legislature or the judiciary. *See also Stiens v. Fire & Police Pension Ass'n*, 684 P.2d 180, 184 (Colo. 1984) (holding that the legislature intended the benefit provisions of a pension act to be severable from the act's unconstitutional funding provisions despite the inseverability provision).

This chapter on components is our last on intrinsic sources. It might have surprised you that components, for the most part, are less relevant to interpretation than are the linguistic canons and other intrinsic sources; however, England's influence in this area continues to have an impact. Next, we turn to the first of our extrinsic sources, those sources related to timing.

D. Mastering This Topic

Return to the hypothetical ordinance provided in Chapter 1. Remember our question: "An ambulance entered Pioneer Park to pick up and take to the hospital a man who has just suffered a heart attack. Did the ambulance driver violate the Pioneer Park Safety Ordinance (PPSO)?" Assuming first that you have concluded that the statute is ambiguous or absurd, how might the components of the ordinance help you resolve the ambiguity or absurdity?

First, let's look at the beginning section components, specifically the titles. The long title of the ordinance is "To Prohibit Motor Vehicles in Pioneer Park." This long title offers no interpretive help. In contrast, the short title of the ordinance is located in section 1: "the Pioneer Park Safety Ordinance." This short title suggests that the purpose of the ordinance is to protect the safety of those using the park. Because allowing an occasional ambulance into the park to assist those needing medical care would not jeopardize the safety of the individuals using the park and, indeed, might increase their safety because they would get access to medical care more quickly if injured, the short title suggests that ambulances should not be included within the ordinance's ban.

Let's turn to findings, purpose, or policy clauses. There are none in this ordinance, so these clauses can offer no interpretive guidance. Consider, however, how it might have helped your interpretation had the council included the legislative facts that led to the ordinance's enactment. The legislative history noted, "The ordinance will address the recent concerns created by a spat of accidents in Pioneer Park. In two of these accidents, a car struck a pedestrian and another struck a bicyclist on park roads. In the third, a motorcyclist drove off road and hit a pedestrian." Had these legislative findings been included in the ordinance, you might conclude that the purpose of the ordinance is to further safety and exclude the ambulance from the ordinance's reach. Note that a strict textualist would need to have the findings included within the ordinance itself, not the legislative history, and that all textualists would first need to find the language ambiguous or absurd to consider the findings, while the other theorists would not.

Finally, you should consider whether there are any definitions. Unfortunately, there are no definitions, though it would have been helpful had the council defined "motor vehicle."

Next, let's turn to the purview and consider whether any of these components aid interpretation. You already know the general rule from the operative section: "No cars, motorcycles, or other motor vehicles may enter or remain in Pioneer Park …." You found the relevant language in this operative section. Notably, there are two provisos; one in section 2—"except as provided in section 3 hereof" and one in section 4, the enforcement provision,—"provided no injuries occurred." Further, there is an exception in section 3 for vehicles used by authorized groups to maintain the park and set up barricades. You may want to argue that ambulances help maintain the park, but you must remember that provisos and exceptions are narrowly construed. Thus, if this exception is narrowly interpreted, ambulances should be prohibited from driving within the park. Yet the enforcement proviso suggests again that the purpose of the ordinance is to further safety; no one was injured when the ambulance drove in the park; indeed, someone's safety was enhanced.

Finally, note that the ordinance does not contain the following provisions: saving clause, sunset clause, or severability or inseverability provisions. It does have an effective date provision. Regardless, none of these provisions would likely assist in interpretation.

Checkpoints

- Federal slip laws are published chronologically in the *Statutes at Large* and include the entire act, not just the components that are codified.

- Acts are rearranged and published in a topical code. Codification is the process of inserting sections of the act into a code.

- Acts have a variety of components; some components are required while others are optional. Some components are relevant to meaning, others are not.

- In the beginning section, the heading comes first. It identifies the sponsor of the bill, the bill number, and the activity taken on the bill.

- All bills have long titles, which precede the enacting clause and, thus, are not codified. Some bills also have short titles, which follow the enacting clause and may be codified. Most bills also have section titles, which are usually codified. The canon for all three is the same: titles cannot control clear text.

- Similarly, preambles, findings, and purpose clauses cannot control clear text.

- When the legislature defines a word or phrase in an act that definition controls.

- Following the beginning section is the purview. Interpretative issues arise in the purview, which includes operative provisions, exceptions and provisos, administrative provisions, and enforcement provisions.

- Exceptions and provisos, which are provisions that exclude something from a statute's reach or qualify something within a statute, are narrowly construed.

- The closing section follows the purview and may include several provisions generally not relevant to interpretation, such as effective date provisions, saving clauses, sunset clauses, and severability/inseverability provisions.

- Severability provisions allow for the remaining sections of an act to remain valid, while inseverability provisions require that an act as a whole be held invalid if any one section is unconstitutional.

- Because acts are presumed severable, courts construe sections of an act as severable, even when the legislature includes an inseverability provision.

Chapter 9

Canons Based on Extrinsic Sources: Timing & the Legislative Process

---

Roadmap

- Learn how courts resolve issues involving statutes that conflict: specific statutes trump general statutes and later enacted statutes trump earlier enacted statutes.

- Learn what repeal by implication is and that it is disfavored.

- Understand when statutes can have retroactive effect and what that means.

- Discover that legislatures often borrow statutory language from other states and jurisdictions or use model or uniform acts.

A. Introduction to This Chapter

In this chapter, we turn from the intrinsic sources to the first of the extrinsic sources: conflicting statutes, implied repeals, retroactivity, and borrowed statutes. We cover these extrinsic sources first because their use is less controversial than those sources in the next chapter, which relate to legislative history. This chapter covers topics related to the timing of the legislative process. The canons based on the timing of the legislative process are presumptions based on how a legislature normally or ideally operates. The canons presume that the legislature intended to act "normally," unless there is evidence that it intended to act otherwise. For example, if two statutes both address an issue, the statute that was enacted last controls unless there is evidence that Congress would have wanted the earlier statute to control. Similarly, if one state copies another state's statute, the copying, or borrowing, state also presumptively borrows the judicial interpretations of that statute from the lending state *up to the date of enactment.* But again, if the borrowing legislature is clear that it did not intend to adopt the judicial interpretations of the other state, then the judicial interpretations do not accompany the borrowed statute. The topics covered in this chapter share one concept: timing. Let's start with conflicting statutes. What happens when multiple statutes address the same issue?

B. Extrinsic Sources

Before we begin this discussion, a brief reminder might be in order; extrinsic sources are those sources outside of the official act, but within the legislative process that created the act. In other words, these are sources intimately related to the enactment process, such as legislative history, purpose, administrative regulations, and the like; but they are separate from the text.

C. Conflicting Statutes

Sometimes, two sections of one statute or, more commonly, two different statutes conflict. For example, assume that statute A provides that all criminal defendants are entitled to parole, while statute B provides that only non-violent criminal defendants are entitled to parole. These hypothetical statutes conflict. When a judge is faced with two conflicting statutes or sections of an act, the judge will first see if the conflict between the two can be reconciled, because the judge will assume that the legislature, when it passed the second act, did not intend to interfere with or abrogate any existing laws relating to the same topic. This policy of reconciling first is based on the assumptions that the legislature (1) was aware of all relevant statutes when it enacted the new one, (2) would have expressly repealed or amended an existing statute had it wanted the new statute to replace the existing one, and (3) failed to repeal the existing statute because the legislature intended for both statutes to exist in harmony. These assumptions fail to reflect reality: a legislature cannot possibly know every law that exists when it enacts legislation. And even if the legislature was aware of a conflicting, existing statute, the conflict between the existing statute and the new statute may not have been apparent when the second statute was enacted. At times, conflicts only appear after a statute has been applied to a particular set of facts. Finally, as we have seen, it is difficult to pass legislation. There are many reasons why the legislature might have chosen not to amend or repeal a conflicting, existing statute. Yet despite the reality, the assumptions remain.

When conflict cannot be reconciled, judges apply three canons to reconcile the conflict: (1) specific statutory language controls general statutory language, (2) later enacted statutes control earlier enacted statutes unless the earlier statute is more specific, and (3) repeal by implication is disfavored. Stated simply,

> [i]f statutes appear to conflict, they must be construed, if possible, to give effect to each. If the conflict is irreconcilable, the later enacted statute governs. However, an earlier enacted specific, special, or local statute prevails over a later enacted general statute unless the context of the later enacted statute indicates otherwise.

Unif. Statute & Rule Constr. Act, § 10a (1995). Let's explore each of these canons in more detail, starting with specific and general statutes. If two statutes so conflict that, despite a judge's best attempts to reconcile them, they are irreconcilable, what should a judge do? How does a judge know which statute was meant to be repealed, wholly or partially, and which was meant to apply? These next sections resolve these questions.

1. Specific Statutes Trump General Statutes

The first canon seems simple: a specific statute governs a general statute. This canon has special force when Congress has enacted a comprehensive statutory scheme, deliberately targeting specific problems with specific solutions. The general-specific canon is often applied to statutes in which a specific prohibition or permission contradicts a general permission or prohibition. To eliminate the contradiction, the specific provision is construed as an exception to the general one, because "the presumption is that the legislature intended the specific provision to be an exception to the general [provision]." RONALD B. BROWN & SHARON J. BROWN, STATUTORY INTERPRETATION: THE SEARCH FOR LEGISLATIVE INTENT 90–91 (2002). But the canon applies equally as well to statutes in which a general authorization and a more limited, specific authorization can exist side-by-side. "There the canon avoids not contradiction but the superfluity of a specific provision that is swallowed by the general one, 'violat[ing] the cardinal rule that, if possible, effect shall be given to every clause and part of a statute.'" *RadLAX Gateway Hotel, LLC v. Amalgamated Bank*, 132 S. Ct. 2065, 2070–71 (2012). The general-specific canon is not absolute; however, it is merely a strong indication of statutory meaning that textual indications pointing in the other direction can overcome.

When two statutes conflict, courts ask first whether one of the two statutes is more specific than the other. What is the difference between a general and specific statute? General statutes apply universally, while specific statutes apply only in certain situations. Thus, a statute regulating domesticated animals would be general, while one regulating swine would be specific. But determining whether a statute is general or specific can be more difficult than it might seem. The case of *Williams v. Commonwealth*, 829 S.W.2d 942 (Ky. Ct. App. 1992), illustrates how judges struggle with this determination. In that case, a state statute directed the trial judge to consider whether a criminal defendant was entitled to community service as an alternative to prison *in every case. Id.* at 944 (citing KY. REV. STAT. ANN. § 500.095) (the "community service statute"). This statute was mandatory in that it required a judge to consider community service for every criminal case. A second statute prohibited defendants who used a gun from being eligible for "probation ... or conditional discharge" at all. *Id.* (citing KY. REV. STAT. ANN. § 533.060(1)) (the "gun statute"). This statute was also mandatory, for it prevented a judge from considering probation for any defendant who used a gun during the commission of a crime. The two statutes conflicted; it was unclear whether the judge should have considered community service for a defendant who used a gun in the commission of a crime. To resolve the conflict, the court tried to determine whether one statute was more specific than the other statute.

The court concluded that both statutes were specific; thus, the general-specific canon was inapposite. *Id.* at 945. This conclusion seems wrong. The community service statute is more general; it applies to all criminal defendants. The gun statute is more specific; it applies only to defendants who used a gun. The court could simply have determined that the gun statute, being the more specific statute, applied to the defendant's situation; thus, no parole. To resolve the conflict, however, the court turned to a second canon: the last-in-time (or later enacted) canon, which we will study in more detail in a moment.

In another case, the Florida Supreme Court addressed the same question— when is a statute specific and when is it general? *Palm Beach Cnty. Canvassing Bd. v. Harris*, 772 So. 2d 1220 (Fla. 2000). This case was one of the many cases that addressed the 2000 election battle between then presidential contenders, Republican George W. Bush and Democrat Vice-President Albert Gore, Jr. The election in Florida was extremely close. An automatic recount was triggered and was conducted. *Id.* at 1226 (citing FLA. STAT. ANN. § 102.141(4) (2000)). After the recount, the vote was still extremely close, so the Florida Democratic Executive Committee requested that sample manual recounts of a percentage of the vote be conducted in certain counties. The manual recounts narrowed

George Bush's lead. *Id.* Based on these recounts, several of the county canvassing boards determined that the sample manual recounts showed potential error, which could affect the outcome of the election. *Id.* Based on this determination, several canvassing boards voted to conduct countywide manual recounts pursuant to Florida's election law. *Id.* (citing FLA. STAT. ANN. § 102.166(5)(c) (2000)).

The problem was that Florida law required that all county returns be certified by 5 p.m. on the seventh day after an election; the recounts simply could not be done within that time frame. So, one canvassing board sought an advisory opinion from the Division of Elections as to whether this deadline applied. *Id.* The Division of Elections concluded that the deadline was firm. *Id.* Relying upon this advisory opinion, the Florida Secretary of State, Republican Katherine Harris (the "Secretary"), said that she would ignore returns from the manual recounts received after the deadline. The canvassing boards sued seeking a declaratory judgment and injunctive relief that the Secretary should count all late returns.

The trial court held that the deadline was mandatory, but that the Secretary could consider, in her discretion, amended returns that came in after the deadline. *Id.* at 1227. The amended returns were filed. But the Secretary, exercising her discretion, refused to consider them. *Id.* As a result of her refusal to consider the returns, the Florida Democratic Party and Al Gore, in a separate action, filed a motion seeking to compel the Secretary to accept the amended returns. *Id.* The trial court denied that motion. Both cases were consolidated for appeal to Florida's Supreme Court.

There were many issues before the court. The relevant one here was whether the Secretary was required to consider the returns when the returns were received after the seven-day deadline set forth in sections 102.111 and 102.112 of Florida's election law. *Id.* at 1228. Florida law provided that "any candidate whose name appeared on the ballot ... or any political party whose candidates' names appeared on the ballot may file a written request with the county canvassing board for a manual recount" accompanied by the "reason that the manual recount is being requested." *Id.* at 1231–31 (quoting FLA. STAT. ANN. § 102.166(4)(a) & (b)). This statute further provided that the written request had to be made prior to the time the Canvassing Board certified the returns or within seventy-two hours after the election, whichever occurred later. *Id.* The recount would likely take some time, but the statute did not identify a time frame within which the recount had to be completed. Thus, the recount provision conflicted with Florida law sections 102.111 and 102.112, which required the boards to submit returns to the Elections Canvassing Commission by 5:00 p.m. on the seventh day following the election or face a penalty. *Id.* at 1233. What penalty had to be imposed was unclear because 102.111 and 102.112 conflicted: 102.111 *required* the Division of Elections to ignore late returns, while 102.112 *allowed* the Division of Elections to ignore late returns but required it to impose a fine. *Id.* at 1234. In other words, 102.111 was mandatory, while 102.112 was permissive regarding whether the Division of Elections could ignore the late returns.

To resolve the conflict, the court turned first to the general-specific canon. *Id.* at 1234. Finding that 102.111 (the mandatory statute) was the more general statute, the court held that 102.112 (the permissive statute) controlled the issue of whether the returns could be considered when filed after the deadline because it was more specific:

> First, it is well-settled that where two statutory provisions are in conflict, the specific statute controls the general statute. In the present case, whereas section 102.111 in its title and text addresses the general makeup and duties of the Elections Canvassing Commission, the statute only tangentially addresses the penalty for returns filed after the statutory date, noting that such returns "shall" be ignored by the Department. Section 102.112, on the other hand, directly addresses in its title and text both the "deadline" for submitting returns and the "penalties" for submitting returns after a certain date; the statute expressly states that such returns "may" be ignored and that dilatory Board members "shall" be fined. Based on the precision of the title and text, section 102.112 constitutes a specific penalty statute that defines both the deadline for filing returns and the penalties for filing returns thereafter and section 102.111 constitutes a non-specific statute in this regard. The specific statute controls the non-specific statute.

Id. at 1234. Because the permissive statute was specific, the court held that it controlled in this conflict. Ultimately, the United States Supreme Court stopped the recount altogether. *Bush v. Gore*, 531 U.S. 98 (2000) (holding that the Florida Supreme Court's method for recounting ballots was unconstitutional and that no alternative method could be established within the time limits established by the statute). Had the Supreme Court not stepped in, then the specific-general canon may have decided the 2000 election!

Thus, when two statutes conflict and cannot be reconciled, the starting point for the court should be to determine whether one of the two statutes is more specific. While determining whether one statute is more specific can be challenging, generally, where one statute has a broader application, it is the more general statute. When the general-specific inquiry fails, however, courts apply a second canon: the last-in-time, or later enacted, canon.

2. Later Enacted Statutes Trump Earlier Enacted Statutes

If both statutes are specific or general, then judges apply a different tie-breaking canon: the newer statute (or provision) generally trumps the older one (the last-in-time canon). The more recently enacted statute is viewed as the clearest and most recent expression of legislative intent. This last-in-time canon respects the power of each legislature: legislatures have the power to enact laws only while in office. One legislature cannot bind the ability of a future legislature to enact statutes; thus, subsequent legislatures can always amend, repeal, modify, or leave alone a statute. Hence, the later enacted statute controls to the extent of any inconsistency between it and an existing statute, unless the legislature intended otherwise. Often these two canons—specific versus general and last-in-time—are examined serially in judicial opinions.

For example, in the first case in the last section, *Williams v. Commonwealth*, 829 S.W.2d 942 (Ky. Ct. App. 1992), the court had to reconcile two, apparently inconsistent (and specific) statutes. One statute, the "community service statute," directed the trial judge to consider whether a criminal defendant was entitled to community service as an alternative to prison *in every case. Id.* at 944 (citing Ky Rev. Stat. Ann. § 500.095). A second statute, the "gun statute," prohibited judges from considering "probation ... or conditional discharge" for defendants who used a gun during the commission of their crime. *Id.* (citing Ky Rev. Stat. Ann. § 533.060(1)).

Remember that the majority concluded that both statutes were specific. *Id.* at 945. Prior to reaching that result, however, the majority first considered whether the community service statute should trump the gun statute because the community service statute was enacted later. Concluding that if the community service statute were controlling it would "make a nullity of the [gun statute]," the court rejected the result the last-in-time canon suggested. *Id.* at 945. In contrast, the dissent concluded that, because the mandatory statute was enacted later than the gun statute, the mandatory statute should have controlled. *Id.* at 947 (Huddleston, J., concurring in part and dissenting in part).

Ultimately, in *Williams*, none of the timing canons helped the majority resolve the issue. First, the majority could not reconcile the statutes, second, the majority rejected the last-in-time canon, and third, the majority rejected the general versus specific canon. The majority had to turn to the linguistic canon *in pari materia* to resolve the issue; the court looked at other, related statutes that the parties did "not otherwise present[] or argue[] in [the] appeal." *Id.* at 945. Looking at the comprehensive scheme presented by all the statutes, the majority concluded that the gun statute applied; thus, the court held that the trial court correctly refused to consider community service. *Id.* at 946.

Notably, the majority applied these two canons in the wrong order. A court should look first to whether one statute is more specific than the other, and only when that canon fails should the court turn to the last-in-time canon. This order better allows courts to give effect to both statutes, rather than find that one trumps the other.

The majority in *Williams* did not approach the canons in the correct order. But in *Palm Beach County Canvassing Board*, the court approached this inquiry properly. In that case, the court addressed the timing of the statutes only after addressing their specificity. According to the court, "the provision in section 102.111 stating that the Department 'shall' ignore returns was enacted in 1951 .... On the other hand, the penalty provision in section 102.112 stating that the Department 'may' ignore returns was enacted in 1989 .... The more recently enacted provision may be viewed as the clearest and most recent expression of legislative intent." *Palm Beach Cnty. Canvassing Bd.*, 772 So. 2d at 1234.

Sometimes, neither of these two canons resolves the conflict. Then the issue is whether one statute or provision impliedly repealed the other.

3. Repeal by Implication Is Disfavored

New statutes should be interpreted harmoniously with existing statutes whenever possible. But sometimes, harmony is simply not possible. When two statutes cannot be reconciled, one way to address the conflict is to conclude that the later statute repealed the earlier statute either explicitly or implicitly. Judges presume that a legislature would not go through the legislative process without intending to change existing law in some way. Thus, every new act should change the status quo, by adding to, modifying, or repealing existing law. But while modification is to be expected, outright repeal is not. Normally, when a legislature wants to repeal a statute or a section of a statute, it does so expressly. Thus, in the absence of an express repeal, it is likely the legislature did not intend any repeal at all. When a legislature intends to repeal a statute, it should say so clearly; repeals should not be implied. Thus, courts apply a canon of negative presumption: repeals—full or partial—by implication are disfavored. This canon rests on the potentially flawed presumption that the legislature was aware of the conflict with the existing statute and specifically opted not to repeal it. Hence, this presumption yields when there is evidence that the legislature intended for the second statute to repeal the first. For example, if the new statute comprehensively covers the entire subject matter of the existing statute and is complete in itself, then the legislature likely intended the new statute to supersede any existing statutes on the subject. Also, if the new statute is completely incompatible with an existing statute, repeal may be appropriate.

In statutory interpretation cases, this issue arises when a judge finds (1) a statute conflicts with an existing statute, (2) the conflict is irreconcilable, and (3) the legislature did not explain how the conflict should be resolved. If there are two reasonable interpretations, the judge should choose the interpretation that does not repeal the existing statute or any part of it. If there is irreconcilability, then the second statute is only repealed to the extent of the irreconcilability; if any part of the earlier statute can exist in harmony with the later statute, that part of the earlier statute is not repealed.

Sometimes, Congress repeals an existing statute with a later statute and then later repeals the later statute. In the past, courts had held that when this happened, the earlier statute was revived, or became effective, again. But Congress and many state legislatures have abolished this old common law canon. 1 U.S.C. § 108. Hence, today, an express or implied repeal of one statute does not revive an earlier statute. The original statute remains repealed.

Also, just because a statute is no longer necessary does not mean it is automatically repealed. For example, state sodomy laws were not repealed as society's mores changed. Rather, state legislatures would have to repeal any existing statutes. For this reason, sodomy laws remain on the books in many states, although they are unconstitutional under *Lawrence v. Texas*, 539 U.S. 558 (2003).

One of the more well-known cases addressing implied repeal is *Morton v. Mancari*, 417 U.S. 535 (1974). This case involved the irreconcilability of two statutes: the Indian Reorganization Act of 1934 ("IRA") and the Equal Employment Opportunity Act of 1972 ("EEO"). The earlier Act, the IRA, provided that "qualified Indians shall hereafter have the preference to appointment to vacancies in [the Bureau of Indian Affairs ('BIA')]." *Id.* at 538 (citing 25 U.S.C. § 472). But the EEO, which was enacted subsequently, specifically provided, "[a]ll personnel actions affecting employees of applicants for employment ... [with] the Federal Government ... shall be made free from any discrimination based on race color, religion, sex, or national origin." *Id.*

at 540 (citing 42 U.S.C. § 2000e-16(a)). The EEO did not expressly repeal the IRA. Plaintiffs, who were non-Indian, BIA employees, challenged the agency's hiring preference adopted under the IRA. *Id.* at 535. Although the district court held that the EEO impliedly repealed the IRA, the Supreme Court disagreed. Citing the presumption against implied repeal, the Court said, "[i]n the absence of some affirmative showing of an intention to repeal, the only permissible justification for a repeal by implication is when the earlier and later statutes are irreconcilable. Clearly, this is not the case here." *Id.* at 550 (citing *Georgia v. Penn. R.R. Co.*, 324 U.S. 439, 456–57 (1945)). Somewhat disingenuously, the Court concluded that a specific provision aimed at furthering Native American self-government could exist harmoniously with a general rule prohibiting employment discrimination based on race. *Id.* In essence, the BIA preference became an implied exception to the EEO; generally, employers cannot discriminate on the basis of race, except when the employer is the BIA and the race is Native American. In this case, the Court heralded the canon disfavoring repeal by implication to reach this result; additionally, the Court turned to the canon that directs that specific statutes, like the IRA, trump general statutes, like the EEO.

There is a related aspect to this implied repeal canon: the presumption against repeal is especially strong when the second bill is an appropriations (or budget) bill. The presumption is stronger because appropriations bills have a limited and specific purpose: providing funds for authorized programs. These types of bills are supposed to be purely fiscal in nature and not make substantive changes to the law; hence, courts consider it highly unlikely that a legislature would repeal existing law through an appropriations bill. But as with all canons, this presumption can be overcome with specific evidence that the legislature did intend to repeal the existing law impliedly through the later appropriations bill.

The quintessential case rejecting such an argument is *Tennessee Valley Authority v. Hill*, 437 U.S. 153 (1978). *Tennessee Valley* is well-known in the environmental arena because the Court permanently enjoined construction of the Tellico Dam, which was virtually complete, to protect the snail darter, a very small and non-descript species of fish. Construction on the dam started in 1967. In 1973, Congress passed the Endangered Species Act, which authorized the Secretary of the Interior (the "secretary") to declare animal species "endangered" and to identify any "critical habitat" of that species. *Id.* at 159–60 (citing 16 U.S.C. § 1531 *et seq.* (1976)). The secretary was further authorized to take "such action necessary to insure that *actions* authorized, funded, or carried out by [the federal government] do not jeopardize the continued existence of [an] endangered species ... or result in the destruction or modification of habitat of such species ...." *Id.* at 160 (quoting 16 U.S.C. § 1536 (1976)) (emphasis added). The issue in the case was whether the word "actions" in the Act included almost completed projects.

In late 1975, the secretary identified the snail darter as endangered and declared that the area the Tellico Dam would affect was the snail darter's "critical habitat." The secretary then directed the Tennessee Valley Authority, which was building the dam, to stop construction. *Id.* at 161–62. Litigation ensued. While the litigation was pending and despite the secretary's order, Congress continued to appropriate funds for the dam's completion: "The [House Committee on Appropriations] directs that the project ... should be completed as promptly as possible ...." *Id.* at 164 (citing H.R. REP. No. 94-319, at 76 (1975)).

Meanwhile, the litigation was winding its way through the courts. Because the dam was so close to completion, the district court refused to stop the dam construction, despite agreeing with the secretary that completion of the dam would completely destroy the fish's habitat. *Id.* at 165–66. But the Sixth Circuit and a majority of the Supreme Court disagreed. Both held that the language of the Endangered Species Act permitted no exceptions, even for projects near completion. *Id.* at 169.

As for the fact that Congress had continued to provide appropriations for the Tellico Dam, the Supreme Court majority cited *Morton v. Mancari*, 417 U.S. 535 (1974), for the cardinal rule that repeals by implication are disfavored. *Tennessee Valley*, 437 U.S. at 189. The majority further explained that "the [canon] applie[d] with even *greater* force when the claimed repeal rests solely on an Appropriations Act." *Id.* The majority identified the rationale behind this canon as follows: when voting to approve appropriations bills, legislators should be able to assume that the funds earmarked in the bill will be devoted to projects that are lawful. Without such an assurance, every appropriations measure might alter substantive legislation, repealing by implication any prior statute that conflicted with the expenditure. Thus, members of Congress would need to exhaustively review every appropriation in excruciating detail before voting on it. *Id.* Moreover, a House Rule specifically prohibited appropriations bills from "changing existing law ...." *Id.* at 191 (citing House Rule XXI(2)). Hence, the Supreme Court ordered construction on the dam to halt.

Justice Powell dissented. Powell believed that the word "actions" in the Endangered Species Act did not apply to projects that were completed or substantially so, for such an interpretation would be absurd and not what Congress likely intended. *Id.* at 196 (Powell, J., dissenting). Rather, he believed that the language in the statute applied only to *prospective* actions. As for the appropriations bill argument, Powell agreed that appropriations acts are not entitled to significant weight, but in this case the bills and the statements made during their enactment simply confirmed the original congressional intent: that the dam be completed. *Id.* at 210 (Powell, J., dissenting). Interestingly, Powell concluded his dissenting opinion with a statement that Congress would likely soon rectify the majority's error. Powell was correct. In 1980, after prolonged fighting, Congress added a rider to another appropriations bill that authorized the Tennessee Valley Authority to continue construction on the dam despite the Endangered Species Act. Energy and Water Development Appropriation Act of 1980, Pub. L. No 96-69, tit. IV, 93 Stat. 437, 449 (1979). Thus, Congress expressly limited the Endangered Species Act as it applied to the Tellico Dam in an appropriations act.

In summary, when two statutes conflict and the conflict cannot be reconciled, courts ask first whether one statute is specific and the other general. If that distinction does not resolve the dispute, courts look next to whether one statute was enacted later than the other because the last in time should control. Finally, if neither of these tiebreakers resolves the issue, the court will determine whether one statute expressly or impliedly repealed part or all of the other statute. Generally, implied repeals are disfavored, especially when the later, conflicting statute is an appropriations act.

D. Retroactive Statutes

Another timing-related issue is retroactivity. In addition to addressing conflicts among statutes, judges must also determine whether a particular statute was meant to apply to past behavior. Legislatures have the power to amend statutes and to decide that the amended statute applies to events occurring before the statute's effective date. But for a variety of reasons — most notably that statutes that apply retroactively may violate due process — legislatures normally enact statutes with prospective effect, meaning that the statute will apply only to future conduct.

But retroactivity provisions can serve legitimate purposes. For example, such provisions allow a legislature to respond to emergencies, to correct mistakes, to prevent circumvention of a new statute in the interval immediately preceding its passage, and to give comprehensive effect to a new law. The requirement that a legislature clearly state its intention to make a statute retroactive helps ensure that the legislature actually thought about this issue and concluded that the benefits of retroactivity outweighed the potential for disruption or unfairness.

The applicable canon thus states that statutes are applied prospectively rather than retroactively absent a retroactivity provision or clear legislative intent to the contrary. In other words, prospective application is the default. *Landgraf v. USI Film Products*, 511 U.S. 244, 286 (1994) (Scalia, J., concurring) ("[A] legislative enactment affecting substantive rights does not apply retroactively absent [a] *clear statement* to the contrary.") The basis for prospective application being the default is that "[e]lementary considerations of fairness dictate that individuals should have an opportunity to know what the law is and to conform their conduct accordingly; settled expectations should not be lightly disrupted." *Id.* at 265. The *ex post facto* clause of the U.S. Constitution flatly prohibits retroactive application of *penal* legislation; thus, retroactivity issues should arise only in civil actions. We will explore the retroactive effect of penal statutes in more detail in Chapter 12; this section is limited to the application of this canon in civil statutes.

Let's look at the canon at work. In *Landgraf*, an employee sued her former employer for a co-worker's sexual harassment and retaliation. *Id.* at 248. At the time she sued, Title VII did not authorize any recovery of damages even though the plaintiff had been injured. *Id.* at 250. While the action was pending, however, the Civil Rights Act of 1991 was enacted, which created a right to recover compensatory and punitive damages for violations of Title VII and provided for jury trial when such damages were claimed. *Id.* at 249. Plaintiff argued that the Act applied retroactively to her case. Applying the canon, the Court disagreed and held that the Act did not apply to cases pending on appeal when it was enacted. *Id.* at 286.

Before deciding whether a statute is *impermissibly* retroactive, a court must ask first whether the effect of a statute is retroactive. A statute has retroactive effect when the statute defines the legal significance of actions or events that occurred prior to the statute's enactment. The Maryland Court of Appeals applied this test in *State Ethics Commission v. Evans*, 855 A.2d 364 (Md. 2004). Before the facts giving rise to the case occurred, the defendant had been convicted of nine counts of wire and mail fraud. Thirteen months later and in direct response to the defendant's actions, the Maryland legislature amended its government code to permit the State Ethics Commission (the "commission") to revoke the registration of any lobbyist who had been convicted of bribery or similar crimes. *Id.* at 365–66. After serving his prison sentence, the defendant registered as a lobbyist. Relying on the amendment, the commission revoked his registration. *Id.*

The majority and dissent disagreed as to whether the revocation of the defendant's registration based on a criminal conviction that had occurred prior to the effective date of the statute constituted a retroactive or prospective application of the law. Further, they disagreed over the appropriate test for determining whether a statute was retroactive. The dissent offered a two-factor test for retroactivity: (1) whether the commission's action impaired a vested right, or (2) whether it changed the legal significance of a completed transaction. *Id.* at 374 (Cathell, J., dissenting). The dissent said that, in this case, the commission's action did neither; hence, the statute had only prospective effect. *Id.*

In response to the dissent's analysis, the majority stated that it was "hard-pressed to understand" how a statute that, for the first time, permitted the commission to revoke a lobbyist's registration solely on the basis that the lobbyist had been convicted of certain criminal offenses did not change the legal significance of a conviction that occurred prior to the effective date of the statute. *Id.* at 373. In any event, the majority disagreed with the dissent's vested-rights prong of the test because that prong conflated retroactivity with *constitutionally impermissible* retroactivity. *Id.* at 374. The majority described the test as whether the statute " 'purports to determine the legal significance of acts or events that [] occurred prior to the statute's effective date ....' " *Id.* (quoting *St. Comm'n on Human Rel. v. Amecom Div.*, 360 A.2d 1, 3 (Md. 1976)).

Simply because a statute is retroactive does not make it *impermissibly* retroactive. Retroactive statutes are allowable in certain situations. A statute may apply retroactively when (1) there is clear evidence that the legislature intended retroactive effect, and (2) no vested right is impaired. *Id.* The first caveat is a statutory interpretation caveat, while the latter caveat is a constitutional one. *Id.* Looking only at the first caveat, the majority in *Evans* found that, even though the statute had been amended specifically in response to the defendant's actions, that fact alone did not rebut the presumption against retroactivity. *Id.* A clearer statement from the legislature was needed. The majority never reached the constitutional issue of whether this statute impaired a vested right. *Id.*

As noted, evidence that the legislature intended retroactive effect can rebut this presumption of future effect, but such evidence is not found easily. For example, in *McClung v. Employment Development Department*, 99 P.3d 1015 (Cal. 2004), the Supreme Court of California rejected an argument that a statutory amendment was retroactive despite language in the amendment that the amendment was meant to clarify a prior statute. *Id.* at 1021. The facts of the case are largely irrelevant, but the procedural history is central. In an earlier case, *Carrisales v. Department of Corrections*, 988 P.2d 1083 (1999), the court had interpreted a California statute prohibiting employment discrimination to impose liability on employers, but not on nonsupervisory employees. The state legislature did not agree with *Carrisales'* holding. Thus, following the *Carrisales'* decision, the state legislature amended the statute to impose personal liability on nonsupervisory employees who committed harassment. Importantly, the legislature added language to the amendment that said it was "declaratory of existing law." *McClung*, 99 P.3d at 1017 (citing CAL. GOV'T CODE § 12940(j)(2)). The issue for the court was whether the amendment should have retroactive effect (1) when the amendment stated that it simply declared existing law, but (2) when the amendment conflicted with an existing judicial interpretation of that statute.

The court noted that if the amendment merely stated existing law then the issue of retroactivity would not be presented because a statute that merely clarifies existing law and does not change existing law would have no retroactive effect even if applied to circumstances predating its enactment. *Id.* at 1019. In other words, liability would have attached at the time the act became law; the later amendment would not have changed liability. In contrast, when an amendment changes the law, then issues related to retroactivity do arise. In *McClung*, the court then asked two questions: First, did the amendment merely clarify the law or change it? And second, if the amendment changed the law, did that change apply retroactively? *Id.*

Holding that *Carrisales* stated the law because the judiciary is charged with interpreting statutes, the court held that the later amendment changed rather than clarified the law because the amendment conflicted with *Carrisales's* holding. *Id.* at 1021. As a side point, the plaintiff had argued that because *Carrisales* postdated the actions in the lawsuit in question, even the court's interpretation should pose retroactivity issues. But the court disagreed and explained that judicial interpretations may always apply retroactively because "a judicial construction of a statute is an authoritative statement of what the statute meant before as well as after the decision of the case giving rise to that construction." *Id.* In other words, courts interpret statutes as of the enactment date forward; hence, there is no retroactivity issue when courts interpret statutes.

The court then turned to the question of whether the amendment could apply retroactively. The court noted that prospective application is the presumption, but this presumption can be overcome with a showing that the legislature intended otherwise. *Id.* Finding nothing in the statute or legislative history to overcome the presumption, the court held that the amendment was prospective only. *Id.* The court rejected plaintiff's argument that subsection 12940(j)(2) showed such an intent because that subsection predated *Carrisales* and was inserted in reference to another change to the statute. *Id.* at 1022. The dissent disagreed with the second step of the majority's analysis and argued that subsection 12940(j)(2) showed clear legislative intent for retroactive effect. *Id.* at 1024 (Moreno, J., concurring and dissenting).

In summary, courts presume that statutes apply prospectively. For civil statutes, the presumption can be rebutted with clear evidence that the legislature intended the statute to apply retroactively if retroactive application will not impair a vested right. And a statute has retroactive effect when that statute defines the legal significance of acts or events that occurred prior to the statute's enactment. In contrast, criminal statutes never apply retroactively without violating the *ex post facto* clause. Chapter 12 addresses this issue in detail, for the prohibition against penal statutes applying retroactively is constitutionally based.

E. Statutes from Other Jurisdictions

The next two subsections address two issues that cross jurisdictions. What relevance should judicial interpretations from other jurisdictions, whether state or federal, have on the interpretation of a statute? For common law decisions, the judicial interpretations of other jurisdictions are merely persuasive, never more than that. But when statutory interpretation is involved, judicial interpretations are important in two situations: when a state borrows a statute from another jurisdiction and when a state enacts a uniform or model act.

1. Modeled & Borrowed Statutes

A legislature may model one statute after an existing statute; modeling happens intra-jurisdictionally. For example, the Age Discrimination in Employment Act ("ADEA") was modeled after three acts: the National Labor Relations Act, the Fair Labor Standards Act ("FLSA"), and Title VII of the Civil Rights Act. When Congress models, courts will look to the modeling statute (the existing statute) and its settled judicial interpretations for guidance on interpreting the modeled statute (the new statute). Thus, in *Lorillard v. Pons*, 434 U.S. 575 (1978), the Supreme Court looked at FLSA to determine whether ADEA provided a right to jury trials because ADEA specifically provided that it be interpreted in accordance with the "powers, remedies, and *procedures*" of FLSA. *Id.* at 579 n.5 (quoting 29 U.S.C. §626(b)). Because FLSA provided such a right, the Court held that ADEA did as well. *Id.* at 579.

Similarly, states routinely borrow statutes, in whole or in part, from other jurisdictions; borrowing occurs inter-jurisdictionally. States borrow because it is simpler than creating a statute anew. When a state legislature borrows a statute from another jurisdiction—whether state or federal—courts assume that the borrowing legislature took not only the statutory language, but also any settled judicial opinions interpreting that statute from the highest court in the patterning jurisdiction at the time of the adoption. *Zerbe v. State*, 583 P.2d 845, 846 (Alaska 1978) (refusing to adopt the judicial opinion of a lower court). This canon is based on the presumptions that the borrowing legislature (1) was aware of the judicial interpretations in the patterning jurisdiction, and (2) intended those interpretations to guide its own judiciary. But after the borrowing occurs, subsequent judicial opinions in the patterning jurisdiction are simply informative; the borrowing state's judiciary remains free to reject the later interpretations.

For example, in *Van Horn v. William Blanchard Co.*, 438 A.2d 552 (N.J. 1981), the plaintiff sued two defendants, a general contractor and a subcontractor, after he fell at his workplace. *Id.* at 553. The jury found that the plaintiff was 50% at fault, the general contractor was 30% at fault, and the subcontractor was 20% at fault. The state's comparative negligence statute barred recovery when a plaintiff's negligence was "greater than the negligence of *the person* against whom recovery is sought." *Id.* at 554 (quoting N.J. STAT. ANN. §2A:15-5.1) (emphasis added). In this case, because the plaintiff's negligence was greater than the *individual* negligence of either of the joint tortfeasors, the trial court entered judgment for the defendants. The plaintiff argued that the court should have taken an aggregate, rather than an individual, approach to the determination: if the plaintiff's negligence was less than the defendants' *combined* negligence, the plaintiff should be able to recover. *Id.* at 553–54.

The New Jersey Supreme Court disagreed. In doing so, the court noted that the New Jersey statute was borrowed "nearly verbatim" from Wisconsin; therefore, it applied the borrowing presumption. The court reasoned that when the New Jersey legislature borrowed the statutory language from Wisconsin, it also borrowed the settled jurisprudence. Because the court believed that Wisconsin applied the individual approach, this court had to as well. *Id.* at 555–56.

The dissent did not dispute the majority's description of the general borrowing presumption. Instead, the dissent pointed out that it was unclear whether Wisconsin was the sole patterning state; the legislative history was unclear on this issue. *Id.* at 559 (Handler, J., dissenting). Thus, "[t]he decisions of the Wisconsin Courts do not constitute persuasive evidence of the intent of the New Jersey Legislature on this facet of the Act." *Id.* at 563. He noted that other possible patterning jurisdictions applied the aggregate approach. Because there was no clear patterning state, the dissent reasoned that the court's hands were not bound, and it could decide which approach the New Jersey legislature intended. Perhaps the dissent was right; a mere year later, the New Jersey Legislature amended the statute to require the aggregate approach. N.J. STAT. ANN. §2A:15-5.3. You might also note that the majority ignored the canon that the plural can include the singular (*see* Chapter 5).

2. Model & Uniform Acts

Uniform and model acts are similar to borrowed acts, but these acts are borrowed from another source altogether. The National Conference of Commissioners on Uniform State Laws, the American Law Institute, and other institutional drafters develop model and uniform acts. Uniform Acts are proposed state laws that the National Conference of Commissioners on Uniform State Laws ("Conference") or another institutional actor drafts. The Conference was established in 1892 and is made up of lawyers, judges, and law professors. Members of the Conference draft laws on a variety of subjects and propose them for enactment within the states, the District of Columbia, the U.S. Virgin Islands, and Puerto Rico. The Conference has no legislative power; rather, the proposed uniform acts become law only when they are adopted in a particular state. Thus, proposed uniform acts serve as guidelines, or samples, for the state legislatures. The United States is a country with one federal system of law and fifty or more state systems of law. The purpose of the Conference is to help encourage uniformity across state lines, particularly in areas where state boundaries are essentially irrelevant. For example, the Uniform Commercial Code, which has been widely adopted among the states, unifies the law regarding the sale of goods. There are currently more than 100 different uniform acts, including one on statutory interpretation.

Both types of acts are created to address multijurisdictional issues, such as interstate commerce or child custody. Some familiar examples of these acts include the Uniform Commercial Code, the Model Business Corporation Act, the Uniform Child Custody Jurisdiction and Enforcement Act, and the Model Penal Code. Interestingly, Nevada appears to have adopted the most model and uniform acts with the least number of changes.[1] In addition to the web, model and uniform acts can be found in the Uniform Laws Annotated, which is a set of books that includes the laws and annotations showing where the laws have been adopted, interpreted, and cited.

---

1. American Law Sources On-Line, *Uniform Law and Model Acts*, AMERICAN LAW SOURCES, http://www.lawsource.com/also/usa.cgi?usm. (last visited July 15, 2012).

The principal difference between model and uniform acts is the importance of uniform adoption and interpretation. For *uniform acts*, uniformity is essential. *Pileri Indus., Inc. v. Consolidated Indus., Inc.*, 740 So. 2d 1108, 1114 (Ala. Civ. App. 1999) (Crawley, J., dissenting). The Commissioners draft a uniform act in two situations: (1) when they anticipate enactment in a large number of jurisdictions, and (2) when they have uniformity among the various jurisdictions as a principal objective. NATIONAL CONFERENCE OF COMMISSIONERS ON UNIFORM STATE LAWS, STATEMENT OF POLICY ESTABLISHING CRITERIA AND PROCEDURES FOR DESIGNATION AND CONSIDERATION OF ACTS (2001). Thus, the Commissioners encourage state legislatures to adopt a uniform act in its entirety with as few changes as possible. The Commissioners' principal goal when drafting a uniform act is to obtain immediate uniformity, not uniqueness, among the states on a particular legal subject. This goal affects interpretation in that the judicial interpretations from other states are always strongly persuasive, regardless of when they occur.

> While opinions by courts of sister states construing a uniform act are not binding upon this court, we are mindful that the objective of uniformity cannot be achieved by ignoring utterances of other jurisdictions .... This does not mean that this court will blindly follow decisions of other states interpreting uniform acts but, this court will seriously consider the constructions given to comparable statutes in other jurisdictions and will espouse them to maintain conformity when they are in harmony with the spirit of the statute and do not antagonize public policy of this state.

Holiday Inns, Inc. v. Olsen, 692 S.W.2d 850, 853 (Tenn. 1985). In *Holiday Inns*, the court agreed with other states that had interpreted the term "business earnings" in the Uniform Division of Income for Tax Purposes Act. The court thereby rejected the state tax department's interpretation of the statute.

When courts conform their interpretations of uniform acts to those of other states, courts help ensure that the construction of such acts remains standard and uniform. *Blitz v. Beth Isaac Adas Israel Congregation*, 720 A.2d 912, 918 (Md. 1998) (interpreting the word "disbursements" in the Uniform Arbitration Act to include attorney's fees, in part, because other states had done so even though the text of the Act suggested that attorney's fees should not be included).

In contrast, uniformity is less central for model acts. The Commissioners choose to draft a model act in two situations: (1) when uniformity is desirable but not primary, and (2) when the purposes of an act can be substantially achieved even though the act is not adopted in its entirety by every state. NATIONAL CONFERENCE OF COMMISSIONERS ON UNIFORM STATE LAWS, STATEMENT OF POLICY ESTABLISHING CRITERIA AND PROCEDURES FOR DESIGNATION AND CONSIDERATION OF ACTS (2001). A model act may develop new or unusual approaches to particular legal problems; the effectiveness of these approaches will likely become clearer with time. Model acts are intended as guidelines that states may adapt to best address their unique circumstances. Hence, uniformity of interpretation and application, which is so important for uniform acts, is less critical for model acts. While uniformity is less critical, it is still a guiding principle when the model act has been widely adopted. "When the words of a statute are materially the same and where the reasoning of another court interpreting the statute is sound, we do not sacrifice sovereign independence, nor undermine the unique character of Wyoming law, by relying upon the precedent of a foreign jurisdiction." *Brown v. Arp & Hammond Hardware Co.*, 141 P.3d 673, 680 (Wyo. 2006) (internal quotation marks omitted).

Sometimes a uniform act is adopted in fewer states than was originally expected. When this happens, the Commissioners may either formally or informally relegate such an act to *model-act* status; the Uniform Construction Lien Act was one such act. Such a change illustrates simply that the act was less popular than originally expected. Importantly, state legislatures are not always clear that they are adopting a model or uniform act. Hence, it may be necessary to check the legislative history to determine whether it was intended to be one or the other.

3. The Uniform Statute & Rule Construction Act

The Conference drafted the Uniform Statute and Rule Construction Act ("the Act") in an attempt to unify the process of statutory interpretation. The Conference approved the Act in 1993 and recommended enactment in the states. The Act represents a compromise among the various conflicting preferences in the field of statutory construction. For example, in Chapter 4, this text describes various theories, or approaches, of statutory interpretation, including textualism — which focuses on the text — and purposivism — which focuses on the text together with the purpose of the statute. The drafters of the Act claimed not to have adopted any theory. The Act does emphasize the primacy of the text, but it also recognizes non-textual sources such as legislative history from which purpose may be discerned. The Act thus takes a middle-ground approach to this philosophical and academic debate. Additionally, the

Act makes clear that its "rules" are not rules in the typical legal sense, but rather are simply a "hierarchy of values" for the interpreter to follow as the circumstances allow. UNIF. STATUTE & RULE CONSTR. ACT § 18 cmt. at 71 (West Supp. 1995). After all, statutory interpretation is not an exact science governed by legal rules; rather, it is an art: a patchwork of contradictory and competing canons.

To date, only the state of New Mexico has adopted the Act. However, the Act offers an easy reference guide and a succinct articulation of many of the canons we will be covering. Thus, this text often refers to relevant sections of the Act.

The canons in this chapter all relate to the timing of legislative enactments. Courts make certain assumptions about how legislatures would expect legislation to be interpreted based on the legislative process. Hence, later statutes generally control earlier ones, specific statues generally control general ones, implied repeals are generally disfavored, and jurisdictions often borrow statutes and the judicial opinions that interpreted the patterning statute up to the point of the adoption. In the next chapter, we explore other canons related to the legislative process—those canons related to context.

F. Mastering This Topic

Return to the hypothetical ordinance provided in Chapter 1. Remember our question: "An ambulance entered Pioneer Park to pick up and take to the hospital a man who has just suffered a heart attack. Did the ambulance driver violate the Pioneer Park Safety Ordinance (PPSO)?" The hypothetical did not provide an issue relating to conflicting statutes, nor any of the other issues in this chapter; however, let's assume that another ordinance provided as follows:

An Ordinance
To Exempt Emergency Vehicles from Traffic Regulations
Be it enacted by the Council of the City of Pioneer assembled,
(1) As used in this section the term "emergency vehicle" means any vehicle used for emergency purposes by:
   (a)   The Pioneer City Police;
   (b)   A rescue squad;
   (c)   An emergency management agency if it is a publicly owned vehicle;
   (d)   The Pioneer City Fire Department; and

(e)   An ambulance service or medical first-response provider licensed by the Pioneer Board of Emergency Medical Services, for any vehicle used to respond to emergencies or to transport a patient with a critical medical condition.

(2) Traffic regulations set forth in the Pioneer Revised Ordinances do not apply to emergency vehicles in the following circumstances:

(a)   When responding to emergency calls; or

(b)   To police vehicles when in pursuit of an actual or suspected violator of the law; or

(c)   To ambulances when transporting a patient to medical care facilities; and

(d)   The driver thereof.

(3) No portion of this subsection shall be construed to relieve the driver of the duty to operate the vehicle with due regard for the safety of all persons using public property.

(4) The driver of an emergency vehicle, when responding to an emergency call, or of a police vehicle in pursuit of an actual or suspected violator of the law, or of an ambulance transporting a patient to a medical care facility and giving the warning, upon approaching any red light or stop signal or any stop sign shall slow down as necessary for safety to traffic, but may proceed past such red or stop light or stop sign with due regard for the safety of persons using the street or highway.

(5) The driver of an emergency vehicle, when responding to an emergency call, or of a police vehicle in pursuit of an actual or suspected violator of the law, or of an ambulance transporting a patient to a medical care facility and giving warning required by subsection (5) of this section, may drive on the left side of any highway or in the opposite direction of a one-way street provided the normal lanes of traffic are blocked and he does so with due regard for the safety of all persons using the street or highway.

(6) The driver of an emergency or public safety vehicle may stop or park his vehicle upon any street or highway, provided that, during the time the vehicle is parked at the scene of an emergency, at least one warning light is in operation at all times.

Effective: July 15, 1980.

The first question you should ask is whether this second hypothetical ordinance ("the traffic regulation exception") applies at all. While the traffic regulation exception explicitly applies to emergency vehicles including ambulances, it exempts such vehicles only from "traffic regulations." Is the

PPSO (the other ordinance) a traffic regulation? Using the skills you've learned to date, determine whether the PPSO is a traffic regulation. You should be able to do this step on your own.

Assuming that you conclude that the PPSO is a traffic regulation (or that the traffic regulation exception would apply in this situation regardless), you now have two ordinances that conflict. The traffic regulation exception exempts ambulances from traffic regulations, although it makes clear that "No portion of this subsection shall be construed to relieve the driver of the duty to operate the vehicle with due regard for the safety of all persons using public property." The PPSO prohibits all motor vehicles from entering and driving in Pioneer Park. Can you reconcile these two ordinances? Perhaps. You might say that the PPSO applies in all cases in which there is no emergency and that the traffic regulation exception applies when there are emergencies. Such an analysis would make the traffic regulation exception an implied exception to the PPSO.

Perhaps, instead, you conclude that the conflict cannot be so easily reconciled. In that case, you must apply the rules relating to conflicting statutes: specific controls general and later controls earlier. Which ordinance is more specific? The traffic regulation exception is specific to emergency vehicles, while the PPSO applies to all motor vehicles (with identified exceptions). One might argue then that the more specific traffic regulation ordinance controls over the PPSO; thus, the driver should not be cited. However, arguably the PPSO is the specific ordinance, while the traffic regulation exception is the general ordinance: the PPSO is specific as to location — it applies only to Pioneer Park — while the traffic regulation exception applies to all locations. Lastly, both ordinances might be specific: the PPSO is specific as to location — it applies only to Pioneer Park — while the traffic regulation exception is specific as to vehicles — it applies only to emergency vehicles. Here, you see the difficulty with trying to determine whether one statute is specific and another general. You might thus conclude that this canon does not resolve the conflict

Moving onto the second canon — that the later enacted ordinance controls the earlier — you would conclude that the PPSO has an effective date of August 15, 1998, while the traffic regulation exception has an effective date of July 15, 1980. Because the PPSO was enacted after the traffic regulation exception, the PPSO should control; thus, the driver should be cited.

Does such a result mean that the Pioneer Council impliedly repealed all or a portion of the traffic regulation ordinance? You will remember that implied repeals are disfavored, and here there is no clear evidence of legislative intent suggesting that the Council thought about the existing ordinance at all, let alone intended to repeal any portion of it. Thus, you should conclude that the PPSO did not implicitly repeal the traffic regulation exception.

Ultimately, you probably see that these canons are not terribly helpful in resolving this issue. If you were inclined to cite the driver, you have an argument to do so: the PPSO, as the later enacted statute, controls. If you were inclined not to cite the driver, you have an argument to do so: the traffic regulation exception is more specific to ambulances. Subjectivity continues.

Checkpoints

- Reminder: extrinsic sources are those sources outside of the enacted act but within the legislative process that created the act.

- When two statutes or sections of a statute conflict, a judge will first see if the conflict between the two can be reconciled, meaning that the statutes can be harmonized.

- Where two statutes are in conflict and the conflict cannot be reconciled, a specific statute controls a general statute. If neither statute is specific, then the later enacted statute controls the earlier enacted statute. These canons can both be overcome with evidence that the legislature did not intend for the conflict to be resolved as the canons direct.

- If conflict remains, then a judge will check to see if one statute repealed, in whole or in part, the other. But repeals by implication are disfavored. When a legislature wishes to repeal an existing statute, the legislature should be clear.

- Statutes are applied prospectively rather than retroactively absent a retroactivity provision or clear legislative intent to the contrary.

- When a state legislature borrows a statute from another jurisdiction—whether state or federal—courts assume that the borrowing legislature took not only the statutory language, but also any settled judicial opinions interpreting that statute from the highest court in the patterning jurisdiction at the time of the adoption as well.

- When a state legislature enacts a *uniform act*, uniformity is essential. Thus, the interpretations of other jurisdictions are always persuasive, regardless of when they occur. When a state legislature enacts a *model act*, uniformity is less important, unless the model act is widely adopted.

Chapter 10

Canons Based on Extrinsic Sources: Legislative History & Purpose

---

Roadmap

- Learn to use what occurred *prior to* and *during* the enactment process.
- Understand what legislative history is.
- Learn where to find legislative history, how to use it, and how to criticize its use.
- Understand how to find purpose and discover its relevance to interpretation.

A. Introduction to This Chapter

In this chapter, we continue with our examination of extrinsic sources and turn to enactment context. Legislative intent and purpose can often be found by understanding what motivated the legislature to act, by knowing what information the legislature considered when it acted, and by knowing what was said during the enactment process. This chapter will explore the canons related to legislative context, including using legislative history and *unexpressed* statutory purpose to discern meaning.

B. Using What Occurred
Prior to & During Enactment

1. Context

Knowing why a legislature chose to enact a statute may help a judge interpret that statute. *Contextualism* is the process of using context to determine why a legislature acted in order to understand what a statute means. There are different types of context, including social and historical events (social or historical context), the legal and political climate (legal or political context), economic or market factors (economic context), and even textual and linguistic patterns (textual context). We already looked at textual and linguistic context in preceding chapters (*see* Chapters 5–8).

In this chapter, we move to other sources of context. A judge's interpretative theory determines which, if any, of these other contexts are relevant to that judge (*see* Chapter 4). For example, textualists will look at textual, legal, and linguistic context to understand the way that a particular legislature may have used words and phrases. In contrast, purposivists will look at social, historical, legal, economic, and political context, any one of which may help them identify the statutory purpose. These types of context can help reveal the purpose of the act by showing how events of the time might have impacted a legislature's choices. For example, consider how the contexts of the following statutes may be germane to meaning:

- *Social and historical context*—the Patriot Act, which was enacted in response to the terrorist attacks of 9-11;
- *Political context*—the McCain-Feingold Act, which was enacted in response to perceived illegal political spending;
- *Legal context*—an appropriation provision that was included in a budget bill to continue building the Tellico Dam and which was enacted during the pendency of litigation to shut down construction of the Dam; and
- *Economic context*—statutes enacted during the New Deal, which were enacted in response to the Great Depression.

Intentionalists will look at social, historical, legal, economic, and political context, which may help them identify the specific legislative intent. But most relevant to intentionalists is the enactment process itself. As we have seen, a statute is often the result of political compromise; contextualism allows intentionalist judges to interpret the statute so as to promote that compromise thereby furthering legislative intent. *Mohasco Corp. v. Silver*, 447 U.S. 807, 819–20 (1980).

For some judges, context can overcome ordinary meaning. For example, a federal statute prohibited citizens from bringing into the United States "*any* false, forged, or counterfeit coin or bar." *United States v. Falvey*, 676 F.2d 871, 872 (1st Cir. 1982) (quoting 18 U.S.C. §§ 485, 486) (emphasis added). The three defendants owned counterfeit Krugerrands, which are coins from South Africa and which were not in circulation in the United States. The ordinary meaning of the statute was clear: the defendants were guilty because they brought counterfeit coins into the United States. However, the court did not find the defendants guilty because earlier drafts of the bill and its legislative history demonstrated that "the only foreign coins covered by the [statute were] those 'current ... or in actual use and circulation as money within the United States.'" *Id.* at 873 (quoting the lower court opinion). Thus, in this case the drafting history overcame ordinary meaning.

Similarly, in *D.C. Federation of Civic Ass'ns v. Volpe*, 308 F. Supp. 423 (D.D.C.), *rev'd*, 434 F.2d 436 (D.C. Cir. 1970), the District Court for the District of Columbia rejected the ordinary meaning of a procedural requirement in the Federal-Aid Highway Act of 1968. That provision specifically directed the government of the D.C. to commence work on the bridge as soon as possible, subject to specific planning and public hearing requirements. *Id.* at 424. The statute required the government to act "in accordance with all applicable provisions of title 23 of the United States Code." *Id.* The District Court narrowed the language, interpreting it to apply only to activities that addressed actual construction and not activities that involved planning for construction. *Id.* at 425. The court reasoned that because Congress had legislatively overruled a prior case enjoining construction of the bridge, Congress intended the bridge be built promptly. Not surprisingly given the clarity of the language, the court was reversed on appeal. *D.C. Federation*, 434 F.2d at 437.

Historical, social, economic, and legal context can be found in many places, such as newspapers that were current at the time. Most commonly, however, judges turn to the legislative history of the bill at issue, including draft versions of the bill, as the First Circuit did in *Falvey*. Judges vary in their willingness to consider legislative history, and even in their willingness to consider all forms of legislative history, some forms of legislative history are believed to be more trustworthy than other forms. Also, some forms of legislative history are considered to be more relevant than other forms. Let's explore these issues in more detail.

2. Legislative History

Legislative history can be defined as the written record of deliberations surrounding and preceding a bill's enactment. Legislative history includes all the documentation that was generated during the enactment process, including committee reports and hearing transcripts, floor debates, recorded votes, conference committee reports, presidential signing statements, veto messages, and more. Most legislative history is generated at the chokeholds, or vetogates, within the legislative process. (See Chapter 2 for a discussion of vetogates.)

At one point routine, today the use of legislative history to discern meaning is highly controversial. As a litigant, you need to be aware of what legislative history is relevant, how relevant it is, how to find it (see Appendix E), how to use it, and how to criticize its use. This next section will explore the relevance of legislative history to interpretation.

a. The Legislative History Hierarchy

As mentioned above, legislative history includes everything developed during the legislative process, including committee reports, floor debates, conference committee reports, executive signing and veto statements, override memos, hearing transcripts, and even statements from sponsors. A search through all of the available documentation for the gold nugget of meaning can be burdensome, expensive, and time-consuming. Because not all legislative history has the same relevance, a savvy litigant should focus the search, especially when time and cost constraints matter. Some types of legislative history are more relevant than others; in other words, there is a legislative history hierarchy, and smart litigants know how to focus their search.

At the top of that hierarchy is the conference committee report. This report is, perhaps, "the most persuasive evidence of congressional intent, next to the statute itself." *United States v. Salim*, 287 F. Supp. 2d 250, 340 (S.D.N.Y. 2003). You may remember from Chapter 2 that commonly the House and Senate pass different versions of a bill and that the conference committee — an ad hoc committee of select senators and representatives — meets, discusses the differences in the bill, resolves those differences, recommends action, and writes a report analyzing its work. This report is considered very good evidence of what the legislature wanted as a whole because it is the only report members from both chambers generate. It truly identifies the compromises that led to the bill's passage. But even a conference committee report may not overcome clear text. In *In re Sinclair*, 870 F.2d 1340 (7th Cir. 1989), the plaintiffs identified a conference committee report that contradicted the ordinary meaning of the language in the statute. Writing for the majority, Judge Easterbrook, a textualist, refused to consider the report because the language of the statute was clear. *Id.* at 1344.

Next on the hierarchy are committee reports. Committee reports are also considered reliable evidence of meaning because the committee primarily responsible for drafting, amending, considering, and reporting the bill to the full chamber generates them. The committee or committees (or its staff) that had jurisdiction over the bill write committee reports. Generally, a committee report summarizes the bill and identifies the committee's recommendations and actions. Theoretically, all members of the committee read the report (or at least a summary of it) and vote based on the content of the report. The report follows the bill to the floor of the House or Senate, where it is expected that all members of the chamber will read the report. For these reasons, judges often consider committee reports. *See, e.g., Church of the Holy Trinity v. United States*, 143 U.S. 457, 464 (1892) (relying on a committee report to hold that Congress intended the word "labor or service" to mean manual labor only).

Former Justice Scalia initiated his assault on legislative history generally and on committee reports specifically while he was still on the D.C. Circuit. *Hirschey v. FERC*, 777 F.2d 1 (D.C. Cir. 1985). In a footnote in *Hirschey*, Scalia quoted an exchange between members of the Senate who were debating a tax bill. In the exchange, the chair of Senate Committee on Finance admitted that he did not yet read his committee's report. "It is not a best seller, but I am working on [reading] it." *Id.* at 7 n.1.

If you would like to see what a simple committee report looks like, you will find a section of the Senate Report for the sample bill we explored in Chapter 8 (actually it is for the Senate's companion bill) in Appendix C. You may recall that the sample bill would have established a loan forgiveness program for lawyers who became public defenders and prosecutors. The Senate Report identifies a concern of at least two members of the Senate: the high cost of law school. Had the bill become law, this report may have aided a court with subsequent interpretive issues.

There is another form of legislative history that should be distinguished from committee reports called "committee prints." Committee prints are documents created for a congressional committee about topics related to that committee's legislative or investigatory responsibilities. Studies by committee staff members or experts on the subject matter of a proposed bill, committee rules, and summaries of the legislative history of earlier failed bills are all examples. Committee prints are drafted for the committee's internal use and are not always available publicly.[1] Because committee prints vary significantly in content, are not always forwarded to the full chambers, and may not reflect the intent of the legislature, they play a minimal role in interpretation. RONALD BENTON BROWN & SHARON JACOBS BROWN, STATUTORY INTERPRETATION: THE SEARCH FOR LEGISLATIVE INTENT 133–34 (2d ed. 2011).

Another potentially relevant source of legislative history is earlier drafts, or versions, of the bill and rejected amendments to it. The enactment process frequently involves numerous drafts as the bill language is refined with time. It can be instructive to see what the committee, subcommittee, or full chamber changed. Thus, earlier versions and rejected amendments might help explain what a legislature intended when it adopted the enacted language. To illustrate, the dissent in *NLRB v. Catholic Bishop*, 440 U.S. 490, 515 (1979) (Brennan, J., dissenting), found rejected amendments informative.

It is less clear whether bills that were never enacted are relevant at all. If a prior legislature refused to enact a bill, that fact should have no relevance for interpreting bills that are subsequently enacted. But if a legislature rejects one bill and instead adopts a compromise bill, the rejected bill might help a judge discern legislative intent for the compromise bill. RONALD BENTON BROWN & SHARON JACOBS BROWN, *supra* 146–47. Moreover, judges might consider the rejected bill to be evidence that the legislature acquiesced in, or agreed with, an earlier judicial interpretation of an act (*see* Chapter 11).

Some argue that the most relevant statements are the drafter's commentary because that commentary is prepared before the bill is subject to legislative manipulation by either those in favor or those opposed to the bill's passage. For example, the comments on the Uniform Commercial Code (UCC) that the National Conference of Commissioners on Uniform State Laws, the American Bar Association, and the American Law Institute prepared jointly are generally found to be very relevant to that Act's meaning. These drafters are considered experts in the area; they had tremendous knowledge of the bill and its purpose. Given that they are academics and practicing attorneys, their comments were deliberate and thoughtful, rather than political. Additionally, when Congress enacted the UCC, it likely considered the comments and intended that the UCC be interpreted as the comments recommended. Had Congress wanted a different interpretation, Congress would likely have changed the language of the bill, which it was free to do.

---

1. *See U.S. Government Publishing Office, About Congressional Committee Prints* https://www.gpo.gov/help/about_congressional_committee_prints.htm.

Thus, in certain circumstances, drafters' commentary can aid interpretation. *See, e.g., United Steelworkers v. Weber*, 443 U.S. 193, 231–44 (1979) (Rehnquist, J., dissenting) (considering statements from both the Senate and House sponsors to argue that Title VII of the Civil Rights Act was color-blind).

Others, however, argue that statements from a drafter or sponsor (the legislator or legislators proposing the bill to the legislature) are not relevant to meaning because the critical intent is not that of the individual or individuals; rather, the critical intent is that of the legislature as a whole. Additionally, staff members or lobbyists may draft bills, and the intent of these individuals is irrelevant. Regardless of these criticisms, some judges will still consider drafter and sponsor statements. "[N]o one can gainsay the overwhelming judicial support for the proposition that explanations by sponsors of legislation during floor discussion are entitled to weight when they cast light on the construction properly to be placed upon statutory language." *Overseas Educ. Ass'n, Inc., v. Fed. Labor Relations Auth.*, 876 F.2d 960, 967 n.41 (D.C. Cir. 1989) (citing more than ten cases relying on sponsor statements). In contrast, lobbyist materials are usually not considered relevant to interpretation.

Statements, remarks, and debates that take place in either the Committee of the Whole or on the floor of either chamber are low on the legislative hierarchy. There are a few problems with relying on these types of colloquy. One problem is that they reflect only one legislator's intent, not the intent of the legislature as a whole. Because each legislator may have a unique reason for voting for a particular bill, one legislator's intent shows little. "The floor statements of individual legislators are larded with remarks which reflect a political ('sales talk') rather than a legislative purpose." *In re Virtual Network Servs. Corp.*, 98 B.R. 343, 349 (Bankr. N.D. Ill. 1989).

A second problem is that remarks could be added to the debate record without ever having been spoken on the floor for other legislators to hear. For example, in *City of Harrisburg v. Franklin*, 806 F. Supp. 1181 (M.D. Pa. 1992), the court refused to consider a legislator's written statements, which were made after the bill was passed and were "*never actually spoken on the floor of the legislature.*" *Id.* at 1184. Importantly, a relatively recent rule has required that these statements be clearly marked in the extension of remarks section of the legislative history; thus, this concern has lessened, but it should be kept in mind for statutes enacted less recently.

Another potential problem is that legislators do not always attend or hear all debates; sometimes, speeches are made to empty chambers for political or other reasons. And even if they are heard, some people question whether the remarks were influential. There is simply no way to know. If not influential, should they matter? Wouldn't this rule set up a requirement that legislators respond to all floor comments with which they disagree? Would such a rule be efficient?

Next on the hierarchy are floor debate comments offered by those opposed to the legislation. These carry even less weight than statements from those in agreement. "[S]peeches by opponents of legislation are entitled to relatively little weight in determining the meaning of the Act in question." *United States v. Pabon-Cruz*, 391 F.3d 86, 101 (2d Cir. 2004).

For all these reasons, floor debate statements, both pro and con, are generally not considered as reliable as the other forms of legislative history. Despite these concerns, judges still rely on these statements when interpreting statutes. Most famously in *United Steelworkers v. Weber*, 443 U.S. 193 (1979), the majority and dissent both relied on different parts of the floor debates to prove that their interpretation of the word "discriminate" in Title VII of the Civil Rights Act was accurate.

Finally, we reach the tail end of the hierarchy: executive signing statements and veto messages. Signing statements are actually *subsequent* history for they generally follow the bill's enactment (presidents typically sign the bill and then issue a signing statement). Moreover, neither is *legislative* history in the sense that neither comes from the legislature, but instead both come from the executive. But they are similar enough to the other forms of legislative history to be addressed here. As noted in Chapter 2, signing statements may indicate how an executive intends to implement a law. The relevance (if any) these statements should have on interpretation is unclear. Those advocating for their use argue that signing statements illustrate the executive's position in negotiating with the legislature. Supporters further argue that, because the executive has a constitutional role to play in enactment, the statements are germane to meaning. Those opposed to the use of these statements argue that the legislature, and only the legislature, has the constitutional power to enact law. Only the enacting legislature's intent is relevant; the executive's understanding or misunderstanding is irrelevant.

Further, those opposed to the use of these statements fear that the executive has an incentive to alter meaning when writing signing statements, a fear which recent presidents have proved to be founded. Thus, opponents argue that signing statements should be irrelevant, even though the executive has to sign the bill before it becomes law. The majority took this approach in *Hamdan v. Rumsfeld*, 548 U.S. 557 (2006), when it gave no weight to President Bush's memorandum regarding his understanding of the Detainee Treatment Act of 2005.

Regardless of whether they play any role in interpretation, presidents have increasingly included such statements. For example, former President George W. Bush regularly used signing statements to limit the reach of some laws. In July 2006, a task force of the American Bar Association challenged his use of the statements in this way as "contrary to the rule of law and our constitutional system of separation of powers."[2] President Obama also issued signing statements regularly to indicate his disagreement with portions of a bill. The ABA was similarly critical.[3] While it is too early to confirm that President Trump is following suit, it is likely he too will use such statements to limit the interpretation of statutes with which he is concerned.

b. Using Legislative History

Now that you know what to look for, you might ask: What do I do with it? Typically, judges use legislative history for one of two reasons: (1) to shed light on the specific intent of the enacting legislature, or (2) to identify one or more unexpressed statutory purposes. This section will focus on the first reason, finding the specific intent of the enacting legislature; we will look at the second reason later in this chapter. Generally, when judges use legislative history to find specific intent, they are looking to discover whether the legislature had a specific idea about the precise issue before the court.

Generally, textualist judges refuse to look at legislative history unless the language is ambiguous, absurd, or contains a scrivener's error. But non-textualist judges are willing to use legislative history to confirm the ordinary meaning of a clear language and, in some cases, to defeat the ordinary meaning of a statute. One could say that there is a continuum regarding a judge's willingness to use legislative history. Some judges are almost never willing to use legislative history (former Justice Scalia and Justice Thomas, for example); other judges are always willing to use legislative history (Justice Breyer and former Justice Stevens, for example). Most judges today, however, are willing to use legislative history when the language is ambiguous, absurd, raises a constitutional question,

---

2. American Bar Association, *Blue-Ribbon Task Force Finds President Bush's Signing Statement Undermine Separation of Powers* (July 24, 2006), https://americanbarassociation.wordpress.com/2006/07/24/blue-ribbon-task-force-finds-president-bushs-signing-statements-undermine-separation-of-powers/.

3. American Bar Association, *Letter from William Robinson to President Barack Obama*, (December 30, 2011) http://www.americanbar.org/content/dam/aba/administrative/litigation/materials/sac_2012/52-5_agr_2011_12_30_aba_letter_to_obama_re_signing_statements. authcheckdam.pdf.

or has a scrivener's error. A number of judges are willing to use legislative history to confirm the meaning of clear text. Less common today are judges willing to use legislative history to overcome the clear text. Here is a graphic that depicts this continuum:

Judicial Willingness to Use Legislative History

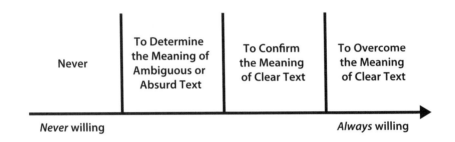

For example, in the following two bankruptcy cases, the judges differed in their willingness to look at legislative history in the face of clear text. In one case, the court refused to look at legislative history at all. In *In re Sinclair*, 870 F.2d 1340 (7th Cir. 1989), the debtors had filed a bankruptcy action under Chapter 11. Subsequently, Congress enacted Chapter 12, specifically for small farmers like the debtors. *Id.* at 1341. The debtors moved to convert their Chapter 11 proceeding to a Chapter 12 proceeding, which was a more favorable proceeding for debtors. *Id.* Chapter 12 provided, "The amendments made by subtitle B of title II *shall not apply* with respect to cases commenced under title 11 of the *United States Code* before the effective date of this Act." *Id.* (quoting Pub. L. No. 99-54) (emphasis added). Despite this clear text, a Conference Committee report suggested that conversion was possible:

> It is not intended that there be routine conversion of Chapter 11 ... cases, pending at the time of enactment, to Chapter 12. Instead, it is expected that courts will exercise their sound discretion in each case, in allowing conversions only where it is equitable to do so.
> Chief among the factors the court should consider is whether there is a substantial likelihood of successful reorganization under Chapter 12.

Id. The bankruptcy judge denied the debtors' motion to convert, and the Seventh Circuit affirmed, basing its decision on the clarity of the statute's text. *Id.* at 1344–45. Because the court found the statute clear, the court refused to consider the conference committee report at all. In so doing, the court indicated that legislative history should be used only to clarify ambiguous or absurd text because of the constitutional allocation of powers. "Legislative history helps us learn what Congress meant by what it said, but it is not a source of legal rules competing with those found in the U.S. Code." *Id.* at 1344. It will likely not surprise you that the author of *Sinclair* was Judge Easterbrook, a strong advocate of textualism.

In contrast, in the second case, the court found the text clear, but still looked at the legislative history to see if it offered additional insight. *In re Idalski*, 123 B.R. 222 (Bankr. E.D. Mich. 1991). In *Idalski*, the court found the text of another bankruptcy statute clear, but the court still looked to see if the legislative history suggested that a different meaning was intended. *Id.* at 225. In this case, a debtor had voluntarily paid money into an ERISA retirement account while she was employed. *Id.* at 223. At the time she had invested, the ERISA plan prohibited any voluntary or involuntary alienation of the plan benefits to creditors. *Id.* at 223–24. In other words, creditors could not attach the ERISA plan funds for any reason. The money in the account was subsequently returned to her after she left her employment and filed for bankruptcy. *Id.* at 223. The bankruptcy trustee sought to add the money refunded to the debtor to the bankruptcy estate to distribute to the debtor's creditors. The debtor claimed the money was exempt (meaning she could keep it) under the statute. *Id.*

The relevant statute provided, "A restriction on the transfer of a beneficial interest of the debtor in a trust that is enforceable under applicable *nonbankruptcy law* is enforceable in a case under this title." *Id.* (quoting 11 U.S.C. § 541(c)(2)) (emphasis added). The issue for the court was whether an ERISA plan was created under a nonbankruptcy law. The court held that it was. The court based its decision on the ordinary meaning of the text; ERISA laws are not bankruptcy laws. *Id.* at 225. Despite the clarity of the text, the court turned to the legislative history of the bankruptcy statute. Despite looking at the legislative history, the court found it to be unhelpful because it was unclear. Thus, the court adopted the ordinary meaning.

In looking at the legislative history, the *Idalski* court disagreed with the *Sinclair* court that legislative history was only relevant when text was ambiguous. Rather, the court said, "the [plain meaning] rule should be applied [only] where the statutory construction urged by a party is so inherently improbable that it defies common sense." *Id.* at 228. In all other cases, a court should "consider evidence that may substantiate a statutory construction which a party claims most accurately reflects the legislative intent[.]" *Id.* at 227. The judge in *Idalski* believed that legislative history was almost always relevant.

Interestingly, both bankruptcy judges discussed the consistency of the Supreme Court's use of legislative history over the years. The judge in *Sinclair* claimed the Court had been consistent. *Sinclair*, 870 F.2d at 1341. The judge in *Idalski* claimed the Court had not been consistent. *Idalski*, 123 B.R. at 225. The *Idalski* judge is correct. As the Court's membership and preferred statutory theory have changed over time, the willingness of the justices to consider legislative history has also changed. While the justices routinely looked at legislative history before Justice Scalia joined the Court, that practice has modified slightly with his textualist influence. Lower courts have followed suit. Let's explore that history now as we discuss the ways you can critique your opponent's use of legislative history.

c. Criticizing Your Opponent's Use of Legislative History

i. Understanding the Supreme Court's Use of Legislative History

Recall from Chapter 4 that prior to 1965, judges in England refused to consider legislative history under the exclusionary rule. Our judicial system is based on the English common law system; however, the United States rejected the exclusionary rule in 1892. In *Church of the Holy Trinity v. United States*, 143 U.S. 457 (1892), the Court considered the legislative history. In that case, the Court had to decide whether a statute that prohibited the importation of foreigners to perform "labor or service of any kind" applied to ministers. Despite the relative clarity of the text (rectoring is labor and service), the Court examined the legislative history of the bill and concluded that the enacting legislature had intended to stem the influx of cheap, manual labor from China. Because the purpose of the bill was to stem cheap Chinese labor, the Court held that "labor or service" included manual labor only. *Id.* at 464. Following *Holy Trinity*'s approach, courts began regularly to consider legislative history to discern legislative intent.

Over time, the Court's willingness to consider legislative history has waxed and waned. As the preferred statutory interpretation theory has changed, the use of legislative history has changed accordingly. When purposivism was popular, so was the Court's use of legislative history. At that time, the Court did not need a reason to look at legislative history, such as ambiguity or absurdity. Legislative history was considered regardless of the clarity of the text. "When aid to the construction of the meaning of words, as used in the statute, is available, there certainly can be no 'rule of law' which forbids its use, however clear the words may appear on 'superficial examination.'" *United States v. Am. Trucking Ass'ns, Inc.*, 310 U.S. 534, 543–44, 60 (1940) (footnotes omitted). Similarly, when members of the Warren court preferred intentionalism, legislative history was central to the justices' analyses. *See, e.g., Chevron, U.S.A. Inc. v. Natural Resources Defense Council, Inc.*, 467 U.S. 837 (1984) (examining legislative history among other sources).

The justices' approach changed, however, when Justice Scalia joined the Court in 1986 and refocused the statutory interpretation discourse on the text. As a result of his efforts, text reemerged as primary to the inquiry. In refocusing the inquiry, Justice Scalia directly assaulted the other justices' use of legislative history. For example, in *Koons Buick Pontiac GMC, Inc. v. Nigh*, 543 U.S. 50 (2004), Justice Scalia said:

> Needless to say, I also disagree with the Court's reliance on things that the sponsors and floor managers of the 1995 amendment failed to say. I have often criticized the Court's use of legislative history because it lends itself to a kind of ventriloquism. The Congressional Record or committee reports are used to make words appear to come from Congress's mouth which were spoken or written by others (individual Members of Congress, congressional aides, or even enterprising lobbyists.)

Id. at 73 (Scalia, J., dissenting). While a few judges, such as former Justice Scalia, Justice Thomas, and Judge Easterbrook, are unwilling to consider legislative history at all, most judges generally allow lawyers some opportunity to "prove" the correctness of their interpretation with evidence from the legislative history. For example, the remaining members of the Rehnquist Court did not agree that legislative history should always be out-of-bounds. In *Wisconsin Public Intervenor v. Mortier*, 501 U.S. 597 (1991), they rejected Justice Scalia's position on legislative history. "Our precedents demonstrate that the Court's practice of utilizing legislative history reaches well into its past. We suspect that the practice will likewise reach well into the future." *Id.* at 610 n.4 (internal citation omitted). Under the Roberts Court, most of the justices continue to consider legislative history; however, their use is more limited than in the past.

There can be no doubt that Justice Scalia's criticisms had an effect on the use of legislative history in judicial interpretation. Judges today are far less likely to rely significantly on legislative history than in the past. And for some judges, litigants must first show that the statute as written is absurd, ambiguous, or has a scrivener's error before suggesting that the legislative history is relevant. But not all members of the judiciary have embraced moderate textualism.

ii. The Criticisms of Using Legislative History

There are many criticisms of judicial use of legislative history, including the following: (1) constitutionality issues, (2) accessibility and cost considerations, and (3) reliability concerns. This section will explore those criticisms.

First, critics argue that reliance on legislative history is unconstitutional for a few reasons. State and federal constitutions provide a process for enactment: passage by both chambers in identical form (bicameral passage) and presentment to the executive for approval or veto (presentment). Legislative history does not follow this process; only the text of the bill does. Hence, legislative history is not law and should not be consulted.

Moreover, critics reason that the Constitution delegates law-making power to the legislature as a whole — not to committees or individual legislators. For this reason, statements made in committee reports and floor debates, which are only the statements of individual legislators, should not be cited as evidence of the whole legislature's intent. Complicating the issue further is the fact that staff members or lobbyists and not legislators regularly draft committee reports and other legislative documents. Justice Scalia once said:

> As anyone familiar with modern-day drafting of congressional committee reports is well aware, the [language was] … inserted, at best by a committee staff member on his or her own initiative, and at worst by a committee staff member at the suggestion of a lawyer-lobbyist; and the purpose of [that language] was not primarily to inform Members of Congress about what the bill meant, … but rather to influence judicial construction.

Blanchard v. Bergeron, 489 U.S. 87, 98–99 (1989). Thus, strict textualists point out that the intent of staffers and lobbyists regarding the meaning of a law is simply irrelevant and, arguably, unconstitutional.

Additionally, they note that due process requires that citizens have notice of the law. If judges cannot understand what a statute means without perusing the legislative history, how can an ordinary citizen, who is unlikely to have access to such history, know what a statute means?

Second, critics argue that legislative history is not equally accessible and available to all. Legislative history is often voluminous (or non-existent), obscure, hard to find, and poorly indexed, especially at the state level. It can be expensive and time-consuming to examine all of it. The dissent in *Pepper v. Hart* made this same point. Lawyers are trained to search exhaustively for the "smoking gun." Doing so in this context may cost a client a lot of money. Many clients cannot afford to pay for such a search, putting them at a disadvantage.

Third, critics argue that legislative history may be unreliable. Legislators simply do not read every report or attend every debate. In *Hirschey v. FERC*, 777 F.2d 1, 7 n.1 (D.C. Cir. 1985), then Judge Scalia included a snippet from a Senate floor debate to underscore this point:

> Several years ago, the following illuminating exchange occurred between members of the Senate, in the course of floor debate on a tax bill:
>
> **Mr. ARMSTRONG.** . . . My question, which may take [the chairman of the Committee on Finance] by surprise, is this: Is it the intention of the chairman that the Internal Revenue Service and the Tax Court and other courts take guidance as to the intention of Congress from the committee report which accompanies this bill?
>
> **Mr. DOLE.** I would certainly hope so. . . .
>
> **Mr. ARMSTRONG.** Mr. President, will the Senator tell me whether or not he wrote the committee report?
>
> **Mr. DOLE.** Did I write the committee report?
>
> **Mr. ARMSTRONG.** Yes.
>
> **Mr. DOLE.** No; the Senator from Kansas did not write the committee report.
>
> **Mr. ARMSTRONG.** Did any Senator write the committee report?
>
> **Mr. DOLE.** I have to check.
>
> **Mr. ARMSTRONG.** Does the Senator know of any Senator who wrote the committee report?
>
> **Mr. DOLE.** I might be able to identify one, but I would have to search. I was here all during the time it was written, I might say, and worked carefully with the staff as they worked. . . .
>
> **Mr. ARMSTRONG.** Mr. President, has the Senator from Kansas, the chairman of the Finance Committee, read the committee report in its entirety?
>
> **Mr. DOLE.** I am working on it. It is not a bestseller, but I am working on it.
>
> **Mr. ARMSTRONG.** Mr. President, did members of the Finance Committee vote on the committee report?

Mr. DOLE. No.

Mr. ARMSTRONG. Mr. President, the reason I raise the issue is not perhaps apparent on the surface, and let me just state it:.... The report itself is not considered by the Committee on Finance. It was not subject to amendment by the Committee on Finance. It is not subject to amendment now by the Senate....

If there were matter within this report which was disagreed to by the Senator from Colorado or even by a majority of all Senators, there would be no way for us to change the report. I could not offer an amendment tonight to amend the committee report.

[F]or any jurist, administrator, bureaucrat, tax practitioner, or others who might chance upon the written record of this proceeding, let me just make the point that this is not the law, it was not voted on, it is not subject to amendment, and we should discipline ourselves to the task of expressing congressional intent in the statute.

128 CONG. REC. S8659 (daily ed. July 19, 1982).

Id.

And even if read, comments made within committee reports and during legislative hearings may not reflect the understanding of every legislator. For example, in *Amalgamated Transit Union Local 1309 v. Laidlaw Transit Servs., Inc.*, 435 F.3d 1140 (9th Cir. 2006), the court relied on a Senate report to discern the purpose of the Class Action Fairness Act. However, that particular report was not submitted until after the House and Senate had voted on the bill and the President had signed it into law. *Amalgamated Transit Union Local 1309 v. Laidlaw Transit Servs., Inc.*, 448 F.3d 1092, 1096 (9th Cir. 2006) (Bybee, J., dissenting) (order denying en banc rehearing). The report could have had no influence whatsoever on the legislators' decisions, yet it influenced the court's interpretation.

Similarly, in *Hamdan v. Rumsfeld*, 548 U.S. 557 (2006), Senators Jon Kyl and Lindsey Graham filed an amicus brief in which they offered a colloquy from *The Congressional Record* as evidence that Congress was aware that the Detainee Treatment Act would strip the Supreme Court of jurisdiction to hear cases the Guantanamo detainees filed. *Id.* at 580 n.10. The Justice Department relied on this legislative history to argue that its interpretation of the Act was the correct one. *Id.* at 576. Yet the majority rejected this particular colloquy because it was inserted into *The Congressional Record* after the Senate debate. *Id.* at 580 n.10. In other words, members of Congress never considered the comments nor had an opportunity to disagree with them. The majority did consider floor debates and other legislative history that were a part of the enactment process, but not these after-the-fact insertions into the record.

As you might imagine, Justice Scalia was not happy with the majority's willingness to consider any of the legislative history:

> The Court immediately goes on to discount numerous floor statements by the [Act's] sponsors that flatly contradict its view, because "those statements appear to have been inserted into the Congressional Record after the Senate debate." Of course this observation, even if true, makes no difference unless one indulges the fantasy that Senate floor speeches are attended (like the Philippics of Demosthenes) by throngs of eager listeners, instead of being delivered (like Demosthenes' practice sessions on the beach) alone into a vast emptiness. Whether the floor statements are spoken where no Senator hears, or written where no Senator reads, they represent at most the views of a single Senator.

Id. at 665–66.

Critics raise another criticism of the use of legislative history: it often includes contradictory statements. When contradictory legislative history exists, which history counts? This issue was at the forefront of the debate in *United Steelworkers v. Weber*, 443 U.S. 193 (1979). In that case, the justices used different aspects of the legislative history to support their interpretation that Title VII did or did not allow affirmative action programs. *Weber* illustrates a problem with using legislative history; litigants tend to rely on the history that supports their interpretation while ignoring or minimizing the history that contradicts that interpretation. In *Weber*, the justices can be faulted for doing the same.

The facts of the case are straightforward. In 1974, Kaiser, the defendant's employer, and the United Steelworkers of America, a labor union, agreed that Kaiser would create a new training program in response to the employer's historical discrimination of African American workers. *Id.* at 197–98. According to the collective bargaining agreement, Kaiser would admit one African American into the program for every African American that applied until the percentage of African American workers in the program was equal to the percentage of African American workers in the local work force. *Id.* at 198. Weber was a Caucasian employee who sued when he was not selected for a place in the program, while other African American workers with less seniority were chosen instead. *Id.* at 199.

The issue for the Court, as framed by the majority, was whether Title VII of the Civil Rights Act forbade Kaiser from adopting this *voluntary* affirmative action program to remedy past discrimination against African American workers. *Id.* at 200. Title VII prohibited employers from *"discriminat[ing]* against any individual ... because of such individual's race." *Id.* at 199–200 n.2 & 3 (quoting 42 U.S.C. § 2000e-2(a), (d)). The majority held that Kaiser's program was permitted precisely because it was a *voluntary* program aimed at correcting past discrimination. *Id.* at 208.

In reaching this holding, the majority agreed that the word "discriminate" was not ambiguous but suggested that a literal construction of the text would be misplaced. *Id.* at 201 (citing *Church of the Holy Trinity v. United States,* 143 U.S. 457, 459 (1892)). Title VII must "be read against the background of the legislative history ... and the historical context from which the Act arose." *Id.* Reasoning that the purpose of this section was to remedy "the plight of the Negro in our economy," the majority held that Title VII's prohibition did not apply when an employer *voluntarily* enacted an affirmative action program to remedy past discrimination and forestall future litigation. *Id.* at 202, 208. Note that the majority used legislative history to find the general purpose of the statute, and not to find the specific intent of the legislature.

To find this general purpose, the majority looked to various parts of the legislative history. First, the majority cited the Senate floor debate comments of Senator Humphrey, who worked tirelessly to move the bill through the Senate. *Id.* at 202. During the floor debates, Senator Humphrey said, "The rate of Negro unemployment has gone up consistently as compared with white unemployment for the past 15 years. This is a social malaise and a social situation which we should not tolerate. That is one of the principal reasons why the bill should pass." *Id.* at 202 (quoting 110 CONG. REC. 7220 (1964) (statement of Sen. Humphrey)). During the debates, Senator Humphrey had specifically indicated that without well-paying jobs past discrimination could not be corrected. " 'The crux of the problem [was] to open employment opportunities for Negroes in occupations which have been traditionally closed to them.' " *Id.* at 203 (quoting 110 CONG. REC. 6548 (1964) (statement of Sen. Humphrey)). Additionally, the majority noted that the House Report accompanying the bill when it was sent to the Senate stated that the bill would *"create an atmosphere conducive to voluntary or local resolution of other forms of discrimination."* *Id.* at 204 (quoting H.R. REP. No. 914, at 18 (1963)). The majority suggested that Congress was concerned about the plight of African American workers and wanted to remedy that "mischief." *Id.*

In response to one of the dissent's primary arguments, the majority suggested that another section of the Act (section 703(j)) was specifically included to protect employers from being *required to* implement affirmative action programs, not to stop them from *choosing to* implement such programs. *Id.* at 205–06. The majority suggested that Congress could easily have included language in section 703(j) that would not "permit" employers to remedy past discrimination. Because Congress chose not to do so, voluntary programs were permissible. *Id.* at 206–07.

According to the majority's understanding of this legislative history, Congress wanted a law that would not only prevent discrimination in the future but would allow past discrimination to be voluntarily remedied. *Id.* at 204. This history suggested to the majority that the purpose of Title VII was to help African American workers secure jobs by increasing employment opportunities. *Id.* Because the statute was enacted to help African American workers, it would be ironic, the majority believed, were it to become the legal impediment to voluntary attempts to correct past discrimination. *Id.*

The dissent disagreed with the majority's characterization and selection of relevant legislative history. According to the dissent, the text and legislative history were abundantly clear: Congress intended to limit all forms of discrimination, not just prohibit discrimination against African American workers. *Id.* at 228–29 (Rehnquist, J., dissenting).

Unlike the majority, which looked for the general purpose of the statute, the dissent looked for and found specific legislative intent. To so do, the dissent detailed the passage of Title VII of the Civil Rights Act in excruciating detail. *Id.* at 231–52. The Civil Rights Act was originally introduced in the House, where it was immediately sent to the Judiciary Committee. *Id.* at 231. The Judiciary Committee amended the bill by adding Title VII and later reported the Act to the House floor with both majority and minority committee reports accompanying it. *Id.* The majority report "advanced a line of attack which was reiterated throughout the debates in both the House and Senate and which ultimately led to passage of § 703(j)." *Id.* The minority concern was that employers would be forced to address past discrimination under the language of the amendment because "discriminate" was not defined. The minority report included hypotheticals, including one in which an employer was forced to hire non-Caucasians to racially balance its workforce. *Id.* Note that the legislature specifically discussed the meaning of the language at issue in this case: "discriminate."

In response to the concerns raised in the minority report, the sponsor of the bill and chair of the Judiciary Committee, Representative Celler, said that the "Bill would do no more than prevent employers from discriminating against or *in favor of* workers." *Id.* at 233 (quoting 110 CONG. REC. 1518 (1964) (statement of Rep. Celler)). The battle-lines were drawn, but ultimately the bill with the amendment was passed in the House by a vote of 290 to 130. The bill was then sent to the Senate where the longest debate in that body's history took place. *Id.* at 234. The Senate voted to address the bill directly and not forward it to any of the committees, which was highly unusual. *Id.* at 237.

During the ensuing debate, many senators remained concerned that employers would be expected to correct past discrimination by requiring quotas despite the colloquy from the House. *Id.* at 238. Senator Humphrey, a strong proponent of the bill, repeatedly assured those who were concerned that "not only does Title VII not require use of racial quotas, *it does not permit their use.*" *Id.* But the senators were not as easily persuaded as the representatives had been, and the debate continued.

While the debate in the Senate raged, a bipartisan coalition drafted an amendment, which included a new subsection — section 703(j) — to allay the racial-quota concern. *Id.* at 243. That subsection provided, " 'Nothing contained in [Title VII] shall be interpreted to require any employer ... to grant preferential treatment to any individual or to any group because of the race ... of such individual or group on account of' a racial imbalance in the employer's work force." *Id.* at 244 (quoting 42 U.S.C. § 2000e-2(j)). Remember that the majority had suggested that this language prohibited only *required* affirmative action programs, not *voluntary* affirmative action programs. *Id.* at 206–07 (majority opinion). The dissent was incredulous:

> Not once during the 83 days of debate in the Senate did a speaker, proponent or opponent, suggest that the bill would allow employers *voluntarily* to prefer racial minorities over white persons. In light of Title VII's flat prohibition on discrimination "against any individual ... because of such individual's race," § 703(a), 42 U.S.C. § 2000e-2(a), such a contention would have been, in any event, too preposterous to warrant response. Indeed, speakers on both sides of the issue, as the legislative history makes clear, recognized that Title VII would tolerate no voluntary racial preference, whether in favor of blacks or whites. The complaint consistently voiced by the opponents was that Title VII, particularly the word "discrimination," would be interpreted by federal agencies such as the [Equal Employment Opportunity Commission] to require the correction of racial imbalance through the granting of preferential treatment to minorities. Verbal assurances

that Title VII would not require—indeed, would not permit—
preferential treatment of blacks having failed, supporters of H.R. 7152
responded by proposing an amendment carefully worded to meet,
and put to rest, the opposition's charge. Indeed, unlike §§ 703(a) and
(d), which are by their terms directed at entities—*e. g.*, employers,
labor unions—whose actions are restricted by Title VII's prohibitions,
the language of § 703(j) is specifically directed at entities—federal
agencies and courts—charged with the responsibility of interpreting
Title VII's provisions.

Id. at 244–46 (Rehnquist, J., dissenting). Finally, the dissent concluded, "In
light of the background and purpose of § 703(j), the irony of invoking the
section to justify the result in this case is obvious." *Id.* at 246. The legislative
history was overwhelmingly clear to the dissent: Title VII was meant to be
racially blind. Because affirmative action programs, whether voluntary or
involuntary, discriminate against Caucasian workers, such programs were
prohibited under the Act.

Who was right? Critics of the *Weber* holding note that Justice Rehnquist's
dissent more faithfully explored and characterized the legislative history. The
enacting Congress likely did intend a race-blind act. Thus, the majority can
be criticized for missing (or perhaps ignoring) the specific intent of the enacting
legislature. But Justice Rehnquist is not without fault. His opinion failed to
take into account critical facts in the case. Title VII was enacted in 1964. More
than ten years later, the workforce at the Kaiser plant where Weber worked was
still 98.2% Caucasian even though the local workforce was 39% African
American—"fishy numbers ten years after Title VII had prohibited race
discrimination . . . ." WILLIAM N. ESKRIDGE, JR., ET AL., CASES AND MATERIALS
ON LEGISLATION: STATUTES AND THE CREATION OF PUBLIC POLICY 218 (3d ed.
2001). Likely, the enacting Congress anticipated that employment decisions
after the Act's passage would not be based on race. But what if they were? The
legislative history could not address the issue of what to do about employers
that refused to abide by Title VII after its passage, yet those were precisely the
facts in the *Weber* case. "This [omission] undermines Justice Rehnquist's specific
intent argument: It is not clear that Congress considered affirmative action in
the context of Weber's case." *Id.* Thus, the majority's purposivist approach
better addresses these facts.

Perhaps the most accurate approach was that of Justice Blackmun who, in
concurrence, considered both factors. *Weber*, 443 U.S. at 214–15 (Blackmun,
J., concurring). While he shared many of Justice Rehnquist's concerns about

the specific intent of the enacting legislature, he ultimately sided with the majority's general purpose argument because circumstances had changed since Title VII had been passed:

> The bargain struck in 1964 with the passage of Title VII guaranteed equal opportunity for white and black alike, but where Title VII provides no remedy for blacks, it should not be construed to foreclose private affirmative action from supplying relief. It seems unfair for respondent Weber to argue, as he does, that the asserted scarcity of black craftsmen in Louisiana, the product of historic discrimination, makes Kaiser's training program illegal because it ostensibly absolves Kaiser of all Title VII liability. Absent compelling evidence of legislative intent, I would not interpret Title VII itself as a means of "locking in" the effects of segregation for which Title VII provides no remedy.

Id.

Those who criticize the use of legislative history point to cases like *Weber* to demonstrate that legislative history can be manipulated to support any result a judge or litigator wants. Judge Harold Leventhal has said quite famously, "the trick is to look over the heads of the crowd and pick out your friends." ANTONIN SCALIA, A MATTER OF INTERPRETATION: FEDERAL COURTS AND THE LAW 36 (1997). Some critics have even suggested that legislators may insert language into legislative history for the sole purpose of influencing later judicial interpretations. The facts of *Hamdan v. Rumsfeld* lend some weight to this argument. 548 U.S. 557, 580 n.10 (2006) (refusing to consider legislative colloquy that was inserted into *The Congressional Record* after the Senate debate). Thus, for these reasons, critics argue that the reliability of legislative history can be problematic.

All of these concerns are valid and are ones that you or your opponent should be aware of and be able to articulate. But rather than prohibit the use of legislative history entirely, these concerns merely show that legislative history should be relegated to a non-leading role in interpretation. Legislative history is certainly not law, but legislative history can offer insight into what some or all of the legislators may have been thinking when the act, which did go through the constitutional process, was enacted. Thus, legislative history offers context for the enactment process of a particular act. A skilled litigant will know where to find legislative history, how to use it, and how to criticize an opponent's use of it.

iii. The "Dog Does Not Bark" Canon: When Congress Is Silent

What if the legislative history is silent on a particular issue? Ordinarily, "[s]ilence in the legislative history about a particular provision ... is not a good guide to statutory interpretation and certainly is not more persuasive than the words of a statute." *America Online, Inc. v. United States*, 64 Fed. Cl. 571, 578 (2005). However, silence can sometimes be illuminating. Suppose, for example, that a statute on its face makes a radical and controversial change in the law— one that you would expect Congress would have discussed and debated. Yet the legislative history is silent; Congress did not mention the change at all. Under these circumstances, wouldn't silence speak volumes? Generally, the answer is no; occasionally, the answer is yes.

To illustrate, in *Harrison v. PPG Industries, Inc.*, 446 U.S. 578 (1980), the issue for the Court was whether a general catch-all term— "any other final action"— in the Clean Air Act meant *any* final agency action or just actions similar in nature to the specific actions preceding the general catch-all. *Id.* at 587, 592. In other words, the question was whether the other surrounding, listed actions narrowed the general catch-all, as *ejusdem generis* would suggest. A broad interpretation would dramatically shift responsibility for reviewing the Environmental Protection Agency's actions under this Act from the district courts to the courts of appeals. *Id.* at 585. For this reason, the Fifth Circuit found it unlikely that Congress would have intended such a major jurisdictional shift without expressly addressing this anticipated change during the enactment process. For the court, "[t]he 'most revealing' aspect of the legislative history of [the subsection at issue] ... was the complete absence of any discussion of such a 'massive shift' in jurisdiction." *Id.* at 585 (citing *PPG Industries, Inc. v. Harrison*, 587 F.2d 237 (5th Cir. 1979)).

On appeal, the Supreme Court rejected this "silence speaks volumes" argument. "In ascertaining the meaning of a statute, a court cannot, in the manner of Sherlock Holmes, pursue the theory of the dog that did not bark." *Id.* at 592.[4]

---

4. The Court was referring to A. CONAN DOYLE, SILVER BLAZE, *in* THE COMPLETE SHERLOCK HOLMES 289 (1927), in which the following exchange took place: "Is there any point to which you would wish to draw my attention?" asked the Scotland Yard Detective. To which Holmes responded, "To the curious incident of the dog in the night-time." Detective: "The dog did nothing in the night-time." "That was the curious incident," replied Sherlock Holmes.

Despite strong rhetoric in *PPG Industries* against the-dog-did-not-bark argument, this argument can, at times, be persuasive; hence, it should not be ignored. For example, in *Chisom v. Roemer*, 501 U.S. 380 (1991), the majority found legislative silence informative. In that case, the Court had to determine whether Section Two of the Voting Rights Act, which protects individuals' rights to elect "*representatives*," applied to the election of state judges. *Id.* at 384. The petitioners, African American voters, alleged that Louisiana's method of electing two justices to the State Supreme Court at-large from the New Orleans area impermissibly diluted the minority vote; the state responded that the Act did not apply to the election of state judges because judges are not representatives. *Id.* at 385, 390.

The legislative history was telling precisely because it was not telling. Congress had amended Section Two of this Act in 1982. *Id.* at 393. Prior to the amendment, there was no question that judges were covered. *Id.* at 392. With the amendment, Congress had responded to a prior judicial interpretation of the statute that had required proof of intent to discriminate. *Id.* at 393. Congress had eliminated this judicially imposed intent requirement. *Id.* The majority concluded that had Congress intended, by using the word "representatives," to exclude vote dilution claims involving judges: "Congress would have made it explicit in the statute, or at least some of the Members would have identified or mentioned it at some point in the unusually extensive legislative history of the 1982 amendment." *Id.* at 396. The Court reasoned that because no legislator had ever suggested that judges would no longer be covered, Congress must have meant to maintain the status quo in this regard despite its choice of the term "representatives." *Id.* at 399. Thus, silence spoke volumes.

Justice Scalia, in dissent, chastised the majority's dog-does-not-bark analysis:

> Finding nothing in the legislative history affirming that judges were excluded from the coverage of § 2, the Court gives the phrase "to elect representatives" the quite extraordinary meaning that covers the election of judges.
>
> As method, this is just backwards, and however much we may be attracted by the result it produces in a particular case, we should in every case resist it. Our job begins with a text that Congress has passed and the President has signed. We are to read the words of that text as any ordinary Member of Congress would have read them ... and apply the meaning so determined. In my view, that reading reveals that § 2 extends to vote dilution claims for the elections of representatives only,

and judges are not representatives.... Apart from the questionable
wisdom of assuming that dogs will bark when something important is
happening, we have forcefully and explicitly rejected the Conan Doyle
approach to statutory construction in the past.

Id. at 40506 (Scalia, J., dissenting) (citations omitted). For another example,
see *Mississippi Poultry Association, Inc. v. Madigan*, 992 F.2d 1359, 1378 (5th
Cir. 1993) (Reavley, C.J., dissenting) (arguing that it was inconceivable that
Congress would enact a statute that effectively created a trade barrier without
talking about "why a barrier was justified, what it was supposed to accomplish,
or how its effectiveness would be monitored."), *aff'd on reh'g*, 31 F.3d 293 (5th
Cir. 1994) (en banc), *overruled by* 21 U.S.C. § 466(d)(1) (1994), amended
through Pub. L. 103465, § 431 (k)(1) (1994).

Despite the reality that Congress is unlikely to make a radical shift in law or
policy without some discussion during the enactment process, the presumption
remains that legislative silence during enactment is not relevant to meaning. If
the legislature did not mean what it wrote, then the legislature, not the court,
should fix the error, as it did after the *Mississippi Poultry Association* case.

We have now surveyed the various types of legislative history, examined the
Supreme Court's use of legislative history over time, explored the criticisms of
using legislative history, and explored the relevance of silence during the
enactment process. We turn now to another way to use legislative history: to
identify unexpressed statutory purpose.

3. Finding & Using Purpose

While statutory interpretation may center on the language in the text,
understanding language is more than simply identifying the ordinary meaning
of those words using dictionaries. Statutes consist of a body and soul: "[T]he
letter of the law is the body of the law, and the sense and reason of the law is
the soul of the law." William N. Eskridge, Jr., *All About Words: Early
Understandings of the "Judicial Power" in Statutory Interpretation, 1776–1806*,
101 COLUM. L. REV. 990, 1000 (quoting *Eyston v. Studd*, 75 Eng. Rep. 688,
695). In other words:

Legislation has an aim; it seeks to obviate some mischief, to supply
an inadequacy.... That aim ... is not drawn, like nitrogen, out of the
air; it is evinced in the language of the statute, as read in the light of
other external manifestations of purpose.

Felix Frankfurter, *Some Reflections on the Reading of Statutes*, 47 COLUM. L. REV. 527, 538–39 (1947). We turn now to the soul of the law: purpose. Below you will learn first how to find it, then you will learn how to use it.

a. Finding Purpose

In Chapter 8, we examined preambles, findings, and purpose clauses. When Congress includes one of these, finding purpose is easier. Whether purpose can be used if it is located in one of these clauses was also explored in Chapter 8. But many acts, particularly older acts, do not have preambles, explanatory findings, or other indicia of purpose. And because of the political nature of the legislative process, even when acts contain such clauses, the clauses may be incomplete or unhelpful. When acts have no such clause or incomplete clauses, one area from which you can derive purpose is from the text. Discerning an act's purpose from text alone can be challenging, but it is the first place to start. "There is, of course, no more persuasive evidence of the purpose of a statute than the words by which the legislature undertook to give expression to its wishes. Often these words are sufficient in and of themselves to determine the purpose of the legislation." *United States v. Am. Trucking Ass'ns*, 310 U.S. 534, 543 (1940).

In 1584, the quintessential purpose case was decided in England, *Heydon's Case*, 76 Eng. Rep. 637 (Ex. 1584). The facts were few: King Henry VIII adopted a statute that specified which property interests would be invalidated if used to avoid the King's ability to seize property. The particular property owner used copyhold interests (an ancient form of landownership), which were not expressly identified in the statute. Thus, the court had to decide whether to expand the statute to include these types of property interests — even though they were not explicitly included within the text — and give the King more property or whether to limit the statute to its words — even though this interest had likely been omitted inadvertently. To decide whether these interests should be included, the court identified a four-step process: *first*, identify the law as it existed prior to a statute's enactment; *second*, identify the "mischief" that the legislature wished to remedy by enacting the statute; *third*, identify the remedy the legislature devised to correct that mischief; *finally*, interpret the statute to further that remedy and minimize that mischief. This four-step process is known as the *Mischief Rule*. Applying this four-step process in *Heydon's Case*, the court extended the statute to include the omitted property interest because this interpretation would correct the "mischief," *i.e.* people evading royal property confiscations. *Id.* at 638.

How does one identify the mischief and remedy? Professors Henry Hart and Albert Sachs simplified the rule in *Heydon's Case* as follows:

In interpreting a statute a court should:
(1) Decide what purpose ought to be attributed to the statute ... ;
and then
(2) Interpret the words ... to carry out the purpose as best it can,
making sure, however, that it does not give the words ...
(a) a meaning they will not bear....

WILLIAM N. ESKRIDGE, JR. & PHILIP P. FRICKEY, INTRODUCTION TO HENRY M.
HART, JR. & ALBERT M. SACKS, THE LEGAL PROCESS (1994) 1374 (William N.
Eskridge, Jr. & Philip P. Frickey, eds., 1994).

In our modern era, judges often turn to legislative history to find the statutory
purpose, especially when the text is unhelpful. Knowing why a law was enacted
can explain the purpose behind the legislation. The seminal case in this area,
Church of the Holy Trinity v. United States, 143 U.S. 457 (1892), was one of the
first cases in which American judges used legislative history to discern purpose.

In that case, Holy Trinity Church had paid a rector to come over from
England to serve as the church's pastor. A federal statute prohibited the church
from importing "any alien ... into the United States ... to perform *labor or
service of any kind*." *Id.* at 458 (emphasis added). The Supreme Court conceded
that "the act of the corporation [was] within the letter of this section, for the
relation of rector to his church is one of service, and implies labor on the one
side with compensation on the other." *Id.* But the Court rejected this
interpretation. Stating the infamous phrase, "[i]t is a familiar rule that a thing
may be within the letter of the statute and yet not within the statute, because
not within its spirit, nor within the intention of its makers," the Court turned
to the legislative history of the statute. *Id.* at 459. According to the Court, the
legislative history, specifically the committee reports and floor debates, was
clear that the mischief Congress had tried to stem was the influx of "cheap,
unskilled labor ... not brain toilers." *Id.* at 464. Hence, the statute was
inapplicable to the rector because including rectors would not further the
statutory purpose. *Id.* at 465. Thus, in this case, the Court looked to legislative
history to find the statute's purpose and narrowly interpreted the broad statutory
language. As a side note, the rector did not stay in the United States for long.
Shortly after the Court's decision, he left New York claiming that it was an
"immoral place to be."

Thus, when a statute does not include a purpose clause or the clause is
unhelpful, purpose may be found in the text of the statute, in its legislative
history, or even in the social and historical context surrounding a law's
enactment. Once you find unexpressed purpose, how do you use it?

b. Using Purpose

Judges use purpose in many ways. Judges may use purpose to confirm ordinary meaning, to resolve ambiguity, and to provide guidance in the case of absurdity. For example, in *Ohio Division of Wildlife v. Clifton*, 692 N.E.2d 253 (Ohio Mun. Ct. 1997), the state court judge relied on the purpose of a state statute to overcome the government's absurd interpretation.

The facts in the case are as follows. A squirrel fell out of a tree. Ms. Clifton saved its life and kept it for a pet. She contacted the state agency responsible for managing the state's wildlife and was incorrectly told she did not need to get a license to keep the animal. She named the squirrel Angele Daniel Nicole and let it roam freely in her house. The squirrel even slept in her bed. Around Halloween, the defendant entered the squirrel in the local pumpkin parade and won first prize for most unusual pet. A picture of the squirrel appeared in the local paper. Shortly thereafter, two state officers from the Division of Wildlife appeared on her doorstep to take the squirrel. She asked if she could let the squirrel live in her backyard, but was told no. She was cited when she refused to hand over the squirrel to certain death. *Id.* at 254.

The state statute broadly allowed "'(a)ny person' [to] 'apply' for a license 'to have … game quadrupeds, or fur-bearing animals in captivity.'" *Id.* However, the statute further provided that "*except as provided by law*, no person shall possess … fur-bearing animals." *Id.* at 255 (emphasis added). The statute included three exceptions. One exception allowed for commercial propagating licenses; a second allowed for noncommercial propagating licenses; the third allowed for catch-and-release licenses. *Id.* at 254–55. None of the exceptions applied in this case because the defendant had no plans to propagate or release Angele Daniel Nicole.

In addition to prohibitions in the statute, the State Division of Wildlife, a state agency, had issued regulations prohibiting people from taking animals from the wild for any purpose other than for hunting. Violating the law carried a maximum fine of $500 and 60 days in jail. *Id.* at 254. Thus, the statute and regulations were clear; Clifton had broken the law.

Despite the clarity of the text, the trial court dismissed the case, chastising the state for wasting resources prosecuting a Good Samaritan. *Id.* at 258. The court admitted that the law was clear: Clifton could only own a squirrel if she could get a license, and the statute and regulations did not provide any way for her to get a license. The court seemed to find this interpretation absurd, saying "[e]ven a child can see there is no justice in this result." *Id.* Using purposivism, the court reasoned that the purpose of the statute and criminal justice generally would not be furthered by incarcerating or fining Clifton. *Id.*

at 257–58. The court reasoned that the legislature could not have intended to allow wild animals to been taken from the wild only to be killed. "No one could be so myopic as to believe that the legislature was so ambivalent toward the protection of wild animals as to have legislated an Act that requires, manifestly, that all animals found in whatever location defined under the statute must be thereafter killed …." *Id.* at 256. Thus, the court considered the purpose of criminal laws generally (justice) and the purpose of this statute (general public safety from wild animals) to dismiss the defendant's citation. *Id.* at 259. *See also Church of Scientology v. Dep't of Justice*, 612 F.2d 417, 424–25 (9th Cir. 1979) (turning to the purpose as found in the legislative history to confirm the statute's clear text).

In addition to using purpose to resolve ambiguity, absurdity, and confirm the meaning of clear text, some judges use purpose to overcome clear text. For example, in *Holy Trinity*, the Court stated first that the language at issue was not ambiguous and included rectoring (although that concession is debatable) and then used purpose, which the Court found in the legislative history, to reject the ordinary meaning. *See also King v. Burwell*, 135 S. Ct. 2480, 2497 (2015) (holding that the phrase "an Exchange established by the State" meant "an Exchange established by the State or federal government" to further the purpose of the Affordable Care Act).

Similarly, the Ninth Circuit used purpose to hold that "less" actually meant "more." In *Amalgamated Transit Union Local 1309 v. Laidlaw Transit Servs., Inc.*, 435 F.3d 1140 (9th Cir. 2006), the court rejected the ordinary meaning of the text of the Class Action Fairness Act. That Act provided that "a court of appeals may accept an appeal … denying a motion to remand a class action to the State court from which it was removed if application is made to the court of appeals *not less than 7 days* after entry of the order." *Id.* at 1142 (quoting 28 U.S.C. § 1453(c)(1)) (emphasis added). The ordinary meaning of the text of the statute imposed a seven-day waiting period but contained no upper time limit for appealing. The Ninth Circuit found this ordinary meaning "illogical" but not necessarily absurd. *Id.* The court then turned to the legislative history of the Act (specifically a Senate committee report) to discern the purpose of the Act and concluded that Congress had intended the Act to impose a *time limit* for appealing rather than a waiting period to appeal. *Id.* at 1146. A textualist court could have reached this same result using the scrivener's error doctrine.

One member of the Ninth Circuit, Judge Bybee, was so upset with the majority's decision that he *sua sponte* called for an en banc rehearing, which was denied. *Amalgamated Transit Union Local 1309 v. Laidlaw Transit Servs., Inc.*, 448 F.3d 1092 (9th Cir. 2006). Judge Bybee then dissented from the order denying the rehearing, which is also very unusual. *Id.* at 1094 (Bybee, J., dissenting). In his dissent, Judge Bybee chastised the majority for rejecting the ordinary meaning of the statute when the text was so clear. According to Judge Bybee, none of the reasons for avoiding the plain meaning canon applied. The statute was not absurd or ambiguous, there was no scrivener's error, and there was no constitutional question. Hence, if there was an error, then Congress, not the courts, should correct it. *Id.* at 1096–98. Judge Bybee was particularly concerned that the majority relied on a Senate committee report that "was not submitted until eighteen days after the Senate had passed the bill, eleven days after the House had passed the bill, and ten days after the President signed the bill into law." *Id.* at 1096. In Judge Bybee's opinion, the majority relied on legislative history that no member of Congress or the President had considered to interpret the statute to mean the exact opposite of what the statute actually said. *Id.*

Was Judge Bybee correct? Regardless of the relevance of the committee report, consider just the text. Could Congress truly have meant to enact a statute identifying an appeal timeline that created a waiting period rather than a time limit? And assuming not, who should fix the error? Consider the implications of waiting for Congress to fix its mistake. Textualists would say the legislature must correct its own errors, while purposivist and intentionalists would say the courts should fix the error when a mistake is so clear. Would the scrivener's error doctrine have been appropriate here?

The debate between the majority and dissent in this case illustrates nicely the impact that a judge's theory of interpretation can have on meaning. In *Amalgamated Transit Union* and in *Holy Trinity*, the judges were willing to look beyond clear text to statutory purpose, as found in the legislative history, to interpret the relevant statute as Congress likely intended but certainly did not say. In contrast, the dissent in *Amalgamated Transit Union* was unwilling to look beyond the text because no exceptions applied, even though it was likely that Congress never intended the statute to mean what it actually said. When text is clear, purpose generally plays a supporting, not leading, role. "To let general words draw nourishment from their purpose is one thing. To draw on some unexpressed spirit outside the bounds of the normal meaning of words is quite another." *Addison v. Holly Hill Fruit Prods., Inc.*, 322 U.S. 607, 617 (1944).

Sometimes a statute has more than one purpose. When multiple purposes of a statute conflict and are impossible to reconcile, which purpose should control? There is no easy answer to this question. One approach is to try to further more of the purposes. By furthering as many purposes as possible, the court does not elevate one purpose at the expense of others. *See, e.g., Office Planning Group, Inc. v. Baraga-Houghton-Keweenaw Child Development Bd.*, 697 N.W.2d 871, 894 (Mich. 2005) (Kelly, J. dissenting) (arguing that implying a private right of action would better further a second purpose while not adversely affecting the statute's primary purpose).

Sometimes the purpose of an exception in a statute conflicts with the statute's general purpose. When this occurs, which purpose should matter: the purpose of the statute as a whole or the purpose of the statute's exception? Currently, there is no agreed answer to this question. Generally, a court will try first to find an interpretation that furthers more of the purposes, but when the court cannot reconcile the purposes, the court should read the exception's purpose narrowly, much like a proviso (*see* Chapter 8). *See, e.g., Church of Scientology*, 612 F.2d at 424–25 (in which the majority relied on the purpose of the exception while dissent relied on the purpose of the Act as a whole).

What if two related statutes have purposes that conflict? Which should control? Generally, courts try to reconcile both statutes' purposes, but when that is not possible, the purpose of the applicable statute controls. This approach mirrors the courts' approach to conflicting statutes: reconcile if at all possible. *See, e.g., Kentucky Off-Track Betting, Inc. v. McBurney*, 993 S.W.2d 946 (Ky. 1999) (comparing the purposes of an earlier existing statute and later enacted amendments).

In conclusion, with the renewed focus on the text, unexpressed purpose seems to have become less relevant to many judges than in years past. Perhaps the days in which purpose can trump ordinary meaning have ended. But wholesale rejection of purpose is not appropriate either. Like legislative history, purpose has a role in interpretation, albeit only a supporting one.

In this chapter, we explored the role that legislative history and unexpressed purpose play in interpretation. In the next chapter, we turn to the role that subsequent legislative action plays in interpretation.

C. Mastering This Topic

Return to the hypothetical ordinance provided in Chapter 1. The first question that was asked was the following: "An ambulance entered Pioneer Park to pick up and take to the hospital a man who had just suffered a heart attack. Did the ambulance driver violate the Pioneer Park Safety Ordinance (PPSO)?" How should you, as prosecutor, attempt to answer that question using what you've learned in this chapter?

Let's start with the legislative history to see if we can find specific intent regarding whether the legislators intended to allow ambulances (or other emergency vehicles) in the park. We have three pieces of legislative history: the Public Park Committee Report (the equivalent of a Senate or House committee report), a summary of the floor debates (generally, the floor debates of Congress are not summarized, as was done here), and the Mayor's signing statement (the equivalent of a presidential signing statement). From our review of the legislative history hierarchy, we know that the committee report carries the most weight. Looking at that report, we see that there is no evidence of specific intent regarding ambulances or even emergency vehicles. (Note that the report does show specific intent regarding parade vehicles, but that is not the issue you are researching at this time.)

We turn next to the summary of the floor debates. Again, the summary provides no evidence that the council members had a specific intent about ambulances or emergency vehicles; however, if we had a question about water skiing, we would have specific intent and, thus, guidance. Finally, we look at the Mayor's signing statement. It provides no evidence of a specific legislative intent (as a statement from the executive, query whether a signing statement ever could). Generally, signing statements carry little weight, which we will see in Chapter 14. Thus, in this case, the legislative history provides no evidence of specific intent on this issue.

Let's turn to purpose. The ordinance does not include a purpose or findings clause, so we must search for unexpressed purpose. We begin with the text. Section 4 of the ordinance increases the fines for anyone violating the ordinance and causing injury while doing so: "If any injury occurred, the fine shall be doubled." This section suggests that one possible purpose for the ordinance was to improve safety for those using the park. This purpose could suggest either that ambulances should be allowed in the park because ambulances help injured people receive treatment sooner or that ambulances should not be allowed in the park because they can injure pedestrians and others as easily as cars and motorcycles. The text in the case is ambiguous regarding purpose.

Let's apply the mischief rule. First, we need to identify the law as it existed prior to the ordinance's enactment. Here, motor vehicles of all kinds were permitted to enter the park. Second, we need to identify the "mischief" that the council wished to remedy by enacting the ordinance. Here, the "mischief" that the council wanted to remedy, according to the committee report, was injuries cars and motorcycles caused by striking pedestrians and bicyclists. Moreover, the summary of the debate suggests that noise and pollution were also of concern. Also, as noted above, the ordinance increases the penalty for anyone causing injury while violating the ordinance. Third, we need to identify the remedy the council devised to correct that mischief. Here, the remedy was to prohibit all motor vehicles from coming into the park with specific exceptions for maintenance and parade vehicles. Lastly, we need to interpret the statute to further that remedy and minimize that mischief. Here, the mischief rule would suggest that ambulances should not be permitted. They might strike pedestrians or bicyclists, and they are noisy and cause pollution. Thus, the unexpressed purpose of this ordinance, as found in the text and legislative history, suggests that ambulances should not be allowed to enter the park and that the driver should be cited. Arguably, this interpretation is absurd, which we examined earlier in Chapter 6.

Checkpoints

- Contextualism is the process of using context to determine what a statute means.

- Context includes a range of things including social and historical events, legal and political climate, economic and market factors, and even textual and linguistic context.

- Legislative history is the written record of deliberations surrounding and preceding a bill's enactment. Judges vary in their willingness to consider legislative history.

- Typically, judges use legislative history for one of two reasons: (1) to shed light on the specific intent of the enacting legislature, or (2) to identify the unexpressed statutory purpose.

- Some judges refuse to consider legislative history at all, but most are willing to consider legislative history to resolve ambiguity, absurdity, or scrivener's error. Some are willing to consider legislative history to confirm a statute's ordinary meaning.

- The use of legislative history has been criticized for many reasons, including the following: (1) constitutionality concerns, (2) reliability issues, and (3) accessibility and cost considerations.

- Legislative silence during the enactment process is generally not a good guide to meaning; however, sometimes, silence may have meaning pursuant to the "dog did not bark" canon.

- Judges may use unexpressed purpose in many ways: to resolve ambiguity and absurdity, to confirm ordinary meaning, and to overcome ordinary meaning.

Chapter 11

Canons Based on Extrinsic Sources: Post-Enactment Legislative & Judicial Context

---

Roadmap

- Learn to use what occurred in the legislature *after* the enactment process.
- Understand the *stare decisis* effect of judicial interpretations.
- Learn the relationship between super strong *stare decisis* and legislative acquiescence.
- Understand the role of subsequent legislative action, including new enactments, subsequent legislative history, reenactments, and affidavits from legislators.

A. Introduction to This Chapter

In this chapter, we continue with our examination of extrinsic sources and context. We move from an exploration of what happens during the legislative process to an examination of what occurs afterward. Subsequent events may shed light on what a statute means. This chapter will explore the canons related to subsequent actions of the legislature and the judiciary. In Chapter 14, we will look at the subsequent actions of the executive, namely signing statements and agency interpretations.

B. Using What Occurred
Subsequent to Enactment

If using what occurred prior to and during enactment can be controversial, using what occurred after enactment is even more so. If the goal of interpretation is discerning the intent of the enacting legislature, regardless of whether that is accomplished by finding purpose or intent, then anything that happens after passage should be irrelevant. Similarly, if discerning the common understanding of words when the text was originally adopted is the goal, subsequent events should be irrelevant. Yet complete irrelevancy is not the presumption. While some subsequent acts are generally considered irrelevant (*e.g.*, affidavits of legislators and subsequent legislative history), most are relevant at times (*e.g.*, legislative acquiescence and subsequent enactments), and others (*e.g.*, executive subsequent acts, such as agency interpretations) are not only relevant, but may well be conclusive.

1. Subsequent Judicial Action: Super
Strong *Stare Decisis*

In Latin, *stare decisis* means to stand by things decided. In law, it means that courts are reluctant to overturn prior judicial decisions absent a good reason to do so. *Stare decisis* furthers certainty in the law and faith in the judicial system. It also gives the appearance of objectivity; judges decide cases based on legal precedents rather than based on political leanings and personal preferences.

There are two aspects to *stare decisis*. First, the decisions of higher courts bind lower courts within the same jurisdiction. This aspect is not controversial. Second, a court should not overturn its own precedents without good reason. This aspect is neither controversial nor absolute: when an existing judicial opinion is clearly wrong, courts will overturn it. The most famous example of this latter aspect is the Supreme Court's decision in *Brown v. Board of Education*, 347 U.S. 483 (1954). In *Brown*, the Supreme Court overturned *Plessy v. Ferguson*, 163 U.S. 537 (1896), in which the Court had held that racial segregation in public accommodations was constitutional.

For cases involving statutes, the Supreme Court (and some lower courts) applies a heightened form of *stare decisis* known as "super strong *stare decisis*." This concept simply means that judicial decisions interpreting statutes should be overruled even less easily than judicial decisions refining the common law because Congress is the more appropriate body to correct erroneous interpretations of statutes. Under super strong *stare decisis*, even when a prior decision is clearly wrong, courts are reluctant to overrule it.

A federal case illustrating super strong *stare decisis* is *Faragher v. City of Boca Raton*, 524 U.S. 775 (1998). In that case, a female lifeguard, who worked for the City of Boca Raton, was sexually harassed by her supervisors. She sued her the supervisors and the City under Title VII of the Civil Rights Act of 1964, which provided,

> [i]t shall be an unlawful employment practice for an employer ... to fail or refuse to hire or to discharge any individual, or otherwise to discriminate against any individual with respect to his compensation, terms, conditions, or privileges of employment, because of such individual's race, color, religion, sex, or national origin.

Id. at 786 (citing 42 U.S.C. § 2000e-2(a)(1)).

In an earlier case, the Court had held that sexual harassment so "severe or pervasive" so as to "'alter the conditions of [the victim's] employment and create an abusive working environment'" violated Title VII. *Id.* at 786 (quoting *Meritor Savings Bank, FSB v. Vinson*, 477 U.S. 57, 67 (1986)). The issue for the Supreme Court in *Faragher* was whether the City should be liable for the actions of its employee-supervisor. The Court answered the question affirmatively. In its reasoning, the Court explained:

> We are bound to honor *Meritor* on this point not merely because of the high value placed on *stare decisis* in statutory interpretation, ... but for a further reason as well. With the amendments enacted by the Civil Rights Act of 1991, Congress both expanded the monetary relief available under Title VII to include compensatory and punitive damages and modified the statutory grounds of several of our decisions. The decision of Congress to leave *Meritor* intact is conspicuous. We thus have to assume that in expanding employers' potential liability under Title VII, Congress relied on our statements in *Meritor* about the limits of employer liability. To disregard those statements now (even if we were convinced of reasons for doing so) would be not only to disregard *stare decisis* in statutory interpretation, but to substitute our revised judgment about the proper allocation of the costs of harassment for Congress's considered decision on the subject.

Id. at 804 n.4 (internal citations omitted).

Super strong *stare decisis* may make sense in situations like *Faragher*, where Congress bases future legislation on the Court's existing interpretation. But sometimes the Court's unwillingness to overturn a prior decision for this reason makes little sense. Most notably, in *Flood v. Kuhn*, 407 U.S. 258 (1972), the Court examined the issue of whether baseball should be exempt from federal antitrust laws. Curtis Flood had been the center fielder for the St. Louis Cardinals. He missed a fly ball in the 7th inning of the 1968 World Series with Detroit. His error cost his team the series. Not surprisingly, the following year St. Louis traded him, along with six other players, to the Philadelphia Phillies. Flood did not want to go to Philadelphia, for a variety of reasons. He wrote to the Commissioner of Baseball and asked the Commissioner to let other teams know of his availability. The Commissioner refused. Flood sued, claiming the Commissioner's action violated federal antitrust laws. *Id.* at 265.

The issue for the Court was whether baseball was an interstate trade or commerce. In two of its earlier cases, *Federal Baseball Club v. National League*, 259 U.S. 200 (1922), and *Toolson v. New York Yankees, Inc.*, 346 U.S. 356 (1953), the Court had held that baseball was not an interstate trade or commerce, which was required for federal antitrust laws to apply. In 1922, the Court may have been correct that baseball did not affect interstate commerce, but by 1972, it was clear that baseball did have such an effect. Yet the majority in *Flood*, while acknowledging that these earlier cases were wrongly decided, refused to overturn them. 407 U.S. at 279. The majority reasoned that because of the long-standing nature of the opinions, Congress should make the change. *Id.* at 283–84. The Court was concerned, in part, that baseball had developed during these fifty years under the assumption that it was exempt from the antitrust laws. To change the rules now would be unfair because judicial interpretations of statutes apply retroactively while legislative changes usually apply only prospectively.

The dissent disagreed, arguing that the earlier cases were wrong and that it was time to overturn them. "This is a difficult case because we are torn between the principle of *stare decisis* and the knowledge that the decisions in *Federal Baseball Club* ... and *Toolson* ..., are totally at odds with more recent and better reasoned cases." *Id.* at 290 (Marshall, J., dissenting). As Justice Marshall explained:

> We do not lightly overrule our prior constructions of federal statutes, but when our errors deny substantial federal rights, like the right to compete freely and effectively to the best of one's ability as guaranteed

by the antitrust laws, we must admit our error and correct it. We have done so before and we should do so again here.

Id. at 292–93. In Justice Marshall's opinion, it was enough that the prior decisions were wrong and that the holdings deprived a litigant of a "substantial federal right[]." *Id.* at 292.

Who was right? Justice Marshall's standard for reversing Supreme Court precedent is perhaps too light, while the majority's unwillingness to reexamine and correct interpretations that are wrong and at odds with the rest of the Court's jurisprudence also seems wrong. In this case, Flood, an African American, "was profoundly offended by the reserve clause, which resembled slavery in some ways and would result in his being forced move to a less tolerant community." WILLIAM N. ESKRIDGE, JR., ET AL., CASES AND MATERIALS ON LEGISLATION 278 (2000). Particularly given this background, the Court's refusal to change an interpretation that no longer made any sense seems unjustifiable. *Stare decisis* is important for many reasons noted above, but it should yield when time proves the earlier decisions to be wrong under modern standards. Given the realities of the legislative process, it can be extremely difficult for Congress to change precedent and fix its own mistakes; here, the Court was asking Congress to go one step further and correct the Court's mistake. Fixing its own mistakes should be the Court's job. For all these reasons, many academics urge that super strong *stare decisis* be relaxed so that opinions interpreting statutes can be afforded ordinary *stare decisis*.

In 1998, Congress finally did respond to *Flood* by enacting The Curt Flood Act of 1998, 15 U.S.C. § 26b. The Act did not alter the bargaining relationship between players and management in Major League Baseball. However, the socio-economic and political concerns surrounding the Curt Flood Act did impact that bargaining relationship. *See* J. Gordon Hylton, *Why Baseball's Antitrust Exemption Still Survives*, 9 MARQ. SPORTS L.J. 391 (1999). Then in 2015, the Ninth Circuit rejected an invitation to reconsider *Flood*. In *City of San Jose v. Office of the Commissioner of Baseball*, 776 F.3d 686 (9th Cir. 2015), *cert. denied*, 136 S. Ct. 36 (2015), the court held that Major League Baseball's franchise relocation policies were exempt from antitrust laws under *Flood*. Although San Jose had argued that *Flood* applied only to baseball's reserve system, and its holding had been legislatively overruled, the court disagreed: "antitrust claims against MLB's franchise relocation policies are in the heartland of those precluded by *Flood*'s rationale." *Id.* at 691. The Supreme Court denied cert.

In sum, the rule remains that *stare decisis* plays a heightened role in statutory interpretation cases; indeed, cases can be wrong, but still be right, as *Flood* demonstrates. But *stare decisis* is not an absolute rule. Typically, the Supreme Court overrules at least one statutory interpretation case each term. William N. Eskridge, Jr., et al., *supra* at 281.

2. Subsequent Legislative Inaction: Legislative Acquiescence

Closely related to super strong *stare decisis* is the doctrine of legislative acquiescence. By far the most common legislative response to a judicial interpretation of a statute is silence. Some judges reason that a legislature's silence to an interpretation means acquiescence, or agreement, with that interpretation. One basis for finding silence to mean legislative acquiescence is the notion of super strong *stare decisis*. As you learned in the last section, super strong *stare decisis* refers to the heightened *stare decisis* effect given to court opinions from the highest court in a jurisdiction that interprets statutes. Pursuant to super strong *stare decisis*, courts presume that these statutory precedents are correct. Once the Supreme Court has authoritatively construed a federal statute or the state's highest court has construed a state statute, judges believe that the legislature is the more appropriate body to change the interpretation if there is any error. If the legislature disagrees with the court's interpretation, then the legislature should change the interpretation. "When a court says to a legislature: 'You (or your predecessor) meant X,' it almost invites the legislature to answer: 'We did not.'" Guido Calabresi, A Common Law for the Age of Statutes 31–32 (1985). The fact that the legislature did not change the interpretation suggests that it agreed with the decision.

Legislative acquiescence is appropriate when the deciding court was the highest court within a jurisdiction, rather than a lower court, because there is still a chance that the highest court will correct the lower court's error. But in fact, a majority of the circuits apply the canon to appellate court opinions as well.[1]

---

1. *See, e.g., In re Zurko*, 142 F.3d 1447, 1457-58 (Fed. Cir. 1998) (en banc), *rev'd on other grounds sub nom. Dickinson v. Zurko*, 527 U.S. 150, 165 (1999); *Bath Iron Works Corp. v. Dir., Office of Workers' Comp. Programs*, 136 F.3d 34, 42 (1st Cir. 1998); *Chicago Truck Drivers v. Steinberg*, 32 F.3d 269, 272 (7th Cir. 1994); *Critical Mass Energy Project v. Nuclear Regulatory Comm'n*, 975 F.2d 871, 875-76 (D.C. Cir. 1992) (en banc); *Owen v. CIR*, No. 78-1341, 1981 WL 16570, at *9 (6th Cir. June 23, 1981); *Cottrell v. CIR*, 628 F.2d 1127, 1131 (8th Cir. 1980) (en banc); *Gen. Dynamics Corp. v. Benefits Review Bd.*, 565 F.2d 208, 212 (2d Cir. 1977).

Does legislative acquiescence reflect reality? At times, the legislature probably does acquiesce to an interpretation by not acting in response. But more often, the political reality is that such silence means little. There is a multitude of reasons the legislature could have failed to amend the statute. The legislature could be unaware of the judicial opinion; the legislature might be unable to act in response to the interpretation; the legislature might have more pressing business; or the legislature might, indeed, agree with the decision.

Another criticism of legislative acquiescence is that when interpreting statutes, courts generally focus on finding the intent or purpose of the *enacting* legislature, not of a subsequent legislature. The legislature that silently approves the interpretation is most likely a different legislature than the legislature that enacted the statute. Silence from a subsequent legislature should have absolutely no relevance to the meaning the enacting legislature intended.

Finally, legislative acquiescence bypasses the constitutional process for enacting legislation; silence is neither passed bicamerally nor presented to the president. If silence is accepted as a legislative action, then Congress can effectively legislate in a way the Constitution does not contemplate. For this reason, textualists are particularly loath to rest an interpretation on legislative acquiescence. At bottom, "legislative acquiescence [is] focused on the wrong legislature and it may be unreliable. On close analysis, it may even be unconstitutional [sic]. But it is frequently invoked ...." RONALD BENTON BROWN & SHARON JACOBS BROWN, STATUTORY INTERPRETATION: THE SEARCH FOR LEGISLATIVE INTENT 164 (2002).

Perhaps the best case for finding legislative acquiescence, if it should ever be found, is *Flood v. Kuhn*, 407 U.S. 258 (1972), which we studied earlier in this chapter. Remember in that case, the Supreme Court examined the issue of whether baseball was exempt from federal antitrust laws. *Id.* at 265. The issue for the Court was whether baseball, specifically its reserve system, affected interstate commerce. The issue would have been simple to resolve were it not for two earlier cases, *Federal Baseball Club v. National League*, 259 U.S. 200 (1922), and *Toolson v. New York Yankees, Inc.*, 346 U.S. 356 (1953). In these cases, the Court had held that baseball was not an interstate trade or commerce, which was required for federal antitrust laws to apply.

Shortly after these decisions, the Court had recognized that professional sports did impact interstate commerce and, thus, held that the antitrust laws applied to other professional sports, such as wrestling and football. In doing so, the Court specifically expressed concern with its conflicting precedent and invited Congress to legislatively overrule *Federal Baseball Club* and *Toolson*.

Flood, 407 U.S. at 273. In response, more than fifty bills were introduced in Congress; however, none of those bills were enacted. Of those bills that either the House or Senate passed, most would have expanded, rather than narrowed, the *Toolson* exception to apply to other professional sports. *Id.* at 281–82. Thus, Congress was not silent in response to *Federal Baseball Club* and *Toolson*; rather, Congress was simply unsuccessful at legislatively changing the outcome.

Because of this legislative acquiescence, the majority in *Flood* refused to overturn the Court's earlier holdings. *Id. at* 279. The majority was loath to overturn the cases when "Congress, by its *positive inaction*, ... ha[d] clearly evinced a desire not to disapprove them legislatively." *Id.* at 283-84. (emphasis added). Despite recognizing the error of its earlier holdings, the majority refused to correct its mistake because Congress's "positive inaction" suggested acquiescence to the judicial decision. The majority suggested that *Flood* was not a case of legislative acquiescence; rather it was "something other than mere congressional silence and passivity." *Id.* at 283. The majority's position is unsupportable: Congress had not acted, at least not successfully; hence, legislative acquiescence really did serve as the basis for the majority's holding.

The dissent was ready to correct the prior mistaken holdings. In response to the majority's legislative acquiescence argument, the dissent suggested that because the Court had, in prior decisions, treated other sports differently than baseball, Congress may not have been motivated to act. *Id.* at 290 (Marshall, J., dissenting). In any event, the dissent saw no reason to continue to uphold its prior erroneous precedent when substantial rights were affected.

If *Flood* is a case in which legislative acquiescence could reasonably have been found because Congress indicated its awareness of the judicial holdings and tried but failed to act to expand those holdings, *Bocchino v. Nationwide Mutual. Fire Insurance, Co.*, 716 A.2d 883 (Conn. 1998), is a case in which legislative acquiescence should not have been found. In that case, the plaintiff sued his insurance company after his house burned to the ground. The insurance policy, pursuant to a state statute, had required the plaintiff to file his lawsuit within one year of the date of the loss. *Id.* at 884. He did, but then, because of a computer error on the court's part, the suit was mistakenly dismissed. *Id.* at 889 (Berdon, J., dissenting). In response to the court's error, plaintiff re-filed within one year of the court's dismissal. But this refiling occurred more than one year from date of the loss. *Id.* at 884 (majority opinion). A state failure-of-suit statute permitted a plaintiff to file a new action "[i]f any action, commenced within *the time limited by law*, has failed one or more times to be tried on its merits ...." *Id.* at 883 n.2 (quoting CONN. GEN. STAT. § 52-592) (emphasis added).

The trial court dismissed the action as not being filed within the one-year time limitation. *Id.* at 884. The Connecticut Supreme Court affirmed, holding that the "time limited by law" exception did not apply to contractual limitations periods even when those provisions were required to be included in a contract because of a state law. *Id.* at 885. Although the court acknowledged that the language in the failure-of-suit statute was ambiguous, the court reasoned that the ambiguity had been resolved by two of its prior decisions, *Chichester v. New Hampshire Fire Insurance Co.*, 51 A. 545 (Conn. 1902), and *Vincent v. Mutual Reserve Fund Life Ass'n*, 51 A. 1066 (Conn. 1902). In these two prior opinions, the court had held that the failure-of-suit statute applied only to actions barred by a statute of limitations and not to actions limited contractually. The decisions in these cases were reaffirmed in *Monterio v. American Home Assurance Co.*, 416 A.2d 1189 (Conn. 1979). Because the legislature was silent in response to these opinions, the *Bocchino* majority assumed that legislature acquiesced in the holdings. Because the court determined that the time frame was contractual rather than required by law, the court affirmed the dismissal. *Bocchino*, 716 A.2d at 886–87.

Bocchino is poorly reasoned. Unlike the *Flood* case, in *Bocchino* there was absolutely no proof that the legislature was aware of these old opinions. Moreover, the opinions addressed civil procedure issues, issues typically of more concern to the judiciary than to the legislature. And further, the prior holdings did not actually address the precise issue before the *Bocchino* court. Rather, in *Chichester*, the plaintiff's suit had been tried on the merits and failed; he was then precluded from bringing a second action. *Chichester*, 51 A. at 545. In *Monterio*, the plaintiff had commenced his action more than one year from the date he suffered the loss because his attorney was seriously ill. *Monterio*, 416 A.2d at 1189. For these reasons, the *Bocchino* dissent disagreed with the majority. The dissent argued that even if the opinions the majority cited actually were on point, the dissent would have overruled them. The language in the statute was clear: The filing time was in the statute because a state law required it to be; hence, the time to file "was limited by law." *Bocchino*, 716 A.2d at 891 (Berdon, J., dissenting). Given that the legislature was not likely aware of the prior opinions and that legislative acquiescence should be an exception in interpretation, not a rule, the dissent would have reversed.

If *Flood* presents one situation where Congress may have acquiesced, it is perhaps the only such case. Judges should find legislative acquiescence only rarely. It is, perhaps, legitimate to say that Congress acquiesced when it tried, but failed, more than fifty times to overturn a prior precedent. It is quite another thing to say that silence *in all cases* means that the legislature agreed with the opinion:

> It is perhaps too late now to deny that, legislatively speaking as in ordinary life, silence in some instances may give consent. But it would be going even farther beyond reason and common experience to maintain, as there are signs we may be by way of doing, that in legislation any more than in other affairs silence or nonaction always is acquiescence equivalent to action.

Cleveland v. United States, 329 U.S. 14, 22–24 (1946) (Rutledge, J., concurring). Silence can mean any number of things; judges should not presume silence always means agreement.

One final case of note: in *FDA v. Brown & Williamson Tobacco Corp.*, 529 U.S. 120 (2000), the Supreme Court considered whether the Food and Drug Administration ("FDA") had authority to regulate tobacco as a "drug" under the Food, Drug, and Cosmetic Act. For years, the FDA had refused to regulate tobacco and, in fact, claimed it lacked jurisdiction under the Act to do so. *Id* at 125. Eventually, when a new president came to office, the FDA reversed course and began to regulate. The tobacco companies sued, claiming the FDA's new interpretation was *ultra vires*. *Id* at 129. The majority agreed. The majority reasoned that against the FDA's repeated assertions that it lacked authority to regulate, Congress had enacted six separate pieces of "tobacco-specific" legislation to "creat[e] a distinct regulatory scheme for cigarettes and smokeless tobacco." *Id* at 155. With this distinct regulatory scheme, Congress evidenced its intent that it and not the FDA regulate this significant issue. *Id* at 155–56.

Justice Breyer in dissent noted that the subsequent legislative activity was ambiguous at best and accused the majority of resting its decision on legislative acquiescence alone. *Id* at 181–82 (Breyer, J., dissenting). The majority responded, "We do not rely on Congress' failure to act—its consideration and rejection of bills that would have given the FDA this authority—in reaching this conclusion. Indeed, this is not a case of simple inaction by Congress that purportedly represents its acquiescence in an agency's position." *Id* at 155.

Who was right? If the majority based its holding in *Brown & Williamson* on legislative acquiescence, the holding is extremely problematic because it is not actually a case of legislative acquiescence to a prior judicial interpretation, even accepting the reasons the majority offered. The Supreme Court had never determined whether the relevant act covered cigarettes and tobacco. Only the executive agency in charge of food and drugs, the FDA, had done so. The FDA initially said that cigarettes and tobacco were not covered then later changed its interpretation when a new executive came into office. Thus, if Congress acquiesced to anything, it acquiesced to the *FDA's* interpretation of a statute, not to the Supreme Court's interpretation of it. It is not clear that the legislative acquiescence doctrine is appropriate when Congress acquiesces to an agency interpretation of a statute because this doctrine rests on concerns about *stare decisis* and separation of powers. *Stare decisis* has no application when there is no underlying judicial opinion to overturn. And the separation of powers issue relates not to the balance of power between the judiciary and legislature, but rather it relates to the balance of power between the executive and legislature. An agency should not be able to limit or expand a grant of authority from Congress, yet this opinion allowed an agency to do precisely that. Further, an agency should not be able to bind Congress to a particular interpretation of an act: courts yes (as we will see in Chapter 15), but Congress no. Further, if the interpretations of a prior administration that later prove unwise in light of changing economic, technologic, and political realities bind Congress and agencies, then executive flexibility may well be sacrificed. For all of these reasons, the legislative acquiescence aspect of this case is very troubling. However, what about the six subsequent legislative actions? Should they be relevant to interpretation? We explore that issue next.

3. Subsequent Legislative Action

The previous section explored subsequent legislative *inaction*. This section explores subsequent legislative *action*. After a statute is enacted, legislatures and legislators act in ways that could be relevant to an existing statute's meaning. For example, legislatures may enact subsequent legislation or discuss existing statutes during the legislative enactment of a new bill. In addition, legislators may testify or offer affidavits to "prove" a statute's meaning. This section explores the relevance of each of these in turn.

a. Subsequent Acts

Enactment of a subsequent act may affect the meaning of an existing act. *Franklin v. Gwinnett Cnty. Pub. Sch.*, 503 U.S. 60 (1992). For example, in *Franklin*, the Supreme Court had to decide whether, under Title IX's implied causes of action, a plaintiff could recover money damages in addition to injunctive relief.

The plaintiff in the case, a student at the public high school, was the subject of inappropriate and unwanted sexual advances by one of her teachers. *Id.* at

64. By the time the case was heard, both the student and teacher had left the school. Hence, injunctive relief would not have benefitted this student. As for the remedy, the legislative history was silent, which makes sense given that the cause of action was not express but was implied. The silence did not trouble the Court. "Since the Court ... concluded that this statute supported no express right of action, it is hardly surprising that Congress also said nothing about the applicable remedies for an implied right of action." *Id.* at 71.

Thus, the Court turned to another source to resolve the issue: subsequent legislative acts. In two related acts (the Rehabilitation Act Amendments of 1986 and the Rehabilitation Act of 1973), Congress broadly defined the express remedies available under those acts to include all forms of damages. *Id.* at 73. The majority and concurrence both found Congress's subsequent legislation to be "a validation of [the court's earlier] holding" and "an implicit acknowledgment that damages [were] available." *Id.* at 78 (Scalia, J., concurring). Thus, subsequent acts may provide insight into the contours of an existing act.

Let's return to *Brown & Williamson.* Recall that the FDA claimed it lacked jurisdiction to regulate tobacco for thirty-five years. During this time, Congress was not inactive. Some legislators attempted to amend the Act to give the FDA explicit authority to regulate tobacco, but their efforts proved unsuccessful. *Brown & Williamson,* 529 U.S. at 147. Congress did, however, enact "six separate pieces of legislation" regulating the advertising of tobacco and requiring warning labels. *Id.* at 155. Congress also moved promptly to take away jurisdiction when another agency, the Federal Trade Commission (the "FTC"), tried to regulate. *Id.* at 145. Thus, members of Congress were unsuccessful at expanding the FDA's jurisdiction to regulate tobacco but were successful at limiting the FTC's jurisdiction and enacting some oversight.

When President Bill Clinton was elected the political climate changed, at least within the executive branch. The FDA reversed course, declaring tobacco to be a "drug" and cigarettes to be "combination products" that delivered nicotine to the body. *Id.* at 127. The FDA enacted regulations to control the sale and distribution of both cigarettes and tobacco. Not surprisingly, the tobacco companies quickly challenged the FDA's regulations.

The majority rejected the FDA's attempt to regulate despite the ordinary meaning of the text: tobacco was a "drug" and cigarettes were "combination products." *Id.* at 133. The majority reasoned that against the backdrop of the FDA's repeated statements that it lacked jurisdiction to regulate, Congress had enacted various "tobacco-specific statutes" to "creat[e] a distinct regulatory scheme for cigarettes and smokeless tobacco." *Id.* at 155. Because Congress legislated, albeit in another area, deference to the FDA's changed interpretation was inappropriate.

The dissent disagreed, finding the language of the statute clear and determining that the FDA's inclusion of cigarettes as drugs supported the general purpose of the Act. *Id.* at 191 (Breyer, J., dissenting). In response to the majority's arguments, the dissent noted that the subsequent legislative activity was ambiguous at best. *Id.* at 186. First, the failure of the legislature to enact legislation granting the FDA express authority to act proved only that Congress did not have enough votes to pass the bills. *Id.* at 183. Second, that Congress moved quickly to take away jurisdiction from other agencies that tried to assert jurisdiction in this area might have shown, as the majority asserted, that Congress "resented agency assertions of jurisdiction in an area it had reserved for itself." *Id.* But if so, the dissent wondered, why then had Congress not immediately reacted when the FDA changed course and asserted jurisdiction over tobacco? *Id.* If Congress were opposed to any agency assuming jurisdiction, then Congress should have acted immediately in response to the FDA's claim of authority. *Id.* Third, the dissent noted that the statutes that were enacted limited the authority of another agency, the FTC, not the FDA. The dissent questioned "[w]hy would one read the [labeling act's] pre-emption clause ... so broadly that it would bar a different agency from engaging in any other cigarette regulation at all?" *Id.* at 185.

This opinion is interesting for a number of reasons. First, the textualists on the bench signed onto a decision that ignored the ordinary meaning of relatively clear text and did so by relying on legislative acquiescence, all while claiming not to have done so. Similarly, the dissenting purposivists and intentionalists focused heavily, albeit not exclusively, on the text. This is one case in which the justices appear to have rejected their preferred theoretical approaches in favor of their preferred policy outcome.

In sum, subsequent acts may provide insight into the contours of an existing act.

b. "Subsequent Legislative History"

Sometimes, while enacting a new law, the legislature will comment on an existing act. This *subsequent legislative history*, as it is called, should be irrelevant. (Note the irony in the title: How can subsequent events ever be historical?) While the legislature's comments might be relevant to the interpretation of the new act, those comments are generally not relevant to the interpretation of the existing act. "[S]ubsequent legislative history will rarely override a reasonable interpretation of a statute that can be gleaned from its language and legislative history prior to its enactment." *Consumer Prod. Safety Comm'n v. GTE Sylvania*, 447 U.S. 102, 117–18 n.13 (1980). Use of these comments for interpreting a

statute is extremely controversial, but done, for the reasons identified by Justice
Scalia below:

> The legislative history of a statute is the history of its consideration
> and enactment. "Subsequent legislative history"—which presumably
> means the *post*-enactment history of a statute's consideration and
> enactment—is a contradiction in terms. The phrase is used to smuggle
> into judicial consideration legislators' expressions *not* of what a bill
> currently under consideration means (which, the theory goes, reflects
> what their colleagues understood they were voting for), but of what
> a law *previously enacted* means ....
>
> In my opinion, the views of a legislator concerning a statute already
> enacted are entitled to no more weight than the views of a judge
> concerning a statute not yet passed. In some situations, of course, the
> expression of a legislator relating to a previously enacted statute may
> bear upon the meaning of a provision in a bill under consideration—
> which provision, if passed, may in turn affect judicial interpretation
> of the previously enacted statute, since statutes *in pari materia* should
> be interpreted harmoniously. Such an expression would be useful, if
> at all, not because it was subsequent legislative history of the earlier
> statute, but because it was plain old legislative history of the later one.
>
> Arguments based on subsequent legislative history, like arguments
> based on antecedent futurity, should not be taken seriously, not even
> in a footnote.

Sullivan v. Finkelstein, 496 U.S. 617, 631–32 (1990) (Scalia, J., concurring).
In other words, comments made during the enactment of a new act do not
reflect what the enacting legislature intended or what the words meant when
an existing act was enacted. Thus, any such comments would show no more
than what a later legislature believed an earlier legislature thought. Any other
balance would elevate the intent of the second legislature above that of the
enacting legislature.

Occasionally, however, a court will find subsequent legislative history
relevant. To illustrate, in *Montana Wilderness Ass'n v. U.S. Forest Service*, 655
F.2d 951 (9th Cir.), *cert. denied*, 455 U.S. 989 (1981), the court addressed
the issue of whether a railroad had a right of access across federal lands. The
parties disputed whether subsection 1323(a) of the Alaska National Interest

Lands Conservation Act ("the Alaska Act") applied to the country as a whole or just to Alaska. *Id.* at 953. The Alaska Act required the Secretary of Agriculture to provide access to nonfederally owned land "within the boundaries of the *National Forest System*" in certain situations. *Id.* (citing Pub. L. No. 96-487, § 1323(a), 94 Stat. 2371 (1980)) (emphasis added). The next subsection of the Act, subsection (b), was expressly limited to lands situated in the National Forest System *in Alaska. Id.* at 953–54 (citing Pub. L. No. 96-487, § 1323(b), 94 Stat. 2371 (1980)). There was no similar express limitation in the subsection at issue — subsection (a).

The issue for the court was whether "National Forest System" as used in subsection (a) meant only national forests in Alaska or all national forests within the United States. *Id.* at 954. Looking at the sections *in pari materia,* the court agreed that the two subsections seemed to apply just to Alaska because the limitation in the second subsection (b) could be read to limit the first subsection (a). *Id.* at 954–55. But the court did not stop its analysis after applying this linguistic canon. The court reviewed the Alaska Act's legislative history, which it found to be unilluminating. *Id.* So, the court turned to the legislative history of an act passed *three weeks after* the Alaska Act, the Colorado Wilderness Act. *Id.* at 956. The conference committee report from this subsequent act showed that the members of the same Congress that had enacted the Alaska Act believed that subsection (a) applied nationwide. *Id.* at 955 n.6. The court acknowledged that, generally, subsequent legislative history is not entitled to "great weight," but suggested that subsequent legislative history would be entitled to significant weight when it was clear that the subsequent conference committee (1) had carefully considered the issue, and (2) had relied on a specific interpretation of the first act when drafting the second act. *Id.* at 957. Thus, the court held that subsection (a) of the Alaska Act applied to lands nationwide despite the strong *in pari materia* argument that it did not. *Id.*

Montana Wilderness represents the exception to the rule that subsequent legislative history is irrelevant to interpretation; when a legislature crafts a new law based on an interpretation of an existing law, then it may well make sense to give the prior law the subsequent meaning if only to harmonize both acts. Generally, however, subsequent legislative history is not relevant to the interpretation of a previously enacted act. Were the rule different, legislators could use after-the-fact statements to manipulate the interpretation process relatively easily. Moreover, the enacting legislature's intent and purposes would take a back seat to those of the new legislature.

The dog was going to bark scenario

c. The Reenactment Canon

You will remember that codification refers to the insertion of sections of an act into the relevant section of the code, whether state or federal. Codification was covered in detail in Chapter 8. Recodification simply means to codify again. Reenactment means, essentially, the same thing.

Occasionally, legislatures recodify or reenact the whole or portions of a code. Legislatures recodify for many reasons, including to simplify and consolidate statutes, to eliminate defects in the original enactment, to remove inconsistencies and obsolete provisions, to expand titles to permit past or future growth, and to reorganize to make provisions easier to find. For example, Congress recodified the criminal code in 1948. When it did so, Congress changed some statutory language, but left other language intact. When a legislature recodifies a code, the presumption is that the recodification clarified the law, but did not make substantive changes, unless the new language unmistakably indicates the legislature's intent to make substantive changes. *Fourco Glass Co. v. Transmirra Products Corp.*, 353 U.S. 222, 227 (1957).

When the text is changed, new interpretations will likely follow. But when a statute is reenacted in identical or similar form (for example, when code sections are simply renumbered), there is a presumption that the legislature knew of any existing judicial or administrative interpretations of that statute and intended to continue those interpretations. *Lorillard v. Pons*, 434 U.S. 575, 580–81 (1978). Otherwise, the presumption continues, the legislature would have amended the text. The reenactment canon is stated simply as follows: when a legislature reenacts or recodifies a statute that a court or an agency had previously interpreted judges presume that the legislature intended to continue that interpretation. This canon is similar to the super strong *stare decisis* canon discussed above. Yet the reenactment canon is also broader because it applies not only to the decisions of the highest court in a jurisdiction but also to agency and lower court interpretations.

This presumption is bolstered when there is evidence that the reenacting legislature was aware of the specific interpretation. For example, Congress reenacted the Voting Rights Act on two separate occasions. Both times the legislative history was clear that Congress agreed with earlier interpretations of the Act. Thus, those interpretations survived reenactment. "When a Congress that re-enacts a statute voices its approval of an administrative or other interpretation thereof, Congress is treated as having adopted that interpretation, and this Court is bound thereby." *United States v. Bd. of Comm'rs of Sheffield,*

Ala., 435 U.S. 110, 134 (1978). This presumption can be overcome with evidence that the legislature was unaware of or did not intend the existing interpretation.

d. Testimony by & Affidavits from Legislators & Staff Members

Least relevant of all to interpretation are testimony and affidavits from legislators or staff members. Sometimes, during litigation, one party will introduce the testimony or affidavit of a legislator or staff member who was present when the statute was enacted. This "evidence" of intent is generally considered irrelevant to the meaning of the statute, even when the affidavit comes from the drafter of the bill. "[E]vidence of a … draftsman of a statute is not a competent aid to a court in construing a statute." *S.D. Educ. Ass'n v. Barnett*, 582 N.W.2d 386, 400 (S.D. 1998) (Zinter, J., concurring in part and dissenting in part) (quoting *Cummings v. Mickelson*, 495 N.W.2d 493, 499 n. 7 (S.D. 1993)).

There are three reasons why such evidence is ignored. First, these affidavits indicate only one specific legislator's or, even worse, a lobbyist or staffer's understanding of the meaning and not the intent of the legislature as a whole. "Views of individuals involved with the legislative process as to intent [are of] no assistance … [for] it is the intent of the legislative body that is sought, not the intent of the individual members who may have diverse reasons for or against a proposition …." *American Meat Inst. v. Barnett*, 64 F. Supp. 2d 906, 916 (D.S.D. 1999).

Second, such affidavits are created to support one party's position in litigation after the legislative process has concluded. Memories may be inaccurate, incomplete, or intentionally wrong. Giving these statements weight could encourage gamesmanship. Finally, allowing such evidence of meaning would set legislators as rivals against one another and might give an individual legislator too much power to determine the meaning of a statute a legislature enacts. Despite these concerns, affidavits may be useful in limited situations. When the affidavit is "provided as background as to the nature of the problem and why and how the Legislature sought to address it," these concerns disappear. *S.D. Educ. Ass'n*, 582 N.W.2d at 397 (Gilbert, J., concurring).

In this chapter, we have discussed the role of subsequent judicial and legislative actions in interpretation. In the next chapter, we turn from the canons based on extrinsic sources to the canons based on policy-based sources.

C. Mastering This Topic

Return to the hypothetical ordinance provided in Chapter 1. The first question that was asked was the following: "An ambulance entered Pioneer Park to pick up and take to the hospital a man who has just suffered a heart attack. Did the ambulance driver violate the Pioneer Park Safety Ordinance (PPSO)?"

Is there anything is this chapter that could help you attempt to answer that question? Sadly, no. But that should not be surprising. In general, subsequent legislative acts, whether they be affidavits from legislators or silence from the legislature, are generally irrelevant to meaning. Thus, even if you had such information, it should play little, if any, role. For example, assume there was an earlier case in your jurisdiction that had held that firefighters were not exempt from the penalties in the PPSO. Assume further that, after this holding was issued, the council did not respond. Would the council's silence signal legislative acquiescence to the idea that emergency personnel were exempted from the PPSO's coverage? Certainly not. It is unlikely this council would have been aware of the decision, let alone had the time and or inclination to act on the interpretation. Unlike *Flood* and *Brown & Williamson*, there is simply no evidence of "positive inaction." Further, statements from the council members would not be relevant, the PPSO was not a recodified ordinance, and there are no subsequently enacted laws to consider. Simply put, this chapter is mostly useless to you; however, it has helped you learn the weakness of your opponent's arguments should your opponent raise arguments based on subsequent legislative action or inaction.

Checkpoints

- Using subsequent events from the legislative branch to discern the meaning of a statute is highly controversial.

- Under super strong *stare decisis*, a heightened form of *stare decisis*, judges are reluctant to overrule a judicial interpretation of a statute even when it is wrong.

- The most common legislative response to a judicial interpretation of a statute is silence. Silence can mean many things, including that the legislature agreed with the judicial interpretation.

- Legislative acquiescence is the doctrine that allows a court to presume the legislature's agreement with prior statutory interpretations.

- Legislative acquiescence rests on *stare decisis* and separation of powers concerns. It should be invoked rarely.

- Subsequent acts may provide insight into the contours of an existing act.

- Generally, subsequent legislative history of later enacted acts is irrelevant to the interpretation of a previously enacted act.

- When Congress reenacts or recodifies a statute that a court or an agency had previously interpreted, judges presume that Congress intended to continue the interpretation.

- Testimony by and affidavits from legislators and staff members is generally considered irrelevant to the meaning of a statute, even when the statement comes from the drafter of the bill.

Chapter 12

Canons Based on Policy-Based Considerations: Constitutional & Prudential

---

Roadmap

- Identify the canons based on constitutional and prudential considerations.
- Understand how the Constitutional Avoidance Doctrine applies.
- Learn the rule of lenity and its role in penal cases.
- Understand when clear statements are necessary.
- Explore the canons regarding remedial statutes and statutes in derogation of common law.
- Understand implied causes of action and implied remedies.

A. Introduction to This Chapter

We have finished examining the intrinsic and extrinsic sources with the exception of subsequent executive actions. We will cover that in Chapters 13–15. In this chapter, we turn to the third and final source of meaning: policy-based sources. You will remember from Chapter 4 that policy-based sources are sources that are extrinsic both to the statute and to the legislative process. They reflect important social and legal choices derived from the Constitution, social policy, and prudential ideals. These canons protect fundamental constitutional rights, such as due process, and advance particular policy objectives, such as requiring Congress to be clear when it impacts states' rights.

There are two types of policy-based sources: those based on constitutional considerations and those based on prudential considerations. This chapter will explain the former first and the latter second.

B. Review: Policy-Based Sources

Policy-based sources can play a fundamental role in interpretation. Your education in statutory interpretation would be incomplete without a discussion of these sources and the canons developed to further them. While you will gain an overview of these canons in this chapter, it is critical for you as a lawyer to research the role these canons play within your particular jurisdiction, for jurisdictions vary in their willingness to embrace or reject these sources.

Unlike the canons we have looked at so far, these canons do not claim to be neutral; rather, they value one consideration at the expense of another. For example, the rule of lenity directs judges to adopt the least penal interpretation of an ambiguous criminal statute or civil statute with a penal component. Here, fair notice trumps penalizing bad behavior.

Because these canons are non-neutral, their use may seem activist. Consider, for example, the 2000 Bush versus Gore election debacle. A Florida canon, derived from that state's constitution, directed Florida judges to construe election statutes so that the right of Florida voters to participate fully in the federal electoral process would be protected. *Palm Beach Cnty. Canvassing Bd. v. Harris*, 772 So. 2d 1220, 1237 (Fla. 2000). Hence, the court ordered the Florida Secretary of State to accept some amended returns. *Id.* at 1240. To some, this outcome appeared activist because it favored Democrat Al Gore over Republican George Bush.

Judges' willingness to use a particular policy-based source changes over time and across jurisdictions. For example, the rule of lenity, which arises from constitutional due process concerns about providing adequate notice of penal conduct, has been relegated to a rule of last resort in many states as a result of society's current focus on penalizing criminals. *See, e.g., United States v. Sanchez*, No. 08-CR-0017, 2008 WL 1926701 at *6–7 (E.D.N.Y. Apr. 30, 2008) (stating that "the court may resort to the rule of lenity as a last resort") (internal quotations omitted). Indeed, some state legislatures, such as California's, have attempted to abolish the rule of lenity entirely. *See* CAL. PENAL CODE § 4. However, because the rule of lenity flows from procedural due process, the California courts have had difficulty discarding it, even though there is a statute directing them to do so. *See, e.g. Wooten v. Superior Court*, 93 Cal. App. 4th

422, 432 (Cal. App. 4th Dist. 2001) (applying the rule of lenity to determine that a customer's observation of sexual contact between two exotic dancers was not a "lewd act" for purposes of a prostitution statute and failing to mention CAL. PENAL CODE § 4).

C. Law's Hierarchy

Before we detail the various canons based on the Constitution, we first need to review the legal structure of the United States. Some of the policy-based canons are based on the hierarchy of laws within the United States. As you are no doubt aware, the U.S. Constitution is the highest source of law. No statute passed by Congress or any state legislature can conflict with the U.S. Constitution. Statutes that do so are unconstitutional. Thus, to avoid declaring statutes unconstitutional, courts avoid interpreting statutes when possible in a way that would raise a constitutional issue.

The historical development of judicial review is informative. In early England, Parliament (the legislature) enjoyed almost unlimited power. In 1610, a "physician" was jailed for practicing medicine without a license. *The Case of the College of Physicians*, 8 Co. Rep. 107a, 77 Eng. Rep. 638 (C.P. 1610) (known as *Bonham's Case*). He sued for false imprisonment. In its defense, the Royal College of Physicians argued that a statute allowed the doctor to be imprisoned and fined. The Chief Justice, Sir Edward Coke, held for the doctor and said in dicta, "[W]hen an Act of Parliament is against common right or reason, or repugnant, or impossible to be performed, the common law will controul it and adjudge such Act to be void." *Id.* at 118a, 77 Eng. Rep. at 652. Despite what some thought at the time, *Bonham's Case* did not actually make English common law supreme over statutory law. *Hurtado v. California*, 110 U.S. 516, 531 (1884) ("[N]otwithstanding what was attributed to Lord Coke in *Bonham's Case* ... the omnipotence of parliament over the common law was absolute ... for English liberty against legislative tyranny was the power of a free public opinion represented by the commons.").

However, Coke's dictum set the stage for the acceptance of judicial review of legislation in America by "providing an early foundation for the idea that courts might invalidate legislation that they found inconsistent with a *written* constitution." *Seminole Tribe of Florida v. Florida*, 517 U.S. 44, 162 n.56 (1996) (Souter, J., dissenting). Judicial review was, of course, adopted in this country in *Marbury v. Madison*, 5 U.S. (1 Cranch) 137 (1803). As a result, our judiciary has the power to determine whether statutes are constitutional.

The second highest source of law is federal law, first statutes then federal common law. While you may have heard that there is no federal common law, this statement is not quite accurate. It is true that there is no federal common law in areas traditionally reserved to state courts, such as torts and contracts. But there are two basic areas where federal common law exists. The first area of federal common law includes those areas in which Congress has given federal courts the power to develop substantive law (for example, in admiralty, antitrust, bankruptcy, interstate commerce, and civil rights). The second area of federal common law includes those areas in which a federal rule of decision is necessary to protect interests that are uniquely federal. *Clearfield Trust Co. v. United States*, 318 U.S. 363 (1943) (identifying a three-step test for determining whether a federal common law rule is necessary to protect a significantly important federal interest). Thus, federal common law does exist, but it exists only so long as Congress allows it to exist.

Next on the hierarchy are federal regulations. Federal regulations are legislative-like rules that federal administrative agencies promulgate. First, Congress enacts a statute granting an agency the power to regulate, called the enabling statute. This enabling statute defines the boundaries of the administrative agency's regulatory power. Second, the agency promulgates a regulation to exercise its delegated power. So long as the agency stays within the boundaries of its delegated power, the regulations are generally valid. When an agency steps outside of its parameters, however, any regulations are *ultra vires*, or invalid. Linda D. Jellum, *Dodging the Taxman: Why Treasury's Anti-Abuse Regulation Is Unconstitutional*, 70 MIAMI L. REV. 152, 204 (2015) (describing the difference between unconstitutional and *ultra vires*). For example, the Environmental Protection Agency (EPA) has the power to regulate environmental issues. However, the EPA has no power to regulate international trade or taxes. Any attempt to do so would be *ultra vires*. Federal agencies also issue non-legislative laws known collectively as guidance documents. We will study these in Chapters 13–15.

Federal law of any kind trumps state law. The U.S. Constitution explicitly places federal law above state law, even state constitutions. Under the Supremacy Clause of the Constitution, federal law "preempts" state laws that conflict with it. U.S. CONST., art. 6, cl. 2. Thus, for example, if a federal statute required gasoline to be lead-free, a state law that permitted the sale of leaded gasoline would conflict with federal law, be preempted, and be unconstitutional. *But see Oxygenated Fuels Ass'n Inc. v. Davis*, 331 F.3d 665 (9th Cir. 2003) (rejecting preemption claim when California banned a chemical used to reduce gasoline emissions).

Although it occupies a lower tier on the legal hierarchy, state law is the overwhelming source of most rights and obligations. Virtually all tort law, contract law, and property law come from state statutes and case law. State law comes in four forms: constitutions, statutes, common law, and regulations. Each state has its own constitution. Many of them differ in important respects from the U.S. Constitution, often by providing for greater protection than the federal one. State constitutions can legitimately provide more protection to state citizens than the U.S. Constitution; however, state constitutions cannot provide less protection.

Just as all federal statutes must be constitutional under the U.S. Constitution, each state statute must be constitutional under that state's constitution. A state statute that conflicts with its state's constitution is unconstitutional. Accordingly, state courts endeavor to interpret state statutes to be constitutional, just as federal courts endeavor to interpret federal statutes to be constitutional. And like federal agencies, state agencies have the power to enact rules. State law creates one additional issue that seldom arises in connection with construing federal statutes: State statutes can conflict with state common law. Thus, courts must determine how to interpret state statutes that conflict with state common law. The next sections explore how courts interpret statutes in light of these hierarchies, starting with the constitutional avoidance doctrine.

D. Canons Based on the Constitution

1. The Constitutional Avoidance Doctrine

The constitutional avoidance doctrine is a statutory canon that respects this hierarchy. We studied it in Chapter 6, because it is one doctrine that allows judges to reject the ordinary meaning of clear text. You should reread that chapter if you have forgotten the doctrine's relevance. In this section, we explore the role that this doctrine plays in respecting separation of powers and the Constitution. Pursuant to this canon, when there are two reasonable interpretations of statutory language, one which raises constitutional issues and one which does not, the statute should be interpreted in a way that does not raise the constitutional issue. *Murray v. Schooner Charming Betsy*, 6 U.S. (2 Cranch) 64, 118 (1804). Simply put: "A statute or rule is construed, if possible, to: ... avoid an unconstitutional ... result." UNIF. STATUTE & RULE CONSTR. ACT, § 18(a3) (1995). When the court faces a question about the constitutionality of a statute, even if serious constitutional doubt is raised, the court will first ascertain whether another construction of the statute is *fairly possible* so that the constitutional question can be avoided.

This canon serves two purposes: first, it protects separation of powers. The court avoids declaring an act of Congress unconstitutional unless the court must do so. The rationale here is simple and reflects judicial respect for the legislature. Judges presume that Congress intended to enact a constitutional statute. They further presume that Congress did not intend to enact a statute that would raise questions about constitutional boundaries absent clear evidence that Congress meant to challenge those boundaries.

Second, this canon furthers judicial economy. If a court need not determine whether a statute is constitutional, why should it bother? Note that this canon does not require a court to first find that one interpretation violates the constitution before adopting another interpretation; rather, this canon requires a court to find only that one interpretation would require the court to consider the constitutionality of the statute in question:

> [W]here a statute is susceptible of two constructions, by one of which grave and doubtful constitutional questions arise and by the other of which such questions are avoided, our duty is to adopt the latter. This "cardinal principle," which "has for so long been applied by the Court that it is beyond debate," requires merely a determination of serious constitutional *doubt*, and not a determination of *unconstitutionality*. That must be so, of course, for otherwise the rule would "mea[n] that our duty is to first decide that a statute is unconstitutional and then proceed to hold that such ruling was unnecessary because the statute is susceptible of a meaning, which causes it not to be repugnant to the Constitution."

Almendarez-Torres v. United States, 523 U.S. 224, 250 (1998) (internal citations omitted). Thus, a judge need not first, indeed should not first, address the constitutional question. Rather, the constitutional issue need simply appear and then be avoided. This distinction is fundamental and often confuses judges, some of whom address the constitutionality of one interpretation before adopting another interpretation.

How exactly does this canon work? In *United States v. Marshall*, 908 F.2d 1312, 1335 (7th Cir. 1990) (en banc), *aff'd sub nom. Chapman v. United States*, 500 U.S. 453 (1991), the court had to interpret the federal sentencing guidelines, which set mandatory minimum terms of imprisonment for individuals who were caught selling drugs. According to the guidelines, anyone selling more than ten grams of a "mixture or substance containing a detectable amount" of a drug would be sentenced to a minimum of ten years, while those selling less than ten grams would be subject to a minimum of five years. *Id.* at 1315. The defendant was convicted of selling more than ten grams of LSD and was sentenced to twenty years. *Id.* at 1314. The issue for the court was whether the language of the statute—"mixture or substance containing a detectable amount of"— meant that the weight of a carrier mixed with the drug was included. *Id.* at 1315. Unlike other drugs such as cocaine, LSD is sold in a very heavy carrier such as orange juice or gelatin cubes. *Id.* If the weight of the carrier were included, then LSD dealers would be subject to the higher penalty even if they sold a smaller total amount of the drug than other drug dealers. In fact, LSD dealers would be sentenced entirely based on the weight of the carrier because the weight of LSD itself is so small in comparison to its carrier. *Id.*

The defendant argued that this interpretation of the statute would raise two constitutional questions: (1) whether the statute violated substantive due process because it penalized individuals without regard to the severity of the crime, and (2) whether the statute violated equal protection because it treated drug dealers differently based on a nonsensical distinction in the weight of drugs sold. *Id.* at 1320, 1322. The majority refused to apply the constitutional avoidance doctrine because the language of the statute was clear: "mixture" did not mean pure drug. *Id.* at 1318. Yet you should remember that the avoidance canon is used precisely to avoid clear language when another interpretation is fairly possible. However, the majority did not find that another interpretation was fairly possible and, thus, adopted the interpretation that raised the constitutional questions. *Id.* at 1318–20, 1324. The majority then dismissed defendant's constitutional concerns. *Id.* at 1326.

In contrast, the dissent argued that the majority should have avoided the constitutional questions altogether by interpreting the language to exclude the carrier. *Id.* at 1337 (Posner, J., dissenting). Although admitting that his interpretation was not the *best* interpretation of the language, the dissent concluded that Congress likely did not understand how LSD was sold and, thus, probably did not intend to raise the constitutional issues that the majority's interpretation raised. *Id.* at 1331. Thus, the dissent believed that another interpretation was fairly possible.

This case raises an important point. In theory, the constitutional avoidance canon should apply only if there are two *reasonable* and *fair* interpretations of a statute. Limiting the choice to interpretations that are fair and reasonable prevents the judiciary from rewriting the statute in a way the legislature did not intend. This limit confines the judiciary to its proper constitutional role of construing statutes so as to give effect to congressional intent and words. But in reality, judges often "do interpretive handsprings to avoid having even to *decide* a constitutional question." *Id.* at 1335. Here, the majority refused to consider an interpretation that while not the best reading of the statute was certainly fairly possible.

In contrast, in many cases, judges actually seem to adopt any possible interpretation to avoid a constitutional issue, not just fair interpretations. For example, in *NLRB v. Catholic Bishop of Chicago*, 440 U.S. 490 (1979), the majority refused to adopt an interpretation of the National Labor Relations Act that might violate the Constitution "if any other *possible construction* remain[ed] available." *Id.* at 500 (emphasis added). In *Catholic Bishop*, the Court was asked to determine whether an agency, specifically the National Labor Relations Board, had jurisdiction over lay teachers who taught at church-operated schools. *Id.* at 491. By its terms, the Act applied to all "employer[s]," defined as "any person acting as an agent of an employer, directly or indirectly …." *Id.* at 510 (Brennan, J., dissenting) (quoting 29 U.S.C. § 152(2)). Refusing to adopt the ordinary meaning of "employer" to include the church-operated schools, the majority required "a clear expression of Congress' intent to [raise Constitutional questions involving] the First Amendment Religion Clauses." *Id.* at 507. Finding no such clear expression, the majority concluded that "employer" must mean all employers *except* church-operated schools. *Id.* at 499. In sum, the majority refused to reach the constitutional question absent clear direction from Congress that it wanted the question addressed; hence, the majority read an implied exception into the statute's coverage, an interpretation that strained the fair meaning of the statute's text.

Critics of the constitutional avoidance canon suggest that when judges fail to adopt fair and reasonable interpretations, judges can be accused of rewriting the statute rather than interpreting it. This problem prompted Judge Easterbrook, a textualist, to write that the canon "is a closer cousin to invalidation than to interpretation," because a court can significantly alter a statute's meaning by avoiding clear text. *Marshall*, 908 F.2d at 1318. Yet despite the criticism of this canon, it remains a powerful tool for avoiding the ordinary meaning of a clear statute.

2. The Rule of Lenity & Penal Statutes

While the constitutional avoidance doctrine is based on concerns about the Constitution as a whole, the next canon, the rule of lenity, is based on concerns about one particular provision in the Constitution: the Fifth (and Fourteenth) Amendment's guarantee of procedural due process—specifically, the right to fair notice. Pursuant to the *rule of lenity*, judges should strictly interpret penal statutes, which are statutes that impose a criminal fine or imprisonment to punish citizens. Why? Historically, the rule of lenity flourished in seventeenth- and eighteenth-century England as a result of regulatory and statutory proliferation. Citizens grew nervous about the expansion of parliamentary power. English judges took on the role of guardians of individual liberty against legislative intrusions. One way in which judges could limit this expansion was by narrowly construing the language of criminal statutes.

In this country, the U.S. Constitution (and all state constitutions for that matter) requires notice before the government can deprive a person of a protected interest involving life, liberty, or property. If a statute does not clearly and unambiguously target specific conduct, an individual should not be penalized, because that individual would not have had notice prior to the deprivation. Thus, the rule of lenity furthers the Constitution's promise that people should have fair warning of crimes before they are penalized. "[I]ndividuals should not languish in prison unless the legislature has clearly articulated precisely what conduct constitutes a crime." *United States v. Gonzalez*, 407 F.3d 118, 125 (2d Cir. 2005).

> When language which is susceptible of two constructions is used in a penal law, the policy of this state is to construe the statute as favorably to the defendant as its language and the circumstance of its application reasonably permit. The defendant is entitled to the benefit of every reasonable doubt as to the true interpretation of words or the construction of a statute.

Wooten v. Superior Court, 93 Cal. App. 4th 422, 429 (2001). Although ignorance of the law is no defense, in this country, those accused of crimes should be able to know what the law is should they bother to check.

The rule of lenity also furthers a second consideration, one that relates to the power distribution between the judiciary and the legislature. Congress defines crimes in statutes; judges have no power to determine that an activity not clearly criminalized by a statute should be penalized. In other words, if judges included activity not explicitly covered in the statutory language, they would be expanding the statute's reach. *United States v. Bass*, 404 U.S. 336, 347–48 (1971) ("[L]egislatures and not courts should define criminal activity."). In this quote, the California appellate court identified both points:

> Application of the rule of lenity ensures that criminal statutes will provide fair warning concerning conduct rendered illegal and strikes

the appropriate balance between the legislature, the prosecutor, and the court in defining criminal liability. (Citation omitted in original.) ("[B]ecause of the seriousness of criminal penalties, and because criminal punishment usually represents the moral condemnation of the community, legislatures and not courts should define criminal activity"). (Citation omitted in original.) [C]riminal penalties, because they are particularly serious and opprobrious, merit heightened due process protections for those in jeopardy of being subject to them, including the strict construction of criminal statutes.

Wooten, 93 Cal. App. 4th at 429.

Like the constitutional avoidance doctrine, this canon also requires that the two interpretations be *fair* or *reasonable* constructions of the statute. "[A]n appellate court should not strain to interpret a penal statute in defendant's favor if it can fairly discern a contrary legislative intent." *People v. Avery*, 38 P.3d 1, 6 (Cal. 2002). However, in *Keeler v. Superior Court*, 470 P.2d 617 (Cal. 1970), the court said, "It is the policy of this state to construe a penal statute as favorably to the defendant as its language and the circumstances of its application may reasonably permit ... [T]he defendant is entitled to the benefit of every reasonable doubt as to the true interpretation of words or the construction of language used in a statute." *Id.* at 624. This is a very defendant-friendly description of the rule of lenity. The Supreme Court of California applied the rule of lenity and refused to interpret the term "human being" to include fetuses because at the time the law was enacted, the legislature did not intend to criminalize feticide (as opposed to abortion). *Id.* at 622. The court reached this result despite the existence of an earlier statute from 1872 that directed California courts not to construe criminal statutes narrowly. *Id.* at 625.

Typically, the rule of lenity applies in criminal cases because of the penal component. For example, in *McNally v. United States*, 483 U.S. 350 (1987), the majority relied on the rule of lenity to reverse convictions of the defendants, who allegedly violated the federal mail fraud statute. That statute prohibited individuals from using the mail for "any scheme or artifice to defraud [individuals of] money or property ...." *Id.* at 352 (quoting 18 U.S.C. § 1341). The government claimed that the defendants' alleged participation in a self-dealing patronage scheme defrauded the citizens and the state of the right to have the state's affairs conducted honestly. *Id.* The issue for the Court was whether the mail fraud statute, which explicitly protected money and property, also protected an intangible right of the citizenry to good government. Applying the rule of lenity, the majority held that it did not: "[W]hen there are two rational readings of a criminal statute, one harsher than the other, we are to choose the harsher only when Congress has spoken in clear and definite language." *Id.* at 360 (citing *Bass*, 404 U.S. at 347; *United States v. Universal C.I.T. Credit Corp.*, 344 U.S. 218, 221–22 (1952)).

The dissent strongly disagreed. Arguing that the purpose of the mail fraud statute resolved any ambiguity, the dissent claimed that the rule of lenity was inapplicable. *Id.* at 375 (Stevens, J., dissenting). Because there was no ambiguity, the rule of lenity should not be applied. Oddly, in a footnote, the dissent implied that the rule of lenity might apply differently to educated defendants because they would be more likely to read statutes accurately. *Id.* at 375 n.9. While Justice Stevens might be correct that educated defendants are better able to understand the meaning of statutes, judges should not determine criminality based on class or education.

While defendants have attempted to argue that the rule of lenity should apply in civil cases that have a penal component, so far, they have been largely unsuccessful. For example, in *Modern Muzzleloading, Inc. v. Magaw*, 18 F. Supp. 2d 29 (D.D.C. 1998), the defendant manufactured and distributed 30,000 Knight Disc Rifles without a license, believing that the Gun Control Act excluded them as "antique firearms." The agency charged with interpreting the Act determined that the rifles were not antique firearms. Modern Muzzleloading sued for a declaratory judgment that the rifles were exempt antiques. The court denied the relief, reasoning that the statute was not "*grievously ambiguous.*" *Id.* at 33. The plaintiff argued that, because the statute was penal in nature, the rule of lenity required that any ambiguity should be resolved in its favor. The court disagreed and refused to apply the rule of lenity at all. According to the court, the plaintiff overstated the canon. *Id.* The point at which a judge should turn to the rule of lenity is when all other sources fail to resolve the ambiguity. In this case, the court resolved the ambiguity by using *in pari materia* and by looking at the statute as a whole. *Id.*

And in *Babbitt v. Sweet Home Chapter of Communities for a Great Oregon*, 515 U.S. 687 (1995), the Supreme Court rejected a rule of lenity challenge in another administrative penalty case. In *Babbitt*, the Court interpreted the Endangered Species Act, which penalized the "taking" of an endangered species. *Id.* at 690 (quoting 16 U.S.C. § 1532(9)(a)(1)). The term "take" was defined in the statute to mean "harass, *harm*, pursue, hunt, shoot, wound, kill, trap, capture, or collect, or to attempt to engage in any such conduct." *Id.* at 690– 91 (quoting 16 U.S.C. § 1532(9)(a)(1)) (emphasis added). The Secretary of the Interior, the head of the agency in charge of implementing the Act, promulgated a regulation defining "harm" to include "significant habitat modification or degradation where it actually kills or injures wildlife." *Id.* at 691 (quoting 50 C.F.R. § 17.3 (1994)).

Logging companies and landowners in the Northwest sued, alleging that the Secretary's interpretation of the word "harm" was unlawful. They argued that the rule of lenity should apply because the civil statute imposed criminal penalties for violations. If the rule of lenity were applied, the plaintiffs contended that the Court would find that the word "harm" was ambiguous and consequently adopt the plaintiffs' interpretation; one that would minimize criminal penalties. The majority rejected this argument and held that the rule of lenity should not apply in this case. "We have never suggested that the rule of lenity should provide the standard for reviewing facial challenges to administrative regulations whenever the governing statute authorizes criminal enforcement." *Id.* at 704 n.18.

The question of exactly when to apply the rule of lenity is subject to some controversy. Should a defendant "win" from the start if ambiguity appears on the face of the statute or should all evidence of intent be explored first? In other words, should the canon be a rule of first or last resort? While the canon may have been applied as a rule of first resort in the past, today other sources of meaning are usually explored before the canon is applied. The canon "is not a catch-all maxim that resolves all disputes in the defendant's favor—a sort of juristical 'tie goes to the runner.'" *United States v. Gonzalez*, 407 F.3d 118, 125 (2d Cir. 2005). Instead, many courts apply the canon, not when the statutory text is ambiguous, but only when the ambiguity remains after the court has examined all other sources of meaning, including legislative history and statutory purpose. *Reno v. Koray*, 515 U.S. 50, 65 (1995). The canon is reserved "for those situations in which a reasonable doubt persists about a statute's intended scope even *after* resort to the language and structure, legislative history, and motivating policies of the statute." *Moskal v. United States*, 498 U.S. 103, 108 (1990).

However, applying the canon solely as a method of last resort is problematic. Had the statute in *Modern Muzzleloading* been clear, the plaintiff would likely have complied: Why incur unnecessary fines? If the basis for the canon is fair notice, it appears disingenuous to require criminal defendants to read legislative history and determine statutory purpose to understand the meaning of the language used.

Judges and legislatures are less enthusiastic about the rule of lenity today than in the past. The rule of lenity has fallen so out of favor that some state legislatures, such as New York and California, have attempted to abrogate it by statute. For example, California's statute provides, "The rule of the common law, that penal statutes are to be strictly construed, has no application to this Code." Cal. Penal Code §4 (West 2013). But because the rule of lenity rests on constitutional concerns, courts are understandably reluctant to eliminate it entirely. Thus, in New York, the Court of Appeals cautioned that "[a]lthough [the anti-lenity statute] obviously does not justify the imposition of criminal sanctions for conduct that falls beyond the scope of the Penal Law, it does authorize a court to dispense with hypertechnical or strained interpretations ...." *People v. Ditta*, 422 N.E.2d 515, 517 (N.Y. 1981). Similarly, the California courts have explained that "while ... the rule of the common law ... has been abrogated ... it is also true that the defendant is entitled to the benefit of every reasonable doubt, whether it arises out of a question of fact, or as to the true interpretation of words or the construction of language used in a statute." *People ex rel. Lungren v. Superior Court*, 926 P.2d 1042, 1056 (Cal. 1996) (internal citations omitted). As noted above, in *Keeler*, the California Supreme Court applied the rule of lenity in a murder case, despite a statute from 1872 directing state courts not to construe criminal statutes narrowly. 470 P.2d at 623. Applying the rule of lenity to a case where the defendant kicked his wife in the stomach after learning she was pregnant, the court refused to interpret the term "human being" to include fetuses. *Id.* at 618, 622.

In contrast, the South Carolina Supreme Court refused to apply the rule of lenity to the word "child" in a child abuse and endangerment statute. *Whitner v. State*, 492 S.E.2d 777 (S.C. 1977). In that case, the mother had been convicted for smoking crack in her third trimester. The statute criminalized neglect of a "child," which was defined in another section of the children's code as "a person under the age of eighteen"; thus, the issue for the court should have been whether a fetus was a "person" under age eighteen. However, the majority focused on the word "child" instead, found it to be clear and unambiguous after a thorough analysis, and, therefore, refused to apply the rule of lenity. *Id.* at 784. The dissent found the language was ambiguous and argued that the majority should have applied the rule of lenity: "I cannot accept the majority's assertion, that the child abuse and neglect statute unambiguously includes a 'viable fetus.' If that is the case, then why is the majority compelled to go to such great lengths to ascertain that a 'viable fetus' is a 'child?' " *Id.* at 787–88 (Fine, C.J., dissenting).

Even Congress has attempted to limit the rule of lenity's reach. The federal Racketeer Influenced and Corrupt Organization Act specifically directs that its "provisions ... be liberally construed to effectuate [the bill's] remedial purposes ...." Pub. L. No. 91-452, §904(a), 84 Stat. 922 (1970). However, like the state courts, the federal courts have refused to apply this "anti-lenity" provision broadly, instead limiting its application to the civil aspects of the Act. *Keystone Ins. Co. v. Houghton*, 863 F.2d 1125, 1128 (3d Cir. 1988) ("[A]pplicability of the liberal construction standard has been questioned in *criminal* RICO cases in view of the general canon of interpretation that ambiguities in criminal statutes are to be construed in favor of leniency . . . .") (emphasis added). Thus, at least in the criminal context, the rule of lenity can provide some powerful arguments for a criminal defendant facing an ambiguous statute. A good prosecutor should be aware of the rule's limitations and its current use as a canon of last resort.

3. Retroactive Criminal Statutes: *Ex Post Facto* Laws

While the Constitution does not prohibit retroactive civil laws, the Constitution does prohibit retroactive criminal laws, known as *ex post facto* laws. Like the rule of lenity, this canon is based on one specific section of the U.S. Constitution: Congress shall pass "[no] . . . ex post facto law." U.S. CONST. art. I, §9, cl. 3. In Chapter 9, we discussed retroactivity in regard to civil cases. This section addresses retroactivity in regard to criminal cases.

Ex post facto is Latin for "something done afterwards." An *ex post facto* law is impermissible if it is both retroactive and disadvantageous to a defendant. An *ex post facto* statute is a statute that changes the legal consequences of an action after the action has occurred, specifically, by redefining criminal conduct or by increasing the penalty for criminal conduct. There are four types of *ex post facto* statutes: (1) those criminalizing actions that were legal when they were committed, (2) those altering the nature of a crime so that it is categorized more severely than when it was committed, (3) those increasing the punishment prescribed for a crime than when it was committed, and (4) those altering the rules of evidence to make conviction easier. *Calder v. Bull*, 3 U.S. (3 Dall.) 386 (1798). The two purposes behind the *ex post facto* prohibition are to prevent legislatures from enacting vindictive laws to punish individuals and to ensure that statutes give fair notice of their legal effect. The canon shares this latter purpose with the rule of lenity.

Retroactive effect is not enough to make a law unconstitutional. A law may have *retroactive* effect and still not be an impermissible *ex post facto* law. To be an impermissible *ex post facto* law, the statute must punish defendants for their prior actions. For example, the Adam Walsh Child Protection and Safety Act of 2006, Pub. L. No. 109-248, 120 Stat. 587 (2006), requires convicted sex offenders to register in a database. When enacted, the Act applied retroactively, meaning those already adjudged as sex offenders had to register. In *Smith v. Doe*, 538 U.S. 84 (2003), the Supreme Court held that the Act did not violate the *ex post facto* clause because compulsory registration was not a punishment. *Id.* at 105.

Similarly, the Domestic Violence Offender Gun Ban of 1996, 18 U.S.C. § 922(g)(9), prohibits persons who are convicted of misdemeanor domestic violence and who are subject to a restraining order from owning guns or ammunition. When enacted, this Act also applied retroactively. Persons convicted of violating the Act could be sentenced to up to ten years for possessing a firearm, regardless of whether they legally possessed the weapon at the time the law was passed. In *United States v. Brady*, 26 F.3d 282 (2d Cir.), *cert. denied*, 513 U.S. 894 (1994), the Second Circuit denied an *ex post facto* challenge because the Act was considered regulatory, not punitive—in other words, violation of the Act was a status offense, not a punishment.

You can see that determining whether a statute is an *ex post facto* law, meaning it has punitive effect, is challenging. Even judges do not always agree. In *People v. Leroy*, 828 N.E.2d 769 (Ill. App. Ct. 2005), the Illinois Court of Appeals addressed this issue in determining whether a statute that limited where convicted sex offenders could live was an *ex post facto* law. *Id.* at 775, 778–79. As a child, the defendant had been convicted of a sexual offense. *Id.* at 775. He later pled guilty for failing to register as a sex offender and was sentenced to one year's probation. While on probation, he lived in his mother's house, which was located near an elementary school. *Id.* A statute, which was enacted after his underlying criminal conviction, prohibited convicted sex offenders from "knowingly resid[ing] within 500 feet of a playground or a facility providing programs or services exclusively directed toward persons under 18 years of age." *Id.* (quoting 720 Ill. Comp. Stat. 5/11-9.4(b-5)). The State sought to revoke his probation because he violated this statute. *Id.*

The defendant admitted violating the statute but argued that the statute was an unconstitutional *ex post facto* law because the statute increased the penalty he received for his underlying conviction. *Id.* at 779. The appellate court disagreed, holding instead that (1) the legislature intended to enact a regulatory scheme, not to punish individuals, and (2) the effect of the law was not so punitive that it prevented the State from creating civil restrictions. *Id.* at 779, 782. Therefore, the statute was not an impermissible *ex post facto* law. *Id.* at 782. Disagreeing, the dissent claimed that "a punitive effect unquestionably flow[ed] from this enactment [and violated the] constitutional guarantee against the imposition of *ex post facto* punishment." *Id.* at 785 (Kuehn, J., dissenting).

A question arises when a court subsequently changes its prior interpretation of a criminal statute. Does doing so violate the *ex post facto* clause? In *Michigan v. Schaefer*, 703 N.W.2d 774 (Mich. 2005), the Michigan Supreme Court tackled this question in a consolidated case. One of the defendants struck and killed an eleven-year-old girl who suddenly emerged on her bike in front of his car.

Id. at 779. Defendant was driving drunk. *Id.* He was charged with operating a motor vehicle while under the influence of liquor and causing death, among other charges. *Id.* At the preliminary hearing, the prosecutor's expert testified that the accident was unavoidable, so it was irrelevant that the defendant was drunk. *Id.* at 779. Hence, the district court dismissed the driving drunk charge because the state failed to show that defendant's intoxicated driving was a substantial cause of the victim's death. *Id.* at 780. The court required such evidence because in an earlier case the Michigan Supreme Court had held that "the people must establish that the particular defendant's decision to drive while intoxicated produced a *change in that driver's operation of the vehicle* that caused the death of the victim." *Id.* at 781–82 (quoting *People v. Lardie*, 551 N.W.2d 656, 668 (Mich. 1996)).

On appeal to the Michigan Supreme Court, the State argued that *Lardie* should be overruled. The majority agreed, finding that the language of the statute stated clearly that "the defendant's *operation* of the motor vehicle ... must cause the victim's death, not the defendant's 'intoxication.'" *Id.* at 783. Despite changing its interpretation of the statute, the majority did not find an *ex post facto* concern because the court concluded that it was merely correcting its prior, erroneous interpretation. *Id.* at 789 n.80. The correct interpretation should have been clear from the statute's face. "[I]t is not 'indefensible or unexpected' that a court would ... overrule a case that failed to abide by the express terms of a statute." *Id.*

The concurring judge disagreed about whether the change implicated *ex post facto* concerns. He argued that the court had already interpreted the statute in such a way that the majority's new interpretation criminalized behavior that was not criminal when performed. *Id.* at 793 (Cavanagh, J., concurring in part and dissenting in part). Thus, he would have held that the new interpretation violated the *ex post facto* clause. *Id.* at 794. Acknowledging that the *ex post facto* clause does not apply to the judiciary, he argued that the principles are applicable by analogy through the Due Process Clauses. *Id.* at 794 n.1. "When a defendant is deprived of due process, and, thus, is subjected to a punishment not available at the time of his or her conduct, this treatment is precisely what is contemplated, and prohibited, under ex post facto principles." *Id.* The majority responded, "[the concurrence's] ex post facto and due process concerns are misplaced. As the United States Supreme Court has held, 'The *Ex Post Facto Clause*, by its own terms, does not apply to courts. Extending the Clause to courts through the rubric of due process thus would circumvent the clear constitutional text.'" *Id.* at 789 n.80 (quoting *Rogers v. Tennessee*, 532 U.S. 451, 460 (2001)).

Hence, the legislature cannot enact statutes that have retroactive punitive effects without violating the *ex post facto* clause of the U.S. Constitution; however, courts can. The challenge, of course, is determining exactly when a statute has a punitive, rather than regulatory, effect.

4. Clear Statement Rules

When a statute can be interpreted to abridge long-held individual or states' rights, or when it appears that a legislature has made a large policy change, courts will generally not interpret the statute to abridge those rights or make that change unless the legislature was clear about its intention. The requirement of a clear, or plain, statement is based on the simple assumption that a legislature would not make major policy changes without being absolutely clear about doing so. Thus, courts require clear statements to encourage the legislature to indicate explicitly that it wants a change in the status quo.

Courts tend to require clear statements to maintain under-enforced constitutional traditions. Above, we saw two examples of when courts require clear statement rules: the constitutional avoidance doctrine and the rule of lenity. Below, we turn to four additional areas of important concern: federalism, preemption, American Indian rights, and sovereign immunity. We will look at each in turn. You should be aware, however, that clear statement rules have a role in many areas of statutory interpretation. We are looking at just a few of those areas so that you understand what a court means when the court requires the legislature to be clear about what it intends.

a. Federalism

Our nation is made up of one federal government and fifty state governments. At times, the laws of the two sovereign governments conflict. The principle of federalism respects the sovereignty of each state from federal intrusion. Judges will not interpret statutes to burden state sovereignty unless Congress clearly expresses its intent to do so. The requirement of a clear statement respects federalism because Congress must be clear when it wishes to impact areas of traditional state power, such as land management and taxation:

> Federal statutes impinging upon important state interests "cannot ...
> be construed without regard to the implications of our dual system of
> government .... [W]hen the Federal Government takes over ... local

radiations in the vast network of our national economic enterprise and thereby radically readjusts the balance of state and national authority, those charged with the duty of legislating (must be) reasonably explicit."

BFP v. Resolution Trust Corp., 511 U.S. 531, 544 (1994) (quoting Felix Frankfurter, *Some Reflections on the Reading of Statutes*, 47 COLUM. L. REV. 527, 539–40 (1947)).

For example, "[r]egulation of land [and water] use ... is a quintessential state and local power." *Rapanos v. United States*, 547 U.S. 715, 738 (2006). If Congress wants to encroach on this traditional and primary state power, then Congress should say so very clearly. In 1972, Congress enacted the Clean Water Act, which made it illegal to discharge dredged or fill material into "navigable waters" without a permit. *Id.* at 722–24. "Navigable waters" are defined as "the waters of the United States, including the territorial seas." *Id.* at 760 (quoting 33 U.S.C. §§ 1362(7) & (12)). The Army Corps of Engineers had interpreted "the waters of the United States" very broadly to include not only waters that were navigable but also "[t]ributaries of such waters" and "'wetlands' adjacent to such waters and tributaries." *Id.* at 724 (quoting 33 CFR §§ 328.3(a)(5) & (7)). In essence, the Corps interpreted the language broadly to include any waters that might ultimately enter navigable waters.

In *Rapanos*, the Supreme Court had to consider whether four Michigan wetlands, which lay near ditches and man-made drains that would eventually empty into traditional navigable waters constituted "waters of the United States" within the meaning of the Act. The majority rejected the Corps's interpretation as unreasonable. *Id.* at 738. The Court in *Rapanos* noted that it ordinarily required a "'clear and manifest'" statement from Congress to authorize an unprecedented intrusion into traditional state authority. "[And t]he phrase 'the waters of the United States' hardly qualifie[d]." *Id.*

b. Preemption

Clear statements are also required in the area of preemption. Judges presume that state law is not preempted absent a clear statement from Congress to this effect. Preemption is the displacing effect that federal law has on conflicting or inconsistent state law. Preemption occurs because the Supremacy Clause in the Constitution states that "[t]he Laws of the United States, (which shall be made in Pursuance to the Constitution), shall be the supreme Law of the land." U.S. CONST. art. VI, § 2. Thus, if there is a conflict between state and federal law, federal law preempts state law.

Preemption is an enormously complicated area of law, which we need not delve into too deeply here. It is sufficient for you to know that there is a presumption in favor of the applicability of state law and against preemption. Courts presume that Congress generally does not intend to preempt state law when enacting a federal law; thus, Congress must provide a clear statement that it intended to preempt state law:

> In all pre-emption cases, and particularly in those in which Congress has 'legislated ... in a field which the States have traditionally occupied,'... we 'start with the assumption that the historic police powers of the States were not to be superseded by the Federal Act unless that was the clear and manifest purpose of Congress.'

Medtronic, Inc. v. Lohr, 518 U.S. 470, 485 (1996) (quoting *Rice v. Santa Fe Elevator Corp.*, 331 U.S. 218, 230 (1947)).

Sometimes, Congress includes a specific preemption clause in the act at issue, which makes the preemption question relatively easy. For example, the Supreme Court held that the Medical Device Amendments Act of 1976 preempted state common-law claims challenging the safety and effectiveness of any medical device approved by the Federal Drug Administration. *Riegel v. Medtronic, Inc.*, 552 U.S. 312 (2008). The Act contained a clause that expressly preempted state requirements that differed from federal law. *Id.* at 330 (citing 21 U.S.C. § 360k(a)(1)).

But Congress is not always so clear about its intent. What then? When possible, courts generally try to reconcile seemingly inconsistent state and federal laws. But reconciliation is not always possible. For example, in *Wyeth v. Levine*, 555 U.S. 555 (2009), the Supreme Court had to determine whether the federal Food, Drug, and Cosmetic Act ("FDCA"), which did not include a preemption provision, impliedly preempted state tort law. *Id.* at 560–61. The plaintiff in the case had lost her arm after she was injected with the defendant's anti-nausea drug. *Id.* at 558. Although the label warned of this risk, the plaintiff argued that under state tort law the defendant should not have allowed the drug to be used intravenously, even with the labeling. *Id.* at 559–60. The FDCA outlined a comprehensive process for approving drug labels. The drug manufacturer-defendant argued that the FDCA's labeling process preempted state tort law for two reasons. First, the defendant raised the issue of "impossibility preemption" and argued that it was impossible to comply with both the labeling requirements and state tort law. *Id.* at 568. The Court rejected this argument, noting that the defendant "failed to demonstrate that it was impossible for it to comply with both federal and state requirements." *Id.* at 574–75.

Second, the defendant argued that the state tort claims were preempted because allowing state tort claims to apply would interfere with "Congress's purpose to entrust an expert agency to make drug labeling decisions that strike a balance between competing objectives." *Id.* at 574. The Court similarly rejected this argument, in part, because Congress had enacted a preemption provision in a related area, the Medical Device Amendments Act:

> The case for federal pre-emption is particularly weak where Congress has indicated its awareness of the operation of state law in a field of federal interest, and has nonetheless decided to stand by both concepts and to tolerate whatever tension there [is] between them.

Id. at 575 (quoting *Bonito Boats, Inc. v. Thunder Craft Boats, Inc.*, 489 U.S. 141, 166–67 (1989) (internal quotation marks omitted). In sum, the Court held that the FDCA's regulatory approval process did not preempt state tort law. *Id.* at 581.

Disliking this second analysis, Justice Thomas wrote separately to criticize the majority for routinely invalidating state laws based on perceived conflicts with broad federal policy objectives, legislative history, and statutory purposes that are not contained within the text of federal law. *Id.* at 582 (Thomas, J., concurring). For Justice Thomas, preemption can be implied only through a textual analysis.

Lastly, even in the absence of a clear statement that Congress intended to "occupy the field" of a particular area, courts will be more likely to find that federal law preempts state law if the state law touches upon an area that has historically implicated a strong federal interest, such as banking, interstate commerce, or foreign affairs.

c. American Indian Treaty Rights

Clear statements are also required when Congress impacts American Indian treaty rights by diminishing native lands. Not only are we a nation with various state sovereigns, we are a nation within a nation. American Indian lands should be protected from unnecessary federal intrusion and diminishment. The *diminishment doctrine* was established to distinguish between those statutes that removed lands from a reservation from those statutes that merely made surplus lands available for settlement within a reservation. Courts require a clear statement when Congress "diminishes" reservation boundaries by statute. *Hagen v. Utah*, 510 U.S. 399, 411 (1993).

Further, when there are two possible interpretations, the non-diminishment interpretation should govern. Courts presume that Congress would not have wanted to diminish the reservation boundaries without being explicit. For example, in *Solem v. Bartlett*, 465 U.S. 463 (1984), the Supreme Court held that there was no such clear statement to reduce the Cheyenne River Sioux Reservation in the Cheyenne River Act, despite language describing opened areas as being in "the public domain" and describing unopened areas as comprising "the reservation thus diminished." *Id.* at 475–76. This language simply was not clear enough to imply diminishment. Additionally, the Court reasoned that the Act had been enacted at a time when the word "diminished" was not yet a term of art in American Indian law. *Id.* at 476 n.17. Finally, the Court found that there was no clear congressional purpose to reduce the reservation. *Id.* at 476.

d. Sovereign Immunity

Clear statement rules are also used to protect sovereign immunity. Sovereign immunity is a judge-made doctrine that dates from the beginning of our nation's birth. The doctrine is fairly straightforward: the federal government, or sovereign, may not be sued without its consent. To further this doctrine, federal courts developed two statutory interpretation principles to determine whether a statute waives immunity. The first principle is that a statutory waiver of sovereign immunity must be definitely and unequivocally expressed. In other words, Congress must provide a clear statement that Congress intended to waive *sovereign immunity*. The second principle is that if a waiver is found, a court must construe the waiver narrowly in favor of the government.

These presumptions are so strong that they can trump other canons. For example, in *Burch v. Secretary of Health & Human Services*, No. 99-946V, 2001 WL 180129 (Fed. Cl. Feb. 8, 2001), the administrative judge refused to give the word "received" its ordinary meaning because the language at issue came from a statute implicating sovereign immunity. In that case, a child was allegedly injured when her mother received a vaccine while the child was *in utero*. A statute allowed anyone who had "received" a vaccine and been injured as a result to sue the federal government. *Id.* at *1 (citing 42 U.S.C. § 300aa-11(c)(1)(A)). Although the parties stipulated that the vaccine could have caused the child's injuries, the judge denied the claim. Despite the fact that Congress waived immunity very clearly for anyone injured as a result of receiving a vaccine, the judge interpreted the term "received" in the statute very narrowly. *Id.* at *2. According to the judge, the narrow interpretation was warranted pursuant to the second principle of this doctrine: statutes that waive sovereign immunity must be interpreted narrowly in favor of the government. *Id.* at *5.

Thus, when a statute could be interpreted to abridge federalism, to preempt state law, to diminish American Indian lands, or to waive sovereign immunity, courts generally require the statute to express clearly the legislature's intention to impact these rights. Additionally, courts require clear statements in other situations not explored here. Clear statement rules place the burden on Congress to be clear in its drafting, but such rules can also frustrate Congress's intent by requiring such meticulousness. It is questionable whether the Supreme Court has the power to demand clear statements when the Constitution does not require Congress to write laws in this way.

E. Canons Based on Prudential Considerations

We move now away from the constitutional-based considerations and into the prudential-based considerations. Here, the constitution is not the star; rather, concerns about the interplay between the common law and statutes are front and center. We will begin with two related canons: (1) courts should narrowly construe statutes in derogation of the common law, and (2) courts should broadly construe remedial statutes. These rules sound easy in theory, but it can be difficult to tell whether a statute is remedial or in derogation of the common law. These two canons have particular force in states because there is limited federal common law.

1. Statutes in Derogation of the Common Law

Courts should strictly construe statutes in derogation of the common law. A statute is in derogation of the common law when the statute partially repeals or abolishes existing common law rights or otherwise limits the scope, utility, or force of that common law right. BLACK's LAW DICTIONARY 476 (8th ed. 2004).

For example, statutes that alter existing property rights are in derogation of the common law. Similarly, wrongful death statutes are in derogation of the common law. Before wrongful death statutes existed, the common law did not recognize the existence of a wrongful death claim because claims died with the victim. There was no way to compensate a dead victim. Thus, under the common law, surviving family members could not seek damages from the person who caused their relative's death. But this common law rule led to odd results — a tortfeasor would be off the hook if her victim died, but not if her victim lived. For this reason, England enacted Lord Campbell's Act in 1846: the first "wrongful death statute" that allowed relatives who were damaged by the death of the victim to sue the tortfeasor even though the victim died.

American states quickly followed suit. But these wrongful death statutes were in derogation of the common law; thus, early judicial thought was that the statutes should be strictly construed. For example, in *Boroughs v. Oliver*, 64 So. 2d 338 (Miss. 1953), the Mississippi Supreme Court narrowly construed the word "parent" in its wrongful death statute to prevent adoptive parents from suing a tortfeasor for the negligent death of their son. *Id.* at 314. Shortly after that case, the Mississippi legislature corrected this absurdly narrow interpretation. MISS. CODE ANN. § 11-7-13 (2004) ("Any rights which a blood parent or parents may have under this section are hereby conferred upon and vested in an adopting parent or adopting parents surviving their deceased adopted child, just as if the child were theirs by the full blood and had been born to the adopting parents in lawful wedlock.").

But a bigger question is why should statutes in derogation of the common law be strictly construed? Basically, the answer to this question is power. Before the 1900's, common law was more prevalent than statutory law. Hence, statutes were viewed with suspicion:

> Statutes then were not created from common law methodology. Indeed, 18th century judges felt them rather subject to tyrannical majorities and shifting whims. England had suffered through the civil wars of the Seventeenth Century and the abuses of unchecked majorities in Parliament. The beheading of Charles I was followed by the post-restoration instability leading to the Glorious Revolution in 1685. [Judges] viewed the common law as a source of social stability, cast from the wisdom of the ages and forged in cases evolving over the long sweep of history. Statutes often emerged from ephemeral, narrow and parochial interests, but the common law was eternal and universal.

Blankfeld v. Richmond Health Care, Inc., 902 So. 2d 296, 305 (Fla. Dist. Ct. App. 2005) (Farmer, C.J., concurring).

Not only were statutes viewed with suspicion, but those statutes that did exist were either very narrow, were limited exceptions to existing common law, or were narrow corrections of common law. Hence, judges developed the canon that statutes in derogation of the common law should be strictly construed. A common articulation of the canon from that time is as follows: "No statute is to be construed as altering the common law, farther than its words import." *Shaw v. Merchants' Nat. Bank*, 101 U.S. (11 Otto) 557, 565 (1879). Thus, the derogation canon is best understood as reflecting the early reluctance of American courts to allow legislatures to restrict common law rights. Because there is very little federal common law, this canon is commonly implicated when state statutes modify state common law.

In the twentieth century, a power struggle ensued. Wishing to increase their lawmaking power, legislatures enacted more statutes. Wishing to maintain the power it had, the judiciary limited the breadth of those statutes with the derogation canon. If the legislature failed to clearly address an issue, then that issue fell into the judiciary's jurisdiction. Eventually, the legislature won the battle; today, statutes create most rights and responsibilities, while common law acts as the gap filler. As a consequence, the usefulness of the derogation rule of statutory construction has waned.

Thus, many states have abolished the derogation canon. For example, a Kentucky statute provides: "All statutes of this state shall be liberally construed with a view to promote their objects and carry out the intent of the legislature, and the rule that statutes in derogation of the common law are to be strictly construed shall not apply to the statutes of this state." KY. REV. STAT. ANN. § 446.080(1) (West 2008). Thus, this canon is less useful to litigants than it once was. In contrast, the remedial canon, which we will address next, remains more firmly a factor.

2. Remedial Statutes

One purpose of the derogation canon was to prevent a legislature from unintentionally abrogating rights the common law granted. Remember, prior to the twentieth century, legislatures focused on running the government, not making law. So, when a legislature did enact statutes, those statutes were mainly designed to remedy errors in the common law. These statutes were specific, narrow, and limited in application. A statute passed to repair the common law was not *in derogation* of the common law, but rather was *in aid* of the common law. Hence, courts did not view such statutes with suspicion because common law remained supreme. Courts interpreted these "remedial statutes," as they were known, liberally, not narrowly, to achieve the statute's purpose. *Chisom v. Roemer*, 501 U.S. 380, 403 (1991); *Smith v. Brown*, 35 F.3d 1516, 1525 (Fed. Cir. 1994).

In addition to corrective statutes, remedial statutes include those statutes that create new rights or expand remedies that were otherwise unavailable at common law. For example, a tax statute is not remedial, while a statute intended to protect civil rights is. While this definition seems clear, in reality the distinction between remedial and non-remedial is more elusive. "[I]t is not at all apparent just what is and what is not remedial legislation; indeed all legislation might be thought remedial in some sense—even massive codifications." *Ober United Travel Agency, Inc. v. DOL* 135 F.3d 822, 825 (D.C. Cir. 1998). For example, if we return to the wrongful death cases above, a wrongful death statute may be remedial as to a plaintiff because it adds a cause of action or measure of damages otherwise lost, but non-remedial as to the defendant, who would have been exempt from liability under common law. Thus, some states consider wrongful death statutes to be remedial, such as Wyoming and Rhode Island. *See, e.g., Corkill v. Knowles*, 955 P.2d 438, 442 (Wyo. 1998); *O'Sullivan v. Rhode Island Hosp.*, 874 A.2d 179, 183 (R.I. 2005). Other states, such as Arkansas and Maryland, consider wrongful death statutes to be in derogation of the common law. *See, e.g., Cockrum v. Fox*, 199 S.W.3d 69, 73 (Ark. 2004) (Thornton, J., dissenting); *Cohen v. Rubin*, 460 A.2d 1046, 1056 (Md. Ct. Spec. App. 1983).

Because many statutes today are remedial in nature—enacted to solve a problem a legislature identified—this canon now has particular force. Indeed, some states have codified this canon. *See, e.g.,* OHIO REV. CODE ANN. § 1.11 ("Remedial laws and all proceedings under them shall be liberally construed in order to promote their object and assist the parties in obtaining justice. The rule of the common law that statutes in derogation of the common law must be strictly construed has no application to remedial laws; but this section does not require a liberal construction of laws affecting personal liberty, relating to amercement, or of a penal nature."); TEX. GOV'T CODE ANN. § 312.006(a), (b) ("The Revised Statutes are the law of this state and shall be liberally construed to achieve their purpose and to promote justice. The common law rule requiring strict construction of statutes in derogation of the common law does not apply to the Revised Statutes.").

Yet interpreting remedial statutes broadly may conflict with the plain meaning canon or with other canons. For example, in *Burch v. Secretary of Health & Human Services*, No. 99-946V, 2001 WL 180129 (Fed. Cl. Feb. 8 2001), the administrative judge rejected the ordinary meaning of the word "received" and refused to interpret the statute broadly despite the remedial nature of the act at issue because another canon urged a narrow reading of the statute. In that case, the plaintiff-mother had been given a vaccine through injection while she was pregnant that allegedly injured her child. *Id.* at *1. The judge acknowledged that pursuant to the ordinary meaning of "received," the child had received the vaccine. *Id.* at *8. Moreover, the judge concluded that the statute was remedial. *Id.* at *7. Despite these two findings, the judge denied the claim, narrowly construing the statute because it implicated sovereign immunity. *Id.*

3. Implied Causes of Action & Remedies

Our next topic is, in many ways, confounding to textualists. Implied causes of action and remedies are just that, implied; neither is explicitly set forth in a statute. As such, the current trend is to deny the existence of new implied actions and restrict the reach of those already in existence, as we will see below.

a. Implied Causes of Action

An implied cause of action exists when a court determines that even though a statute does not expressly grant private parties the right to sue, the statute implicitly does so. In early English common law, private lawsuits were the primary method of enforcing common law and statutes. WILLIAM ESKRIDGE, JR., ET AL., CASES AND MATERIALS ON LEGISLATION: STATUTES AND THE CREATION OF PUBLIC POLICY 1110 (3d ed. 2001). Early American courts adopted this presumption. When Congress drafted a statute protecting important interests, courts readily assumed private individuals had the ability to enforce those rights in court regardless of whether the statute said so.

But after the New Deal, Congress delegated to agencies the responsibility of enforcing many of these rights; thus, private rights of action became less necessary and, over time, courts rejected implied rights claims more easily. Over the past half century, the Supreme Court has taken three different approaches to implied causes of action; each approach has more severely limited the availability of implied causes of action.

J.I. Case Co. v. Borak, 377 U.S. 426 (1964), illustrates the first, and most liberal, approach. In that case, the Supreme Court had to decide whether the Securities Exchange Act of 1934 allowed a private right of action when none was expressly provided in the Act. Examining the Act's legislative history and purposes, the Court held that a private right of action should be implied. The Court believed that it was "the duty of the courts to be alert to provide such remedies as are necessary to make effective the congressional purpose." *Id.* at 433.

This case was decided in 1964, long before new textualism refocused attention on statutory text. The case also offered a somewhat simplistic rationale, "for it assume[d] that more enforcement is always better." ESKRIDGE ET AL., CASES

AND MATERIALS ON LEGISLATION, *supra,* at 1111. Beginning in 1975, the Court began its retreat from this simplistic approach. In *Cort v. Ash,* 422 U.S. 66 (1975), the Supreme Court retreated from the broad language of *Borak.* The issue in *Cort* was whether a civil cause of action existed under a criminal statute prohibiting corporations from making contributions to a presidential campaign. The Court held that a civil action should not be implied. In doing so, the Court identified four factors for courts to consider when deciding whether a statute implicitly included a private cause of action. *Id.* at 78. These factors included the following:

(1) Whether the plaintiff was one of the class of persons "for whose especial benefit" the statute was enacted,
(2) Whether the legislative history showed that Congress intended to create or deny a private cause of action,
(3) Whether an implied cause of action would be consistent with the underlying purposes of the statute, and
(4) Whether the issue would be one that is traditionally left to state law.

Id.

For several years after *Cort,* the Supreme Court applied this four-factor test and generally refused to create implied causes of action. A notable exception was the case of *Cannon v. University of Chicago,* 441 U.S. 677 (1979), in which the Court recognized an implied cause of action for claims brought under Title IX of the Education Amendments of 1972. *Id.* at 695. Justice Powell, in dissent, criticized the majority's decision and the creation of implied causes of action in general. Powell believed that the Court's test for implied causes of action violated separation of powers. *Id.* at 730 (Powell, J., dissenting). Because Congress, not the judiciary, has the power to create causes of action, "[a]bsent the most compelling evidence of affirmative congressional intent, a federal court should not infer a private cause of action." *Id.* at 731. In essence, Justice Powell required a clear statement for implied causes of action.

Despite Powell's heartfelt dissent, *Cannon's* four-factor test was mentioned again in *Jackson v. Birmingham Board of Education,* 544 U.S. 167 (2005), in which the Supreme Court allowed a private individual to sue for sex-based *retaliation* under Title IX, which prohibits discrimination based on "sex." One might question whether the Court created a new implied cause of action or simply expanded an existing one. In *Cannon,* the plaintiff was discriminated against because of her sex, or gender. In contrast, in *Jackson,* the male plaintiff was discriminated against because of *other people's* gender, namely the members of the women's basketball team. Apparently, the majority believed that it was merely determining the contours of an existing cause of action, for the majority never discussed *Cort* or *Alexander* (*see* below).

Soon after *Cannon* was decided, the Supreme Court again modified its approach to implying causes of action in *Touche Ross & Co. v. Redington*, 442 U.S. 560 (1979). The issue before the Court was whether a provision in the Securities Exchange Act of 1934 had an implied cause of action. While the Court mentioned all the *Cort* factors, it suggested that the first three were relevant only because they showed legislative intent. "The ultimate question is one of congressional intent, not one of whether this Court thinks that it can improve upon the statutory scheme that Congress enacted into law." *Id.* at 576. Thus, the *Cort* factors continued to be relevant, but only to the extent that they demonstrated congressional intent to include private causes of action.

In 1986, former Justice Scalia joined the Supreme Court. Subsequently, the Court refined the implied rights doctrine once more. In *Alexander v. Sandoval*, 532 U.S. 275 (2001), the Court held that there was no private cause of action to enforce disparate-impact regulations promulgated under Title VI of the Civil Rights Act of 1964. *Id.* at 285. Justice Scalia, writing for the majority, reiterated *Touche's* focus on legislative intent; however, he added his own twist: "We therefore begin (and find that we can end) our search for Congress's intent with the text and structure of Title VI." *Id.* at 288. In other words, even though the statute at issue had been enacted during a time when the Court easily implied private rights of action (the *Borak* era), even though the enacting Congress might thus have anticipated that the Court would imply a cause of action in the statute, and even though implied rights are by their very nature *non-explicit*, Justice Scalia used a textualist approach to determine whether Congress intended the act in question to allow private causes of action. *Id.* at 287. In essence, Justice Scalia obliterated the concept of *implied* private causes of action. In his dissent, Justice Stevens noted: "[T]oday's decision is the unconscious product of the majority's profound distaste for implied causes of action rather than an attempt to discern the intent of the Congress that enacted Title VI of the Civil Rights Act of 1964." *Id.* at 317 (Stevens, J., dissenting).

The current tension amongst justices in this area is demonstrated in *CBOCS West, Inc. v. Humphries*, 553 U.S. 442 (2008). In this case, the plaintiff alleged that he was fired after he complained that another employee was fired because of his race. The relevant statute, section 1981 of the Civil Rights Act, provides that all persons "shall have the same right in every State and Territory to make and enforce contracts ... as is enjoyed by white citizens." *Id.* at 445 (quoting

42 U.S.C. § 1981(a)). Employment is considered a contract, so the Act covered the employee who was fired because of his race. However, this case raised the question of whether an employee who was fired for whistleblowing could bring a claim for *retaliation* under section 1981. Relevantly, in an earlier case the Court had held that a companion statute to section 1981, 42 U.S.C. § 1982 ("section 1982"), included a prohibition against retaliation for advocating for the rights of those whom section 1982 protects. *Sullivan v. Little Hunting Park, Inc.*, 396 U.S. 229, 237 (1969). Because sections 1981 and 1982 were enacted together, the plaintiff argued that the statutes should be interpreted similarly (*in pari materia*). *See CBOCS West*, 533 U.S. at 445–46. The majority agreed and held that section 1981 did encompass retaliation claims. *Id.* at 451.

Not surprisingly, the textualists on the Court, Justices Thomas and Scalia, dissented from the majority decision finding an implied cause of action. *Id.* at 456–47. (Thomas, J., dissenting). Indeed, during oral argument Justice Scalia criticized the Court's earlier approach to implied causes of action: "We inferred that cause of action [for section 1982] in the bad old days, when we were inferring causes of action all over the place." Transcript of Oral Argument at 45, *CBOCS West, Inc. v. Humphries*, 553 U.S. 442 (2008).

Given the relatively recent addition of two more conservative justices to the Supreme Court (Gorsuch and Kavanaugh), it seems likely that the Court will continue to apply the textualist approach to deny implied causes of action.

b. Implied Remedies

"[A] right without a remedy is not a right at all." *Doe v. Cnty. of Centre, PA*, 242 F.3d 437, 456 (3d Cir. 2001). Thus, once a court finds an implied cause of action, the court must determine which, if any, remedies are available. After *Cannon* was decided, the Supreme Court addressed the issue of whether the remedy for Title IX's implied cause of action included recovery of money damages or was limited to injunctive relief. *Cannon*, 441 U.S. at 686–88. In a later case, the Court held that monetary damages were recoverable. *Franklin v. Gwinnett Cnty. Pub. Sch.*, 503 U.S. 60, 66 (1992). The Court indicated that it would "presume the availability of all appropriate remedies unless Congress has expressly indicated otherwise." *Id.* (internal citations omitted). It might be hard to find that "Congress has expressly indicated otherwise" when Congress does not expressly grant a private cause of action in the first place!

The plaintiff in *Franklin*, a student at the public high school, was the subject of inappropriate and unwanted sexual advances by one of her teachers. The student claimed that the school failed to take any action other than discouraging her from filing charges. *Id.* at 64. By the time the case was heard, both the student and the teacher had left the school. *Id*. Hence, injunctive relief would not have helped this particular student. In holding that all forms of relief were available unless Congress had indicated otherwise, the *Franklin* majority was quick to distinguish its evolving test for finding implied remedies: "[T]he question whether a litigant has a 'cause of action' is analytically distinct and prior to the question of what relief, if any, a litigant may be entitled to receive." *Id*. at 69 (internal quotation marks omitted). Because the Court had implied a cause of action in *Cannon*, the legislative silence surrounding available remedies did not trouble the *Franklin* majority. *Id*. at 71. "Since the Court in *Cannon* concluded that this statute supported no express right of action, it is hardly surprising that Congress also said nothing about the applicable remedies for an implied right of action." *Id*.

So the Court turned to another source to resolve the issue: subsequent legislative acts. In two subsequent, related acts (the Rehabilitation Act Amendments of 1986 and the Rehabilitation Act of 1973), Congress had eliminated the states' Eleventh Amendment immunity from suit. *Id*. at 72–73. In doing so, Congress broadly defined the available remedies to include all forms of damages. *Id*. at 73. The *Franklin* majority and the concurrence interpreted Congress's subsequent legislation as "a validation of *Cannon's* holding" and "as an implicit acknowledgment that damages are available." *Id*. at 78 (Scalia, J., concurring). Even Justice Scalia, a firm critic of implied causes of action, was willing to grant all available remedies once the cause of action was implied. *Id*. at 78. Thus, if the Court is willing to imply a cause of action, the court should be willing to award both equitable and legal remedies. For example, relying on the *Franklin* presumption—that all remedies are available absent congressional intent to the contrary—the Fourth Circuit held that a plaintiff could seek punitive damages under section 504 of the Rehabilitation Act. *Pandazides v. Virginia Bd. of Educ.*, 13 F.3d 823, 830–32 (4th Cir. 1994).

There is a different, but related, issue regarding implied remedies. When a statute expressly provides a private cause of action, are the explicitly identified remedies in the statute exclusive? Let's return to our discussion of wrongful death statutes and punitive damages. If a wrongful death statute does not specifically say that punitive damages are recoverable, should a court interpret the statute to allow them? What about equitable relief? Should a statute that provides for monetary damages be interpreted to provide equitable relief as well?

As you might imagine, the decision of whether to expand a statute with some remedies identified to include remedies not specifically identified turns on the judge's particular approach to statutory interpretation. Judges who follow a purposivist approach to this issue consider whether the identified remedy will further the purpose of the statute. For example, in *Orloff v. Los Angeles Turf Club, Inc.*, 180 P.2d 321, 324 (Cal. 1947), the court held that equitable relief should be implied. In that case, the plaintiff was repeatedly kicked out of a horse racing track because of his race. *Id.* at 321. A state statute provided that anyone who was denied access to a public facility would be entitled to recover either actual damages or one hundred dollars. *Id.* at 322 (citing CAL. CIVIL CODE § 54). Because he was not hurt, plaintiff would have been limited to an award of one hundred dollars. *Id.* at 323. Because of the inadequacy of the available damages, the plaintiff sought equitable relief, specifically an injunction. *Id.* at 322. The court held that injunctive relief was necessary to effectuate the purpose of the statute: to prevent the exclusion of persons from certain places based on their race. *Id.* at 325. However, this is a very old case and might be decided differently today with the emphasis on text and the linguistic canons. In this case, *expressio unius* counsels a different result.

It is less likely that a court today would expand remedies beyond those explicitly provided in the statute. Indeed, in *Snapp v. Unlimited Concepts, Inc.*, 208 F.3d 928, 934 (11th Cir. 2000), the court held that the Fair Labor Standards Act's anti-retaliation provision for general damages did not include punitive damages. The Act allowed "such *legal* or equitable *relief* as may be appropriate to effectuate the purposes of section 215(a)(3) of this title, including without limitation employment, reinstatement, promotion, and the payment of wages lost and an additional equal amount as liquidated damages." *Id.* at 933 (quoting 29 U.S.C. § 216(b)) (emphasis added). Because the types of damages specifically enumerated in this section and in other sections of the Act were all "meant to *compensate* the plaintiff," the court determined that punitive damages were inappropriate. *Id.* at 935.

These two areas of law—implied causes of action and implied remedies— demonstrate the impact that textualism has had on statutory interpretation. The doctrines have been altered in ways that make little sense. How will it ever be possible to find an implied cause of action using textualism? If courts will consult only the text, then unless Congress expressly includes such a cause of action, courts will not imply one. This tension between the power of the legislature to say what the law is and the power of the judiciary to say what the law means underscores every aspect of statutory interpretation, but it is most visible in this area. The two most recent additions to the Supreme Court, Justice Gorsuch and Justice Kavanaugh, will play a huge role in shaping the Court's doctrine and approach to statutory interpretation. Sit back and relax. It should be an interesting show!

F. Mastering This Topic

Return to the hypothetical ordinance provided in Chapter 1. The first question that was asked was the following: "An ambulance entered Pioneer Park to pick up and take to the hospital a man who had just suffered a heart attack. Did the ambulance driver violate the Pioneer Park Safety Ordinance (PPSO)?" How should you, as prosecutor, attempt to answer that question using what you've learned in this chapter? Let's apply the canons you learned in this chapter. First, the ordinance does not raise a constitutional avoidance issue. However, the ordinance has penal implications, so the rule of lenity is definitely implicated. Remember that the rule of lenity directs that when there are two or more fair and reasonable interpretations of a penal statute, the interpretation that is less penal should be favored. Alternatively, you might say that penal ordinances should be strictly construed.

Applying the rule of lenity, you note that there are two reasonable interpretations: ambulances are either motor vehicles or they are not. Because the less penal interpretation should govern, you would likely find that the ambulance driver did not have fair enough notice that driving an ambulance into the park to rescue someone would be criminal. However, you should remember that the rule of lenity is disfavored in some jurisdictions, and other jurisdictions require a court to exhaust all other sources of meaning before adopting the less penal alternative. Both of these approaches might suggest that the rule of lenity is not applicable here.

Turning to the other topics, you note that the ordinance does not raise *ex post facto* issues. The ordinance did not criminalize or increase the penalty on prior legal behavior; the ordinance was enacted before the ambulance driver made the fateful drive. If the city council were to amend the statute to require anyone who *had in the past* been convicted of violating the statute to surrender his or her driver's license, then an *ex post facto* issue would be raised.

Further, this ordinance does not raise federalism, federal preemption, American Indian, or sovereign immunity issues, so the clear statement canon is not applicable. However, if there were a state statute that specifically permitted emergency vehicles to travel wherever necessary to aid injured individuals (as suggested in the hypothetical analysis in Chapter 9), then the statute and ordinance would conflict. In this scenario, the state statute would essentially "preempt" the local ordinance, although we don't typically use preemption language in this situation. While the state statute likely did not contain a clear statement that it preempted all local conflicting laws, preemption would be implied given the irreconcilable conflict.

Additionally, the ordinance is neither in derogation of the common law—there is no common law right to drive in public parks—or remedial—the ordinance does not create new rights or expand remedies.

Finally, for the hypothetical offered, there are no issues involving implied causes of action and implied remedies. But assume that the ambulance driver had hit someone while driving through the park. Could the injured person successfully argue that this ordinance included an implied cause of action allowing victims to sue drivers who violated the ordinance (for purposes of this hypothetical, ignore the likelihood that state tort law would be applicable)?

Assuming that the current test for implying causes of action is to look for legislative intent by considering the *Cort* factors, you should consider each of the four factors. The first factor—whether the victim was within the class of persons "for whose especial benefit" the ordinance was enacted—seems to be met here. The city council enacted the ordinance to further safety and protect individuals in the park from getting hurt. The second factor—whether the legislative history showed that the city council intended to create or deny a private cause of action—seems not to be met. The city council did not address the issue in any way. Because it would be unusual to add a cause of action for this type of ordinance, likely the city council would have at least discussed the issue (the "dog does not bark" canon). The third factor—whether an implied cause of action would be consistent with the underlying purposes of the statute—seems to be met. Imposing civil liability on top of criminal liability in this situation would likely discourage individuals from driving in the park and promote safety. Finally, the fourth factor—whether the issue would be one that is traditionally left to "local" law—also seems not to be met. Tort liability is generally a matter of state rather than local law. However, the Supreme Court seems hostile to finding implied causes of actions. Should this fact impact your analysis?

Assuming a court implied a cause of action, what remedies would the court imply? Generally, courts will presume the availability of all appropriate remedies unless the legislating body has expressly indicated otherwise.

Checkpoints

• Policy-based sources reflect important social and legal choices derived from both the Constitution and prudential ideals.

• The constitutional avoidance doctrine directs that when there are two reasonable interpretations of statutory language, one of which raises constitutional issues and one of which does not, the statute should be interpreted in a way that does not raise the constitutional issues.

• The rule of lenity directs judges to interpret penal statutes strictly; penal statutes are those statutes that punish citizens by imposing a criminal fine or imprisonment. It is less clear that the rule of lenity applies to cases purely involving administrative fines.

• *Ex post facto* laws violate the U.S. Constitution. An *ex post facto* law is a law that redefines criminal conduct or increases the penalty for criminal conduct.

• Where a statute could be interpreted to abridge federalism, to preempt state law, to impact American Indian rights, or to waive sovereign immunity, courts generally require the legislature to be clear about its intention. The requirement of a clear statement is based on the assumption that a legislature would not make such important changes without being absolutely clear about doing so.

• Statutes in derogation of the common law should be strictly construed. A statute is in derogation of common law when it partially repeals or abolishes existing common law rights or otherwise limits the scope, utility, or force of that law. This canon is currently disfavored.

• Remedial statutes are those that create new rights or expand remedies. They should be liberally, not narrowly, construed to achieve their statutory purpose.

• Implied causes of action are not expressly provided for in the statute; rather, a court must imply them. Whether a court will do so is a question of congressional intent. Currently, the court looks to the *Cort* factors to make that determination. Once a court implies a cause of action, generally the court will interpret the statute to include all statutory remedies, unless the statute specifically includes a list of remedies.

Chapter 13

The Administrative State: An Introduction to Administrative Agencies

---

Roadmap

- Learn what agencies are and what they do.
- Examine how agencies fit within our constitutional structure.
- Understand the direct and indirect ways that the legislature and executive exert control over agency actions.

A. Introduction to This Chapter

In Chapter 11 we covered post-enactment context: what happens after enactment. You may have noticed that we covered both subsequent judicial action and subsequent legislative action but did not address subsequent executive action. Before we can begin that discussion, you need to understand agencies: what they are and what they do. Only then will you be able to understand the role they play in turning general statutory directives into concrete requirements or prohibitions governing the public. So this chapter will introduce you to agencies.

We proceed as follows. First, you will learn *what* agencies are. What makes an authority of the government an agency? Is anyone working for the government an agency? Next, you will learn *why* agencies regulate. Why, you might ask, do we need agency regulation at all? After learning why agencies regulate, we turn to the question of *how* agencies regulate. Agencies can regulate in a variety of ways, from issuing rules, to adjudicating cases, to inspecting businesses. We will examine all of these actions in some detail because the way that an agency regulates plays a role in the deference a court will give an agency when it interprets a statute. Finally, we will conclude this chapter by learning *where* agencies fit within our constitutional structure. Agencies have executive, quasi-legislative, and quasi-adjudicatory powers. Yet they are located within the executive branch. Under separation of powers, how can agencies legitimately exercise any power other than executive?

B. What Agencies Are

The Administrative Procedures Act (APA), 5 U.S.C. §551 *et. seq.*, governs agencies and identifies their procedural law, which we call *Administrative Law*. The APA defines "agency" as "each authority of the Government of the United States ... not includ[ing Congress, the courts, state governments, etc.]." 5 U.S.C. §551(1). For purposes of the APA, the term "agency" includes all governmental authorities including administrations, commissions, corporations (*e.g.*, the Federal Deposit Insurance Corporation), boards, departments, divisions, and agencies. The definition is very broad. Indeed, the Supreme Court held that Amtrak is a governmental entity because of the government's oversight of and involvement with the corporation. *DOT v. Ass'n of Am. R.R.*, 135 S. Ct. 1225, 1233 (2015).

There are a couple of things to note about the APA's definition of an agency. First, it does not define the term "authority." Second, the definition lists specific exclusions but does not exclude the president. Surprisingly, the issue of whether the president is an agency subject to the APA did not come before the Supreme Court until 1992. Is the president an agency? *Expressio unius* would suggest so given that there is no catch-all; however, the Supreme Court rejected the *expressio unius* argument that the president should be considered an agency because the executive was not specifically excluded from the definition, while Congress and the judiciary were. *Franklin v. Massachusetts*, 505 U.S. 788, 796 (1992). Despite the strong statutory interpretation argument in favor of finding the president to be an agency, the Court held that the president was not an agency due to concerns regarding separation of powers; the justices all agreed that they lacked power to order a sitting president to act. "It is a commentary upon the level to which judicial understanding—indeed, even judicial awareness—of the doctrine of separation of powers has fallen, that the District Court entered this order against the President without blinking an eye. I think it clear that no court has authority to direct the President to take an official act." *Id.* at 826 (Scalia, J., concurring).

Moving beyond the APA's definition, Congress has created two types of agencies: *independent agencies* and *executive agencies*, although these two types lie along a spectrum, rather than dividing neatly into two categories. Independent agencies are thought to be less subject to the president's influence because they are often headed by multimember groups from both political parties. Further, these agency heads serve specific terms, rather than at-will, and can only be removed for cause. Examples of independent agencies include the Securities and Exchange Commission, the Federal Trade Commission, the Federal Election Commission, the Equal Employment Opportunity Commission, and the National Labor Relations Board.

In contrast, executive agencies are usually headed by individuals (generally called secretaries or administrators), whom the president appoints, with the advice and consent of the Senate, and who serve at the discretion of the president. Examples of executive agencies include the Department of Treasury, the Department of Agriculture, and the Department of Labor. The largest and most influential executive agencies are called *departments*; departments contain a host of sub-agencies. A few examples of departments include the Commerce Department, the Justice Department, the Department of Energy, the Department of Education, and the Department of Homeland Security. Sub-entities within the Department of the Interior include the Fish and Wildlife Service, the National Park Services, the Bureau of Indian Affairs, the Bureau of Reclamation, and the Bureau of Land Management. The heads of the departments are known collectively as the Cabinet. While presidents turned to the Cabinet for advice in the past, more recently, presidents seek advice from other entities and individuals.

C. Why Agencies Regulate

A government may regulate, or affect behavior, in numerous ways. Legislatures regulate by enacting statutes. Courts regulate by issuing judicial opinions. And the executive regulates by promulgating rules and issuing orders. Executive regulation, or agency regulation, has advantages over legislative and judicial regulation. Generally, agencies have the flexibility to act more quickly than either the legislature or courts, and agencies can act with more detail and expertise. In short, the legislature and courts simply cannot do it all quickly and thoroughly enough. *Mistretta v. United States*, 488 U.S. 361, 372 (1989) ("[The Court's] jurisprudence has been driven by a practical understanding that in our increasingly complex society ... Congress simply cannot do its job absent an ability to delegate power.").

Importantly, agencies have specialized and relevant expertise in their area of responsibility. The modern administrative state is vastly complex. Consider the U.S. Department of Veterans' Affairs (VA), the Environmental Protection Agency (EPA), and the Food and Drug Administration (FDA). Each of these agencies has experts and specialists trained in their relevant field. Legislators have various backgrounds and judges are generalists with expertise in law, not in the environment or food safety. Hence, it simply makes more sense for medical personnel within the VA to determine disability benefits for veterans, for scientists within the EPA to determine acceptable levels of pollutants in the air, and for nutritionists within the FDA to determine the safety of food additives.

Moreover, agencies may be more responsive to the electorate than the judiciary would be, although perhaps less responsive than legislators. National goals and policies change as society evolves. Agency administrators are accountable to the public via the Office of the President and, therefore, will be more likely to conform their policies to match populist expectations. Federal judges, in contrast, are appointed for life and are, thus, more insulated from political backlash. They tend to protect minority interests, rather than represent the majority position.

Today, many of us take for granted that our regulated world is safe. But are we really better off with agency regulation? Could market forces serve the same function, perhaps without the costs of regulation? *Regulated entities* (the general term for those institutions and people that agencies regulate) and others argue that overregulation raises the cost of doing business, increasing the price consumers must pay thus hurting the economy. If regulation is too strict, these individuals argue, companies may be forced to close their doors, depriving workers of jobs and consumers of the things they wish to buy.

If agencies stopped regulating, only market forces would be left to protect the public. Market forces are generally assumed to limit the abuses of companies operating in competitive markets. When an individual can choose among many companies, each of those companies has strong incentives to keep prices low and quality high—otherwise, no one will buy their products. And technology can help, with reputation aggregators like Yelp or Amazon.com reviews allowing potential buyers to envision what their world will be like if they make the purchase. However, not every market works perfectly, and not every market is competitive, meaning there are many sellers. Can market forces adequately and efficiently protect the public in these markets? Consider the following example.

Prior to 1938, drugs were largely unregulated in the United States. Then more than 100 people died from one drug. That drug, sulfanilamide, had been safely used to treat streptococcal infections for some time in both tablet and powder form. But there was a growing demand for a liquid form. In response to this market demand, the chief chemist and pharmacist from S.E. Massengill Company[1] experimented and found that sulfanilamide dissolved in diethylene glycol. The chemist lab tested his new liquid mixture for flavor, appearance, and fragrance. However, he did not test for toxicity. Diethylene glycol is a chemical that is normally used as antifreeze; it is deadly.

After the liquid mixture passed the taste and smell test, Massengill immediately sent 633 shipments of its new drug to doctors and pharmacists throughout the country. The drug had a pleasant, raspberry flavor that was particularly appealing to children. More than 100 people died after taking the drug; many of those who died were children being treated for sore throats. After taking the drug, the victims were sick for seven to ten days and experienced symptoms characteristic of kidney failure, including the inability to urinate, severe abdominal pain, nausea, vomiting, stupor, and convulsions. These individuals suffered intense and unrelenting pain. One mother described the heartache she experienced at the loss of her daughter:

> The first time I ever had occasion to call in a doctor for [Joan] and she was given Elixir of Sulfanilamide. All that is left to us is the caring for her little grave. Even the memory of her is mixed with sorrow for we can see her little body tossing to and fro and hear that little voice screaming with pain and it seems as though it would drive me insane.... [2]

A doctor described his own distress at prescribing the medicine:

> Nobody but Almighty God and I can know what I have been through these past few days. I have been familiar with death in the years since I received my M.D. from Tulane University School of Medicine with

---

1. Massengill was a pharmaceutical company started in 1898 by Samuel Evans Massengill. Samuel graduated from the University of Nashville Medical School but decided to manufacture drugs rather than practice medicine. The company employed more than 200 people in Bristol, Tennessee, including six pharmaceutical chemists. It operated as a family owned company until 1971, when it was acquired by another company. Most recently, it merged with Prestige Brands Holdings, Inc.

2. Carol Ballentine, *Taste of Raspberries, Taste of Death: The 1937 Elixir Sulfanilamide Incident*, FDA Consumer Magazine, June 1981, available at https://www.fda.gov/about-fda/histories-product-regulation/sulfanilamide-disaster.

the rest of my class of 1911. Covington County has been my home. I
have practiced here for years. Any doctor who has practiced more than
a quarter of a century has seen his share of death.

But to realize that six human beings, all of them my patients, one
of them my best friend, are dead because they took medicine that I
prescribed for them innocently, and to realize that that medicine which
I had used for years in such cases suddenly had become a deadly poison
in its newest and most modern form, as recommended by a great and
reputable pharmaceutical firm in Tennessee: well, that realization has
given me such days and nights of mental and spiritual agony as I did
not believe a human being could undergo and survive. I have known
hours when death for me would be a welcome relief from this agony.[3]

Although Massengill quickly discovered that the drug was toxic, the
company was in no hurry to recall it. Instead, Massengill merely sent telegrams
to its salesmen, druggists, and doctors asking them to return the drug. The
telegrams provided little explanation: they failed to mention the urgency of
the situation or even that the drug was lethal. Only after insistence from
governmental officials did the company finally send out a second set of
telegrams that warned of the danger. Even so, Massengill admitted no
responsibility: Dr. Samuel Evans Massengill, the company's owner, said: "My
chemists and I deeply regret the fatal results, but there was no error in the
manufacture of the product. We have been supplying a legitimate professional
demand and not once could have foreseen the unlooked-for results. I do not
feel that there was any responsibility on our part."[4] Yet "[a] few simple tests
on experimental animals would have demonstrated the lethal properties of
the elixir. Even a review of the currently existing scientific literature would
have shown that" diethylene glycol was toxic and could cause kidney damage
or failure.[5] Massengill's chemist, the person who created the formula, must
have felt more culpable. He committed suicide.

Under the law in effect at the time, the U.S. Department of Agriculture
(USDA) had almost no power to seize the drug or to prosecute Massengill
for distributing a deadly drug. The USDA focused its early efforts on

---

3. Letter from Dr. A.S. Calhoun (October 22, 1937), available at http://www.fda.gov/
aboutfda/whatwedo/history/productregulation/sulfanilamidedisaster/default.htm.
4. *Id.*
5. *Id.*

convincing the company to help find and destroy the drug. Ultimately, the USDA charged Massengill for drug misbranding. The USDA argued that by using the term "elixir" in its product description Massengill had implied that the product was an alcoholic solution. However, the product contained no alcohol. At that time, misbranding was only a fineable offense. Had Massengill called the product a "solution" instead of an "elixir," the USDA would have had no legal authority to penalize the company or even to seize the drug. Undoubtedly, many more people would have died.

Why did the USDA have no authority to act? The Pure Food and Drug Act of 1906 was obsolete. That Act together with the Meat Inspection Act were Congress's response to the public outcry from Upton Sinclair's 1905 book, *The Jungle*—an exposé about the Chicago meat-packing industry— and from articles about the widespread adulteration of drugs and food. When it was enacted, the Pure Food and Drug Act of 1906 was the federal government's most significant intrusion into industry through the interstate commerce clause. Although other federal agencies could regulate prices and workplace safety, Congress gave the USDA the power to regulate the manufacture, sale, and advertising of food, drugs, and medicines.

The Act provided, in relevant part:

> An Act—For preventing the manufacture, sale, or transportation of adulterated or misbranded or poisonous or deleterious foods, drugs, medicines, and liquors, and for regulating traffic therein, and for other purposes ....
>
> [Section 2] That the introduction into any State or Territory or the District of Columbia ... of any article of food or drugs which is adulterated or misbranded, within the meaning of this Act, is hereby prohibited ....
>
> [Section 4] That the examinations of specimens of foods and drugs shall be made in the Bureau of Chemistry of the Department of Agriculture, or under the direction and supervision of such Bureau, for the purpose of determining from such examinations whether such articles are adulterated or misbranded within the meaning of this Act.

Federal Food and Drugs Act of 1906, 21 U.S.C. §§ 1–15 (1934), *repealed by* 21 U.S.C. § 329 (a) (1938).

While this Act was a significant first step, it actually provided little protection to the public. The Act did not prohibit the sale of dangerous, untested, or poisonous drugs, nor did it require that safety studies be done on new drugs before they entered the marketplace. While selling toxic drugs was, undoubtedly, bad for business, it was not illegal. By the 1930s it was widely recognized that this Act needed amendment; however, Congress was at an impasse to effect change until the "Elixir Sulfanilamide" incident described above. After that disaster, Congress quickly enacted the Federal Food, Drug, and Cosmetic Act, giving authority to the Food and Drug Administration (FDA), which is within the USDA, to regulate food, cosmetic, and drug safety. This new Act required manufacturers to demonstrate to the FDA the safety of new drugs prior to making them available to the public. Twenty-five years after its enactment, this Act saved the United States from another potential drug tragedy — the thalidomide disaster. The FDA had prevented that drug from being approved in the United States, but it was used widely in Europe with devastating effects. Today, the Food and Drug Act continues to be the basis for FDA regulation of these products.

Supporters of regulation acknowledge that the Food and Drug Act is not perfect and offer this story as an example of the failure of market forces, alone, to safely and adequately protect our nation. Regulation skeptics typically also acknowledge that there are times when markets fail to protect individuals and the public. But they suggest that reputational factors can be combined with modern tort liability to discipline companies so that regulation is largely unnecessary. For example, in the case of sulfanilamide, thalidomide, and other drugs, catastrophic failure of the product today would lead to massive tort liability that could bankrupt the company (consider the opioid crisis). Knowledge of that likely possibility would have made the sulfanilamide tragedy far less likely, according to regulation skeptics.

Regulation skeptics also point out that, over time, regulated entities begin to exert significant power over their regulators. If their efforts are successful, regulation stops protecting the public and begins to protect industry. This theory of regulation — known as "agency capture theory," or "rent-seeking" in public choice economics, is hotly contested. But there is some evidence to indicate, for example, that drug companies exert strong influence on the drug approval process, that the food industry dominates food-related FDA decisions, and that large banks control the banking regulators.

Proponents of regulation have largely won the day, but a certain level of skepticism remains regarding the efficacy and efficiency of regulation. Accepting that some regulation is desirable, we, as a society, have to decide what level of agency regulation is desirable. Once we have done that, the next question is how do agencies regulate? We now turn to that question.

D. How Agencies Regulate

Legislatures delegate power to agencies to regulate specific conduct or run programs. For example, federal agencies regulate private conduct, administer entitlement programs, collect taxes, deport aliens, issue permits, run the space program, manage the national parks, and so on. Simply put, agencies run the functions we think of as government, whether state or federal. Of more interest to us is *how* agencies regulate.

Let's look at an example of congressional delegation coupled with agency action. In 2011, Congress enacted the Food Safety Modernization Act (an amendment to the Food, Drug, & Cosmetic Act) to address the problem of foodborne illness. Within this Act, Congress targeted the intentional adulteration of food. 21 U.S.C. § 350d. Congress specifically directed the Secretary of the FDA to "promulgate regulations to implement this subsection." 21 U.S.C. § 350d(b)(5)(A) (addressing suspension of registration for facilities that likely caused serious adverse health consequences or death to humans or animals).

In 2016, pursuant to this rulemaking authority, the FDA promulgated a rule requiring a factory, warehouse, or establishment that manufactures, processes, or holds food to implement food defense measures to protect against the intentional adulteration of food. 21 C.F.R. §§ 11, 121 (2019). One subsection of that regulation requires these facilities to create and implement a food defense plan. 21 C.F.R. § 121.126 (2019). That plan must identify vulnerabilities and actionable process steps, mitigation strategies, and procedures for food defense monitoring, corrective actions, and verification. *Id.* Thus, Congress enacted a statute to further a general goal: make our food safer and protect against intentional adulteration. In doing so, Congress delegated authority to the FDA to develop rules that would help Congress achieve its goals. The FDA then promulgated a binding rule in the form of a regulation. Note the statute itself does not require facilities to create food defense plans, only the regulation requires it. Yet if a facility fails to comply, serious consequences ensue. Hence, even though Congress did not require food defense plans, the FDA's regulation has the force and effect of law.

This last example shows an agency acting via rulemaking. But agencies can also act by adjudicating or by investigating. Agencies act like courts when they adjudicate, like legislatures when they make rules, and like the police when they investigate. For an agency to have any power to act, the legislature must enact a statute that both creates the agency (if it does not already exist) and identifies the agency's powers and regulatory agenda. This statute is known as the *enabling*, authorizing, or organic act (all three names are used). In an enabling act, the legislature commonly authorizes an agency to use one or more of the powers identified above: rulemaking, adjudication, or investigation. This next section explores each power in more detail, beginning with rulemaking. We will confine our discussion to federal agencies; state agencies may operate differently.

1. Rulemaking

The APA defines rulemaking as the "agency process for formulating, amending, or repealing a rule." 5 U.S.C. § 551(5). A rule is "an agency statement of general ... applicability and future effect designed to implement, interpret, or prescribe law or policy." 5 U.S.C. § 551(4). In short, rules, like statutes, are laws that when *promulgated*, or enacted, apply prospectively to large numbers of regulated entities.

Academics divide the world of agency rulemaking into two types: legislative rulemaking and non-legislative rulemaking, although these terms are not used in the APA. Let's look at each and how they differ.

a. Legislative Rules & Rulemaking

Legislative rules are rules that have legal (or binding) effect, meaning if a regulated entity violates the rule, the entity will be subject to penalty. Agencies promulgate legislative rules, or regulations, through three different processes. These processes differ in their degree of procedural formality.

The most formal process is formal rulemaking; however, it is almost never used today. The procedures for formal rulemaking can be found in sections 556 and 557 of the APA. In short, formal rulemaking includes a hearing with civil, trial-like procedures. Entities and individuals the rule might impact have a right to notice of the hearing, and they have a right to participate in the hearing in some fashion. 5 U.S.C. § 554(b), (c). The rules of evidence do not apply. *See* 5 U.S.C. § 556(c)(3) (instructing hearing officers to receive relevant evidence). A hearing officer, known as an administrative law judge (ALJ), compiles the record and makes either an initial decision or recommendation to the agency head. 5 U.S.C. § 554(d). The agency head then either adopts the ALJ decision or issues a final decision. That decision is subject to judicial review. 5 U.S.C. § 706(2).

The procedures used in formal rulemaking are better suited for resolving adjudicative facts (*e.g.*, who is telling the truth) rather than for resolving legislative facts (*e.g.*, what degree of arsenic in the soil is safe). Partly for this reason, formal rulemaking is not common. Moreover, the APA requires agencies to use formal rulemaking only "[w]hen rules are required by statute to be made on the record after opportunity for an agency hearing." 5 U.S.C. § 553(c). While Congress may have intended formal rulemaking to occur more often, the Supreme Court took a literal approach to interpreting this language in *United States v. Florida E. Coast Ry. Co.*, 410 U.S. 224 (1973). In that case, the Court held that enabling statutes that merely require an agency to issue a rule "after hearing" do not trigger formal rulemaking. *Id.* at 238. If Congress wants agencies to use formal rulemaking, Congress must be explicit (essentially, Congress must provide a clear statement). Thus, for formal rulemaking to be required, the enabling statute must require both a hearing *and* that the proceeding be on the record. As a result, formal rulemaking is quite rare at the federal level. It is, however, more commonly used in the states; for example, the Minnesota legislature frequently requires formal rulemaking.

The next most formal process is notice-and-comment rulemaking (also known as informal rulemaking). Like its name suggests, notice-and-comment rulemaking requires an agency to publish notice of its proposed rule in the Federal Register (notice) and to solicit and respond to comments from the public and others about the proposed rule (comment). 5 U.S.C. § 553(b), (c). At the conclusion of this notice-and-comment process the agency typically promulgates a regulation.

While Congress likely intended notice-and-comment rulemaking to be a relatively quick process, it has become much more procedurally burdensome as the courts and executive have added requirements beyond those found in the APA. For example, Executive Order 12,866, which is discussed in detail below, requires agencies to conduct a cost-benefit analysis on all proposed rules that are "significant." Exec. Order No. 12,866, 58 Fed. Reg. 51,735 (1993). Additionally, the Regulatory Flexibility Act requires agencies to create a Regulatory Flexibility Analysis for any proposed rule that will significantly impact a substantial number of small businesses, organizations, or governments. 5 U.S.C. § 601 *et seq.* And the Unfunded Mandates Reform Act requires agencies to prepare a statement assessing the effect of any proposed regulation that will cause state, local, or tribal governments to incur more than $100 million annually. 2 U.S.C. § 1501 *et seq.*

Additionally, in an enabling statute, Congress may require an agency to use procedures in addition to those the APA requires. For example, Congress may require an agency to hold public hearings. Alternatively an agency may choose to use procedures in excess of those the APA and its enabling act require. Indeed, the number and variety of these additional procedures has led commentators to lament the slowing-down, or "ossification," of the rulemaking process.

However, while Congress, the president, and agencies can impose additional rulemaking procedures to those the APA requires, courts cannot do so. In a landmark case, the Supreme Court held that courts cannot require procedures other than those the APA, the Constitution, or a statute require. *Vermont Yankee Nuclear Power Corp. v. Natural Resource Defense Council, Inc.*, 435 U.S. 519, 524 (1978).

Because agencies must follow time-consuming, detailed procedures to enact a regulation, notice-and-comment rulemaking is informal in name only. And the APA is only the starting point for procedural requirements. It is not the ending point.

Finally, the least formal process is publication rulemaking. The APA exempts some legislative rules from both formal and notice-and-comment procedures: (1) rules relating to military and foreign affairs; (2) rules relating to agency management and personnel; (3) rules relating to public property, loans, grants, benefits, and contracts; (4) rules for which the agency has "good cause" reason to avoid notice-and-comment rulemaking; and (5) rules of agency organization, procedure, and practice. 5 U.S.C. § 553(a), (b)(3)(A), (b)(3)(B). Rules within these five categories together account for a tremendous number of rules. For example, if you have a federal student loan, the agency rules related to your loan need not be promulgated with notice-and-comment or formal rulemaking procedures. If you visit federal parks, the agency rules related to your use of the parks need not be promulgated with notice-and-comment or formal rulemaking procedures. Importantly, however, while the agency need not use notice-and-comment or formal rulemaking procedures, the APA does require that the agency publish these rules in the Federal Register or provide actual notice to anyone against whom the agency wishes to enforce a rule. 5 U.S.C. § 552 (a)(1). Hence, these types of rules may be called "publication rules." Peter L. Strauss, An Introduction to Administrative Justice in the United States, 222–24 (2d. ed. 2002).

b. Non-Legislative Rulemaking

Unlike legislative rules, non-legislative rules do not have independent legal effect. Rather, the legal effect they have, if any, comes from pre-existing legislative rules (whether from Congress or the agency). Academics and practitioners collectively call non-legislative rules "*guidance documents.*" Guidance documents are rules that are exempt from the formal and notice-and-comment procedures, but not from publication procedures. 5 U.S.C. § 553(b)(3)(A). They are not publication rules, however, because they do not have independent legal effect.

The APA specifically identifies two types of guidance documents: (1) *interpretative (or interpretive) rules*, and (2) *general statements of policy. Id.* Interpretive rules are self-describing; they are rules interpreting language in an existing statute or regulation. In contrast, policy statements are statements from an agency that prospectively advise the public and agency personnel on the way in which the agency plans to exercise discretionary power in the future. Agencies may issue policy statements to announce new duties the agency plans to adopt in a future adjudication or rulemaking. Note that there is no such thing as an "interpretive statement" or a "policy rule."

Agencies use non-legislative rules for many reasons. For example, assume that after an agency has enacted a regulation, questions arise about how the agency will interpret that regulation. Lower level administrators may seek guidance from senior level administrators about how to implement the new regulation, or regulated entities may seek clarification about their responsibilities under the new rule. In response, agency administrators may develop a list of "frequently asked questions," update an agency manual, or provide guidance in some other form. To illustrate, the Army Corps of Engineers maintains Regulatory Guidance Letters, which are issued to field personnel to interpret or clarify existing regulatory policy. Similarly, the Internal Revenue Service issues letter rulings, which are written statements issued to taxpayers that interpret tax laws. There are examples of the many different ways that an agency might issue a non-legislative rule. Because agencies do not go through a procedurally prescribed process, such as formal or notice-and-comment rulemaking, when they issue these rules, the rules are easily modifiable.

Non-legislative rules play a legitimate and important role in agency policy-making. They help agencies apply law consistently across field offices by affording guidance to both the public and lower level agency personnel. Non-legislative rules ensure greater and faster compliance than legislative rules alone, because legislative rules may lack specificity and clarity. Finally, non-legislative rules also help agencies develop a flexible policy quickly and easily, while still giving the regulated entities and the public advance notice of new policies. From an agency's perspective, non-legislative rules are "law" in a practical sense, because they influence the conduct of regulated entities and, thus, regulate behavior. But legally, non-legislative rules are not truly "law," because they are not legally binding alone. If an agency wants a rule to legally bind regulated entities, the agency must use formal, notice-and-comment, or, for specific rules, publication procedures. The flowchart on the following page shows the types of rulemaking available to agencies.

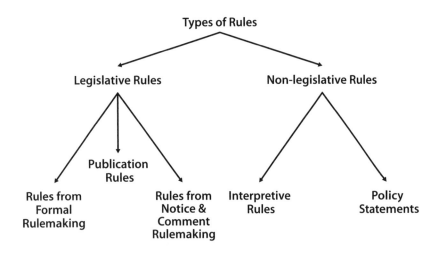

You need not fully understand the differences in the various processes described above at this point. What should be clear, however, is that an agency can act with varying degrees of procedural formality. Let's turn now to adjudication.

2. Adjudication

The APA defines "adjudication" as the "agency process for the formulation of an order." 5 U.S.C. § 551(7). An "order" is "the whole or a part of a final disposition ... of an agency in a matter other than rule making." 5 U.S.C. § 551(6). Collectively, these definitions are so broad that agency activity that is not rulemaking or investigating would seem to be adjudication (including the granting of a permit). Note, however, that the definition requires a "final disposition." Hence, many agency activities are neither rulemaking nor adjudication. For example, investigations and advising the public about regulatory matters are neither adjudication nor rulemaking.

An "adjudication" is the agency process for formulating a decision of "particular" applicability and "present" effect. *Id.* While agency rulemaking is akin to a legislature enacting legislation, agency adjudication is akin to a court conducting a trial or hearing. When using rulemaking, an agency crafts a general rule to address a general problem, which will apply to all regulated entities and take effect after the rule's promulgation and publication. In contrast, when using adjudication, an agency crafts an order to address a specific problem, which will apply to only the specific regulated entities before the agency in the administrative proceeding. The order has retroactive and future effect. Years ago, I had a student submit a drawing depicting the difference between adjudication and rulemaking. For rulemaking, the student drew a bus heading down the freeway with all the passengers looking forward. For adjudication, the student drew a Volkswagen bug, stopped on the road with its driver, alone, looking backward.

While administrative adjudication is similar to judicial adjudication, there are three important differences. First, volume differs. Federal agency adjudication takes place millions of times each year, as compared to the thousands of cases courts hear. This volume requires simpler and faster procedures than are typical for a court.

Second, agencies use adjudication to accomplish different things; the purpose is not simply to resolve a dispute among parties, as it is in court. Here are just a few examples of when an agency might use adjudication:

- An agency wants to stop a regulated entity allegedly engaged in unlawful activity.
- An agency must decide whether to grant or deny a benefit to a regulated entity.
- An agency must decide whether to allow a regulated party to engage in conduct.

These different types of adjudications present different problems to resolve. The differences affect whether the parties will be adversarial, whether the disputed issues will focus more on legislative facts or adjudicative facts, and whether the consequences of the adjudication will affect anyone other than the parties. Hence, these differences may require different hearing processes.

Third, the person making the final decision in agency adjudication is rarely the neutral generalist judge presiding in a courtroom. The adjudicatory design must guarantee the parties meaningful hearings and objective decision-making while at the same time allowing the agency to bring its technical expertise and political mission into the process. Hence, agencies ultimately decide the issues directly, but most use Administrative Law Judges (ALJs) to make the initial decision (the trial court equivalent, if you will).

Despite these differences, administrative and judicial adjudications have much in common, including similar goals. Both seek factual accuracy. Both seek to be cost-effective. And both seek to be perceived as fair, rational, and open.

Like rulemaking, there are two kinds of adjudication in the APA: formal adjudication and informal adjudication. The APA does not require formal adjudicative procedures in every adjudication. Instead, the APA provides that an agency must use formal procedures "in every case of adjudication required by statute to be determined on the record after opportunity for an agency hearing." 5 U.S.C. § 554(a). Hence, in the agency's enabling statute, Congress must specify that formal adjudication is or is not required. Typically, unless Congress includes very clear language that a hearing and decision on the record are mandatory, an agency may use informal APA procedures. *Dominion Energy Brayton Point, LLC v. Johnson*, 443 F.3d 12, 16 (1st Cir. 2006) (overruling an earlier case establishing a presumption in favor of formal adjudication); *Chemical Waste Mgmt., Inc. v. EPA*, 873 F.2d 1477, 1482 (D.C. Cir. 1989) (deferring to the agency's decision that its enabling statute did not require formal adjudication procedures). Although Congress may impose requirements in addition to those the APA requires and often does, the discussion below will focus only on the APA requirements.

Let's start with formal adjudication. The procedures an agency must use for formal adjudication are the same procedures it must use for formal rulemaking. 5 U.S.C. §§ 554, 556. Because formal adjudication is more common than formal rulemaking, we will look at the process in more detail here than we did in the rulemaking section.

The APA requires agencies to notify "[p]ersons entitled to notice of an agency hearing" of when and where the hearing will occur. 5 U.S.C. § 554(b). Importantly, the APA does not define who is entitled to notice; rather, other statutes and the Due Process Clause of the U.S. Constitution identify these persons. The APA further requires that the notice be timely and identify the matters of fact alleged, the relevant law and legal authority, and the agency's jurisdiction to hold the hearing. *Id.* Notice is adequate when it is sufficient to fairly apprise interested parties of an agency action that will affect their interests. *Southwest Sunsites, Inc. v. FTC*, 785 F.2d 1431, 1435 (9th Cir. 1986); *NLRB v. Local Union No. 25*, 586 F.2d 959, 961 (2d Cir. 1978). In other words, notice is sufficient when the regulated entity knows what it did wrong and can respond to the agency's allegations. *See, e.g., John D. Copanos & Sons, Inc. v. FDA*, 854 F.2d 510, 521 (D.C. Cir. 1988) (holding that notice was sufficient despite coming "perilously close to ... denying the applicant a meaningful opportunity to respond" to the agency's allegations). All interested parties, not just those litigating, have the right to submit facts, arguments, and settlement offers, so long as time and the public interest permit. 5 U.S.C. § 554(c).

Formal administrative hearings resemble a civil trial with many of the same procedural accoutrements, including the right to notice, a hearing, a record, and a (mostly) neutral decision-maker. Let's look at some of these requirements in more detail.

The APA gives *any interested person*, not just the parties, the right to appear before the agency to discuss any issue involved in a "proceeding," whether that proceeding be an adjudication, a licensing, or a rulemaking. 5 U.S.C. § 555(b). The only explicit limitation in this section is that the person's right to appear may not impair the "orderly conduct of public business." *Id.* Note, however, there is no requirement that the agency notify interested persons of a proceeding.

Parties and witnesses compelled to testify have a right to be "accompanied, represented, and advised" by counsel or a representative. 5 U.S.C. § 555(b). This is also true for informal adjudications.

The proponent of a rule or order has the burden of proof—both production and persuasion. 5 U.S.C. § 556(d). Typically, then, the agency bears the burden; however, when a private party seeks a license or other benefit, that party would have the burden.

The federal rules of evidence do not apply in administrative adjudications. However, because ALJs are trained as lawyers, most prefer to follow the rules of evidence even though the APA gives agencies significant discretion. Moreover, the federal rules of evidence provide a framework for resolving evidentiary questions. For example, 5 U.S.C. § 556(d) provides that "[a]ny oral or documentary evidence may be received, but the agency as a matter of policy shall provide for the exclusion of irrelevant, immaterial, or unduly repetitious evidence." Further, "[a] sanction may not be imposed or rule or order issued except on consideration of the whole record ... [which is] supported by and in accordance with the reliable, probative, and substantial evidence." 5 U.S.C. § 556(d). The rules of evidence help explain what evidence would be irrelevant, immaterial, unduly repetitious, reliable, probative, and substantial. But there is one critical difference. Unlike in judicial trials, hearsay is commonly admitted in administrative hearings. Because there is no jury and the ALJ is legally trained, the admission of hearsay evidence is less troubling in the administrative context. An agency's final decision must be supported by "substantial evidence." 5 U.S.C. §§ 556(d), 706(2)(E).

Additionally, there is no absolute right either to cross-examination at all or to unlimited cross-examination. Parties may conduct cross-examination *if necessary*. 5 U.S.C. § 556(d). The courts have held that a party seeking cross-examination has the burden to show that cross is required for a "full and true disclosure of the facts." *Citizens Awareness Network, Inc. v. United States,* 391 F.3d 338, 354 (1st Cir. 2004). Cross-examination is usually allowed, however.

Like judicial trials, *ex parte* communications are generally not allowed, but the rules depend on who is deciding the case and who is communicating *ex parte*. An ALJ cannot discuss the *facts* of the case with any person or party inside or outside of the agency, except in the presence of all other parties. 5 U.S.C. § 554(d)(1). This section does not prohibit the agency itself from having internal communications. Further, an ALJ or other agency decisionmaker cannot discuss the *merits* of the case (facts, policy, or law) with *interested parties* outside of the agency. 5 U.S.C. § 557(d)(1); *Prof'l Air Traffic Controllers Org. v. FLRA*, 685 F.2d 547, 570 (D.C. Cir. 1982) (describing interested parties as anyone who has an interest in a proceeding that is greater than the interest a general member of the public would have). The APA defines *ex parte* communications as communications not on the public record and to which notice to all parties is not given, but the definition excludes status reports. 5 U.S.C. § 551(14).

ALJs generally preside over formal agency adjudications, although the person or persons in charge of the agency may choose to preside instead. 5 U.S.C. § 556(b). ALJs have the power to administer oaths, issue subpoenas, receive evidence, hold settlement conferences, dispose of procedural requests, take official notice of facts, and, most importantly, decide the case either by making an initial decision or by making a recommendation to the agency. 5 U.S.C. § 557(b). When the APA was first adopted, ALJs were known as "hearing examiners" and were expected only to assemble the record for the agency head; the term was changed to administrative law judges in 1978 to elevate their status and increase their impartiality. But if you understand that their initial role was simply to create the record, you might better understand some of what follows.

The ALJ is an employee of the agency for which he or she works. 5 U.S.C. § 3105. To ensure that ALJs retain as much independence and neutrality as possible, agencies may not evaluate, discipline, reward, punish, or remove their ALJs; instead, the Merit Systems Protection Board (an independent agency) makes these decisions. 5 U.S.C. § 7521.

Further, pursuant to a provision known as the separation of functions provision, the APA ensures that the agency officials who perform investigative or prosecutorial functions do not supervise or oversee ALJs: An ALJ "may not ... be responsible to or subject to the supervision or direction of an employee or agent engaged in the performance of investigative or prosecuting functions for an agency." 5 U.S.C. § 554(d)(2). Also, the APA prohibits prosecutors and investigators from participating or advising the ALJ in decisionmaking unless the prosecutor or investigator is a participant in the hearing itself. *Id.* This restriction applies not only to the specific case but also to any "factually related" cases, meaning different cases arising out of the same set of facts. *Id.* The APA thus separates the functions of decisionmakers, investigators, and prosecutors, with three exceptions: (1) proceedings involving applications for initial licenses;

(2) proceedings involving the validity or application of rates, facilities, or practices of public utilities or carriers; and (3) proceedings involving the agency or a member or members of the body comprising the agency as the decision maker. 5 U.S.C. § 554(d)(2)(A)–(C).

As a result of an adjudication, a record is compiled. The APA provides that "[t]he transcript of testimony and exhibits, together with all papers and requests filed in the proceeding, constitutes the exclusive record for decision." 5 U.S.C. § 556(e). This "exclusive record" ensures the hearing is "on the record." Assuming an ALJ presided at the hearing, then after the hearing concludes the ALJ will make a "recommended" or "initial decision." 5 U.S.C. §§ 554(d), 557(b). Typically, the ALJ will both preside at the hearing and make an initial decision. However, if an agency prefers to retain the power to make the initial decision, it can elect to have an ALJ preside at the hearing and make a "recommended" decision. 5 U.S.C. § 557(b). The ALJ's initial decision "becomes the decision of the agency" if there is no appeal. *Id.*

An ALJ must rule "on each finding, conclusion, or exception presented." 5 U.S.C. § 557(c)(3). All decisions, initial and otherwise, must include a statement of the "findings and conclusions, and the reasons or basis therefor, on all the material issues of fact, law, or discretion presented on the record; and the appropriate rule, order, sanction, relief, or denial thereof." 5 U.S.C. § 557(c)(3)(A), (B). This section ensures that the ALJ and agency respond to the parties' arguments so that that the reviewing court will know what the decisions were based upon.

Similar to trial court decisions, agency adjudications are subject to judicial review. 5 U.S.C. § 706(2). To appeal an ALJ's initial decision—which includes findings of fact, conclusions of law, the basis for the findings, and the order— a party must appeal first to the agency itself. Unlike appeals in a court of law, appeals to the agency are reviewed using a *de novo* standard of review: "the agency has all the powers which it would have in making the initial decision." 5 U.S.C. § 557(b). This distinction is important and not intuitive to lawyers: The APA allows the agency to give little to no deference to the ALJ's initial decision. And agencies do reverse ALJ decisions.

Despite this *de novo* standard of review, a reviewing court will be less likely to reverse an agency's final decision that defers to an ALJ's findings regarding witness credibility. Why? Because the reviewing court will evaluate the agency's factual findings to see if there is "substantial evidence" in the record to support those findings. 5 U.S.C. § 706(2)(E). The ALJ's initial opinion is part of the "whole record" that the reviewing court will examine. *Universal Camera Corp. v. NLRB*, 340 U.S. 474, 493 (1951). In those cases where the demeanor of the witnesses is critical to the outcome, the reviewing court will consider the

ALJ's demeanor findings because the ALJ actually observed the witnesses. When an agency rejects an ALJ's credibility findings without sufficient explanation, a reviewing court may reject the agency's final decision finding it to be unsupported by substantial evidence. *Id.* at 497. Thus, while an agency may reject an ALJ's decision, the agency's success on appeal will be affected by how persuasively the agency explains its rejection of an ALJ's findings relating to credibility.

The appeal process is similar to an appeal in court; the parties submit written briefs and may argue orally. If the agency rules against itself (its prosecuting arm), there is no further appeal. If, however, the agency rules in favor of itself, the losing party may appeal to a court of law, usually an appellate court. Judicial review concludes the formal adjudication process.

While formal adjudication resembles a civil trial, informal adjudication is altogether different. In a typical APA informal adjudication, the agency may provide no hearing at all. Indeed, the APA requires few procedures; an agency need only promptly decide an issue and notify the affected party. 5 U.S.C. § 555(e). Informal adjudications can be as simple as an agency approving an individual's application for a permit. If you have ever received a driving, hunting, fishing, or business license, you have been involved in an informal adjudication (albeit at the state level).

The APA only provides for these two adjudicative processes; however, agencies often provide adjudications that offer more procedures than informal but less than formal adjudication. You should be aware that there is a vast amount of adjudication that falls in between the extremes of formal and informal adjudication, but we will not talk about them further here.

Although the APA requires few procedures for informal adjudications, the U.S. Constitution or the agency's enabling statute may require more. In cases involving the deprivation of life, liberty, or property rights, the Due Process Clause of the U.S. Constitution requires some form of a hearing. The hearing need not be elaborate; rather, the required procedures for that hearing vary in accordance with the competing interests. To determine whether an agency provided sufficient procedures to an individual who was deprived of a life, liberty, or property interest, a court will balance (1) the private interest being affected, (2) the risk of erroneous deprivation of this interest through the procedures the agency used, and (3) the administrative and fiscal burden to the agency of using of additional procedures (the government's interest). *Mathews v. Eldridge*, 424 U.S. 319, 335 (1976). Moreover, absent a really good reason, the government must offer a pre-deprivation hearing (rather than post-deprivation), although an abbreviated form is sufficient if the agency offers a post-deprivation hearing that comports with the *Mathews'* requirements. *Cleveland Bd. of Educ. v. Loudermill*, 470 U.S. 532, 542 (1985). In sum, compared to formal adjudication, informal adjudication procedures are generally minimal, and the process is much faster.

One last point: Agencies may choose to regulate using either rulemaking or adjudication. So long as an agency has authority to act using either process (check the enabling act), the decision of whether to proceed through rulemaking or adjudication is vested, primarily, in the informed discretion of the agency. *SEC v. Chenery Corp.*, 332 U.S. 194, 202–03 (1947) (saying that an agency "may not have had sufficient experience with a particular problem to warrant rigidifying its tentative judgment into a hard and fast rule. Or the problem may be so specialized and varying in nature as to be impossible of capture within the boundaries of a general rule."). In *Chenery II* (as it is known), the Supreme Court recognized that, although an agency should consider making policy as much as possible using rulemaking, agencies must have flexibility to deal with regulatory problems in the manner they deem most appropriate.

Although the decision whether to proceed through rulemaking or adjudication is primarily vested in the informed discretion of the agency, courts may set aside an agency's order if the agency's decision to use adjudication amounts to an abuse of discretion. For example, were an agency to impose a substantial penalty or liability on a regulated person or entity for violating a legal principle that had not been previously announced, the agency's order would likely be set aside. *See, e.g., NLRB v. Bell Aerospace Co. Div. of Textron Inc.*, 416 U.S. 267, 295 (1974). A regulated entity's substantial reliance on the agency's prior practice may, in some cases, also warrant the setting aside of an agency order.

3. Investigation

Investigation is typically a function of the executive; thus, it should come as no surprise that Congress may grant agencies investigatory powers. To effectively regulate, agencies need information and lots of it. To believe that its government is acting legitimately, the public demands transparency. Hence, information flows in both directions: from the public to the agency and from the agency to the public. The APA does not address an agency's ability to seek information from those it regulates; rather, the agency's enabling act and the Fourth and Fifth Amendments to the U.S. Constitution regulate this area. Similarly, the APA does not address an agency's duty to provide information to the public. Rather, other statutes do so, such as the Freedom of Information

Act, 5 U.S.C. §552; the Government in Sunshine Act, 5 U.S.C. §552b; the Federal Advisory Act, 5 U.S.C. app. 2 §1 *et seq.*; and the Privacy Act, 5 U.S.C. §552a, among others.

Let's examine the rules relating to an agency's ability to seek information from those entities it regulates. Agencies inspect facilities, require regulated entities to file reports and provide information, and issue subpoenas for a variety of reasons, including to ensure that regulated entities are complying with the law. Agencies may need information to set policy through the promulgation of rules, to keep Congress advised of their regulatory agenda, to gain information to enforce regulatory requirements, and to prosecute regulated entities for civil and criminal violations. For example, state health inspectors need the ability to enter and inspect restaurants to ensure that they are meeting applicable health standards. Also, when a state welfare agency receives a complaint that a child's parents are abusing or neglecting a child, the welfare officials may need to enter and inspect the home to determine whether the complaint is valid. Federal Occupational Safety and Health Administration inspectors must visit worksites to ensure that the employers are providing safe working environments for their employees. And the Federal Trade Commission may require corporations to submit information in a report. Must an agency obtain a warrant before seeking such information?

You likely know that the U.S. Constitution requires that the government obtain a warrant based on probable cause prior to searching citizens' property for evidence of criminal activity. U.S. Const. amend. IV. It also requires the government obtain a warrant to search citizens' property for evidence of administrative violations. However, the probable cause standard for administrative searches is significantly less stringent than for criminal searches. *Marshall v. Barlow's, Inc.*, 436 U.S. 307, 320 (1978) (explaining that the "probable cause justifying the issuance of a warrant [in the administrative context] may be based not only on specific evidence of an existing violation but also on a showing that reasonable legislative or administrative standards for conducting an ... inspection are satisfied.") (internal quotations omitted); *See v. Seattle*, 387 U.S. 541, 545– 46 (1967); *Camara v. Municipal Court of San Francisco*, 387 U.S. 523, 538 (1967).

In *Camara*, the Court held that inspectors did have to get a warrant before they could search an apartment for violations of a city housing code. 387 U.S. at 538. The inspectors did not have to show cause that they would find violations at the particular apartment complex they wanted to inspect; rather, the inspectors had to show that "reasonable legislative or administrative standards for conducting an area inspection are satisfied with respect to a particular dwelling." *Id.* The Court explained that such standards, which will vary with the administrative program being enforced, may be based upon the passage of time, the nature of the building, or the condition of the entire area. Further, the standards will not necessarily depend upon specific knowledge of the condition of the particular dwelling. In other words, an inspection can occur without evidence of wrongdoing. The Court reached this conclusion because a search under these circumstances would be reasonable: the warrant procedure is designed to guarantee that a decision to search private property is justified by a reasonable governmental interest. "If a valid public interest justifies the intrusion contemplated, then there is probable cause to issue a suitably restricted search warrant." *Id.* at 539.

Note, however, that Congress cannot simply provide in an act that an agency has the authority to conduct a warrantless search. *Marshall*, 436 U.S. at 316 (holding that the agency did not have power to conduct warrantless searches despite an explicit grant to do so in the statute). The Fourth Amendment limits Congress's authority to allow warrantless, administrative searches.

Although the Fourth Amendment requires an agency to obtain a warrant based on probable cause before the agency conducts an administrative inspection, few inspections are actually based on a warrant. Rather, individuals and businesses often give consent. Indeed, many trade and industry groups advise their members to consent to searches absent unusual circumstances that might justify refusal. For this reason, unless there is an emergency, an inspector may wish to seek consent prior to seeking a warrant. In addition, when an inspector has the business's consent to search, the inspector can inspect more broadly than a warrant would have allowed. Searches based on a warrant are limited to areas and items identified in the warrant.

While administrative searches of ordinary businesses require a warrant, searches of businesses that are closely, or "pervasively," regulated do not require a warrant because these businesses have lower expectations of privacy. *New York v. Burger*, 482 U.S. 691, 702–03 (1987). Such businesses have a long tradition of being closely supervised by the government. Hence, warrants are unnecessary. The closely regulated exception to the warrant requirement is essentially an outgrowth of the waiver/consent doctrine: by voluntarily engaging in a heavily regulated business, business owners voluntarily give up or waive their privacy expectations.

While the Fourth Amendment applies, it does not require either a warrant or probable cause. *Id.* Instead, the standard for a valid warrantless search of a closely regulated business is threefold: (1) the regulatory scheme has to be justified by a substantial governmental interest, (2) warrantless inspections must be necessary to further that regulatory scheme, and (3) the terms of the inspection must provide a constitutionally adequate substitute for a warrant. *Id.* This third element requires that the scheme be detailed enough to put regulated entities on notice that they will be subject to periodic inspections, and the scheme must limit the inspector's discretion, requiring the inspector to act reasonably. *Id.*

To date, only a few businesses have been found to be closely regulated. *Colonnade Catering Corp. v. United States*, 397 U.S. 72, 77 (1970) (liquor dealers); *United States v. Biswell*, 406 U.S. 311, 315 (1972) (weapon dealers); *Donovan v. Dewey*, 452 U.S. 594, 602–03 (1981) (mining companies); *Burger*, 482 U.S. at 707 (junkyards engaging in vehicle dismantling). Importantly, when an agency conducts an administrative search as a pretense to search for evidence of criminal activity, the agency must obtain a warrant and meet the criminal probable cause standard. *Burger*, 482 U.S. at 716–17 n.27 (saying that an administrative inspection cannot be used as a "pretext" for a traditional law enforcement search for evidence of a crime).

In sum, absent an exception to the warrant requirement (including consent), agencies must obtain a warrant prior to an administrative search, even when a statute provides authority to the agency to conduct searches. Indeed, if the statute did not provide the agency with authority to search, then even if the agency obtained a warrant, the search would likely be invalid because the agency would not have been delegated this authority.

E. Delegation & Nondelegation

As you just saw, Congress often enacts a broad act and authorizes an agency to regulate to further the purposes of that act; in other words, Congress delegates regulatory authority to an agency. The agency then regulates, using rulemaking or adjudication. Delegation has virtues. One virtue is that agencies have expertise and experience that Congress and the president do not. Agency employees are less political than members of Congress and the president. Finally, agencies can respond more quickly than Congress. So some agency regulation is good; however, whether agency regulation is a good thing is a different question from whether agency regulation is constitutional.

As we saw in Chapter 3, the U.S. Constitution anticipates a legislature, an executive, and a judiciary, and it defines each of their powers. Agencies are not mentioned. Moreover, the Framers certainly did not foresee their proliferation during the twentieth century. Yet the administrative state is here to stay despite some conservative challenges to its constitutionality.

In the next two sections, we examine the constitutional limits the Supreme Court has placed on legislative and adjudicative delegation. As you read these sections, you will find that the Court's doctrine in both areas is unsatisfactory at best and result-oriented at worst. Do not expect clarity.

1. Delegating Legislative Power

The U.S. Constitution, Article I vests in Congress "[a]ll legislative Powers herein granted." U.S. Const. art. 1, §1. And Article II vests the "executive Power ... in a President of the United States of America." U.S. Const. art. 2, §1, cl. 1. Congress makes law and policy; the executive executes that law and policy.

Under a formalist interpretation of the vesting clauses, Congress cannot delegate policymaking power to an agency because it operates within the executive branch. This limitation is known as the *nondelegation doctrine*. The nondelegation doctrine comes from agency law (as in agency and partnership law, not administrative law) and provides that an agent may not subdelegate its power to an assistant. Thus, because Congress is the agent of the people who elected it, Congress may not subdelegate its policymaking power to an agency, its assistant.

Yet we know that agencies promulgate rules, which are similar to statutes that Congress or a state legislature enacts. Agency rules make conduct illegal or require people and businesses to act in specific ways. For example, the Federal Aviation Administration (FAA) has the authority to enact a regulation that would require all airlines to inspect airplanes for fuselage cracks at specific intervals. If the FAA required yearly inspections, then airlines that failed to comply could be subject to a fine or other penalty. Why is such agency rulemaking constitutional?

While the nondelegation doctrine does not permit an agent to subdelegate power to an assistant, the doctrine does permit an agent to tell its assistants how to carry out tasks to accomplish the agent's responsibilities, so long as the agent itself remains in control of the decisions. In other words, the assistant can "fill up the details" so long as the agent remains in control of the important choices. *Wayman v. Southard*, 23 U.S. (10 Wheat.) 1, 43 (1825).

The Supreme Court has struggled to create a coherent nondelegation doctrine to apply in the administrative context, one that places some limits on Congress's ability to delegate legislative power to agencies while also acknowledging that some delegation is inevitable, necessary, and beneficial. Indeed, Congress has delegated to agencies since our founding. *See, e.g.*, Act of Sept. 29, 1789, 1 Stat. 95 (authorizing payment of military pensions "under such regulations as the President of the United States may direct").

Pursuant to the *intelligible principle doctrine*, Congress may delegate legislative power to agencies pursuant to the Necessary and Proper Clause, U.S. Const. art. I, § 8, so long as Congress provides intelligible principles, or standards, to guide agencies' exercise of that delegated power. *J.W. Hampton, Jr. & Co. v. United States*, 276 U.S. 394, 409 (1928); *see also Whitman v. American Trucking Ass'ns, Inc.*, 531 U.S. 457, 474–76 (2001). As long as Congress makes policy, agencies can legitimately "'fill up the details' by the establishment of administrative rules and regulations." *United States v. Grimaud*, 220 U.S. 506, 517 (1911) (quoting *Wayman*, 23 U.S. at 43); *Loving v. United States*, 517 U.S. 748, 771 (1996) (stating that "[t]he intelligible-principle rule seeks to enforce the understanding that Congress may not delegate the power to make laws and so may delegate no more than the authority to make policies and rules that implements its statutes"). The Court attempted to reconcile nondelegation principles with the reality that agency policy implementation was essential, but as will become clear in a moment, reality won the day.

So here is the fiction the Court has wrought. When Congress delegates legislative power to an agency and provides intelligible principles, Congress transforms legislative power into executive power. As the Supreme Court explained when it invalidated the legislative veto:

> Congress protests that affirming the Court of Appeals in this case will sanction "lawmaking by the Attorney General .... Why is the Attorney General exempt from submitting his proposed changes in the law to the full bicameral process?" To be sure, some administrative agency action — rule making, for example — may resemble "lawmaking." ... This Court has referred to agency activity as being "quasi-legislative" in character. Clearly, however, "[i]n the framework of our Constitution, the President's power to see that the laws are faithfully executed refutes the idea that he is to be a lawmaker." When the Attorney General performs his duties pursuant to [the statute at issue in this case], he does not exercise "legislative" power .... The constitutionality of the Attorney General's execution of the authority delegated to him by [this statute] involves only a question of delegation doctrine. The courts, when a case or controversy arises, can always "ascertain whether the will of Congress has been obeyed," and can enforce adherence to statutory standards. It is clear, therefore, that the Attorney General acts in his presumptively Art. II capacity when he administers the Immigration and Nationality Act. Executive action under legislatively delegated authority that might resemble "legislative" action in some

respects is not subject to the approval of both Houses of Congress and the President for the reason that the Constitution does not so require.

INS v. Chadha, 462 U.S. 919, 953 n.16 (1983) (citations omitted). Perhaps, as former Justice Stevens once suggested, the Court should "frankly acknowledge[]" that the power being delegated is legislative, but the intelligible principles in the statute adequately restrain it. *Whitman v. American Trucking Ass'ns*, 531 U.S. 457, 488 (2001) (Stevens, J., concurring) ("I am persuaded that it would be both wiser and more faithful to what we have actually done in delegation cases to admit that agency rulemaking authority is 'legislative power.' ").

Returning to our hypothetical, we can see that before the FAA could enact the regulation identified above, Congress would first have to enact a law delegating authority to the FAA to set safety standards for airlines and airplanes. Within this enabling act, Congress would delegate broad authority to the FAA to regulate air safety in general, but Congress must also provide intelligible principles to guide the agency's policy choices. So long as Congress places some boundaries on agency authority, delegation is legitimate. The Court presumes that if Congress sufficiently and explicitly constrains an agency's policy-making choices, then the agency is not making law; rather, the agency is implementing congressionally made law. Only when the delegation is too broad is the delegation unconstitutional. But what is too broad?

a. Historical Doctrine

Apparently, very little. As one scholar put it: the nondelegation doctrine had one good year: 1935. Cass R. Sunstein, *Nondelegation Canons*, 67 U. Chi. L. Rev. 315, 322 (2000).

The 1930s represented a time of great turmoil for the United States because of the Great Depression, among other things. During this time, President Franklin Delano Roosevelt was elected into office after promising to improve the economy. Just five days after his election, Congress was called into session and enacted five major acts after only forty hours of debate. This enactment speed and breadth was unprecedented. And the expansive delegation of power to agencies had never before been seen. The federal judiciary's reaction to the power grab was hostile, to say the least; lower federal courts soon found four major pieces of legislation unconstitutional and issued numerous injunctions. These cases made their way to the Supreme Court. The conservatives on the Court were largely hostile to what they perceived to be an increase in size and scope of the administrative state. These cases provided an avenue for them to express their displeasure.

In the first case, *Panama Refining Co. v. Ryan*, 293 U.S. 388 (1935) (known as the "Hot Oil Case"), the Court struck down a provision of the National Industrial Recovery Act ("NIRA") that allowed the president to prohibit the interstate transportation of oil in excess of that allowed by state law. *Id.* at 420–21. Under the NIRA, Congress wanted to prevent oil producers from evading state laws limiting the amount of oil they could sell (hence, "hot" as in illegal oil). Striking down the statute, the Court held that Congress did not provide sufficient standards to limit the executive's exercise of power. The Court stated, "As to the transportation of oil production in excess of state permission, the Congress has declared no policy, has established no standard, has laid down no rule. There is no requirement, no definition of circumstances and conditions in which the transportation is to be allowed or prohibited." *Id.* at 430. In other words, Congress had not provided an intelligible principle to guide the executive's exercise of its delegated power.

In the second case, *A.L.A. Schechter Poultry Corp. v. United States*, 295 U.S. 495 (1935) (known as the "Sick Chicken Case"), the Court struck down another provision in the NIRA that allowed the president to approve codes for "fair competition" that would be established jointly with the chicken industry. *Id.* at 538–39. The Court struck down the provision, stating that the President's authority was not sufficiently limited:

> [The provision] supplies no standards for any trade, industry or activity. It does not undertake to prescribe rules of conduct to be applied to particular states of fact determined by appropriate administrative procedure. Instead of prescribing rules of conduct, it authorizes the making of codes to prescribe them. For that legislative undertaking, section 3 sets up no standards, aside from [general aims]. In view of the scope of that broad declaration, and of the nature of the few restrictions that are imposed, the discretion of the President in approving or prescribing codes, and thus enacting laws for the government of trade and industry throughout the country, is virtually unfettered.

Id. at 541–42. Justice Cardozo, who dissented in the Hot Oil Case, agreed and eloquently stated that "[t]his [was] delegation running riot." *Id.* at 553 (Cardozo, J., concurring).

The statute at issue in the third case allowed certain mine owners and miners the authority to set maximum labor hours, which would be binding on other mine owners and miners. *Carter v. Carter Coal Co.* 298 U.S. 238, 279 (1936) (citing 15 U.S.C.A. §§ 801 to 827). The Court struck down this third party delegation and stated:

> The power conferred upon the majority is, in effect, the power to regulate the affairs of an unwilling minority. This is legislative delegation in its most obnoxious form; for it is not even delegation to an official or an official body, presumptively disinterested, but to private persons whose interests may be and often are adverse to the interests of others in the same business.

Id. at 311. *Carter Coal* held that delegations to third parties are unconstitutional. While we will see in a moment that the delegation doctrine of today has no teeth, the *Carter Coal* holding remains vibrant. *DOT v. Ass'n of Am. R.Rs.*, 135 S. Ct. 1225, 1238 (2015) (stating that "handing off regulatory power to a private entity is 'legislative delegation in its most obnoxious form.'" (quoting *Carter v. Carter Coal Co.*, 298 U.S. 238, 311 (1936)).

b. Modern Doctrine

As you might imagine, President Roosevelt was less than thrilled with the Court's attacks on his New Deal legislation. To influence future decision-making, he proposed adding an additional justice to the Supreme Court for each justice over the age of 70 (the "Court Packing Plan"). Although the plan was never adopted, the threat of adoption achieved the desired effect. Since *Panama Refining* and *Schecter*, the Court has never again struck down an act of Congress as violating the nondelegation doctrine, even though Congress has enacted numerous statutes that are equally expansive in delegating legislative power with minimal guiding principles.

For example, in *Whitman v. American Trucking Ass'ns, Inc.*, 531 U.S. 457 (2001), the Court reviewed the constitutionality of a section of the Clean Air Act that directed the EPA "to set primary ambient air quality standards 'the attainment and maintenance of which ... are requisite *to protect the public health.*'" *Id.* at 465 (quoting 42 U.S.C. § 7409(b)(1)) (emphasis added). The issue for the Court was whether the language "to protect the public health" sufficiently constrained the delegation; the Court held that it did. *Id.* at 472–73. *See also Touby v. United States*, 500 U.S. 160, 167–68 (1991) (upholding as constitutional a law that directed the attorney general to designate certain drugs as controlled substances for purposes of criminal enforcement if doing so was "necessary to avoid an imminent hazard to the public safety") (*quoting*

21 U.S.C. §811(h)); *Industrial Union Dept., ALF-CIO v. American Petroleum Inst.*, 448 U.S. 607, 639 (1980) (upholding as constitutional a provision in the Occupational Safety and Health Act requiring the agency to "set the standard which most adequately assures to the extent feasible, on the basis of the best available evidence, that no employee will suffer any impairment of health") (*quoting* 29 U.S.C. §655(b)(5)); *Lichter v. United States*, 334 U.S. 742, 785–86 (1948) (upholding delegation to an agency to recoup "excessive profits" on war contracts); *American Power & Light Co. v. SEC*, 329 U.S. 90, 104 (1946) (upholding as constitutional a statute that allowed the agency to modify the structure of holding company systems to ensure that they are not "unduly or unnecessarily complicate[d]" and do not "unfairly or inequitably distribute voting power among security holders.") (*quoting* Public Utility Act of 1935, 49 Stat. 803); *National Broadcasting Co. v. United States*, 319 U.S. 190, 225–26 (1943) (upholding delegation to an agency to allocate broadcasting licenses in "the public interest, convenience, and necessity"). And most recently, the Court held that a statute containing no guiding principles within its text did not violate the nondelegation doctrine because "[t]he text, considered alongside its context, purpose, and history, makes clear that the Attorney General's discretion extends only to considering and addressing feasibility issues." *Gundy v. United States*, 2019 WL 2527473, at *4 (June 20, 2019). The standards in these cases were no more constraining than "fair competition." Thus, the nondelegation doctrine is little more than a time-honored sound bite to give legitimacy to delegation that raises constitutional concerns for some while being essential to a functioning government for others.

Finally, although the nondelegation doctrine has no teeth, the Supreme Court has found another way to narrow broad delegations: statutory interpretation. As the Court said, "In recent years, our application of the nondelegation doctrine principally has been limited to the interpretation of statutory texts, and, more particularly, to giving narrow constructions to statutory delegations that might otherwise be thought to be unconstitutional." *Mistretta v. United States*, 488 U.S. 361, 373 n.7 (1989). Constitutional avoidance, anyone?

For example, in the *Benzene* case, the relevant statute delegated to the Occupational Safety and Health Administration the responsibility of developing standards regarding workplace hazards "which most adequately assures, *to the extent feasible*, on the basis of the best available evidence, that no employee will suffer any impairment of health or functional capacity even if such employee has regular exposure to the hazard dealt with by such standard for the period of his working life." *Industrial Union Dept., ALF-CIO v. American Petroleum*

Inst., 448 U.S. 607, 612 (1980) (emphasis added). The phrase "to the extent feasible" transformed an otherwise legitimate intelligible principle into no limiting principle at all.

The Court should have held that the statute violated the nondelegation doctrine and was unconstitutional; however, the Court did not. Instead, a plurality added a limitation that Congress had not explicitly included, specifically, that the agency find a "significant risk" to employee health before adopting a safety standard. *Id.* at 639. The plurality found this limiting principle in the act's definition of "occupational health and safety standard." The act defined that phrase to mean a standard that is "reasonably necessary or appropriate to provide safe or healthful employment and places of employment." *Id.* at 612 (quoting 29 U.S.C. § 652(8)). Thus, the Court adopted an interpretation of the act that while not the best interpretation, was reasonable and saved the act from being unconstitutional.

But while it is fine for courts to narrowly interpret acts to avoid declaring them unconstitutional, agencies cannot save an act from unconstitutionality. *Whitman v. American Trucking Ass'ns, Inc.*, 531 U.S. 457, 475 (2001) (rejecting the lower court's holding that the agency could "extract a determinate standard on its own" to remedy the constitutional infirmity) (quoting *American Trucking Ass'ns, Inc. v. EPA*, 195 F.3d 4, 7 (D.C. Cir. 1999)).

2. Delegating Judicial Power

If the Court's non-delegation doctrine barely constrains legislative delegation, what about judicial delegation? Article III, § 1 of the U.S. Constitution provides that "all judicial power of the United states shall be vested in one Supreme Court and such inferior courts as the Congress may from time to time ordain and establish." U.S. Const. art. 1, § 3. Adjudication by non-Article III judges violates this provision. Yet agencies adjudicate disputes regularly. How can agency adjudication be constitutional?

The Supreme Court's jurisprudence in this area is even less cohesive than it is for legislative delegation. Early on, the Court distinguished between claims involving public and private rights. Private rights involve the liability of one individual to another, whereas public rights involve the liability of the government to its citizens. The Court reasoned that non-Article III courts could adjudicate claims involving public rights because the government does not have to agree to be sued at all under the doctrine of sovereign immunity. So if the government did agree to be sued, the government could set the parameters of being sued, including that the suit occur before a non-Article

III tribunal. *Murray's Lessee v. Hoboken Land & Improvement Co.*, 59 U.S. (18 How.) 272 (1855); *see* Peter L. Strauss, *The Place of Agencies in Government: Separation of Powers and The Fourth Branch*, 84 COLUM L. REV. 573, 632 (1984) (stating that "the whole point of the 'public rights' analysis was that no judicial involvement at all was required—executive determination alone would suffice").

In contrast, the Court has held that adjudication involving private rights must be heard by an Article III court or at least be subject to Article III judicial review. *See Crowell v. Benson*, 285 U.S. 22, 51 (1932) (holding that an agency could constitutionally adjudicate a case involving purely private rights because the agency made only factual findings, which were subject to judicial review by an Article III court).

Let's look at an example. Prior to 1978, federal district courts served as bankruptcy courts, appointing referees to conduct the hearings. In 1978, Congress enacted the Bankruptcy Act of 1978, which created bankruptcy courts and eliminated this referee system. Although called courts, bankruptcy courts are actually administrative agencies. They are known as Article I Courts, because Congress created them pursuant to its powers under Article I of the U.S. Constitution. Other Article I courts include the United States Court of Appeals for Veterans Claims, the United States Court of Military Appeals, the United States Court of Federal Claims, and the United States Tax Court, to name just a few. These are agencies, not Article III courts. Do not let their names confuse you.

The Bankruptcy Act provided that the president, with the advice and consent of the Senate, would appoint bankruptcy judges for fourteen-year terms. Northern Pipeline Construction Company filed for Chapter 11 bankruptcy. In its bankruptcy case, Northern included a number of purely private state law claims against Marathon Pipe Line Company. Marathon moved to dismiss the claims, arguing that the Act unconstitutionally conferred Article III powers on administrative judges who lacked constitutional protections, including lifetime tenure and salary protections. The plurality agreed. *Northern Pipeline Construct. Co. v. Marathon Pipe Line Co.*, 458 U.S. 50, 87 (1982). The Court explained that an Article I court could not hear purely private claims. *Id.* at 77.

But in 1986, the Court appeared to retreat from its private-public rights distinction in *Commodity Futures Trading Comm'n v. Schor*, 478 U.S. 833 (1986). *Schor* involved an act that allowed customers of federal securities brokers to seek reparations from a broker who violated federal commodities law. The Commodity Futures Trading Commission, a federal agency, adjudicated the case. Schor, a customer, sued his broker for a debt balance; the broker counter-claimed for money it claimed Schor owed it. *Id.* at 837. This second claim was a private state law claim. Although the broker had originally filed the claim in district court under diversity jurisdiction, Schor demanded that the broker bring the claim before the Commission. *Id.* at 838. So the broker voluntarily dismissed the district court claim and brought the counterclaim before the Commission. *Id.* When Schor lost, he argued, for the first time, that the Commission lacked jurisdiction to hear the counterclaim against him. *Id.* at 840. Given these facts, it should not be too surprising that the plurality ruled against Schor even though the counterclaim involved purely private rights.

The Court said, "Our precedents ... demonstrate ... that Article III does not confer on litigants an absolute right to the plenary consideration of every nature of claim by an Article III court." *Id.* at 848. Invoking functionalism, the Court explained that the inquiry regarding "the constitutionality of a given congressional delegation of adjudicative functions to a non-Article III body ... is guided by the principle that practical attention to substance rather than doctrinaire reliance on formal categories should inform application of Article III." *Id.* at 847–48 (internal quotations omitted). Because Schor had "expressly demanded" that the broker's counterclaim be brought in the administrative proceeding, he had "indisputably waived any right he may have possessed to [a] full trial ... before an Article III court." *Id* at 849. The Court distinguished *Northern Pipeline*, noting that the statute in *Schor* left "far more of the essential attributes of judicial power to Article III courts than did [the act] found unconstitutional in *Northern Pipeline.*" *Id.* at 852. In *Schor*, the Court reasoned that because "the decision to invoke this forum [was] left entirely to the parties and [because] the power of the federal judiciary to take jurisdiction of these matters [was] unaffected ... separation of powers concerns [were] diminished." *Id.* at 855.

However, *Shor*'s new functionalist test was short-lived. In *Stern v. Marshall*, 564 U.S. 462 (2011), the Court revived its private-public rights distinction. Prior to *Stern*, Anna Nicole Smith married wealthy 89-year-old millionaire J. Howard Marshall II. While he was still alive, she sued in a Texas state probate court, alleging that Marshall's youngest son, Pierce, had induced his father to sign a living trust that excluded her even though Marshall had promised her half his estate for marrying him. *Id.* at 470. After Marshall died, Smith filed a bankruptcy petition in the Central District of California. Meanwhile, Pierce filed a complaint in that bankruptcy proceeding, contending that Smith had defamed him. *Id.* Smith counterclaimed, alleging that Pierce had tortiously interfered with Marshall's promise to give her half of the estate. *Id.*

The probate court resolved the case in Pierce's favor, while simultaneously the bankruptcy court awarded Smith more than $425 million. *Id.* at 470–71.

In other words, the district court and the bankruptcy court reached opposite results. On appeal from the bankruptcy court opinion, the court of appeals held that the bankruptcy court did not have authority to issue a final judgment regarding Smith's tortious interference claim. *Id.* at 472. Smith's estate appealed to the Supreme Court. The question presented was whether the bankruptcy court could constitutionally enter a final judgment on a non-core tort compulsory counterclaim. There were two issues for the Court: first, whether the Bankruptcy Act provided the bankruptcy court with jurisdiction on this issue, and second, if it did, whether jurisdiction was constitutional. *Id.* at 469.

The first issue was a question of statutory interpretation; the second issue was a question of constitutionality. For the first issue, the majority (and dissent) held that the Bankruptcy Act permitted the bankruptcy court to enter final judgment on Smith's counterclaim (the jurisdiction question). *Id.* at 475–78. For the second issue, the majority held that the jurisdiction provision violated Article III of the Constitution. *Id.* at 482–95. The majority reasoned that the Constitution vested "[t]he judicial power of the United States" in life-tenured and salary-protected judges. Non-Article III bankruptcy judges, who do not have this protection, may not exercise the general judicial power of the United States and, therefore, may not finally resolve controversies that are not within the core Article I bankruptcy power Congress relied upon in creating the current system of bankruptcy jurisdiction. The majority distinguished *Schor*, in part, by characterizing Smith's counterclaim as purely private in nature, thus reviving the private-public distinction. *Id.* at 492.

As a result of this case, Smith's estate lost any right to recover from Marshall's estate. In other words, she married the octogenarian for naught. Moreover, the Court returned to its private versus public rights distinction for the time being.

F. Mastering This Topic

Return to the hypothetical ordinance provided in Chapter 1. The first question that was asked was the following: "An ambulance entered Pioneer Park to pick up and take to the hospital a man who had just suffered a heart attack. Did the ambulance driver violate the Pioneer Park Safety Ordinance (PPSO)?" How should you, as prosecutor, attempt to answer that question using what you've learned in this chapter? You may recall that the Commission of Parks ("Commission"), an agency, promulgated a regulation interpreting the

PPSO regarding whether certain vehicles were permitted in Pioneer Park. As you know, the law described in this chapter is federal law and applies to federal agencies, not state agencies or local agencies. For educational purposes, however, let's ignore that fact and assume that this chapter identifies the applicable law that this jurisdiction would follow.

Your first question should be whether the City Council (the legislature in this hypothetical) delegated legislative or quasi-legislative authority to the Commission to promulgate rules related to this ordinance, and, if so, whether the City Council provided intelligible principles to guide the Commission's exercise of that authority. The ordinance provides, "The Commission of Parks shall have the power to issue rules to implement this ordinance as necessary to protect public safety." You confirm that the City Council delegated legislative authority to the Commission. Moreover, the limiting principle in this language to guide the Commission in the exercise of its rulemaking power is "as necessary to protect public safety." Arguably, that limiting language provides a sufficient intelligible principle under the modern delegation doctrine. You can simply compare it to the list of intelligible principles the Supreme Court has already approved.

Second, you should determine whether the City Council delegated judicial or quasi-judicial authority to hold hearings, and, if so, whether that delegation is constitutional under the public-private rights doctrine. The ordinance provides, "The Commission of Parks shall have the power to ... hold hearings regarding any violations of its provisions." Thus, the City Council delegated judicial power to the Commission. Further, the adjudications involve fines for violating local laws; hence, these adjudications do not involve disputes between private parties; hence, the delegation is likely constitutional.

Third, you would want to determine whether the Commission properly exercised its rulemaking authority under the APA. The hypothetical notes that the Commission promulgated a regulation but does not describe whether the Commission used formal or informal procedures in doing so. From this information, you can determine that the agency used rulemaking procedures to promulgate a binding rule. While you do not know which procedures the agency used, you do know that there are three possibilities:

- formal rulemaking — requiring trial-like hearings,

- informal rulemaking — requiring notice-and-comment procedures, and

- publication rulemaking — requiring publication procedures

Alternatively, you should consider whether the agency could have used non-legislative procedures to issue the rule in the form of guidance (then it likely would not be called a regulation). In this case, the agency interpreted a phrase in a statute: "motor vehicle." Hence, the agency could have issued its "interpretative rule" without using formal or informal rulemaking procedures under § 553 of the APA. In the real world, you would want to identify which procedure the agency used and determine whether the agency followed the APA requirements for that procedure, but this hypothetical does not provide enough information for you to do so.

Finally, you note that the relevant regulation (33 C.F.R. § 2300(1)) defines a "motor vehicle" as "a road vehicle driven by a motor or engine used or physically capable of being used upon any public highway in this state in the transportation of persons or property." How strongly, if at all, would a court defer to the agency's definition? You do not know yet but will shortly; stay tuned.

Checkpoints

• Agencies are defined under the Administrative Procedures Act as any authority of the Government of the United States, excluding Congress, the courts, state governments, and others. The president is not an agency pursuant to common law.

• There are two types of agencies: independent agencies and executive agencies. Independent agencies are less subject to the president's influence because they are generally headed by multi-member, bi-partisan boards, serving terms.

• The judiciary is not the only branch that interprets statutes. Administrative agencies within the executive branch regularly interpret statutes as they regulate.

• The act that creates an agency, authorizes the agency to act, and identifies the agency's agenda is known as the enabling, or organic, act. It is the first law to search when trying to determine whether an agency has the power to act at all.

• Agencies act in three ways: by adjudicating, by rulemaking, and by investigating. The APA provides specific procedures for agencies to follow.

• The APA further divides rulemaking and adjudication into other categories, including formal rulemaking, formal adjudication, notice-and-comment rulemaking, informal adjudication, publication rulemaking, and guidance.

• Congress has the authority to delegate legislative or quasi-legislative power to agencies pursuant to the Necessary and Proper Clause, U.S. Const. art. I, § 8, so long as Congress provides intelligible principles, or standards, for agencies to use when exercising their delegated power.

• Congress has the authority to delegate judicial or quasi-judicial power to agencies so long as the agency adjudicates only public, not private, rights.

Chapter 14

The Administrative State: Legislative & Executive Oversight of Agencies

---

Roadmap

- Learn the ways that Congress controls agency actions, including enacting other relevant legislation and funding agencies.

- Learn the ways the executive controls agency actions, including appointment and removal, executive orders and directives, and signing statements.

- Understand that the president appoints principal officers with the advice and consent of the Senate and can generally remove such officers at will.

- Understand that Congress can give the president, the courts of law, or the heads of departments the power to appoint inferior officers.

- Consider whether Congress may limit a president's ability to remove agency officials who perform quasi-judicial or quasi-legislative activity.

- Learn that inferior officers are subordinate to principal officers.

- Note that inferior officers, unlike mere employees, exercise significant authority pursuant to the laws of the United States.

- Learn that signing statements are largely irrelevant to interpretation.

A. Introduction to This Chapter

In the last chapter, we learned what agencies do, why they do it, how they do it, and that they are constitutional. In this chapter, we examine legislative and executive oversight of agencies. Because agencies wield so much delegated power, it is not surprising that Congress and the president—the elected branches—would want to control how agencies exercise that power. This chapter explains some of the ways that Congress and the president control agency decision making. We begin with legislative oversight, then move to executive oversight. After learning how the legislature and executive exert control over agencies in this chapter, in the next chapter we will learn about the role agencies play in interpretation, particularly the interpretation of statutes.

Much of the information in this chapter builds on our earlier discussion of the U.S. Constitution and separation of powers, which we discussed in Chapter 3. You may wish to review that section before we begin.

B. Legislative Control over Delegated Power

As you learned in the last chapter, agencies have only the power that a legislature delegates to them. Legislatures control agency activity by broadly or narrowly delegating authority. In particular, Congress has an interest in ensuring that federal agencies are faithful to congressional intent when they exercise delegated authority. To ensure such faithfulness, Congress uses a number of tools. This section explores those tools, starting with provisions within enabling acts and moving outward.

1. Enabling Legislation

In a number of agencies' enabling acts, Congress has required more procedures than the APA requires. Rulemaking pursuant to such additional procedures is known as "*hybrid rulemaking.*" Congress may also include additional procedures for adjudication. Hybrid rulemaking and adjudication are neither formal nor informal but are somewhere in between these extremes.

For example, the APA does not require that agencies hold oral hearings for rulemaking. But the Occupational Safety and Health Act requires a public hearing when an interested person requests one. 29 U.S.C. § 655 (b)(3). Also, the Federal Trade Commission must allow cross-examination in some informal adjudications. 15 U.S.C. § 57a(c); *see also* 15 U.S.C. § 78f(e) (similarly requiring the Securities and Exchange Commission to allow cross-examination in some adjudications). And in the Clean Air Act, Congress required the Environmental Protection Agency to include the following information in a proposed rule: "a summary of the factual data on which the proposed rule is based; the methodology used in obtaining the data and in analyzing the data; and the major legal interpretations and policy considerations underlying the proposed rule." 42 U.S.C. § 7607(d)(3)(a)-(c). In all of these examples, Congress required the agency to do more than the APA requires; hence, we call these hybrid rulemaking and hybrid adjudication.

2. Other Legislation

Additionally, Congress may control agency rulemaking by amending or repealing the enabling act or by enacting other statutes subsequently. Specifically, Congress can narrow or revoke authority it has given to an agency. For example, after a tremendous public outcry regarding the Food and Drug Administration's decision to ban saccharin, the only alternative sweetener at the time, Congress suspended regulatory action in this area and required a warning label to replace the proposed ban. Saccharin Study, Labeling and Advertising Act, Pub. L. No. 95-203, 91 Stat. 1451 (1977).

With subsequent legislation, Congress may also require an agency to follow new procedures. Here are just a few examples. In 1969, Congress required all agencies to consider the environmental impact of major decisions with the National Environmental Policy Act, 42 U.S.C. §4321 *et seq.* Congress also enacted the Regulatory Flexibility Act of 1980, 5 U.S.C. §601 *et seq.*, which requires agencies to consider and minimize the economic effects of regulations on small businesses. And with the Unfunded Mandates Reform Act of 1995, 2 U.S.C. §1501 *et seq.*, Congress directed agencies to consider the impact of their regulations on state governmental agencies and adopt the least burdensome alternative that would further the agency's objectives or explain why another option was chosen.

Also, in 1990, Congress added sections 561–70 to the APA, which authorize agencies to accomplish some aspects of the rulemaking process by negotiation. Negotiated rulemaking (reg-neg as it has come to be called) involves convening a group of major stakeholders — those parties principally affected by the contemplated rule — to see if a consensus about the new rule can be developed. A draft rule worked out pursuant to this process is published as a proposed rule, and the usual public comment process ensues. Supporters believe that negotiated rulemaking produces technically better rules that more clearly identify the diverse concerns of those constituents the rule affects, leads to simpler enforcement, and results in less judicial review. The concept has, however, generated controversy. Critics worry that some affected interests will not be invited to the party. Others are concerned that the system transfers too much power to the private sector.

Congress may also reject an agency's rule altogether using the Congressional Review Act ("CRA"). 5 U.S.C. §801 *et seq.* The CRA provides a process for Congress to reject a rule a federal agency promulgates. Congress enacted the CRA in 1996 as part of the Small Business Regulatory Enforcement Fairness Act. Congress carefully designed the CRA to comply with the bicameralism and presentment requirements in the U.S. Constitution because the Supreme Court had earlier rejected Congress's attempt to retain for itself the power to veto actions of the executive. *INS v. Chadha*, 462 U.S. 919, 951 (1983) (holding that a one-house, legislative veto violated separation of powers). We will examine the legislative veto more in a moment, for now, let's stay with the CRA.

Pursuant to the CRA, both independent and executive agencies must submit a report to each house of Congress and to the Comptroller General before a rule can take effect. This report contains a copy of the proposed rule; a concise general statement of the proposed rule, including whether it is a major rule; and the effective date of the proposed rule. Any "major rules" are stayed for sixty days, rather than the thirty the APA requires. 5 U.S.C. § 553(d). A major rule is one whose annual economic impact is greater than $100 million. The Office of Information and Regulatory Affairs (OIRA) determines which rules are major, not the agency. Non-major rules go into effect after thirty days but may be reversed later. The CRA defines "rule" to include interpretive rules and general statements of policy. 5 U.S.C. § 804(3).

After receiving the agency's report on a proposed rule, Congress has a limited time to propose and vote on a joint resolution of *dis*approval. If both houses pass the joint resolution, it is sent to the president for signature or veto. If the president vetoes the resolution, Congress can override the veto. If there is no override, the rule becomes effective. If the president signs the resolution or Congress effectively overrides a veto, the "rule shall not take effect (or continue)." 5 U.S.C. § 801(b)(1). Even non-major rules that had become effective would be retroactively negated.

Importantly, the CRA further provides that an agency may not issue a rule in "substantially the same form" as the disapproved rule unless subsequent law specifically authorizes the substantially similar rule. 5 U.S.C. § 801(b)(2). Unfortunately, the CRA does not define "substantially the same form," which will likely lead to litigation at some point.

Until 2017, Congress had used the CRA to disapprove of only one agency rule (a 2001 Clinton-era OSHA ergonomics regulation); however, after the 2016 election, the Republicans took control of Congress and the White House. President Trump and Congress used the CRA to roll back more than fifteen Obama-era regulations, including one from an independent agency. In 2018, the Democrats regained control of the House, and the CRA has laid relatively dormant since.

The 2017 high rate of disapproval is unlikely to reoccur. The CRA is a useful tool for a new political party to overturn the regulations of its predecessor, as occurred when Trump took office after Obama. But the CRA is less useful for Congress to overturn current agency regulations because the president must sign the disapproval resolution or Congress must override a presidential veto. Because agencies typically implement presidential policy, presidential vetoes should be the norm and override the exception. Indeed, in 2015 and 2016, President Obama vetoed five such resolutions, and Congress was unable to override any of his vetoes. Thus, because the CRA essentially requires a supermajority of the members of Congress to override agency rules, it is a less effective tool than it might otherwise seem to be.

President Trump's administration has further weaponized the CRA. In 2019, Office of Management and Budget (OMB) issued a memorandum providing guidance on agency compliance with the CRA.[1] In the past, independent agencies had not been expected to comply with this act. Moreover, OMB did not review agency guidance, just legislative rules. OMB's latest memo changed both of these norms.

Criticism has come with the Republican's heavy use of the CRA. On May 16, 2017, Senators Cory Booker and Tom Udall introduced S. 1140, a bill to repeal the CRA and to slow Republican deregulation. The bill was referred to the Committee on Homeland Security and Governmental Affairs, where no further action has been taken.

3. Appropriation (Funding) Legislation

Now, back to the legislative veto. Congress inserted its first *one-house* legislative veto in 1932 in a law allowing then President Hoover the power to reorganize the executive branch. 31 U.S.C. § 1535. The one-house legislative veto allowed the House of Representatives to reject an executive action without Senate or presidential involvement. Ironically, the House exercised its veto power when Hoover lost re-election and then tried to issue a reorganization plan.

By the early 1980s, Congress had inserted legislative veto provisions, both one-house and dual, in more than 320 different acts as a way to maintain control over its broad delegations to agencies. The legislative veto was perceived as a method for Congress to rein in an out-of-control presidency. *See generally* ARTHUR SCHLESINGER, JR., THE IMPERIAL PRESIDENCY (1973).

In 1983, the Supreme Court held that one-house veto provisions violated the bicameralism and presentment clauses of the U.S. Constitution. *INS v. Chadha*, 462 U.S. 919, 951 (1983). To the extent that a joint-house provision

---

1. Russell T. Vought, *Memorandum for the Heads of Executive Departments and Agencies,* OFFICE OF MGMT. & BUDGET, (April 11, 2019), https://www.whitehouse.gov/wp-content/uploads/2019/04/M-19-14.pdf.

does not allow the president an opportunity to veto the resolution, it too would be unconstitutional. Despite being unconstitutional, however, legislative veto provisions remain on the books (the remedy for an unconstitutional provision is generally to sever the specific provision, but these provisions are not removed from the code). More surprisingly, Congress sometimes includes such veto provisions in new statutes or says in a committee report that an agency must seek congressional approval before using its delegated authority. *See, e.g.*, H.R. REP. No. 98-916 (1984) (requiring NASA to receive permission from the Appropriations Committees to exceed spending caps). While such provisions and restrictions are legally unenforceable, practically speaking, an agency may choose to comply because Congress can make the agency's life much more difficult in other ways. For example, Congress holds the purse strings, meaning Congress authorizes funding.

Agencies need funding to operate. To receive funding, the agency's enabling act (or another act) must authorize legislative appropriations. Legislative authorizations may be limited by time or purpose, have a ceiling, or be unlimited. Assuming such an authorization is included in its enabling act, agencies must submit annual budget requests to the OMB, which the president oversees. After OMB adjusts the budget request, it is forwarded to the House and Senate appropriations committees, which hold hearings and allocate funding accordingly. Finally, Congress provides funding as part of its annual budget. Note that a few agencies are funded primarily by fees levied on regulated entities, such as the Federal Reserve and the Consumer Financial Protection Bureau. This funding arrangement increases agency independence from Congress.

Funding amounts are up to Congress, and its decisions do not always make sense. For example, Congress can choose to enact sweeping legislation, then underfund the agency authorized to implement the new legislation. Or Congress might choose to underfund an agency to show disapproval. For example, during President Obama's tenure, the Republican Congress underfunded the Treasury Department, in part, as retaliation for the agency's perceived targeting of conservative groups. Alternatively, Congress might increase funding to an agency to encourage it to do more. For example, in 2018, Congress increased the Department of Energy's nuclear energy budget by $121 million. In short, Congress expresses its legislative intent and impacts agency behavior through funding decisions. *Cf. Tennessee Valley Authority v. Hill*, 437 U.S. 153 (1978) (rejecting the lower court's argument that appropriation bills funding a dam project were relevant to congressional intent regarding whether there was an exception in the Endangered Species Act).

Congress affects agency behavior with funding in other ways. During the budget process, Congress may enact substantive provisions known as *riders* to restrict an agency's authority to act in specific ways. Generally, these provisions are controversial and would be unlikely to be passed through the normal legislative process. For example, members of Congress have offered riders to defund Planned Parenthood and to repeal the Affordable Care Act. The rider approach is effective because appropriations bills are more likely than other bills to become law because the government shuts down when it is not funded. Once a rider passes, it may be in effect until someone sues. Thus, riders can control the agency's behavior unless or until a court finds them to be invalid.

Congress can even withhold funding altogether and has done so. In 1964, Congress enacted the Administrative Conference Act, which established the Administrative Conference of the United States ("ACUS"). ACUS is an independent federal agency dedicated to improving the administrative process and federal agency procedures. In 1995, rather than repeal the Administrative Conference Act, Congress simply refused to fund ACUS; it is not clear why. Oddly, Congress then reauthorized the Act in 2004 and 2008 and even expanded ACUS's powers, all while still refusing to fund it. Congress finally restored funding in 2009 when President Obama took office.

4. Hearings, Investigation & Audits

In addition to these direct methods of control, Congress has indirect methods of control. One indirect method of control is Congress's power to *investigate* agencies. Any congressional committee that has jurisdiction over an aspect of an agency's program may hold hearings and investigate the agency's implementation of its authority. Often, these hearings are publicized to mobilize public and political pressure. For example, in 2012, the House Judiciary Committee held hearings regarding the Bureau of Alcohol, Tobacco, Firearms and Explosives' Fast and Furious program, which was intended to track firearms that were transferred to high-level drug traffickers in Mexican cartels, with the hope that tracking would lead to arrests and the dismantling of the cartels. The program was unsuccessful; the government lost track of the guns. After a series of public hearings, Congress held Attorney General Eric Holder in criminal contempt for refusing to provide documents to the House Judiciary Committee. President Obama invoked executive privilege to prevent the disclosure. More recently, President Trump has invoked executive privilege to prevent the Department of Justice from releasing an unredacted version of the Mueller report to the House Judiciary Committee. Whether he will be successful remains to be seen.

There are other indirect methods of control as well. Congress has established other organizations to help oversee agencies, including the Congressional Research Service and the Governmental Accountability Office (previously known as the General Accounting Office (GAO)). These agencies are both located within the executive. For this reason, this method of oversight is indirect for Congress, while it is direct for the executive. While the GAO was created originally to oversee the use of agency budgeting and funding, its authority to oversee agency program implementation has been expanding, as we will see below.

C. Executive Oversight

In addition to Congress, the president also exerts control over agencies, albeit in ways that differ from those Congress uses. Methods of executive control include appointment, removal, executive orders, centralized agency review, presidential directives, and signing statements.

Because agencies are part of the executive branch, the president must control those who implement his or her policy choices. After all, the people elected the president to accomplish an agenda. To do so, the president needs help. Agencies provide the person-power to get the job done. But a president will want loyalty and allegiance. Next, we discuss the way a president tries to obtain loyalty, allegiance, and oversight.

1. Appointment

Perhaps the president's strongest form of direct executive control is the power to appoint and remove agency personnel. Although the president has the power to appoint and remove government officials, the power is not absolute. The U.S. Constitution places a number of limitations on the president's appointment and removal power. The Constitution gives the president the power to appoint *principal officers*, subject to Senate approval. U.S. CONST. art. II, § 2, cl. 2. The Constitution gives Congress the power to vest the appointment power of *inferior officers* in the president, the courts of law, or in heads of departments. *Id.*

Unfortunately, the Constitution does not define who is a principal and who is an inferior officer. Further, the Supreme Court has never clearly defined the difference between a principal and inferior officer; however, the Court has offered some guidance. For example, in *Morrison v. Olson*, 487 U.S. 654 (1988), the Supreme Court held that Congress could give the judiciary the power to appoint an *inferior* executive officer. At issue in that case was the Ethics in Government Act, 28 U.S.C. §49 *et seq.*, which authorized a special division of the United States Court of Appeals for the District of Columbia to appoint an independent counsel to investigate and prosecute high-ranking executive officials. *Id.* at 661. The independent counsel would perform executive functions. *Id.* at 691. Although the Act empowered the judiciary to appoint and oversee an officer who would be performing executive functions, the Court did not invalidate the Act. Instead, using a functionalist approach, the Court concluded that the independent counsel performed only limited investigative and prosecutorial work for a set period of time; hence, the officer was an inferior officer, not a principal officer. *Id.* at 671–72. Because the Constitution allows Congress to delegate the appointment of inferior officers to the judiciary, the appointment provision in the Act was constitutional. *Id.* at 673–74. Justice Scalia dissented.

Nine years later, in *Edmond v. United States*, 520 U.S. 651 (1997), Justice Scalia, writing for the majority, rejected *Morrison*'s multi-factor test for determining whether a government employee was a principal officer. In *Edmond*, the issue was whether military trial judges were principal or inferior officers. Justice Scalia concluded that military judges were "inferior officers" because "[g]enerally speaking, the term 'inferior officer' connotes a relationship with some higher ranking officer or officers below the President: [w]hether one is an 'inferior' officer depends on whether he has a superior." *Id.* at 662. For now, then, the difference between principal and inferior officers is based on whether the officer has a superior between herself and the president.

The line between officer and mere employee is less bright-lined than that between principal and inferior officer. For the former, the Supreme Court established a two-part test. First, a court looks to see whether the individual holds a "continuing" position established by law. *United States v. Germaine*, 99 U.S. 508, 511–12 (1878). The position must be "continuing and permanent," rather than "occasional or temporary." *Id.* This prong of the test is generally easy to resolve because the statute is readily ascertainable. Second, a court must determine whether the individual exercises significant authority pursuant to the laws of the United States. *Buckley v. Valeo*, 424 U.S. 1, 126 (1976). This prong of the test is more difficult to resolve because the Supreme Court has not clearly explained what "significant authority" means. The Court has merely decided the issue in individual cases. For example, the Court has found many lesser functionaries to be inferior officers, including a district court clerk, *Ex parte Hennen*, 38 U.S. (13 Pet.) 230, 258 (1839); a federal marshal, *Ex parte Siebold*, 100 U.S. 371, 397 (1879); and special trial judges ("STJs") of the United States Tax Court, *Freytag v. Comm'r*, 501 U.S. 868, 881 (1991).

In *Freytag*, the Court held that Tax Court "STJs" were inferior officers. *Id.* at 881–82. The Tax Court is an Article I court with judges who are appointed for limited terms. Congress authorized the Chief Judge of the Tax Court to appoint STJs to hear specific tax cases. For some of these cases, the STJ could resolve the case directly, but for others, the STJ could make a recommended decision only. *Id.* at 873. A judge from the Tax Court would review the STJ's recommended decision and make the final decision. Freytag's case was one of the latter, requiring review and adoption by a Tax Court Judge. *Id.* at 877.

Freytag challenged the validity of the judgment against him, arguing, in part, that the appointment of STJs by the Chief Judge of the Tax Court violated the Appointments Clause. The government argued that the STJs were merely employees who did no more than assist the regular Tax Court Judges in taking evidence and preparing proposed findings and an opinion. *Id.* at 880–81. The justices unanimously rejected this argument and held that the STJs were inferior officers. To find that STJs were inferior officers and not merely employees, the Court considered multiple factors. *Id.* at 882. First, the Court noted that the office of special trial judge is "established by Law" and that the statute lays out the "duties, salary, and means of appointment for that office." *Id.* at 881.

Second, the Court focused on the types of duties and level of discretion STJs had. STJs "perform more than ministerial task[s]"; they take testimony, conduct trials, rule on the admissibility of evidence, and enforce compliance with discovery orders. *Id.* at 881–82. In the course of performing these tasks, STJs "exercise significant discretion." *Id.* at 882. Third, the Court added that "[e]ven if the duties of [STJs] were not as significant as ... we have found them to be," there are circumstances where "they exercise independent authority," and they cannot be "inferior Officers" for some purposes and not others. *Id.* Fourth, and almost as an aside, the Court pointed out that STJs were authorized to decide cases *in some instances,* even if in other instances STJs only proposed findings and orders, while the regular Tax Court judge rendered the final decision. Notably, the Court specifically rejected the argument that officials who "lack authority to enter into a final decision" must be employees and not inferior officers, because that argument "ignores the significance of the duties and discretion that special trial judges possess." *Id.* at 881. In 2018, the Supreme Court relied on these factors to hold that ALJs who work for the Securities and Exchange Commission are also inferior officers. *Lucia v. SEC,* 138 S. Ct. 2044, 2053–54 (2018).

The distinctions between (1) principal officers and inferior officers, and (2) inferior officers and employees are relevant not only to appointment but also to removal.

2. Removal

Appointment and removal challenges often occur together, yet appointment issues may be easier. While the Constitution explicitly provides for the appointment of principal and inferior officers, it does not explicitly provide for their removal. Rather, the Constitution contains only one removal provision, which provides that "all civil officers of the United States [may] be removed from office on impeachment for, and conviction of, treason, bribery, or other high crimes and misdemeanors." U.S. CONST. art. II, §4. The impeachment process is seldom used, yet officers are removed regularly. How is that possible?

The answer is that the Supreme Court has concluded that the Constitution vests removal power in the president *implicitly*. According to the Court, the president has the power to remove executive officers because that power was not "'expressly taken away'" from the president in the Constitution. *Free Enterprise Fund v. Public Co. Accounting Oversight Bd.*, 561 U.S. 477, 492 (2010) (citing *Letter from James Madison to Thomas Jefferson (June 30, 1789)*, 16 DOCUMENTARY HISTORY OF THE FIRST FEDERAL CONGRESS 893 (2004)). Further, the Constitution provides that "[t]he executive Power shall be vested in a President of the United States of America." U.S. CONST. art. II, §1, cl. 1. As Madison stated on the floor of the First Congress, "if any power whatsoever is in its nature Executive, it is the power of appointing, overseeing, and controlling those who execute the laws." 1 Annals of Cong. 463 (1789).

When Congress tries to limit the president's power to remove an agency official, the limit may be unconstitutional. For example, in *Myers v. United States*, 272 U.S. 52 (1926), the Supreme Court struck down a statute that required the president to obtain the advice and consent of the Senate prior to removing the postmaster general. *Id.* at 106–18, 176. The Court reasoned that the power to remove a federal officer necessarily accompanies the constitutionally granted power to appoint that officer because the power to remove compliments the power to appoint. *Id.* at 126. The Court rejected the argument that the power to remove flowed from the Senate's ability to advise on and consent to appointments. *Id.* at 126–27.

But the president's removal power is not unlimited. The Supreme Court has upheld removal protections designed to further an agency's independence. Recall that one difference between independent and executive agencies is that independent agencies are often headed by multi-member boards. Each member of these boards is often removable only for cause. In contrast, the heads of executive agencies generally serve at the president's pleasure, meaning they are removable at will.

In *Humphrey's Executor v. United States,* 295 U.S. 602 (1935), the Court upheld a provision in the Federal Trade Commission Act that permitted the president to dismiss a commissioner of the Federal Trade Commission (FTC), a principal officer, only for "inefficiency, neglect of duty, or malfeasance in office." *Id.* at 622 (quoting 15 U.S.C. §41). The Court distinguished its holding in *Myers* by noting that the postmaster general performed purely executive functions and had to be responsible to the president while the FTC member performed quasi-legislative or quasi-judicial powers and had to be independent of the president. *Id.* at 627–28. *See also Wiener v. United States,* 357 U.S. 349, 350 (1958) (limiting the president's ability to remove a commissioner of the War Claims Commission, which had only a three-year existence, even though the relevant statute was silent regarding removal because Congress intended to insulate the Commission from presidential interference). In *Humphrey's Executor,* the Court limited *Myers*'s holding — that the president's removal power could not be limited — to "all purely executive officers." 295 U.S. at 628.

However, this purely executive distinction did not last long. In *Morrison v. Olson,* 487 U.S. 654, 689 (1988), the Court upheld a for-cause removal limitation on a "purely executive" *inferior* officer, an independent counsel. The Court said, "the determination of whether the constitution allows Congress to impose a 'good cause'-type restriction on the President's power to remove an official cannot be made to turn on whether or not that official is classified as 'purely executive.'"*Id.* The Court reasoned that the most important question was whether the removal restriction "impede[d] the President's ability to perform his constitutional duty" to ensure that the laws are faithfully executed.*Id.* at 691. The Court then reasoned that because the independent counsel (1) was an inferior officer, (2) had limited jurisdiction, (3) did not have tenure, (4) lacked policymaking power, and (5) did not have significant administrative authority, the for-cause removal provision was a reasonable restriction on the president's removal authority. However, *Morrison*'s rejection of the *Myers/ Humphrey*'s distinction was short-lived.

In *Free Enterprise Fund v. Public Co. Accounting Oversight Bd.,* 561 U.S. 477 (2010), the Court resurrected the distinction to hold that dual for-cause removal provisions are unconstitutional because the president cannot "'take care that the Laws be faithfully executed' if he cannot oversee the faithfulness of the officers who execute them."*Id.* at 484. Prior to *Free Enterprise,* Congress had created the Public Company Accounting Oversight Board (the Board) in the Sarbanes–Oxley Act of 2002 (the Act). *Id.* The Board has five members. *Id.* The Commissioners of the Securities and Exchange Commission (SEC), an independent agency, appointed those members. *Id.* The Board was modeled on private self-regulatory organizations in the securities industry that investigate and discipline their own members subject to SEC oversight. Unlike those private organizations, however, the Board is a federal agency that has expansive powers to govern an entire industry. The Act gave the SEC oversight of the Board, but the SEC Commissioners could not remove Board members absent "good cause shown" and "in accordance with" specified procedures. *Id.* at 486 (quoting 15 U.S.C. § 7211(e)(6)). This was removal layer one. Moreover, the parties stipulated that the SEC Commissioners could not themselves be removed by the president except for inefficiency, neglect of duty, or malfeasance in office (*i.e.* for cause). *Id.* at 487. This was removal layer two. (The relevant statute was actually silent on this issue, but the parties believed that *Humphrey's Executor* compelled this stipulation.)

Petitioners sued, arguing that the two layers of for-cause tenure protection insulated the Board members from presidential control. *Id.* The District Court granted summary judgment to respondents. *Id.* at 488. The Court of Appeals affirmed, holding that dual for-cause restrictions on the Board members' removal were constitutional.

The Supreme Court reversed. *Id.* at 514. The majority held that the dual for-cause limitations on the removal of the members of the Board contravened the U.S. Constitution's separation of powers because the president could not faithfully execute the law if he did not have removal power over those executing the law on his behalf. *Id.* at 492. Rather than invalidate the Act, the majority simply severed the removal provision of the Act to remedy its constitutional infirmity.

A percolating issue is whether the dual for-cause removal provisions protecting ALJs who work for independent agencies are similarly unconstitutional. ALJs cannot be removed from their position except for cause, and the heads of these agencies are similarly protected from at-will removal. *Free Enterprise* suggests that two levels of for-cause removal protection are invalid. Yet Congress included these removal provisions to protect the independence of the ALJs, who exercise quasi-judicial authority. So *Humphrey's Executor* suggests that at least one level of protection would be permissible, but which: the protection for the ALJs or the protection for the agency heads? And what about the point that even if an agency head recommends that an ALJ be removed, the ALJ is then entitled to a formal adjudication before the Merit Protection Review Board, which is an independent agency whose ALJs and members are also protected from removal? For a discussion of this topic, see Linda D. Jellum, *You're Fired! Why the ALJ Multi-Track Dual Removal Provisions Violate the Constitution & Possible Fixes*, 26 GEO. MASON L. REV. ____ (forthcoming 2020).

3. Executive Orders

Appointment and removal are two very important tools for a president to control those who work for her. But the president uses other methods, including *executive orders*. An executive order is a directive issued by a president to implement or interpret federal law. Executive orders are printed in the Federal Register.

Presidents have issued executive orders since 1789. Presidents have used executive orders to suspend habeas corpus, implement affirmative action requirements for government contractors, slow stem cell research, and authorize citizen surveillance. Why do presidents like them?

> In contrast to legislation or agency regulation, there are almost no legally enforceable procedural requirements that the president must satisfy before issuing (or repealing) an executive order.... That, no doubt, is central to their appeal to presidents. They rid the president of the need to assemble majorities in both houses of Congress, or to wait through administrative processes, such as notice-and-comment rulemaking, to initiate policy.

Kevin M. Stack, *The Statutory President*, 90 Iowa L. Rev. 539, 552–53 (2005).

Although there is no constitutional provision, act, or statute that explicitly permits the president to issue executive orders, presidents assumed this power pursuant to their authority to "take Care that the Laws be faithfully executed." U.S. Const. art. II, §3, cl. 5. Presidents generally use executive orders to guide federal agencies and officials in their execution of statutory authority. However, presidents use executive orders in other ways as well. For example, presidents may use proclamations, a special type of executive order, for ceremonial or symbolic messages, such as when the president declares *National Take Your Child to Work Day*. Also, presidents issue National Security Directives, which concern national security or defense issues.

Executive orders are somewhat controversial because the U.S. Constitution gives Congress the power to make law, albeit with the executive's assistance. When a president issues an executive order, it might appear as if the president is making law unilaterally. Often, when a president from one party attempts to influence policy using an executive order, members of Congress who are in the other party accuse the president of exceeding constitutional authority. For example, the Republican Party was highly critical of President Obama's executive orders addressing gun sales, deportation deferrals, and minimum wages. Former House Speaker John Boehner said, "President Obama has overstepped his constitutional authority—and it is the responsibility of the House of Representatives to defend the Constitution.... Congress makes the laws; the president executes them. That is the system the Founders gave us. This is not about executive orders. Every president issues executive orders. Most of them, though, do so within the law."[2]

Was President Obama unique? Simply put, no. All presidents issue executive orders. Former President Roosevelt issued the most (3,728) as the country dealt with the Great Depression and World War II. Herbert Hoover issued 995. More recent presidents have issued fewer. Jimmy Carter issued 319 (in only four years); George W. Bush issued 291; Bill Clinton issued 364; Barack Obama issued 276; and Donald Trump issued 92 in the first two years of his presidency.[3] Many important policy and legal changes have occurred through executive orders. For example, President Lincoln emancipated slaves; President Truman integrated the armed forces; President Eisenhower desegregated schools; Presidents Kennedy and Johnson barred racial discrimination in federal housing, hiring, and contracting; President Reagan barred the use of federal funds for abortion advocacy (which President Clinton reversed); President Clinton fought a war in Yugoslavia; President Obama closed "the gun show loophole"; and President Trump sought to repeal the Affordable Care Act. All of these significant events occurred because of an executive order.

Some executive orders are legitimate exercises of executive power. Congress gives agencies considerable leeway in implementing and administering federal statutes and programs. This leeway leaves gaps for the executive to fill and ambiguities for the executive to interpret. When Congress fails to spell out the details of how a law should be executed, the door is left open for a president to provide those details, and executive orders are one way a president does so.

However, when a president deviates from "congressional intent" or exceeds the constitutional powers delegated to the executive, the executive order is not a legitimate exercise of executive power. For example, when President Truman seized control of the nation's steel mills in an effort to settle labor disputes that arose after World War II, the Supreme Court held that the seizure was unconstitutional and exceeded presidential powers because neither the

---

2. John Boehner, *We're Defending the Constitution,* USA TODAY (July 27, 2014), http://www.usatoday.com/story/opinion/2014/07/27/president-obama-house-speaker-john-boehner-executive-orders-editorials-debates/13244117/ (explaining a congressional resolution to sue the president for extending a deadline in the Affordable Care Act).

3. John Woolley and Gerhard Peters, *Executive Orders: Washington—Obama,* THE AMERICAN PRESIDENCY PROJECT (January 20, 2016), http://www.presidency.ucsb.edu/data/orders.php.

Constitution nor any statute authorized the President to seize private businesses to settle labor disputes. *Youngstown Sheet & Tube Co. v. Sawyer*, 343 U.S. 579 (1952). Notably, this outcome was unusual. Generally, the Court is fairly tolerant of executive orders. *See, e.g., Korematsu v. United States*, 323 U.S. 214 (1944) (upholding the constitutionality of E.O. 9066, which ordered Japanese Americans into internment camps during World War II); *see generally* Erica Newland, Note, *Executive Orders in Court*, 124 YALE L.J. 2026 (2015) (examining 700 cases from the Supreme Court and D.C. Circuit Court addressing the validity of various executive orders).

4. Executive Order 12,866 & Centralized Agency Review

Let's look more closely at a specific executive order. In 1980, President Reagan campaigned on a platform of deregulation. Once elected, he issued Executive Order 12,291. This executive order directed all executive agencies to perform a regulatory analysis assessing the costs and benefits of any "major" proposed regulations. Exec. Order No. 12,291, 3 C.F.R. §127 (1982). One of Reagan's purposes for issuing this executive order was to limit what he considered to be excessive regulation. (Similarly, President Trump issued the Two-For-One, Exec. Order No. 13,771, requiring federal agencies to repeal two regulations for each new regulation.)

Although this executive order came from a Republican president, each president since Reagan has reissued this same order, albeit with slight changes. Former President Clinton issued Executive Order (E.O.) 12,866, which mostly mirrored President Reagan's order; however, he changed the phrase "major rule" to "significant action." Next, former President George W. Bush adopted Clinton's order, but also issued two additional executive orders that slightly amended E.O. 12,866; importantly, one of these orders added guidance documents to the order's coverage. Exec. Order No. 13,422, 72 Fed. Reg. 2763 (Jan. 23, 2007). When President Obama took office, he repealed the two Bush orders, Exec. Order No. 13,497, 74 Fed. Reg. 6113 (Feb. 4, 2009), and amended E.O. 12,866 to allow agencies to consider not only monetary costs and benefits of "significant actions," but "human dignity" and "fairness" as well. Today, centralized agency review is now a fixture of executive agency rulemaking, as E.O. 12,866 has been reissued by each president since Reagan.

E.O. 12,866 provides guiding principles that executive agencies (independent agencies are not currently included, but the Trump administration is trying to change that) must follow when developing regulations that will have an economic effect of at least one hundred million dollars. Pursuant to the order, agencies may promulgate regulations only when the regulations are "required by law," "necessary to interpret the law," or "are made necessary by compelling public need, such as material failures of private markets to protect or improve the health and safety of the public, the environment, or the well-being of the American people." Exec. Order No. 12,866 § 1(a), 58 Fed. Reg. 51,735 (October 4, 1993). Pursuant to E.O. 12,866, agencies must follow specific procedural steps when developing regulatory priorities, including the following: (1) identifying the problem the regulation was intended to address, including "the failures of private markets or public institutions that warrant new agency action"; (2) determining whether the problem could be addressed through modifications to existing regulations or laws; (3) assessing alternatives to regulation, such as economic incentives; (4) considering "the degree and nature of the risks posed by various substances or activities" within the agency's jurisdiction; (5) fashioning regulations "in the most cost-effective manner"; (6) assessing the costs and benefits, such that benefits justify the costs; (7) basing decisions "on the best reasonably obtainable scientific, technical, economic, and other information"; (8) recommending performance-based solutions rather than behavioral ones, when possible; (9) consulting with state, local, and tribal governments and assessing the impacts of regulations on these local governments; (10) avoiding duplications and inconsistencies among federal agencies; (11) minimizing the burdens; (12) considering the cumulative costs of regulation; and (13) writing all regulations in language that the general public can easily understand. Exec. Order No. 12,866 § 1(b)(1)–(12), 58 Fed. Reg. 51,735 (October 4, 1993).

Most importantly, in deciding whether regulation is necessary, agencies must assess the costs and benefits of the alternatives, "including the alternative of not regulating." Exec. Order No. 12,866 § 1(a), 58 Fed. Reg. 51735 (October 4, 1993). "[U]nless [the] statute requires another regulatory approach," agencies must choose the regulatory path that maximizes net benefits. *Id.* Once an agency has completed its analysis, the agency submits the proposed regulation along with its analysis of that regulation to the Office of Information and Regulatory Affairs (OIRA). OIRA is responsible for overseeing the Federal Government's regulatory, paperwork, and information resource management activities and is located within the OMB. OMB is located within the executive office and is very closely aligned with the president and his or her policies. OIRA will review the agency's proposed rule and analysis to ensure compliance with E.O. 12,866; in simple terms, OIRA acts as gatekeeper for the promulgation of all significant regulations.

Additionally, E.O. 12,866 imposes regulatory planning measures. All agencies, including independent agencies, must produce a semi-annual *regulatory agenda* of all regulations under development or review. Pursuant to another executive order, E.O. 12,291, the agencies provide their agenda in April and October of each year, a requirement that Congress partially codified in the Regulatory Flexibility Act. 5 U.S.C. § 602(a). Each regulatory agenda includes a summary of the action to be taken, the agency's legal authority for acting, legal deadlines if any, and an agency contact. Exec. Order No. 12,866 § 1, 58 Fed. Reg. 51735 (October 4, 1993). An example of the 2012 Department of Health and Human Services regulatory agenda can be found at 77 Fed. Reg. 7946 (Feb. 13, 2012), available at http://www.gpo.gov/fdsys/pkg/FR-2012-02-13/pdf/2012-1647.pdf.

In addition, pursuant to E.O. 12866, all agencies must produce a *regulatory plan*, which identifies the most significant regulatory activities the agency has planned for the upcoming year. Exec. Order No. 12,866 § 4(c), 58 Fed. Reg. 51735 (October 4, 1993). While the regulatory *agenda* includes *all* proposed actions, the regulatory *plan* includes only the most important proposed actions. The agency must explain how the action relates to the president's priorities, determine anticipated costs and benefits, provide a summary of the legal basis for the action, and include a statement of why the action is needed. Regulatory plans are forwarded to OIRA on June 1 of every year. OIRA reviews the plans for consistency with the president's priorities, the requirements of E.O. 12,866, and the regulatory agendas of other agencies.

OIRA publishes the regulatory agendas and plans together in the Unified Agenda, which is available to the public online: http://reginfo.gov. Each edition of the Agenda includes the regulatory agendas from all federal agencies that currently have regulations under development or review. In addition, the fall edition of the Agenda includes the agencies' regulatory plans. The Agenda is an integral part of the federal regulatory process. Its semiannual publication enables regulated entities, the public, companies, and other interested persons to understand and prepare for new rules that are planned or under development. The Agenda provides important information to agency heads, centralized reviewers, and the public at large, thereby serving the values of open government.

Finally, at the beginning of each planning period, the director of OMB convenes a meeting with the regulatory advisors and agency heads to coordinate regulatory priorities for the coming year. Exec. Order No. 12,866 § 4(a), 58 Fed. Reg. 51735 (October 4, 1993).

While E.O. 12866 is the most prominent executive order requiring regulatory analysis, it is by no means the only analysis requirement to come from the executive office. Over the years, presidents have required agencies to perform many different analyses. *See, e.g.,* Exec. Order No. 12,372, 47 Fed. Reg. 30959 (July 16, 1982) (requiring agencies to analyze the impact of proposed and final regulations on state and local governments); Exec. Order No. 13,175, 65 Fed. Reg. 67249 (Nov. 9, 2000) (requiring agencies to analyze the impact of proposed and final regulations on tribal governments).

This form of executive oversight amends, delays, or stops regulatory action. What if the president wants an agency to act? We turn to that issue next.

5. Presidential Directives

Congress typically delegates authority to the head of agencies rather than the president. Such delegations will often direct the agency administrator to adopt necessary regulations to implement the purposes of the enabling act. *See, e.g.,* 26 U.S.C. § 7805(a) ("Except where such authority is expressly given by this title to any person other than an officer or employee of the Treasury Department, the Secretary shall prescribe all needful rules and regulations for the enforcement of this title, including all rules and regulations as may be necessary by reason of any alteration of law in relation to internal revenue."); *cf.* 40 U.S.C. § 121(a) ("The President may prescribe policies and directives that the President considers necessary to carry out this subtitle.").

For example, the Clean Water Act delegates authority to the EPA administrator to carry out many of its provisions. 33 U.S.C. § 1251(d). Yet former President Clinton issued a presidential directive telling a number of agencies to work harder on improving water quality. Memorandum on Clean Water Protection, 2 Pub. Papers 857–58 (May 29, 1999). President Clinton used such directives aggressively, especially when Congress turned Republican. Indeed, Justice Kagan, who served as a senior advisor to President Clinton, explained that he used such directives as his "primary means ... of setting an administrative agenda." Elena Kagan, *Presidential Administration*, 114 Harv. L. Rev. 2245, 2290 (2001).

Presidential directives are similar to executive orders, although perhaps less formal. *See* Legal Effectiveness of a Presidential Directive, as Compared to an Executive Order 24 Op. O.L.C. 29 (2000). They are easily issued and rescinded, but are they legally binding on agencies? Does the president have any ability to tell agencies how to exercise their discretion when Congress delegated that authority to the agency? And what if the agency given discretionary power is an independent agency rather than an executive agency (one expected to be freer from the president's influence)? Unfortunately, there is no good answer to these questions. Some believe the president, pursuant to the take care clause, has inherent authority to direct agency officials regarding the lawful exercise of their discretion. *See, e.g.,* Steven G. Calabresi & Saikrishna B. Prakash, *The President's Power to Execute the Laws,* 104 YALE L.J. 541, 583 (1994). Others argue that the president has the power to oversee an agency's decision-making process but not an agency's exercise of discretionary authority. Peter L. Strauss, *Overseer, or "The Decider"? The President in Administrative Law,* 75 GEO. WASH. L. REV. 696, 751–57 (2007).

The U.S. Constitution places all executive power in a president. "The idea of a 'plural executive,' or a President with a council of state, was considered and rejected by the Constitutional Convention." *Sierra Club v. Costle,* 657 F.2d 298, 405 (D.C. Cir. 1981). For this reason, the president likely has the legal authority to tell agencies what to do so long as the action would be lawful, although there is little case law on this issue. *See Center for Auto Safety v. Peck,* 751 F.2d 1336, 1368 (D.C. Cir. 1985) (noting that the court would be concerned if "the President directed the agency, in the course of [an investigation], to disregard the statutory criteria controlling its actions.").

Finally, pragmatically, the argument above may be irrelevant. Executive administrators serve at the president's pleasure. A president may be none too pleased if an administrator ignores his or her preferences. And even those administrators who can be removed only "for good cause" may prefer to work cooperatively with the president rather than to force a judicial decision on whether ignoring a presidential directive constitutes good cause.

6. Signing Statements

In this section, we turn to a less direct method of executive control: signing statements. As mentioned in Chapter 2, when a president signs legislation that the president does not like but does not want to veto, the president may include a limiting *signing statement.* Because these statements often indicate how the executive intends to implement the law, they are another way that the executive oversees agencies. The question is whether signing statements have any effect beyond oversight. As we noted, these statements have become controversial, in part, because presidents have begun to use them to influence statutory interpretation.

President Reagan's administration persuaded West Publishing Company to include signing statements in the *United States Code Congressional and Administrative News,* specifically to influence statutory interpretation. Courts, however, do not appear to have turned to signing statements in the manner that the administration wished. The Constitution specifically identifies the role that presidents have in enacting legislation — signing a bill into law or vetoing it. For example, the Constitution allows a president to note objections when vetoing a bill, but the Constitution does not require a president to announce the reasons for approving a bill. Moreover, if a president vetoes a bill, Congress, pursuant to a constitutionally prescribed procedure, is permitted to respond to the veto and raise objections in an attempt to override it. In contrast, there is no prescribed process for Congress to respond to presidential objections contained in signing statements. While this dichotomy does not require courts to ignore signing statements, it suggests that presidential signing statements that conflict with congressional intent should be discounted.

Relatedly, a president has the constitutional authority to approve or veto a bill only in its entirety. Signing statements, however, often contain objections to specific statutory provisions, making them akin to line-item vetoes. The president does not possess line-item veto authority, and Congress cannot grant the president such authority. *Clinton v. City of New York*, 524 U.S. 417, 447–49 (1998).

Whether for these or other reasons, the courts give little to no weight to signing statements. For example, in *DaCosta v. Nixon*, 55 F.R.D. 145, 146 (E.D.N.Y. 1972), the court rejected President Nixon's signing statement, which claimed that a provision in a statute did not "represent the policies of this Administration" and was "without binding force or effect." The court explained that a signing statement "denying efficacy to the legislation could have [n]either validity or effect." *Id.* And in *Hamdan v. Rumsfeld*, 548 U.S. 557 (2006), the majority completely ignored President Bush's signing statement when it held that the Detainee Treatment Act did not apply to pending habeas petitions of Guantanamo detainees. In a dissenting opinion (joined by Justice Alito, Surprise!), Justice Scalia criticized the majority for using legislative history while ignoring the President's signing statement. *Id.* at 666 (Scalia, J., dissenting) ("Of course in its discussion of legislative history the Court wholly ignores the President's signing statement, which explicitly set forth his understanding that the [act] ousted jurisdiction over pending cases."). Lastly, in *United States v. Stevens*, 559 U.S. 460 (2010), the Court noted that President Clinton's signing statement, which promised to limit prosecutions under an animal cruelty statute only to those cases of "wanton cruelty to animals designed to appeal to a prurient interest in sex," did not save an otherwise unconstitutionally overbroad statute. *Id.* at 480. As these cases show, signing statements generally have no relevance in court.

There are times, however, when a signing statement might provide limited judicial guidance. When a president has worked closely with Congress in developing legislation and when the enacted version of the bill addresses the president's veto concerns, then a court might consider an ensuing signing statement as evidence of the political compromises that were reached. In these situations, signing statements might help explain rather than negate congressional action. For example, former President Franklin Roosevelt issued a signing statement during World War II contesting the constitutionality of section 304 of the Urgent Deficiencies Appropriations Act of 1943, ch. 218, 57 Stat. 431, 450 (1943). He indicated that he felt that he had no choice but to sign the bill "to avoid delaying our conduct of the war." *United States v. Lovett*, 328 U.S. 303, 313 (1946) (quoting H.R. Doc. No. 78-264 (1943)). When the statute was challenged, the Court struck down the provision, citing the signing statement in its reasoning.

The growing use of signing statements to influence interpretation has attracted the attention of Congress. A few bills have been introduced to stop this practice. For example, Senator Arlen Specter introduced the Presidential Signing Statements Act of 2006, which would have prohibited courts from considering signing statements. Presidential Signing Statements Act of 2006, S. 3731, 109th Cong. § 4 ("In determining the meaning of any Act of Congress, no State or Federal court shall rely on or defer to a presidential signing statement as a source of authority."). The bill died in committee. *See also* Congressional Lawmaking Authority Protection Act of 2007, H.R. 264, 110th Cong. § 4 ("For purposes of construing or applying any Act enacted by the Congress, a governmental entity shall not take into consideration any statement made by the President contemporaneously with the President's signing of the bill or joint resolution that becomes such Act.").

Although signing statements are not generally relevant to interpretation in court, such statements nonetheless greatly affect the actions of administering agencies. The president oversees agencies and sets administrative policy. While the executive's interpretation of a statute does not bind judges, it binds agency personnel. Moreover, as we will see in the next chapter, courts generally defer to agency interpretations of statutes that are made during rulemaking or other formal processes. To the extent that a signing statement impacts an agency's interpretation of a statute, that signing statement will impact interpretation, albeit indirectly. Thus, while signing statements may not have had the interpretive impact former Attorney General Meese (and Justice Alito) would have liked, there is no question that they are having at least some impact.

D. Mastering This Topic

Return to the hypothetical ordinance provided in Chapter 1. The first question that was asked was the following: "An ambulance entered Pioneer Park to pick up and take to the hospital a man who had just suffered a heart attack. Did the ambulance driver violate the Pioneer Park Safety Ordinance (PPSO)?" How should you, as prosecutor, attempt to answer that question using what you've learned in this chapter?

The hypothetical includes the mayor's signing statement. You may have wondered how relevant executive signing statements are to interpretation. The discussion above should make clear that the proper role of signing statements in interpretation is far from settled, but that generally, signing statements are considered irrelevant in courts. Nevertheless, the signing statement may inform the relevant agency regarding the executive's preferences regarding enforcement. As a prosecutor for the city, you work for the executive; thus, you may wish to consider the executive's preferences when choosing to bring an enforcement action. Does the mayor's statement give you any guidance regarding whether you should prosecute the ambulance driver? What about the other drivers in the hypothetical questions? The mayor seemed very concerned with pollution and noisy vehicles. An ambulance would not seem to fit within these concerns. Likely, you would choose not to prosecute in this situation, even though you know that this signing statement would have little impact in court.

While it may have little impact in court, your choice may affect your ability to keep your job. Can you be fired if you refuse to follow the mayor's preferences? Assuming hypothetically that federal law applies, you would want to determine whether you are a principal officer, inferior officer, or employee. Unless you are the head prosecutor reporting directly to the executive, you are not a principal officer. However, you do exercise significant authority pursuant to the laws of the city; thus, you are likely not a mere employee. Can the executive fire inferior officers? Yes, so long as the legislature has not protected that officer with for-cause removal protection. In short, you may want to check with your boss, who can check with the executive for guidance on prosecuting alleged violators of this ordinance.

Checkpoints

- Congress controls agency exercise of delegated power to ensure agencies follow legislative intent.

- Congress has a number of ways to oversee agency behavior. Congress may broadly or narrowly grant an agency rulemaking authority or subsequently broaden or narrow such authority.

- Congress can also require an agency to follow new procedures either in the enabling act or in a subsequent statute, such as the Congressional Review Act.

- Congress holds the power of the purse and may also hold hearings to investigate agencies.

- The president also has a number of ways of controlling agency behavior, including appointment and removal, executive orders and directives, and signing statements.

- The Constitution places limits on the appointment of agency officials. Principal officers, like agency heads, must be appointed by the president with the advice and consent of the Senate. Inferior officers, like other higher-level agency officials, must be appointed by the president, the courts of law, or the head of the department.

- Principal officers report directly to the president while inferior officers exercise significant authority pursuant to the laws of the United States.

- A president's removal power is implied in the U.S. Constitution, but Congress can limit it in cases involving agency independence.

- Executive Order 12,866 is the most prominent executive order and requires agencies to perform cost-benefit analyses on all proposed regulations that will have a significant impact on the economy.

- Signing statements have little impact on statutory interpretation but may greatly impact agency behavior.

Chapter 15

The Administrative State: Judicial Review of Agency Decisions

---

Roadmap

- Understand the differences among questions of law, application, fact, and policy.

- Understand the difference between standard of review and scope of review.

- Learn the standard of review that courts apply to agency findings of law and law application.

- Understand *Chevron*'s two-step test, *Skidmore*'s power-to-persuade test, and *Auer*'s plainly-wrong test.

- Learn the standard of review that courts apply to agency findings of fact and policy.

- Understand substantial evidence and arbitrary and capricious review.

A. Introduction to This Chapter

In the last two chapters, you learned about agencies: what they are, what they do, and how the executive and legislature oversee their activities. As you now know, agencies are entrusted to implement complicated regulatory schemes. Congress delegates the power to regulate to agencies. With delegation comes the power to make rules and adjudicate.

Whether agencies make rules or adjudicate, they decide questions of law, fact, and policy. Courts often have to review those decisions when they are challenged in court. In this chapter, we explore the standard and scope of review courts use to review agency decisions. The standard of review refers to the particular review standard used (*e.g.*, *Auer* deference) while the scope of review refers to the breadth of that standard (*e.g.*, very differential).

As you know, agencies have expertise that informs their resolution of these questions. Moreover, to be able to respond to economic, technological, and political changes, agencies must have flexibility to change their decisions. You will learn that the standard of review changes depending on the nature of the question being reviewed and the importance of agency expertise and flexibility to the resolution of that question. Generally, judicial review is less exacting when agencies bring expertise to the issue and more exacting when courts are equally, if not better, able to resolve the issue. But this topic is substantially more complex than that and hotly debated in judicial, legislative, and academic circles.

B. Intensity of Judicial Review Generally

The regulatory state grew exponentially in the last decades. With this growth came a substantial delegation of basic policy-making power from elected officials (members of Congress) to unelected administrators (agency officials). While members of Congress are accountable to the public through elections, agency officials are not. To increase accountability, oversight is necessary to keep agency officials faithful to congressional preferences. We learned the ways that Congress and the president oversee agencies in the last chapter. We did not discuss judicial oversight. We do so now.

Judicial review is the most obvious and, in some senses, the most final judicial oversight mechanism. When agencies lose in court, they generally must start their regulatory process all over again. The possibility that the courts will review their decisions thus serves an oversight function even if such review never actually takes place. Agencies will think about how to best accomplish their objectives, knowing that their decisions may be subject to judicial review.

As we will see, judicial review allows courts to determine the legality of agency action while simultaneously preventing courts from interfering with congressional delegation and agency expertise. If the scope of a judicial review standard is too intensive, then federal judges will make policy. However, federal judges have neither technical expertise nor political accountability. In contrast, if the scope of a judicial review standard is not intensive enough, then agency policies may not sufficiently adhere to congressional delegation and may not sufficiently follow the rule of law. Hence, in developing the standards of review, courts have sought balance.

Before we talk about the standards that apply in the administrative law context, let's look first at some standards of review that apply in the non-administrative law context. Low-intensity review is review in which a judge is highly deferential to the trier of fact's views. For example, when an appellate court reviews a lower court's opinion using the clear error standard of review, that is a low intensity review standard.

At the other end of the spectrum, high-intensity review is review in which a judge substitutes her own views for that of the trier of fact. The *de novo* standard of review is a form of high intensity review, perhaps even the highest form. There are gradations in the middle of the spectrum. See the figure below. While the differences among the various judicial review standards are far too subtle to be captured on a single linear spectrum, thinking about the standards in this way will give us a start on understanding the scope of the different judicial review standards. After our discussion of standards of review in the administrative context, we will revisit this figure and locate the administrative law standards accordingly.

Conventional Standards of Review

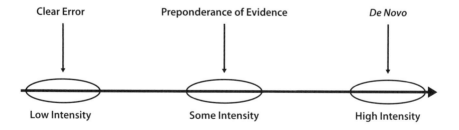

C. Intensity of Judicial Review in Administrative Law

1. Types of Questions Subject to Judicial Review

Now let's return to the administrative context. Agency actions are generally reviewable in court, although you may need to address questions about the availability of judicial review before determining the applicable standard of review. The availability of judicial review involves questions about standing, finality, and exhaustion of administrative remedies, among other issues. It is a topic well beyond the scope of this text.

To find the appropriate standard of review, you should look first to the enabling act. Congress includes judicial review provisions in most enabling acts. If Congress has provided a specific standard in the enabling act, that standard applies. If Congress has not provided a specific standard, the APA contains a default provision. 5 U.S.C. § 706(2). This subsection identifies five possible standards of review. Which standard applies depends on the issue before the court, the process the agency used to decide that issue, and common law factors.

Assume a regulated entity challenges an agency's decision in an Article III court. That challenge will attack one or more of the agency's resolution of questions of law, questions of law application, questions of fact, or questions of policy. In this section, we will consider the two questions of law categories: pure questions of law and questions of law application. In the next section, we will consider questions of fact and policy.

A pure question of law is one in which the resolution of the question does not require knowledge of the facts. A statement of law is an assertion about legal effect that can be advanced with *little* to no knowledge of the facts in a particular case. "Little" because you need to know some basic facts, such as the actors and the situation, but you do not need to know the individual facts. Let's look at a non-agency example. Assume that there was a car accident. During the investigation, the accident investigator noted that the speed limit was 30 mph on the road where the accident took place. This assertion would be a statement of law. The facts are irrelevant: it does not matter whether someone was speeding or drinking or texting. The speed limit on that road in that location is invariable in each case.

In contrast, a question of law application, or a mixed question of law and fact, requires knowledge of both the law and the specific facts. In our car accident example, assume the investigator concluded that the defendant must have exceeded the speed limit because the skid marks were unusually long. This determination involves applying the relevant law (the speed limit) to the specific facts in a particular case (the unusually long skid marks) to reach a conclusion (the defendant was speeding).

Let's turn back to our world of agencies. Agencies must determine the boundaries of their delegated authority and the meaning of the laws within their authority. Questions related to these types of issues are pure questions of law. Agencies often resolve questions of law during rulemakings, although they may also do so during adjudications. For example, assume an act required certain "states to establish a permit program regulating new or modified major stationary sources of air pollution." Assume further that Congress delegated to the Environment Protection Agency (EPA) the authority to issue rules and regulations to implement this act. The EPA begins a rulemaking to define "major stationary sources." The EPA has choices: a major stationary source may be any device in a manufacturing plant that produces pollution, or it may be the entire plant as a whole. This is a question of law; the individual facts of each plant are irrelevant to the EPA's resolution of this question.

In contrast, agencies typically resolve questions of law application during adjudications when they determine whether a particular law applies to a given set of the facts. For example, assume that an agency must decide whether people who deliver newspapers are employees of a particular newspaper company or are independent contractors. If they are employees, then the refusal of their employer to bargain might constitute an unfair labor practice, depending upon the facts relating to the refusal. Resolving this question involves both the facts and the law. Hence, this is a mixed question of law and fact.

Now let's define a pure question of fact. A question of fact is one in which the resolution of the question does not require an application, or knowledge, of the law. Thus, a statement of fact "is an assertion that a phenomenon has happened or is or will be happening independent of or anterior to any assertion as to its legal effect." LOUIS L. JAFFE, JUDICIAL CONTROL OF ADMINISTRATIVE ACTION 548 (1965). In short, the facts are mostly irrelevant when resolving pure questions of law, and the law is mostly irrelevant when resolving pure questions of fact.

Let's return to our non-agency example: the car accident. Assume that during the investigation, the accident investigator noted that the skid marks on the pavement were forty-six feet long. This would be a finding of fact. The law is irrelevant. Findings of fact answer questions about who did what to whom and with what effect.

Let's turn back to our world of agencies. Agencies must make factual findings regularly. For example, an agency may have to determine whether one witness or another is telling the truth. The agency may have to determine whether someone was fired in the way he claimed. These types of facts—who said what, who did what, and when—are adjudicatory facts. Agencies may also have to decide whether a pesticide is safe for human consumption. These types of facts are legislative facts. Agencies typically make findings of adjudicatory facts during adjudications and findings of legislative facts during rulemakings.

Finally, agencies resolve questions of policy. Courts do not make policy decisions, so there is no comparable non-agency example, as there was for our car accident example. Earlier we defined a mixed question of law and fact as one in which the agency applies the relevant law to the specific facts in an adjudication to reach a conclusion. A question of policy similarly involves resolution of both law and facts, but questions of policy generally arise during rulemakings rather than during adjudications. The relevant facts are legislative facts.

For example, suppose an agency must decide on the location for a new highway, how many parts per million of a certain chemical will be injurious to human health, what kinds of safety features should be required in passenger cars, or what level of protection should be afforded workers in factories. Resolution of these kinds of issues involves policy decisions—decisions requiring value choices that are not fully resolved by the legislative facts (though these help) or the legal standards. In making policy, the agency must consider the legislative facts in light of its delegated authority, for example, "to make drinking water safe," to arrive at its policy choice. The legislative facts (arsenic is never safe) help the agency resolve the policy question (absolutely no arsenic in the water supply).

Thus, there are four types of agency findings that courts review: (1) pure questions of law; (2) questions of law application, or mixed questions; (3) pure questions of legislative or adjudicative fact; and (4) questions of policy. Before you can determine which standard of review applies, you must first determine which kind of question the court is reviewing. We turn now to the appropriate standards of review.

2. Standard of Review for Pure Questions of Law

Agencies interpret statutes and regulations as part of their day-to-day implementation and enforcement of legislatively delegated power. When an agency's interpretation of a statute is challenged in court, the court confronts a complicated question involving the intersection of legislative, executive, and judicial powers. Who should interpret the statute initially? Who should have the final say? Further, when agencies interpret regulations they have promulgated, should courts simply trust the agency's interpretation or look at the regulation *de novo*?

Answering these questions is not easy. The appropriate standard and scope of review is one of the most challenging, and certainly the most discussed, issues in administrative law right now. Moreover, the appropriate standard has changed over time. Thus, to understand where the law has landed today, we must begin with the past.

a. Statutory Interpretation: Standards of Review Pre-Chevron

In the 1940s and early 1950s, the Supreme Court used two different deference standards: "no deference" (or a *de novo* standard) and "limited deference." While the deference world was never black and white, the standard the Court used seemed to depend on the type of question that was presented. When an agency interpretation involved a pure question of law, the Court used the "no deference" standard. *See, e.g., Gray v. Powell*, 314 U.S. 402, 414–17 (1941) (refusing to defer to the agency's determination that coal that was transported from one entity to another without a title transfer constituted coal that was "sold or otherwise disposed of" within the meaning of the Bituminous Coal Act of 1937); *NLRB v. Hearst Publications*, 322 U.S. 111, 124–29 (1944) (refusing to defer to the agency's determination that newsboys were "employees" under the National Labor Relations Act); *O'Leary v. Brown-Pacific-Maxon, Inc.*, 340 U.S. 504, 506 (1951) (refusing to defer to the agency's interpretation of the term "course of employment" in the Longshoremen's and Harbor Workers' Compensation Act).

In contrast, when an agency interpretation involved a question of law application, the Supreme Court used the "limited deference" standard. *See, e.g., Gray*, 314 U.S. at 410–13 (deferring to the agency's finding that a specific plaintiff was a coal producer); *O'Leary*, 340 U.S. at 507–08 (deferring to the agency's finding that a particular rescue occurred during the course of an employee's employment). For application questions, the Court afforded the agency interpretation some deference because of the agency's expertise and express congressional delegation. *Hearst Publications*, 322 U.S. at 120; *Gray*, 314 U.S. at 412 ("Congress ... found it more efficient to delegate [these issues] to those whose experience in a particular field gave promise of a better informed, more equitable" resolution of the issues).

Thus, when the issue involved law application, courts deferred because of the agency's expertise and the likelihood that Congress intended to delegate resolution of the issue to the agency. However, when the agency interpretation involved a pure question of law, the Court did not defer to the agency interpretation at all because judges were as competent, if not more so, than agencies to determine the intended meaning of ambiguous statutory language. Pursuant to this bifurcated deference, or two-tracked, approach, judges retained the primary responsibility for interpreting statutes by reviewing questions of law *de novo* and by reviewing questions of law application more deferentially, giving the agency's interpretation some level of deference but not full deference. This bifurcated deference approach made sense and was consistent with the judicial review approach used in civil litigation. In civil cases, appellate judges determine questions of law *de novo*. Because appellate judges are experts at interpreting law, no deference is due when trial courts resolve questions of law. This approach was also consistent with the APA, which provides, "the reviewing court shall decide all relevant questions of law, [and] interpret constitutional and statutory provisions." 5 U.S.C. § 706.

In contrast, questions of law application were reviewed under a more deferential standard because agencies had more experience understanding how the statute should apply in any given situation and Congress would thus likely prefer that the agency resolve the issue.

However, while courts deferred to agency resolutions involving law application, the scope of that deference was unclear. In 1944, the Supreme Court decided two cases that addressed the scope. In the first case, *Hearst Publications, Inc.*, the Court held that as long as an agency interpretation had "warrant in the record and a reasonable basis in law," a court should not substitute its own interpretation for that of the agency entrusted with administering the statute. 322 U.S. at 131 (internal quotations omitted). In this case, the Court addressed the appropriate level of deference to give a National Labor Relations Board's (NLRB) determination that the word "employee" in the National Labor Relations Act applied to newsboys. *Id.* at 120–23. Because the NLRB had "familiarity with the circumstances and backgrounds of employment relationships in various industries," the Court held that determining the scope of the term "employees" "belongs to the usual administrative routine of the [NLRB]." *Id.* at 130. (internal citations omitted). Thus, the Court sustained the Board's interpretation under this "reasonable basis in the law" deference standard.

In the second case, *Skidmore v. Swift & Co.*, 323 U.S. 134 (1944), the Court explained that agency interpretations should be given deference when they are persuasive, meaning they had "all those factors which give [the agency interpretation] power to persuade, if lacking power to control." *Id.* at 140.

Skidmore involved the appropriate level of deference for a court to give an *interpretive* rule, a form of guidance. The issue in this case was whether certain employees of Swift & Co. were entitled to overtime pay under the Fair Labor Standards Act of 1938 ("FLSA"). The employees were paid for the work they performed during the day but were not paid overtime for their "in-active duty," or on-call time, during which they were required to remain on company premises even when not working. *Id.* at 138. Without using notice-and-comment procedures, the Department of Labor issued an "interpretive bulletin," which offered the Department's interpretation of FLSA on this issue. *Id.* at 138. Both lower courts ignored the bulletin entirely, deciding the issue *de novo*, and held that no overtime pay was warranted. The Supreme Court reversed and remanded, directing the Fifth Circuit to consider the agency's interpretation. *Id.* at 140.

> Under *Skidmore*'s power-to-persuade test, an agency's interpretation is entitled to deference when (1) the agency interprets the language consistently over time, (2) the agency thoroughly considers the issue, and (3) the agency offers sound reasoning to support the interpretation.

In so doing, the Court made clear that the agency had "accumulated a considerable experience in the problems of ascertaining working time in employments involving periods of inactivity and a knowledge of the customs prevailing in reference to their solution." *Id.* at 137–38. The Court noted that the agency's interpretation should not be ignored because the agency had expertise in this area. *Id.* at 139–40. Further, the weight to give an agency's interpretation should depend on "all those factors which give it power to persuade, if lacking power to control." *Id.* at 140. According to the Court, the factors giving an agency's interpretation "power-to-persuade" include the following: (1) the consistency in the agency's interpretation over time, (2) the thoroughness of the agency's consideration, and (3) the soundness of the agency's reasoning. *Id.* In other words, the more thoroughly considered and reasoned an agency interpretation is, the more a court should defer to that interpretation.

The Court reasoned that deference was appropriate because agencies are experts in their field and familiar with the industry customs surrounding certain issues. Hence, their expertise could inform a court's interpretation. Under *Skidmore*'s "power-to-persuade" test, agencies are akin to expert judicial advisors offering expertise in an area of judicial uncertainty; however, courts retain the majority of the interpretive power. Thus, a court reviewing an agency's interpretation would be free to use the traditional tools of interpretation, which are identified throughout the rest of this text. *Skidmore*'s "power-to-persuade" test simply added an agency's interpretation as another source for the court to consider during the interpretive process.

While *Skidmore*'s "power-to-persuade" test afforded agency interpretations some deference, the exact amount was unclear and indeterminate. The more consistent, thorough, and considered agency interpretations were, the more likely a court would defer to them. Agency interpretations that were persuasive received deference; those that were not persuasive received little or no deference. Whereas some deference would be accorded, the amount of deference would vary depending on the circumstances surrounding the agency's interpretation in each case. In effect, agencies faced a balancing test: under *Skidmore*, deference was earned, not automatic. But under *Skidmore*, certainty was lost.

b. Statutory Interpretation: Chevron

In 1984, after forty years of *Skidmore*, the Court adopted a new deference standard. In one of the most cited Supreme Court cases of all time, *Chevron U.S.A., Inc. v. National Resources Defense Council, Inc.*, 467 U.S. 837 (1984), the Court flipped the bifurcated deference standard it had been using, in which agencies played almost an advisory role while courts were the final arbiters of what an ambiguous statute meant.

Chevron involved a question about the Clean Air Act and addressed the level of deference appropriate for legislative — specifically notice-and-comment — rulemaking. The provision of the Act at issue required plants to obtain a permit when that plant wished to modify or build a "major stationary source[]" that emitted air pollution. *Id.* at 840. The term "major stationary source" was not defined in the Act. *Id.* at 841. Thus, the EPA, the agency in charge of administering the Act, had to interpret the term. The EPA issued two regulations interpreting "major stationary source." The first regulation, issued while President Carter was in office, defined "major stationary source" as the construction or installation of any new or modified equipment that emitted air pollutants. *Id.* at 840 n.2. But the following year, when President Reagan came to office, the EPA repealed that regulation and issued a new one that expanded the definition to encompass a plant-wide or "bubble concept" definition. *Id.* at 858. The bubble concept definition allowed a plant to offset increased air pollutant emissions at one part

Chevron's two-step deference framework:
• *Step one*: a court should determine "whether Congress has directly spoken to the precise question at issue."
• *Step two*: if Congress has not spoken, then a court must accept any "permissible," or "reasonable," agency interpretation.

of its plant with reduced emissions at another part of the plant. So long as total emissions at the plant remained constant, no permit was required. *Id.* at 852. Because this interpretation was less protective of the environment, environmentalists sued. The issue for the court was whether the EPA's interpretation of "stationary source" in the Clean Air Act was a valid interpretation of the statute. Applying the bifurcated approach, the D.C. Circuit said no, using a *de novo* standard of review for this pure question of law. *Id.* at 842.

The Supreme Court reversed, upholding the agency's interpretation. *Id.* at 842. In so doing, the Court ignored *Skidmore*'s power-to-persuade test and instead created a new two-step deference framework, based in part on its holding from *Hearst Publications.* Pursuant to the first step, a court should determine "whether Congress has directly spoken to the precise question at issue." *Id.* In other words, a court should ask whether Congress's intent is clear or whether there is a gap or ambiguity for the agency to fill. According to the Court, courts should resolve this issue by "employing traditional tools of statutory construction." *Id.* at 843 n.9. Under this first step, courts should not defer to agencies at all. Rather, "[t]he judiciary is the final authority on issues of statutory construction . . . ." *Id.* This step mirrors the *de novo* standard courts were already using for pure questions of law.

Assuming Congress's intent is not clear at step one, however, under step two, a court must accept any "permissible," or "reasonable," agency interpretation, even if the court believes a different interpretation would be better. *Id.* at 843. While Justice Stevens used the word *permissible* for step two, courts today typically use the word *reasonable* instead. Deferring at step two is called *Chevron* deference. This step mirrors the deferential standard courts applied for questions of law application: some deference, but not complete. As we will see, the rationale for deference at this step rests on agency expertise and implicit congressional delegation. This step was new and didn't exist under the bifurcated approach for pure questions of law.

At step two, courts must defer to "reasonable" interpretations. Professors John Manning and Mathew Stevenson explained what the Court meant by reasonable using a visual similar to the one on the next page. JOHN F. MANNING & MATTHEW C. STEPHENSON, LEGISLATION AND REGULATION 763 (2d ed. 2013). Notice that an agency's interpretation is reasonable so long as it stays within the range of reasonableness, even if the interpretation does not match the court's preferred interpretation. If, for example, the language being interpreted is "black" and the agency interprets black to include dark grey, that interpretation would likely be reasonable. But if the agency interprets "black" to include lime green, that interpretation would likely be unreasonable.

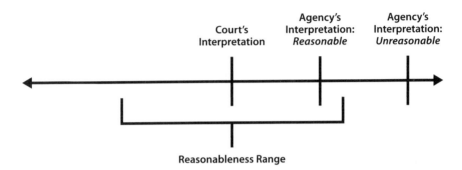

While some law professors' and even courts' opinions have suggested that *Chevron*'s second step is simply arbitrary and capricious review, others disagree. *See, e.g., Michigan v. EPA*, 135 S. Ct. 2699, 2707 (2015) (using a one-step analysis that jumbled together *Chevron* and arbitrary and capricious review); Mark Seidenfeld, *A Syncopated* Chevron: *Emphasizing Reasoned Decision-Making in Reviewing Agency Interpretations of Statutes*, 73 Tex. L. Rev. 83, 129–30 (1994); Ronald M. Levin, *The Anatomy of* Chevron: *Step Two Reconsidered*, 72 Chi.-Kent L. Rev. 1253, 1254–55 (1997). As we will see in a moment, arbitrary and capricious review is the standard that courts apply to review agency findings of fact and policy in informal rulemakings and adjudications. While arbitrary and capricious review and reasonableness review are similar, what the agency, and thus the court, are reviewing is different. For arbitrary and capricious review, a court reviews the record to determine whether there is a "rational connection between the facts found and the choice made." *Motor Vehicle Mfrs. Ass'n v. State Farm*, 463 U.S. 29, 43 (1983); *see also Citizens to Preserve Overton Park v. Volpe*, 401 U.S. 402, 416 (1971) (describing such review as whether the agency's findings were based on a consideration of irrelevant factors or whether the agency made a clear error of judgment). In contrast, for reasonableness review, an agency and the court examine the agency's interpretation to determine whether it is a reasonable construction of the statute in light of the statutory text, legislative history, and purpose.

When a court reaches *Chevron*'s second step, an agency is much more likely to win the legal challenge. Indeed, in the past, if a litigant challenged an agency interpretation and lost at step one, that litigant would likely lose the case. According to one empirical study that is now somewhat dated (1995–96), agencies prevail at step one 42% of the time and at step two 89% of the time. Orin S. Kerr, *Shedding Light on* Chevron: *An Empirical Study of the* Chevron *Doctrine in the U.S. Courts of Appeals*, 15 YALE J. REG. 1, 31 (1998) (finding that courts uphold agency interpretations 73% of the time; of all those decisions rejecting the agency's interpretation, 59% failed step one, 18% failed step two, and 23% failed a conflated step one and two, a one-step review for reasonableness.).

In *Chevron*, the Court offered three reasons to justify its decision to defer to agency interpretations at step two. First, the Court continued *Skidmore*'s rationale that agency personnel are experts in their field while judges are not. *Chevron*, 467 U.S. at 865. Congress entrusts agencies to implement law in a particular area because of this expertise. For example, scientists and analysts working for the Food and Drug Administration (FDA) are more knowledgeable about food safety and drug effectiveness than are judges. Because agencies are specialists in their field, they are in a better position to implement effective public policy. Courts are more limited in both knowledge and reasoning methods. While agencies can develop policy using a wide array of methods, courts are limited to the adversarial process. Hence, deferring to these experts makes sense.

Second, Congress simply cannot legislate every detail in a comprehensive regulatory scheme. Gaps and ambiguities are inevitable; an agency must fill and resolve these gaps and ambiguities to regulate. The *Chevron* Court presumed that by leaving these gaps and ambiguities, Congress impliedly delegated the authority to the agency to resolve them. *Id.* at 843–44. Finally, administrative officials, unlike federal judges, have a political constituency to which they are accountable. "[F]ederal judges—who have no constituency—have a duty to respect legitimate policy choices made by those who do." *Id.* at 866. Thus, the Court provided three reasons for its new standard: agency expertise, implied congressional delegation, and democratic theory. Deference, which had been earned by agencies through reasoned decision-making under *Skidmore*, became essentially an all-or-nothing grant of power from Congress under *Chevron*. Either Congress was clear when it drafted the statute and the judiciary should not defer to the agency's interpretation at all, or Congress was not clear and the judiciary should defer completely to an agency's reasonable interpretation.

Shortly after the case was decided, however, debate arose regarding the nature of the inquiry at the first step. The debate centered around two questions. First, was step one a search for congressional intent or textual clarity: meaning, was the search at step one to be broad and include a review of legislative history, statutory purpose, and other sources of statutory meaning, or was it to be narrow and focus primarily, if not exclusively, on the text? *Chevron* was indecisive on this question. When the Court created its two-step approach, the Court did not explain clearly how ambiguity should be resolved at step one. Justice Stevens described this step as a search for congressional intent that "employ[s] traditional tools of statutory construction," but he did not explain which tools of statutory construction were appropriate and "traditional." *Id.* at 843 n.9. Moreover, the opinion contained language suggesting that only the text was relevant at step one: "[If] the statute is silent or ambiguous with respect to the specific issue, the question for the court is whether the agency's answer is based on a permissible construction of the statute." *Id.* at 843. Yet the Court approached the interpretive process in a decidedly non-textualist way, starting with the legislative history, then turning to the text. *Id.* at 851.

As you should know by now, the appropriate tools and approaches have changed throughout history as different theories of statutory interpretation have held favor. Because Justice Stevens used an intentionalist approach in *Chevron* and because he referenced the traditional tools of statutory construction, it seemed that he anticipated step one to be intentionalist. Indeed, many of the justices on the bench when *Chevron* was decided were intentionalists or, at least, were willing to look at legislative history and purpose to discern meaning.

Thus, *Chevron* streamlined the analysis into two straightforward steps: first, a court should look to see if Congress had decided the issue; if not, the court should defer to the agency's interpretation so long as it was reasonable. But the Court soon chipped away at *Chevron*'s broad deference by limiting its application.

c. Statutory Interpretation: Standards of Review Post-Chevron

When the Court decided *Chevron*, it appeared to streamline the analysis into two straightforward steps: first, a court looked to see if Congress had an intent as to the specific issue before the court; if not, the court adopted the agency's interpretation so long as it was reasonable. But *Chevron* does not apply to every agency interpretation. Before a court can apply *Chevron*, the court must make sure that the interpretation is one deserving of *Chevron*. Sometimes *Chevron* is not the correct standard of review. In these next sections, you will learn that *Chevron* does not apply unless an agency interprets a statute that the agency administers. Moreover, assuming an agency interprets a statute that the agency administers, *Chevron* still may not apply (1) when an agency interprets a statute using a process that does not involve force of law procedures, (2) when the issue is simply too important to the national landscape to trust to agency resolution, or (3) when an agency interprets a statute differently from a preexisting court interpretation.

i. Choosing between *Chevron* & *Skidmore*

Chevron applies only when the agency interprets a statute it administers using force of law procedures. This analysis is exceedingly complex. But if you break the analysis into its sub-questions, the analysis is at least approachable. Here are the sub-questions: (1) *What* did the agency interpret? (2) *Which* agency did the interpreting? (3) *How* did the agency do its interpreting? And (4) *Can* this agency interpret the statute? Below, we explore each question in more detail.

1. WHAT DID THE AGENCY INTERPRET?

Chevron analysis is applicable only when an agency interprets a specific type of legal text. To illustrate, *Chevron* does not apply when agencies interpret the Federal Constitution, court opinions, and legal instruments such as contracts. Similarly, *Chevron* does not apply when agencies interpret other agencies' regulations. Indeed, in these situations, courts do not defer at all.

When an agency interprets its own regulation, a different form of deference may apply: *Auer* deference, or *Seminole Rock* deference. The former term refers to the Supreme Court case of *Auer v. Robbins*, 519 U.S. 452 (1997), which came after *Chevron* and confirmed that *Seminole Rock* deference had survived *Chevron*. *Id*. at 461–63. In *Bowles v. Seminole Rock & Sand Co*., the Supreme Court held that an agency's interpretation of its own ambiguous regulation was entitled to "controlling weight unless [the interpretation was] plainly erroneous or inconsistent with the regulation." 325 U.S. 410, 414 (1945). The Court reasoned that when Congress delegates authority to promulgate regulations, it also delegates authority to interpret those regulations; such power is a necessary corollary to the former. Because judicial deference is based on congressional intent to delegate, the agency's interpretation must be authoritative and official, not ad hoc. *Kisor v. Wilkie*, 2019 WL 2605554, at *9 (June 26, 2019). Further, the agency's interpretation must reflect a "fair and considered judgment" and must be based on its substantive expertise. *Id*. (internal quotations omitted). Courts should not defer to agency interpretations that are merely "convenient litigating position[s] or post hoc rationalizatio[ns] advanced to defend past agency action against attack." *Id*. (internal quotations omitted).

> Under *Auer*, courts defer to an agency's interpretation of its own regulation unless the interpretation is "plainly wrong."

Moreover, courts should not defer under *Auer* when agencies merely parrot statutory language in their regulation and then, in a later regulation, claim they are interpreting the first parroting regulation rather than the statute. Courts should not defer because the agency is actually interpreting the statute, rather than the regulation. *Gonzales v. Oregon*, 546 U.S. 243, 257 (2006) (refusing to defer to the Attorney General's interpretive rule that physician-assisted suicide was not a legitimate medical purpose for prescribing medication when the regulation merely paraphrased the language in the statute).

Auer deference has been criticized on a number of grounds. First, separation of powers: to separate lawmaking from law interpreting, we should prevent the writer of a law from being the person who determines that law's meaning. Pursuant to separation of powers, Congress cannot determine the final meaning of a statute; that task was given to the courts. However, granting such deference to an agency's interpretation of its own regulations allows agencies to function both as law writers and law interpreters. In addition, too much deference to agency interpretations may limit public participation in new policy development. Agencies are not required to use notice-and-comment procedures when issuing interpretative rules. 5 U.S.C. § 553(b)(3)(A). Former Justice Scalia and Justices Thomas and Alito seem to have embraced these concerns, even though Justice Scalia wrote the *Auer* opinion. *See, e.g.*, *Perez v. Mortgage Bankers Ass'n*, 135 S. Ct. 1199, 1212 (2015) (Scalia, J. concurring) (stating that *Auer* deference should be jettisoned altogether as inconsistent with separation of powers).

Although legal challenges to *Auer* are percolating up though the lower courts, for now, *Auer* remains good law. Indeed, in *Kisor*, the Supreme Court refused to overrule *Auer* despite widespread anticipation of just this outcome. Instead, the Court confirmed that courts should defer to an agency's reasonable interpretation of its own *genuinely ambiguous* regulation after the court first exhausts all the "'traditional tools' of construction." 2019 WL 2605554, at *8 (quoting *Chevron U.S.A. Inc. v. Natural Resources Defense Council, Inc.*, 467 U.S. 837, 843, n.9 (1984)). When "genuine ambiguity" remains, the court should defer so long as the agency's interpretation is reasonable. *Id.* More on this two-step approach in a moment.

In summary, *Chevron* applies only when an agency (1) *interprets a statute.*

2. WHICH AGENCY INTERPRETED THE STATUTE?

But it is not enough that an agency interprets the correct type of legal text, a statute. *Chevron* applies only when the agency that interprets the statute "administers" that statute. While the Court has never clearly articulated what it means to "administer" a statute, lower court cases that have addressed this issue suggest that agencies administer a statute when they have a special and unique responsibility for that statute. *See, e.g., Wagner Seed Co. v. Bush*, 946 F.2d 918, 925–26 (D.C. Cir. 1991) (Williams, J., dissenting) (arguing that the Environmental Protection Agency did not administer the reimbursement provisions of the Superfund Amendments and Reauthorization Act of 1986). Moreover, when more than one agency administers a statute, *Chevron* is generally inappropriate. *See Lawson v. FMR LLC*, 571 U.S. 429, 477 (2014) (Sotomayor, J., dissenting) (stating that "if any agency has the authority to resolve ambiguities in § 1514A with the force of law, it is the SEC, not the Department of Labor."); *Rapaport v. U.S. Dep't of the Treasury*, 59 F.3d 212, 216–17 (D.C. Cir. 1995) (declining to apply *Chevron* where the agency shared responsibility for the administration of the statute with another agency); *Illinois Nat'l Guard v. Fed. Labor Relations Auth.*, 854 F.2d 1396, 1400 (D.C. Cir. 1988) (declining to apply *Chevron* deference); *cf. CF Indus., Inc. v. FERC*, 925 F.2d 476, 478 n.1 (D.C. Cir. 1991) (stating in a footnote that there "might well be a compelling case to afford deference if it were necessary for decision [where] both agencies agree as to which of them has exclusive jurisdiction.").

For example, although multiple agencies interpret the Internal Revenue Code, it is generally only the Department of Treasury that is authorized to administer tax statutes; thus, only the Treasury should receive *Chevron* deference for interpretations of such statutes. *See, e.g., Mayo Found. for Med. Educ. & Research v. United States*, 562 U.S. 44, 55 (2011) (applying *Chevron* deference to review the Department of Treasury's interpretation of a tax statute). Note, however, that some statutes in the tax code are not just tax statutes. *See, e.g.,* Affordable Care Act Patient Protection and Affordable Care Act, Pub. L. No. 111-148, 124 Stat. 119 (2010). What then?

Agencies also must interpret generally applicable statutes, such as the Administrative Procedure Act (5 U.S.C. § 500 *et seq.*), the Regulatory Flexibility Act (5 U.S.C. §§ 601–12), and the Freedom of Information Act. (5 U.S.C. § 552). For such generally applicable statutes, no agency's interpretation is entitled to *Chevron* deference. *See, e.g., Association of Am. Physicians & Surgeons, Inc. v. Clinton*, 997 F.2d 898, 913 (D.C. Cir. 1993) (interpreting the Federal Advisory Committee Act *de novo*); *FLRA v. U.S. Dep't of Treasury*, 884 F.2d 1446, 1451 (D.C. Cir. 1989) (refusing to apply *Chevron* to the Federal Labor Relation Authority's interpretation of the Freedom of Information Act or the Privacy Act because "[the agency] is not charged with a special duty to interpret [these statutes]"); *Reporters Comm. for Freedom of the Press v. U.S. Dep't of Justice*, 816 F.2d 730, 734 (D.C. Cir. 1987) (stating that no deference would be given to an agency's interpretation of the Freedom of Information Act because "it applies to all government agencies, and thus no one executive branch entity is entrusted with its primary interpretation"), *rev'd on other grounds,* 489 U.S. 749 (1989).

In summary, *Chevron* applies only when an agency (1) interprets a statute (2) *that the agency administers.*

3. How Did the Agency Interpret the Statute?

But it is not enough that an agency interpret a statute that it administers. As you have learned, agencies act in a variety of ways. Some of these ways require more procedural formality and deliberation than others.

For example, an agency might interpret a statute as part of a notice-and-comment rulemaking process, like the EPA did in *Chevron.* Also, an agency might interpret a statute during a formal adjudication. Or, an agency might interpret a statute when drafting an internal policy manual or when writing a letter to a regulated entity. *See, e.g., Christensen v. Harris County*, 529 U.S. 576, 580–81, 586–89 (2000) (interpreting a statute in response to a letter inquiry from the county); *see also United States v. Mead Corp.*, 533 U.S. 218, 221–27 (2001) (interpreting a tariff classification ruling).

For formal rulemaking, formal adjudication, and notice-and-comment rulemaking, Congress has given the agency the authority to act with the force of law, and the agency has used that authority to act. If Congress has given the agency the authority to take action of that significance, Congress likely intended that agency legal interpretations should be respected by the courts. In contrast, for non-legislative rulemaking, Congress has not given the agency the authority to act with the force of law.

Moreover, formal rulemaking, formal adjudication, and notice-and-comment rulemaking typically involve more procedural protections and are more deliberative than informal adjudication and non-legislative rulemaking. If one purpose of judicial review is to cure procedural shortfalls that limit neutral and fair decision-making, limiting *Chevron*'s applicability to more formal processes make sense. If an agency chooses to make a determination informally where the protections of neutral and fair decision-making are limited, then a more intensive judicial review standard would seem appropriate. If instead the agency has followed a more formal procedure, one that facilitates neutral and fair decision-making, then there should be less need for intensive judicial review. Deference is appropriate.

In *Chevron*, the Supreme Court did not indicate, expressly or implicitly, whether the deliberateness of the agency's procedures affected the applicability of the two-step analysis. Before the Court decided *Chevron*, however, the Court factored the deliberative nature of the agency's interpretive process into the analysis. Under *Skidmore*'s power-to-persuade test, interpretations that were made through a more deliberative process, such as notice-and-comment rulemaking, were considered more persuasive than interpretations made through a less deliberative process, such as non-legislative rulemaking.

Immediately after the Court decided *Chevron*, the Court did not distinguish between deliberative agency decision-making and non-deliberative agency decision-making. Rather, the Court applied its two-step analysis to all types of agency interpretations, regardless of the procedure involved. So, for example, in *Reno v. Koray*, 515 U.S. 50, 61 (1995), the Court held that *Chevron* should apply to an interpretation contained in an agency's internal guideline, a non-legislative rule. And in *NationsBank of North Carolina. v. Variable Annuity Life Insurance Co.*, 513 U.S. 251, 256–57, 263 (1995), the Court applied *Chevron* to an agency's decision to grant an entity's application to act as an agent and sell annuities, an informal adjudication. *See also National R.R. Passenger Corp. v. Boston & Me. Corp.*, 503 U.S. 407, 417 (1992) (applying *Chevron*'s framework to an agency's interpretation made informally); *Federal Deposit Ins. Corp. v. Philadelphia Gear Corp.*, 476 U.S. 426, 439 (1986) (suggesting that *Chevron* should apply to an agency's longstanding "practice and belief"). But with time, the type of procedure gained importance.

Beginning in 2000, the Supreme Court decided a trilogy of cases that limited *Chevron*'s application based on the procedures the agency used to make the interpretation. In *Christensen*, 529 U.S. at 576, *Mead Corp.*, 533 U.S. at 218, and *Barnhart v. Walton*, 535 U.S. 212 (2002), the Court substantially checked *Chevron*'s applicability based, in part, upon the type of procedure the agency used to reach the interpretation being challenged. Let's start with *Christensen*.

In *Christensen*, the Supreme Court began its retreat from a *Chevron*-only deference world. At issue in *Christensen* was whether the United States Department of Labor's Wage and Hour Division (the Division) should receive *Chevron* deference for an interpretation the agency expressed in an opinion letter. 529 U.S. at 587. The defendant in the case, Harris County, had been concerned about the fiscal consequences of having to pay its employees for accrued but unused compensatory time. *Id.* at 578. For this reason, the County wrote to the Division and asked whether the County could require its employees to take, rather than continue to accrue, their unused compensatory time. *Id.* at 580–81. Responding by letter, the Division told the County that absent an employment agreement to the contrary, the Fair Labor Standards Act of 1938 ("FLSA") prohibited an employer from requiring employees to use accrued compensatory time. *Id.* at 581. The County ignored the letter and forbade its employees from accumulating more compensatory time than it deemed reasonable. *Id.* The employees sued, arguing that the County's policy violated FLSA. *Id.*

The issue for the Supreme Court was whether the agency's interpretation of FLSA, which was contained in an informal opinion letter, was entitled to *Chevron* deference. *Id.* at 586–87. For the first time since *Chevron* had been decided, the Court directly addressed whether the agency process mattered in the deference analysis; in other words, did a different deference standard apply when an agency acted with less deliberation and process.

For the first time, the majority found the level of process to be determinative. The majority reasoned that the agency's opinion letter was not entitled to *Chevron* deference because it lacked the "force of law." *Id.* at 587. Agency interpretations have the "force of law" when "Congress has delegated legislative power to the agency and ... the agency ... exercise[d] that power in promulgating the rule." *American Mining Cong. v. Mine Safety & Health Admin.*, 995 F.2d 1106, 1109 (D.C. Cir. 1993) (defining "force of law"). In other words:

> An interpretation will have the force of law when the agency has exercised delegated power, as to both subject matter and format, reflecting congressional intent that such an interpretation is to bind. "Force of law" ... merely connotes the binding effect given the kinds of agency interpretations that Congress through its delegations *intends* to bind the courts. And that binding effect (force of law) means simply that the courts may not subject the interpretations to independent judicial review, but rather must accept them subject only to limited review for reasonableness and consistency with the statute. Thus, an interpretation carrying the force of law gets only limited review because by definition it is covered by delegation that contemplates only limited review.

Robert A. Anthony, *Which Agency Interpretations Should Bind Citizens and the Courts?*, 7 YALE J. ON REG. 1, 39 (1990) (footnotes omitted).

According to *Christensen*, procedurally prescribed actions, such as formal adjudication and notice-and-comment rulemaking, have the "force of law," while less procedurally prescribed actions, such as "opinion letters ... policy statements, agency manuals, and enforcement guidelines ... lack the force of law." *Christensen*, 529 U.S. at 587. The Court explained that "interpretations contained in [informal] formats such as opinion letters are 'entitled to respect' under our decision in *Skidmore...*, but only to the extent that those interpretations have the 'power to persuade.'" *Id.* at 587 (citation omitted).

Thus, *Christensen* seemingly divided agency interpretations into two well-defined categories: those subject to *Chevron* analysis—the "force of law" category—and those subject to *Skidmore* analysis—the no-"force of law" category. This was a simple, albeit, formalistic test: courts should apply *Chevron* deference to an agency's interpretation of a statute when an agency used relatively formal procedures (including formal adjudication, formal rulemaking, and notice-and-comment rulemaking), and courts should apply *Skidmore* deference when an agency used less formal procedures (including issuing interpretive rules, policy statements, and ruling letters). This test would have been relatively simple for judges to apply: simply look to the agency action and apply the appropriate analysis, *Chevron* or *Skidmore*.

> Under **Christensen's** "force of law" test, an agency's interpretation is entitled to **Chevron** deference when arrived at through a more procedurally prescribed process and to **Skidmore** deference when arrived at through a less procedurally prescribed process.

Alas, nothing remains so simple, and the Court refined *Christensen*'s simple force of law test a year later in *Mead Corp.*, 533 U.S. at 218. The issue in *Mead* was whether the U.S. Customs Service's ("Customs") informal ruling letters (which do not go through legislative rulemaking procedures) were entitled to *Chevron* or *Skidmore* analysis. *Id.* at 221. The plaintiff imported day planners. Although Customs had classified the planners as duty-free "day planners" for several years, it changed its interpretation and issued a ruling letter classifying them as "bound diaries." *Id.* at 225. Importantly, bound diaries were subject to tariff, while day planners were not. The letters described the goods being imported and identified the amount of tariff to be paid. *Id.* at 223. Customs issued ruling letters without much procedure, did not publish them, and indicated they were non-binding.

The majority held that *Skidmore* rather than *Chevron* analysis was appropriate, which should not be surprising or confusing given the absence of any formalized procedures. *Id.* at 227. In reaching its holding, the majority reaffirmed *Christensen*'s holding by explaining that *Chevron* applies when an agency acts with force of law, which occurs "when it appears that Congress delegated authority to the agency generally to make rules carrying the force of law and that the agency interpretation claiming deference was promulgated in the exercise of that authority." *Id.* at 226–27. Had the Court stopped at this point, it would not even warrant a footnote. Unfortunately, the Court did not stop at this point.

The Court added a wrinkle to *Christensen*'s force of law test by saying that "[d]elegation of such authority may be shown in a variety of ways, as by an agency's power to engage in adjudication or notice-and-comment rulemaking, *or by some other indication of a comparable congressional intent.*" *Id.* at 227 (emphasis added). The Court added, "[A]s significant as notice-and-comment is in pointing to *Chevron* authority, the want of that procedure here does not decide the case, for we have sometimes found reasons for *Chevron* deference even when no such administrative formality was required and none was afforded." *Id.* at 231 (citing *NationsBank of N.C.,* 513 U.S. at 256–57, 263). The Court did not explain what these reasons were but did find that there were no such reasons in *Mead* because (1) the face of the statute gave no indication that Congress intended to delegate authority to Customs to issue classification rulings with the force of law, (2) Customs regarded the classification decisions as conclusive only between itself and the importer to whom it was issued, and (3) forty-six different Customs' offices issued 10,000 to 15,000 classifications each year. *Id.* at 233. In other words, there were simply too many classification rulings each year for Customs to be able to carefully consider the issue. Hence, the Court held that *Skidmore,* not *Chevron,* was appropriate.

Prior to *Mead,* the test was bright-lined: *Chevron* applied when the agency acted with "administrative formality," and *Skidmore* applied when the agency acted with less administrative formality. Now, the bright line was blurring. Using administrative formality provided the agency with a *Chevron* safe harbor. In other words, when an agency used one of the three procedures identified above to interpret a statute, *Chevron* analysis applied. Now, however, even when an agency used one of the other processes described above, *Chevron* analysis might still apply. But we did not know when or why. The Court in *Mead* simply stated, without elaborating, that some agency actions might qualify for *Chevron* analysis even though the agency used less formal procedures. Exactly what types of "other indications" would be sufficient to trigger *Chevron* analysis was not readily apparent from this case alone. However, in the following year, Justice Breyer tried to explain what such "other indications" were.

In *Barnhart,* the Social Security Administration (SSA) determined that the plaintiff, who was unable to work for eleven months, was not eligible for disability benefits. 535 U.S. at 215. The SSA had enacted a regulation, using notice-and-comment procedures (apparently in response to the pending litigation), which stated that a claimant was not disabled if that claimant could engage in "substantial gainful activity." *Id.* at 214. In doing so, the SSA "codified" an existing, non-legislative rule. In addition to codifying the non-legislative rule, the SSA subsequently interpreted this new regulation to mean that the claimant was not disabled if "within 12 months after the onset of an impairment ... the impairment no longer prevent[ed] substantial gainful activity." *Id.* at 217 (quoting 65 Fed. Reg. 42,772 (2000)). All parties agreed that the second regulation, as an interpretation of the new regulation, was entitled to *Auer* deference. *Id.* at 217. However, the parties disagreed about whether the new regulation governed because it was enacted during and in response to the litigation or whether the non-legislative rule governed because it existed prior to the litigation. *Id.* at 221–23. If the new regulation governed, *Chevron* analysis would be the appropriate standard of review under *Mead* and *Christensen.* If the non-legislative rule governed, likely *Skidmore* analysis would be the appropriate standard of review.

Writing for the majority, Justice Breyer held that the new regulation controlled despite its timing and thus *Chevron* analysis was appropriate. *Id.* at 217. Given the level of procedure that was used (notice-and-comment rulemaking), that result should not be surprising. But once again, Justice Breyer did not stop when he should have; instead, he rejected the "force of law" formality dichotomy by saying that "the fact that the [SSA] previously reached its interpretation through means less formal than 'notice and comment' rulemaking does not automatically deprive that interpretation of the judicial deference otherwise its due." *Id.* at 221. *Mead,* he said, had made clear that there was no bright-line deference dichotomy based on how the agency arrived at its interpretation. *Id.* Thus, Justice Breyer reaffirmed the dicta in *Mead,* stating that some interpretations contained in non-legislative rules might receive *Chevron* analysis.

Which agency interpretations deserve *Chevron,* rather than *Skidmore,* analysis depends on Congress. Justice Breyer explained that the *Skidmore* and *Chevron* cases articulated different rationales for judicial deference to agency interpretations. In *Skidmore,* the Court reasoned that deference was appropriate because of agency expertise, while in *Chevron,* the Court reasoned that deference was appropriate because of implicit congressional delegation. Applying this understanding in *Barnhart,* Justice Breyer explained that *Chevron* applies whenever Congress intended the courts to defer to an agency's interpretation. *Id.* at 220–22. To determine whether Congress intended for courts to defer, a court must consider the following five factors: (1) the interstitial nature of the legal question, (2) the relevance of the agency's expertise, (3) the importance of the question to administration of the statute, (4) the complexity of the statutory scheme, and (5) the careful consideration the agency had given the question over a long period of time. *Id.* at 222.

While it was helpful that he provided factors for a court to consider in deciding which standard of review to apply, the factors meld elements from both *Skidmore* (agency expertise and careful consideration) and *Chevron* (implied delegation as shown by the interstitial nature of the legal question and the importance of the question to the administration of the statute), while adding an entirely new consideration: the complexity of the statutory scheme. In short, the test is exceedingly ineffective. Indeed, since *Barnhart* was decided, the Supreme Court has not applied *Chevron* analysis to an agency interpretation that was made without force of law procedures. However, some lower courts have done so. *Compare Schuetz v. Banc One Mortg. Corp.*, 292 F.3d 1004, 1011–13 (9th Cir. 2002) (holding that *Chevron* applied to a HUD Statement of Policy), *and Kruse v. Wells Fargo Home Mortg., Inc.*, 383 F.3d 49, 61 (2d Cir. 2004) (same), *with Krzalic v. Republic Title Co.*, 314 F.3d 875, 879 (7th Cir. 2002) (holding that *Chevron* did not apply to an HUD Statement of Policy).

Whether *Chevron* or *Skidmore* analysis is appropriate is exceedingly complex. It has become colloquially known as either *Chevron* Step Zero or the *Mead* Mess. Cass R. Sunstein, Chevron *Step Zero*, 92 VA. L. REV. 187, 211 (2006); Lisa Bressman, *How* Mead *Has Muddled Judicial Review of Agency Action*, 58 VAND. L. REV. 1443 (2005) (coining the phrase "Mead Mess"). Professor Sunstein put it bluntly: "the power to act with the force of law is taken as a sufficient, even if not necessary condition for *Chevron* deference." Sunstein, *supra* at 224. Thus, *Chevron* always applies when Congress vests an agency with rulemaking or formal adjudication authority *and* the agency uses that authority to promulgate its interpretation. Always. *City of Arlington v. FCC*, 569 U.S. 290, 306 (2013). But the reverse cannot be said—that *Skidmore* always applies when the agency does not use that authority to promulgate its interpretation.

The best that can be said at this point is that the appropriate standard of review depends on congressional intent. If Congress intends that an agency receive judicial deference for interpretations, then courts should apply *Chevron* regardless of how the agency reached its interpretation. In these situations, *Chevron* is appropriate because Congress intended for the agencies, not the courts, to develop this area of law. In contrast, if Congress does not so intend, then the agency is deserving of only *Skidmore* at best. In this situation, Congress intended the courts to be the final interpreters, but an agency's expertise can inform a court's decision.

There is no doubt that Justice Scalia said it best. He criticized the Court's *Mead* decision as "one of the most significant opinions ever rendered by the Court dealing with the judicial review of administrative action ... and almost uniformly bad." *Mead*, 533 U.S. at 261 (Scalia, J., dissenting).

In summary, *Chevron* applies only when an agency (1) interprets a statute (2) that the agency administers (3) *while using force of law procedures.*

4. CAN THE AGENCY INTERPRET THE STATUTE?

However, it is not enough that an agency interprets a statute the agency administers while using force of law procedures. In the midst of deciding the *Christensen/Mead/Barnhart* trilogy, the Supreme Court issued more cases in this area that only added to the complexity. This further *Chevron* carve-out is known as the *major questions doctrine.*

In *Chevron*, the Court rationalized deference to an agency's interpretation by suggesting that when Congress enacts statutes with gaps and ambiguities, Congress *implicitly* intends to delegate interpretive authority to the agency. But in two cases, *FDA v. Brown & Williamson Tobacco Corp.*, 529 U.S. 120 (2000), and *King v. Burwell*, 135 S. Ct. 2480 (2015), the Court rejected, or at least narrowed, this rationale. In each of these cases, the Court reasoned that in some instances, despite statutory ambiguity, Congress did not intend to delegate rulemaking authority to the agency at all. As the Court explained:

> Deference under *Chevron* to an agency's construction of a statute that it administers is premised on the theory that a statute's ambiguity constitutes an implicit delegation from Congress to the agency to fill in the statutory gaps. In extraordinary cases, however, there may be reason to hesitate before concluding that Congress has intended such an implicit delegation.

Brown & Williamson, 529 U.S. at 159 (internal citations omitted). Those "extraordinary cases" comprise the court's important question doctrine: some issues are so important to the national economy that Congress could not have intended to delegate interpretive authority to a mere agency.

For example, in *Brown & Williamson*, the majority rejected the Food and Drug Administration's (FDA) decision to regulate tobacco. *Id.* at 161. The relevant statute authorized the FDA the authority to regulate "drugs" and "devices." *Id.* at 126 (citing 21 U.S.C. § 321(g)–(h)). The FDA had known for years that tobacco was deadly but chose not to regulate tobacco, fearing that Congress would reject its action. The tobacco companies had, and still have, an extremely powerful lobby in Washington. Presidents Reagan and Bush would not have supported the FDA's attempt to regulate tobacco. However, in 1993, Bill Clinton assumed the office of president. President Clinton was anti-tobacco. He appointed Dr. David Kessler to head the FDA and indicated a willingness to support the FDA's attempt to regulate tobacco. Armed with Clinton's support, the FDA interpreted cigarettes and tobacco products to be "drugs." In response, the tobacco companies sued.

Under the relevant statute, the FDA was authorized to regulate "drugs," "devices," and "combination products." *Id.* at 126 (citing §21 U.S.C. §321(g)–(h)). The statute defined these terms as "articles ... intended to affect the structure or any function of the body." *Id.* (quoting 21 U.S.C. §321 (g)(1)(C)). The FDA interpreted this language as allowing it to regulate tobacco and cigarettes.

Despite the fact that the language of the statute alone was broad enough to support the agency's interpretation, the majority concluded, after applying *Chevron*'s first step "that Congress ha[d] directly spoken to the issue here and precluded the FDA's jurisdiction to regulate tobacco products." *Id.* at 133. The majority supported its holding by noting that Congress had (1) created a distinct regulatory scheme for tobacco products in subsequent legislation, (2) squarely rejected proposals to give the FDA jurisdiction over tobacco, and (3) acted repeatedly to preclude other agencies from exercising authority in this area. *Id.* at 159–60. The majority suggested that this was "hardly an ordinary case," because of the importance of the tobacco industry to the American economy and Congress's oversight of this area. *Id.* at 159. Hence, while Congress may not have spoken to the precise issue when enacting the relevant statute, Congress had subsequently spoken broadly enough on related questions to prevent the agency from acting at all. *Id.* at 159–60.

The Court concluded that regulation of tobacco was too important for the national economy for Congress to have delegated its resolution to the FDA. *Id.* at 160. Thus, the Court resolved this case at *Chevron*'s first step and never reached its second. Usually the Court applies *Chevron*'s first step, or *de novo* review, to these cases; in at least one case, the Court applied *Skidmore* analysis rather than *Chevron. See e.g., Gonzales,* 546 U.S. at 267 (applying *Skidmore* analysis rather than *Chevron* because "[t]he idea that Congress gave [the Attorney General] such broad and unusual authority through an implicit delegation in the [Controlled Substances Act] registration provision is not sustainable.").

The Supreme Court would return to this "too important for the national economy" limitation on agency delegation fifteen years later in *King,* 135 S. Ct. at 2489. At issue in this case was whether language in the Affordable Care Act, "exchange established by the State," meant "exchange established by the

State" only or whether it also included exchanges established by the Federal Government. *Id.* at 2487. The Department of the Treasury issued a regulation using notice-and-comment procedures adopting the latter interpretation. *Id.* at 2487–88. Because the Treasury used force of law procedures, under *Christensen/Mead/Barnhart, Chevron* analysis should have applied. Had the Court applied *Chevron*, the majority likely would have found that the text pointed in one direction, while the statutory purpose pointed in another. Hence, Congress did not speak directly to the precise issue before the Court. Assuming the Court then reached step two, the Court should have found the Treasury's interpretation was reasonable given the conflict between the text and the statutory purpose, although this is a closer question.

But the Court refused to apply *Chevron* analysis at all. *Id.* at 2488–89. Instead, the majority reasoned that universal health care was simply too important for Congress to have intended to delegate to the Treasury without saying so clearly. *Id.* The Court refused to apply *Chevron* at all. Instead, the Court applied *de novo* review and agreed with the Treasury's interpretation. *Id.* at 2495–96. As you might imagine with such clear text, former Justice Scalia dissented vociferously, calling the majority's opinion "absurd" and noting that "the Court's 21 pages of explanation make it no less so." *Id.* at 2496 (Scalia, J., dissenting).

In these cases, the Supreme Court significantly limited the implied-delegation rationale. The Court held that Congress did not implicitly delegate interpretive power to the agency despite statutory ambiguity. The holdings in these cases are at odds with *Chevron*'s implicit-delegation rationale, which states that "[d]eference under *Chevron* to an agency's construction of a statute that it administers is premised on the theory that a statute's ambiguity constitutes an implicit delegation from Congress to the agency to fill in the statutory gaps." *Brown & Williamson*, 529 U.S. at 159. Notably, in none of the applicable statutes did Congress expressly say that it was not delegating to the agency. Rather, the Court inferred Congress's intent not to delegate based on other factors, including the existence of other legislation (*Brown & Williamson*) and the importance of the issue to the national economy (*Brown & Williamson* and *Burwell*).

> Under ***Brown & Williamson*** and ***Burwell***, when an issue is too important for Congress to delegate to an agency without a clear statement to that effect, then the agency's interpretation is entitled to ***de novo*** review.

In summary, *Chevron* applies only when an agency (1) interprets a statute (2) that the agency administers (3) while using force of law procedures, (4) *so long as Congress intended to delegate interpretive power to the agency.* You have now mastered *Chevron* step zero and the major questions doctrines.

ii. Applying *Chevron* Step Zero

At this point, you may well be wondering how to apply these doctrines. Let me suggest the following process. First, ask whether the agency is interpreting a statute and whether the agency has the sole or primary authority to administer that statute. If the agency is interpreting its own regulation, *Auer* analysis may be appropriate; if the agency is interpreting anything else, no deference is due.

Second, ask whether Congress intended to delegate the specific issue to the agency at all (the major questions doctrine). If the issue is one of such major importance to the national economy that Congress would not have intended to delegate authority, then the agency likely has no power to interpret the statute. To date, tobacco, health care, and assisted suicide are the only examples of issues too important to the national economy. However, if the issue you are resolving is similar to one of these three, then look for a clear statement in the enabling act delegating interpretive power to the agency. Such a finding will be rare. Assuming no such statement, *de novo* review is appropriate. This step is based on *Brown & Williamson*'s and *Burwell*'s holdings.

Third, if Congress intended to delegate interpretive authority to an agency, you should determine whether Congress intended courts to defer to that particular agency's interpretation. To do so, look first to the type of agency action at issue; in other words, look to see if the agency acted with force of law, a safe harbor for *Chevron* analysis. If the agency interpreted the statute during notice-and-comment rulemaking, formal rulemaking, or formal adjudication, then *Chevron* analysis would be appropriate. This step is based on *Mead*'s and *Christensen*'s holdings.

Fourth, determine whether *Chevron* analysis is appropriate even though force of law procedures were not used. To do so, determine whether Congress intended courts to defer to agency interpretations by applying the *Barnhart* factors. Those factors include the following: (1) the interstitial nature of the legal question, (2) the relevance of the agency's expertise, (3) the importance of the question to administration of the statute, (4) the complexity of the statutory scheme, and (5) the careful consideration the agency has given the question over a long period of time. If these factors suggest that Congress did not intend for courts to defer, then *Chevron* analysis is inapplicable. If *Chevron* analysis is inapplicable, then you should apply *Skidmore* analysis. This step is based on the holdings from *Mead* and *Barnhart*. But if the *Barnhart* factors suggest that Congress did intend for the courts to defer, you should apply *Chevron* analysis.

Fifth, apply the standard of review that you just determined was appropriate. If you determined at step three or four that *Chevron* analysis should apply, then, using traditional tools of statutory interpretation, ask whether Congress has spoken to the precise issue before the court. This is *Chevron*'s first step. If Congress has so spoken, then your analysis is complete, for Congress has the authority to interpret its own statutes when it so chooses. But if Congress has not directly spoken to the precise issue or if Congress has left a gap or impliedly delegated to the agency then proceed to *Chevron*'s second step: ask whether the agency's interpretation is reasonable in light of the underlying statute. Compare the agency's interpretation with the language of the statute, the legislative history, and the purpose of the statute. If the agency's interpretation is unreasonable when compared to these sources, then no deference is due. If the agency's interpretation is reasonable, then full deference is due. Understandably, some overlap between the analyses at step one and step two will result. Consider whether to apply arbitrary and capricious review in addition to, or instead of, reasonableness review. Arbitrary and capricious review is explained later in this chapter.

If, instead, you determined at step four that *Skidmore* analysis should apply, then apply *Skidmore*'s power-to-persuade test to the agency's interpretation. An agency's interpretation is entitled to deference based on the following factors: (1) the consistency in the agency interpretation over time; (2) the thoroughness of the agency's consideration; and (3) the soundness of the agency's reasoning. Deference under this standard is earned, not automatic.

Understanding the difference between deference earned under *Chevron* and *Skidmore* is not always so easy. However, Professor Gary Lawson offered a way of thinking of the difference, which he defines as the difference between legal deference and epistemological deference. Gary Lawson, *Mostly Unconstitutional: The Case Against Precedent Revisited*, 5 AVE MARIA L. REV. 1, 2–10 (2007). Legal deference is deference earned solely based on the identity of the interpreter and the method of interpretation. *Id.* at 9. For example, lower courts must defer to interpretations of higher courts within the same jurisdiction but need not defer to interpretations from courts in other jurisdictions. The decision of whether to defer depends entirely on the identity of the interpreter. *Chevron* deference is a form of legal deference: agencies earn deference simply because they are agencies interpreting statutes using a particular process.

In contrast, epistemological deference is deference earned because of the persuasiveness of the reasoning. *Id.* at 10. Courts in neighboring jurisdictions need not follow each other's opinions but can choose to do so because the reasoning is persuasive. The decision of whether to defer depends entirely on the persuasiveness of the reasoning; the identity of the interpreter is irrelevant. *Skidmore* deference is a form of epistemological deference; agencies earn deference based on the soundness of their reasoning, not because they are agencies interpreting statutes.

Not all academic administrative law experts would agree that this simplified, five-step process completely or even accurately captures the analysis. Rightly, they would note that the interaction of these cases is extremely complex and constantly changing. To illustrate, during listserv discussions, one scholar stated that the "force of law" phrase is one of the most confusing in administrative law. Another stated that *Mead* is not particularly coherent and raises tough issues regarding when *Chevron* should apply. These comments show that even the experts disagree on exactly how to understand and reconcile these cases. Unfortunately, *Chevron*'s application is a mess and may eventually lead to its demise.

iii. Agency Interpretations That Conflict with Judicial Interpretations

In the last section, we addressed what level of deference, if any, a court should give to an agency interpretation when there are no pre-existing judicial interpretations of the same statute. The next obvious question is: what if there is a prior judicial opinion? Should a court defer to an agency interpretation of a statute that varies from an existing judicial interpretation? Prior judicial interpretations exist when a court defers to an agency interpretation or interprets the meaning of a statutory provision because an agency has not yet interpreted it. The question is whether thereafter an agency is bound to follow this prior judicial interpretation or whether the agency is free to make its own interpretation. At issue is flexibility—the ability for an agency to adjust policy and statutory interpretations over time. On the one hand, flexibility is essential to effective operation regulation as technology and economics advance and administrative priorities change with time and with new administrations. If agencies were unable to alter their interpretations over time, flexibility would be significantly hindered, and agencies would be less effective at responding to changes. On the other hand, too much change can lead to unpredictability, uncertainty, and, potentially, unfairness. Similarly situated litigants expect the government to treat them similarly.

The Supreme Court addressed this issue in *National Cable & Telecommunications Ass'n v. Brand X Internet Services*, 545 U.S. 967 (2005). In that case, the Court chose flexibility over certainty by holding that, if a prior court had determined that a statute was clear under *Chevron*'s first step, then that judicial interpretation would bind the agency. *Id.* at 985. But if the court did not decide that the statute was clear under *Chevron*'s first step, then the prior interpretation would not bind the agency. *Id.* In other words, a prior judicial interpretation does not eliminate a pre-existing ambiguity. The prior interpretation merely reflects a determination that either there is no ambiguity or that there is ambiguity. If there is no ambiguity, then Congress has spoken and the agency, as well as the courts, must follow Congress's intent. But if there is ambiguity, then regardless of whether a court issues the first interpretation of an ambiguous statute or an agency does, the interpretation does not bind the agency.

This approach is intuitively appealing and seems to flow from *Chevron*'s analysis; however, judges are not always clear about whether an adopted interpretation rests on a finding that Congress was ambiguous at *Chevron*'s first step, especially for cases that predate *Chevron*. Justice Scalia eloquently summarized this point:

> In cases decided pre-*Brand X*, the Court had no inkling that it *must* utter the magic words "ambiguous" or "unambiguous" in order to (poof!) expand or abridge executive power, and (poof!) enable or disable administrative contradiction of the Supreme Court. Indeed, the Court was unaware of even the utility (much less the necessity) of making the ambiguous/nonambiguous determination in cases decided pre-*Chevron*, before that opinion made the so-called "Step 1" determination of ambiguity *vel non* a customary (though hardly mandatory) part of judicial-review analysis. For many of those earlier cases, therefore, it will be incredibly difficult to determine whether the decision purported to be giving meaning to an ambiguous, or rather an unambiguous, statute.

United States v. Home Concrete & Supply, 566 U.S. 478, 493–94 (2012) (Scalia, J., concurring in part).

In *Home Concrete*, the Court had to resolve the meaning of a tax statute. The statute allowed the IRS to assess a deficiency against a taxpayer within "3 years after the return was filed." *Id.* at 480 (quoting 26 U.S.C. § 6501(a). The statute further provided that the three-year period would be extended to six years when a taxpayer "omit[ed] from gross income an amount properly includible therein which is in excess of 25 percent of the amount of gross income stated in the return." *Id.* (quoting 26 U.S.C. §6501(e)(1)(A)). I realize your eyes may be rolling to the back of your head, but hang in there.

The question for the Court was "whether this latter provision applied (and extended the ordinary 3-year limitations period) when the taxpayer overstate[d] his basis in property that he had sold, thereby understating the gain that he received from its sale." *Id.* at 480 (emphasis omitted). Basis in property is generally the purchase price of an asset or its value. *Id.* at 481–82.

But the IRS was not writing on a clean slate. In an earlier case, the Court had held that taxpayer statements overstating the basis in property did not fall within the scope of the statute. *Colony, Inc. v. Commissioner*, 357 U.S. 28, 32 (1958). Despite *Colony*'s holding, the IRS enacted a regulation interpreting the relevant language in the statute to *include* basis misstatements. *Id.* at 487.

When challenged in court, the IRS argued that it was entitled to deference under *Chevron* for its contrary interpretation because the *Colony* Court had stated that the tax statute was "not unambiguous." *Id.* at 487–89. The IRS argued that the meaning of this double negative phrase was that the statute was ambiguous. The majority disagreed. It observed that *Colony* had been decided long before *Chevron* was decided. *Id.* Thus, the majority continued, the *Colony* Court was likely not thinking in first step/second step terms. *Id.* at 488. The majority pointed out that the *Colony* Court had said that the taxpayer had the better textual argument, had found that the legislative history supported the interpretation, had concluded that the government's interpretation would create a patent incongruity in the tax law, and had believed its interpretation to be in harmony with the 1954 Tax Code. *Id.* at 487–89. For the majority, these findings resolved any ambiguity at *Chevron*'s first step. These are all traditional tools of statutory interpretation.

Not surprisingly, Justice Scalia vehemently disagreed. Because the *Colony* Court had stated that the statute was "not unambiguous," Scalia argued that the majority could only reject the agency's later interpretation under *Brand X* if the interpretation were unreasonable under *Chevron*'s second step. *Id.* at 494 (Scalia, J. concurring). Calling for *Brand X*'s death, Justice Scalia lamented, "*Colony* said unambiguously that the text was ambiguous, and that should be an end of the matter .... Rather than making our judicial-review jurisprudence curiouser and curiouser, the Court should abandon the opinion that produces these contortions, *Brand X*." *Id.* at 496.

It looks like Justice Scalia got this case right. On July 31, 2015, Congress enacted H.R. 3236, Surface Transportation and Veterans Health Care Choice Improvement Act of 2015. Section 2005 of the Act amended 26 U.S.C. § 6501(e)(1), which is the exception to the three-year statute of limitations at issue in *Colony* and *Home Concrete*. The amendment provides: "An understatement of gross income by reason of an overstatement of unrecovered cost or other basis is an omission from gross income." In short, the amendment legislatively overruled both *Colony* and *Home Concrete & Supply*.

3. Standard of Review for Mixed Questions

The last sections described the complex analysis for determining the appropriate standard of review for pure legal questions: interpretations of statutes and regulations. This next section describes the standard of review applicable to mixed questions of law and fact. This section is substantially shorter for the simple reason that the standard is currently unclear. Some courts treat the question as a pure question of law, while others treat the question as one of fact. *See, e.g., O'Leary*, 340 U.S. at 507 (treating as a question of fact the issue of whether the death of a federal worker "arose out of and in the course of employment").

In one landmark case, the Supreme Court accepted an agency's resolution of a mixed question because it had "warrant in the record" and "a reasonable basis in the law." *NLRB v. Hearst Publications*, 322 U.S. 111, 131 (1944). Many believe that Justice Stevens was attempting to restate the standard from *Hearst Publications* when he wrote *Chevron*. Indeed, he cited the earlier case to support his explanation: "We have long recognized that considerable weight should be accorded to an executive department's construction of a statutory scheme it is entrusted to administer, and the principle of deference to administrative interpretations." *Chevron*, 467 U.S. at 844 (citing *NLRB v. Hearst Publications, Inc.*, 322 U.S. 111, 131 (1944)).

> Under *Hearst Publication*'s "reasonable-basis-in-the-law" test, an agency's interpretation is entitled to deference because agencies are experts in the field and Congress delegates authority to them to administer these programs.

Possibly *Hearst* still applies; however, *Hearst* is rarely cited today for the appropriate standard of review in these cases (it is probably time for administrative law textbooks to remove it). Instead, courts break the mixed question into its component parts: questions of law and questions of fact.

To the extent that the issue primarily involves a question of law, the analysis above applies. To the extent that the issue involves primarily a question of fact, the analysis that follows applies.

4. Standard of Review for Questions of Fact & Policy

For judicial review of questions of fact that agencies resolve, reviewing courts use two standards of review. Assuming that Congress has not provided a different standard in the enabling act, then the APA's default provision applies. The default provisions identify two standards of review for agency factual findings: the substantial evidence standard and the arbitrary and capricious standard. 5 U.S.C. § 706(2). The appropriate standard depends on the procedure the agency used, just as it did for pure questions of law.

The APA provides that for findings and conclusions from *formal* proceedings (formal adjudications or rulemakings required to be conducted on the record after a hearing), a reviewing court must use the "substantial evidence" standard to review the factual adequacy of an agency's findings. 5 U.S.C. § 706(2)(E). In contrast, the APA provides that for *informal* proceedings (notice-and-comment rulemaking and informal adjudications), a reviewing court must apply the "arbitrary and capricious" standard to review the factual adequacy of an agency's factual findings. 5 U.S.C. § 706(2)(A). The next sections explain these two standards and how they differ, if at all.

For judicial review of questions of policy that agencies resolve, reviewing courts use the arbitrary and capricious standard of review. This is true regardless of the formality of the procedure. The APA directs that courts "hold unlawful and set aside agency action, findings, and conclusions found to be arbitrary, capricious, an abuse of discretion, or otherwise not in accordance with law." 5 U.S.C. § 706(2)(A). Because agencies exercise discretion when making policy decisions, this "abuse of discretion" standard—which we also call arbitrary and capricious review—makes sense.

Below, each standard is explained, and then the two are compared.

a. Substantial Evidence Review

When an agency makes a factual determination during formal procedures (most commonly during a formal adjudication), the APA directs reviewing courts to review those findings using the substantial evidence standard of review. 5 U.S.C. § 706(2)(E). Substantial evidence has been defined as follows:

> "(S)ubstantial evidence is more than a mere scintilla. It means such relevant evidence as a reasonable mind might accept as adequate to support a conclusion."... [I]t "must do more than create a suspicion of the existence of the fact to be established.... it must be enough to justify, if the trial were to a jury, a refusal to direct a verdict when the conclusion sought to be drawn from it is one of fact for the jury."

Universal Camera Corp. v. NLRB, 340 U.S. 474, 477 (1951) (internal citations omitted). Pursuant to this standard, judges should not substitute their judgment for that of the agency. Rather, a judge should review the evidence in the record to confirm that a reasonable person could make the same factual finding that the agency made. In other words, the question is whether the determination is well reasoned given the administrative record, not whether the finding is correct. Thus, the task of the reviewing court is to examine each of the agency's findings to see if there is evidence in the record supporting that finding. In making this determination, the reviewing court must take into account not only the evidence supporting the agency's findings but also any evidence that "fairly detracts" from that finding. *Id.* at 487.

For example, suppose an agency denied an individual's claim for disability; in doing so, the agency relied on the testimony of its medical expert, who stated that the claimant could stand for seven or eight hours in a workday. The claimant had testified he could stand only for short periods. Based on this evidence, the agency determined that the claimant was not disabled because he could stand for seven or eight hours per day. The claimant appealed and challenged the finding that he could stand for seven or eight hours per day. A reviewing court would likely find the agency's finding should be sustained under the substantial evidence standard. Although there is evidence on both sides of the factual issue, after examining the record, "a reasonable mind" would accept the agency's factual finding—that the individual could stand for seven or eight hours per day.

Let's change the hypothetical. Assume instead that there were other medical experts who testified that the claimant could stand only for short periods. Assume further that these medical experts actually examined the individual, while the agency's medical expert merely reviewed the individual's medical records. The agency again determined that the claimant was not disabled, ignoring the medical experts who disagreed. The claimant appealed and challenged the finding that he was not disabled. This time, a reviewing court would likely find that the agency's finding should not be sustained under the substantial evidence standard. The evidence in favor of the agency's finding is minimal; in other words, after reviewing the record, "a reasonable mind" would *not* accept the agency's finding.

Thus, the substantial evidence standard is fairly deferential to an agency's factual findings. Similar to the civil context, courts use a deferential standard for these questions because the trier of fact, the agency, has expertise that the reviewing court does not. But to be clear, the standard is not the same as in a civil context, which is the preponderance of the evidence test. A reviewing court's job is to decide whether the agency's findings were well reasoned given the record in the case, not whether they were right.

b. Arbitrary & Capricious Review

Courts use the substantial evidence standard to review the sufficiency of findings of fact agencies make during *formal* proceedings or when Congress specifies this standard of review in an enabling act. For reviewing the sufficiency of findings of fact that agencies make during *informal* proceedings, the reviewing court applies arbitrary and capricious review. 5 U.S.C. § 706(2)(A). Additionally, for findings of policy made during formal or informal proceedings, courts also use this standard, as noted above.

The APA provides that the reviewing court shall hold unlawful and set aside agency findings that are "arbitrary, capricious, [or] an abuse of discretion." *Id.* Combined, these terms are understood to mean arbitrary and capricious review.

Originally, arbitrary and capricious review was understood to be very deferential to agencies. However, in 1971, the Supreme Court gave the standard unexpected teeth in *Citizens to Preserve Overton Park, Inc. v. Volpe*, 401 U.S. 402 (1971). This case involved judicial review of an agency's policy decision rather than a finding of fact, but the standard is the same.

The statute at issue in *Overton Park* prohibited the Federal Highway Administration from providing public funds to build a highway through a public park unless no feasible and prudent alternative existed. *Id.* at 407. The State of Tennessee requested funds to build a highway that would cut through the middle of a local park in Memphis. The Secretary of Transportation approved the funds, stating that he agreed with the State that the highway should be built through the park. Local citizens sued, claiming that his approval was unlawful. *Id.* at 406.

The Supreme Court applied arbitrary and capricious review, describing it in the following way:

To make [a finding that the actual choice made was not arbitrary, capricious, an abuse of discretion, or otherwise not in accordance with law] the court must consider whether the decision was based on a consideration of the relevant factors and whether there has been a clear error of judgment. Although this inquiry into the facts is to be searching and careful, the ultimate standard of review is a narrow one. The court is not empowered to substitute its judgment for that of the agency.

Id. at 416. Thus, for arbitrary and capricious review, courts determine whether "the [agency's] decision was based on a consideration of the relevant factors and whether there has been a clear error of judgment." *Id.* Moreover, the agency's decision must not be pretextual. *Department of Commerce v. New York*, 2019 WL 2619473, at *16 (June 27, 2019) (stating that agencies must offer genuine justifications for their decisions).

Similarly, in *Motor Vehicles Mfrs. Ass'n v. State Farm*, 463 U.S. 29 (1983), using arbitrary and capricious review, the Court struck down an agency's policy choice. *State Farm* came about after President Reagan was elected and promised to roll back regulations. Under the Carter administration, the Department of Transportation ("Department") had adopted a rule requiring car manufacturers to phase in passive restraints, such as automatic seatbelts and airbags. With the new administration, the newly appointed Secretary of Transportation undertook a new notice-and-comment rulemaking to rescind the phase-in rule. The evidence at the time was clear: seatbelts and airbags saved lives. So the insurance industry sued, claiming that the new rule was arbitrary and capricious.

In holding that the Department had acted arbitrarily and capriciously in revoking its prior rule requiring seatbelts or air bags in passenger cars, the Court reaffirmed that arbitrary and capricious review is "narrow" and that a court should not substitute its judgment for the agency's decision. Yet one might argue that the Court did just that: substituted its judgment for the agency's.

The Court specifically confirmed that arbitrary and capricious review is more intensive than the minimum rationality test used for reviewing the constitutionality of statutes: "We do not view [arbitrary and capricious review] as equivalent to the presumption of constitutionality afforded legislation drafted by Congress ...." *Id.* at 43, n.9. The Court described arbitrary and capricious review of an agency's policy decisions as follows:

[T]he agency must examine the relevant data and articulate a satisfactory explanation for its action including a "rational connection between the facts found and the choice made." In reviewing that explanation, we must "consider whether the decision was based on a consideration of the relevant factors and whether there has been a clear error of judgment." Normally, an agency rule would be arbitrary and capricious if the agency has relied on factors which Congress has not intended it to consider, entirely failed to consider an important aspect of the problem, offered an explanation for its decision that runs counter to the evidence before the agency, or is so implausible that it could not be ascribed to a difference in view or the product of agency expertise.

Id. at 43 (citations omitted). In short, "[the rule must be] the product of reasoned decisionmaking." *Id.* at 52.

In *State Farm*, the Department had justified the rule change by claiming that the car manufacturers would choose to put in automatic seatbelts rather than airbags and that individuals would then unhook those seatbelts; hence, the rule would not improve safety. *Id.* at 52–53. Rejecting this argument, the Court reasoned that the Department had failed to consider an important aspect of the problem, namely, a rule that required the car manufacturers to include air bags only. *Id.* at 53. Further, the Court found that the agency's explanation for its decision ran counter to the evidence: the evidence did not support the agency's finding that people detach automatic seatbelts at the same rate as they fail to use manual seatbelts. The agency had ignored inertia (otherwise known as laziness). *Id.* at 54.

State Farm demonstrates what happens when scientific findings (seatbelts and air bags unquestionably save lives) run into (a) public perceptions about the sanctity of the private automobile, (b) political attitudes about regulation, (c) stiff industry opposition, (d) insurance company interests, and (e) the normal complications of the legislative process. Even though we had seatbelt and air-bag technology in the 1960s, these complicating factors resulted in twenty years of delay in regulations requiring their use, at a cost of 12,000 lives annually.

State Farm is not a great example of arbitrary and capricious review. The Court rejected the agency's policy decisions as unreasonable thus substituting the Court's policy choices for those of the agency. Instead, the Court should have decided whether the agency's decision-making process was sufficient.

Perhaps the majority believed that the real reason for the change in the rule was the newly elected president's preference for deregulation. If true, then Justice Rehnquist had a response:

> The agency's changed view of the standard seems to be related to the election of a new President of a different political party. It is readily apparent that the responsible members of one administration may consider public resistance and uncertainties to be more important than do their counterparts in a previous administration. A change in administration brought about by the people casting their votes is a perfectly reasonable basis for an executive agency's reappraisal of the costs and benefits of its programs and regulations. As long as the agency remains within the bounds established by Congress, it is entitled to assess administrative records and evaluate priorities in light of the philosophy of the administration.

Id. at 59 (Rehnquist, J., concurring and dissenting).

Should a change in the executive be enough to support an agency's change in policy? In *FCC v. Fox*, the Court debated whether an agency needs to justify a rule change with more than the fact that the president had changed. 556 U.S. 502, 504 (2009). *Fox* involved broadcasts with fleeting, indecent language. *Id.* at 510. The Federal Trade Commission had for many years prohibited fleeting expletives only when the offending words were used multiple times in one broadcast. *Id.* at 507–08. When President George W. Bush came to the White House, the Commission changed its rule to prohibit a single use of an offending word. *Id.* at 508. The Commission chose not to impose fines right away for violations because the rule changed. *Id.* at 510. When two celebrities swore on a program on Fox, the Commission sent violation notices to the broadcaster. Fox sued, claiming the new rule was arbitrary and capricious. The Second Circuit held that the Commission's change of policy was inadequately explained; hence, it was arbitrary and capricious. *Id.* at 511–12.

The Supreme Court reversed. *Id.* at 530. There were six different opinions in the case, making it difficult to know what the Court actually held. Justice Scalia, writing for the plurality, found the Commission's explanation for the change sufficient. *Id.* at 520–21. Justice Scalia said an agency can change policy but must explain why it is changing policy; however, the agency is under no duty to prove to a court that the new policy is better than the old. *Id.* at 513. But all an agency needs to do is establish that the new policy is rational and within its authority. *Id.* at 514. If the new policy results from changes in facts, laws, or policies on which the old policy rested, those changes should be identified and explained. *Id.* at 514–15.

Dissenting, Justice Breyer defined the duty to explain as more encompassing:

> [T]he agency must explain why it has come to the conclusion that it should now change direction. Why does it now reject the considerations that led it to adopt that initial policy? What has changed in the world that offers justification for the change? What other good reasons are there for departing from the earlier policy?

Id. at 550 (Breyer, J., dissenting) (emphasis omitted). So, does an agency need to explain a policy change by saying anything more than "We have a new president and she believes a new policy is preferable"? We really do not know.

Today, arbitrary and capricious review of policy decisions is called "hard look" review. Not only should a court be sure the agency took a hard look at the problem, but the court itself should take a hard look at the agency's policy choice and explanation for that choice. With this change, arbitrary and capricious review moved up on the intensity scale.

5. A Difference in Name Only

Today it is unclear whether there is any difference between these two standards. A generation ago, practitioners challenging discretionary decisions made during formal proceedings frequently invoked the substantial evidence standard of review. *See, e.g., State Farm*, 463 U.S. at 36 (applying arbitrary and capricious review despite challengers' argument that the substantial evidence standard applied). They had a good reason for doing so. At that time, substantial evidence review was believed to be significantly tougher than arbitrary and capricious review.

Because of cases like *Overton Park*, *State Farm*, and *Fox*, arbitrary and capricious review has become better defined, and the difference in intensity between the two has been narrowed or eliminated. Thus, when former Justice Scalia was a circuit court judge, he explained that the two tests were essentially identical because "it is impossible to conceive of a 'nonarbitrary' factual judgment supported only by evidence that is not substantial in the APA sense." *Association of Data Processing Serv. Orgs. v. Board of Governors of Fed. Reserve Sys.*, 745 F.2d 677, 684 (D.C. Cir. 1984).

Others argue that subtle differences do exist; substantial evidence requires the court to conduct a slightly more searching inquiry. There is some support for this argument; after all, Congress specifically identified two different standards in the APA. *Expressio unius*, the identical words presumption, and the rule against surplusage would all tell us that these standards must mean different things.

Further, Congress sometimes requires the substantial evidence standard in an enabling act when the arbitrary and capricious standard would be the default, suggesting that Congress does not consider the standards interchangeable. For example, the Occupational Safety and Health Administration, the Consumer Product Safety Commission, and the Federal Trade Commission all have enabling statutes requiring a court to apply the substantial evidence standard when reviewing factual decisions made during informal proceedings. *See* 29 U.S.C. § 660(a); 15 U.S.C. § 2060(c); 15 U.S.C. § 45(c). The legislative history of these statutes suggests that Congress intended courts to more closely supervise the adequacy of the factual decisions from these agencies.

In sum, whether the two standards truly reflect different intensity standards, the language differs; be sure you use the right standard and the corresponding test.

6. Putting It All Together

We have now reviewed all of the standards of review that courts apply when reviewing agency decisions. To summarize, when determining which standard of review a court will apply to review an agency's finding, you must first determine what type of finding is involved: one of law, one of application of law to fact, one of fact, or one of policy. Then you must determine what procedure the agency used to reach its determination. For questions of law, the standard of review will vary based on what the agency was interpreting, a statute or its own regulation, and how the agency reached its interpretation, by legislative or non-legislative rulemaking. For questions of law application, break the questions into parts and follow the appropriate standard for each subpart.

For questions of policy, the standard of review is arbitrary and capricious review. Finally, for questions of fact the standard of review will vary based on

Judicial Standard of Review Flowchart

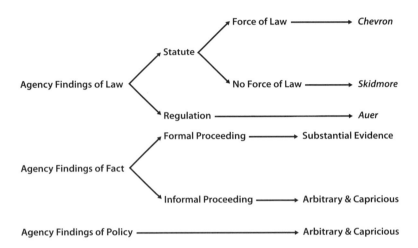

whether the agency used formal or informal procedures. But be aware that these standards of review are inexact. Even within a particular standard of review, the intensity of one judge's review may vary from the intensity of another judge's review. Here is a very simplified flowchart:

Administrative Law Standards of Review

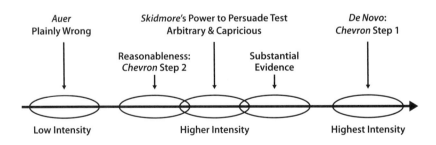

Returning to our discussion of the intensity spectrum for scope of review, let's replace the conventional judicial standards of review with the standards of review used in administrative law, assuming that there is some difference between arbitrary and capricious review and substantial evidence review. Our revised figure might look something like this.

Note that the standards are not set points on the spectrum. Rather, judges apply varying levels of intensity even when using the same standard of review. Other factors may nudge the intensity of the review further in one direction or the other. For example, the quality of an agency's decision-making process nudges the standard. One would expect less intensive review of agency decision-making that is thorough, fair, and complete. Additionally, a judge's view of the appropriate judicial role may nudge the standard. One would expect more intensive review from judges who doubt the efficacy of political controls on agencies and who regard courts as effective and legitimate instruments for imposing such controls.

D. Mastering This Topic

Return to the hypothetical ordinance provided in Chapter 1. The first question that was asked was the following: "An ambulance entered Pioneer Park to pick up and take to the hospital a man who had just suffered a heart attack. Did the ambulance driver violate the Pioneer Park Safety Ordinance (PPSO)?" How should you, as prosecutor, attempt to answer that question using what you've learned in this chapter?

You may recall that the Commissioner of Parks ("Commissioner"), an agency, promulgated a regulation interpreting the PPSO regarding whether certain vehicles were permitted in Pioneer Park. How does the agency's regulation affect your determination of whether an ambulance is a vehicle?

For your information, you should know that the standards of review discussed in this chapter apply only to federal agencies, not state agencies or local agencies. While some states do apply these standards, others do not. In practice, you should determine the law for your own jurisdiction. For educational purposes, however, let's assume that this chapter identifies the applicable law that your jurisdiction would follow.

Returning to the problem, you should first identify the type of question the agency resolved. Because the agency interpreted language in a statute, you know that the agency resolved a question of law. You would next search the statute for a specific standard of review for these types of questions. You would come up empty handed.

The operative language in the statute, as we identified long ago, is "motor vehicle." The relevant regulation (33 C.F.R. §2300(1)) defines a motor vehicle as follows:

> "Motor vehicle" in the PPSO means a road vehicle driven by a motor or engine used or physically capable of being used upon any public highway in this state in the transportation of persons or property, except vehicles operating wholly on fixed rails or tracks and electric trolley buses.

Would a court defer to this agency's interpretation, or definition? Let's apply *Chevron's* step zero process to see whether a court would defer and, if so, which deference standard would apply, *Chevron* or *Skidmore*.

First, you should confirm that the Commissioner interpreted an ordinance— for our purposes the equivalent of a statute—that the agency administers. Second, you should ask whether the City Council intended to delegate the specific issue to the Commissioner at all. If the issue is one of such major importance that the Council would never have intended to delegate, then the Commissioner likely has power to interpret the ordinance. In this case, it is unlikely that the City Council would consider this issue too important for the Commissioner's interpretation.

Second, ask whether the City Council intended to delegate interpretive authority to the Commissioner. To do so, look first to the type of agency action at issue; in other words, look to see if the Commissioner acted with the force of law. If the Commissioner interpreted the statute during notice-and-comment rulemaking, formal rulemaking, or formal adjudication, then *Chevron* deference is appropriate. In this case, the Commissioner promulgated a regulation and not a guidance document, although we do not know whether it was by notice-and-comment procedures or by formal procedures. We do not need to resolve the latter question because either type of procedure is considered force of law and, thus, *Chevron* applies.

Third, note that step four above is inapplicable because the Commissioner acted with force of law procedures. Hence, you have determined that the applicable standard is *Chevron*, so you will apply that standard. Using traditional tools of statutory interpretation, ask first whether the City Council has spoken to the precise issue—what the term "motor vehicles" means. You have already resolved this question as you have worked though this hypothetical in preceding chapters. For example, in Chapter 6, you concluded that the text was either ambiguous or absurd. In Chapter 7, you considered whether the linguistic canons helped resolve the ambiguity or absurdity. In Chapter 10, you considered the legislative history and the purpose of the ordinance. Perhaps at one of these steps, you concluded that the City Council had spoken, intending the term "motor vehicle" to include or not include ambulances. If so, then your analysis ended at that point, for the Council as the legislative body has the authority to determine what its ordinances mean.

But if you did not conclude that the Council had definitively resolved this issue and that ambiguity or absurdity remained, then you would proceed to *Chevron*'s second step and ask whether the Commissioner's interpretation is reasonable. To do so, you must compare the interpretation in the regulation with the language of the ordinance, with its legislative history, and with its purpose.

When we compare the text in the ordinance to the text in the regulation, we would see that they are compatible. The ordinance prohibits motor vehicles from entering the park, and the regulation defines motor vehicles broadly to include all vehicles that typically are driven on roads.

When we compare the regulation to the ordinance's legislative history, we would see that these two are also consistent. The City Council members seemed concerned about safety and wished to ban all vehicles that could injure people. The interpretation in the regulation is consistent with this intent.

Finally, when we compare the regulation to the purpose of the ordinance — to increase safety and decrease noise pollution — we see that they are similarly consistent. Likely, you would find that the Commissioner's interpretation of the ordinance is reasonable compared to these factors; hence, deference is due. You would now apply the regulation to the ambulance. Had you concluded that the regulation was unreasonable, then the ordinance would apply to the situation.

For educational purposes, let's assume that the Commissioner had issued this interpretation via a non-legislative, interpretive rule (a form of guidance). Would the result be different? Return to the process above. This time at the third step, note that you would conclude that the Commissioner did not use force of law procedures. Hence, application of *Chevron* is not automatic.

Instead, you must now determine whether *Chevron* is appropriate even though force of law procedures were not used. To do so, determine whether the City Council intended *Chevron* to apply as shown by the *Barnhart* factors. Those factors include the following: (1) the interstitial nature of the legal question; (2) the relevance of the agency's expertise; (3) the importance of the question to administration of the statute; (4) the complexity of the statutory scheme; and (5) the careful consideration the agency has given the question over a long period of time. You will remember that the more difficult the issue and the regulatory scheme are, the more experience the agency has in the particular area, the more important resolution of this issue is to the agency's ability to administer the program, and finally, the more carefully the agency considered the interpretation, the more likely that the lawmaking body would have intended for courts to defer to the agency's interpretation using *Chevron*.

In this case, the issue and regulatory scheme are not complex and do not seem to need special expertise to resolve. Further, there is no indication that the Commissioner considered the issue carefully or that the Commissioner needed to resolve this issue to take care of the parks. Thus, because the *Barnhart* factors suggest that the City Council did not intend for courts to defer, *Chevron* would be inapplicable. Instead, you should apply *Skidmore*'s power-to-persuade test. Under *Skidmore*'s power-to-persuade test, the Commissioner's interpretation would be entitled to some deference based on the following factors: (1) the consistency in its interpretation over time, (2) the thoroughness of its consideration, and (3) the soundness of its reasoning. In this case, this is the first time the Commissioner has interpreted this ordinance; there is no indication regarding how thoroughly the Commissioner considered the issue; and there is no reasoning offered for the interpretation. Applying *Skidmore*'s power-to-persuade test, you might conclude that the Commissioner's interpretation is not persuasive. Alternatively, you might conclude that the interpretation is consistent enough with the ordinance to be persuasive. If you conclude the interpretation is persuasive and, thus, applies, you must next apply it.

If you decided that the Commissioner's interpretation is unpersuasive, then you must next determine how the ordinance applies to the ambulance driver without regard to the Commissioner's definition (*i.e.*, you must apply the "statute" to the facts of the case). If you decided that the Commissioner's interpretation is persuasive, you must determine whether the ordinance as refined by the regulation applies to the ambulance (*i.e.*, you must apply the "regulation" to the facts of the case). Do you prosecute, or bring an enforcement action?

Assume your office brings an enforcement action against the driver, using formal adjudication. At the hearing, the driver testified that he did not simply drive the ambulance through the park for an afternoon ride; rather, he drove slowly and carefully into the park to pick up an individual who needed medical attention. On this record, the ALJ finds that the driver violated the ordinance, and the agency affirms this finding. The driver appeals. What standard of review will the reviewing court apply to the agency's finding? You must first determine what kind of finding this is. You should conclude it is a mixed question of law to fact: the driver, who was driving an ambulance, drove through the park, which violated the ordinance. Recall that the appropriate standard to apply to mixed questions of law and fact is currently unclear. Some courts accept an agency's decision if it has "warrant in the record" and "a reasonable basis in law." Here, the records support a finding that the driver drove an ambulance into the park (warrant in the record) and that an ambulance is a motor vehicle (a reasonable basis in law).

Alternatively, some courts break a mixed question into its component parts—questions of law and questions of fact. The question of fact in this case is whether the ambulance driver drove the ambulance into the park. The question of law is whether the ordinance covers ambulances.

Questions of fact are reviewed under different standards pursuant to section 706(2) of the APA. For agency findings of fact made during informal rulemaking, the relevant standard is whether the agency's findings are arbitrary and capricious. 5 U.S.C. § 706(2)(A). Applying the arbitrary and capricious standard, a court would determine whether the agency's findings were based on a consideration of irrelevant factors or whether the agency made a clear error of judgment. For agency findings of fact made during formal rulemaking, the standard is whether the agency's findings are supported by substantial evidence. 5 U.S.C. § 706(2)(E). Applying the substantial evidence standard, a court would determine whether the record contains "such evidence as a reasonable mind might accept as adequate to support a conclusion." *Consolidated Edison Co. v. NLRB*, 305 U.S. 197, 229 (1938).

Because the decision here was made during a formal adjudication, the substantial evidence standard is appropriate. Applying that standard, a court would sustain the agency's finding of fact because a reasonable mind would likely conclude from this record that the driver drove into the park.

Above we addressed the legal question and its standard of review. We concluded *Chevron* applied. We then applied *Chevron* and deferred to the Commissioner's interpretation at step two.

In this case, the Commissioner's interpretation did not significantly help you resolve the ambulance hypothetical. Does this mean that agency interpretations are generally unhelpful? Not at all. Consider whether the Commissioner's interpretation would help you resolve the other hypothetical questions, notably the helicopter and airplane questions.

Checkpoints

- Judges use different standards of review in administrative law, which depend on the type of issue involved and the procedure used to resolve the issue.

- For questions of law, judges apply one of three standards: *Chevron*, *Skidmore*, or *Auer*.

- Courts apply *Chevron* analysis to agency interpretations of statutes that the agency administers when the agency made the interpretation using force of law procedures, such as formal rulemaking, notice-and-comment rulemaking, and formal adjudication.

- At *Chevron* step one, a court should determine "whether Congress has directly spoken to the precise question at issue," which is not the same as whether the statute is textually ambiguous.

- At *Chevron* step two, if Congress has not spoken, then a court should accept any "permissible," or "reasonable," agency interpretation.

- Under *Skidmore's* power-to-persuade test, an agency's interpretation of a statute made during non-legislative rulemaking is entitled to deference when (1) the agency consistently interprets the language over time, (2) the agency thoroughly considers the issue, and (3) the agency offers sound reasoning to support its interpretation.

- Under *Auer*, courts defer to an agency's interpretation of its own regulation unless the interpretation is "plainly wrong." This standard has been criticized as violating separation of powers.

- For questions of fact, a court applies the substantial evidence standard when the agency reached its finding via a formal proceeding.

- For questions of fact, a court applies the arbitrary and capricious standard when the agency reached its finding via an informal proceeding.

- For questions of policy, a court applies the arbitrary and capricious standard regardless of how the agency exercised its discretion.

- Substantial evidence and arbitrary and capricious review may differ very little today.

Chapter 16

Summary: The Linear Approach to Interpretation

There are many ways to approach the process of interpreting a statute (or any legal text). Textualism is an interpretative approach that relies heavily on the intrinsic, or text-based, sources to determine meaning. Former Justice Scalia, Justices Thomas, Kagan, Alito, Gorsuch, and Kavanaugh, and Judge Easterbrook are textualists. Next, intentionalism is an interpretative approach that searches all sources, particularly an act's legislative history, to discern the enacting legislature's specific intent for enacting the act. Former Justices Rehnquist, Stevens, and O'Connor, and Justice Ginsburg are intentionalists. This approach is less popular today than it was during the years of the Rehnquist Court. Finally, purposivism is an interpretative approach that searches all of the sources to discern the enacting legislature's general intent, or purpose, and then harmonizes the text and purpose of the statute. Chief Justice Roberts, Justices Breyer and Sotomayor, and Judge Posner are purposivists.

While there are many ways to approach interpretation, the linear approach appeals to textualists, intentionalists, and purposivists alike. This approach offers a process for approaching statutory interpretation that begins with the text and moves outward from concrete sources linked to the text to abstract sources based on policy. The linear approach provides a step-by-step method, or even a checklist, for you to use to analyze statutory language so you can convince a court to interpret the statute in a way that would benefit your client. Further, it shows the depth of possible arguments that you or your opponent may use to persuade a court about a statute's meaning. Below you will find this checklist, with cases illustrating the concepts. They are included in the footnotes to avoid interruption of the outlined text.

The Linear Approach

- **STEP 1:** Identify the specific language of at issue
  - The language of the statute is always the starting point for interpretation
    - Start with the operative section of the statute
    - Then move to other sections as needed
  - Ask: what does your client want the language to mean?[1]
    - Be specific: *e.g.,* "use a firearm" means to shoot a gun or to use it as a weapon
  - Ask: what does your opponent want the language to mean?
    - Be specific: *e.g.,* "use a gun" means to use it in any way, including trading it for drugs

- **STEP 2:** Determine whether Congress intended the language to have its ordinary or technical meaning
  - To determine which meaning was intended
    - Look at the audience of the statute, and
    - Look at the other words within the statute
    - Ordinary meaning is generally intended

  - Grammar & Punctuation Canons
    - Grammar and punctuation are intrinsic sources
    - When used properly, grammar and punctuation are generally considered when finding ordinary/technical meaning
    - When used improperly, they are considered later in the interpretive process

  - Finding ordinary meaning
    - Plain meaning canon: directs that words and phrases shall be construed according to the commonly approved usage of the language
      - Ordinary meaning differs from definitional meaning
        - Ordinary meaning, the meaning most people would give the language, is narrower than dictionary meaning
          - Use a gun as a weapon is the ordinary meaning of "use a gun"
      - Dictionary meaning includes all ways words are used and is broader

---

1. *See, e.g.,* Smith v. United States, 508 U.S. 223, 240 (1993) (Justice O'Connor held that "use" of a firearm during a drug trafficking crime included trading the gun for drugs, while former Justice Scalia, dissenting, said "use" of a firearm meant using it as a weapon). *Cf.* Watson v. United States, 552 U.S. 74, 83 (2007) (holding that accepting a gun for drugs was not "use" of a firearm).

- Use a gun in any way, including as an item of barter, is a dictionary meaning of "use" (notice the word "gun" is omitted to broaden the meaning)
  - Places to find the ordinary meaning of a word
    - Dictionaries[2]
      - Consider which dictionary to use, one in effect when the statute was written or in effect today[3]
      - Newspapers, magazines, literature, songs, pop culture[4]

- Finding technical meaning
  - Technical meaning canon directs that technical words and phrases as have acquired a peculiar and appropriate meaning shall be construed accordingly
    - Word must be used in its technical context, so look to the statute's audience
      - E.g., tomato is a vegetable, not a fruit, because the statute taxing tomatoes was written for merchants, not botanists[5]
  - Technical meaning is rarely intended because most audiences are not technical
    - Exception: words with legal meaning[6]
      - E.g., statute of limitations, conviction,[7] assault[8]

---

2. Nix v. Hedden, 149 U.S. 304, 307 (1893) (saying that dictionary definitions are offered "not as evidence, but only as aids to the memory and understanding of the court.").

3. Chisom v. Roemer, 501 U.S. 380, 410 (1991) (Scalia, J., dissenting) (saying that a dictionary in effect at the time legislation was drafted would be appropriate). In *MCI Telecomms. Corp. v. American Tel. & Tel. Co.*, 512 U.S. 218 (1994), former Justice Scalia, for the majority, identified a number of different dictionaries with similar definitions of the word at issue: "modify." While the majority of dictionaries suggested that "modify" meant a modest change, one dictionary, Webster's Third New International Dictionary, suggested that "modify" could mean either a modest or substantial change. *Id.* at 225–26.

4. *See, e.g.*, Muscarello v. United States, 524 U.S. 125, 128, 140 (1998) (in which the majority and dissent turned to each of the sources to discern ordinary meaning).

5. *Nix*, 149 U.S. at 306.

6. *See, e.g.*, Dickens v. Puryear, 276 S.E.2d 325, 446 (N.C. 1981) (interpreting the term "assault" to have its legal, tortious meaning, specifically freedom from the apprehension of a harmful or offensive contact).

7. *But see* St. Clair v. Commonwealth, 140 S.W.3d 510, 568 (Ky. 2004) (interpreting the term "prior record of conviction" in its ordinary rather than legal sense).

8. *But see* Patrie v. Area Coop. Educ. Serv., 37 Conn. L. Rptr. 470 (Conn. Super. Ct. 2004) (interpreting the term "assault" in its ordinary sense because the statute was written for educators rather than lawyers).

- **STEP 3:** Determine whether the language is ambiguous, meaning there are multiple interpretations
  - If so, court will examine sources beyond the text of the statute, such as legislative history
  - Definitions of ambiguity:
    - Easier definition to meet: 2 or more reasonable people disagree[9]
    - Harder definition to meet: 2 or more equally plausible meanings[10]
      - There is no agreement on the definition of ambiguity, so use an easier definition if you want the court to find ambiguity and a harder definition if you do not want the court to find ambiguity[11]

- **STEP 4:** Determine whether there is a reason to reject the ordinary meaning for another fair interpretation
  - Absurdity
    - Definitions of absurdity
      - Easier definition: would frustrate purpose/intent
      - Harder definition: would shock the general moral/common sense[12]
    - There is no agreement on the definition of absurdity, so use an easier definition if you want the court to find absurdity and a harder definition if you do not want the court to find absurdity

  - Scrivener's (drafting) error
    - Definition: an obvious drafting error
      - This is a very narrow exception[13]

---

9. In re Unknown, 701 F.3d 749, 760 (5th Cir. 2012), *cert. granted in part sub nom. and vacated*, 133 S. Ct. 2886 (2013).

10. Florida Dept. of Revenue v. Piccadilly Cafeterias, Inc., 554 U.S. 33, 41 (2008).

11. *See, e.g.*, Goswami v. American Collections Enters., Inc.,377 F.3d 488, 492 (5th Cir. 2004) ("In interpreting statutes we do not look beyond the plain meaning of the statute unless the statute is absurd or ambiguous.").

12. In *King v. Burwell*, Justice Scalia defined an absurd result as "a consequence 'so monstrous, that all mankind would, without hesitation, unite in rejecting the application.'" 135 S. Ct. 2480, 2505 (2015) (Scalia, J., dissenting) (quoting Sturges v. Crowninshield, 17 U.S. (4 Wheat.) 122, 203 (1819)); Mayor of Lansing v. Michigan Pub. Serv. Comm'n, 680 N.W.2d 840, 847 (Mich. 2004) (explaining why the "reasonable people disagree" standard cannot be accurate).

13. United States v. Granderson, 511 U.S. 39, 68 (1994) ("It is beyond [a court's] province to rescue Congress from its drafting errors, and to provide for what [it] might think ... is the preferred result.").

- It permits judges to correct obvious clerical or typographical errors[14]

- Constitutional avoidance doctrine[15]
  - Definition: two interpretations are "fairly possible" and one raises doubt about the constitutionality of the statute
    - Note that the two interpretations need not be equally plausible, just fairly possible (otherwise, ambiguity would be a way to avoid ordinary meaning)[16]
  - Caution: a court does not actually determine that the statute is unconstitutional; rather, the court avoids having to determine constitutionality by adopting an alternate interpretation

- **STEP 5:** Determine whether intrinsic sources (other than text) are relevant to meaning
  - **Intrinsic sources** are materials that are part of the official act being interpreted, such as text, grammar, etc.

- Grammar & Punctuation
  - General Rule
    - Statutes are interpreted as punctuated using ordinary rules of grammar unless either contradicts the ordinary meaning[17]
  - Specific Rules for resolving ambiguity and absurdity
    - Commas

---

14. *See, e.g.,* U.S. Nat'l Bank of Or. v. Indep. Ins. Agents of Am., Inc., 508 U.S. 439, 462 (1993) (correcting misplaced punctuation); United States v. Coatoam, 245 F.3d 553, 557 (6th Cir. 2001) (correcting an incorrect cross-reference to another section in the statute); United States v. Scheer, 729 F.2d 164, 169 (2d Cir. 1984) (changing the word "request" to "receipt" where language in statute provided that a certificate would be furnished "upon *request* of the … request").

15. *See, e.g.,* Public Citizen v. DOJ, 491 U.S. 440, 455 (1989); Green v. Bock Laundry Mach. Co., 490 U.S. 504, 510 (1989).

16. United States v. Marshall, 908 F.2d 1312, 1318 (7th Cir. 1990), *aff'd sub nom.* Chapman v. United States, 500 U.S. 453 (1991).

17. In England, "until 1849 statutes were enrolled upon parchment and enacted without punctuation. No punctuation appearing upon the rolls of Parliament such as was found in the printed statutes simply expressed the understanding of the printer." Taylor v. Caribou, 67 A. 2, 4 (Me. 1907). Congress passes bills with the punctuation included; hence, "[t]here is no reason why punctuation, which is intended to and does assist in making clear and plain the meaning of all things else in the English language, should be rejected in the case of the interpretation of [American] statutes." *Id.*

- Doctrine of last antecedent[18]
  - Directs that words and phrases modify only the immediately preceding noun or noun phrase in a list of items
  - Exception: if the drafter includes a comma between the modifier and the last antecedent, then all of the nouns or noun phrases are modified
- And v. Or
  - Generally, the word "and" has a conjunctive meaning, while the word "or" has a disjunctive meaning
  - However, when context dictates, courts will interchange these two words[19]
- Singular v. Plural
  - For ease of drafting, statutes are typically written in the singular[20]
  - But for statutory interpretation, the legislature's use of the singular is assumed to include the plural, and the legislature's use of the plural is assumed to include the singular unless context directs otherwise[21]
- Masculine v. Feminine
  - For ease of drafting, statutes are typically written in the masculine
  - The masculine pronoun is generally interpreted to include the feminine or neuter[22]

---

18. *See, e.g.,* Barnhart v. Thomas, 540 U.S. 20, 26 (2003) (applying the doctrine and explaining its limitations); Commonwealth v. Kelly, 64 Mass. (10 Cush.) 69, 71 (1852) (applying the doctrine to hold that hotel owners could not sell alcohol after eleven).

19. *See, e.g.,* Comptroller of Treasury v. Fairchild Industries, Inc., 493 A.2d 341, 343–44 (Md. 1985).

20. Homebuilders Ass'n v. Scottsdale, 925 P.2d 1359, 1366 (Ariz. Ct. App. 1996) ("The historical purpose of construing plural and singular nouns and verbs interchangeably is to avoid requiring the legislature to use such expressions as 'person or persons,' 'he, she, or they,' and 'himself or themselves.' Under this principle, the plural has often been held to apply to the singular in a statute, absent evidence of contrary legislative intent.").

21. *See, e.g.,* 1 U.S.C. § 1 ("In determining the meaning of any Act [or resolution] of Congress, unless the context indicates otherwise[,] words importing the singular include and apply to several persons, parties, or things; words importing the plural include the singular …."). For an example of a case in which the rule was ignored, see *Van Horn v. William Blanchard Co.,* 438 A.2d 552, 554 (N.J. Sup. Ct. 1981).

22. *See, e.g.,* 1 U.S.C. § 1 (providing that "words importing the masculine gender include the feminine as well"); Commonwealth. v. Henninger, 25 Pa. D. & C.3d 625, 626 (Pa. Ct. Com. Pl. 1981) (interpreting "he" in a statutory rape statute to include female defendants).

- The feminine pronoun may be interpreted to include the male or neuter, but this is less common[23]
- Mandatory & Discretionary
  - Generally
    - "Shall" is mandatory[24]
    - "May" is discretionary[25]
    - "Must" is considered mandatory when a condition precedent is present
    - "Should" is considered discretionary[26]
  - Sometimes not[27]

- Linguistic Canons: Canons regarding word usage
  - *In pari materia*
    - Where a court may look for help in interpreting a statute
    - Means "of the same material"
    - Judges will look at an entire act and related statutes to determine meaning[28]
      - Whole act aspect: the entire act is relevant to interpretation[29]

---

23. *See, e.g.,* In re Compensation of Williams, 635 P.2d 384, 386 (Or. Ct. App. 1981) (refusing to interpret the word "woman" to include men because "woman" was not a word used "in the *masculine* gender"), *aff'd,* 653 P.2d 970 (Or. 1982).

24. *See, e.g.,* Escondido Mut. Water Co. v. La Jolla Indians, 466 U.S. 765, 772 (1984) ("The mandatory nature of the language chosen by Congress [shall] appear[] to require that the Commission include the Secretary's conditions in the license even if it disagrees with them.").

25. *But see* Fink v. City of Detroit, 333 N.W.2d 376, 379 (Mich. App. 1983) (holding that "may" was mandatory).

26. Daniel v. United Nat'l Bank, 505 S.E.2d 711, 716 (W. Va. 1998).

27. Jersey City v. State Bd. of Tax Appeals, 43 A.2d 799, 803–04 (N.J. 1945) (refusing to interpret "shall" in a statute to be mandatory); Cobb Cnty. v. Robertson, 724 S.E.2d 478, 479 (Ga. App. 2012) ("Even though the word 'shall' is generally construed as mandatory, it need not always be construed in that fashion.").

28. *See, e.g.,* Fla. Dep't of Highway Safety & Motor Vehicles v. Hernandez, 74 So. 3d 1070, 1076 (Fla. 2011) (noting that a statute that allowed the state to suspend the driver's license of any person who refused to submit to a "lawful" breath test must be read *in pari materia* with a different statute that defined the parameters of a lawful breath-alcohol test).

29. *See, e.g.,* Rhyne v. K-Mart Corp., 594 S.E.2d 1, 20 (N.C. 1994) (interpreting the words "a defendant" in a punitive damages statute to mean each defendant or each verdict because in the same section of the act being interpreted, the legislature also referred to "*a* verdict" and to "*the* award.").

- Whole code aspect: acts with similar purposes may be relevant to interpretation[30]
- Helps ensure consistency within acts, across acts, and even within the code as a whole
- The presumption of consistent usage and meaningful variation (also called the identical words presumption)[31]
  - Directs that when the legislature uses the same word in different parts of the same act, the legislature intended those words to have the same meaning (consistent usage)[32]
  - Also directs that, if the legislature uses a word in one part of the act, then changes to a different word in the same act, the legislature intended the different words to have different meanings (meaningful variation)
- *Noscitur a sociis*
  - Means "it is known from its associates"
  - Used for words within a list, not the catch-all[33]
  - Listed words have a commonality that should be shared by all
  - Directs that when a word has more than one meaning, the appropriate meaning should be gleaned from the textual context (meaning the surrounding words in the statute or act)[34]
- *Ejusdem generis*
  - Means "of the same kind, class, or nature"
  - Used for general words & catch-alls, not words within a list
    - Subset of *noscitur a sociis*

---

30. *See, e.g.*, Smith v. City of Jackson, 544 U.S. 228, 233 (2005) (interpreting the ADEA and the Civil Rights Act *in pari materia*); Commonwealth v. Smith, 728 N.E.2d 272, 278–79 (Mass. 2000) (discussing whether an incest statute and rape statute were *in pari materia*).

31. *See, e.g.*, Robinson v. City of Lansing, 782 N.W.2d 171, 182 (2010) ("[U]nless the Legislature indicates otherwise, when it repeatedly uses the same phrase in a statute, that phrase should be given the same meaning throughout the statute.").

32. *See, e.g.*, Travelscape, LLC v. S.C. Dept. of Revenue, 705 S.E.2d 28, 33–35, 40 (2011) (in which the majority and dissent argue about whether the words "furnished" and "furnishing" in a state tax statute should have the same meaning).

33. Babbitt v. Sweet Home Chapter Communities, 515 U.S. 687, 720 (1995) (Scalia, J., dissenting) (noting that the agency incorrectly identified the appropriate canon).

34. *See, e.g.*, G.C. Timmis & Co. v. Guardian Alarm Co., 662 N.W.2d 710, 713 (Mich. 2003) (discussing whether *noscitur a sociis* is applied intuitively by English speakers); People v. Vasquez, 631 N.W.2d 711, 714 (Mich. 2001) (applying *noscitur a sociis* to determine whether a defendant who lied to a police officer about his age "obstruct[ed], resist[ed], oppose[d], assault[ed], beat, or wound[ed]" that officer).

- Directs that when general words or catch-alls are near specific words or listed words, the general words and catch-alls should be limited to include only things similar in nature to the specific words[35]
- The rule against surplusage, or redundancy
  - Directs that the proper interpretation of a statute is the one in which every word, phrase, section, etc. has independent meaning; nothing is redundant or meaningless[36]
  - Disfavored canon because it does not reflect legal drafting
- *Expressio unius est exclusio alterius*
  - Means the expression of one thing excludes the inclusion of other similar things[37]
  - Directs that when the legislature includes some things explicitly, courts should conclude that the legislature intentionally omitted other similar things that would logically have been included
  - Disfavored canon because it does not reflect legal drafting[38]

- Statute's Components (other than operative provisions)
  - Titles
    - Three types
      - Long titles, precede enacting clauses
      - Short titles, may follow enacting clauses
      - Section titles
    - The canon for all is the same: titles cannot control clear text but can be used where there is ambiguity or absurdity[39]

---

35. *See, e.g.*, Yates v. United States, 135 S. Ct. 1074, 1081 (2015); Ali v. Federal Bureau of Prisons, 552 U.S. 214, 225, 231 (2008) (majority refused to apply the canon while the dissent found it dispositive).

36. Begay v. United States, 553 U.S. 137, 143 (2008) (applying the canon to limit the meaning of "violent felony" to not apply to felony drunk driving).

37. *See, e.g.*, Dickens v. Puryear, 276 S.E.2d 325, 330 n.8 (N.C. 1981).

38. National Petroleum Refiners Ass'n v. FTC, 482 F.2d 672, 676 (D.C. Cir. 1973) ("[*Expressio unius*] is increasingly considered unreliable, for it stands on the faulty premise that all possible alternative or supplemental provisions were necessarily considered and rejected by the legislative draftsmen.").

39. Brotherhood of R. R. Trainmen v. Baltimore & O. R. Co., 331 U.S. 519, 529 (1947) (stating that section titles "are but tools available for the resolution of a doubt. But they cannot undo or limit that which the text makes plain."); Caminetti v. United States, 242 U.S. 470, 490 (1917) ("[T]he name [or short title] given to an act by way of designation or description ... cannot change the plain import of its words."); Church of the Holy Trinity v. United States, 143 U.S. 457, 462 (1892) ("The title of an act cannot control its words, but may furnish some aid in showing what was in the mind of the legislature.").

- Definitions
  - One of the first places to look after finding the relevant language in an operative section of the act
  - When the legislature defines a word or phrase in a statute, that definition is controlling even if it makes no sense[40]
- Preambles, findings, purpose clauses
  - Included in acts more commonly today than in the past
  - Preambles, findings, and purpose clauses cannot contradict clear text but can aid meaning where there is ambiguity or absurdity[41]
- Provisos & exceptions
  - Defined: provisions that exclude something from a statute's reach or qualify something otherwise within a statute
  - Construed narrowly
  - There is a presumption against creating exemptions in a statute that has none explicitly provided
- Non-severability & severability clauses
  - Severability provisions allow for the remaining sections of an act to remain valid with the invalid provision excised
    - Rebuttable presumption of validity[42]
    - Common, generally followed even though added as boilerplate language
  - Inseverability provisions require that an act as a whole be held invalid if any one section is invalid
    - Rebuttable presumption of validity[43]

---

40. *See, e.g.*, Commonwealth v. Plowman, 86 S.W.3d 47, 49 (Ky. 2002) (holding that a defendant who set fire to a bulldozer started a fire "with intent to destroy or damage a building" because the statute defined "building" to include "any … automobile, truck, watercraft, aircraft, … or other … vehicle.…"). For a fun fictional case, see *Regina v. Ojibway*, 8 Crim. L.Q. 137 (Toronto 1965) (interpreting the term "bird" to include a pony covered in feathers).

41. Sutton v. United Air Lines, Inc., 527 U.S. 471, 484 (1999) (examining a findings provision to limit the reach of the Americans with Disabilities Act ("ADA")).

42. Alaska Airlines, Inc. v. Brock, 480 U.S. 678, 686 (1987) (stating such a clause is merely a rebuttable presumption that can be overcome by "strong evidence that Congress intended otherwise.").

43. Biszko v. RIHT Fin. Corp., 758 F.2d 769, 773 (1st Cir. 1985) ("[A] non-severability clause cannot ultimately bind a court, it establishes [only] a presumption of non-severability.").

- Less common, generally not followed even though they arguably show legislative intent better than severability provisions[44]

- **STEP 6:** Determine whether extrinsic sources are relevant to meaning
  - **Extrinsic sources** are sources outside of the enacted act but within the legislative process that created the act, *e.g.*, legislative history, purpose
  - Other acts and statutes that conflict with the statute at issue
    - For conflicts within a jurisdiction
      - Harmonize if possible, but if not, follow these steps in this order:
        - Specific statutes trump general statutes[45]
        - Later-enacted statutes trump earlier-enacted statutes[46]
        - Repeal by implication is disfavored[47]
          - Especially for appropriation bills[48]
    - For conflicts across jurisdictions
      - When a federal statute conflicts with a state statute
        - Preemption: federal law controls state law[49]
          - Express preemption[50]

---

44. Farrior v. Sodexho, U.S.A., 953 F. Supp. 1301, 1302 (N.D. Ala. 1997) ("A non-severability [provision] is almost unheard of and constitutes a legislative finding that every section [of an act] is so important to the single subject that no part of the act can be removed without destruction of the legislative purpose.").

45. *See, e.g.*, Palm Beach Cnty. Canvassing Bd. v. Harris, 772 So. 2d 1220, 1234 (Fla. 2000) ("First, it is well-settled that where two statutory provisions are in conflict, the specific statute controls the general statute.").

46. Williams v. Commonwealth, 829 S.W.2d 942, 947 (Ky. Ct. App. 1992) (Huddleston, J., concurring in part and dissenting in part); Palm Beach Cnty. Canvassing Bd., 772 So. 2d at 1234 ("The more recently enacted provision may be viewed as the clearest and most recent expression of legislative intent.").

47. Morton v. Mancari, 417 U.S. 535, 550 (1974) ("In the absence of some affirmative showing of an intention to repeal, the only permissible justification for a repeal by implication is when the earlier and later statutes are irreconcilable. Clearly, this is not the case here."). There is a related aspect to this implied repeal canon: the presumption against repeal is especially strong when the second bill is an appropriations (or budget) bill.

48. Tennessee Valley Authority v. Hill, 437 U.S. 153, 189 (1978) (noting that "the [canon] applies with even *greater* force when the claimed repeal rests solely on an Appropriations Act.").

49. U.S. Const. art. VI, cl. 2.

50. *See, e.g.*, Medtronic, Inc. v. Lohr, 518 U.S. 470, 485 (1996) (refusing to find preemption even though the statute provided that "no State ... may establish ... any requirement ... which is different from, or in addition to, any [federal] requirement ....").

- Implied preemption[51]
  - Field preemption (rare)[52]
  - Conflict preemption (more common)[53]
    - Found when it is impossible for an entity to comply with both laws, or
    - When the state law stands as an obstacle to the accomplishment of the federal objective
- When one state's statute impacts another state's statute
  - Modeled & Borrowed Acts
    - Directs that when Congress *models* one act based on an existing act, the modeling act and its settled judicial interpretations are relevant to interpretation[54]
    - Directs that when a state legislature *borrows* a statute from another jurisdiction—whether state or federal—courts assume that the borrowing legislature took not only the statutory language, but also any settled judicial opinions interpreting that statute from the highest court in the patterning jurisdiction *at the time of the adoption* as well[55]
      - Subsequent judicial interpretations are only persuasive[56]
  - Uniform Acts
    - When a state legislature enacts a uniform act, uniformity across jurisdictions is essential[57]

---

51. Wyeth v. Levine, 555 U.S. 555, 565 (2009) (explaining that preemption turns on congressional intent).

52. *See* Rogers v. Yonce, 2008 WL 2853207, at *10 (N.D. Okla., July 21, 2008) (identifying the three times the Supreme Court has found field preemption: (1) the Labor Management Relations Act; (2) the Employee Retirement Income Security Act, and (3) the National Bank Act).

53. Pulkkinen v. Pulkkinen, 127 So. 3d 738, 742 (Fla. Dist. Ct. App. 2013).

54. Lorillard v. Pons, 434 U.S. 575, 579 n.5 (1978) (examining FLSA to determine whether ADEA provided a right to jury trials because ADEA specifically provided that it be interpreted in accordance with the "powers, remedies, and *procedures*" of FLSA) (quoting 29 U.S.C. § 626(b)).

55. Zerbe v. State, 583 P.2d 845, 846 (Alaska 1978) (refusing to adopt the judicial opinion of a lower court).

56. Van Horn v. William Blanchard Co., 438 A.2d 552, 555–56 (N.J. 1981).

57. Pileri Indus., Inc. v. Consolidated Indus., Inc., 740 So. 2d 1108, 1114 (Ala. Civ. App. 1999) (Crawley, J., dissenting); Blitz v. Beth Isaac Adas Israel Congregation, 720 A.2d 912, 918 (Md. 1998) (interpreting the word "disbursements" in the Uniform Arbitration Act to include attorney's fees, in part, because other states had done so even though the text of the Act suggested that attorney's fees should not be included); Holiday Inns, Inc. v. Olsen, 692 S.W.2d 850, 853 (Tenn. 1985).

- Interpretations of uniform acts from jurisdictions are strongly persuasive, regardless of when or where they occur
  - Contrary to borrowed statutes canon above

- Model Acts
  - When a state legislature enacts a model act, uniformity is less important, unless the model act is widely adopted
  - Interpretations of a model act from other jurisdictions are informative, but not controlling[58]

- Timing of enactment
  - Using pre-enactment context (what occurred before enactment)
    - Legislative history
      - Identifying legislative history
        - Conference committee reports[59]
        - Committee reports[60]
        - Bill drafts and amendments[61]
        - Committee hearings
        - Floor debates[62]

---

58. Brown v. Arp & Hammond Hardware Co., 141 P.3d 673, 680 (Wyo. 2006) ("When the words of a statute are materially the same and where the reasoning of another court interpreting the statute is sound, we do not sacrifice sovereign independence, nor undermine the unique character of Wyoming law, by relying upon the precedent of a foreign jurisdiction.") (internal quotation marks omitted).

59. United States v. Salim, 287 F. Supp. 2d 250, 340 (S.D.N.Y. 2003) (identifying the conference committee report as "the most persuasive evidence of congressional intent, next to the statute itself.").

60. Church of the Holy Trinity v. United States, 143 U.S. 457, 464 (1892) (relying on a committee report to understand which of two meanings the legislature intended for the word "labor" (manual labor or all labor)); *but see* Blanchard v. Bergeron, 489 U.S. 87, 98–99 (1989) (Scalia, J., concurring in part and concurring in the judgment) (criticizing the use of committee reports).

61. NLRB v. Catholic Bishop of Chicago, 440 U.S. 490, 515 (1979) (Brennan, J., dissenting) (finding rejected amendments informative).

62. United Steelworkers v. Weber, 443 U.S. 193, 202 (1979) (citing floor debates); In re Virtual Network Servs. Corp., 98 B.R. 343, 349 (Bankr. N.D. Ill. 1989) ("The floor statements of individual legislators are larded with remarks which reflect a political ('sales talk') rather than a legislative purpose.").

- Sponsor statements[63]
- Silence:[64] The dog does not bark canon: if the act would cause significant change, it is unlikely a legislature would have intended such a change and not discussed it[65]
- Presidential signing statements & veto messages
  - Not "legislative" history at all
  - Generally not relevant to interpretation[66]
- Using legislative history
  - To find the purpose, or spirit, of the act[67]
  - To find specific congressional intent
  - Judges vary in their willingness to consider legislative history at all[68] and specific types of legislative history
- Criticism of the use of legislative history

---

63. United Steelworkers, 443 U.S. at 231–44 (1979) (Rehnquist, J., dissenting) (referring to statements from both the Senate and House sponsors to argue that Title VII of the Civil Rights Act was color-blind); Overseas Educ. Ass'n, Inc., v. Federal Labor Relations Auth., 876 F.2d 960, 967 n.41 (D.C. Cir. 1989) (citing more than ten cases relying on sponsor statements).

64. America Online, Inc. v. United States, 64 Fed. Cl. 571, 578 (2005) ("Silence in the legislative history about a particular provision ... is not a good guide to statutory interpretation and certainly is not more persuasive than the words of a statute.").

65. Harrison v. PPG Indus., Inc., 446 U.S. 578, 585 (1980) ("The 'most revealing' aspect of the legislative history of [the subsection at issue] ... was the complete absence of any discussion of such a 'massive shift' in jurisdiction.").

66. Hamdan v. Rumsfeld, 548 U.S. 557, 623 (2006) (ignoring President Bush's signing statement); United States v. Stevens, 559 U.S. 460, 480 (2010) (ignoring President Clinton's signing statement); DaCosta v. Nixon, 55 F.R.D. 145, 146 (E.D.N.Y. 1972) (ignoring President Nixon's signing statement); but see United States v. Lovett, 328 U.S. 303, 313 (1946) (citing President Roosevelt's signing statement).

67. United Steelworkers v. Weber, 443 U.S. 193, 201, 217 (1979) (in which the majority used legislative history to identify purpose while the dissent used it to find congressional intent).

68. Wisconsin Public Intervenor v. Mortier, 501 U.S. 597, 610 n.4 (1991) ("Our precedents demonstrate that the Court's practice of utilizing legislative history reaches well into its past. We suspect that the practice will likewise reach well into the future."); United States v. American Trucking Ass'ns, Inc., 310 U.S. 534, 543–44 (1940) ("When aid to construction of the meaning of words, as used in the statute, is available, there certainly can be no 'rule of law' which forbids its use, however clear the words may appear on 'superficial examination.'"); Koons Buick Pontiac GMC, Inc. v. Nigh, 543 U.S. 50, 73 (2004) (Scalia, J., dissenting) (criticizing the use of legislative history); see, e.g., In the Matter of Sinclair, 870 F.2d 1340, 1344 (7th Cir. 1989) (refusing to consider a conference committee report because it contradicted the ordinary meaning of the statute).

- Unconstitutional
- Unreliable
- Not accessible to all
- Expensive to research
- Unexpressed statutory purpose
  - Finding purpose
    - Within the text[69]
      - *Heydon*'s Case: the Mischief Rule[70]
        - Identify the law prior to the enactment,
        - Identify the mischief and defect, or the problem, the legislature wanted to correct,
        - Identify the remedy the legislature chose,
        - Interpret the statute to advance the remedy and suppress the mischief
    - Within purpose & findings clauses
    - Within legislative history
    - Within historical context
  - Using purpose
    - To confirm ordinary meaning,[71] and
    - To overcome ordinary meaning[72]
      - When there is ambiguity, absurdity, scrivener's error, or constitutional question

- Using post-enactment context (using what occurred after enactment)
  - Subsequent legislative acts
    - Subsequent legislatures can always change an existing act
    - The reenactment canon: recodification clarifies law, does not make substantive changes[73]

---

69. American Trucking Ass'ns, Inc., 310 U.S. at 543 ("There is, of course, no more persuasive evidence of the purpose of a statute than the words by which the legislature undertook to give expression to its wishes. Often these words are sufficient in and of themselves to determine the purpose of the legislation.").

70. 76 Eng. Rep. 637 (Ex. 1584).

71. Church of Scientology v. United States, 612 F.2d 417, 426 (9th Cir. 1979).

72. Amalgamated Transit Union Local 1309 v. Laidlaw Transit Servs., Inc., 435 F.3d 1140, 1145 (9th Cir. 2006) (finding a statute that imposed a waiting period to appeal rather than a time limit). *Cf.* Addison v. Holly Hill Fruit Prods., Inc., 322 U.S. 607, 617 (1944) ("To let general words draw nourishment from their purpose is one thing. To draw on some unexpressed spirit outside the bounds of the normal meaning of words is quite another.").

73. Fourco Glass Co. v. Transmirra Prods. Corp., 353 U.S. 222, 227 (1957).

- "Subsequent" legislative history[74]
  - Use of subsequent legislative history is highly controversial because the enactment of a subsequent act does not show the enacting legislature's intent regarding the existing act[75]
  - However, subsequent acts may provide insight into the contours of an existing act
- Super strong *stare decisis*
  - A heightened form of stare decisis
  - Directs that even when a judicial interpretation of a statute is "wrong," judges should be reluctant to overrule that interpretation because of the possibility of legislative acquiescence[76]
- Legislative acquiescence[77]
  - Directs a court to presume that through silence a legislature agreed with a prior statutory interpretation because the legislature did not amend the act in response
    - Legislative acquiescence is based on *stare decisis* and separation of powers
  - Criticisms:
    - Silence can mean many things, including (as legislative acquiescence presumes) that the legislature agreed with the judicial interpretation
    - The most common legislative response to a judicial interpretation of a statute is silence
    - Legislative acquiescence should be invoked rarely, if at all
- Subsequent executive acts: deference to agency interpretations of statutes & regulations
  - Agency interpretation of language in regulations
    - Standard of Review: *Auer* = plainly wrong[78]

---

74. Consumer Prod. Safety Comm'n v. GTE Sylvania, 447 U.S. 102, 117–18 n.13 (1980) ("[S]ubsequent legislative history will rarely override a reasonable interpretation of a statute that can be gleaned from its language and legislative history prior to its enactment.").

75. Sullivan v. Finkelstein, 496 U.S. 617, 632 (1990) (Scalia, J., concurring) ("Arguments based on subsequent legislative history, like arguments based on antecedent futurity, should not be taken seriously, not even in a footnote."); *but see* Montana Wilderness Ass'n v. U.S. Forest Serv., 655 F.2d 951, 957 (9th Cir. 1981) (relying on a conference committee report from a subsequent act).

76. Faragher v. City of Boca Raton, 524 U.S. 775, 804 n.4 (1998); Flood v. Kuhn, 407 U.S. 258, 279 (1972) (acknowledging that its earlier opinions holding that baseball was not interstate commerce was wrong but leaving the correction to Congress).

77. *Flood*, 407 U.S. at 283.

78. Auer v. Robbins, 519 U.S. 452, 461 (1997).

- Agency interpretation of language in statutes
  - Steps to find Standard of Review
  - First: *Chevron* step zero
    - Determine whether agency used "force of law" procedures
      - Force of law = formal rulemaking, informal rulemaking, and formal adjudication
      - Non force of law = all other procedures, *e.g.*, interpretive rules, policy statements, informal adjudications, Q & As
  - Second: for interpretations without force of law
    - Because of the lack of "force of law," courts presume that Congress did not intend courts to defer to agency interpretations
    - Standard of Review: *Skidmore* = power-to-persuade test[79]
      - Agency interpretation is given deference based on its power to persuade as determined by these factors:
        - The agency consistently interprets the language over time,
        - The agency thoroughly considered the issue, and
        - The agency offers sound reasoning to support the interpretation
  - For interpretations made with force of law
    - Presume that Congress intended courts to defer to agency interpretations
    - Standard of Review: *Chevron* = two step analysis[80]
      - Has Congress spoken to the precise issue before the court?
      - If not, is the agency interpretation reasonable?
  - Exception: Major Questions Doctrine
    - When the issue is too important to believe that Congress implicitly delegated interpretive power to the agency, courts require a clear statement from Congress before deferring[81]

---

79. Skidmore v. Swift & Co., 323 U.S. 134, 139–40 (1944).

80. Chevron v. National Resources Defense Council, Inc., 467 U.S. 837, 842–844 (1984).

81. FDA v. Brown & Williamson Tobacco Corp., 529 U.S. 120, 159 (2000) ("Deference under *Chevron* to an agency's construction of a statute that it administers is premised on the theory that a statute's ambiguity constitutes an implicit delegation from Congress to the agency to fill in the statutory gaps. In extraordinary cases, however, there may be reason to hesitate before concluding that Congress has intended such an implicit delegation.") (internal citations omitted); *see also* King v. Burwell, 135 S. Ct. 2480, 2489 (2015) ("Whether those [health care] credits are available on Federal Exchanges is thus a question of deep 'economic and political significance' that is central to this statutory scheme; had Congress wished to assign that question to an agency, it surely would have done so expressly.").

- For interpretations that conflict with prior judicial interpretations
  - Non force of law interpretations
    - This area of the law is unsettled, but it would seem that the agency has no power to interpret a statute differently than a court
  - Force of law interpretations
    - The agency has the power to interpret a statute differently than a court does when the court decided the meaning of the statute at *Chevron*'s step 2[82]

- **STEP 7:** Determine whether policy-based sources are relevant to meaning
  - **Policy-based sources** are extrinsic both to the statutory act and to the legislative process; they are based on the U.S. Constitution or policy preferences

  - Canons based on the Constitution
    - Clear Statement Rules
      - When courts require a legislature to include a clear statement when the legislature wishes to impact important areas of the law
      - Courts assume that a legislature would not make such important changes without being absolutely clear that it was doing so
      - Clear statements are required in many areas, including
        - Federalism[83]
        - Preemption[84]
        - American Indian lands[85]
        - Sovereign immunity[86]
        - Criminal statutes (*see* below, rule of lenity)

    - Penal Statutes
      - The rule of lenity[87]

---

82. National Cable & Telecomms. Ass'n v. Brand X Internet Servs., 545 U.S. 967, 980 (2005).

83. BFP v. Resolution Trust Corp., 511 U.S. 531, 544 (1994).

84. Medtronic, Inc. v. Lohr, 518 U.S. 470, 485 (1996).

85. Hagen v. Utah, 510 U.S. 399, 411 (1994); Solem v. Bartlett, 465 U.S. 463, 477–78 (1984).

86. Burch v. Secretary of Health & Human Servs., 2001 WL 180129, at *11 (Fed. Cl. Feb. 8, 2001).

87. McNally v. United States, 483 U.S. 350, 375 (1987) (Stevens, J., dissenting); United States v. Universal C.I.T. Corp., 344 U.S. 218, 221–22 (1952).

- Penal statutes[88] are those that punish citizens by imposing a fine or imprisonment
  - Whether the rule of lenity applies when statutes imposing administrative penalties are interpreted is currently unclear
- Directs that judges should strictly interpret penal statutes because the Due Process Clause requires that citizens have notice of criminal activity[89]
  - Former Justice Scalia applied the rule of lenity early in the interpretive process
  - Most judges apply the rule of lenity after all other sources of meaning have been considered and have not resolved the interpretation[90]
  - Some states have tried to abolish the rule of lenity by statute but have had limited luck due to the constitutional underpinnings
- *Ex post facto* prohibition[91]
  - *Ex post facto* laws defined[92]
  - Redefine criminal conduct or
  - Increase the penalty for criminal conduct
  - *Ex post facto* laws violate the U.S. Constitution
- Canons based on prudential considerations
  - Statutes in derogation of the common law[93]
    - Defined: statutes that partially repeal or abolish existing common law rights or otherwise limit the scope, utility, or force of that law
    - Such statutes should be narrowly construed
  - Remedial statutes[94]
    - Defined: statutes that create new rights or expand remedies

---

88. Babbitt v. Sweet Home Chapter, 515 U.S. 687, 704 n.18 (1995) (rejecting the rule of lenity argument in a case imposing regulatory fines); Modern Muzzleloading, Inc. v. Magaw, 18 F. Supp. 2d 29, 33 (D.C. 1998).

89. Keeler v. Superior Court, 470 P.2d 617, 626 (Cal. 1970).

90. United States v. Gonzalez, 407 F.3d 118, 125 (2d Cir. 2005); Reno v. Koray, 515 U.S. 50, 65 (1995).

91. U.S. Const. art. I, § 9, cl. 3.

92. Calder v. Bull, 3 U.S. (3 Dall.) 386, 390 (1798).

93. Behrens v. Raleigh Hills Hosp., 675 P.2d 1179, 1184 (Utah 1983); Cohen v. Rubin, 460 A.2d 1046, 1055 (Md. Ct. Spec. App. 1983).

94. Chisom v. Roemer, 501 U.S. 380, 403 (1991); Smith v. Brown, 35 F.3d 1516, 1525 (Fed. Cir. 1994).

- Such statutes should be broadly, not narrowly, construed to achieve their remedial purpose
  - *E.g.*, the Americans with Disabilities Act
- Implied causes of action & remedies[95]
  - Implied causes of action are not expressly provided for in the statute; rather, they are implied by a court[96]
    - Under today's more textualist approach to interpretation, implied causes of action are found less often
    - Whether a cause of action should be implied is one of congressional intent
    - Once a cause of action is implied, generally all statutory remedies will similarly be implied[97]

- **STEP 8:** Determine whether substantive canons unique to particular areas of law are relevant to meaning
  - Some examples:
    - **Contracts**: construe ambiguities against the drafter
    - **Tax**: tax statutes should be strictly construed, and if any ambiguity is found to exist in a tax statute, that ambiguity should be resolved in favor of the taxpayer.
    - **Veteran's Law**: *Gardner's* Presumption: interpretive doubt should be resolved in the veteran's favor
    - **Antitrust**: statutes should be liberally interpreted
    - **Immigration**: interpret ambiguities in favor of aliens
    - **International Law**: national statutes must be construed so as not to conflict with international law
    - **American Indians**: statutes are to be construed liberally in favor of Indians with ambiguous provisions interpreted to their benefit

---

95. Jackson v. Birmingham Bd. of Educ., 544 U.S. 167, 182 (2005) (reaffirming *Cannon*); Cannon v. University of Chicago, 441 U.S. 677, 711–12 (1979) (finding an implied cause of action).

96. Alexander v. Sandoval, 532 U.S. 275, 285 (2001) (identifying the Court's current approach to implying causes of action); CBOCS West, Inc. v. Humphries, 553 U.S. 442, 445 (2008); Transcript of Oral Argument at 45, CBOCS West, Inc. v. Humphries, 553 U.S. 442 (2008) (No. 06-1431) ("We inferred that cause of action [for section 1982] in the bad old days, when we were inferring causes of action all over the place.").

97. Doe v. County of Centre, PA, 242 F.3d 437, 456 (3d Cir. 2001); Franklin v. Gwinnett Cnty. Pub. Sch., 503 U.S. 60, 66 (1992).

Chapter 17

Master Checklist

The following outline reflects the topics covered in each chapter. A good understanding of the overall material requires detailed knowledge of each of these topics.

Chapter 1 — Preliminary Matters
- Learn what interpretation is and what it is not.
- Understand why most laws work as intended and interpretation is unnecessary.
- Use a hypothetical to help identify your current beliefs.

Chapter 2 — The Legislative Process
- Understand how a bill becomes a law.
- Learn about bicameralism and presentment.
- Understand the role of the various players in the legislative process.
- Learn how legislative history is created during the legislative process.
- Compare direct democracy processes.

Chapter 3 — Separation of Powers
- Learn what "separation of powers" is.
- Learn the formalist and functionalist approaches to this doctrine.
- Understand the role that separation of powers plays in statutory interpretation.

Chapter 4 — Statutory Interpretation:
Sources & Theories
- Identify the three sources of evidence judges use to interpret statutes: intrinsic sources, extrinsic sources, and policy-based sources.
- Study the three main theories judges use to interpret statutes: textualism, intentionalism, and purposivism.
- Learn about other theories, such as imaginative reconstructionism, dynamic interpretation, and Alaska's sliding scale approach.

- Discover how the states and other countries approach statutory interpretation.
- Learn that constitutional interpretation differs from statutory interpretation.
- Question whether theory really matters.

Chapter 5 — Canons Based on Intrinsic Sources: The Text, Grammar, & Punctuation

- Understand the plain meaning rule and its corollary, the technical meaning rule.
- Learn the difference between ordinary, definitional, and technical meanings.
- Understand that grammar and punctuation matter, except when they do not matter.
- Understand the basic grammar and punctuation rules.
- Understand special punctuation rules, such as the Doctrine of Last Antecedent.
- Learn special grammar rules relating to "and" and "or," singular and plural words, mandatory and permissive words, and masculine and feminine words.

Chapter 6 — Canons for Choosing or Avoiding Ordinary Meaning

- Learn how judges define and resolve ambiguity.
- Understand that the ordinary meaning may be absurd or raise a constitutional question.
- Learn how judges define and resolve absurdity.
- Learn how judges resolve interpretations that contain a scrivener's error or raise a constitutional question.

Chapter 7 — Canons Based on Intrinsic Sources: The Linguistic Canons

- Learn *in pari materia*: both the whole act and whole code aspects.
- Learn the linguistic canons including the presumption of consistent usage and meaningful variation, the rule against surplusage, *noscitur a sociis*, *ejusdem generis*, and *expressio unius est exclusio alterius*.
- Understand that the linguistic canons are simply rules reflecting commonly understood agreements about language usage.

Chapter 8 — Canons Based on Intrinsic Sources: The Components

- Learn the codification process.
- Identify the three parts of the bill, including the beginning provisions, the purview, and the closing provisions.
- Understand that the operative and enforcement sections include the general rule, any exceptions to that rule, and methods for enforcing the rule.
- Learn to start the interpretive process by finding language within the purview.
- Learn that the other components, such as headings, titles, enacting clauses, preambles, and definitions, may aid interpretation but do not establish rights, duties, or legal obligations.

Chapter 9 — Canons Based on Extrinsic Sources: Timing & the Legislative Process

- Learn how courts resolve issues involving statutes that conflict: specific statutes trump general statutes and later enacted statutes trump earlier enacted statutes.
- Learn what repeal by implication is and that it is disfavored.
- Understand when statutes can have retroactive effect and what that means.
- Discover that legislatures often borrow statutory language from other states and jurisdictions or use model or uniform acts.

Chapter 10 — Canons Based on Extrinsic Sources: Legislative History & Purpose

- Learn to use what occurred *prior to* and *during* the enactment process.
- Understand what legislative history is.
- Learn where to find legislative history, how to use it, and how to criticize its use.
- Understand how to find purpose and discover its relevance to interpretation.

Chapter 11 — Canons Based on Extrinsic Sources: Post-Enactment Legislative & Judicial Context

- Learn to use what occurred in the legislature *after* the enactment process.
- Understand *stare decisis* effect of judicial interpretations.
- Learn the relationship between super strong *stare decisis* and legislative acquiescence.

- Understand the role of subsequent legislative action, including new enactments, subsequent legislative history, reenactments, and affidavits from legislators.

Chapter 12 — Canons Based on Policy-Based Considerations: Constitutional & Prudential

- Identify the canons based on constitutional and prudential considerations.
- Reexamine how the Constitutional Avoidance Doctrine applies.
- Learn the rule of lenity and its role in penal cases.
- Understand when clear statements are necessary.
- Explore the canons regarding remedial statutes and statutes in derogation of common law.
- Understand implied causes of action and implied remedies.

Chapter 13 — The Administrative State: An Introduction to Administrative Agencies

- Learn what agencies are and what they do.
- Examine how agencies fit within our constitutional structure.
- Understand the direct and indirect ways that the legislature and executive exert control over agency actions.

Chapter 14 — The Administrative State: Legislative & Executive Oversight of Agencies

- Learn the ways that Congress controls agency actions, including enacting other relevant legislation and funding agencies.
- Learn the ways the executive controls agency actions, including appointment and removal, executive orders and directives, and signing statements.
- Understand that the president appoints principal officers with the advice and consent of the Senate and can generally remove such officers at will.
- Understand that Congress can give the president, the courts of law, or the heads of departments the power to appoint inferior officers.
- Consider whether Congress may limit a president's ability to remove agency officials who perform quasi-judicial or quasi-legislative activity.
- Learn that inferior officers are subordinate to principal officers.
- Note that inferior officers, unlike mere employees, exercise significant authority pursuant to the laws of the United States.
- Learn that signing statements are largely irrelevant to interpretation.

Chapter 15 — The Administrative State:
Judicial Review of Agency Decisions

- Understand the differences among questions of law, application, fact, and policy.
- Understand the difference between standard of review and scope of review.
- Learn the standard of review that courts apply to agency findings of law and law application.
- Understand *Chevron*'s two-step test, *Skidmore*'s power-to-persuade test, and *Auer*'s plainly-wrong test.
- Learn the standard of review that courts apply to agency findings of fact and policy.
- Understand substantial evidence and arbitrary and capricious review.

Appendix A

Glossary

While this glossary defines many of the new words you will encounter learning this subject, it is not a substitute for looking up unfamiliar words on your own. Part of learning the law is learning its language. Even words that may look familiar to you may take on a different meaning to someone with legal training.

Absurdity Doctrine — when interpreting a statute according to its ordinary meaning would lead to absurd results, courts can avoid the ordinary meaning

Act — a law that Congress has passed and the president has signed; acts originate as bills and become acts when enacted

Adjudication — agency action that is similar to civil litigation; can be very informal

Administrative Conference of the United States (ACUS) — an independent federal agency dedicated to improving the administrative process and federal agency procedures

Administrative Law — the law governing the procedures that agencies use

Administrative Procedures Act (APA) — the statute that governs the procedural activities of federal agencies

Administrative Provisions (or Sections) — sections of an act that address the creation, organization, powers, and procedures of the governmental organization that will enforce or adjudicate the law

Adversarial Legal System — a system to resolve legal disputes which is based on two sides vigorously arguing for their side with a neutral decision-maker, as in the United States

Agency — as defined in 5 U.S.C. § 551(1): "each authority of the Government of the United States ... not includ[ing Congress, the courts, state governments, etc.]"

Ambiguity — when reasonable people understand words to have more than one meaning

Amendment — a change or addition to a bill or legal document

Amendment by Implication—when the legislature does not indicate expressly that it is amending a statute, but the judiciary assumes that the legislature intended to amend the existing statute

Appropriations Bill—a bill that authorizes the government to spend money

A Priori—Latin for "relating to"; referring to something that is based on a theoretical deduction rather than an empirical deduction

Arbitrary & Capricious Review—the standard of review that courts apply when reviewing agency policy decisions and factual findings that are made during informal rulemakings and adjudications

Article I Court—administrative agencies that Congress creates pursuant to Article I of the U.S. Constitution to adjudicate specific disputes, e.g., the United States Court of Federal Claims

Article III Court—federal courts that Congress creates pursuant to Article III of the U.S. Constitution

Articles of Confederation—the original constitution of the United States, which was ratified in 1781 and was replaced by the US Constitution in 1789

***Auer* (Seminole Rock) Analysis**—the standard of review courts apply when reviewing agency interpretations of their own regulations

***Auer* Deference**—deference by a court to an agency's interpretation of a regulation because it is not plainly wrong

Avoidance Canon—another name for the constitutional avoidance doctrine

Bargaining Theory—a legislative process theory that focuses on furthering the compromises that lead to a bill's passage

Bicameral—a system of government involving a legislative branch that has two branches or chambers

Bicameral Passage—the Constitutional requirement that both chambers of Congress pass a bill in identical form before it can become law; also required in almost all states

Bill—a law that Congress or the President has or is considering but has not yet enacted; if enacted, a bill becomes an act

Borrowed Statutes—statutes that are taken, in whole or in part, from another jurisdiction

Cabinet—the collective heads of the Departments who have served to guide the president in years past

Canons of Interpretation—rules of thumb, or guides, judges use when interpreting statutes

***Chevron* Analysis**—the standard of review courts apply when reviewing agency interpretations of statutes they administer; requires that the court look first to see if Congress has spoken on the issue, and then if not, to defer to any reasonable agency interpretation

Chevron **Deference**—deference by a court to an agency's interpretation of a statute under Chevron's second step

Chevron **Step Zero**—the doctrine that before a court applies Chevron analysis, the court must determine whether the agency used force of law procedures when issuing its interpretation or whether Congress provided some other indication that it wished the courts to defer to the agency's interpretation

Civil Law—general principles laid out in a code for courts to use to guide decision-making

Classical Avoidance Canon—a stronger version of the constitutional avoidance doctrine, which requires a court to find the statute unconstitutional before adopting another, fair interpretation

Clause (Provision)—generic name for a section or part of a statute; can be used interchangeably with "provision"

Clear Statement Rules—when courts require the legislature to make a clear or plain statement when a statute will impact important rights, such as federalism, because the court assumes that a legislature would not make such a major change without being absolutely clear

Closed Rule—a type of process for consideration of bills in the House that prohibits members from offering amendments to the bill; voted on by the members

Cloture—the process in which sixty senators agree to defeat a filibuster

Code—a collection of statutes or regulations

Code of Federal Regulations—the codified rules and regulations of federal administrative agencies; divided into fifty different titles

Codification—the process of consolidating statutes into subjects, forming a legal code

Committee of the Whole—the largest committee in the House, which is made up of all representatives and was formed to debate proposed bills

Committee Report—a document produced by the House and Senate committees that address legislative and other policy issues, investigations, and internal committee matters; they are uniquely identified by a standardized citation that includes the Congress, chamber (House or Senate), and report number

Common Law—law developed in incremental fashion by courts, as opposed to law made by a legislative or regulatory body

Conference Committee—an ad hoc committee, which is usually composed of senior members of the standing committees of each chamber that originally considered the legislation, formed to resolve differences in the two bills

Conference Committee Report—a document the Conference Committee produces to propose and explain amending language to a bill

Conflicting Statutes—statutes that cannot exist harmoniously

Constitutional Avoidance Canon/Avoidance Canon—the doctrine that allows judges to avoid the ordinary meaning of the statute when there are two reasonable interpretations of statutory language and one meaning does not raise constitutional doubt

Contextualism—the process of using the context to determine why the legislature acted or to determine what a statute means

Definitional Meaning—the many ways a word might be used, which dictionaries show

Definitions Provisions (or Sections)—the sections in an act that define words and phrases within the act

Delegation Doctrine, the—the doctrine by which the Supreme Court determines whether intelligible principles sufficiently constrain legislative or quasi-legislative power delegated to agencies from Congress

De Novo—Latin for "starting from the beginning, or anew"; meaning to give no deference to what was decided below

Derogation of the Common Law—a statute that partially repeals or abolishes existing common law rights or otherwise limits the scope, utility, or force of that law

Discretionary Language—the use of the word "may" or "should" in a statute means that the action is not required

Dog Does Not Bark Doctrine—the canon that directs that silence in the legislative history about a particular subject is generally not a good guide to meaning

Due Process—a fundamental principle located in the Fifth and Fourteenth Amendments of the federal Constitution, which protects individual rights during adjudication in accordance with fundamental principles of justice. Notice and the right to an unbiased adjudicator are examples.

Due Process Clause—clauses within the Fifth and Fourteenth Amendments of the federal Constitution, which protect individual rights during adjudication

Dynamic Interpretation—a theory of interpretation that encourages judges to be flexible and consider what the enacting legislature would have wanted, given modern day realities

Ejusdem Generis—the linguistic canon that general words should be limited to include only things similar in nature to the specific words near the general words

Enabling Act & Statute—the act creating an agency, if it did not already exist, and identifying the agency's regulatory authority

Enacting Clause—a section of a bill that is statutorily required. Components following enacting clauses are codified. Components preceding enacting clauses are not codified.

En Banc—Latin for "the full court"; used when all judges of a particular court hear a case

Engrossed Bill—a bill that one chamber of Congress has passed and forwarded to the other chamber

Enrolled Bill—a bill that both chambers of Congress have passed in identical form and have forwarded to the president for signature

Enrolled Bill Rule—the rule that once a bill is filed, it is conclusively presumed to have been validly adopted

Exception Provision—provisions that exclude something from a statute's reach or qualify something within a statute; see proviso below

Exclusionary Rule—a rule of statutory interpretation used in England by which judges refuse to consider the legislative history of a statute for any reason

Executive Agency—a federal agency that is very much subject to presidential control because the head serves at the pleasure of the president

Executive Order—written statements from a president or governor directing agencies and officials in the execution of legislatively granted authority

Ex Parte—involving one side or one party only

Ex Post Facto **Law**—a law that redefines what is criminal conduct or increases the penalty for criminal conduct; the Ex Post Facto Clause of the U.S. Constitution prohibits such laws

Expressio (Inclusio) Unius (Est Exclusio Alterius)—the linguistic canon of negative implication such that the inclusion of one thing means the exclusion of another; see also inclusio unius

Ex Rel.—Latin for "on the relation of"; when used in the case caption, the party named after "ex rel." is the party on whose information the suit is brought

Extrinsic Sources of Meaning—materials outside of the official act but within the legislative process that created the act

Federalism—a system of government in which entities such as states or provinces share power with a national government

Federalist Papers — eighty-five essays written by Alexander Hamilton, James Madison, and John Jay in the late 1780s to persuade the voters of New York to adopt the Federal Constitution

Federal Register — a daily publication from the federal government that includes proposed and final regulations from administrative agencies

Filibuster — generally a prolonged speech offered by a senator as a delaying tactic to obstruct the legislative progress

Five-Minute-Rule — the House rule that in theory limits debate for and against an amendment offered in the Committee of the Whole to ten minutes, five minutes in support and five minutes in opposition

Formalism — an approach the Supreme Court uses in separation of powers cases to maintain three distinct branches of government with constitutionally defined powers

Framers — the drafters of the United States Constitution

Functionalism — an approach the Supreme Court uses in separation of powers cases to balance the inevitable overlap among the branches

Funnel of Abstraction — a V-shaped diagram generated by Professors Eskridge and Frickey that depicts the sources of interpretation on one side of the V and the concreteness of that source on the other side of the V to explain pragmatic theory

General Assemblies — the name for state legislatures in some states

General Intent — another term for the purpose of a statute, often determined by using the Mischief Rule; used by purposivists

Germane — relevant to a subject under consideration

Germaneness Rule — the rule in the House that permits amendments to bills only if the amendments are germane to the bill being considered

Golden Rule Exception — the absurdity doctrine; the idea that if interpreting a statute according to its ordinary meaning would lead to absurd results, a court can avoid the ordinary meaning

Grandfather (Saving) Clauses — provisions that limit the application of the new law by exempting certain activity from the new law's reach

Guidance & Guidance Documents — non-legislative, non-binding rules that agencies issue that advise the public about the agency's interpretation of a statute or regulation or that indicate the agency's plans regarding its approach to regulating, including interpretive rules and policy statements

Horizontal Hierarchy of Law — the understanding that some sources of law within a jurisdiction trump other sources of law from that same jurisdiction: a constitution is superior to legislation, which is superior to regulation, which is superior to common law

House of Representatives (or House) — the lower house of the United States Congress

Hybrid Rulemaking & Adjudication — agency rulemaking and adjudication subject to procedures in addition to those the APA requires

Identical Words Presumption (Presumption of Consistent Usage and Meaningful Variation) — the linguistic canon directing that when the legislature uses the same word in different parts of the same act or a related act, the legislature intended those words to have the same meaning (consistent usage), and that if the legislature uses a word in one part of an act or a related act, then changes to a different word in another part of the same or related act, the legislature intended to change the meaning (meaningful variation)

Imaginative Reconstructionism — a theory of interpretation in which a judge would try to imagine what the enacting legislature would have intended had the precise factual problem before the court been raised during the enactment process

Implied Causes of Action and Remedies — causes of action and remedies that are not expressly provided for in the statute, but that the court implies based on the goals of the legislature

Inclusio (Expressio) Unius (Est Exclusio Alterius) — another name for expressio unius, the linguistic canon of negative implication such that the inclusion of one thing means the exclusion of another

Independent Agency — a type of agency that is more independent from the president because it is headed by a multi-member, bi-partisan board, serving terms

Inferior Officer — an agency official who has a superior who reports directly to the president

In Haec Verba — Latin for "in these words," meaning to include the exact language of an agreement in a complaint or other pleading rather than attaching a copy as an exhibit

Initiative Process — a form of direct democracy in which a certain minimum number of registered voters sign a petition to force a public vote on a proposed issue

In Pari Materia — a linguistic canon that identifies the statutory material that judges can legitimately look at to discern meaning, including the entire act and other statutes with similar purposes

Inquisitorial Legal System — a system to resolve legal disputes in which the judge is actively involved rather than a neutral decision-maker

Inseverability Provision—a provision in a bill or act that indicates a legislature's expectation that if any provision in the act is unconstitutional, the act as a whole must fail

Intelligible Principle Doctrine—the doctrine that Congress cannot constitutionally delegate policymaking power to an agency unless Congress provides a guiding standard, or intelligible principle, with the delegation

Intentionalism—a theory of statutory interpretation that focuses on finding the specific intent of the enacting legislature

Intentionalist—one who uses the intentionalism theory of interpretation

Inter Alia—Latin for "among other things"

Interpretive (Interpretative) Rule—a non-legislative rule issued by an agency that interprets language in a statute or regulation

Intrinsic Sources of Meaning—sources of meaning from the official act being interpreted; sometimes called textual sources

Journal Entry Rule—a rule in states that allows judges to determine whether constitutional enactment requirements were met by looking at the bill's journal entry

Last Antecedent, Doctrine of—a grammar canon that directs that a limiting or restrictive clause in a statute is generally construed to restrict the immediately preceding clause unless a comma separates the two

Last Enacted Rule—the doctrine that when two statutes conflict and cannot be harmonized, the last in time controls

Legislative Acquiescence—the reasoning that the legislature's failure to take action in response to a judicial interpretation of a statute means that the legislature agreed with or acquiesced to the judicial interpretation

Legislative History—the written record of deliberations surrounding and preceding a bill's enactment, including committee reports and hearing transcripts, floor debates, recorded votes, conference committee reports, presidential signing and veto messages, etc.

Legislative Inaction—when the legislature takes no action in response to a judicial interpretation of a statute

Legislative Intent, General—the purpose of the enacting legislature for enacting a bill

Legislative Intent, Specific—the intent of the enacting legislature on the specific issue before the court

Legislative Rules—rules an agency enacts that have binding effect (legislative rulemaking is the process of enacting legislative rules)

Legislative Supremacy—the notion that the policy decisions of the legislature must be respected because the Constitution grants the legislature all legislative power

Legislative Veto—a provision in a statute that allows one or both bodies of Congress to issue a resolution to overturn a rulemaking or other action taken by an executive agency; one house legislative vetoes are unconstitutional

Legislator—a member of a state or federal legislative body

Lenity, Rule of—a canon of interpretation based on due process concerns that judges should strictly interpret penal statutes

Lexical Ambiguity—occurs when a word or phrase has multiple meanings, such as "bay," "pen," and "suit"

Linguistic (Semantic) Canons—common-sense rules that reflect shared assumptions about the way English speakers and writers use language and grammar

Lobbyists—individuals who are generally paid to represent a particular point of view for a specific industry or organization

Major Questions Doctrine—the doctrine in which a court does not apply Chevron analysis to an agency's interpretation of a statute because the issue is too important to the national economy

Majority Party Leader—the lead speaker for the majority party, who develops the calendar and assists the President of the Senate or Speaker of the House with policy

Mandatory Language—the use of the word "shall" in a statute means that the action is required to occur; similarly, the use of the word "must" makes the statute mandatory when a condition precedent has been satisfied

Minority Party Leader—the lead speaker for the minority party, who develops the minority position and negotiates with the majority party

Mischief Rule—the idea that statutes should be interpreted to further their purpose or to limit the mischief the statute was designed to remedy

Model Acts—proposed acts that the National Conference of Commissioners on Uniform State Laws or the American Law Institute developed to address multijurisdictional issues; uniformity is not central

Moderate Textualism—a form of textualism that prohibits consideration of extrinsic and policy-based sources absent a threshold finding of ambiguity or absurdity

Moderate Textualist—one who uses the textualism theory of interpretation

Modified Closed Rule—a type of process for consideration of bills in the House that allows members to offer limited amendments to the bill; voted on by the members

Necessary and Proper Clause—Article I, section 8 of the U.S. Constitution, which provides that Congress may make all laws that are necessary and proper for executing its enumerated and other powers

New Textualism—a form of textualism that focuses on the legislative compromises as they are evidenced by the text

New Textualist—one who follows the new textualism theory of interpretation

Nondelegation Doctrine—the idea that Congress cannot delegate legislative power under the U.S. Constitution unless the delegation includes limiting principles called intelligible principles

Non-legislative Rule—a rule an agency issues that does not have binding effect (non-legislative rulemaking is the process of issuing a non-legislative rule)

Noscitur a Sociis—the linguistic canon that that when a word has more than one meaning, the appropriate meaning should be gleaned from the words surrounding the word being interpreted; generally used when the statute contains a list of words

Notice-and-Comment Rulemaking—another name for informal rulemaking required under the Administrative Procedures Act; an agency publishes notice of a proposed rule, then seeks public comment on the rule

Open Rule—a type of process for consideration of bills in the House that allows members to offer any germane amendments to the bill; voted on by the members

Operative Provisions (or Sections)—the sections of an act that (1) identify the rights, duties, powers, and privileges being created, and (2) address the creation, organization, powers, and procedures of the governmental organization that will enforce or adjudicate the law

Ordinary Meaning—the commonly understood meaning of a word or phrase, generally narrower than dictionary meanings

Originalism—a theory of constitutional interpretation that looks for the Framers' original intent and does not consider the document to be a living document

Originalists—adherents of the theory of originalism, such as former Justice Scalia

Override—Congress's ability to overcome a president's veto of a bill; requires 2/3 positive vote from each chamber of Congress

Penal Statute—a statute that has a punitive effect

Plain Meaning Rule (or Canon)—a canon, or rule of thumb, that allows judges to presume that words in a statute have their "plain," or "ordinary," meaning

Plain Meaning Theorists—adherents of the plain meaning theory of interpretation

Plain Meaning Theory—another name for textualism that recognizes the role that the plain meaning canon plays in interpretation; proponents are willing to consider non-textual sources of meaning even when the statute is not ambiguous or absurd

Pluralist Theories—theories of legislative process that focus on the role special interest groups play in setting legislative policy, such as bargaining theory and public choice theory

Pocket Veto—if the president does not sign an enrolled bill for ten days during which Congress adjourns, the bill is vetoed

Points of Order—a query during a legislative debate regarding whether the correct procedure is being followed

Policy-Based Sources of Meaning—sources of meaning that are extrinsic to both the statutory act and the legislative process; generally based on the Constitution or policy considerations

Policy Statement & General Statement of Policy—a non-binding statement an agency issues to advise the public about its thoughts on an issue or to give guidance

Post Hoc—Latin for "occurring after an event"

Pragmatism—a theory of constitutional interpretation that allows for the Constitution to evolve as a living document

Pragmatists—adherents of the theory of pragmatism, such as Justice Breyer

Preambles—a component in a bill that often precedes the enacting clause and explains the reason the statute is being enacted

Preemption—the displacing effect that federal law has on conflicting or inconsistent state law

Presentment—the Constitutional requirement that a bill be presented to the president and be signed before it becomes law

President Pro Tempore—the most senior senator in the majority party who presides when the vice president is absent from deliberations

Presidential Directive—written or oral direction from the president, generally to federal agencies, regarding actions to be taken or not taken

Presiding Officer of the Senate—the person who presides over the Senate, maintains order, recognizes members to speak, and interprets the Senate's rules, practices, and precedents; typically the vice president, but the president pro tempore may fill this role in the vice president's absence

Presumption of Consistent Usage and Meaningful Variation (Identical Words Presumption)—the linguistic canon directing that when the legislature uses the same word in different parts of the same act or a related act, the legislature intended those words to have the same meaning (consistent usage), and that if the legislature uses a word in one part of an act or a related act, then changes to a different word in another part of the same or related act, the legislature intended to change the meaning (meaningful variation)

Principal Officer — an agency official who reports directly to the president

Provision (Clause) — generic name for a section or part of a statute; can be used interchangeably with "clause"

Proviso — a clause in a statute that creates an exception to or otherwise limits the effect of another provision; provisos often start with "provided that," "except for," and "provided however"

Public Choice Theory — a legislative process theory that statutes are the result of compromises among legislators and various competing private interest groups

Purpose — the reason the statute was enacted, the mischief that was designed to be remedied; also called the spirit of the law

Purposivism — a theory of statutory interpretation that focuses on the purpose of the statute and looks at all sources of meaning

Purposivist — one who uses the purposivism theory of interpretation

Reenactment Canon — the presumption that the recodification clarified the law but did not make substantive changes, unless the new language unmistakably indicates the legislature's intent to make substantive changes

Recodification — to codify again, see reenactment

Recommits — the process of referring a bill back to committee

Reenactment — to codify again, see recodify

Referendum — a popular form of democracy that allows voters to approve or reject legislation a legislature passes

Regulation — a rule an agency promulgates via its rulemaking procedures

Regulated Entity — a general term for those entities that agencies regulate

Remedial Statutes — statutes that are in aid of the common law or create new rights and remedies rather than being in derogation of the common law

Repeal by Implication — when the legislature does not indicate expressly that it is repealing a statute, but the judiciary assumes that the legislature intended to repeal the existing statute because it cannot exist in harmony with a conflicting statute

Representative — a person who serves in the House of Representatives

Resolution, Concurrent and Simple — proposed laws that regulate procedure or express Congress's opinion on a relevant issue

Retroactive—statutes that govern both past and future conduct; generally statutes only govern future conduct

Rider—a provision added to an appropriations bill typically to affect agency action

Rule against Surplusage (Superfluity)—the linguistic canon that a statute should be construed so that effect is given to all its words and phrases, so that no part will be inoperative or superfluous, void or insignificant

Rules Committee—the committee in the House or Senate that determines the rules governing debate on proposed bills

Saving (Grandfather) Clauses—provisions that limit the application of the new law by exempting certain activity from the new law's reach

Scrivener's Error—a doctrine that permits judges to correct obvious clerical or typographical errors

Semantic (Linguistic) Canons—common-sense rules that reflect shared assumptions about the way English speakers and writers use language and grammar

Senate—the upper house of the United States Congress or state legislature

Senator—a person who serves in a state or federal senate

Separation of Powers—the notion that the powers of government should be split among the various branches of government

Session Laws—legislative enactments for an annual period that have been bound chronologically. Federal session laws can be found in the Statutes at Large

Severability Provision—a provision in a bill or act that indicates a legislature's expectation that if any one section of an act is unconstitutional, then it shall be severed so that the rest of the act may be saved

Signing Statements—statements a president or governor issues when a bill is passed, often to impact the law in some way

Single Subject Rule—the rule in most state constitutions that bills may only include one subject

Skidmore **Analysis**—the standard of review courts apply when reviewing agency interpretations of statutes that do not receive Chevron deference; agency interpretations receive deference under Skidmore to the extent that they have the power-to-persuade the court; known as the Power-to-Persuade test

Skidmore **Deference**—deference by a court to an agency's interpretation of a statute under Skidmore analysis

Slip Laws—a legislative enactment that is published separately and promptly after passage, which can be used and cited in temporary form until it is published in a more permanent form by the Government Printing Office or state equivalent

Sovereign Immunity—a judge-made doctrine that a government or sovereign may not be sued without its consent

Speaker of the House—the leader of the House of Representatives

Specific Intent—the expectation an enacting legislature may have had regarding an interpretive issue before the court; used by intentionalists

Spirit of the Law—the purpose of the statute

Sponsor of a Bill—the legislator or legislators proposing a bill to the legislature

Standard/Scope of (Judicial) Review—the standard a court will use to review an issue; standard of review refers to the particular review used, such as abuse of discretion, while the scope of review refers to the breadth of that standard, such as very deferential

Stare Decisis—the policy of the court to respect prior precedent (see super strong stare decisis below)

Statute—a written law enacted by a legislative body and the executive; used for either one section or piece of an act or multiple sections or pieces

Statutes at Large (U.S.)—a chronological compilation of all enacted acts; includes the slip laws

Statutory Construction—another name for statutory interpretation

Statutory Interpretation—the process of determine the meaning of language in a statute

Steering Committee—a committee in the House that assigns fellow party members to other House committees and advises party leaders on policy; each party has its own committee

Strict Construction—a theory of interpretation similar to textualism that strictly construes words in the statute

Structural Ambiguity—when a sentence or phrase can be interpreted in more than one way due to ambiguous structure, such as "visiting relatives can be boring"

Sub Nom.—Latin for "under another name"; used in case citations when the case name changes during appeal

Subsequent Legislative History—comments made during the legislative enactment of a later act addressing an earlier act

Sub Silentio—Latin for "in silence"; used when something is implied but not expressly stated

Substantial Evidence Standard—the standard of review that courts apply when reviewing agency findings of fact during formal rulemaking or adjudication

Substantive Provisions (or Sections)—sections of an act that identify the rights, duties, powers, and privileges being created

Sunset Provision—a clause that provides that an act or some of its provisions shall no longer have effect after a specific date, unless further legislative action is taken to extend the act

Super Strong *Stare Decisis*—a heightened form of stare decisis the Supreme Court (and occasionally lower courts) uses for its statutory interpretation decisions

Technical Meaning Rule (or Canon)—a corollary to the plain meaning rule; the technical meaning rule directs that a word or phrase that has acquired a technical or particular meaning in a particular context has that meaning if it is used in that context

Textualism—a theory of statutory interpretation that focuses on the text and intrinsic sources of meaning

Textualist—one who uses the textualism theory of interpretation, most commonly modern textualism

Title Canon—titles of statutes are not controlling, but may be relevant to meaning in some situations

Ultra Vires—without legal authority to act

Unicameral—a system of government involving a legislative branch having one branch or chamber

Uniform Acts—proposed acts developed by the National Conference of Commissioners on Uniform State Laws or the American Law Institute to address multijurisdictional issues; uniformity is central across jurisdictions

Uniform Statute & Rule Construction Act—a uniform act drafted by the National Conference of Commissioners on Uniform State Laws to unify statutory interpretation

United States Code—the official compilation and codification of all federal laws, which contains 44 titles

Vertical Hierarchy of Law—the idea that law from higher sources trumps laws from lower sources: federal law is superior to state law, which is superior to local law

Veto—the president's rejection of a bill

Vetogate—a term Professors Eskridge and Frickey coined to describe the chokepoints in the legislative process that can prevent a bill from becoming law, such as committee votes

Veto Messages—written messages from the executive explaining the reasoning behind a veto

Whip—legislators who try to ensure that their party's members vote as the party leadership desires

Whole Act Aspect—a component of the in pari materia canon that a court may look to the entire act when construing a statute

Whole Code Aspect—a component of the in pari materia canon that a court may look to the entire code, so long as the statutes have similar purposes, when construing a statute

Appendix B

House Bill 916

Union Calendar No. 88

110TH CONGRESS   H. R. 916
1ST SESSION

[Report No. 110-148]

To provide for loan repayment for prosecutors and public defenders.

————

IN THE HOUSE OF REPRESENTATIVES
FEBRUARY 8, 2007

Mr. SCOTT of Georgia (for himself, Mr. GORDON of Tennessee, Mr. LEWIS of Georgia, Mr. PAYNE....) introduced the following bill; which was referred to the Committee on the Judiciary

MAY 14, 2007

Additional sponsors: Mr. LINCOLN DAVIS of Tennessee, Mr. COOPER, Mr. CHANDLER, Mr. UDALL of Colorado....

MAY 14, 2007

Reported with an amendment, committed to the Committee of the Whole House on the State of the Union, and ordered to be printed

————

A BILL

To provide for loan repayment for prosecutors and public defenders.

Be it enacted by the Senate and House of Representatives of the United States of America in Congress assembled,

SECTION 1. SHORT TITLE.

This Act may be cited as the "John R. Justice Prosecutors and Defenders Incentive Act of 2007".

SEC. 2. LOAN REPAYMENT FOR PROSECUTORS AND DEFENDERS.

Title I of the Omnibus Crime Control and Safe Streets Act of 1968 (42 U.S.C. 3711 et seq.) is amended by adding at the end the following:

"PART JJ—LOAN REPAYMENT FOR PROSECUTORS AND PUBLIC DEFENDERS

499

"SEC. 3111. GRANT AUTHORIZATION.

"(a) PURPOSE. — The purpose of this section is to encourage qualified individuals to enter and continue employment as prosecutors and public defenders.

"(b) DEFINITIONS. — In this section:

"(1) PROSECUTOR. — The term 'prosecutor' means a full-time employee of a State or local agency who—

"(A) is continually licensed to practice law; and

"(B) prosecutes criminal or juvenile delinquency cases (or both) at the State or local level, including an employee who supervises, educates, or trains other persons prosecuting such cases.

"(2) PUBLIC DEFENDER. — The term 'public defender' means an attorney who—

"(A) is continually licensed to practice law; and

"(B) is—

"(i) a full-time employee of a State or local agency who provides legal representation to indigent persons in criminal or juvenile delinquency cases (or both), including an attorney who supervises, educates, or trains other persons providing such representation;

"(ii) a full-time employee of a non-profit organization operating under a contract with a State or unit of local government, who devotes substantially all of such full-time employment to providing legal representation to indigent persons in criminal or juvenile delinquency cases (or both), including an attorney who supervises, educates, or trains other persons providing such representation; or

"(iii) employed as a full-time Federal defender attorney in a defender organization established pursuant to subsection (g) of section 3006A of title 18, United States Code, that provides legal representation to indigent persons in criminal or juvenile delinquency cases (or both).

"(3) STUDENT LOAN. — The term 'student loan' means—

"(A) a loan made, insured, or guaranteed under part B of title IV of the Higher Education Act of 1965 (20 U.S.C. 1071 et seq.);

"(B) a loan made under part D or E of 20 title IV of the Higher Education Act of 1965 (20 U.S.C. 1087a et seq. and 1087aa et seq.); and

"(C) a loan made under section 428C or 23 455(g) of the Higher Education Act of 1965 (20 U.S.C. 1078-3 and 1087e(g)) to the extent that such loan was used to repay a Federal Direct Stafford Loan, a Federal Direct Unsubsidized Stafford Loan, or a loan made under section 428 or 428H of such Act.

"(c) PROGRAM AUTHORIZED.—The Attorney General shall, subject to the availability of appropriations, establish a program by which the Department of Justice shall assume the obligation to repay a student loan, by direct payments on behalf of a borrower to the holder of such loan, in accordance with subsection (d), for any borrower who—

"(1) is employed as a prosecutor or public defender; and

"(2) is not in default on a loan for which the borrower seeks forgiveness.

"(d) TERMS OF LOAN REPAYMENT.—

"(1) BORROWER AGREEMENT.—To be eligible to receive repayment benefits under subsection (c), a borrower shall enter into a written agreement with the Attorney General that specifies that—

"(A) the borrower will remain employed as a prosecutor or public defender for a required period of service of not less than 3 years, unless in voluntarily separated from that employment;

"(B) if the borrower is involuntarily separated from employment on account of misconduct, or voluntarily separates from employment, before the end of the period specified in the agreement, the borrower will repay the Attorney General the amount of any benefits received by such employee under this section; and

"(C) if the borrower is required to repay an amount to the Attorney General under subparagraph (B) and fails to repay such amount, a sum equal to that amount shall be recoverable by the Federal Government from the employee (or such employee's estate, if applicable) by such methods as are provided by law for the recovery of amounts owed to the Federal Government.

"(2) REPAYMENT BY BORROWER.—

"(A) IN GENERAL.—Any amount repaid by, or recovered from, an individual or the estate of an individual under this subsection shall be credited to the appropriation account from which the amount involved was originally paid.

"(B) MERGER.—Any amount credited under subparagraph (A) shall be merged with other sums in such account and shall be available for the same purposes and period, and subject to the same limitations, if any, as the sums with which the amount was merged.

"(C) WAIVER.—The Attorney General may waive, in whole or in part, a right of recovery under this subsection if it is shown that recovery would be against equity and good conscience or against the public interest.

"(3) LIMITATIONS.—

"(A) STUDENT LOAN PAYMENT AMOUNT.—Student loan repayments made by the Attorney General under this section shall be made subject to the availability of appropriations, and subject to such terms, limitations, or conditions as may be mutually agreed upon by the borrower and the Attorney General in an agreement under paragraph (1), except that the amount paid by the Attorney General under this section shall not exceed—

"(i) $10,000 for any borrower in any calendar year; or

"(ii) an aggregate total of $60,000 in the case of any borrower.

"(B) BEGINNING OF PAYMENTS.—Nothing in this section shall authorize the Attorney General to pay any amount to reimburse a borrower for any repayments made by such borrower prior to the date on which the Attorney General entered into an agreement with the borrower under this subsection.

"(e) ADDITIONAL AGREEMENTS.—

"(1) IN GENERAL.—On completion of the required period of service under an agreement under subsection (d), the borrower and the Attorney General 7 may, subject to paragraph (2), enter into an additional agreement in accordance with subsection (d).

"(2) TERM.—An agreement entered into under paragraph (1) may require the borrower to remain employed as a prosecutor or public defender for less than 3 years.

"(f) AWARD BASIS; PRIORITY.—

"(1) AWARD BASIS.—The Attorney General shall provide repayment benefits under this section—

"(A) subject to the availability of appropriations; and

"(B) in accordance with paragraph (2), except that the Attorney General shall determine a fair allocation of repayment benefits among prosecutors and defenders, and among employing entities nationwide.

"(2) PRIORITY.—In providing repayment benefits under this section in any fiscal year, the Attorney General shall give priority to borrowers—

"(A) who, when compared to other eligible borrowers, have the least ability to repay their student loans (considering whether the borrower is the beneficiary of any other student loan repayment program), as determined by the Attorney General; or

"(B) who—

"(i) received repayment benefits under this section during the preceding fiscal year; and "(ii) have completed less than 3 years of the first required period of service specified for the borrower in an agreement entered into under subsection (d).

"(g) REGULATIONS.—The Attorney General is authorized to issue such regulations as may be necessary to carry out the provisions of this section.

"(h) REPORT BY INSPECTOR GENERAL.—Not later than 3 years after the date of the enactment of this section, the Inspector General of the Department of Justice shall submit to Congress a report on—

"(1) the cost of the program authorized under this section; and

"(2) the impact of such program on the hiring and retention of prosecutors and public defenders.

"(i) GAO STUDY.—Not later than one year 1 after the date of the enactment of this section, the Comptroller General shall conduct a study of, and report to Congress on, the impact that law school accreditation requirements and other factors have on the costs of law school and student access to law school, including the impact of such requirements on racial and ethnic minorities.

"(j) AUTHORIZATION OF APPROPRIATIONS.—There is authorized to be appropriated to carry out this section $25,000,000 for each of the fiscal years 2008 through 2013."

Appendix C

Companion Senate Bill to H.R. 916

John R. Justice Prosecutors and Defenders Incentive Act of 2007
(Reported in Senate)

S 442 RS

Calendar No. 113
110th CONGRESS
1st Session
S. 442
[Report No. 110-51]
To provide for loan repayment for prosecutors and public defenders.

IN THE SENATE OF THE UNITED STATES
January 31, 2007

Mr. DURBIN (for himself, Mr. SPECTER, Mr. LEAHY, Mr. SMITH, Mr. KERRY, Ms. COLLINS, Ms. LANDRIEU, Ms. SNOWE, Mr. BIDEN, Mr. COCHRAN, Mr. KENNEDY, Mr. FEINGOLD, Mrs. FEINSTEIN, Mr. SCHUMER, Mr. WHITEHOUSE, Mr. COLEMAN, Mr. KOHL, and Mr. HARKIN) introduced the following bill; which was read twice and referred to the Committee on the Judiciary

April 10, 2007

Reported by Mr. LEAHY, with amendments
[Omit the part struck through and insert the part printed in italic]

————

A BILL

To provide for loan repayment for prosecutors and public defenders.
Be it enacted by the Senate and House of Representatives of the United States of America in Congress assembled,

SECTION 1. SHORT TITLE.

This Act may be cited as the "John R. Justice Prosecutors and Defenders Incentive Act of 2007".

SEC. 2. LOAN REPAYMENT FOR PROSECUTORS AND DEFENDERS.

Title I of the Omnibus Crime Control and Safe Streets Act of 1968 (42 U.S.C. 3711 et seq.) is amended by adding at the end the following:

"PART JJ—LOAN REPAYMENT FOR PROSECUTORS AND PUBLIC DE-FENDERS

"SEC. 3111. GRANT AUTHORIZATION.

"(a) Purpose—The purpose of this section is to encourage qualified individuals to enter and continue employment as prosecutors and public defenders.

"(b) Definitions—In this section:

"(1) PROSECUTOR—The term "prosecutor" means a full-time employee of a State or local agency who—

"(A) is continually licensed to practice law; and

"(B) prosecutes criminal *or juvenile delinquency* cases at the State or local level*(including supervision, education, or training of other persons prosecuting such cases).*

"(2) PUBLIC DEFENDER—The term "public defender" means an attorney who—

"(A) is continually licensed to practice law; and

"(B) is—

"~~(i) a full-time employee of a State or local agency or a nonprofit organization operating under a contract with a State or unit of local government, that provides legal representation to indigent persons in criminal cases; or~~

"*(i) a full-time employee of a State or local agency who provides legal representation to indigent persons in criminal or juvenile delinquency cases (including supervision, education, or training of other persons providing such representation);*

"*(ii) a full-time employee of a nonprofit organization operating under a contract with a State or unit of local government, who devotes substantially all of his or her full-time employment to providing legal representation to indigent persons in criminal or juvenile delinquency cases, (including supervision, education, or training of other persons providing such representation); or*

"(ii)*(iii)* employed as a full-time Federal defender attorney in a defender organization established pursuant to subsection (g) of section 3006A of title 18, United States Code, that provides legal representation to indigent persons in criminal *or juvenile delinquency* cases.

"(3) STUDENT LOAN—The term "student loan" means—

"(A) a loan made, insured, or guaranteed under part B of title IV of the Higher Education Act of 1965 (20 U.S.C. 1071 et seq.);

"(B) a loan made under part D or E of title IV of the Higher Education Act of 1965 (20 U.S.C. 1087a et seq. and 1087aa et seq.); and

"(C) a loan made under section 428C or 455(g) of the Higher Education Act of 1965 (20 U.S.C. 1078-3 and 1087e(g)) to the extent that such loan was used to repay a Federal Direct Stafford Loan, a Federal Direct Unsubsidized Stafford Loan, or a loan made under section 428 or 428H of such Act.

"(c) Program Authorized—The Attorney General shall establish a program by which the Department of Justice shall assume the obligation to repay a student loan, by direct payments on behalf of a borrower to the holder of such loan, in accordance with subsection (d), for any borrower who—

"(1) is employed as a prosecutor or public defender; and

"(2) is not in default on a loan for which the borrower seeks forgiveness.

"(d) Terms of Agreement—

"(1) IN GENERAL—To be eligible to receive repayment benefits under subsection (c), a borrower shall enter into a written agreement that specifies that—

"(A) the borrower will remain employed as a prosecutor or public defender for a required period of service of not less than 3 years, unless involuntarily separated from that employment;

"(B) if the borrower is involuntarily separated from employment on account of misconduct, or voluntarily separates from employment, before the end of the period specified in the agreement, the borrower will repay the Attorney General the amount of any benefits received by such employee under this section;

"(C) if the borrower is required to repay an amount to the Attorney General under subparagraph (B) and fails to repay such amount, a sum equal to that amount shall be recoverable by the Federal Government from the employee (or such employee's estate, if applicable) by such methods as are provided by law for the recovery of amounts owed to the Federal Government;

"(D) the Attorney General may waive, in whole or in part, a right of recovery under this subsection if it is shown that recovery would be against equity and good conscience or against the public interest; and

"(E) the Attorney General shall make student loan payments under this section for the period of the agreement, subject to the availability of appropriations.

"(2) REPAYMENTS—

"(A) IN GENERAL—Any amount repaid by, or recovered from, an individual or the estate of an individual under this subsection shall be credited to the appropriation account from which the amount involved was originally paid.

"(B) MERGER—Any amount credited under subparagraph (A) shall be merged with other sums in such account and shall be available for the same purposes and period, and subject to the same limitations, if any, as the sums with which the amount was merged.

"(3) LIMITATIONS—

"(A) STUDENT LOAN PAYMENT AMOUNT—Student loan repayments made by the Attorney General under this section shall be made subject to such terms, limitations, or conditions as may be mutually agreed upon by the borrower and the Attorney General in an agreement under paragraph (1), except that the amount paid by the Attorney General under this section shall not exceed—

"(i) $10,000 for any borrower in any calendar year; or

"(ii) an aggregate total of $60,000 in the case of any borrower.

"(B) BEGINNING OF PAYMENTS—Nothing in this section shall authorize the Attorney General to pay any amount to reimburse a borrower for any repayments made by such borrower prior to the date on which the Attorney General entered into an agreement with the borrower under this subsection.

"(e) Additional Agreements—

"(1) IN GENERAL—On completion of the required period of service under an agreement under subsection (d), the borrower and the Attorney General may, subject to paragraph (2), enter into an additional agreement in accordance with subsection (d).

"(2) TERM—An agreement entered into under paragraph (1) may require the borrower to remain employed as a prosecutor or public defender for less than 3 years.

"(f) Award Basis; Priority—

"(1) AWARD BASIS—Subject to paragraph (2), the Attorney General shall provide repayment benefits under this section on a first-come, first-served basis, and subject to the availability of appropriations.

"(2) PRIORITY—The Attorney General shall give priority in providing repayment benefits under this section in any fiscal year to a borrower who

"(f) Award Basis; Priority—

"(1) AWARD BASIS — Subject to paragraph (2), the Attorney General shall provide repayment benefits under this section —

"(A) giving priority to borrowers who have the least ability to repay their loans, except that the Attorney General shall determine a fair allocation of repayment benefits among prosecutors and public defenders, and among employing entities nationwide; and

"(B) subject to the availability of appropriations.

"(2) PRIORITY — The Attorney General shall give priority in providing repayment benefits under this section in any fiscal year to a borrower who —

"(A) received repayment benefits under this section during the preceding fiscal year; and

"(B) has completed less than 3 years of the first required period of service specified for the borrower in an agreement entered into under subsection (d).

"(g) Regulations — The Attorney General is authorized to issue such regulations as may be necessary to carry out the provisions of this section.

"*(h) Study — Not later than 1 year after the date of enactment of this section, the Government Accountability Office shall study and report to Congress on the impact of law school accreditation requirements and other factors on law school costs and access, including the impact of such requirements on racial and ethnic minorities.*

"~~(h)~~(i) Authorization of appropriations — There are authorized to be appropriated to carry out this section $25,000,000 for fiscal year 2008 and such sums as may be necessary for each succeeding fiscal year."

Calendar No. 113

Appendix D

Senate Report 110-051

PROVIDING FOR LOAN REPAYMENT FOR PROSECUTORS AND PUBLIC DEFENDERS

VIII. ADDITIONAL VIEWS

ADDITIONAL VIEWS OF SENATORS KYL AND HATCH

While the bill reported by this Committee will help reduce the burden of the heavy law-school student loans borne by many young prosecutors and public defenders, this legislation treats only the symptoms, not the source, of this problem. The source of the problem—the cause of the excessive cost of becoming eligible to practice law in the United States today—was identified in testimony before this Committee by George B. Shepard, an associate professor of law at Emory University School of Law. In his testimony on February 27, Professor Shepard endorsed the John R. Justice Act, but went on to note that:

> [W]e need to recognize that passage of the Act is necessary partly because of the [law-school] accreditation system; without the accreditation system, many more students would graduate from law school with no loans or much smaller ones, so that they would not need to use the benefits that the Act provides. With the accreditation system, the Act will, in effect, transfer much taxpayers' money from the federal government to overpriced law schools.

> Professor Shepard went on to describe exactly how the American Bar Association's law-school accreditation rules substantially and unnecessarily increase the cost of becoming eligible to practice law:

> The ABA's accreditation requirements increase the cost of becoming a lawyer in two ways. First, they increase law school tuition. They do this by imposing many costs on law schools. For example, accreditation standards effectively raise faculty salaries; limit faculty teaching loads; require high numbers of full-time faculty rather than cheaper part-time adjuncts; and require expensive physical facilities and library collections. The requirements probably cause law schools' costs to more

than double, increasing them by more than $12,000 per year, with many schools then passing the increased costs along to students by raising tuition. The total increase for the three years of law school is more than $36,000.

The impact of the increased costs from accreditation can be seen by comparing tuition rates at accredited schools and unaccredited schools. Accredited schools normally charge more than $25,000 per year. Unaccredited schools usually charge approximately half that amount. One example of the many expensive accreditation requirements is the ABA's requirement that an accredited school have a large library and extensive library collection. Insiders confirm that the ABA requires a minimum expenditure on library operations and acquisitions of approximately $1 million per year. This is more than $4,000 per student in an averaged-sized school.

The second way that the ABA requirements increase students' cost of entering the legal profession is as follows. The ABA requires students to attend at least six years of expensive higher education: three years of college and three years of law school. Before the Great Depression, a young person could enter the legal profession as an apprentice directly after high school, without college or law school. Now, a person can become a lawyer only if she can afford to take six years off from work after high school and pay six years of tuition.

The requirement of six years of education is expensive. The sum of the tuition payments and foregone income can easily exceed $300,000, or more. For example, a conservative estimate is that attending a private college and law school for six years would cost approximately $25,000 per year for a total of $150,000. In addition, let's assume conservatively that a student who could qualify for college and law school would have earned only $25,000 per year if the student had not attended college and law school. The amount of income that the student sacrifices for six years to become a lawyer is $150,000. The total is $300,000.

In addition to the John R. Justice Act, there are two other means by which the problem of the excessive cost of becoming eligible to practice law in this country could be addressed. First, the states themselves could liberalize their law-school accreditation requirements. This would directly reduce the cost of becoming a lawyer in all cases, not just for prosecutors and public defenders. In his February 27 testimony, Professor Shepard recommended that:

[T]he accreditation system's restrictions should be loosened. For example, law schools might be permitted to experiment with smaller libraries, cheaper practitioner faculty, and even shorter programs of two years rather than three, like business school. Or the requirements might be eliminated completely; students without a degree from an accredited law school would be able to practice law.

Removing the flawed, artificial accreditation bottleneck would not in fact be a drastic change, and it would create many benefits but few harms. The current system's high-end qualities would continue, while a freer market for variety would quickly open up. To Rolls-Royce legal educations would be added Buicks, Saturns, and Fords. The new system would develop a wider range of talent, including lawyers at $60, $40, and even $25 an hour, as well as those at $300 and up. This would fit the true diversity of legal needs, from simple to complex. With cheaper education available to more people, some lawyers for the first time would be willing and able to work for far less than at present.

The addition of many more lawyers would produce little additional legal malpractice or fraud, and the quality of legal services decline little, it at all. Private institutions would arise within the market for legal services to ensure that each legal matter was handled by lawyers with appropriate skills and sophistication. For example, large, expensive law firms would continue to handle complicated, high-stakes transactions and litigation. However, law companies that resembled H&R Block would open to offer less-expensive legal services for simple matters. Accounting and tax services are available not only for $300 per hour at the big accounting firms, but also for $25 per hour at H&R Block. The new law companies would monitor and guarantee the services of their lawyer-employees.

Elimination of the accreditation requirement is a modest, safe proposal. It merely reestablishes the system that exists in other equally-critical professions, a system that worked well in law for more than a century before the Great Depression. Business and accounting provide comforting examples of professions without mandatory accreditation or qualifying exams. In both professions, people may provide full-quality basic services without attending an accredited school or passing an exam. Instead, people can choose preparation that is appropriate for their jobs. A person who seeks to manage a local McDonald's franchise or to prepare tax returns need not attend business school or become a CPA first. Yet there is no indication that the level of malpractice or fraud is higher in these fields than in law. Likewise, there is no indication that malpractice and fraud were any more frequent during the century before accreditation and the bar exam, when lawyers like Abraham Lincoln practiced. Lincoln never went to law school.

Second, in response to those who have turned to Congress to address this problem, I would note that Congress already *has* acted. It acted in 1868, by enacting the Privileges and Immunities Clause of the Fourteenth Amendment. That Clause was understood at the time of the nation's founding 'to refer to those fundamental rights and liberties specifically enjoyed by English citizens and, more broadly, by all persons.' *Saenz* v. *Roe*, 526 U.S. 489, 524 (Thomas, J., dissenting) — a meaning that carried over to the Fourteenth Amendment as well, see *Id.* 526–27. Legal scholars and civil-rights organizations such as the Institute for Justice have in the past presented compelling arguments that the fundamental rights and liberties protected by the Privileges and Immunities Clause include a right to pursue a career or profession. And that right is in clear tension with the apparently protectionist nature of the current accreditation regime. As Professor Shepard noted in his testimony:

> Strict accreditation requirements are a relatively recent phenomenon, having begun in the Great Depression. What seems normal now after 70 years was in fact a radical change from a much more open system that had functioned well for more than a century before then. Until the Great Depression, no state required an applicant to the bar to have attended any law school at all, much less an accredited one. Indeed, 41 states required no formal education whatsoever beyond high school; 32 states did not even require a high school diploma. Similarly, bar exams were easy to pass; they had high pass rates.

* * * * * * *

During the Depression, state bar associations attempted to eliminate so-called 'overcrowding' in the legal profession; they felt that too many new lawyers were competing with the existing ones for the dwindling amount of legal business. They attempted to reduce the number of new lawyers in two ways. First, they decreased bar pass rates. Second, they convinced courts and state legislatures to require that all lawyers graduate from ABA-accredited law schools.

The protectionist nature of the current accreditation regime not only is at odds with the Privileges and Immunities Clause; it also has a disproportionate impact on the very minority groups that the Fourteenth Amendment was originally designed to protect. Several of the witnesses who testified before the Committee emphasized the negative effects that escalating tuition costs have on minority participation in the legal profession and on access to legal services in minority communities. Jessica Bergeman, an Assistant State's Attorney for Cook County, Illinois, stated:

> I truly believe that it is good for the communities of Chicago to see Assistant State's Attorneys of color. Unfortunately, it is often we who are most burdened with educational debt. People like me who are forced to leave the office because they cannot afford to stay cannot be categorized as just a personal career set-back, but rather it has the potential to further the divisions between the prosecutors and so many of the people they prosecute.

Professor Shepard seconded this point in his testimony, noting that 'the system has excluded many from the legal profession, particularly the poor and minorities. It has raised the cost of legal services. And it has, in effect, denied legal services to whole segments of our society.'

Simple legal planning plays an important role in individuals' efforts to provide for their families, start businesses, and plan for their economic futures. Lower and middle-income citizens' lack of access to legal services makes it more difficult for them to make the informed choices that will improve their lives. And existing law-school accreditation requirements play a significant role in driving up the cost of legal services. Recognizing the significance of these phenomena, the Committee adopted an amendment to this legislation that will require the Government Accountability Office to report to Congress on the impact that law-school accreditation requirements have on law-school tuition, including the effect that the elevated cost of legal services has on members of minority groups.

The bill reported by this Committee addresses a real problem. It is a problem, however, that should also be addressed by other, more direct means.

JON KYL.
ORRIN G. HATCH.

Appendix E

Finding Legislative History

This appendix explores text-based resources. Good online sources include Duke Law Library,[1] Georgetown Law Library,[2] and the Law Library of Congress.[3]

Before beginning your research, you should know the following pieces of information: (1) the public law citation (*e.g.*, Pub. L. No. 106-23) or the *Statutes at Large* citation (*e.g.*, 121 Stat. 3), and (2) the bill number and the Congress that enacted the law (*e.g.*, H.R. 3162 from the 107th Congress). If you look at the sample bill included in Appendix D, you should see that the bill number is H.R. 916 and that the Congress is the 110th. The companion bill included in Appendix E is bill number S. 442 also from the 110th Congress. Neither bill has a public law citation or *Statutes at Large* citation because neither was enacted, although President Obama signed an identical bill into law as part of the Higher Education Opportunities Act (Pub. L. No. 110-315, section 952).

If you know only the popular name of the statute (*e.g.*, No Child Left Behind Act), you may check the Popular Names Table included with the *United States Code, United States Code Annotated*, or the *United States Code Service* to find the public law and *Statutes at Large* citation. To find numbers for bills enacted since 1904, check in the *United States Statutes at Large*. The *United States Statutes at Large* is also available in PDF in HeinOnline's *United States Statutes at Large Library* from 1789 to present. Westlaw Edge also contains the *Statutes at Large* from 1789 to 1972.

One starting point for researching legislative history is to begin with compiled legislative histories. A compiled legislative history is a resource that has already researched and collected the relevant legislative documents for a particular act. Because it is very time-consuming (and thus costly) to exhaustively research the legislative history of a particular bill, it can be helpful to rely on history that has already been compiled. Here is one compilation to consider: RONALD E. WHEELER & JENNA E. FEGREUS, SOURCES OF COMPILED LEGISLATIVE HISTORIES: A BIBLIOGRAPHY OF GOVERNMENT DOCUMENTS, PERIODICAL

---

1. Located at https://law.duke.edu/lib/researchguides/fedleg/.
2. Located at http://guides.ll.georgetown.edu/legislative_history.
3. Located at http://www.loc.gov/law/help/leghist.php.

ARTICLES, AND BOOKS, 1ST CONGRESS-114TH CONGRESS (4th ed. 2018). This publication identifies government and commercial sources that contain either the text of or citations to legislative history documents. This publication is also available in HeinOnline's U.S. Federal Legislative History Library dating back to the 1st Congress.

The *United States Code Congressional and Administrative News* ("U.S.C.C.A.N." published by Thomson Reuters) also contains selected House and Senate reports (for most laws, either a House or a Senate report is reprinted), presidential proclamations and executive orders, information on the status of pending legislation, and the full text of the Public Laws signed during the reporting period. Each bound volume has a "contents" page, which lists the following: (1) the identities of the president and cabinet members, (2) the identity of senators and representatives, and (3) congressional committees. The final volume has a series of tables that help researchers find Public Laws (1) by bill number, (2) by reference to the affected section of the *United States Code* and the *United States Code Annotated*, and (3) by popular name. One table identifies the "legislative history" of Public Laws by bill number. Other tables identify administrative regulations, proclamations, executive orders, and major bills that are pending with a record of House and Senate action to date. U.S.C.C.A.N. is an excellent place to begin your research. U.S.C.C.A.N. is available on Westlaw Edge in the Federal Legislative History database. It includes Congressional Committee Reports, Executive Orders, Legislative History Table, Presidential Messages & Signing Statements, Presidential Proclamations, and Public Laws.

The *Congressional Record* is the official source for House and Senate debates. There are four separately paginated sections to *The Congressional Record*: the Proceedings of the Senate, the Proceedings of the House, the Extension of Remarks section, and the Daily Digest. *The Congressional Record*'s page numbers begin with a letter that represents each of these four sections: H for the House; S for the Senate; E for the Extension of Remarks section; and D for the Daily Digest. The Daily Digest is issued each day while Congress is in session. The bound *Congressional Record* is the final, permanent edition. These sections contain summaries of committee meetings, lists of witnesses from committee hearings, legislative action taken on bills, and the Senate and the House debates.

An index to *The Congressional Record* is published every two weeks; the index contains two sections. One section indexes the proceedings by subject and by speaker; the other section indexes the history of bills and resolutions by number. The indexes help researchers trace the progress of legislation through Congress and locate Senate and House debates on legislation. The *Congressional Record* is available on Westlaw Edge under Federal Legislative History. Coverage begins with the First Session of the 99th Congress (1985). It is also available on govinfo from 1994 to present (daily), and 1873-2001, 2005 to 2013 (bound). *ProQuest Congressional* provides the *Congressional Record Permanent Digital Collection* from its inception in 1873.

The *CIS Annual*, which the Congressional Information Services publishes, covers laws from 1970 to the present. This publication is a comprehensive index to legislative history documents. *CIS Annual* abstracts and indexes most congressional information, including House and Senate reports, hearings, and committee prints, with additional citations to *The Congressional Record*. From 1970 to 1983, the *CIS Annual* abstracts contained a condensed "Legislative History" section in the back of each volume, which lists congressional documents by public law number. From 1984 to the present, the *CIS Annual* has separate Legislative History volumes. Also, the CIS provides access to the full text of legislative history documents in microfiche.

The indexes reference *CIS Annual*'s abstracts; while the abstracts contain complete bibliographic information and a summary of the publications. Legislative documents can be located either by bill number, by Public Law number, by report number, by subject, by title, by author, or by witness name.

ProQuest Congressional is the online counterpart to CIS and includes legislative histories for laws from 1969. To easily access the histories for a public law on ProQuest, enter the Public Law number on the Search by Number page, and then narrow to Legislative History on the left. In addition, ProQuest Legislative Insight contains extensive compilation of legislative histories of U.S. public laws enacted from 1789 to the present. Histories include the full text of the public law itself, all versions of related bills, law-specific Congressional Record excerpts, committee hearings, reports, prints, presidential signing statements, and CRS reports. All documents are full-text, searchable PDFs.

Also, the *U.S. Congressional Serial Set*, commonly referred to as the *Serial Set*, contains House and Senate Documents and House and Senate Reports organized by session of Congress. The publication began in 1817 with the 15th Congress. Documents generated before 1817 may be found in the *American State Papers*. In general, the *Serial Set* includes the following: committee reports related to bills and other matters, presidential communications to Congress, treaty materials, certain executive department publications, and certain non-governmental publications. This set is also available in ProQuest Congressional, and on HeinOnline from the 15th through the 113th Congress (1817-2014).

The General Accounting Office's Reports may also be informative. The U.S. General Accounting Office (the "GAO") is an administrative agency within the legislative branch of the government that conducts audits, surveys, investigations, and evaluations of federal agencies and programs. The GAO's findings and recommendations are made public in written form, as written reports to Congress, or in oral form, as testimony to congressional committees. Although GAO reports are not official *legislative* history because they come from the executive, they may be relevant, especially when the GAO contributes to the drafting or review of a bill pending before Congress. For presidential signing statements and veto messages, you should consult the *Weekly Compilation of Presidential Documents.* This compilation is current from 1965 to date. Westlaw Edge contains the U.S. GAO Federal Legislative History database and includes legislative histories for most public laws enacted between 1921 and 1995. Westlaw Edge, Lexis Advance, govinfo, and Congress.gov provide limited online coverage to the C.F.R., although Westlaw Edge, Lexis Advance, and govinfo provide online access to the *Federal Register* from its inception in 1936 to present. However, HeinOnline provides comprehensive coverage for both the C.F.R. and the F.R. It has all the C.F.R. volumes dating back to 1938 in PDF format. The *Federal Register*, also in PDF, is available from its inception in 1936 and is updated on a daily basis on HeinOnline.

Also of note are two additional resources under Westlaw Edge's Federal Legislative History category on the home page:

- U.S. Congressional Testimony—which provides agendas and witness lists for U.S. congressional committee hearings, transcripts of oral statements, and written statements submitted to committees of Congress. Coverage begins with January 1993.
- U.S. Political Transcripts—which provides transcripts of news conferences, press briefings, political speeches, and oral testimony from congressional committee hearings. Coverage begins with February 1994.

While agencies do not enact statutes, at some point, you may need to research the history of the enactment of an agency regulation. To do so, you will need to check the *Federal Register* and the *Code of Federal Regulations.* The Office of the Federal Register, National Archives and Records Administration, publishes the *Federal Register*, which is a daily publication containing newly promulgated regulations, proposed rules, and notices from federal administrative agencies. The notices of proposed regulations often contain detailed information regarding the goal of the agency in developing the regulation, public comments responding to drafts, and other relevant information. The *Federal Register* also contains executive orders and other presidential documents. The *Code of Federal Regulations* (the "C.F.R.") is the codification of the regulations enacted by federal agencies. Like the *United States Code*, the C.F.R. is divided by subject into fifty titles. Each volume of the C.F.R. is updated once each calendar year and is issued on a quarterly basis. It contains no history, only the text of the regulation.

While federal statutes often have extensive legislative history, state statutes often do not. Moreover, the availability of state legislative history is more sporadic. Some states maintain these records (like New York), while others do not (like Georgia). You will need to check your specific state for more information.

Index